PENGUIN BOOKS

# GERMANY AND THE GERMANS

John Ardagh was born in Malawi, East Africa, in 1928, the son of a colonial civil servant. He was educated at Sherborne School and Worcester College, Oxford, where he took an honours degree in classics and philosophy. From 1955 to 1959 he was a staff correspondent of *The Times* in Algeria and in Paris, where he began what has proved to be a long love-hate relationship with the French. Back in England, he was for five years a staff writer on *The Observer*. Fascinated by the deep changes in France during that period, he published in 1968 his first major study of modern France, *The New French Revolution*, later reprinted and revised in Pelican Books as *The New France*. A new edition of this same book, *France in the 1980s*, won the Enid McLeod Prize in 1982. The newest version has been in print with Penguin Books since 1988 as *France Today*.

John Ardagh's other books include *A Tale of Five Cities: Life in Provincial Europe Today* (1979), *Rural France* (1983) and *Writers' France* (1989). In 1987 he widened his European range by publishing *Germany and the Germans*, an anatomy of that country's society; an updated version, taking account of the new united Germany, is in Penguin (1995). Ardagh's most recent book, his third portrait of a modern country, is *Ireland and the Irish* (Penguin, 1995). He is also a freelance journalist, lecturer and broadcaster, and a member of the Franco-British Council. He remains a passionate believer in the battered old ideal of European unity. His other special interests include the cinema and gastronomy (he is continental editor of *The Good Hotel Guide*). He lives in Kensington with his German wife Katharina, who often acts as his research consultant, and he has a son by a previous marriage.

To my son Nicholas

# CONTENTS

## Contents

## Contents

# PREFACE TO THE 1995 EDITION

This book was thoroughly revised in 1991, with a lengthy new chapter on the fall of the GDR regime in 1989 and the huge problems of the east Germans in clearing up its legacy and adapting to the west. I have now added a new introduction, giving a picture of what has happened in Germany between mid-1991 and spring 1995 — the re-election of Chancellor Kohl in 1994, the coming and going of recession, the continued malaise in the east despite economic renewal, the flare-up of racial violence, Berlin's preparation to be again the German capital, and much else. A postscript on page 580 looks at Germany's role in Europe, and in the world, in 1995.

The rest of the book remains unchanged since 1991. It has two long chapters on the east, but it is mostly about the western part of Germany. Here I have loosely used the words 'Germany' and 'Germans' to refer to that part of the country, where life and attitudes are still rather different. And let me stress that this is *not* a book about party politics or foreign policy: like my other Penguin books, *France Today* and *Ireland and the Irish*, it is primarily a study of society and of regional, economic and cultural affairs. Nor is it a history of post-war Germany so much as a portrait of this complicated nation as it is now in the mid-1990s.

This certainly does not mean that I have ignored the major 'German' themes that still make this country something of a special case. The legacy of Nazism and wartime defeat; the forty years' division of the country and the anguished problems of unification; the wary search for a new national identity, after the catastrophe of nationalism before 1945; the remarkable post-war forging of a stable democracy in the west; the clash of generations, values and life-styles, often so sharp in

Germany; the advantages and drawbacks of the Germans' famous thoroughness; the old streak of insecurity and anxiety, assuaged by economic success but also revived by an anxious world climate – these are the leitmotifs running through the book or examined in its final chapters. But I have also tried to look at western Germany at least, not just as a peculiar problem child but as a normal modern society. Fifty years after the war's end, that ought to be possible.

Why should a French specialist of thirty years' standing have turned to Germany, as I did when I started this work in 1984? It seems entirely natural that a francophile Englishman with 'European' convictions should have wished to extend his range to the other main pillar of the European Union; I have always liked and admired the Germans, and been fascinated by Germany. The field research for my book about provincial Europe, *A Tale of Five Cities* (1979), with its long chapter on Stuttgart, had given me a foretaste. If I may intrude a personal note that is most relevant: I began my research as an outsider, with hundreds of contacts and some German friends, but no inside connection. Then in Stuttgart in 1984 I met Katharina (Katinka) Schmitz, who was working there for the Baden-Württemberg tourist board. She was a Berliner, brought up in Munich. We became engaged, and are now married. She worked with me full-time on the book, as co-researcher, consultant, guide to 'the awful German language' (Mark Twain's phrase) and, above all, interpreter of the subtleties and contradictions of her fellow-citizens. She provided me with a perspective I could not have achieved on my own, and an emotional involvement with Germany which is now as great as my long involvement with France.

For our initial field research, we lived for some months in Stuttgart, and spent many weeks each in Munich, Frankfurt, Bonn, Hamburg and other towns, especially Berlin, which I have come to know well and to love. We have been back to Germany constantly. So I have got to know those *Autobahnen* all too intimately, and in my sleep I could retrace every curve of those giddy gradients in the Schwäbische Jura or the hills south of Kassel, with the BMW 700s flashing by. Apart from this hazard, I find Germany – including the east today – a very pleasant and easy place to travel and work in, with cosy little hotels, good honest food well served, and polite people.

The Germans may not be as colourful and amusing as the French. But they are far better at answering letters or telephone calls, and are nearly always frank, helpful and ready to talk. It is easier than in most countries to fix meetings with busy people at short notice.

Their alleged lack of a sense of humour is one foreign myth – if it still exists – that needs exploding. Among friends they are lively and good fun, especially Berliners and Rhinelanders. But to be frivolous or ironic about serious or important subjects, in the British or French manner, can still make them uneasy. This is a trait that goes deep into their past and may be related to an old idealism and love of absolutes, but there may be another explanation, too: because their democratic values and institutions are still relatively recent, and because in a sense they still feel insecure about them, they are not able to be flippant about what others might take for granted. Around a dinner table, there can be plenty of animated jokey conversation on personal matters, and then, if someone mentions a 'serious' topic, the tone changes and lengthy debate ensues. And once a German gets his teeth into a subject of this kind, he likes to worry at it for hours.

This seriousness can be tiresome, but it has its appealing side. Younger Germans in particular, at least the ones I meet, I have found to be more than averagely thoughtful, concerned, gentle and internationally minded. The Germans are less pompous than they used to be. Their old tendency towards arrogance, associated with the Prussian upper classes, took such a punishment from wartime defeat and Nazi shame that until now it has been not much present, at least in their dealings with foreigners from the West, whose good opinion they are keen to cultivate. I have found less arrogance than in Paris, save maybe among some haughty executives of big firms. But I know that many west Germans give a less favourable impression to their brothers in the old GDR, or to many immigrants.

Even a western visitor can find some aggressive instincts lurking behind the surface of this polite new Germany – or that is the impression one gains from observing the German behind his steering-wheel. I repeat that I do not relish the Wagnerian spectacle of those imperious *Autobahnen* that sweep through the rolling fields and forests, their lanes packed with neat-suited executives in their powerful Mercedes, Audis and BMWs. On many motorways there is no speed limit, so if you dare stay in the fast lane at a mere 140 kph, they nose up behind you, lights flashing angrily, then race ahead of you at maybe 250 kph as you meekly move aside. It is unnerving. 'This desire to dominate in a car is stronger than in other countries,' a leading psychologist, Carmen Lakashus, suggested to me. 'And it goes far back into history, this internalised frustration of the German male.' However, in 1994, fears of ozone pollution caused the Social Democrats to propose universal 130 kph speed limits, and some *Länder* to introduce voluntary ones. Many drivers obeyed, while polls showed that 50 per cent of motorists were in favour of limits. So maybe the German male, torn between love of speed and environmental panic, no longer knows where to vent his frustration.

For centuries the Germans have been regarded as an unstable and unpredictable people, even by their own greatest thinkers. 'The Germans', said Goethe, 'make everything difficult both for themselves and everyone else,' while Nietzsche wrote in *Beyond Good and Evil* (1886), 'The German soul has ... caves, hiding-places, dungeons in it; its disorder possesses much of the fascinating and mysterious; the German is acquainted with the hidden paths to chaos.' Foreigners were equally perplexed, especially the neighbouring French. De Gaulle, who had fought the Germans in 1914–18, has a remarkable passage about them in his *Vers l'Armée de métier* (1934): 'A bundle of strong and troubled instincts, born artists without taste, technicians who are still feudal, fathers of families who are warriors, oppressors who want to be loved, separatists who are strictly obedient, knights bearing garlands who vomit beer ... a sublime green ocean where the net hoists a tangle of monsters and treasures.'

And today, in the stable, well-ordered post-war Germany, what does the net hoist up? The contrast between the Germans' passion for orderliness and their tendency towards romanticism and irrationality has long puzzled observers, and the two elements would seem to be inter-related: the Germans, being aware of their 'troubled instincts', feel a special need to impose order and discipline on their society, but this in turn has built up frustrations leading to the kind of outbursts it is designed to prevent. And the Germans seem to be one thing one day, another the next – as the late Luigi Barzini suggested in his book *The Impossible Europeans* (1983), where in a brilliant chapter headed 'The Mutable Germans' he argued that their society has various diverse facets which would come to the fore one by one under differing circumstances. He noted that before 1860 the patchwork of German states seemed to be a peaceful Arcadia, full of picturesque old towns and earnest, moral, tenderly sentimental people. Then the new united Germany under Bismarck emerged as militaristic and aggressive, leading to the 1914–18 war. The ensuing Weimar period, said Barzini, was a bizarre interlude filled with confusion, civil strife, moral decay and freakish exhibitionism, but then all returned to tidy orthodoxy after the Nazis' arrival. Nazism later produced barbarous excesses behind its façade of *Ordnung*: but after the catharsis of defeat in 1945 the Germans swung to the other extreme, turning their heels on heel-clicking and embracing a new democratic ideal. They settled in a very sane, peaceful, bourgeois mould which Barzini found 'Swisslike' and felt to be no new invention but something that had long been hibernating in the German soul. However, the sceptical Milanese wondered whether the youth malaise and anxieties of the 1970s and 1980s – leading to fringe terrorism and the wilder fantasies of some Greens – might not be heralding another mutation. Is the German, he asked, still 'acquainted with the hidden paths to chaos'? After his death, the inter-German bitterness and racial violence of the early 1990s might have added to his doubts. And yet, another answer came from a 1991 poll showing safe, bourgeois Switzerland as the Germans' preferred model of society, by far.

The Germans may seem to have changed radically since their Nazi aberration. But how deep does the change go? In many ways the picture since the war has been most positive. A new and open society has developed, less class-divided than it used to be, or than Britain or France still are; labour relations have blossomed into harmony, and a spirit of reasonable consensus has guided politics, helped by the stability given by economic success. If it has proved a rather conformist society, this has been in part an unconscious result of the attempt to tame the wild streak that led to Nazism. It has proved also a very legalistic society, festooned by a myriad petty rules and regulations, and the need to abide by them. This is by no means a new German trait, but the law-making has intensified since the war: Germans seem to have felt instinctively that the best way to safeguard a fledgling democracy is to hedge it about with laws that direct the citizen on how to behave in it.

However, the trait of automatic obedience has weakened in recent years. Under the impact of the ideas of 1968, society has become a little more socially informal, less deferential to authority, perhaps more tolerant. A new generation has new values; and although some of the wilder ideas of the Greens may be far too fanciful, there is certainly a sympathetic side to many recent trends – the concern for nature and quality of life, the renewed interest in local tradition. The links with the better side of the German heritage were smashed by the Nazi experience, which led to a blanket rejection of the entire past, in a bid for a clean new start. This was understandable, but in the longer term could be harmful. Today, enough time has gone by for there to be a cautious return to tradition. It can be seen in the new vogue for restoring ancient houses, rather than tearing down everything old as happened in the 1950s. Young people, as in other Western countries, have been turning towards private values and feelings, alike to spiritual and hedonistic satisfactions. They want to get more fun out of life, and they reject the work-for-work's sake ethic of their elders. This is sympathetic, but can create problems. Older west Germans remain much attached to their high standards of living, built up so effortfully since the war. And the recession of 1992–3 showed how easily these can be imperilled, if they relax their efforts, in an age of rising world competition.

Today, much has changed since the Berlin Wall came down in November 1989, leading to what Germans call the *Wende*, the great change. The new united Germany is larger, by 17 million people, than the old West Germany. It will become more powerful, though for the present it is still weakened by the costs of restoring the east. For forty years, the western Federal Republic was a model of democratic stability. Since the *Wende* new tensions have arisen, and the Germans have possibly become less predictable – is this another of Barzini's cyclic mutations? The next pages, written early in 1995, examine these problems.

# 1

## INTRODUCTION

### *Introduction to the 1995 edition: the new united Germany in a new era*

In the final months of 1989, the GDR regime collapsed far more suddenly than almost anyone in the West had expected. For some years, westerners had stopped expecting unification, or even regarding it as an important issue. But when the liberated East Germans began clamouring for it, the continued separate existence of their state no longer made much sense. So Chancellor Kohl went all out for as swift a reunion as possible. It was possibly a correct decision, but he and his Government then made some serious tactical mistakes (the detailed story of these events is given in chapter 8).

Politically, the reunion was managed quite skilfully, after the east's first free elections in March 1990. The implantation of west Germany's legal, administrative and political systems into this former Communist society has inevitably had its problems: but east Germans on the whole have easily embraced democracy. Both economically and psychologically, however, unification has been far more traumatic. First, in 1990 Kohl and his advisors seriously under-estimated the cost of rescuing the east's economy, which was already nearing bankruptcy and soon began to collapse: since 1991, the cost to the federal budget of the special aid to the east has been over 150 billion DM a year, equal to half of all German tax revenues. Secondly, Kohl failed to warn his electors frankly of these difficulties, but promised that unification would not demand great sacrifices. He was soon proved wrong – and this provided the basis of the malaise in Germany in the early 1990s, with growing mutual resentments between 'Wessis' and 'Ossis' (as the peoples from the west and east dubbed each other). When they met after their long separation, the two sides found that they did not like each other much and did not have much in common. Wessis, after paying lip service to reunification for so long, now baulked at having to pay for it, and regarded Ossis as lazy and ungrateful. Ossis in turn saw westerners as arrogant and ungenerous. They may not have liked their old regime: but it did give them security and full employment. Many have now lost their jobs. And even those in work have been finding it curiously difficult, mentally, to adapt to a capitalist system. Very few 'want the Wall back' (as the saying goes): but they are disappointed with the free west.

All this, together with world recession, Government scandals at home, growing Euro-scepticism abroad, and the spectre of neo-Nazism as racist violence grew, plunged the Germans into one of their cyclic bouts of *Angst* and self-doubt, even intolerance — and this worried Germany's neighbours, too. The mood was at its worst in 1992–3. Since then, matters have improved a little. But uncertainties remain.

By 1992, the mighty German economy had to struggle not only with helping the east but with the unfortunate coincidence of a sharp recession spreading from America. This had initially been delayed by the artificial boom created at first by unification: the east had been flooded with Deutschmark, provoking a spending spree that led many west German firms to work at full tilt in order to meet this demand. But the spree ended; and by 1993 Germany was engulfed in what was called 'the worst recession since the war': major firms piled up heavy losses, especially in the crucial automobile industry. This and some other factors engendered gloom, and sent Kohl's popularity plummeting.

However, German industry responded to the challenge with a massive, and overdue, programme of rationalisation. It cost many jobs, but financially it bore fruit; and as Europe moved out of recession, so did Germany, turning minus 1 per cent growth in 1993 into plus 2.5 per cent for 1994. The mood brightened — and so did Kohl's own fortunes, in a crucial election year. Having been Chancellor since 1982, he was easily re-elected in 1990 on a wave of post-unification optimism. But in 1993–4 his Christian Democratic Union and its Bavarian sister-party, the Christian Socialist Union, fell behind the Social Democratic Party (SPD) in the opinion polls and local elections. So Kohl's chances of yet another victory looked slim. Yet from spring 1994 this eternal survivor began to pick up, and as the federal elections of October approached, the CDU/CSU and the SPD were level-pegging in the polls. In the event, the ruling coalition, which included the Free Democratic Party, won a majority of just ten votes over the parties of the Left – the Social Democrats, Greens and reformed Communists (PDS). The results for the 672-seat Bundestag were as follows (with 1990 figures in brackets):

|  | Percentage of seats | Number of seats |
| --- | --- | --- |
| CDU and CSU | 41.5 (43.8) | 294 (319) |
| FDP | 6.9 (11.0) | 47 (79) |
| SPD | 36.4 (33.5) | 252 (239) |
| Greens | 7.3 (5.1) | 49 (8) |
| PDS | 4.4 (2.4) | 30 (17) |

Kohl had scraped back home, but with so small a majority that many observers foresaw his coalition not surviving another full four-year term. The liberal FDP, a crucial component, was now a much-reduced force: its popular former leader, Hans-Dietrich Genscher, had resigned from politics in 1992, and his successor, Klaus Kinkel, had not yet proved much of a success. It was thought that the FDP might at some point choose to switch alliances (to the SDP), as it had done before. Kohl, however, expressed cautious triumph about the election result. By autumn 1996 he will have overtaken Adenauer's record fourteen years in office, to become post-war Germany's longest serving Chancellor.

His victory was due not only to the economic up-turn but to his own personality and leadership. After his mid-term unpopularity, he was later able to rally back many voters, to whom he seemed to offer more reassurance than the SPD alternative. A huge, burly Rheinlander with an affable, gregarious manner and a flair for walkabout tours, Kohl has hardly appeared a very exciting leader: but he has been a skilful, even ruthless party organiser, dominating the CDU, using his great bulk as a kind of political weapon. Above all, in the troubled mid-1990s he has represented much that Germans feel they need – continuity, normality, even ordinariness, plus pragmatism, a lack of 'isms', a prudent conservatism and a moral stress on *Leistung* (achievement). Though too staunch a 'European' to be an old-style nationalist, he has sought to give back to his people a sense of pride in being German, and of belonging to a normal, decent nation. His main weakness has been his tendency to brush aside unpleasant problems, hoping that if he bides his time they will simply go away. This has led him into errors, notably over unification.

In the 1994 election, Kohl benefited also from the uninspiring stance of the SPD. This party should have been able to win, under the normal swings of democracy, and after so many Government errors, but since the departure of Helmut Schmidt in 1982, it had failed to throw up any really effective, durable leader. Oskar Lafontaine, its candidate for Chancellor in 1990, was too radical a maverick. The excellent, modern-minded Björn Engholm took the helm in 1991; but in 1993 he resigned after involvement in a minor scandal. It was then the turn of Rudolf Scharping to lead the SPD into the 1994 election: but this dull, decent man proved unable to impress voters. By now the SPD had moved quite close to the CDU on many key issues, and it no longer presented any clear image of its own. Scharping himself seemed little more than a paler, smaller version of Kohl (they even shared the same background, both having been prime minister of Rheinland-Pfalz). However, the SPD does today have a majority in the Bundesrat, the Upper House, which has to approve all legislation; and this gives it much control over Kohl's policies. So government is now proceeding by a kind of combative partnership between the major parties – an aspect of the rule by consensus that has guided West Germany since the war. It has brought much stability, plus some drawbacks.

Two smaller parties of the left did well in the elections. West Germany's Greens returned to the Bundestag, after a difficult period that had included the tragic murder (or suicide) of their charismatic former leader, Petra Kelly. The Greens are today firmly in the hands of their 'Realo' faction, which unlike the 'Fundis' welcomes political power (see p. 545), and they have been making an impact in a ruling coalition with the SPD in Hessen. In a Germany still worried by environmental problems, they will certainly keep an influence. In the east, the Party for Democratic Socialism, made up of former Communists, won 17 per cent of the vote, by crystallising local feelings of protest against Bonn and the west. The far-Right Republikaner party fared very badly.

Germany today seems to remain politically stable, despite its problems. But there have been some disturbing trends. One is the much-discussed *Politikverdrossenheit* (disillusion with politics), so common in Europe today. In Germany, this has expressed itself in the opinion surveys, in lower poll turnouts and in the emergence of local freak parties. It is part of a lowering of confidence in public bodies that has spread to include the big banks, those haughtily superior trustees of the economy. When in 1994 the mighty Deutsche Bank was shown up as having incautiously allowed an alleged swindler, the property developer Jürgen Schneider, to make away with some 9 billion DM, the whole banking world was discredited. And when recession came in 1992–3, some of the grandest firms such as Daimler-Benz, bywords for German industrial power, were revealed as having complacently neglected cost realities for far too long. But they have since made amends.

German industry since the war has generally been excellent at high-quality production and marketing, but poor at innovation and cost reduction. This did not matter so much in the boom years: but recession then exposed its weaker points. The Japanese had been leaping ahead in technology; the proud label, 'Made in Germany', was losing some of its selling power, now that some firms in the Far East, or America, were able to produce the same quality at lower cost; and Germany's share of world trade declined in 1987–93 from 13.5 to 11.4 per cent, sharp evidence of waning competitiveness. In 1993, output in Germany's crucial automobile industry fell by 23 per cent, and losses piled up. Alarm bells rang, and numerous firms, not only carmakers, began a furious offensive to reduce costs and modernise inflexible, inefficient work practices. Porsche even sunk its pride and brought in Japanese consultants, who pronounced the firm thirty years out of date: so Porsche sacked a third of its managers. Daimler-Benz rationalised so ruthlessly that it laid off 75,000 staff and claimed savings of 2 billion DM. Volkswagen followed a similar path. Some 150,000 jobs were shed in the automobile industry, and 30,000 others in chemicals, while overall unit labour costs were cut by 5 per cent. These measures have had some effect, helping Germany to climb out of recession in 1994; and today the economy is again fairly healthy. Inflation is around 3 per cent. Unemployment in the west, at around 8.3 per cent, is well below the EU average (in the east, with its special problems, it is of course much higher).

The Germans are as perplexed as others about how to reconcile competitiveness with high employment. And German firms have one further problem: their high labour costs. In this rich country, not only are wages very good, but employers must help pay for a welfare system that is today widely regarded as too generous: benefits are about 50 per cent above British levels (for what *that* is worth), and the 'safety net' embraces many people who could afford to pay much more themselves. A great debate has been under way, not only on this issue, but on the many rigidities that are seen to impede economic activity in this rule-loving country. These include: a wage-bargaining system that encourages labour harmony but has become too inflexible; a mass of tiny regulations that inhibit innovation and technical change; environmental laws that are maybe *too* severe; and protected markets in fields such as energy. Various experts, including the OECD in its 1994 report, have come down heavily in favour of reform, on these and other matters. But while Kohl has tinkered with deregulation and gone ahead with privatisation, on many of the difficult structural questions he has preferred, characteristically, to wait.

This well-known rigidity of the Germans has certainly made it harder for them to tackle the admittedly stupendous task of rescuing and renewing the east. Germans may be excellent at routine methodical work, but they have little flair for improvisation or innovation (a point I return to in later chapters): yet this is just what the problems of the east have needed. There are no set rules, of the kind the Germans love, for the unprecedented challenge of converting a country and its economy from Communism to the free market. In short, west Germans have the wealth for this job, but not the aptitude.

As I write, four and a half years after unification, the old GDR is still strewn with physical dereliction, yet the signs of renewal are also everywhere. In the towns, the ugly little 'Trabis' have mostly disappeared, replaced by second-hand Audis or BMWs. Historic city centres, as in Erfurt and Schwerin, are being gracefully restored. In Leipzig and Dresden, the once-polluted air is now far fresher. Roads have been rebuilt. New supermarkets, boutiques, hotels and factories, nearly all western-owned, are there by the thousand. Steadily the east is being renovated and aligned with the west: it is only a matter of time, and the process will succeed. But it has proved harder than expected; and it could have been managed better, with less human distress (see chapter 8 for my mid-1991 assessment of the whole situation).

Kohl, in my view, had little choice but to go for rapid unification in 1990. One alternative, then canvassed by left-of-centre groups in the east such as Neues Forum, was a liberalised GDR pursuing its own path to some ideal Socialism; this never became a realistic option and was rejected massively by East Germans at the polls. Once the old regime ended, the GDR lost its *raison d'être*. Rapid unity was also needed to stem the damaging exodus of talent to the west, and to provide a basis for western aid and investment. And as Foreign

Minister Genscher stressed in private, since unification required formal Soviet approval, it was vital to act quickly while friendly rulers were still in power in Moscow. His fears were proved justified by the almost successful coup against Gorbachev in August 1991.

Economically, however, Kohl should have gone more slowly. That is, within political unity, ways should have been found of phasing more gradually the merging of the two economies. As it was, the sudden marriage hastened the collapse of the east's outmoded industries, leading to mass unemployment and added costs.

There were several mistakes. The first, which Kohl later admitted, was a lack of prudence. Promising in 1990 that economic unification would involve few hardships, he offered the easterners 'blossoming landscapes'; and when these failed to flower as soon as expected, resentment grew. He told westerners there would be no need for extra direct taxes. But this then made it harder for him to demand more sacrifices; and when he did put up taxes, it greatly contributed to the drop in his popularity in 1992–3. Either he had knowingly lied, for electoral reasons, or he was badly advised by his experts.

A second mistake was monetary. Under the currency union of July 1990, a generous 1–1 rate was chosen for converting Ostmarks into Deutschmarks. This delighted consumers. But the Bundesbank's president, Karl Otto Pöhl, had argued that a 1–1 rate would gravely overprice eastern industry and deter investors; he proposed a 2–1 rate. Kohl overrode him, and a year later Pöhl resigned, claiming that events had proved him right. Certainly the 1–1 rate hastened the collapse of many eastern firms. A third mistake, arguably, was over property ownership (see pp. 451–3). Those whose former property in the east had been confiscated by the GDR could now claim it back, as many did. But this tended to deter investors, for it was often unclear who really owned land or premises. Later the laws were changed, to allow genuine investors precedence over former owners. This helped, but given the slowness and complexity of the German legal system, the whole issue remained an obstacle to economic renewal. It was not entirely clear, however, what other course the Government could have taken.

One of the worst mistakes, not directly the Government's fault, concerned wage levels in the east, which in 1990 were running at on average 40 per cent of those in the west. Unions and employers in the west then agreed that they should be increased gradually to parity by 1996. But productivity rates were in 1994 still only about 50 per cent of western ones. When some engineering firms claimed that recession made it impossible for them to honour the pay deal, the workers responded with a strike, although it put their own jobs at risk; finally matters were saved by a compromise. Unions and bosses, it would seem, were reckless in allowing eastern wages to rise so much faster than productivity (by 1994 they had reached some 80 per cent of the western ones). It would have been wiser economically, if harder politically, to peg them more directly to increase in output. As it is, like the 1–1 currency rate, the policy added to closures and unemployment, and deterred investors.

Much of the GDR's industry was found to be severely antiquated. It lost its assured east European markets, and could seldom compete on free western ones. So there were massive closures, which only in some cases did the Government try to prevent. Or else firms kept going through drastic staff reductions. Industrial output fell by 65 per cent in 1990–1, with a loss of 2 million jobs by 1993, plus 750,000 others in farming. By 1992, open unemployment was at 17 per cent, but training schemes and early retirement disguised a real figure of more like 30 per cent.

The Government chose privatisation as the prime means of salving the economy, and in 1990 it set up the Treuhandanstalt to deal with this. This agency made a slow start: but by the time its mandate ended in December 1994, it had sold off nearly all the 8,000 former State enterprises put into its charge, while others it closed down. Some 2,000 firms, mostly smaller ones, were bought by east Germans, and about 800 by foreigners, with the French in the lead. The bulk went to west Germans. The Treuhand did its work fairly well; it tried to prevent asset-stripping or excessive lay-offs. But many critics argued that it would have been better if the Government had held on to some larger firms for much longer, modernised them itself, then sold them at a higher price. This could have saved jobs. This however was not in the philosophy of the CDU/CSU, which was prepared to give welfare handouts, but not to spend huge sums on the firms themselves.

Under the Marxist ethos of jobs for all, most GDR firms were hugely overstaffed. Under the new free-market ethos, staff now had to be pared right down: this, more than the actual closures, was the main cause of unemployment. Many of these people were given early retirement, or put on official training schemes; the rest received unemployment benefits, at near-to-western levels. And this whole operation has been the largest item in the more than 150 billion DM that the exchequer has paid for the east each year (the rest has gone mostly on new infrastructure, clearing up pollution, etc.). This above all has fuelled the mutual resentment, as Ossis bemoan their plight, and Wessis begrudge having to pay for it.

In 1991, Kohl did eat his words on no extra taxation, by putting up income tax by 7.9 per cent and slapping heavy new charges on telephones. Then in spring 1993, as costs grew, a new 'solidarity pact' for paying for the east was worked out with the SPD: this included short-term borrowing and more stringent future plans. Notably, the *Finanzausgleichgesetz* (see p. 87), whereby richer *Länder* have always helped to pay for poorer ones, had been suspended after reunification but was to be brought back from January 1995. So the richer *Länder*, i.e. the western ones, must now pay more for the east, but for this they get an extra share of national VAT; and the Government is compensated by a special 7 per cent surcharge on income tax. So Wessis *are* now making the extra small sacrifices that most of them can easily afford. Ever since 1990, they have shown no great sign of fraternal generosity towards their re-found brothers in the east, whom they tend to regard as naive, grasping and ungrateful.

Easterners, in their turn, today still resent the way that the west has simply taken over the east as a kind of colony, imposing its own system and standards, without much regard for local feelings. Wessis are seen as arrogant colonisers: but this is not always fair. Thousands of westerners have come to work in the east, in firms, schools or local governments, and many do it in a genuine spirit of public service and are appreciated: the star case is that of Kurt Biedenkopf, the successful and popular Prime Minister of Saxony. But some, it is true, can be very patronising. I shared a taxi in Schwerin with two senior civil servants from the west who said to me, 'These are very simple people here, they have no idea how to run things, so we have to do it.' The driver, no doubt understanding English, looked furious. This kind of Wessi is dubbed 'Besserwessi' (*Besserwisser* means 'smart-aleck' or 'know-all'). At first many Ossis really did believe the Wessis' claim that they were superior, wiser: but today a new Ossi self-respect, even pride, is asserting itself. 'We are actually better than them, in many ways,' said a senior journalist I met in east Berlin. 'We hate the way they try to tell us what life in the GDR was like, or how we wasted forty years.'

It has to be said that the animosity tends to be general, rather than personal. When they meet as individuals, the two sides tend to get on reasonably well, if warily. 'Ossis on the whole are awful – but Berndt in our office, he's fine,' is the kind of remark you might hear. Even so, there is still not much social mixing, even in Berlin where the two sides live so close: Ossis and Wessis visit the other half of the city for theatre, discos, dining-out, or for their work, but they keep to their own circles of friends. 'I go to the Ku'damm area for its Irish pubs, a new culture for me,' said one young east Berliner, 'but my true pals are all in east Berlin. Those Wessis are too snooty.' Even the east–west school exchanges, which started so hopefully after the *Wende*, have now in many cases lapsed. Although the east's school system is now officially transmuted into that of the west, in practice many eastern schools retain their own approach, not exactly Marxist but authoritarian and deductive. This can deter west Berlin parents from helping the mix by going to live in the east. More significant, the old cross-Wall intellectual contacts of the days before and after the *Wende*, when writers and others would feel a mutual fascination and Wessis would feel it a duty to help Ossi culture, have now dropped off; the two sides no longer find each other so interesting. In short, in Germany today, the brief euphoria of the *Wende* has subsided, not so much into hostility as indifference.

While life in the west has changed hardly at all, easterners have seen their world turned upside down. Much is for the better, as they will admit. But they regret the end of the free kindergartens and cheap subsidised basic goods. Some professors are bitter at losing their jobs through having been in the Party. Many officials are out of work, or have to take jobs far below their qualifications: I met a former army colonel who was now a door guard.

Easterners out of jobs have been urged by the Government to start their own little firms (shades of Tebbit's 'Get on yer bike!'). Many have done so, and a few have succeeded well – like the young man I met in Leipzig who has opened a chain of launderettes, a novelty in the east. But very many of these brave ventures fail. Under the old system, initiative was discouraged; easterners are now learning, but it takes time. They may have the technical skills, but they lack market expertise or the western sense of competition; and so high is the the failure rate that the banks, almost all western, are often wary of giving them credit to get started.

A brighter side of the picture is that 2,400 of the Treuhand's sales have been management buy-outs by local staff, and these often work quite well. But most Ossi employees are in firms that are now western-owned. Here in fact they are generally seen as well qualified, reliable and hard-working (the 'lazy Ossi' myth is dying among those who employ them). Yet many feel alienated in this new capitalist world. It is a pity that Bonn did not follow the example of the Czech Republic and other eastern countries, in offering vouchers or workers' shares to staff. This could have given them a greater sense of participation in their country's renewal. As it is, Bonn chose efficiency, selling the firms to the highest bidder. Much of this new investment is positive: but stories circulate of firms that indulge in asset-stripping or dumping, in defiance of Treuhand rules. Another special problem in the east is farming. The big State collectives have now been turned into free cooperatives, or split into little separate farms regained by their pre-GDR owners. This might seem reasonable. But so over-staffed were the collectives that unemployment on the land is today even higher than in the towns: the workforce has dropped from 850,000 to 180,000. And those still at work are being driven mad by the regulations devised in Brussels, a new nightmare world for them.

This general malaise in the east fuelled the rise in 1993–4 of the Party of Democratic Socialism. This was the reformed version of the GDR's old Communist Party, the SED, and had been launched in December 1989 by some moderate Communist leaders, as a bid to keep Socialism alive in a new, more democratic form. In 1990 it did poorly at the polls, for easterners were still on a honeymoon with Bonn. But then, as Kohl's landscapes failed to blossom, so the PDS grew, under its witty, liberal-minded leader, Gregor Gysi. In December 1993, in a *Land* election in Brandenburg, it took 21 per cent of the vote, ahead of the CDU; next July, it reached almost 30 per cent in city elections in Dresden. Then in the federal elections it scored 17 per cent in the east, but only 1 per cent in the west: this gave it an overall figure of 4.4 per cent. Under Germany's complex semi-proportional system, the PDS was able to avoid the 5 per cent barrier (see p. 514) and take 30 seats in the Bundestag, because in three seats it had come first by direct vote, all of them in east Berlin. One of the PDS's new deputies there was the 81-year-old left-wing writer Stefan Heym, an outspoken dissident under the SED regime who had now rallied to the PDS in protest against Kohl's policies.

There were three strands in PDS support. Many of its voters were the former élites and officials of the GDR regime who had now lost their jobs and identity, and felt aggrieved; hence the party's success in Berlin. Some of these people, but not many, remained ideological Communists. More important, easterners of all kinds were expressing their disillusion with Bonn and the west's take-over: extremely few of them wanted a new GDR-style regime, but they shared in a sharp form the general German *Politikverdrossenheit*. So the PDS is a true regional party, unusual in Germany (Bavaria's CSU is almost a part of the CDU), and it has grown from within the east, not been transplanted from the west like the other parties. In Bonn, the rise of the PDS caused some disquiet – was the east returning to Communism? Kohl and his ministers expressed visible distaste when Heym made a sweet, conciliatory maiden speech in the Bundestag: crafty provocation, they called it. And there was evident political motivation behind the fiscal authorities' bid in November to impose heavy arrears of taxes on the PDS (Gysi and his friends went on brief hunger strike, and the matter was then settled by a compromise). But surely Bonn need not have been too anxious. A 17 per cent vote is no landslide, after all. And the PDS is now an ordinary socialist party, little different from the mild ex-Communists now in power in Hungary and Poland. As many observers have suggested, it may even be a valuable vehicle for subsuming the old Communism into normal democracy.

As is often remarked, the mood in the east today is worse than the outward situation merits. Many people recognise this. They are sunk in a strange collective depression, and yet, as the opinion surveys show, they know that the material prospects are improving, even for them individually. Certainly the vast sums spent on the east are now bringing results, as indeed they should. The most pollutant factories and lignite mines have been closed; more than 3,500 miles of roads have been renewed, more than 800 bridges rebuilt, more than 1,400 miles of rail track re-laid; Leipzig especially is a boom city, with smart new shops; ultra-modern factories have been opened, such as Opel's at Eisenach. Even unemployment has begun to drop at last, from a high of 17 per cent to under 15 per cent by early 1995, according to official claims. And surveys reflect a change in opinion. According to *Die Zeit*, pessimism was at its worst in September 1993, when almost half the sample thought the economic situation 'bad'. A year later, some 65 per cent called their own personal situation 'good', and only 6 per cent said it was 'really bad'. Another 1994 poll found 70 per cent believing that things were improving, and only 20 per cent disagreeing.

So why the sense of protest? While those in work are doing well, some of them *very* well, nearly every family has at least one member with no job (including retrainees and the early retired); and although benefits are adequate, the frustration and boredom are infectious. Many people in their forties know they will never work again. The young may be best at adapting to western work-styles: but even the young share the anti-Wessi resentment (a third of PDS voters are under 25). Many older people look with a false nostalgia at the old days, wilfully overlooking all that was bad; and the initial excitement of their new freedom to travel, or to criticise openly, has worn off. They envy the richer west, comparing Dresden, say, with Düsseldorf, whereas the real comparison should be, say, with Krakow or Bratislava. Thanks to all those Deutschmarks, east Germans are well ahead of their eastern neighbours, materially. But Poles or Slovaks have the pride of a real nationhood; Ossis, still not quite identifying with the Federal Republic, feel adrift. The problem, in short, is less economic than psychological.

A solution will take time, maybe a generation, but it will come. Meantime, the morose mood shows various symptoms. One is the amazing fall in the birth-rate, by 60 per cent in four years. In 1989, there were 199,000 live births in the east; in 1993, 80,000. Among the reasons given for this waning desire to have children are the end of free kindergartens, the fear women have that if they become pregnant they will find it harder to get a job, and the new freedom to travel and buy luxury goods, more exciting than the old GDR option of sitting with the kids in a little flat. The marriage rate has also fallen by 60 per cent. Demographic collapses on this scale are said to be unique in the post-war industrial world. The result, if there is no change, will be a severely ageing population.

Another symptom is xenophobia. The problem has often been exaggerated by the media: but it has brought troubled echoes of the Nazi past, and has done little good to Germany's image abroad. In the west, since the 1950s the millions of immigrant *Gastarbeiter* (guest workers) had often been treated with scorn, even ostracism, but seldom with violence; then in the east, after the GDR regime fell, matters were worse (see pp. 443–5). Unused to foreigners, and disoriented by the collapse of Communist discipline, some young people turned to attacking the few coloured immigrants in their midst, also Poles, Romanian gypsies, and others. The incidents grew, to reach a climax in Rostock in August 1992, when mobs of thugs attacked a big hostel for *Asylanten* (asylum seekers). A crowd stood by and cheered; and the local police, untrained in dealing with such riots, took days to get the situation under control. Many of them were clearly in sympathy with the crowd. The Government probably made a mistake in insisting that the east, so unused to non-Germans, should take its share of the huge number of *Asylanten*. Amazingly, only 3 per cent of Germany's 6.8 million foreigners live there.

Then the trouble spread to the west. The huge Turkish population there had generally been left in peace: but in November 1992 neo-Nazi skinheads attacked Turkish families in the little town of Mölln, near Lübeck, set their houses on fire, and killed three people. Many Germans were by now becoming alarmed at the spectre of violent racism, and over three million people joined candlelit protest marches in several cities. Kohl was at first criticised for not taking quicker action against the rioters, but later he did so: the neo-Nazi National Front was outlawed, some of the Rostock rioters were jailed. Then in June 1993 came the worst incident, when five Turks were killed in an arson attack at Solingen, near Cologne. Some local Turks lost their usual sang-froid and went on the rampage. But the threat of racial mayhem was averted: police measures against skinheads were tightened, and gradually the public alarm subsided. Since Solingen, there have been no more major outrages, though smaller incidents have continued. Coloured people travelling alone at night on the Berlin suburban S-Bahn are sometimes attacked, even thrown out of the train. Many are afraid to go out alone at night. And when Coca-Cola transferred its west Berlin factory to the east, the coloured *Gastarbeiter* on its staff refused to go too.

Fears of immigrants taking German jobs helped to fuel the violence. It was significant that the major attack at Rostock was against a hostel for *Asylanten*, who under the liberal asylum laws (see pp. 290–5) had been pouring into Germany in ever greater numbers. In 1992, 438,000 arrived – 75 per cent of all asylum-seekers in the EC. They came above all from Romania, Bulgaria, Turkey and ex-Yugoslavia (and the figure excluded the genuine war refugees from Bosnia and Croatia, to whom Germany, unlike Britain, was also extremely generous). They pleaded political persecution at home, but almost all were in fact coming for economic reasons; and less than 5 per cent were formally granted the right to stay. During the long waits for their cases to be heard, they were put up in hostels at public expense (this cost over 10 billion DM in 1992); and many who lost their appeal then found ways of staying on illegally. Public indignation grew. But to alter the law, a two-thirds majority in Parliament was needed – and the SPD felt that Germany should still keep an open door, as atonement for Nazism.

Finally, after Rostock, the SPD was persuaded to bend to realism and accept a change. Günter Grass left the party in disgust, claiming that Germany's liberal image was sullied. But in 1993 the law was tightened, so as to exclude the 'economic' *Asylanten*: those coming from a list of 'safe' countries with no sign of political persecution (including Romania and Bulgaria) were no longer allowed to claim asylum, and for others the legal procedures were speeded up and the checks on entry reinforced. As a result, the overall total of asylum-seekers fell to 127,000 for 1994; those from Romania, for example, dropped from 12,586 in April 1993 to 784 in December. Some critics argued that the reform was simply pandering to violence, and might encourage the neo-Nazis to strike harder. But racist violence has in fact fallen off since mid-1993, whatever the reasons.

How strong is the extreme-Right in Germany today? Racist feeling has been growing in other countries too, from France and Belgium to Austria: but in Germany it has been the most violent, and causes most anxiety abroad because of the German past. The Republikaner Party, racist but not violent, began to do well in local elections in the early 1990s, scoring 11 per cent in Baden-Württemberg in 1992. But in the federal election of October 1994 it fell back to under 2 per cent, less than in 1990. The change in the asylum law, plus the arson murders, clearly lost it support. However, the Republikaner are not the same as the neo-Nazi thugs. By advocating racist policies, they provide the thugs with a kind of moral alibi: but they claim to repudiate violence. The so-called neo-Nazis consist of small fringe groups, either stuffed with Nazi ideas or just plain hooligans. Their propaganda success at Rostock encouraged them to parade as heros ('*We* act against immigrants, others merely talk!'). But then the Mölln and Solingen murders so shocked the German public, including many Republikaner voters, that today they appear isolated, enfeebled. And although today there is still a pervasive xenophobia, especially in the east, it would be entirely wrong to compare Germany today with Weimar of around 1930, as many ignorant foreigners do. Politically, the country is now far more stable; economically, it is far better off. And the neo-Nazis have no *Führer*. They are disorganised and marginal, a nuisance, but no grave threat.

If foreigners are to become better accepted in Germany, then it must be made simpler legally for them to integrate. Until now, it has been easy to enter the country and settle there, but hard to become a German (see pp. 287–9). Of the country's 6.8 million foreigners (1.9 million of them Turks), many have been born in Germany or lived there many years, yet only some 30,000 win German nationality each year. This is due to the citizenship laws, which derive from what Neal Ascherson has called 'an old-fashioned view of the nation-state as an ethnic community whose "purity" must be preserved'. That is, the laws for becoming a German citizen are based not on residence but blood. The hordes of recent re-settlers from eastern Europe (see p. 294) can automatically get citizenship, so long as they can prove their ethnic German origin. But a Turk or Indian who has spent his life in Berlin cannot. He has to pass all sorts of tests, wait years, and renounce his original nationality.

Foreign *Gastarbeiter* have welfare rights but cannot vote, and they lack the full protection of the law, so they may feel insecure. Recently, the rules for obtaining citizenship have been simplified. But dual nationality, accepted by countries such as Britain, is still barred, and German ethnicity is still the main test. Pressure had come from liberals to ease this distinction. In 1994 the Government did produce some complex proposals whereby foreign children born in Germany could be regarded as German till the age of eighteen, but must then give up other citizenship. For someone to be a German *and* a non-German seems to offend the German sense of tidiness; and although Germany has become a multi-cultural society, the public does not want to admit it. However, the number of foreigners applying for German citizenship has been rising slowly. Some Turks, who are proud to be Turkish but want to be German too, even cheat the law: to get a German passport, they must prove they have renounced their Turkish one, but then they go to a Turkish consulate and get back their original citizenship, and the German authorities are not to know. This happens in west Berlin, where the large Turkish community is today reasonably well accepted. But it is anxious, for its unemployment level has reached 27 per cent, as about 180,000 easterners are commuting to work into west Berlin each day, and have taken many Turkish jobs.

Berlin, that unique, hypnotic city, is today still in an acute phase of transition, as it prepares to be again Germany's capital and struggles to heal the effects of its forty-year division. The two halves are still very different. In the east, plenty of new offices and western boutiques crowd the central Unter den Linden area, and from here the bright new shops percolate up the main avenues, into districts still dreary with run-down tenement blocks and pot-holed roads. Renovation is sure, but slow. People in the east still dress more dully, in clothes that may be new but are out of fashion; and they are slower, more sullen-looking, than the sprightly west Berliners. As I have said, there is not much social mixing. But of course west and east have always been rather different, the west more bourgeois, the east more proletarian, as in London or Paris.

Today, a new mix *is* appearing, of two kinds: Ossis are now working with Wessis in the new federal and municipal offices east of the old Wall, and many young Wessis are choosing the east for their counter-culture or night entertainment scene. This has been a striking development. Kreuzberg (see pp. 44–5) has declined and the 'scene' has been shifting to the east, where rents are cheaper and empty run-down premises more available. There's even a new inverted chic about it, of the kind young Berliners love. The down-at-heel central area known as Scheunenviertel ('barn quarter'), near Friedrichstrasse, is now lively till late with discos, cabarets, way-out bars and art galleries, and sidewalk prostitutes – all of it crowned by an amazing cooperative 'squat' in a huge derelict department store, Tacheles. This acts as an 'alternative' arts centre and night-time forum. This is in the pre-war Jewish quarter, where the huge Synagogue has been elegantly restored and a number of Jewish galleries and restaurants have opened beside it. But few Jews have yet come back to live in the area.

In the central wasteland where the Wall was, Germany's new capital is now being built – after much delay. The decision to move it from Bonn was taken narrowly by the Bundestag in June 1991: but then followed powerful foot-dragging by politicians and civil servants in Bonn, who for personal reasons did not want to move and claimed geo-political reasons why the transfer would be wrong (see pp. 61–3). The Government dithered; and since costs would be huge, recession made matters no easier. Finally, in 1994, it did set a firm target date of 1999 for the transfer of the key centres of power, Parliament and the Chancellor's Office. However, the Bonn lobby had secured a compromise whereby eight ministries would remain indefinitely in Bonn – including the Ministry of Defence. One unspoken reason was a desire to show the world that this new Berlin would not be a military capital, like Hitler's and the Kaisers'.

As I write in spring 1995, work is at last stirring. Richard von Weizsäcker, very pro-Berlin, had already set the ball rolling when as president of the Republic he formally moved from Bonn to the Schloss Bellevue in the Tiergarten, where his successor, Roman Herzog, is today. Now the Reichstag, after being first 'wrapped' by the zany artist Christo in June–July, will be renovated to the designs of Sir Norman

Foster. Nearby, the new Chancellor's Office will be built; and major ministries will follow later, some in the Wilhelmstrasse area where they used to be. Given the cost and timing, there has been a debate on whether to use some of the old GDR buildings, at least for a while: but this is not popular. The giant bronze—glass Palast der Republik, a proud symbol of the GDR which had housed its Parliament, was found in 1990 to be riddled with asbestos and has been closed ever since. The city Senate would like to pull it down. But the PDS want it kept as a memorial to the old regime, and the city does not want to provoke their feelings. So it stays. A revealing saga.

New commercial investment in the city centre was deterred by the shilly-shallying in Bonn and is now behind schedule. However, at the Potsdamer Platz, former teeming hub of the city and then a blitzed wasteland, cranes and bulldozers are now busy on Europe's biggest building site, where Daimler-Benz and Sony are master-minding two vast complexes of offices, shopping-malls, hotels, cinemas and flats, at a cost of 3 billion DM. Along Friedrichstrasse in the east, formerly the city's Oxford Street, a row of upmarket new department stores and office blocks has gone up fast: but the architecture, here and elsewhere in the new Berlin, is being widely criticised as too heavy and conservative – possibly a missed chance to build a very exciting and elegant new city. The ruling Senate under Mayor Diepgen blames Bonn for delays; but the Senate in turn is blamed for a lack of overall vision or a coherent plan for the much-needed new infrastructure. There are too few east—west main roads to bond the city's two halves and uncertainties persist about a plan for a road and rail tunnel beneath the new government centre.

Five years after the Wall's fall, Berlin today is still in a state of hectic change and confusion. Hence it lost out to Sydney in its bid for the 2000 Olympic Games. But the city in time will come through, as the east as a whole will come through. It will again be the brilliant cultural metropolis of central Europe, capital of a nation that has come such a very long way since 1945.

## *A post-war historical survey: ruins to riches*

In the spring and early summer of 1945, after the final surrender, the cities of Germany lay in ruins. They were pervaded by a strange dazed silence and full of the stench of death, for thousands of bodies lay beneath the piles of rubble that took months to shift. More than three million homes had been destroyed. Many districts were without drinkable water. And the Allied occupation forces authorised only the meagrest of rations – not so much out of vindictiveness as because Germany's transport and distribution systems were crippled, and there was a world food shortage too. While the British and American troops had a daily ration of some 4,000 calories, for German civilians it was only 700 and often less – well below the minimum needed for good health. Many workers were thus too weak and under-nourished to be able to do their jobs properly; thousands of people died each week from malnutrition and some others committed suicide. The Germans were literally stunned by the scale of the defeat and desolation. Some of them raged in silent fury at the Allied bombings: but they also awoke as from a trance to face the enormity of their national guilt in permitting Nazism to happen.

This was the famous *Stunde Null*, or Zero Hour, when Germany was at its bleakest point since the end of the Thirty Years War. And it left the Germans with no other choice but slowly and painfully to make an entirely new start. If their history in the fifty years since then has been mainly such a success story, alike politically and economically, most experts are agreed that one of the principal reasons is precisely this: the sheer magnitude both of the Nazi crime and of the military defeat necessitated a radical break with the past and a total rethink of German values and society, in a way that had never happened after 1918. And, after their initial period of paralysed exhaustion and despair, the Germans found the will and the energy to respond to this challenge.

Long before the war ended, the Allies had begun to address themselves to the task of deciding what to do with a defeated Germany. Stalin, Churchill and Roosevelt all toyed at first with the idea of breaking up the former Reich into four or five separate self-governing states, so that Germany could never again become a major power in Europe. But the plan was soon dropped in favour of a partition between the Allies, for a period of military occupation during which the Germans would be 're-democratized'. The borders of these military zones were decided at a conference in London in 1944. The Americans allowed the British to take the industrialised north-west, including the Ruhr, while allocating themselves the more rural southern regions, including Bavaria, Württemberg and Hessen, and the port of Bremen in the north; the French were later given two strips close to their own borders. The Russians took the east-central part of Germany for their zone, which later became the GDR. As for the areas further east, at the Potsdam Conference of August 1945 the Western Allies agreed 'in principle' that the Königsberg area of East Prussia should come under Soviet control and later be annexed by Russia and that 'pending a peace settlement' Poland should administer southern East Prussia and a large area comprising Silesia and most of Pomerania, as far west as the Oder and Neisse rivers. Poland then annexed these areas *de facto* and expelled their German populations (see pp. 23–4). As a result, today's united Germany covers only 75 per cent of the Germany of 1937. As for Berlin, the London Conference of 1944 decided that it should form an island inside the Russian zone, also to be divided into four zones administered by the four Allied Powers.

The Allies had next to decide what to do with the German people, alike the guilty and the less guilty. At the Nuremberg trials of 1945–6, seven Nazi leaders were given lengthy prison sentences and 12 others were condemned to death by hanging. But a harder task than punishing the leaders was the wider one of dealing with the lesser Nazis and trying to work out who had been truly criminal and who had simply obeyed orders or been seduced by propaganda. After 1945 the Western Allies embarked on a general policy of 'de-Nazification' (see pp. 498–9): but this was carried out clumsily and failed to achieve its true purpose. However, another kind of denazification, also known as 're-democratisation', bore much better results. This was the policy of re-educating the Germans in a free way of life after the years of tyranny. In the Western zones, the Allies rapidly found local personalities with good anti-Nazi records to appoint as mayors of cities – notably, Konrad Adenauer in Cologne – while others were selected to run radio stations and newspapers under Allied supervision. The trade unions and former political parties were helped back on to their feet; the most nazified school-teachers were dismissed, but others were retrained in democracy. This enlightened policy was on the whole carried out sensibly, and it laid the foundation of the new Germany of today.

The next question was what to do with the shattered German economy. With millions near to starvation, it was a heavy liability for the Allies in 1945, and their views differed sharply as to what should be done. The US Treasury Secretary, Henry Morgenthau, had argued for a very tough treatment of Germany after its defeat: he wanted not only forced labour and the mass execution of war criminals, but a 'pastoralisation' of the country, with its larger industries closed down or placed under foreign control. For a while both Churchill and Roosevelt looked sympathetically on these ideas. But other influential voices argued that the Morgenthau plan would be counter-productive: 'Such methods do not prevent war, they breed it,' said Henry Stimson. Finally Churchill and Roosevelt threw their weight behind a more moderate policy, closer to the precept that Churchill later quoted in his memoirs, 'In Victory, magnanimity'. It is true that the Western Allies did enforce some reparations during the first post-war years: but these were modest compared with those of the post-1919 period, or with the Russians' exactions in their zone (see p. 371). The more far-sighted Western leaders were aware of the views expressed by Maynard Keynes and others in the 1930s, that the economic severity of the Versailles Treaty had been directly responsible for the rise of Nazism. In all, only about 5 per cent of German industrial plant was dismantled between 1945 and 1949, and then Adenauer, newly elected Chancellor, managed to persuade the Allies to discontinue the policy.

Before long, Krupp, Thyssen and other industrial barons who had worked for Hitler were back in business. The rapidity of this rehabilitation caused some dismay in the West, and today it seems undeniable that as individuals these men were treated too leniently. Yet in a wider sense it is also clear that the Western Allies showed wisdom and foresight in helping Germany's economy to revive rapidly, so that it could play its part in building the new Europe. When the European Recovery Programme (Marshall Aid) was launched by a generous United States in 1948, West Germany was allowed to benefit from it under the same conditions as the countries that had fought against her.

Even more crucial than Marshall Aid in making the recovery possible was West Germany's famous currency reform of June 1948. Until that date, with Hitler's discredited old Reichsmark still the only legal tender, the economy had been limping along on a barter and black-market basis, and inflation was high. A repetition of the terrifying currency collapses of the 1920s seemed on the cards. Then early in 1948 a Bavarian professor of economics, one Ludwig Erhard, was appointed economic director for the Western zones, and with Allied backing he changed the currency. Overnight on June 20 the Reichsmark was abolished and a new Deutschmark introduced. For their main assets, people were given only one DM for ten old ones, and later the rate was reduced to one to fifteen. Of course reactions were mixed. People were dismayed to see their savings virtually obliterated: but they also found that their modest sums of new money had real purchasing power at last. So the black market vanished, as did the hoarding of stocks, and the shops suddenly became full of things to buy. Erhard also set about dismantling the tight system of wage and price controls, food rationing and trade restrictions, that had survived from the Nazi period. It was a gamble, but it paid off. The lifting of controls initially set prices rising fast: but soon they settled down, and before long the West German inflation rate had fallen to well below British and French levels.

Erhard has been described as 'the father of the economic miracle'. Thanks to his bold policies the economy suddenly took wing. Factory production changed to a higher gear, as did the construction industry: 'Everywhere the noise of new buildings going up replaced the deathly silence of the ruins,' reported one observer. After 1948 the Germans energetically set about rebuilding their devastated cities and providing new homes for the homeless and for the refugees pouring in from the East. In a few towns, such as Nuremberg, picturesque old streets were meticulously restored to their original state: but in most cases a modern town centre was implanted in place of the cleared-away ruins.

The currency reform was quickly extended to West Berlin, where it angered the Russians. By now the two halves of Germany were growing steadily apart, for the Russians from the outset in 1945 had begun to impose their own Communist system in their zone, in breach of the Potsdam Agreement which had stipulated that Germany during the occupation period should be treated as one economic entity. On June 24, 1948, the Russians began to blockade Berlin by sealing off all land traffic leading to the West. In its timing this move was a retort to the currency reform; but it also had a more ambitious objective, for Stalin by now was determined to take control of the Western sectors of the city and thus end this 'nuisance' of a hostile enclave within his territory. But he had reckoned without the firmness of the Allied response and the courage of West Berliners in withstanding the siege throughout a long cold winter. The US and British Air forces immediately began their great airlift, and over the next ten months they brought 1.5 million tons of supplies to the beleaguered city. Finally in April 1949 Stalin admitted defeat and lifted the blockade.

The Western Allies had by now come to realise that there was little hope for reaching agreement with the Russians on a united Germany, and so they laid their own plans for introducing normal political life into their zones. They started in 1947 by sanctioning elections for local parliaments in the eleven *Länder* (see p. 33) of Western Germany. Then in 1948 they gave the signal for the setting up of a separate West German state, by proposing that the *Länder* should elect a constituent assembly to draft a federal constitution. This body completed and approved a lengthy document that was entitled not 'Constitution' but 'Basic Law' (*Grundgesetz*) so as to emphasise its 'provisional' character — for Germans still believed that their country before long would be reunited. Today this same *Grundgesetz* is still the constitution. In August 1949 the West Germans went to the polls to elect the lower house (*Bundestag*) of their new federal parliament, and in September the Bundestag chose Konrad Adenauer, the Christian Democrat leader, then aged 73, as the new Republic's first Chancellor. At the same time, Moscow encouraged the East Germans to match these moves. In May 1949 a 'People's Congress' in East Berlin approved its own constitution, and in October the German Democratic Republic was formally proclaimed. The division of Germany was now complete.

The early 1950s were the first heady years of West Germany's 'economic miracle'. Already by 1950 its GNP had climbed back to the pre-war level, and then in 1950–64 it trebled in real money terms. Income per capita almost doubled between 1950 and 1955, as families equipped themselves with TV sets, new clothes and furniture, and the streets filled up with Volkswagen 'Beetles'. Though loosely described as a 'miracle', this sudden recovery was in fact the result of a combination of several factors (see also pp. 104–5). As well as the Erhard reforms, these included the incentive for renewal after so total a defeat, and the German flair for disciplined hard work and thoroughness. Not least, the millions of refugees from the east helped to provide the labour force that industrial expansion needed.

This exodus of Germans from the eastern territories invaded by the Soviet Army took place amid terrible suffering. Overall it was the greatest migratory movement of modern times, and there were several distinct waves of it. First, at the 1945 Potsdam Conference the West had agreed to the Russian demand for the 'transfer' into Germany of the German populations of Hungary, Poland and Czechoslovakia: this involved some 3.5 million people, mostly from the Sudetenland in Bohemia. But, even before this, as the Red Army advanced some 4 million Germans had already fled from their homelands. Then, after the Russians' arrival, most of the remaining 4.5 million Germans were expelled by force from the areas east of the Oder and Neisse rivers that were to be seized from Germany. All in all, in 1944–6 about 8 million Germans were on the move westward, many of them on foot, straggling along weary and underfed, clutching a few precious belongings. Over a million are estimated to have died en route. The world at large tended to feel, understandably, that this suffering even of the innocent was a part of the just price that Germany must pay for Nazism. But many other Germans felt that the evictions were a gross injustice – and some of them still feel that today.

Most of the refugees moved to the West, where they were joined later by other waves of migrants escaping from the GDR, a total that had reached over 3.5 million by 1961. Altogether, some 13 to 14 million Germans from the east settled in West Germany during the years after the war – and their ultimate integration, not easily achieved, was an amazing saga. Initially, as the cities were so ruined, the vast majority of the newcomers were directed to rural areas, where some were billeted on the inhabitants and others were placed in former barracks or hastily constructed huts. So numerous were they that the population of rural Bavaria rose by 30 per cent and that of Schleswig-Holstein by 60 per cent. This influx was not at all well accepted by the local people: far from welcoming the refugees as fellow-Germans in distress, they tended to look on them as tiresome intruders come to crowd their living space and aggravate their food shortages. In Bavaria, newcomers from Silesia were often insultingly dubbed 'Polacken' – a bitter irony for those who had just been expelled from their homes by the Poles!

Gradually the newcomers became accepted and integrated. 'For us,' said an East Prussian I met in a small town near Stuttgart, 'it took about fifteen years before these stuffy Swabians began to accept us. That's why today I have such sympathy for the Turkish immigrant workers.' From the start, the authorities gave the refugees the same rights as other German citizens, and if they had lost all their goods, they were granted compensation. Many of the refugees displayed the kind of tenacity and adaptability that is so often the hallmark of destitute immigrants. Maybe I shall be suspected of personal bias, seeing that my wife's mother came from Silesia and her father from Dresden: but I have always been forcefully impressed by the fact that so high a percentage of the most cultivated, liberal-minded, intelligent and generally sympathetic Germans I met in the 1980s had come from the eastern areas, above all Silesia and Thuringia. Their contribution to the 'economic miracle' was huge.

The post-war economic resurgence was matched by political recovery too, as West Germany's new democratic institutions found their strength and proved their worth. This too was a remarkable success story — especially in the context of the weakness of earlier democratic tradition in Germany. Whereas the Weimar Republic of the 1920s had proved feeble and unstable and so fell an easy victim to Nazism, the post-1949 Bonn regime turned out to be made of far sterner stuff. Some of the reasons for this I have already mentioned. One was the more positive and sensible treatment by the Western victors after 1945; another, the far more horrific defeat leading to a more radical new start. When they awoke from the paralysing trance of the Nazi period, responsible Germans were so appalled at what had been allowed to happen that they took special pains to build a more effective democratic framework and to keep it running smoothly (see pp. 512–15).

Another reason for the greater success of the Bonn regime was that this time the Germans had the good fortune to find a strong *and* wise leader (albeit an elderly father-figure) to guide them through the difficult post-war years. Konrad Adenauer, who had been mayor of Cologne from 1917 to 1933, provided the firm, patriarchal leadership that Germans tend to like: but he showed that this could be combined with democratic government.

Adenauer was also one of Europe's first post-war leaders to champion the new ideal of European unity, for he believed strongly that the best way to prevent a recrudescence of German nationalism was for Germany to find a new identity within a new kind of European framework. He preached this Europeanism to the German people, and won a strongly favourable response. First, in 1951, Germany joined with France, Italy and the Benelux countries in setting up the European Coal and Steel Community. This helped the German coal and steel industries to find their feet again; more important, it was to prove a valuable dress rehearsal for the Common Market. Adenauer then brought West Germany into the North Atlantic Treaty Organization in 1955. At the same time — in the face of understandable opposition from many Germans of all kinds, not only pacifists — he set about creating a new army, the *Bundeswehr*, as well as navy and air force. West Germany was now integrated into the Western camp as a firm and loyal ally. Then in 1957, with the signing of the Treaty of Rome, it became a founder member of what is now the European Union. After de Gaulle returned to power in 1958, he and Adenauer formed a remarkable rapprochement, and this led in 1962 to the signing of the Franco-

German Treaty of Friendship. It was the Chancellor's crowning achievement. After three Franco-German wars in the preceding hundred years, the hatchet was finally buried and this Paris–Bonn entente was henceforth to be the central pivot of the European Community and the foremost guarantor of stability and unity in Western Europe.

At home the federal elections of 1953 and 1957 brought growing majorities for Adenauer's Christian Democratic Union in partnership with its Bavarian sister-party, the Christian Social Union. But by the end of the 1950s the ageing leader had grown steadily more autocratic. He retired in 1963, to be replaced by Ludwig Erhard, who then proved a somewhat ineffectual Chancellor. In 1966, the Social Democratic Party (*Sozialdemokratische Partei Deutschlands*) agreed to enter into a 'grand coalition' with the CDU/CSU under the chancellorship of the conservative Kurt-Georg Kiesinger, and this lasted until the elections of 1969. The coalition was possible because the SPD had shifted centrewards since the 1950s. Under its first post-war leader, Kurt Schumacher, it had adopted a radical stance as a working-class party favouring nationalisation of industry. But this failed to find much favour with a German electorate then in a conservative mood. So, at a crucial congress in 1959 in the Bonn suburb of Bad Godesberg, the party decided to shed its Marxist dogmas and to assume a social-democratic colouring, in favour of the mixed economy. This led to a period of much consensus in German parliamentary politics. Two extremist parties, the neo-Nazi *Sozialistische Reichspartei* and the Communist Party, had been outlawed in the 1950s on constitutional grounds; and although another extreme-right movement, the *Nationaldemokratische Partei* (NPD), made sudden progress in some *Land* elections in the mid-1960s, bringing fears of a rise of neo-Nazism, it soon fell back and lost all its seats. The mass of German voters in those years showed little desire to experiment with new ideas or policies: they were too preoccupied with extending their new-won affluence, in a society that had become noticeably conformist and even complacent – or so it appeared. And yet, outside party politics, in 1967–8 an entirely new kind of challenge appeared quite suddenly. It came from the left-wing students, teachers and others, who began forcefully to question the whole basis of society and even the validity of parliamentary democracy. The university uprisings of that time were to make a strong impact on the German mood and on German politics.

In the elections of 1969 the SPD did so well that it was able to form a left-of-centre government in alliance with the small 'liberal' centre party, the *Freie Demokratische Partei* (FDP). Willy Brandt, a charismatic idealist who had won renown as a sturdy mayor of Berlin during its crisis years of 1958–61, now became the first SPD chancellor and his first priority was foreign affairs. Believing that it was high time that West Germany normalised its relations with the Soviet bloc (and undeterred by the Russian invasion of Czechoslovakia the year before), he launched his famous *Ostpolitik*, a policy of détente with the East. He opened direct talks with Moscow and Warsaw, and in 1970 became the first West German leader to pay an official visit to the GDR. The result was a treaty with the Soviet Union, and then another with Poland, whereby the Federal Republic agreed to recognise the controversial new Polish and East German frontiers, while not ruling out the possibility of German reunification later on. Brandt was angrily accused of a 'sell-out' by the German Right: but the majority of German opinion appeared to be behind him. His efforts paved the way for a new four-power Agreement on Berlin in 1971, whereby the Russians made the concession of finally accepting the validity of West Berlin and the right of the Western Powers to protect it. And in 1972 a treaty between the two Germanies set the stage for a period of discreet rapprochement. Brandt was awarded the Nobel Peace Prize in 1971. His *Ostpolitik* helped to reduce the tensions of the Cold War.

With his domestic reforms, however, Brandt was less successful. When in 1974 it was discovered that a senior official in his office, Günter Guillaume, was an East German spy, Brandt accepted responsibility and resigned. His successor as SPD chancellor was Helmut Schmidt, a hard-headed pragmatic Hamburger on the right wing of his party, who proved a better manager than Brandt and overall the best chancellor since Adenauer. He dealt effectively with the extreme-Left terrorist wave of the mid-1970s, led by the Baader-Meinhof gang. But after the first oil crisis of 1974 he had to face a worsening world economic situation that put strains on Germany's own economy: 1979–82 were bad years, with very low growth, rising unemployment, and inflation at an unusually high level for Germany. The 'miracle' seemed to be finally at an end. Finally in November 1982 the SPD/FDP coalition collapsed and the CDU/CSU returned to power, this time under Helmut Kohl, who had been the CDU's leader since 1973. He proceeded to govern with the FDP, which had switched alliances.

Kohl continued Brandt's *Ostpolitik* and relations with East Germany became steadily closer. This rapprochement was symbolised by the successful visit of Erich Honecker, the GDR leader, to Bonn in September

1987. The debate in 1983 over the implantation on German soil of new American nuclear missiles served to divide the nation sharply, but a degree of consensus was restored in 1987 when Kohl backed the Soviet-American agreement on dismantling these and other missiles. And in the early 1980s the Greens emerged as a new force in party politics, flag-bearers of a new ecology-minded generation that questioned the entire ethos of Germany's hard-working and materialistic post-war society.

And yet, in 1987 Kohl's coalition was re-elected to power. In the late 1980s, West Germany appeared extremely prosperous and stable, almost boringly so. It was concerned with its own internal problems: but its place in Europe seemed settled, unlikely to change. The two Germanies might improve their relations, but reunification remained out of the question. Meanwhile, however, a revolution was gathering pace in eastern Europe, and in 1989 it spilled over into East Germany, bringing down the Honecker regime. Germany was reunited, and its whole structure changed. Later chapters will examine these momentous events. But first we shall look at one of the most distinctive and successful features of post-war Germany: its federal structure.

# 2

# THE REGIONAL PATCHWORK, AN ANCIENT LEGACY

Germany, it is often said, is very diverse, not so much an integrated nation as a patchwork of different *Länder* and of local identities and loyalties. But this can be overstated. Germany's political history as a united country may be no more than 120 years old: but in terms of temperament and life-style, of culture and geography, I am not at all sure that in western Germany the diversity is any greater than, say, in Britain, France or Italy – is a Hamburger really any more different from a Bavarian than a Scot or Geordie from a Londoner, a Norman from a Provençal, or a Torinese from a Sicilian? It is simply that in Germany the differences tend to be more apparent, or to have more expression, because of political factors – the decentralised federal system of government and, especially before 1989, the absence of one big capital city providing a focus.

Although in 1945–89 Germany was divided in two politically between East and West, culturally and geographically the much older and truer division has long been between north and south. Within a very complicated framework, generalisation is hazardous: but in a few sentences one could summarise by saying that south Germany is hilly and wooded, gentle and picturesque, close in spirit to Austria and very much a part of Central Europe, a land of vineyards and half-timbered houses, baroque churches and old castles on hilltops, while the north is a more austere territory of windy plains and harsh winters, turned towards Scandinavia and to Britain and the open sea. The people of the south, notably the Bavarians, also the Rhinelanders to the west, tend to be Catholic; they have a reputation for extrovert jollity and *Gemüt-lichkeit*, they drink beer heavily, also wine, and sing noisily in their taverns, swaying together, arms linked. This is the Germany of the

[29]

tourist brochures. In the north, the people are mostly Protestant, more stolid and reserved but also possibly more reliable and, in the big cities, more liberal and sophisticated. Compare, for example, the difference in temperament between Hamburg's Helmut Schmidt and the late Franz Josef Strauss of Bavaria.

Look more closely, however, and you see that these broad north-versus-south stereotypes can be misleading, for the true pattern is more complex. In the north, for instance, radical Bremen with its open maritime spirit is a world away from its hinterland in conservative lower Saxony. And the two main peoples of the south, Bavarians and Swabians, longtime rivals, form a clear contrast – Bavarians jovial and mostly Catholic, fun-loving but with touches of brashness and even cruelty, Swabians more kindly and gentle, but slow and solemn, marked by a puritanical Protestantism that is generally untypical of the south. Germany, in short, remains a patchwork, where local patriotism and the sense of belonging are often focused on some quite small, distinct area – such as the Hohenlohe in northern Württemberg, or the Emsland along the Dutch border, or the Hunsrück district east of the Moselle, so lovingly detailed in Reitz's aptly titled film *Heimat*.

In many such areas, indeed throughout western Germany, local and regional dialects survive more actively in daily use than is usual in Europe today. In Bavaria, the dialect of the south is quite different from that of the north, Franconia; some cities, notably Berlin and Cologne, retain their own dialects which a visitor from a village even twenty miles away may find hard to follow; and the *Plattdeutsch* of Friesia by the North Sea is more than just a dialect but a distinct language with its own literature. (In the east, Saxony also has its own dialect.) Today all German children in school are taught the official standard language, *Hochdeutsch*, and they can understand it on radio and television. But in many areas, even in cities, local people still use their dialect for daily speech, and in rural areas they often understand it better than *Hochdeutsch*. Politicians need to take account of this. Strauss made his official speeches in *Hochdeutsch*, but in a strong Bavarian accent of which he was proud; when he got down among his rural electorate he was careful, and glad, to talk to them in dialect. Other leaders do the same.

The variations between dialects are great: for example, 'We have seen it' is '*Wir haben es angesehen*' in *Hochdeutsch*, '*Mir hens a'guckt*' in Bavarian, '*Mr hannet gesäh*' in Swabian, and '*Wir haben's angekiekt*' in Berlin. Small wonder that a German visiting another region may find it hard to follow a conversation in a pub or train – and this helps to explain why some Germans still think of distant parts of their country as alien. Or that is how southerners think of northerners, more than vice versa. North Germans nowadays visit the south so often for their holidays that they have come to accept Bavarians or Swabians as at least vaguely familiar and picturesque, however 'different': but for many a southerner the north remains an unknown world, dour and unwelcoming, peopled by taciturn dullards. A Stuttgart charlady, returning from her son's wedding to a girl in Schleswig, spoke to me as if her daughter-in-law were a Mexican or Australian.

This kind of mutual ignorance used to be far stronger in the old days. But in post-war times it has modified considerably, as shifts of population and other factors – television, modern travel and consumerism – have brought cities and regions closer together and more aware of each other. Perhaps it is just because the different parts of the republic now have more frequent contact with each other that they are now more aware of their differences and continue to cherish the regional stereotypes so fondly, endlessly making music-hall jokes about parsimonious Swabians, thigh-slapping Bavarians, stiff-upper-lipped Hamburgers and the like.

First in the early post-war years came the mass influx of German refugees from the east. As we have seen, they had difficulties at first but are now more or less integrated, and they have brought an enriching new diversity to west German cities: Stuttgart alone has 80,000 Silesians or children of Silesians, and is thus far less homogeneously Swabian than in pre-war days. In addition, the boom years of the 1950s and 1960s created a new mobility among West Germans, as new jobs multiplied and engineers, executives and other professional people (but workers more rarely) moved readily across the country in pursuit of well-paid careers, especially to the south, where economic growth has been fastest. Today amid higher unemployment this movement has slowed right down, but it has left decisive change: western cities are far more varied in their German populations than before the war, and on top of this four million immigrants have arrived from Mediterranean countries. Add again the influence of the networked TV news programmes, the uniformity of modern consumer trends, and the fact that most of the shattered city centres were rebuilt in much the same modern style – all these factors have made west German cities grow to resemble each other more and more. Something important has been lost in the process: but at the same time they have each become more internally variegated, and much more open to the outside world. It is indeed remarkable that each *has* managed to retain so much individuality. This is due in part to the degree of autonomy that German cities enjoy under the decentralised system of government.

Federalism is a natural outcome of German history and tradition. Until the unification of 1866–71, Germany was made up of some thirty kingdoms, duchies and free cities, varying in size from tiny fiefs to the empires of Prussia and Bavaria. Even Bismarck did not remove the local rulers, though he did bring them all under the Prussian umbrella: they survived until 1919, when the Weimar Republic instituted a kind of federal system not so very different from today's. Then the Nazi regime greatly strengthened central government at the expense of *Länder*: but this served to discredit centralism in 1945 and was a major argument then for moving back to an even stronger federalism. Also the victorious Allies felt that a decentralised West Germany of medium-sized units would be less powerful and aggressive. In the event, federalism has proved a source of strength and harmony more than a weakness, and on the whole the system works well.

Today the Federal Republic comprises sixteen *Länder*. Five are the newly constituted eastern *Länder* that joined in October 1990 (see p. 432). A sixth is the new united Berlin (and even before 1989 West Berlin was not juridically a part of the Federal Republic but had a special status). The other ten are the *Länder* into which West Germany was divided after the war, and these we shall now examine. They vary greatly in size and population; and their borders have remained unchanged since 1945, save that in 1951 three smallish *Länder* merged to form Baden-Württemberg. Some *Länder* – notably Bavaria, also Hamburg and Bremen – correspond to historic boundaries and have a genuine historical identity. But others are more hybrid, pieced together from small ancient duchies or bits of the Prussian empire – for example, Hessen, Rhineland-Palatinate and North-Rhine-Westphalia. It is thus inevitable that popular sentiments of *Land* identity and patriotism should vary greatly. They are weak in the more artificial *Länder*, where the stronger attachment is often to a city (e.g. Cologne) or to a former royal domain (Badeners feel that they belong to Baden and they resent Württemberg). But the sentiments are strong in Hamburg and Bremen – and uniquely strong in Bavaria, still vividly conscious of its proud past as a kingdom until 1918, and the only part of Germany that still feels itself to be a separate 'nation', rather as Scotland does. This is a matter of cultural identity more than political fact, for juridically Bavaria today is no more autonomous than any other *Land*. But it

## The regional patchwork, an ancient legacy

| Land (German name in brackets: 'E' indicates new east German Land) | Area (sq. km.) | Population | Capital |
|---|---|---|---|
| Baden-Württemberg | 35,751 | 9,619,000 | Stuttgart |
| Bavaria (Bayern) | 70,554 | 11,221,000 | Munich |
| Berlin (partly E) | 883 | 3,410,000 | Berlin |
| Brandenburg (E) | 29,059 | 2,641,000 | Potsdam |
| Bremen | 404 | 674,000 | Bremen |
| Hamburg | 755 | 1,626,000 | Hamburg |
| Hessen | 21,114 | 5,661,000 | Wiesbaden |
| Mecklenburg-West Pomerania (E) (Mecklenburg-Vorpommern) | 23,838 | 1,964,000 | Schwerin |
| Lower Saxony (Niedersachsen) | 47,344 | 7,238,000 | Hanover |
| North-Rhine-Westphalia (Nordrhein-Westfalen) | 34,070 | 17,104,000 | Düsseldorf |
| Rhineland-Palatinate (Rheinland-Pfalz) | 19,849 | 3,702,000 | Mainz |
| Saarland | 2,570 | 1,065,000 | Saarbrücken |
| Saxony (Sachsen) (E) | 18,337 | 4,901,000 | Dresden |
| Saxony-Anhalt (Sachsen-Anhalt) (E) | 20,445 | 2,965,000 | Magdeburg |
| Schleswig-Holstein | 15,729 | 2,595,000 | Kiel |
| Thuringia (Thüringen) (E) | 16,251 | 2,684,000 | Erfurt |

considers itself different. 'I feel Bavarian first, European second and German third,' one Münchner told me, while a senior Bavarian official said, 'Yes, we have had to give up our formal sovereignty since Bismarck's day, but we are still in many ways masters of our own destiny.' Perhaps this is why so very few Bavarians, unlike the Scots, nourish dreams of separatism: they know that they are better off within the Federal Republic. And visiting Scots (Munich is twinned with Edinburgh) often envy Bavarians their degree of practical autonomy.

The federal system leaves the Land governments in charge of many matters, notably education, culture, justice, and some aspects of economic policy. This decentralisation has advantages. It creates a fertile spirit of competition between the Länder, and it brings decision-making closer to the people – certainly an asset in an age when complex bureaucracy, the world over, has been tending to make government more remote and impersonal. Germany's system is frequently admired and envied, and several of her European partners – Italy, Spain and now even France — have been taking steps in her direction by devolving some power to their regions. But federalism can have drawbacks too; and one, in the case of Germany in the period 1949–89, has been the lack of a proper capital. Bonn, the seat of government but not a large town, has never really fulfilled that role. After unification in October 1990, Berlin was formally made the capital again: then in June 1991 the Bundestag decided by a narrow majority that the Government itself should be transferred there in due course.

### The main cities

Population, 1990, in thousands. NB: these are the populations of the municipality in each case: that of the conurbation is often much larger.

| | | | |
|---|---|---|---|
| Berlin | 3,410 | Düsseldorf | 570 |
| Hamburg | 1,580 | Leipzig | 562 |
| Munich (München) | 1,291 | Stuttgart | 559 |
| Cologne (Köln) | 965 | Duisburg | 540 |
| Essen | 620 | Bremen | 530 |
| Frankfurt | 617 | Dresden | 516 |
| Dortmund | 590 | Hanover (Hannover) | 500 |

The four largest German cities put together, with their suburbs, would be smaller than greater London or greater Paris. Even when it was capital of a unified Germany, in 1866–1945, Berlin never dominated the nation to the same degree as London or Paris. Then in 1949–89 West Germany had several rival cities of roughly equal importance: West Berlin (population 2 million) was equalled by Hamburg and Munich, with Frankfurt close behind, followed by Cologne, Düsseldorf, Stuttgart, Bremen and Hanover (the Ruhr cities, though large, have less influence). Many activities that in Britain or France are centred on the capital are in Germany divided among various towns, each with its own forte. Thus the head offices of the big banks are in Frankfurt; the employers' federation is in Cologne, the trade union federation in Düsseldorf, the film industry in Munich and Berlin; the big weekly magazines, like *Stern, Spiegel* and *Die Zeit* are edited in Hamburg; the second national TV network is run from Mainz, the principal art dealers are in Cologne, the publishing industry is in half a dozen cities, the Goethe Institut (equivalent of the British Council) operates from Munich, capital also for the fashion and high-society worlds; the main consumer defence body is in Berlin . . . and so on. This is not to forget the major federal institutions that have deliberately been spread around the country: the Constitutional Court in Karlsruhe, the Bundesbank in Frankfurt, the employment offices in Nuremberg, and others.

Even if Berlin now assumes a greater role, this pattern may not change so very much, for German decentralisation has deep roots. And the dispersion has some advantages. Towns are in healthy rivalry, especially for cultural life; and the larger cities, many of them *Land* capitals, have more autonomy and often more self-confidence than their British or French equivalents, and can exert more influence on national life. The seven or eight major cities and their rival merits or defects are inexhaustible topics of lively conversation at parties, and many professional people spend much time travelling between one and another; or they live first in one for a few years, then another. But, as there has been no one city that sets a standard and provides a magnet and focus, may not the result be to make all Germany a little provincial? Munich, which likes to call itself '*Weltstadt mit Herz*' (a world city with warmth and soul), is also dubbed '*das Millionendorf*' (the village of more than a million people). It is still too soon to tell whether Berlin will now provide the standard-setting focus that might diminish provincialism, and what the effects of that might be. First, let us look more closely at this new united Berlin, and at the other main cities.

## West Berlin, 1945–89: the buoyant survivor

For more than forty years after the war, West Berlin's situation was highly abnormal. Isolated 120 miles inside East German territory, it depended heavily on financial support from Bonn and was still nominally under Allied military rule. But by the early 1970s access to and along the corridors to the West had become easy, apart from some queuing at checkpoints. As for the Wall that after 1961 divided the city, West Berliners grew so used to it that they hardly noticed it. Their daily life was normal and they lived in a spread-out city with plenty of green space, woods and lakes, far less claustrophobic than its image abroad.

Despite its isolation, West Berlin played a full part in the life of West Germany and had a major cultural role; living standards were just as high as over in the West. Although no longer Germany's capital, it managed to retain some of its old capital-city flavour, quick, mercurial, unconventional, with a society rather more informal, less conformist and materialistic, than in the Federal Republic – one reason why so many young people were attracted to come and live in a town that became the leading German centre of the artistic avant-garde and the 'alternative' scene, a place of cultural innovation, of social mix, sometimes of violence – 'Berlin', it was said, 'lets it all hang out.'

The years after the war were extremely difficult ones. In 1945 Berlin was given a special status and placed under the joint authority of the four Allied Powers, each with its own military sector. But it soon became clear that the aim of the Russians was to gain political control of the whole city. After the failure of their blockade in 1948–9, their pressure continued during the 1950s, and in 1958 Khrushchev issued an ultimatum for the Western Powers to leave the city: but they stood firm. Then in 1958, to halt the growing flight of refugees to the West, the Wall was built that sealed the city in two (see p. 46). Not only were East Berliners now denied access to the West, but West Berliners were no longer able to visit friends and relatives in the East, and many families were severed for years. The 1960s were a sad and lonely time for West Berlin, when it needed all the morale-boosting it could get – it was in this spirit that President Kennedy in June 1963 proclaimed from the balcony of the Rathaus, 'All free men, wherever they may live, are citizens of Berlin. And therefore, as a free man, I take pride in the words, "*Ich bin ein Berliner*."'

After Willy Brandt began to develop his *Ostpolitik* in the late 1960s, a period of détente emerged. In 1971 the three Western Powers succeeded in persuading the Soviet Union to sign a treaty with them that did not alter West Berlin's basic legal status but did greatly alleviate its general situation, for the Russians now formally acknowledged the rights of the Western Powers in the city and agreed to accept its close ties with the Federal Republic; travel between Berlin and the West was to be simplified and guaranteed, and West Berliners were again to be allowed to visit the GDR and East Berlin. This agreement held good, and by strengthening Berliners' feelings of security it proved something of a turning point. Companies gradually became readier to invest in the city, and individuals more willing to settle there. Even so, until 1989 Berlin was to remain an anomaly, caught in the time-warp of 1945 conquest and occupation, the most vivid symbol of the world's division into two ideological blocs.

One obvious aspect of this was the role of the Western Allied forces. Before 1989 there were some 12,000 of them, each in their own sector: 6,000 Americans in the south, 3,000 French to the north – and 3,000 British in the central zone, using as their headquarters the Nazis' pompous old Sport forum in Charlottenburg, right next to the 1936 Olympic stadium and still decked out with Hitlerian nude strength-through-joy sculptures. Legally the Allies were still in Berlin as 'occupiers' under the 1944–5 agreements: in practice their main role was to protect the city, which under those agreements could have no defence force of its own. The protection was mainly psychological, for the surrounding Warsaw Pact forces could have mopped up the city in a few hours if they chose: but that would have started a war. And the Allies scrupulously showed their presence, as a reminder to the Russians: they held a big annual parade in the Tiergarten, near the Wall, and they would go on regular patrols in the eastern sector, as they had a right to do. The Allies of course left the running of the city to its elected government and mayor, and they usually avoided flaunting their occupying status. But they preserved the protocol of their rights.

The Bonn Government paid in full the cost of the Allied forces (some 1.4 billion DM a year by 1989) and it warmly supported their protective presence, as did both the CDU and SPD in Berlin, as well as the vast majority of Berliners, especially older ones who still gratefully remembered the airlift. However, a vocal minority from the younger generation came to resent the Allies. The Alternative List group in the Senate, including the Greens, wanted West Berlin to be neutralised and demilitarised – 'It's an old-style military colony, worse than India under the Raj,' one Green lawyer told me. And some other Berliners, while glad of the Allies' presence, none the less felt that they sometimes exercised their rights too high-handedly. This became quite an issue. For example, in 1984, when the British Army began to build a new firing-range in the quiet woodland suburb of Gatow, local residents discovered that the noise levels might be up to five times the legal limit; unable to appeal to any local court, they took their case to the High Court in London where they sued the Ministry of Defence, but without success. General Gordon Lennox, the British Commander in Berlin, pleaded: 'I am the rightful successor of Doenitz, the last Chancellor of the Third Reich, and I have legal immunity.' Berliners were not impressed with his tact.

The Allies' reserve powers were certainly huge. Of the 6,000 or so military rules that were imposed when Berlin was conquered in 1945, few were ever formally revoked. The Allies, if they wished, could still censor Berliners' mail, tap their telephones, or jail anyone who criticised them (one left-wing paper was fined for printing 'Reagan go home' stickers). Firearms were not permitted, nor even knives. The death penalty, which no longer existed in the Federal Republic, was still in force. Once when I was dining with a mild Berlin housewife (a CDU supporter), she went into her kitchen and returned with a carving-knife: 'For owning this, I could be shot at dawn.' Although the numerous draconian laws were very seldom enforced, their continuing existence irritated many Berliners, who did not like to be reminded of their 'occupied' status. Sensitive to this, the Allies did finally lift some of the rules, including one allowing the death penalty for children. But they argued that for them to alter their legal position in Berlin too blatantly would provide the Soviet Union with an alibi for causing difficulties – something the Allies wanted above all to avoid.

This also explains why West Berlin was never made fully part of the Federal Republic until unification. 'The Russians and East Germans have cheated', explained an official in Bonn, 'by integrating East Berlin totally into the GDR and making it the capital. This is contrary to the 1944–5 agreements which are still in force and lay down that Berlin is a single unit. But if the Russians cheat, that is no reason why we should too. Berlin is still vulnerable, so we should avoid any provocation.' In the meantime West Berlin had no sovereignty and belonged to no one. It had a peculiar role in Bonn, for the deputies it sent to the Bundestag were not directly elected but mandated by the Berlin Parliament, and they could not take part in votes in Bonn. West Berlin citizens had special passports and were not called up for military service. Lufthansa and the other West German airlines did not fly to Berlin, which was served exclusively by Allied airlines: one reason was that the Allies wanted to retain their rights of being guarantors of the air corridors.

In most other respects, however, West Berlin became fully a part of West Germany. It became the home of over sixty federal institutions, and even the President of the Republic retained an official residence there, the Schloss Bellevue. The city was governed as a *Land* on its own, much like Hamburg, with a Parliament that elected a Senate, and a governing mayor who was on a par with the prime ministers of the other *Länder*. The SPD was the ruling party until 1981 (Brandt was mayor in 1957–66). Then the CDU took power under Richard von Weizsäcker, who later became Federal President. He was succeeded in Berlin in 1984 by Eberhard Diepgen, also CDU, who has been mayor of the united city since 1990.

The sense of insecurity in the post-war decades was fuelled by fears that this city cut off from its natural hinterland could not survive economically. Just after the war several major firms, notably Siemens and AEG, moved their headquarters to West Germany, leaving behind only their manufacturing plant, or parts of it. German companies were reluctant to invest in Berlin, so the city failed to share fully in the *Wirtschaftswunder*. It came to depend heavily on subsidies from Bonn – 'Without these', I was told by one senator in 1985, 'I think West Berlin would have collapsed in the fifties or sixties. Before the war, more than half of its revenue came from its functions as capital. Now it has to rely largely on industry – in fact it is still the leading industrial town in Germany, in terms of jobs.' In the 1980s just over 50 per cent of the city's annual budget, which in 1989 totalled 27 million DM, was coming from subsidies and other aid from the Federal Republic.

For some years these inducements had no great effect. But matters began to improve after the 1971 agreement, which gave renewed confidence in West Berlin's future both to its own citizens and to outside investors. Whereas in the 1960s the number of industrial enterprises had dropped by a third, in 1981–7 some 2,000 new firms were set up, 200 of them in high-technology, and in 1984 for the first time for many years more manufacturing jobs were created than lost. Nixdorf, the dynamic computer firm (today owned by Siemens), had set up a plant with 6,000 jobs. In the same year the city's annual growth rate (2.9 per cent) was ahead of that of the Federal Republic.

By the 1980s West Berlin's mood was more optimistic than at any time since the war. It seemed to have survived, by ingenuity, patience and persistence, and had come to terms with its abnormal situation. But the demographic situation, though improved, remained preoccupying. In the early post-war decades there had been a steady emigration, especially of the youthful and ambitious, who felt that long-term prospects were brighter in the Federal Republic. West Berlin's population, 2.1 million in 1949, was then swollen artificially by the refugees from the GDR and had reached 2.3 million by the time the Wall was built: but after this it fell steadily to 1,960,000 in 1986 (East Berlin's population was then 1,160,000, and the whole city before the war had 4,300,000 people). The net emigration had come to a halt: but the population was not being replenished by arrivals from the rural hinterland, as is usual in big cities, and there were more deaths than births each year, owing to the low birth-rate. It was an ageing city: the over-65s accounted for 23 per cent of the population, against a federal average of 15 per cent.

The Bonn Government sought to remedy this situation through inducements for people of working age to stay or settle. Personal income tax was 30 per cent lower than in the Federal Republic; and an 8 per cent bonus on all wages served to push incomes to a level 4 per cent above the federal average. So this was anything but a poor city. The effect of these inducements has been hard to judge. Probably they did less to reduce the population drift than the improved climate since 1971, plus the fact that the absence of military service had enticed some 20,000 young draft-dodgers from the Federal Republic. It was also the high birth-rate among the Turkish immigrant community of some 120,000 that kept the population stable. At any event, whereas until 1985 some 15,000 more Germans each year were leaving the city than arriving in it, in 1986 for the first time since the Wall the German population (Turks apart) actually increased – by some 16,000. Could the main reason for the change have been psychological? It did seem that ordinary middle-class families were at last becoming more prepared to return or settle.

Another inducement for people to settle came via the huge subsidies spent on the city's high-quality cultural life. The Berlin Philharmonic Orchestra under the late Herbert von Karajan, and the Schaubühne theatre when it was directed by Peter Stein, have both been world leaders in their fields, and both have been generously funded. Culture was seen as a means of making Berlin life pleasanter, and also of encouraging trade through promoting the city's image: the large summer arts festival was the brainchild of the Senator for the Economy. And West Berlin's lavish cultural celebrations of the city's 750th birthday, in 1987, attended by Reagan, Queen Elizabeth and Mitterrand, amongst others, cost 220 million DM of which Bonn paid 60 per cent.

Nature, too, helped to make West Berliners' years of isolation much more endurable, and so did the city's wide boundaries. This walled-in city was in fact a place of much spaciousness, of big lakes and rural greenery, and was thus far less tightly claustrophobic than many foreigners imagined. First, Berlin's nineteenth-century expansion had followed a generous grid pattern of broad streets and avenues: in this respect it is truly a city of northern Europe. And the loss of over a quarter of its pre-1939 population had the incidental advantage of providing even greater elbow-room. Secondly, the 1945 division of the city had fortunately preserved its existing broad external boundaries. In the western outskirts, around Spandau, Gatow and Wannsee, you find not only great forests and lakes where Berliners go bathing and sailing, but pastoral woodlands and gentle landscapes with meadows and cottages – you might almost be in Constable's Suffolk. Of all west German registered pleasure-boats, no fewer than half are moored in Berlin. And in the tiny village of Lübars, on the northern edge, in 1985 I visited a quaint old pub amid farmland, right by the Wall with its stern watchtowers. West Berlin's borders comprise scores of small farms.

In most material matters except basic access (and sewage disposal), West Berlin did manage to avoid dependence on the enveloping GDR. But this was not so easy in the case of local rail transport, something of an anomaly. Berlin's complex U-Bahn (metro) system was sliced in two when the city was divided: but one Western line continued to transit under East Berlin, passing through ghost stations (most have today been reopened) on its way from Kreuzberg to Wedding via the Friedrichstrasse entry-point in the east. A more serious problem was posed by the above-ground suburban railway network, the S-Bahn; and the wrangles over this typified the legal absurdities of Berlin's situation. As the S-Bahn belonged not to the city (like the U-Bahn) but to the former German State Railways, the Reichsbahn, the Allies after the war did not allow West Berlin to take over its 110 miles of track in the West. Instead the entire network continued to be operated by the GDR, which had inherited the parts of the Reichsbahn in eastern Germany. But this was hardly very practical. And after 1961, to give vent to their fury about the building of the Wall, the citizens of West Berlin began a spontaneous boycott of the S-Bahn. They were encouraged by the Senate, which laid on special parallel bus lines. So the GDR lost most of its Western revenue from the S-Bahn, whose stations and track became more and more decrepit. Finally, West Berlin acquired its share of the S-Bahn in 1983. Some of the old *art nouveau* stations, much dilapidated, have since been restored to their original nineteenth-century splendour.

The old pre-war heart of the city, where imperial palaces, ministries and great cultural monuments once lined the broad Unter den Linden, was nearly all of it over in East Berlin, across the Wall – another world. Right up until 1989, this central area was an odd mixture of ghost town and grandiose modern capital. The GDR regime had meticulously restored some of the grandest of the old bomb-damaged buildings, including the State Opera House, the Protestant Cathedral and the Pergamon Museum (but the Royal Palace it demolished); and beside them it built some massive new edifices, as symbols of its assertive ambitions as a modern state – notably the towering white rectangle of the Foreign Ministry, and the Palace of the Republic with its gleaming façade of bronze-coloured glass. Today this area round the Unter den Linden and the Marx-Engels-Platz, spacious and monumental if somewhat severe, certainly *looks* more like a dignified capital city than the colourful, messy centre of west Berlin. The huge Alexanderplatz was also rebuilt by the GDR after the war, as East Berlin's main shopping and entertainment centre, hideous but lively – a wide modern piazza with splashing fountain and a curious 'international clock'. Beside it is the 365-metre Television Tower, a dominant landmark with a globe-shaped revolving observation platform, where East Berliners used to go to gaze wistfully at the lights of the forbidden Ku'damm.

Until the 750th anniversary in 1987 (East Berlin celebrated this quite separately, but very grandly), even this historic central part of the city contained much grimy dereliction. But this was then put to rights in some places, just in time for the festivities. The banks of the Spree were neatly grassed over; a new show quarter was built around the Nikolaikirche, with fancy boutiques and cafés that would not disgrace Düsseldorf; and the paved, traffic-free Platz der Akademie, with its colonnaded State theatre and two mighty churches, was made to look most elegant. A few nearby residential streets at last had their façades decently restored. But most others were left to look horribly woebegone, all over this hideously run-down city, victims less of the bombing than of long post-war neglect.

As for west Berlin, despite its current prosperity it has always been something of a jumble, alike physically and socially. Of course it has plenty of well-to-do residential districts with big villas set in gardens, such as Dahlem and Grunewald. But much of the rest of the city still looks a bit tatty (if far less so than the east). This is not surprising, for it was worse bombed than any others except Dresden and maybe Cologne, and was then rebuilt under very difficult conditions, since most of the heavy construction material had to be specially imported from the west.

There is little left physically in west Berlin that suggests a great capital city, apart from the Reichstag, Charlottenburg Palace and a few other scattered buildings. The main focus since the war has been the Kurfürstendamm, a broad avenue of cafés and hotels, shops and cinemas, which was previously the 'West End' entertainment area, well away from the true centre. This Ku'damm (as Berliners call it) and the streets around it are still today the main amusement and shopping district, offering the brash but intriguing spectacle of neon-lit signs, pop-art street decorations and pleasure-bent motley crowds. The grace and dignity of a capital, or of a town like Munich, are markedly absent. And yet, there is something in the air, something hard to define, that still sets Berlin apart . . . You notice it at once, coming from Munich or Hamburg, cities more handsome but somehow less metropolitan. Berlin stays open very late, more so than most north European towns: at 2 a.m. the Ku'damm is thick with crowds and cars, its cafés and eateries full. And all day long the people on the main boulevards are a strange mixture, relatively few of them in normal city dress – coxcomb punks and camera-clutching tourists, bohemian students and trendy mannequins, and wizened old bourgeois ladies in flower-pot hats. Not to mention the more recent influx of drab east Germans, raffish Poles and Romanian gypsies.

Talk to native Berliners, and you find that they preserve something of that sharp, sardonic, restless big-capital-city quality that gives them, temperamentally, more in common with a Parisian or New Yorker than, say, with a Hamburger. Gordon Craig in *The Germans* has summed it up historically: 'Berliners tended to be energetic, ebullient, colourful in their speech, quick at repartee . . . and in time of trouble courageous. They gave the impression of being in perpetual motion.' Visitors are often impressed by Berliners' facility with words, their sense of irony and their quickness of response. In a theatre, they laugh at the jokes more rapidly than in other cities; and I have the impression, though I have never checked, that the traffic-lights change more frequently than elsewhere, perhaps because West Berlin pedestrians would never accept to wait patiently for green like most other Germans! As for their droll sense of humour, this is noticeable in the nicknames they have given to many of their post-war buildings. Thus the lop-sided Kongresshalle in the Tiergarten is known as 'the Pregnant Oyster', or else as 'Jimmy Carter's Grin' because of its façade like an open mouth. And that famous landmark, the gaunt Memorial Church at the top of the Ku'damm, preserved as a ruin, is 'the gaping Tooth', while the new church buildings beside it are 'the Powder Box' and 'the Lipstick Tube'.

Unlike Munich, post-war West Berlin has had little of a smart *Schickeria* set. New arrivals soon discover that the upper ranks of society are remarkably fluid, informal and uncompartmentalised. 'If I go to a big party,' said one businessman, 'I can expect to find not only my own colleagues but actresses, avant-garde sculptors, Allied officers, CDU politicians ... That's common in London, but much less so in Germany.' One explanation is that Berlin for so long has been a melting pot with a tradition of assimilating all sorts; or else that Berliners, despite their differing views and the usual Left/Right tensions, still feel an underlying sense of solidarity, born of the hard years. When I told one CDU senator that I was going to visit the hippy leader of an 'alternative' commune, the UFA-Fabrik, he said, 'Ah yes, my good friend Yupi – give him my regards.' Though the alternative scene is strongest in the Kreuzberg district (see p. 45), it seeps out across the rest of the city too, so that in many areas you see bohemian-looking people (and also a number of sad, broken-looking older ones, shuffling along, survivors of the 1940s nightmares). Values in West Berlin are less materialistic than in the Federal Republic. There is a pleasantly unconventional ambience, noticeable in the many cheerfully informal and arty *Kneipen* (pubs).

Berlin also remains Germany's gay capital, a role it has held since the last century (except under the Nazis, who persecuted homosexuals). A leading figure in this world is the film-maker who calls himself Rosa von Praunheim (see p. 343): he has depicted it vividly in his film about American gays and transvestites in West Berlin, *City of Lost Souls*, and in another about AIDS in the city, *Arses on Fire*. I met him when he was preparing a festival to raise money for Berlin's estimated 20,000 AIDS victims: 'The gay scene has developed a lot, though it's still far smaller and duller than in New York, where I used to live. But I don't care much for the social round of Berlin's sub-culture. As in Munich, there's a lot of false glamour here – a phoney anti-elegant punk glamour, just as Munich has a phoney elegant glamour. Young people come here from other cities, seeking something they don't really find.'

But some perhaps do find it. The alternative, avant-garde and pop scenes, ever diffuse and kaleidoscopic, are much larger and more creative than in any other German cities, though less so than in New York or maybe London. West Berlin is indisputably Europe's rock capital, with over 1,000 groups, some of them officially funded. It also has countless little way-out art galleries, some struggling fringe theatres, innumerable 'happenings' of all sorts, and a remarkable modern art centre in Kreuzberg, the Haus Bethanien, housed in a gigantic neo-Catillian ex-hospital beside the former Wall.

There are reckoned to be over 100,000 people attached to West Berlin's various sub-cultures, living on the margins of 'normal' society –

idealists trying to build an alternative economy around small communes and cooperatives; bohemian artists and intellectuals; punks, drop-outs, drug-addicts and other ne'er-do-wells. The majority have come to Berlin from elsewhere. Some have been drawn by its tradition of permissiveness and experiment, or by the 'glamour' von Praunheim spoke of, or (hitherto) by the chance to avoid military service, or by the chance of finding cheap, semi-derelict housing. Together these factors had a multiplier effect, drawing others in turn, especially to Kreuzberg, which the 'alternative' scene made its citadel. This is a sizeable central district close to the former Wall, full of old tenement blocks and other mixed turn-of-the-century housing. It used to be very run-down but is now being smartened up (see p. 48). In the 1960s Turkish immigrant workers settled here in large numbers with their families, and they now make up 25 per cent of the population. They co-exist easily with the 'alternatives' (see pp. 282–3).

An abandoned factory, known as Mehringhof, was in the 1970s taken over by a network of some thirty small cooperatives of all kinds and has been dubbed 'the Alternative Rathaus'. It has vegetarian stores, a bicycle shop, a sort-of theatre, a sort-of publishing house, a kindergarten run by parents. This is one focal point of a varied Kreuzberg scene that is rich in romantic squalor and quirky self-expression. Provocative graffiti abound – *'Raus mit dem Schweine-Schwanz System'* (away with the swinish penis system) scrawled by feminists at the entrance to an old ballroom offering tango and swing sessions; slogans in support of Palestine and extreme-Left terrorists daubed on the doorways of fancy new blocks of expensive flats beside a tree-lined canal. Blackened bomb-scarred buildings stand next to bright pop-art façades newly painted by squatters. Turkish women in scarves squat on the steps of a neo-Byzantine church. Girls bring their babies and knitting into casual bistros. Nearby, sinister black-jacketed punks hang out around the Kottbusser Tor, while drugged weirdies haunt the night-bars of the Oranienstrasse.

In the late 1970s the presence of so much empty housing enticed squatters to descend in force on Kreuzberg and some other areas (see pp. 552–6). When the police began to evict them, their cause was backed by violent extremist groups who came from as far afield as Holland. There were riots and pitched battles, and window-smashing, car-upturning raids on the Ku'damm area. All this gave the city bad publicity, just when it was trying so hard to attract new business. Finally in 1981–2 the crisis was resolved: the squatters were removed, or legalised and allowed to stay, and the fanatics departed. Calm returned: this was a major reason for the surge of new investment after 1983. And on my own visits to Berlin in 1985–7 I found political tensions very mild. 'We may not care for the *Alternative*,' said one CDU politician, 'but, so long as they are not violent, we recognise that they add spice and colour to the city's life and thus are good for tourism.' On the Ku'damm is a new Beuys-like sculpture of barricades and paving-stones, erected as an 'anti-capitalist' memorial to the squatters' riots of 1981. And who sponsored the artist and placed his work there? The same CDU Senate that had suppressed the riots! Protest no longer comes easy when the hand that feeds you seems to enjoy being bitten.

West Berliners themselves grew used to the Wall, and except for the few thousand who lived close to it, they seldom even noticed it. But it haunted the consciousness of visitors to the city, and remained Europe's most powerful visual symbol of the post-war ideological struggle and the sufferings it caused. Yet though horrifying in what it stood for, the Wall was nothing special to look at. Only twelve feet high, made of whitish concrete topped not with barbed wire but with a concrete bulge affording no grip, it curved and zigzagged through the heart of the city and all around its south and western edges, following the old ward boundaries. In Kreuzberg, unknown artists daubed it with psychedelic frescos, and everywhere along the western side it became inscribed with graffiti in various languages, political, comic or erotic. 'What are you gawping at, haven't you seen a wall before?' and 'Darling, we love each other – why worry about the Wall?' were two of my favourites. In central Berlin the Wall became a major tourist attraction. From observation platforms you could peer over at daily life in the East – same people, same language, same buildings, same city, yet a totally alien world, just one hundred metres away.

Here and there, little crosses were erected – and still stand today – as sad memorials to those shot dead while trying to escape. At the Bernauerstrasse in Wedding, the 1945 demarcation line was drawn down the middle of the street. When in August 1961 militiamen began to build the Wall there, they bricked up the ground-floor doors and windows of the houses on the east side, but a few people managed to jump to freedom from upper floors. One who died in the process was Olga Segler, aged 80, whose cross now stands there.

Next to the now-demolished Checkpoint Charlie, in Kreuzberg, there is a fascinating little privately run museum devoted to the history of post-war Berlin, to the Wall and the various escapes and attempted escapes. It includes souvenirs and documents relating to getaways by tunnelling, by balloon, by diving machine, and in tiny cars or in suitcases fitted together. The most extraordinary story is of a young man in West Berlin whom the building of the Wall had separated from his wife, an East Berliner. She was not allowed to join him. But in West Berlin he managed to find a girl who looked very similar; so he courted her and persuaded her to come with him to the East on a day trip. Here he seized her identity papers, and then hurried round to his wife and easily brought her with him to the West. The poor robbed girl went to the East German police, but she could not prove her identity, and they refused to believe her story. She spent two months in jail and was released only with the help of Western Press publicity. The young man was then put on trial in West Berlin and given seven months in prison for 'damaging human freedom'. But he had won his wife back, the other girl too was free, so all lived happily. Was his venture morally justified? Maybe it was.

The wide vacant area close to the Wall on the west side, running from Checkpoint Charlie to the Reichstag, was until 1989 perhaps the most haunting and disturbing urban landscape in Europe. Before the war it had been the very core of the teeming city: but the Potsdamer Platz, formerly Berlin's Piccadilly Circus, was now just an empty zone dissected by the Wall. The whole area on the west had become a strange lunar landscape, partly pure wasteland, partly a chaos of shacks, dumps and parking lots – and so in a way it still is today, as it awaits redevelopment (see p. 57), though the removal of the Wall has now made it far less sinister, and far busier. Here and there a few old buildings survive as ruins, such as the jagged façade of the former Anhalter railway terminus. Eastwards there stretches a messy jumble, enlivened here and there by giant brightly coloured pop-art murals on blind walls (a Berlin speciality). The skyscraper of the Axel Springer group, built defiantly in 1959 as a beacon of 'freedom' (see p. 364), towers where the Wall was. Close by, cheek by jowl, are: (*a*) the former torture chamber of the Gestapo, now excavated and made into a memorial museum; (*b*) the lovely palace that Martin Gropius built in the happy 1860s, now restored as a modern art centre; and (*c*) the old Prussian Parliament building, looming up just across the old border. 'Here, encapsulated in a hundred square metres, you have the whole history of modern Germany,' said one Berliner.

One small sector just west of the Potsdamer Platz was, it is true, grandiosely replanned in the 1960s and endowed with major new cultural buildings: here are the National Library and Philharmonic Hall (1963), both designed by Sharoun, and the National Gallery (1968), the work of Mies van der Rohe. Why, then, was the rest of the area left unrenovated for so long? Berliners, it was felt, would not want to live or work so close to the Wall; and some bombed spaces had belonged to Jewish families long departed who might yet want to stake a claim. Also hopes lingered – now fulfilled – of a reunified city that could be replanned as one. But even before 1989 some large-scale renewal had begun in western Kreuzberg, prompted by the 750th anniversary. The International Building Exhibition, with forty architects involved, mostly foreign, had started to clean up some façades and to pioneer some intriguingly modernistic blocks of flats and offices, even schools. Tatty old Berlin was getting a new coat of paint at last.

During the hard years there was no joint planning between the two Berlins, save on a few technical matters such as waste disposal. The two mayors never attended each other's receptions. Gradually, however, in the later 1980s the improved relations between the two Germanies – witness Honecker's visit to Bonn in 1987 – became mirrored at the Berlin level. In 1987, although the two Berlins each celebrated the 750th anniversary quite separately, there was some tacit liaison to avoid programme clashes. And semi-official contacts between publishers, art galleries and intellectuals were becoming closer. Mayor Diepgen wanted to go further, and was urging the Allies to let him give greater recognition to East Berlin. When I met him in 1987 he told me apocalyptically, 'Our starting-point today is the idea of Berlin – all Berlin, East and West – as capital of the German nation! We must prepare ourselves for the task of resuming this role.' I was startled, and thought he was being unrealistic. But within three years his prophecy had been fulfilled – quicker than even he had foreseen.

## The new united Berlin, and its victory over Bonn

The fall of the Wall, and the unifying of the city, have put an end to an abnormal situation but brought a new range of problems and challenges. With resilience, courage and ingenuity, West Berliners by 1989 had survived their forty years of isolation and come to terms with it, building for themselves a fairly happy and secure life; East Berliners had survived the much harder ordeal of forty years of Communism, and had also in a way come to terms with it. Now came the task of bonding two different societies and of healing the wounds of division.

It was the unification drama of all Germany enacted within the intimate proximity of one city, where early in 1991 it was still hard to telephone between its two halves, where a doctor or a bricklayer might be earning three times as much as another living a few blocks away, and where the quiet streets of the west had filled up with the ugly, smelly little 'Trabi' cars of the east. Despite a tradition of solidarity between Berliners, tensions between 'Ossis' and 'Wessis' today are often worse in this town than in other parts of Germany where the two species rub shoulders much less closely.

When the Wall was thrown open in 1989, the initial excited euphoria was entirely genuine, on both sides: but it did not last for ever. It was stronger among East Berliners, who could now travel freely and were ridding themselves of an unpleasant regime. For West Berliners, the change was less positive. They could now at last explore their hinterland, for instance make outings to royal Potsdam; and they were proud that their great city might now resume its proper role. But they soon became aware that their old cosy, peaceful isolation had carried certain advantages — at least since the détente of 1971 — whereas they now faced a period of hectic confusion, as their streets filled up with investors and developers, with inquisitve tourists and television crews, with mass migrants from eastern Europe, and above all with the crowds of 'Ossi' day-trippers bent on shopping and sight-seeing. As traffic and property prices swelled, so did tempers.

After the first all-Berlin elections of December 1990, the new Senate faced fearful problems, above all financial. It stood to lose a large part of the old federal subsidy given to compensate for its isolation: yet it now had to help pay for the renewal of east Berlin whose industry and infrastructure shared the plight of all east Germany, and it faced the giant task of replanning the central wasteland astride the old Wall.

After weeks of mounting unrest in the GDR (see pp. 422–5), on the evening of Thursday, November 9, its authorities suddenly announced that citizens were free to leave by any route. People could hardly believe it. But already that night East Berliners in tens of thousands began pouring through the crossing-points such as Checkpoint Charlie, just to take a look at the west: here they were ecstatically greeted by West Berliners who came to meet them. Bliss was it in that dawn . . .

Champagne flowed, strangers kissed and embraced, and in scenes that through television ignited the world's imagination, people danced on the Wall and began to hack at it for souvenirs – under the bewildered but mostly benign gaze of the armed border guards who until a few hours before had orders to shoot at anyone trying to cross.

In the next few days an estimated million or so East Germans flocked to visit the hitherto forbidden paradise of West Berlin, where at first they were greeted with open arms and given all kinds of freebies: buses offered free rides, theatres free tickets, cafés free drinks, while fast-food joints gave discount burgers. If you weren't an Ossi, it was worth pretending to be one (though your clothes and manner usually gave you away). The easterners queued at West Berlin banks for the official 100 DM 'welcome money' that for years had been granted to any immigrant from the GDR; or they changed their paltry Ostmarks on the black market at 11–1 (the official rate was 1–1); and they bought all kinds of luxury novelties, such as bananas, fancy chocolates and Western toys. One special attraction near the Ku'damm was the famous Kaufhaus des Westens (KaDeWe), the Continent's largest and glossiest department store, whose gigantic and super-opulent food section, rivalling Harrods', provided Ossis with the most acute and thrilling form of culture-shock available in the West.

The politicians quickly came to pay their tributes too. The 76-year-old Willy Brandt, mayor of West Berlin when the Wall was built and originator of the 1971 détente, went to the Brandenburg Gate on November 10, and wept with emotion. On November 12, when a wide new crossing in the Wall was punched open at the Potsdamer Platz, the mayors of the two halves of the city, Walter Momper (west) and Eduard Krack (east), went there and cordially shook hands. On December 22 the Brandenburg Gate itself, the city's most powerfully symbolic building, was re-opened in the presence of Chancellor Kohl and the GDR's Prime Minister, Hans Modrow. And finally on June 22 the Western control-hut at Checkpoint Charlie was towed away into 'honourable retirement', at a ceremony attended by all four Allied foreign ministers. 'At long last, we are bringing Charlie in from the cold,' said Douglas Hurd.

Immediately after November 9 the GDR authorities began tearing down bits of the Wall, so as to create more crossing-points. And the souvenir-merchants joined in, some of them lifting out great be-graffiti'd chunks that could be cut up and sold for up to 200,000 DM a piece in New York or Tokyo. On the spot, you could buy a small piece for as little as 5 DM (propping open our attic door in Kensington is a red-green-and-blue bit that we bought in July 1990 from a Turkish stall at the Brandenburg Gate, but I doubt its authenticity). Within a few months, over a hundred roads had been reconnected, all around the city, and most of the Wall had come down. Beside the parts that remained, children now cycled quietly in the once-so-deathly no-man's-land on the eastern side. And at Glienicke, amid the lovely lakes and parkland of the south-west suburbs, walkers could now stroll into Potsdam over the bridge where the spy-swaps were held.

However, by summer 1990 the euphoria had almost vanished and a kind of post-natal depression set in, as the novelty of freedom wore off for Ossis and worries about jobs and money loomed large, while Wessis grew irritated by the bedlam that had invaded their city of serene spaciousness. Various new factors were at work. With the world still mesmerised by Berlin, tourism had shot up 30 per cent and all hotels were booked out – nice for trade, but not for all inhabitants. With Berlin now the hub of most activity for reviving the old GDR, officials and businessmen, many specially arrived from West Germany, were all in a frenzy of overworked pressure, adding to the traffic by racing about non-stop in their cars and taxis (after all, you couldn't easily phone!): I myself found appointments far harder to make than two years previously.

There were other newcomers, too, rather less welcome: migrants looking for work were pouring into West Berlin from countries such as Poland and Bulgaria, as well as from the GDR itself with its crumbling economy, and the city's refugee camps were overflowing. Petty crime soared. Many of the Poles were there on short trading visits, hawking their wares and then carting home bulk supplies in their rickety jalopies – one Grunewald housewife, looking for yoghourt in her local supermarket and finding the dairy shelves empty, was told, 'Oh, it's all gone to Warsaw.' By comparison with these locusts, the settled Turks of Kreuzberg were much more acceptable, and some West Berliners said they now preferred Turks to Ossis. The Poles were tough, alert dealers, while the East Germans were slower, milder, but just as drably dressed. And in what hordes they still came! – either to visit friends and relatives, or for regular shopping, since after the July 1 currency union most ordinary food prices were actually cheaper in West than East Berlin. They crammed the supermarkets, simply transplanting their own habitual queues to the west. And their slow, phut-phutting, exhaust-belching little Wartburgs and Trabants filled the streets, or parked illegally on pavements, or double-parked. West Berlin used to be a motorists' paradise, but it had now caught the parking problems and traffic jams of other huge cities. The trains were fuller too, and the litter worse, while rents rose 30 per cent in six months. The Bahnhof Zoo terminus, long a haunt of sad drug-addicts, was now equally a centre for violent criminal gangs, mostly from eastern Europe. The burglary rate rose fast, too.

Some West Berliners began to whisper half-jokingly, 'If only we could have the Wall back!' But not all were so gloomy. Attitudes to the city's unification were partly a matter of generation: most older people, who remembered pre-war or at least pre-Wall Berlin, felt glad to have their city restored to unity, whereas the younger ones, or people who had arrived more recently, were less likely to feel a sentimental attachment of this kind. Many of the newer immigrants, notably the younger artists or performers, had been drawn to West Berlin just because of its cosily eccentric isolation, a world away from a place like New York or even Munich: and now, seeing it become a big brash metropolis like any other, they felt cheated. In 1990 I talked with the well-known West Berlin rock quartet, Chinchilla Green – two of them from Canada, two from west Germany, all very civilised and up-market – and they said roughly this: 'We came here in 1987 because the Wall lent this city an exotic flavour. It was a cosmopolitan island of exiles escaping the West German rat-race. Flats were cheap, and there weren't too many banks. But now . . . Berlin is becoming over-crowded, full of aggression and xenophobia, a supermarket for eastern Europe. For years it will be just one huge building-site, as the big banks and maybe the ministries move in. And the official subsidies will give priority to this, so that culture will suffer. Yes, it *may* one day become a superb global metropolis of culture, as in the golden twenties – but do we have the patience to stick out the transitional period? Many of our friends feel as we do.' And the Berlin-based transsexual nightclub singer Romy Haag spoke to me just as forcibly, in her provocative way: 'Berlin had only one Wall. Paris and New York, where I've lived and worked, are so cliquey and snobby that each has at least ten walls! Berlin has been cosy and easy-going: *because* of the Wall, people had to get along together without side. But life is now getting hard, and my friends feel nervous and helpless.' Some such people had indeed already left. But another immigrant to Berlin, the film-maker Wim Wenders, born in the Rhineland, was horrified by these views. 'Today Berlin is getting even more exciting, despite the chaos,' he told me; 'its contradictions, its time-warps, its sense of a living past, are all fruitful artistically. The view that it is losing its "cosy little island" charm I find disgusting.'

None feared the new changes more than the *Alternative* of Kreuzberg, who sensed that a golden age was ending. Already before 1989 Kreuzberg had started to become gentrified, like Greenwich Village, as the arty-smarties moved in, flats were renovated, rents rose, and some true bohemians moved out. Now the process seemed set to accelerate, for the fall of the Wall had pitchforked this quiet cul-de-sac into a new central location, a prime site for developers. In 1990 some *Alternative* began moving over to Prenzlauerberg, a burgeoning new mini-Kreuzberg in east Berlin, with similar run-down housing. Here in the 1980s a few bold spirits had discreetly defied the Honecker orthodoxy, and now they came out of the woodwork, opening little alternative cafés, theatres, galleries and bookshops: op-art murals enlivened the gloomy rear courtyards, and some flats were turned into offbeat cafés where bizarre avant-garde art-shows were held. It was all quite excitingly decadent. At least 150 derelict houses, here and elsewhere in east Berlin, were taken over by squatter communities, a few of them extreme-Left, or Neo-Nazi skinhead, and violent clashes occurred. Prenzlauerberg began to look like a re-run of Kreuzberg ten years earlier.

My notes on the east Berlin scene, autumn 1990. The Brandenburg Gate is covered with scaffolding, as it gets a face-lift for its bicentenary. Around its base, where the Wall stood, touristy souvenir-stalls are selling the detritus of the old regime – GDR flags and banners, officers' caps and decorations, and of course bits of Wall ('I never liked that regime, even so it's humiliating to see our country made a mockery of like this,' I hear an east German say). Up the Unter den Linden, right opposite the Soviet Embassy, some posh new Western boutiques are now in place, selling furs, jewellery, Yamaha motorbikes. One smart shoe-shop has clowns, a brass band and free ice-cream for its opening gala; the uniformed local salesgirls stand around awkwardly, as the Western manageress drills them in free-market customer service. On the pavement, where a 'ghost' S-Bahn station has just been re-opened, gipsy women are begging freely (the old regime would swiftly have arrested them). Further up the avenue, the broad park-like Marx-Engels Forum has gone back to its old name of Lustgarten: but the twin statues of the two old Lefties still stand there, maybe wondering where it all went wrong. The bookshop windows are full of authors formerly forbidden. Everywhere Western businessmen with briefcases can be seen inspecting building-sites or hurrying into the newly-opened branches of big Western banks. The traffic, once so light, has grown much heavier here in the east, too, as gleaming Mercedes glide amidst the Trabis. But the restaurants, previously so full that usually you had to queue for ages, have become far emptier since currency union trebled their prices.

Giant Marlboro cigarette hoardings proclaim in English, 'Test the West!' And test it they do, these bewildered, still pallid-looking east Berliners. For all the new activity in the east, the two halves of the city are still very different, in their looks, their economies, their mentalities: people still talk of the other half as *drüben* (over there). Although the east was a national capital while the west was an isolated enclave, west Berliners are inevitably much the more cosmopolitan, assured and international-minded, as well as having more than twice the per capita spending power, far better services and far lower unemployment (some 50,000 east Berliners commute to jobs in the west each day). And yet, just as inevitably, the two halves of Berlin will gradually grow together: the belated provision in 1991 of reasonable cross-city telephone links was a step in that process. The fall of the Wall, even the first all-Berlin elections in December 1990, did not truly make Berlin one city: that will still take some years, but it will happen.

Held on the same day as the first pan-German elections, December 2, 1990, the first pan-Berlin elections resulted in a surprise victory for the CDU, albeit a narrow one. So Eberhard Diepgen again became mayor: but because of the huge tasks ahead he decided to form a 'grand coalition' government including the SPD. With Berlin now fully part of a fully sovereign Germany, the Allies' occupation status ended and their troops withdrew, apart from a few symbolic detachments; and Lufthansa at last began flying into Berlin. The new fifteen-member Senate, which included only three senators from east Berlin, was due in 1991 to leave the ugly old Schöneberg Rathaus, where Kennedy had made his famous speech, and to move back into the towering pre-war city hall near the Marx-Engels-Platz, long known as the 'Rotes Rathaus', more because of its red-brick façade than its politics. The city parliament is due to move in 1992–3 from Schöneberg to Prussia's old parliament building, also in the east.

The tasks confronting the new Senate in 1991 were enormous. Not only did it have to merge and reorganise two city administrations, two police forces, two welfare services and much else – mostly by extending western structures to the east – but it also faced a serious budget crisis. Bonn, not unreasonably, was seeking to reduce the special subsidies that had been granted to West Berlin to assuage its isolation. But it was not providing adequate new funds for dealing with the huge new burden of east Berlin – or so the Senate argued. Bonn wanted to phase out by 1995 the annual 9 billion DM of aid and tax concessions given to firms and individuals. It was allowing the city to retain for the time being the 13 billion DM annual top-up to its own budget, but was saying that this money should be spent on east Berlin. And Diepgen retorted that this was not nearly enough. Not only does nearly all of the east's infrastructure need renewing, and much of its housing, but west Berlin still has its own unsolved housing crisis, whose causes go back to the last century.

As a big city Berlin is relatively young: in 1871 its population was only 900,000, but there followed a period of fast expansion, with numbers more than doubling to reach 1.9 million by 1890. Peasant families poured in to provide a workforce for the new industries, and were housed by none-too-scrupulous authorities in huge apartment blocks, hurriedly built with minimal sanitation and plumbing, in poor districts such as Wedding and Neukölln, as well as in the east. The teeming life of these tenements, where children played in the dark, dank inner courtyards, was poignantly portrayed by Heinrich Zille in his satirical sketches of the 1900–1914 period. Strangely enough, much of this housing survived the bombing. In the east it had crumbled into dilapidation: but even in the west, for various economic and legal reasons, not much of it has been replaced or properly renovated. Many blocks today have absentee landlords, and many owners have been deterred from making improvements by the heavily controlled rents. The slums provide useful shelter for squatters and others: but they have remained a disgrace for the biggest city of a wealthy country where housing standards are so high.

In 1991 a target was set of building 30,000 new homes a year and renovating others. Even so, with the population now rising quite fast, the housing shortage will probably take years to solve. And some major new infrastructure is needed, too, in order to satisfy the city's expanding economic role – a bigger airport, new highways, a proper modern rail terminus in a city that has none, and much new office building. The latter can be privately funded: but for the rest, where will the money come from? 'We can just about manage with our present infrastructure,' said one planner, 'but it doesn't exactly encourage new investors.'

Then there is the vexed question of the cultural subsidies. Until 1989 the governments of the two Germanies, for somewhat different political reasons, each used *its* Berlin as a major cultural showcase, and the level of cultural subsidy in both was probably the world's highest: West Berlin's arts budget for 1990 was 523 million DM, more than that of the Arts Council for the whole of Britain. But today is such priority for culture still justified, especially when east Germany is in such economic crisis? Unification has left Berlin with three full-scale opera houses, more than in any other city in the world, as well as ten orchestras, twenty-seven mainline theatres, and three huge museum complexes. Some of these bodies may now be forced to close or merge, especially in the east. Of course there is no question of tampering with the august Berlin Philharmonic, under its new conductor Claudio Abbado, nor with the west's Deutsche Oper under the great Götz Friedrich, nor with such events as the annual film festival; and late in 1990 Bonn guaranteed the future of the east's two opera houses, and of some leading theatres and orchestras there, for at least another year. But for 1992 and beyond there would probably be large all-round subsidy cuts; and the east's institutions, with their overstaffing and dwindling audiences (see p. 480), were likely to suffer most. This could well include the creaking old Berliner Ensemble, no longer worthy of Brecht who founded it; but probably not the popular Friedrichstadt-Palast, said to be Europe's largest variety theatre. In fact, traditional 1920s variety, with conjurers, chorus-girls and Zarah Leander-style singers in high ostrich-plumes, has been making something of a come-back in a Berlin hungry for nostalgia – but not satiric cabaret.

The rationalisation of Berlin's remarkable museums has been presenting its own problems. Two smallish ones devoted to Berlin's own history, one in the east, one in the west, have agreed to link up and share their material; and the GDR's huge history museum on the Unter den Linden has been taken over by the Federal Government, and its contents will form part of a big new museum of German history likely to be built near the Reichstag. In such cases, where political or social material is involved, an eastern museum usually has first to be 'sanitised' by the removal of its propaganda bias. As for Berlin's greatest museums, they house the distinguished art treasures of the Prussian Cultural Foundation, the heritage of the Prussian kings, which have had a curious history. Until the war all were housed in the group of huge buildings on Museum Island, in the east. Then the Nazis scattered them around Germany where the Americans and Russians confiscated them. In the 1950s these two powers agreed each to give back its own share of this loot to 'its' Germans. So some treasures went back to their now gloomy and decrepit home on the 'island', where the giant Pergamon Altar had luckily survived the bombing; others, including the best of the paintings and the Egyptian bust of Nefertiti, went to spick-and-span buildings in the west Berlin suburbs. A strong lobby in Bonn had wanted the west's share divided up between the *Länder*: but the view prevailed that it should all go back to Berlin, in line with the policy of helping the beleaguered city. In the 1950s, that was a courageous decision. Today the Prussian Foundation in the west has taken charge of the entire heritage and is rearranging it rationally, helped by a 2 billion DM grant that will go towards a needed facelift for Museum Island. Most of the great paintings will stay in Dahlem, in the west. But Nefertiti will return from Charlottenburg to the Bode Museum, to rejoin her husband King Akhnaton, from whom she had been sundered by the fortunes of war. They had previously been together for 3,300 years: so a mere 45 years' separation was bearable for this loving royal couple.

One of the main challenges facing the new Senate is how to rebuild the wide central area on either side of the old Wall and mainly to its east, between the Tiergarten and Friedrichstrasse, between Unter den Linden and western Kreuzberg. This was the pre-war city's vital focus, a place of ministries and embassies, of smart shops and cafés (the Foreign Ministry was on Wilhelmstrasse, renamed Otto-Grotewohl-Strasse by the GDR): today parts of it are a run-down semi-ruin, and parts were razed after bombing and never rebuilt. What an opportunity for intelligent large-scale planning this area presents today! What other world city has so huge a prime site in its very centre, just waiting to be made beautiful? But views vary widely on what should be done, from the Greens' ideas for a park to financiers' visions of lucrative office blocks.

Even before the Wall was opened, some firms were staking claims on the western side — witness the controversial Daimler-Benz affair. It so happens that DB's chairman, Eduard Reuter, is the son of the late and revered Ernst Reuter, who was West Berlin's SPD mayor during the 1949–50 airlift; and in August 1989 mayor Walter Momper (also SPD), partly out of loyalty to the Reuter legacy, partly with an eye to the jobs and profits it would bring, gave a verbal promise to the great man's son that he would sell him a 45-acre empty site right on the Potsdamer Platz, by the Wall. Daimler-Benz wanted to build a mammoth service centre with a staff of 6,000, including some space for shops, cafés, etc. The *Alternative Liste* (Greens included), who were then in Senate, were furious: they had hardly been consulted, although their leader Michaela Schreyer was herself Senator for Planning. And during 1990 they fought hard to get the project cancelled (no contract had yet been signed). They stressed that public money was being wasted, for the land was being sold at one-sixth (93 million DM) of what had now become its market value; also that Daimler-Benz, Germany's leading armaments manufacturer (see p. 112), was a shockingly unsuitable candidate for this key site in what would now be again the city's main square. After Diepgen took power the issue was temporarily shelved. But then the European Commission tacitly took up the Alternatives' cause, alleging that it might be against EC rules for so large and rich a firm to receive such favourable treatment. The EC was due to give its decision late in 1991. The arguments against the project are clear: on the other hand, Berlin badly needs new large-scale investment.

Similar dilemmas will probably colour the overall planning of the central area. In 1990–1 various proposals were being put forward. The Alternatives might like plenty of green space and cultural facilities; others are demanding a major new north–south highway, badly needed, but this could probably go underground; many others want government and commercial office blocks and shopping-centres, in varying proportions. Probably the final plan will be a mix of all these. And it is likely that the Friedrichstrasse, that tawdry eastern thoroughfare, will become a smart shopping and entertainment street, balancing the Ku'damm: Bertelsmann has staked a claim to build a huge media centre there, at the heart of what used to be the publishing district.

Above all, in this mighty debate on central Berlin's future, historians and architects are urging that respect should be paid to the city's history, which should not be swept out of sight, neither the good nor even the bad. 'In a town so shaped by its political upheavals, many of them tragic,' says one academic, 'it is important that the living past remain on view, even the bits we don't like. Even some of those grandiose GDR palaces.' And an American architect has said: 'Commercial sterility should not replace a city essentially spiritual' (I myself would call it cultural rather than spiritual). Some people would like a part of the Wall to be preserved as a memorial, as has been done with many Nazi concentration camps. But it is far from clear what will now happen to Hitler's bunker, still covered by a discreet green mound in the no-man's-land near the Brandenburg Gate.

Active work on a new overall plan first had to await the formation of the new all-Berlin Senate. Then it was held up by other factors. One, as elsewhere in east Germany, was the avalanche of property claims (see p. 451), many from former Jewish or other landowners, evicted either by the Nazis or by the GDR. To name but two: a Swiss bank claimed that it still owned the land where the TV Tower now stands; and the big West German store chain Hertie, previously Jewish-owned, wanted to regain its old head office site east of the Potsdamer Platz. But, more important, the Senate was still awaiting a Federal decision as to whether the Government would be transferred from Bonn to Berlin. If it was, then much of the area around the Reichstag would be needed for new ministries and other such buildings. This stormy issue of Bonn versus Berlin was not finally settled until June 1991.

Why on earth was little Bonn ever chosen as the federal capital in the first place, in 1949, rather than some larger West German city such as Frankfurt? In those days most politicians believed – or paid lip-service to the belief – that Germany before long would be reunified and Berlin would resume its rightful role. So a purely provisional site was needed. Bonn, West Germany's nineteenth town in size, known only for its university and as Beethoven's birthplace, had the advantages of being (*a*) fairly obscure, without pretensions to any permanent role as capital, and (*b*) quite central, neither in north or south Germany. Frankfurt, also central, was seriously considered too, and had many advocates: but it was rejected as being too large and powerful, and too bound up with German history. Hamburg and Munich were excluded for the same reasons; moreover, south Germans would never accept being governed from the far north, nor north Germans from Bavaria's capital. Above all, Bonn was warmly favoured by Chancellor Adenauer, who had his home close by and was CDU deputy for the town, as well as being a native of Cologne. This ageing leader wanted to stay near his *Heimat* – and his voice prevailed. Since then, *c'est le provisoire qui dure* . . . Bonn steadily acquired a large number of solid and expensive government buildings: yet as a capital city it continued to wear a vaguely unreal and makeshift air.

Although the govermental milieu has become livelier and more interesting since the 1989 cataclysm, the town's provincial Rhineland atmosphere remains much the same as evoked in *A Small Town in Germany* (1968) by John Le Carré who served as a diplomat there: he called it 'half as big as the central cemetery in Chicago but twice as dead'. Bonn still keeps its pre-1949 roles – that of quiet residential centre for well-to-do retired people from nearby Cologne and the Ruhr, and of classic university town with an old campus right next to the Altstadt. Just to the south, on what used to be open meadowland beside the Rhine, the main government quarter has been tacked on – a series of discreet modern buildings in side-avenues, all very neat and un-grandiose, almost suburban in flavour. A mile or so further south is Bad Godesberg, formerly a fashionable spa town, now annexed by Bonn and the home of many embassies and diplomatic residences. Some ministries are here, others lie scattered out in the suburbs, so that the city is today rather a sprawl. And beside it there flows the broad Rhine, between green hills crowned by the ruined castles of Godesberg and Drachenfels. It is a pretty setting, and there are pleasant river-walks. But the climate is humid and enervating, causing lethargy, liverishness and bad circulation – not the best recipe for dynamic government, and quite unlike the famously invigorating *Berliner Luft* (Berlin air).

The four distinct societies – bourgeois residential, academic, governmental and diplomatic – do not mix much except for the last two. But if you get away into the older, more down-to-earth districts, you could be in any friendly, unassuming Rhineland town, given over to wine-drinking and jolly jokery. The centre, quite badly bombed, has been rebuilt in the usual antiseptic style, and is now a pedestrian zone of narrow streets converging on a market square where tourists and teenagers loll in open-air cafés and concerts play in summer. Students sit on the grass in the park, and strains of music float out from dignified mansions. It is all quite charming. But Le Carré's darts were directed less at this scene than at the vast milieu of the politicians, bureaucrats and 10,000 diplomats who form a separate world. Many of the senior civil servants have been seconded for a few years from their *Land*, so they do not put down roots, and they tend to return to their home town at weekends, leaving 'official' Bonn deserted and dull. As a capital Bonn still feels neither purely provisional, nor really permanent either, and it seems somewhat cut off from the authentic life of the country (*das Bundesdorf*, the 'federal village', it is called): foreign journalists posted there have often complained how hard they find it to get to grips with the 'real' Germany. Frankfurt, brash and ugly but dynamic and cultured and a true metropolis, would have made a much better capital these past forty years, and Adenauer's choice was wrong, in my view.

By the mid-1980s the 'fiction' of Bonn's provisional status had been tacitly dropped and it was given some solid new buildings more worthy of its status as capital: Parliament was expensively renovated, a new complex of ministries was erected, while the Americans and Russians both invested in huge new embassies. Ironically, this process had just been completed when the Wall came down and unification loomed. In Bonn, where a third of the 300,000 population depended directly on government jobs, panic set in as house prices fell and work on new projects was stopped. Then the Unity Treaty declared that Berlin was the capital but the seat of the government would be decided later, by vote of Parliament. So the rulers of both cities set about massive publicity campaigns to plead their cause: honour and prestige were involved, also jobs and investment. And it soon emerged, perhaps curiously, that despite the lip-service paid to Berlin over the years, Bonn had a strong case and powerful support. Among politicians, von Weizsäcker and Genscher both openly championed Berlin (both had roots in the East); Kohl the Rhinelander was more cautious, but was thought to prefer Bonn. Public opinion polls revealed that some 70 per cent of Germans favoured Berlin as capital: but, significantly, a second question found that 60 per cent of them would be happy for the Government to stay in Bonn. And the vast majority of Bonn civil servants and junior politicians, gripe though they might about the 'boring federal village', found when the chips were down that they simply did not want to change their habits, to be uprooted from their little houses and transplanted to a distant, chaotic metropolis in most cases farther from their own local homelands than so-central Bonn. Dr Karl Zahn, of Baden-Württemberg's permanent delegation in Bonn, put it to me wryly: 'We are all provincials and Bonn, boring and slow, suits our temperament; we'd be out of our depth in Berlin. Bonn is small, convenient, everything is so close; Berlin is too vast, too crime-ridden. And it has only been the capital since 1871. Nothing good has ever come out of it.'

Apart from these reasons of self-interest, involving a few score thousand people, there were other and wider arguments in favour of Bonn. One was the cost of a transfer (many billion DM), at a time when money was more urgently needed for other tasks in east Germany, and when Berlin was physically still in a mess. But the two most crucial arguments concerned (*a*) Berlin's historical reputation, and (*b*) the balance of the federal structure.

As one CDU deputy put it, 'Berlin stands in history for military might, national glory and conflict with other European states; Bonn by contrast represents democracy and European integration.' This lobby pointed out that Berlin, for many people, evoked the aggressive centralism of the Prussians, then of the Nazis, and as seat of power might intensify foreigners' fears of a new too-dominant Germany. Bonn, on the other hand, had been capital during the most stable, prosperous and democratic period in German history, while its geographical closeness to France had helped to underpin the Franco-German entente and German commitment to the EC: might not Berlin distract Germany towards dangerous eastern adventures? In short, Bonn represented the best in Germany, and Berlin some of the worst. But President von Weizsäcker, himself a former mayor of West Berlin, was among those who retorted that this view was absurd. Berlin, he said, also stood for worker movements and resistance to fascism; and others pointed out that Berlin had not been simply an odious stronghold of militarism, but for centuries had also been a home of liberal culture, tolerance, humour and ethnic diversity. And was it not silly to blame Berlin for Germany's past, when Hitler himself had hated the town, much preferring Munich?

The debate over federalism tied in with this historical one. It was striking that all the *Land* governments, except for Berlin itself and one or two of the new ones in the east, were opposed to a transfer away from Bonn. They argued that a strong federal system had played a big part in West Germany's post-war success, and they feared that a more powerful capital might upset this balance, and induce a new centralism that could weaken their autonomy. Bavaria in particular was far keener to be ruled from harmless little Bonn than from its hated Prussian rival. The historian Norman Stone, regius professor at Oxford, backed this view, in his usual provocative way: he wrote in the *Sunday Times*, 'West Germany grew great, in effect, by not having a metropolis ... A great part of its success story is built on the principle of rival cities ... Is Berlin, the German metropolis, then going to kill Germany?' The Berlin lobby replied that the *Länder*'s fears were unfounded. A Government in Berlin would have no greater statutory powers over the *Länder* than when it was in Bonn; and it had been agreed that many federal institutions, including the Bundesbank and Constitutional Court, would remain in other cities. The decentralised tradition would continue.

After months of this debate, the decisive vote by the Bundestag was set for 20 June 1991. It was expected that Bonn would win and that

Berlin would get just a few crumbs, such as periodic parliamentary sessions in the Reichstag. But the deputies voted narrowly for Berlin, by 337 to 320 (even more surprisingly, twelve of the *Land* parliaments, as opposed to their governments, had already expressed a preference for Berlin). The Bundestag formally agreed that parliament and government, including the main ministries, would move to Berlin in stages over the next twelve years, but that Bonn would keep some role as an 'administrative centre'.

Berlin that night was filled with scenes of rejoicing. The Senate was delighted, for legitimate reasons of honour and for economic ones too: in order to pay for the mammoth task of rebuilding, it would now get back in a different form the federal subsidies it had risked losing, and at least 100,000 new jobs would be created in the city. The vast majority of true patriotic Berliners were pleased, too, whatever the doubts of the *Alternative* and some others (as quoted above). And let me declare my own colours: I am also delighted, not only because my wife was born in Berlin. Bonn, as Dr Zahn admitted, stands for the cosy, cautious, provincial side of Germany, and I'm not surprised that so many anxious, security-minded Germans would have preferred to keep it. Berlin is the more daring, ambitious scenario. It is a city where politics and bureaucracy can be dragged out of their dull vacuum, and enriched by close contact with the real world of culture, commerce and social tension. Germany now needs such a true capital.

The new unified Berlin is now certain to increase in cultural and economic importance, not only as Germany's capital but as the *de facto* metropolis of the new free Central Europe. Its geographical position will make it a key centre for dealings with lands further east. Already it is earmarked for the AD 2000 Olympic Games and the new East European training institute; some new galleries, publishers and other firms have been moving there, including a branch of Sotheby's. So the city's longer-term future looks bright, after all its hardships; and the present hectic, crowded time of transition will not last for ever. One Berliner told me: 'So often in the past we've had to adapt to the bad. Now we must adapt to the good, and to the novelty of normality. We've at last become a *normal* big metropolis – like Los Angeles.' Well, I hope *not* like Los Angeles!

Next, a voyage of discovery round some of the other main cities, south to north. They will all keep their special importance: in this federal land, Munich will never dwindle into a mere Manchester or Marseille.

## A diversity of dominant cities: life today in Munich, Stuttgart, Frankfurt, Cologne, Düsseldorf, Hamburg and Bremen

The image of an elegant baroque capital, and the boozy beer-drinking thigh-slapping image, are both of them accurate but only parts of the total reality. Munich is the most smart and stylish of big German cities, the most hedonistic and culture-packed, outwardly the most opulent, and the most exuberant, self-confident and self-congratulatory. Despite Bavarians' relaxed and affable humour, daily business life has a fast, nervous tempo that sometimes reminds me of Paris. Indeed this is the most Paris-like of German cities.

In the decades before unification, this trend-setting city was sometimes described as West Germany's 'secret capital'. The phrase did not mean much, for Munich was never accepted as a capital by other parts of Germany, nor did it 'secretly' govern Germany: Frankfurt has always had more real power. And yet Munich, almost as much as Berlin, does still retain something of the atmosphere of a capital – not of all Germany but of the most assertive of its *Länder*. The spirit of the Wittelsbachs, who ruled here from 1180 to 1918, first as dukes, then as monarchs, is still very much alive. They have bequeathed numerous buildings of regal grandiosity, such as the massive Residenz palace, the Schloss Nymphenburg and the ugly but imposing Parliament that towers on its hill above the river Isar. And Bavarians are sharply aware of this royal legacy and happy to flaunt it. Everywhere the city flies the blue-and-white chequered flag of *Freistaat Bayern*, the 'Free State' of Bavaria; and the head of the Wittelsbach family today, the Duke of Bavaria, is still addressed as 'your Royal Highness' (see pp. 177–8). Bavarians have a fondness for father-figures – hence the great popularity, in his lifetime, of the emperor-like Franz Josef Strauss.

The city has expanded greatly since the war, to reach a population of 1.3 million, and has benefited as much as any from the 'economic miracle'. It was not formerly a very industrial place. But after the war Siemens and some other big companies moved their headquarters here from Berlin; BMW is here too, and MBB, the aerospace firm, and these and other giants have created a spin-off effect, so that Munich now is an expanding centre of electronics and other advanced industries. People of all kinds have flocked in – farm emigrants from depopulating rural Bavaria, and refugees from the lost eastern parts of Germany and elsewhere in eastern Europe — so that most inhabitants of Munich today were not born in the city and 20 per cent are not German. This is also the favoured destination of the newly mobile west German middle classes, and according to opinion polls it is the city that most Germans would prefer to live in if they left their own. People are attracted not only by its own qualities but by the weekend delights of the nearby Alps and lakes and the easy access to Austria and Italy — but less so by the climate, often marred by the *Föhn*, a dry, sultry headache-inducing wind from the mountains.

The suburbs sprawl for many miles: but the *Innenstadt*, the older inner city bound by a ring-road, is very compact, less than a mile across, and this gives Munich a strong sense of cohesion. Here is one of the world's great opera houses, and one of Europe's grandest hotels, the Vier Jahreszeiten. All is sleek and cosmopolitan: and Munich lies securely on the top international circuit for visiting celebrities of all kinds. But if it nonetheless misses the true metropolitan stature of, say, London or Paris, is this because of its smaller size, or its lack of any major political or financial role, or because many of its true original Bavarian inhabitants are still just a little provincial, not quite in tune with its new *Weltstadt* vocation? By no means are they always pleased and flattered by its new popularity and diversity: many of them complain of its being 'de-Bavarianised', and they resent the 'stiff new Prussian influences'. Beneath all the glamour and diversity, this old hard-core Munich still has more than a touch of parochialism about it — as I noted on a visit to *München Leuchtet* ('Munich is shining' — a variation on Thomas Mann's famous phrase 'Munich was shining'), a satirical play-cum-revue that for years in the mid-1980s packed out one of the main theatres. Lovingly self-indulgent, it was a succession of in-jokes and jibes about local politicians, and cosy little send-ups of Munich habits, folklore and myths about itself — and it brought ecstatic applause.

The Bavarians, Münchners especially, are certain they are the best and they constantly say so — they have the best beer, the best music and the best football team, Bayern München. Always grumbling but warm-hearted, rough-tongued but sentimental and great lovers of folksy kitsch, they cultivate a breezy *Gemütlichkeit* that is less sweet and refined than the Austrian brand. Above all, they are great funlovers and hedonists, in contrast to most Germans who, Rhinelanders apart, are not so adept at enjoying themselves. To laugh a lot, to be seen in public to be having fun, to relish your beer, women and song — for this you score high marks in Bavaria.

This rollicking city also has style and stylishness – or rather several styles, for Munich today has many diverse faces. There is rough style of a kind in the traditional popular culture of beer-and-Lederhosen which is not just laid on for tourists but belongs vibrantly to local life. Gladly the Münchners go in big family parties to the annual *Oktoberfest*; and in summer they spread their picnics on the tables in the beer-gardens, where babies squall, students debate, lovers fondle and foaming litre tankards are downed – a Teutonic scene. Then in winter they make for the beer-cellars where thighs are slapped and brass-bands deafen, and the high-piled sausages are as vast, pink and coarse as the faces of the citizens roaring out the choruses, arms linked, swaying together – '*In München steht ein Hofbräuhaus, Eins, Zwei, Gsuffa. . . .*' But this unsophisticated image is only one of the city's faces. It is true that in the streets you still see plenty of veterans in patterned Lederhosen, with hairy knees and feathered green hats – but today in the city centre they are outnumbered by svelte girls from the pages of *Vogue*, for in recent years Munich has asserted itself as the German capital of fashion, high society and *Schick* (see page 184). Here is Germany's Hollywood, also its Mayfair and Madison Avenue, with boutiques in the Maximilianstrasse as smart as any in Paris – and who says the Germans are not smart when they try? Here is the showy world of the *Lodenmantelschickeria*, the smart set of aristocrats, industrialists, film and fashion people, for whom the height of *Schick* is to wear Bavarian *Tracht* (green *Loden* capes and jackets, for men and women) redesigned in stylish cuts by top fashion houses such as Dior. In Munich society, you do best to flaunt your wealth and status, and you are outcast if you do not dress modishly.

A third contrasting face, the bohemian one, is to be found in the Schwabing district, which in the early part of the century was a distinguished centre of European intellectual life – Brecht and Mann, Klee and Kandinsky, Trotsky and Spengler all lived there. Today Schwabing's glory has faded and Munich's true avant-garde has left it to create a new focus in the humbler district of Haidhausen across the Isar. But Schwabing still houses scores of little fringe theatres, art cinemas and arty pubs. The Leopoldstrasse, its main avenue leading up from the university, can be magical on a warm summer night in its own gaudy way – milling youthful crowds, art students hawking their work, and terrace-cafés, unusual for Germany. Just to the east is the Englischer Garten, created by an American, Count Rumford, in 1793, and claiming to be Europe's largest city park, four miles long. Here in summer youth besports itself in the style of the beaches of St-Tropez: this is tolerated (except when girls step naked out of the park into city trams), for Munich itself is today as easy-going as its Catholic rural hinterland is still strait-laced.

Bavaria is often regarded as 'reactionary'. But the heartland of right-wing CSU support is in rural areas and smaller towns, while the capital itself since Wittelsbach has enjoyed a liberal tradition. True, it has known periods of extremism: there was the insurrectionary 'Red' commune of 1918–19, and then in the 1920s Hitler made Munich the headquarters of his Nazi movement and staged his abortive *Putsch* there in 1923. But since the war the city with its new mixed population has been politically moderate, ruled most of the time by the SPD, but often with no overall majority. Today the SPD mayor, Georg Kronawitter, runs the Rathaus in coalition with the Greens, and in 1984–90 his uneasy coalition was with the CSU. This led to the occasional flare-up when the CSU found the SPD's cultural programme too permissive: for instance, in 1985, to mark the 175th *Oktoberfest*, the City Museum, then well known for its provocative Leftist policy, staged a highly critical exhibition, 'The Bavarian National Drunken Frenzy'. The CSU, enraged at this 'affront to national dignity and our cherished traditions', organised a boycott. Such incidents lend local politics a theatrical Latin flavour, agreeably un-German. Another point of controversy has been the council's decision to hire its own police force to patrol the Metro, in a bid to combat crime. These sinister pistol-bearing figures in black leather, dubbed *Schwarze Sheriffe*, may indeed have deterred some muggers: but local radicals and leftists have found them 'fascistic', reviving bitter memories of Munich's guilty past.

There are still various visible traces of this Nazi past. Hitler had some hideous buildings erected in the city, and those that survived the bombing have been allowed to stand as grim memorials. Thus his *Haus der Kunst*, built to enshrine Nazi principles of art, is still in use as a modern art museum, and its swastika patterns are still there on the porch. The gloomy limestone building that now houses the Music School was built by Hitler as his Munich headquarters: here he reviewed parades from its balcony, and here in 1938 Chamberlain signed away the Sudetenland. But, apart from this, Munich has obliterated the Nazi period. Badly bombed in 71 air-raids, many central streets were then hurriedly rebuilt in a somewhat graceless style. But luckily the vast majority of the many fine baroque buildings were spared the bombing, or have since been carefully restored, so that the city still keeps something of its special harmony of lovely façades glowing gold in the sunset. And it is all sparklingly clean and tidy, remarkably so even by German standards.

Post-war planning has mostly been intelligent, avoiding the highrise rash that disfigures Frankfurt and some other cities. Munich allows no downtown skyscrapers. The ugly Arabella/Sheraton towers, built in the 1960s and now much regretted, at least stand two miles out; the strange four-cylinder BMW building, and the nearby 900-foot Olympic Tower, are further out still. Here the 1972 Olympic Games have left the city with the useful legacy of a mammoth sports and leisure complex, adorned with its 18-acre curly roof of acrylic glass, looking like some giant fish-net hung out to dry. All in all the Games were a boon for Munich. They gave it the incentive to build a much-needed modern infrastructure that includes ring motorways and a gleaming super-efficient Metro. A huge new airport is now being completed, after years of delays caused by legal obstruction by Greens and nearby residents, and is due to open in 1992. The modern public transport system, integrating Metro, suburban trains, buses and trams, is one of the best in Europe, about as good as Hamburg's. Parts of the inner city are now a pedestrian zone where broad shopping malls converge on the Marienplatz beside the Rathaus, still the hub of Munich life and all-year-round quite an impromptu carnival scene — one spring Saturday, for instance, young out-of-work musicians playing a classical harp-and-oboe duet while Leftist demonstrators brandished anti-CSU placards. In December the square is given over to the astonishing *Christkindlmarkt*, a huge bizarre bazaar of every kind of Bavarian Christmas kitsch such as marzipan Wise Men and Virgin-and-Child candles. Such is the magic of Munich.

Stuttgart, capital of Baden-Württemberg, has a quaint south German charm of a somewhat different kind. Its best single feature is its physical setting, much the prettiest of any big German city. The others are all on wide plains, but central Stuttgart lies in a hollow, cradled by forested hills; the tidy terraced suburbs rise steeply on either side, and one vineyard slopes up from the main station. This nest-like frame, leafy and bucolic, lends a quality of gentleness to this modern industrial city, home of Bosch and Daimler-Benz. It also makes Stuttgart seem smaller than it is, for its industrial areas sprawl unseen in other valleys. And it gives a feeling of intimacy that chimes in well with the local character of these cosy Swabians, lovers of the twee, for whom even a big mansion is not 'Haus' but 'Häusle' (wee house). A godfearing and, even more, an untidiness-fearing race. The second worst sin is to be seen weeding your garden on the sabbath. The worst sin is not to weed it ever.

Swabian piety and provincialism may irritate, yet this remains my favourite German city – or, at least, I know it far better than the others, and *tout comprendre*. . . . The contrast with Munich is striking – not only the setting, but the atmosphere, more cosy and relaxed; and the people, gentler, kindlier and much less show-off than the Bavarians. These slow Swabians with their big moon faces may be somewhat ponderous and unsophisticated, but they are as solid and dependable as the Mercedes they produce: and they have a pawky sense of humour, typified by Stuttgart's famous mayor, Manfred Rommel, who said when I asked him if pietism was still strong in Swabia, 'Local Protestants used to feel that if they laughed, the Lord would be worried. Today they think better of Him and realise that He too has a sense of humour.'

Stuttgart is the main town of Swabia, which covers a sizeable chunk of south-west Germany from the Black Forest to Augsburg, including most of Württemberg. Once a duchy, Swabia today is not a political unit of any kind: but its people retain a sharp identity, and they tend to be mocked by other Germans for their odd-sounding sing-song accent and ungainly provincial ways. Introduced in the sixteenth century, the Protestant ethic used to be so strong that dance halls were forbidden in some areas, and people seen doing housework on a Sunday might be reported to the police. Today this severity has declined under modern influences, such as the influx of thousands of outsiders, notably Catholics from Silesia. Stuttgart has thus become less Swabian and more tolerant: but in many ways the local character persists. Even more than most Germans, the Swabians are ultra-house-proud, nervous if a cup is left unwashed or a shelf undusted. More than most Germans they have also held on to the old hard-work ethic, which enabled them to build up their famous precision industries with such thoroughness. '*Schaffa, spara, Häusle baua*' ('work, work and build your little house') is their notorious motto. Fortunes are to be made but not seen, for unlike Bavaria this is a society where to display your wealth is considered bad taste – one millionaire factory-owner kept his big Mercedes at home, used it only for weekend motoring and drove to his office each day in a little Volkswagen because he did not want to show off to his workers. So this is the status-symbol society turned on its head, where money is saved or reinvested and thrift sometimes reaches comic proportions: it is told that the late Robert Bosch, founder-owner of Stuttgart's great electrical firm, would go around his factory picking up stray paperclips and complaining, 'Look how you waste my money!'

There is some fascination in the recurrent contrast between Swabians' temperament and life-style and the busy modern surface of their successful and cosmopolitan city, the wealthiest in the EC. As the capital of the third largest *Land*, it enjoys quite a political role; it has world-class industries, not only Bosch and Daimler-Benz but Porsche, Standard Electric Lorenz and German IBM; it has a ballet company of international renown, forty consulates (mostly honorary), restaurants from a score of nations and daily jet flights to the main European centres. Though less metropolitan than Munich, it is all in all quite a place, proud of its world links and happy with its slogan, *'Partner der Welt'*. And yet, it is just a big village — thanks to local character, and geography. Within its sprawling borders it produces more wine than any other German commune, and excellent it is too, light and fruity. There are vineyards everywhere, some just a grape's-throw from the main Mercedes factory, where rows of vines climb neatly Swabian-style over the crests of knobbly hills, like newly-combed hair. Many factory workers still own plots of land and are part-time farmers or vine-growers; in some of the city's suburbs you can still find small unmodernised farms, archaically pastoral. Whereas sleek Munich is sharply different from its rural hinterland, in Stuttgart city and country merge into one and there is little difference in spirit between rural Swabia and its bucolic capital.

It is true that parts of the rebuilt downtown area are the usual modern concrete-and-neon jungle of assertive office-blocks, banks and car showrooms. But through-traffic at least has been kept away from the central area, which is now mostly a pedestrian zone around the wide Schlossplatz — here you can walk for almost a mile through the heart of the city and hardly see a car. There is more sense of open space than in central Munich, and the scene is pleasant and relaxed, with open-air cafés, strolling students, modern sculpture and other splashes of colour. Ducks and swans glide on the Schlossgarten lake, in front of the opera house where John Cranko built the ballet company into one of Europe's finest. Nearby is the palatial Neues Schloss where the kings of Württemberg reigned, just across a noisy main road from the Staatsgalerie museum so controversially redesigned by James Stirling. The small and beautiful Schillerplatz, restored after the bombing, glows gently at night under the floodlights, and just beyond is the unbecoming new Rathaus where Rommel, son of the Desert Fox, rules so benignly – 'I became a general quicker than my father,' he told me, 'and I fight better wars in a better cause.' Stuttgart's elected 'general' is on the liberal wing of the CDU, governing in easy coalition with the SPD. Ever since the war, there has been a stronger spirit of consensus here in politics than in any other major German city, and virtually no corruption as far as is known. That is one of Swabia's many virtues. Out in the suburbs, the Mercedes factories symbolise another Swabian merit: innovation and application in industry. Beside the spa centre in Bad Canstatt you can see the modest shed where in 1883 Gottlieb Daimler, a local engineer, invented the world's first moving vehicle to use an internal combustion engine. And today Stuttgart, along with the Munich area, is one of Germany's two main centres of high-technology. As much as ever, it makes its money from industry – just as Frankfurt's industry is the making of money.

The city of Frankfurt on the river Main began to be a thriving money market in the sixteenth century. Then in the nineteenth it became a major world banking centre, thanks to Rothschild and other financiers, many of them Jewish. Most of the Jews today alas are gone: but the banking remains. This is Germany's commercial capital, site of its main Stock Exchange and of the headquarters of most leading German banks and many insurance and advertising firms. Much of this activity takes place inside one or other of the score or so downtown skyscrapers that have won Frankfurt the nickname of 'Mainhattan' and have made it unique in a Europe where no other city has so many tall office tower-blocks so close together in the centre (the cluster at La Défense, in Paris, is out on the periphery). The newest of them, the 55-storey Messe Turm next to the exhibition grounds, completed in 1991, is said to be the highest office building in Europe (260m). Individually these skyscrapers may not be so lovely: but their harmonious grouping is impressive, and some of them are admired by fans of this kind of modern structure – for example, the new 24-storey Deutsche Bank building with its smooth and gleaming blue-grey façade of glass and steel. But the earlier post-war rebuilding was done hurriedly in a very graceless style, as witness the hideous main shopping mall, the Zeil. And the town's general reputation for mercenary brashness has given it a bad name around the world: it is considered soulless, characterless, too materialistic, too Americanised, especially by older people who remember the pre-war Frankfurt with one of the largest and finest mediaeval centres in Europe. But this adverse image is not entirely deserved. Frankfurt may be no beauty: but it has improved greatly in the past 20 years and today is one of Germany's most lively and exciting cities, teeming with new ideas, new ventures and conflicts, and it has a more active and varied cultural life than any other except Munich and Berlin. It may lack the chic and grace of Munich: but it is pleasingly international and has a real metropolitan flavour quite out of scale with its mere 600,000 population. People who come there to live and work are generally surprised to find it so sympathetic – 'It's a very open, modern society,' said one cultivated banker from Berlin, 'much less cliquey than places like Hamburg and Munich. If you arrive from outside, knowing no one, you are rapidly accepted on your merits. People are competitive, even ruthlessly so, but they are also hospitable and open-minded. Yes, it *is* rather American.' Today Frankfurt has become a little afraid that it may lose some of its high-level financial role to Berlin. However, it has been promised that the Bundesbank, the powerful German central bank, will remain in the city; and this will probably ensure that the headquarters of most other banks do so too. Despite the rise of Berlin, Frankfurt is likely to remain the commercial capital.

The presence of so much high-powered commerce makes Frankfurt a rich city, able to spend lavishly on the arts. And the presence of so many well-to-do-bankers and businessmen, by no means all philistines, helps to provide large audiences for 'established' culture. Until 1977 the city was SPD-run: then, like Stuttgart, it acquired a mayor on the liberal wing of the CDU, Walter Wallmann, and during his 10 years in office he poured money into culture, into new parks, piazzas and other amenities, and into restoring parts of the mediaeval centre around the Römer – all with the additional aim of giving a face-lift to Frankfurt's sorry image. And he was fairly successful. The new museums along the river are remarkable, especially the one devoted to local Jewish history. The Goethe Haus, where the poet was born and lived, and the cathedral where from 1562 to 1808 the Holy Roman emperors were elected and crowned, both serve to make Frankfurt central to German tradition and history. And today it still plays an important role in German intellectual life. Two of Germany's three most influential dailies are published here – the conservative *Frankfurter Allgemeine Zeitung*, strong on the arts as well as on economics and politics, and the radical *Frankfurter Rundschau*. Several leading publishing houses moved here from Leipzig after the war; here too is the celebrated Book Fair, which alas is such a frenetic hurly-burly that it tends to give visiting British and American publishers a jaundiced and distorted view of the city.

The huge and famous university, with 45,000 students, has won a post-war reputation for Leftism, especially in its philosophy and sociology departments. And this brings us to one of the most blatant features of modern Frankfurt: its noisy political polarisation. Can the reason be that so much successful capitalism, some of it with an ugly face, has served to provide the Left with a target for its opposition and has led to a sharpening of its knives? Certainly left-wing protest since the war has been stronger than anywhere else except West Berlin. The student riots of the late 1960s even began four years sooner in Frankfurt than elsewhere, and since then the discontent has rumbled on, taken up by Greens, anarchists and others. It has led to running battles between demonstrators and police, culminating in the great saga of the campaign against the extension of Frankfurt international airport, Germany's largest (see pp. 539–40).

But the Left in Frankfurt is not simply concerned with agitation. New ideas flourish here too. Danny Cohn-Bendit for years has been running an 'alternative' bookshop here; and in 1989 he was elected to the city council on the Greens' list, and was put in charge of 'multi-cultural relations' (i.e. helping *Gastarbeiter*). The city has a small Schwabing-like bohemian quarter, across the river in Sachsenhausen, full of jolly pubs. And the 'alternative' cultural and social scene of little fringe theatres, art centres and communes is livelier than in other towns except Berlin. Some of the fringe drama groups are made up of immigrant workers, notably Italians. Frankfurt has proportionately a larger *Gastarbeiter* population, 22 per cent of the total, than any other German city – and this adds colourfully to its diversity, but also to its problems. Drug-trafficking and other crime are at a higher level here than elsewhere. Near the main station is a sizeable red-light district, smaller than Hamburg's St-Pauli but sleazier and more sinister, operated mainly by Greeks, Turks and south Italians. So, warts and all, this is quite a metropolis. It makes Stuttgart, a city of the same size, seem dozily provincial in comparison. It was a great missed opportunity not to make Frankfurt the federal capital, but to grant that role instead to dull little Bonn.

The two leading Rhineland cities, Cologne and Düsseldorf, are in intense rivalry with each other, part in jest, part in earnest. Cologne is the Rhineland's cultural capital, Düsseldorf its commercial capital and the political one too, for the government of North-Rhine-Westphalia is there. The cities are very different in style – 'Cologne,' said one local observer, 'is more open and friendly; rich and poor jostle and chat together in a jolly, democratic way. Düsseldorf is more uptight, status-conscious and *nouveau riche*, and the social classes keep apart.' That was my own impression too.

Central Cologne was exceptionally badly bombed, then rebuilt in a casual jumble of styles. The traffic-jams are worse than in most big German cities; and a few ungainly high-rise blocks have been allowed to mar the view of the cathedral from some angles. The city's overall appearance is not attractive. Yet scattered here and there one finds a number of individually fine buildings, such as the well-restored Roman-esque churches, and some pleasant surprises and contrasts, such as Roman remains cheek-by-jowl with graceful new glass-and-steel struc-tures, or modern sculptures and gargoyles in old cobbled streets – notably in the restored ancient quarter by the Rathaus. Above this pot-pourri there soars the cathedral, merciful survivor of the worst of the bombing. Visible for miles across the Rhine plain, its twin black spires dwarf the rest of the city and look magical at night, floodlit in a soft silvery light.

The cathedral is the symbol and badge of local identity for the inhabitants, the Kölner, whose city patriotism is as vibrant as any in Germany. A Münchner, though proud of Munich, considers himself foremost a Bavarian: but the Kölner's loyalty is to Cologne far more than to the Rhineland. Phlegmatic Hamburgers may cherish as strong an attachment to their city: but they do not express it in the same extrovert emotional way as the Kölner, with their endless whimsical joking and songfulness. I was reminded of Italy, of the way that Bolognese or Neapolitans sing and joke about their cities. Indeed, Cologne's city-state mentality seems essentially Italian – hardly surpris-ing, maybe, seeing that this was the Romans' leading colony in what is now Germany, and many traces of their imprint have survived, not only in the Roman ruins but, so it is claimed, in the local people themselves, with their dark looks and lively, Latin-like rather un-German temperament. More than most other Rhinelanders, the Kölner are lively, gregarious, talkative, fond of their wine and beer, and more than a little vulgar. Their boisterous whimsy finds its fullest expression at Carnival-time (see p. 226). But it goes on all the year too, especially in the big *Kneipen* (pubs) where the locals drink their mild *Kölsch* beer in slim tall cylindrical glasses and are served by the famous Cologne beer-waiters, known as *Köbes*, whose jokey tradition it is to insult and provoke their customers (if a man in a group of three orders three beers, the *Köbes* may reply, 'Three beers, that's very kind — but what will *you* drink?'). It is a quirky cliquey society, much given to in-jokes told in the strange Kölsch dialect that an outsider can hardly follow; many of the stock jokes centre round the city's two mythical comic characters, little rotund Tünnes and tall bowler-hatted Schäl. Some visitors may find it all somewhat tedious; but it is good-natured. And this is a pleasantly informal, somewhat bohemian town, brimming with culture — some excellent museums, the best German TV station for plays and films, and over 150 art galleries, for this is the leading German city for art-dealers.

Düsseldorf too is a thriving centre of the art trade, more commercially orientated than Cologne. Here everything breathes money. It is the commercial capital of the nearby Ruhr, and its two tallest skyscrapers house the head offices of two of the main Ruhr steel firms, Thyssen and Mannesmann. This is also, after Frankfurt, the leading centre of international banking and finance in Germany with over two thousand foreign firms including 400 from Japan. The Japanese have made this their main trading centre in Europe, and the resident Japanese colony, 6,000, is the largest outside Japan. This wealthy city has a *per capita* income 25 per cent above the German average, and is said to contain more millionaires and big jewellers than any other. In smart society here, more than anywhere else in Germany, you are judged by your money and how well you display it. This can be observed in the Königsallee, known locally as the 'Kö', a fashionable boulevard where luxury cafés and boutiques face on to a central canal. Here some of the ladies are very chic indeed, but in a brittle, hard-faced, almost frightening style, lacking the gentler grace of Munich. The rest of Düsseldorf is mostly dull and ordinary, save for some parkland walks by the Rhine and a few lively Soho-like streets in the Altstadt with cheap outdoor restaurants. All in all, this is my least favourite of big German cities, and I am not alone in this opinion.

Hamburg, by contrast, is a town warmly liked and admired by almost all those who know it. It may possess some of the drawbacks of a northern climate; but it has an extraordinary spaciousness and serenity, a comfortable, confident red-brick quality, at once mercantile and truly cultured. It is Germany's opposite pole from Munich in the far south, its rival (along with Berlin) as leading metropolis. Whereas baroque and showy Munich recalls Austria, even Italy, Hamburg in looks and ambience has something of an English feel, unhurried and gentlemanly. Unlike Bavarians, its citizens seldom burst into song in public; they are heirs to a great liberal and seafaring tradition. Unlike Munich, capital once of a kingdom and now a large *Land*, Hamburg has always been a self-contained city-state and so it remains: it never ruled over its own hinterland, and so when the modern federal structure was created it was allowed to be a smallish *Land* on its own, covering just 748 square kilometres. In the thirteenth century it joined the Hanseatic League of north European trading cities and later became a 'Free and Hanseatic City', a title it still uses. For centuries it was run by its wealthy merchant families who made it immensely influential, the most prosperous of big German towns. In more recent years, its mighty port has run into trouble, partly because after 1945 it was cut off from its natural hinterland to the east (it is only 30 miles from the former GDR border); also some of its older industries such as shipbuilding went into decline, and as an economic pace-setter it began losing out to south Germany. However, German unification and the opening up of eastern Europe now offer brighter prospects to the port. And, despite its difficulties, Hamburg has always retained much manifest wealth. Bred of its long trading tradition, it has an open, outward-looking, world-embracing spirit. It is a most graceful and civilised place.

Water is its element – the huge port, the wide river Elbe, the Alster lake, and the canals. Hamburg holds the world record for bridges – 2,195 of them, compared with London's 850, Venice's 400. No other town in Europe encloses so large a lake right in its centre as the lovely Alster, almost two miles long, the shimmering focus of the city's life. Long-legged Nordic types with capes and scarves go striding along its shore-paths with their bounding, barking dogs, while sails glide against a backdrop of waterside weeping-willows, stately mercantile villas, and the line of spires that are Hamburg's sober skyline. In summer people sit in open-air cafés by the water. In a hard winter, the lake freezes over so firm that cars drive across it: one Sunday, stalls selling hot *Glühwein* were set up on the ice and 4,000 people flocked there for a party, despite police warnings of disaster.

Hamburg has a tidy symmetrical shape. Its downtown business and shopping area lies neatly between the Alster and the port, bounded by a ring-road that follows the line of the old city walls, while residential and factory districts spread out spaciously beyond. One curious paradox is that, while overall it is a handsome, even beautiful town, it contains hardly any individual buildings of real distinction, either old or new.

And this is not just due to the wartime bombing. Long before that, the merchants who built and ruled the city were rather philistine and took little trouble to endow it with fine art treasures, palaces and churches, as did the Wittelsbachs in Munich. They created opulent villas for their own use, but were less concerned with civic splendour. Then in 1842 a great fire destroyed most of the mediaeval nucleus of narrow streets with half-timbered houses, and after this the city was rebuilt on the spacious pattern it still has today. The lavish and pompous Rathaus was erected in 1897 in neo-Renaissance style, its vast interiors and heavy leather furnishings a symbol of the wealth and pride of the city at that time. In 1943, Air Marshal Harris's fire-raids wiped out much of the port and the working-class and factory districts east of the main station: but – a curious if unintended social discrimination – they left almost unscathed the smart bourgeois areas around the Alster and the stately green-roofed buildings that line the smaller Binnenalster in the heart of town.

Post-war reconstruction was better planned and executed than in most German towns devastated on this scale. 'The bombs killed 52,000 civilians, but in one sense were a blessing in disguise,' I was told by the city planning officer, Professor Egbert Kossak, 'for they enabled us to rebuild with much less congestion. Previously, many poorer areas housed 200 to 300 people per acre: now it is 40 to 60 people, and fewer still in the better districts. We have one of the lowest densities of any big European city.' Spacious already, the city has now become even more so. Broad avenues and through-roads have been laid out, where traffic moves easily with an almost total absence of jams. The downtown business area, rebuilt mostly in local red-brick style, is not especially beautiful but lacks the ugly concrete assertiveness of so many German cities. And there are no tall skyscrapers in the centre to mar the graceful skyline of spires. A 25-storey hotel, built in 1968, is at least well away from the inner city where restrictions are now quite strict: 'In 1984 the Springer group wanted to put up an 18-storey block,' said Kossak, 'but we beat them down to nine floors.' In residential areas, one finds streets of brick houses with distinctive Jugendstil wrought-iron balconies, and the odd zany splash of colour from a big modern pop-art mural on a blind wall. Many rebuilt streets still keep their strange ancient names – Ole Hoop, Hopfensack, Dammtordamm.

Today the city is culturally very much alive and has one of the world's finest opera companies (see p. 325). Hamburg is also known as

'Germany's media capital', but this is something of a simplification, for it has no daily paper of the class of those in Frankfurt and Munich. But the TV news programmes are edited here, and so are most of Germany's leading weekly magazines. One of these, *Die Zeit*, typifies the liberal political tradition of this city of free-thinkers that never warmed to Nazism (pro-Hitler rallies were always less enthusiastic here than in other German towns). The merchant class, mainly conservative, has in modern times played little part in governing the city, which has a large working-class population and back in the 1870s was a cradle of German Socialism. Since 1945 this home town of Helmut Schmidt (he was once a senator) has been ruled without a break by the SPD (save in 1953–7, and in coalition with the FDP since August 1987). Its governing body is called the Senate, and as it is both a city and a *Land*, the head of the Senate is both Lord Mayor *and* Prime Minister.

The fact of being also a *Land* gives Hamburg a little more autonomy than most German cities – and it is very well governed, with excellent social services, housing and public transport. But the disadvantage is that it is financially unsupported by its hinterland in adjoining Lower Saxony and Schleswig-Holstein, whose citizens can enjoy its cultural and other amenities but pay no taxes to it. What is more, many industrial firms and well-to-do families have been moving outside its borders into the adjacent *Länder* where land prices and other costs tend to be lower. Hamburg's own population has dropped since 1963 from 1,847,000 to 1,580,000, but that of the conurbation has risen to some 2.5 million. This population drift has now finally been halted, and some younger families are moving back into renovated and subsidised housing in the city centre. But the exodus of industry continues, and this leads to a loss of tax revenue. Hamburg is in financial difficulty, and is beset by a series of handicaps, not all of them its own fault. Not only does it suffer from modern German industry's general preference for settling in the south, but its own traditional industries happen to be those most vulnerable to today's trends. Blohm und Voss, leading Hamburg shipbuilders, have been obliged to shed about a third of their former 6,500-strong workforce and they survive only by diversifying into new fields, including the building of tanks for the German army.

A guided boat-trip round the huge port, one of the tourist highlights of the city, is a fascinating but dispiriting experience. The visitor is dutifully shown the ultra-modern container terminals and dry docks, the 40 miles of quays, the new $2\frac{1}{2}$-mile-long suspension bridge, and the protection walls built against a recurrence of the 1962 floods that claimed 350 lives. But the port, like many in the world today, has been having a tough time. It has to struggle to compete with Rotterdam and Antwerp to the west, better situated for the Atlantic trade, and it suffers from EC tariff regulations that favour road transport to Rotterdam. Today in terms of tonnage handled it is only the fourth port of Europe, below Antwerp and Le Havre, far below Rotterdam. Even so, its traffic has been increasing, from 35 million tons in 1967 to 55 million in 1988, and this enables many merchants and shipowners to remain very rich: but it does not help the employment situation in the docks. This is because Hamburg, in order to compete with other ports, has built very modern terminals that can load or unload very fast, using few dockers, and this speed suits the big container ships, for harbour dues are high (some 100,000 DM for a 50,000-ton vessel to remain berthed for two days). One union leader said ruefully: 'Twenty years ago the port was busy all night and all weekend with big gangs of dockers working overtime. Now the work is done so fast by just a few men and the port is deserted at weekends. No wonder so many dockers are out of work.'

In some other ways, however, the city's economic picture is now improving, after a difficult period. From 1945 to 1989 the GDR and Poland tended to use their own ports in the Baltic, but now these areas are turning to Hamburg again, which is set to regain its traditional role as the major North Sea port for much of central Europe, and to benefit from the increased trade with the east. At the same time, Hamburg's efforts to attract new modern high-tech industries, to replace its old ones, have had some success since the mid-1980s. MBB, the Munich-based aerospace firm, has expanded its local plant where it makes the fuselage for Airbus and now employs 7,000; Philips also has a big new microchips operation. Thanks to these and other ventures, local unemployment fell from 14.3 per cent in 1986 to around 10 per cent in 1991: but it is still above the west German average.

It is widely felt that for years after the war Hamburg lived too easily on its reputation. And when in 1985 I met the then Lord Mayor, Klaus von Dohnanyi (SPD), he blamed this on the merchants: 'For so many centuries,' he told me, 'they had success coming out of their ears: they looked down arrogantly on those "peasants" in Munich and didn't feel they needed to compete. Even a mere twenty years ago the city was actually turning down new investment proposals, one of them from Volkswagen, because it felt it did not need them. This absurd attitude is now changing but it takes time.' There are still plenty of rich merchant families around. Like the gentlemen of the City of London, they have a cautious, traditional way of doing things, and they find it undignified to have to use dynamic tactics to go out and 'sell' their city. This mentality is now on the wane. But merchants and SPD city rulers still cooperate too little: it is symbolic that the Rathaus and the Stock Exchange stand back-to-back, facing in opposite directions.

Despite these difficulties, there is still a great deal of wealth in Hamburg, and it can be seen in the streets, where really smart people are almost as numerous as in Munich. Many of the shop-windows too are dazzling, especially in the five big new shopping-arcades near the Binnenalster, among the most stylish and opulent in Europe. All were built since 1979 and are doing quite well despite the mild recession. Hanseviertel and Galleria are the most strikingly beautiful, with domed glass-and-steel roofs. Their specialised boutiques sell things you do not really need, like rare teas, Tiffany lamps, and clothes and toys for cats and dogs, and their window-displays are the height of colourful arty originality – a jeweller's bedecked with broken eggshells, that sort of thing.

The Hamburgers themselves, less flamboyant than their shops, do not flaunt their wealth like the people of Munich or Düsseldorf. Yet in their own way they have great style. Some are the northern blond type, tall and lean, and they stride the streets in a lordly way; sometimes the men wear those blue Hamburg sailor's caps beloved of Helmut Schmidt. Yet there is very little true *Schickeria* or gossip-column café-society. People prefer to entertain discreetly in their own homes. They are affable and helpful to visitors, but they do not make friends easily and their inner social circles are hard to penetrate. There is less easy informality than in British society today – yet the breezy tolerance and understatement of Hamburg has a decidedly English feel, and it is well known as the most 'English' of German cities, alike in its looks, habits and mentalities. It remains proud of the close historic trade links: 'When it rains in London, Hamburgers put up their umbrellas,' the saying goes. Repeatedly it reminded me of London – a richer, cleaner, tidier London. And more modern too, even though, paradoxically, the strong English influences and affinities relate mainly to the old pre-war England of claret-drinking, beamed pubs, blue blazers and bespoke tailors. Tall brick Victorian-era mansions, set amid lawns and tall trees, recall London. And out in the straggling suburbs there are echoes of old England, even rural England: beyond Altona, within the city borders you find leafy lanes, old timbered farmsteads, country houses with neat gardens, and you might be in mid-Surrey.

The Elbe is now so polluted that little fresh fish is caught locally. But the famous fish-market on the quayside at St-Pauli survives, and gives a lovely idea of the old traditional Hamburg. It is held every Sunday from 5 to 10 a.m., when it must close promptly under an old bye-law forbidding it to compete with church services. Even on a cold winter morning this huge market is lively and crowded with buyers and sellers of all sorts – a brave sight at break of day, with the seagulls flying and the dinghies bouncing on the choppy water. It is now mainly a food-cum-flea market selling anything from rabbits to potplants. But some fish is still sold too – notably by the ebullient 'Eely Dieter' whose loud fast-patter sales line in eels draws the crowds. There are comic Dutch traders too, in clogs and high black hats, and a fruitmonger whose successful sales technique is to pelt his audience with bananas. Late revellers from the nearby night-spots of the Reeperbahn descend on the market in the early hours, blearily sozzled or otherwise sated. Often they make for the big popular Fischerhaus restaurant which does a special early Sunday trade: here, one crisp dawn, in the company of accordionists, tipsy sailors and necking couples in evening dress, I enjoyed a hearty breakfast of beer, soused herring and Hamburg's remarkable eel-plum-and-vegetable soup.

Up the hill is St-Pauli proper, which used to be a fishing-village and working-class district. Since then its notorious main street, the Reeper-bahn, garish and sleazy, has undergone three metamorphoses. First, in the late nineteenth century, when the city's transatlantic passenger trade boomed, a large entertainment district grew up, most of it quite respectable, to cater for the people waiting often several days for their sailings: there were theatres, smart restaurants and terrace-cafés with live orchestras, and a few brothels too of the discreet luxurious kind. In the side-alleys were the sailors' pubs and whorehouses. Then after the war times changed. The big liners vanished; the sailors became fewer as the port modernised and their ships in port turned round so fast; and the Reeperbahn slid down-market into the sex-and-voyeurism industry, catering mainly for provincial businessmen and tourists. In the erotic cabarets, the live sex-act came in every shape and style; in the neat brothels of the Herbertstrasse, the girls sat in ground-floor windows in a lurid pink glow. Some civic worthies were annoyed that the city's popular image around the world should have come to be identified with the Reeperbahn, but they made few moves to curb the excesses. Hamburg, after all, stands for tolerance.

Since the late 1980s, things have changed again, partly under the impact of AIDS. The biggest brothel, the enormous Eros Center, has closed down and become a respectable hotel. The sex-industry is withdrawing into the side-streets, where the Hubertstrasse still just about survives. And the Reeperbahn itself is again mainly an entertainment centre, still very garish and vulgar-looking, though smart restaurants are moving in, as St-Pauli moves back up-market and worker tenements are pulled down to make way for new bourgeois flats. The former Star Club, where the still unknown Beatles performed in the early 1960s, is again a music-hall — but where is today's John Lennon? The famous Café Keese, a survivor since pre-war days, is a big, plushy, very decorous dance-hall for genteel pick-ups mostly middle-aged, with all the thrilling naughtiness of Bournemouth in the 1950s.

St-Pauli's nearby Hafenstrasse, high on a terrace above the Elbe, has also achieved notoriety in recent years: in the mid-1980s some of its half-derelict old houses were occupied by squatters who formed a militant commune and violently resisted all police attempts to evict them. The conflict dragged on for years, making national headlines and polarising local opinion: most Hamburgers were furious at the 'damage' done to the city's image (much more so than in the case of the Reeperbahn, that venerable institution), but the SPD rulers refused to act toughly with the squatters. The latter painted provocative murals and slogans on the blind walls ('We Unite in the Struggle against Renovation, Fascism and the Police State'), clearly visible from any ship entering port. These Leftists were crusading against moves to redevelop this prime site above the river by removing its old working-class inhabitants and building expensive flats and offices. Finally in 1991 the squatters lost the last of their legal appeals, and it seemed that at last they would be evicted.

Germany's other great North Sea port, Bremen, on the river Weser, has no St-Pauli and no Alster; but otherwise it has much in common with its larger rival and neighbour. Like Hamburg it is a Hanseatic free city, very old and very proud, and therefore is likewise allowed to be a *Land* on its own (forming an enclave within Lower Saxony and comprising also the port of Bremerhaven, down on the coast). Like Hamburg, it is a town of seafarers and prosperous merchants, and as at Hamburg the port and shipyards have run into difficulty. Like Hamburg, it has a liberal spirit and strong English connections (there are three daily flights to London). But in some ways the looks and ambience of Bremen are less English than

Dutch or Flemish, and this is noticeable especially in the architecture of the tall gabled town houses, and the weather-beaten looks of the men that stride the cobbled streets — you almost expect them to be wearing clogs.

While Hamburg is somewhat sedate and serious, Bremen has a cheeky quirkiness, a folklorish quality, that I found most appealing. This finds expression in the two curious statues that stand outside the lovely old Gothic Rathaus in the main square — the one, dating from 1404, is a giant 30-foot figure of the knight Roland; the other, entirely modern, is a bronze pyramid of a cock standing on a cat standing on a dog standing on a donkey, and it represents the famous Street Musicians of Bremen from the story by the brothers Grimm. Across the square, I was surprised to find a young man in top hat and tails, sweeping rubbish and confetti from the steps of the cathedral, while a group of other young people stood by laughing and throwing down more rubbish: I was told this is an old Bremen custom, whereby a man still unwed by his 30th birthday must perform this ritual, and then marry the first pretty girl who kisses him. Typical Bremen. In another corner of the square, a chorus of men in nautical dress were singing sea-shanties. Then I explored the adjacent Böttcherstrasse, a delightful red-brick shopping arcade built in the 1920s in *art nouveau* style, lined with highly original boutiques selling hand-made toys and assorted orna-ments of eccentric but clever design. The Ratskeller under the Rathaus, by tradition, sells no beer but only German wine: it has charming little cubicles for private parties, dating from 1600 — and even in today's age the tradition is still observed that a cubicle's door must be left open if a man and a woman are alone in it.

Not that Bremen today is at all puritan or diehard. It has even acquired the reputation of being one of the most avant-garde and 'Red' of German cities, thanks largely to its new and progressive university (see p. 247). Applied to the city as a whole this Leftist reputation is somewhat unjustified, for its own Socialist leaders, who have controlled the council without a break since 1945, are on the moderate wing of the SPD and pride themselves on having better relations with Bremen's conservative merchants than is the case in Hamburg. 'My council and my merchants run my city in a spirit of great solidarity,' I was told by the extraordinary Hans Koschnick, governing mayor and prime minister from 1967 to 1985 — a large, expansive man, eloquent and flamboyant, demagogic but extremely amiable. He had the kind of self-satirising tongue-in-cheek mock arrogance that is very much commoner in France (he even reminded me of the 'emperor' Paul Bocuse) than in a Germany where most politicians are so boringly decorous. Bremen quirkiness, once more.

'My university has now settled down peacefully,' Koschnick went on, 'and my GDP is still high. But my shipyards have been forced to contract, and my unemployment level has risen to 14 per cent. Some 20 per cent of industrial jobs here used to be in shipbuilding: now it's 8 per cent.' There are other problems too: fisheries have slumped badly, and the port, which formerly grew rich on cotton and coffee imports, has run into the same kind of trouble as at Hamburg. The local shipyards, like others in Europe, have been suffering from Japanese and South Korean competition: for many years they also made the mistake of continuing to build large container vessels and tankers for a saturated market, rather than switch in time to more specialised ships. One local firm, AG Weser, closed in 1983. Bremer Vulkan, the largest of all German shipyards, ran into grave deficit about the same time and was forced to shed a third of its workforce. The Thyssen-Bornemisza group, its main owners, lost some 75 million DM in the process and grew so disillusioned with shipbuilding that they sold out 40 per cent of their share, which has now been acquired by the City of Bremen itself. BV is diversifying, and at last seems to be doing better. The German shipbuilding industry as a whole is still the world's third largest, and after a hard period of rationalisation it is now holding its own, but only with the help of large subsidies. As for Bremen itself, it is making an effort to attract new modern replacement industries, in fields such as aerospace and electronics, and with sporadic success. Koschnick himself resigned in June 1985, to move on to politics in Bonn, having sworn to me a month previously: 'I want to stay here in my Rathaus. I'd rather be first in Bremen than fourth or fifth in Bonn. Or rather, I'm second in Bremen – my wife is stronger.'

So ends this tour of the main German cities. It excludes Hanover, a town I do not know well. And it excludes the Ruhr conurbation – but for this see pages 95–103.

# *The* Bund *and the* Länder: *how and why federalism works*

In the large and elegant spa town of Wiesbaden, capital of Hessen, the *Land* government and parliament today inhabit the sumptuous former palace of the Dukes of Nassau, all gilt chandeliers and painted ceiling. Here I attended a session of the *Landtag* (parliament). Amid repeated heckling, CDU and Green orators were engaged in sharp debate about a local nuclear power station; then CDU and SPD crossed swords over the *Land*'s policy on primary schools. Some CDU deputies were quietly reading *Bild Zeitung*; a young Green left her seat to go and flirt gently with an elderly SPD man; behind the Speaker's platform stretched a big tapestry of the ancient Lion of Hessen. All was lively and informal. The *Landtag*'s Americanised young PRO told me that so popular are its debates with the public that seats in the visitors' gallery need to be booked months ahead; I saw several parties of schoolchildren there, and a contingent of *Bundeswehr* conscripts.

The scene may have changed since Nassau days – and so have Hessen's boundaries, for the modern *Land* is composed of several former autonomous states of the old German Confederation, one of them the dukedom of Nassau. But in a town such as Wiesbaden it is easy to see how very much today's federal system is the inheritor of an age-old German tradition. Federalism comes naturally to the Germans, who find it perfectly normal to elect one parliament in Bonn and another in their *Land*; and, although the Constitution sets precise limits on a *Land*'s autonomy, its government is nonetheless a potent reality to its citizens, and is headed by a *Ministerpräsident* (prime minister) who is always a local figure of some power. Some of these men play a major role simultaneously both in their *Land* and in Bonn, though they do not hold ministerial office in both at once. Franz Josef Strauss, a senior minister in Bonn in the 1960s, then became Prime Minister of Bavaria: but as chairman of the CSU he continued to wield great influence in federal politics. Some other prime ministers prefer to devote themselves mainly to their *Land*, yet they always have some voice in Bonn too through their membership of the *Bundesrat* (see p. 88). It is sometimes argued that too much of the best talent tends to stay in the *Länder*, and the quality of Bonn politics suffers accordingly.

Each *Land* has its own sizeable office in Bonn, the *Vertretung* (representation), which acts as a kind of embassy and is headed by a man with the rank of *Land* minister: here it defends its interests by lobbying the Federal Government and trying to influence its policies. At Baden-Württemberg's *Vertretung*, which has a staff of 40, I was told: 'Before 1918, the German dukes and kings each sent a representative to the court of the Emperor in Berlin: our office there was the *Vertretung der Könige von Württemberg*. And that system continues. Federal Canada has a somewhat similar one, but not the United States.' Bonn, on the other hand, has no representative offices in the *Länder*, nothing at all resembling the *préfectures* in France. In Bonn, each *Vertretung* entertains lavishly, rather like an embassy, and vies with the others to stage the best parties or hold the finest concerts. Bavaria's 'embassy', close to the *Bundestag*, has a big beer-cellar in its basement where Bavarian-style parties are held nearly every night – I attended one, to mark some anniversary, and found it packed with people in local costume, swaying to and fro with their foaming tankards as a brass band played. It could have been the Hofbräuhaus. 'We're on foreign soil here,' said one beefy typist, 'so we have to show the flag.' Scots, I felt, might be envious: might it not be nice to have some wee bagpipe-filled corner of Scotland in the heart of Westminster?

Who calls the tune, the Federal Government (*Bund*) or the *Länder*? The share-out of responsibilities between them is a complex business. Under the Constitution, the *Länder* have competence in all matters except those that it has expressly assigned to the *Bund*, and these include, principally, foreign affairs, defence, currency, post and telecommunications, and railways. The *Länder* in turn have almost exclusive responsibility for cultural affairs, education, radio and television, police, environment, and local government and planning. Then there exists a third sector, the so-called 'concurrent tasks', where the Constitution allows the *Bund* a prior right to legislate, leaving the *Länder* to do so where it has not taken up its option: this field includes civil and criminal law, labour law, road traffic, and a number of economic matters. In practice the *Bund* nearly always does exercise its right, so a *Land*'s effective legislative role is limited. However, the *Länder* in many cases have the task of administrating federal laws within their borders, and a *Land* is often able to take its own decisions within the broad framework of a *Bund* law. Thus, for example, the *Bund* lays down the overall policy regarding nuclear power, but a *Land* has the right to ban or authorise any nuclear plant on its territory.

*Bund* and *Länder* derive their incomes from taxes divided between them under a complex set of rules. In a word, personal income tax and corporation tax are shared out fifty-fifty, while the proceeds of turnover taxes go two-thirds to the *Bund* and one-third to the *Länder*. Some tax revenue is passed on to the cities and other local authorities, who also levy their own taxes (see below). All tax legislation is formulated by the *Bund* and applies uniformly throughout the country, so as to avoid imbalances in the tax burden. What is more, since some *Länder* are richer than others and therefore derive more from local taxes, there is an Equalisation Law (*Finanzausgleichgesetz*) that enforces a redistribution whereby no *Land* ends up with a net tax revenue more than 5 per cent above or below the federal average. Hamburg and Bremen are the wealthiest of the *Länder*: this may seem curious, in view of their economic difficulties, described earlier, but it must be remembered that these are city *Länder* without hinterlands, whereas in rural areas the standard of living is lower. Thus Bavaria, despite its new industrial boom, is still below average in wealth. Under the equalisation scheme, Hamburg, Bremen, Baden-Württemberg and Hessen all contribute to the pool, while the six other *Länder* are all recipients (West Berlin was not included, because of its special subsidies). And it is not surprising that the *Länder* are constantly bickering about this share-out, some complaining that they have to pay too much, others that they do not receive enough. Since 1990, the main dispute between them has been over how much each should contribute to the new 150 billion DM fund for helping the five eastern *Länder* (see p. 472). These new *Länder* are not expected to join the main equalisation scheme until 1995 at the earliest, when they will all be major recipients.

The Equalisation Law is just one example of federal control over the *Länder*. In many other matters, too, the *Bund* over the past 30 years has subtly increased its powers (the Constitution has been amended 34 times in this direction) and this is not too popular with the *Länder*. Some of the changes however have been made purely in the interests of greater fairness and efficient standardisation. For example, until fifteen years ago police uniforms were grey in Bavaria, green in Hessen and dark blue in Hamburg (as in Britain) which is what firemen wear elsewhere in Germany. So visitors to Hamburg from other regions often thought its policemen were firemen – very confusing! So the *Bund* stepped in with a new law, and now all German police wear green coats with khaki trousers. Similarly the *Bund* has standardised civil servants' salary scales and pension rights, so as to remove discrepancies that disadvantaged employees in some *Länder*. The *Bund* has also made efforts to induce the *Länder* to harmonise their systems of education – a field where they are sovereign – but this has not proved particularly successful (see p. 237).

More significant has been the recent tendency of the *Bund* to increase, or try to increase, its general control of the economy – a centralising trend common to many other advanced countries. The

*Bund* has allocated generous new funds to the *Länder* for such matters as research and technology, but with the condition that it retains a say in how this money is spent. While glad of the hand-outs, the *Länder* resent the various encroachments on their autonomy: but they are not powerless to defend themselves. For example, in 1984 they succeeded in getting a federal law adopted that bans the *Bund* from interfering in a *Land*'s policy for building and running hospitals. Previously this was a joint responsibility, since much of the money for health services comes from the *Bund*. But now each *Land* receives a lump sum from Bonn and is free to spend it as it wishes. 'This has been quite a victory for us,' I was told in Baden-Württemberg; 'it is the first example for years of the tide of power moving back towards the *Länder*.'

The *Länder* are regularly able to influence federal policy through the *Bundesrat*[1], the Upper House of parliament, which is entirely composed of their delegates. As this chamber has the power to block federal legislation in certain cases, the *Länder* can use it as a weapon. Voting in the *Bundesrat*, as in the *Bundestag*, very often goes on party lines – but not always. Sometimes the *Länder* perceive that they have common interests which override party considerations, and one finds surprising coalitions. Thus in the mid-1980s the four northern *Länder* – Hamburg and Bremen, both SPD, and Lower Saxony and Schleswig-Holstein, then firmly CDU – would vote jointly against measures which they feel are harmful to north Germany.

Inevitably the Federal Government tends to enjoy easiest relations with *Länder* of its own political colour, while with others there may be frictions: one SPD Minister in North-Rhine-Westphalia complained to me, 'This Kohl Government has Thatcherite policies against public spending, and as we cannot fix our own level of taxation, this makes it hard for us to apply measures to reduce unemployment, as we would like.' But it is rare that Bonn goes so far as openly to victimise a *Land* in opposition hands – the Constitution anyway would make this very difficult – and in general a spirit of fair play and cooperation prevails. Never has any *Land* staged an open revolt against Bonn, nor even been as unduly obstructive as it might have the power to be. What is more,

---

1. By mid-1991, although the Government in Bonn was CDU-led, nearly all the western *Länder* were controlled by the SPD, alone or in coalition: only Bavaria, Baden-Württemberg and Rheinland-Pfalz were in CDU/CSU hands. In the east, however, all the new *Länder* except Brandenburg were run by the CDU, and so was Berlin.

in no *Land* is there any separatist movement worth taking seriously, of the kinds found to some degree in Brittany, Scotland or the Spanish Basque provinces.

The federal system indeed works well, and its basic structure is very rarely questioned by Germans in the way that the French, for instance, ceaselessly criticise their own contrasting heritage of centralisation. The *Land*/Bonn power struggles that I have described do not really amount to much more than normal rivalry of interest and they are not destructive. The system is popular with the public and has been getting more so: according to surveys made regularly by the Allensbach Institute, Germany's best-known opinion poll body, the proportion of people wanting to see *Land* governments abolished and all main decisions taken in Bonn fell steadily from 49 per cent in 1952 to 9 per cent in 1980.

The system is popular because it helps to keep government in closer touch with the governed, over a whole range of human welfare matters − education for example − where it is felt that local politicians and bureaucrats will have better understanding of local needs than grey men in far-off Bonn. Federalism has also probably been an advantage to Germany's economic development, for the *Länder* do possess a degree of autonomy in economic planning and subsidies, and this helps local initiative and encourages flexibility − as Baden-Württemberg's former Prime Minister, Lothar Späth, explained to me in the case of agriculture: 'I am able to concentrate on helping the small family farms here in this *Land*, which need a different support system from the bigger ones in the north. Of course we are limited by EC rules, but I do have some freedom of action. Our federal system is in this sense more human.'

In some other respects however the system can sometimes prove a handicap. Elections for the *Bundestag* do not coincide with those for the various *Land* parliaments, nor do these coincide with each other, so that each year there are usually two or three of them. A federal government of any colour therefore has to be careful that its actions do not harm the chances of the party of that same colour in a forthcoming *Land* election. This can be inhibiting to policy-making in Bonn and can sometimes delay the taking of necessary action. And in those fields where the *Länder* hold the responsibility − for example, television (see p. 354) and education (see p. 237) − effective reform or other action can likewise be impeded, for the *Länder* need to coordinate their measures and this, for obvious political reasons, they frequently fail to do. So federalism has its drawbacks. But few doubt that overall it has helped to contribute to Germany's post-war record of good government.

## Benevolent technocrats in the Rathaus

Decentralisation does not stop at *Land* level but goes on down to cities, towns and smaller communes, all of which enjoy rather more autonomy than is usual in most other European countries. The city of Stuttgart has 15,000 full-time municipal employees and an annual budget of over 3 billion DM: it is responsible for its own gas and electricity supplies, for the three largest hospitals, and for many welfare services and cultural activities, and must also pay for much school building. Even a semi-rural commune of 3,000 people will be in charge of its own planning, roads and building policy, and might have a budget of 5 million DM or more.

This German civic tradition can in one sense be traced back to the privileges of the Free Towns of the Middle Ages. In another sense it is quite new, for the municipal system was reconstituted just after the war: when the Allies set out to rebuild democracy, each occupying Power saw fit to impose its own model – and this has remained. The Americans, in the south, set up something close to their own pattern: full-time, fully-salaried professional mayors. The British in the north installed a system rather more similar to their own: the mayor is part-time and has another profession that brings in most of his income, while the main executive work is done by a salaried town clerk. It is thus not easy to generalise about German local government.

In north Germany, the mayor is very often a local businessman, lawyer or teacher. But, although he is not full-time, he is very much more than a mere figurehead chosen annually to preside at banquets and open flower-shows, as in Britain. He may well spend twenty hours or more each week on his mayoral duties, and has much serious policy-making work to do. In an average north German town, local affairs are highly politicised, yet they are run on a coalition basis that makes for a remarkable degree of consensus. If the majority part in the town council is CDU, then it will elect a CDU mayor, but his two deputies may well be from the other parties, FDP and SPD. And the *Oberstadt-direktor* (town clerk) and other senior salaried officials appointed by the council also have declared political affiliations. These posts are shared out between the parties according to their local strengths, and it could even be that the town clerk is of a different political colour from the mayor. This *de facto* coalition system owes nothing to the British model and is not a statutory obligation but very often a gentleman's agreement, worked out pragmatically as the most efficient and democratic way of doing things. In Göttingen, a former mayor told me: 'In the old pre-war Prussian days, officials and councillors tended to be autocratic and very conservative, and there was little real debate. This then made it easier for the Nazis to gain control of local affairs. We feel that our new multi-party coalition system, more open and politically honest, provides checks against such abuses. Of course there are tough debates in the council on many issues: but then comes the vote, where the majority party usually wins, and the officials have to apply the policy whether it suits their views or not.'

In a south German city, the chief mayor (*Oberbürgermeister*) is more of a boss figure. He too is usually a party man: but, highly paid, he doubles up the roles of political leader and chief executive, and can devote his full energies to his job. Moreover, he is directly elected by popular mandate, initially for eight years, with options for renewal. It is a system that puts a strong mayor in a hugely powerful position. He is assisted by five *Bürgermeister*, full-time salaried specialists who are chosen by the city council. This council is sovereign, on budgetary matters and for major new projects: but the mayor, by law, is alone responsible for day-to-day administration, where he cannot be interfered with. In practice it is the mayor who initiates many projects. The council has the right to overrule him, and sometimes does so. But the councillors, unpaid and busy with their own professions, generally defer to the mayor and his salaried deputies with their technical abilities. So a city tends to be run by benevolent technocratic oligarchs who see themselves as business managers, more concerned with getting things done than with wheeler-dealer politics.

This tradition of highly professional city management can sometimes lead to a certain high-handed paternalism — or so it is alleged by some younger critics, Green and others. But it carries undoubted advantages. As mayors and deputy mayors draw handsome salaries and do valuable jobs, the career tends to attract men (or women) of high calibre and qualifications, and senior civic officialdom thus carries higher prestige than, for instance, in Britain. Mayors, often men with a legal background, see themselves as forming a clear-cut profession. Some belong to no party but present themselves to the electorate on their managerial record, as if applying to be head of some big firm; in this spirit they will sometimes seek to move on from one town to a larger one, in search of better pay or prospects. In Konstanz by the Swiss border, Dr Eickmayer comes from Münster in the north: he stood on a non-party ticket and was elected mayor in face of SPD and CDU candidates, both local men, because the citizens knew about him and trusted him. It is a state of affairs that often makes for consensus – in Stuttgart, Mayor Rommel gets on as easily with SPD councillors as with his CDU colleagues – but today it is being contested by Greens newly arrived in councils, who want to shake up the cosy ententes between the older parties (see pp. 546–8).

In smaller towns and rural areas, alike in south and north Germany, the mayor is a part-timer assisted by paid officials. In the industrial townlet of Unterföhring (pop. 2,500), on the edge of the Munich conurbation, the mayor, SPD, is a salesman for an oil company: he told me that he is frequently in conflict with the larger district (*Kreis*) to which the town belongs, for its right-wing CSU-run council manages to block his schemes for low-cost 'social' housing. In Dörpen, a big village of 2,500 souls in Lower Saxony, near the Dutch border, the CDU mayor is a prosperous farmer: he said that his father was mayor before him, and he took on the job 'for idealistic civic reasons'. In the 1970s, the communes (*Gemeinde*) in rural areas were regrouped into larger units, rather as in Britain in the same period, and for the same reasons of administrative efficiency. Western Germany now has some 8,500 communes, against 24,200 before, and few have less than 2,500 inhabitants. All communes, except for the larger towns, are grouped into districts, with an average population of 170,000; in most areas there are thus four levels of government: *Gemeinde, Kreis, Land* and *Bund*. It is costly and bureaucratic, but it works quite smoothly, and few people are in favour of modifying the structure any further.

The financing of local government has recently become a problem. During the boom years West German cities were able to spend lavishly on new projects and even today they are still quite wealthy by British standards. But the money that a city can raise from local taxes is not intended to be adequate for all its needs, and for many of its main activities it either receives further grants from *Land* or *Bund* or it operates in partnership with them. Thus a *Land* helps pay for school building and shares the running costs of opera houses; *Land* and *Bund* pay substantially for new hospitals and bear most of the cost of major new road and traffic schemes. This involves a good deal of joint decision-taking, and of course there are frictions. In particular, Mrs Thatcher's views on the need to cut public spending have been shared to quite an extent by the Kohl Government, which has reduced its level of grants to cities and has tried to induce them to make their own economies. Even if no SPD-led councils have responded with open revolt in quite the Liverpool manner, they have nonetheless grown resentful, for cities have been obliged to cut back their budgets or resort to large bank loans. Nearly all big towns are heavily in debt.

Matters have frequently been aggravated by the tendency of a city's sources of revenue to move out into the nearby towns – as in the case of Hamburg. Well-to-do ratepayers desert the city to build new homes in the suburbs where there is more space and land prices are lower. Industry moves too, for much the same reasons – and this is an economic blow, for a German city's major source of revenue is from the *Gewerbesteuer*, a tax on local industry and business. Towns thus vie with each other to attract new firms. And it is the larger, densely-packed ones that are losing out. In some, notably Cologne, Hanover and Karlsruhe, the *Land* government has enacted laws to force the suburbs to merge with the city into a new larger unit, and the problem is thus solved. But elsewhere this has proved politically impossible.

One such case is Stuttgart. So much of its territory is hilly forest that virtually all available building land has long been used up, and land prices are the highest in Germany: up to 18,000 DM per square metre in central office areas, compared with 1,500 DM or so in a good residential district, and a mere 500 DM outside the town. So house-loving Stuttgarters have been moving out in their thousands: since 1962 the city's own population has fallen from 643,000 to 560,000, while that of the four surrounding *Kreise* has risen by 300,000 to reach 1.9 million. Industry has followed suit: in the past thirty years more than 300 firms left the town to resettle nearby, including the world head office of the mighty Bosch. Several of the towns around Stuttgart have thus grown richer *per capita* than the city itself, and have been able to build themselves luxurious new civic centres, swimming pools and so on. Sindelfingen, home of the largest Daimler-Benz factory, is said to be the richest town in Germany. And Stuttgarters have grown resentful. 'The system penalises us,' says Rommel; 'people from these places freely make use of our own central amenities – opera, museums, hospitals and so on – but the towns refuse to help pay for these directly. They guard their independence jealously and have grown too big and powerful for the *Land* to be able to impose a merger, as it did at Karlsruhe some years ago. Meanwhile Stuttgart is rotting away. I have had to reduce the funding for housing, sports centres, and new town-planning schemes.'

In the early years after the war, the replanning and rebuilding of towns was seldom done very imaginatively. The urgent need was to give shelter to millions still virtually homeless, and then to get the economy moving again. Blocks of flats were thrown up all over the place, and city centres were decked out with ungainly new office buildings. The imperatives of the *Wirtschaftswunder* came before aesthetics. Only a few cities — Hamburg, Munich and Hanover are examples — made any concerted efforts to plan more harmoniously. Many of the others developed into visually characterless places, barely distinguishable one from the other.

Then in the early 1970s there emerged a gradual change of mood. As environmental needs came to the forefront, so the call went out for 'a more humane city', more agreeable to live in. Since then, the centres of many towns have been improved quite remarkably. Shopping streets have been closed to traffic, and pedestrian zones laid out, with flowering shrubs, modern sculpture and outdoor cafés — on a more lavish scale than in most parts of Europe. Handsome old townhouses are no longer being recklessly torn down to make room for more practical modern ones; instead they are now being restored where feasible, even if this adds to costs. My own view is that in the earlier post-war years the Germans were understandably so obsessed with obliterating their terrible past that they tended to abolish many good things along with the bad, in their eagerness to make a clean start. And so they even added to the Allied bombers' toll by pulling down perfectly respectable older houses, undamaged but unpopular simply because they were not new (see p. 205). But this period has ended: nineteenth century downtown blocks are now in some cases being refurbished and modernised, so that their inhabitants, often quite poor and elderly people, can stay there rather than be rehoused in some unfamiliar suburb. And, now that the centres of big towns have been made more attractive, many younger middle-class people have been rediscovering the charms of living centrally, in a smallish flat, rather than emulating their parents' migration to big homes with gardens on the periphery. The trend may be of some comfort to Rommel. But today his main concern is how to catch for Stuttgart as much as possible of that lucrative new high-tech industry that has been flowing into Baden-Württemberg and Bavaria.

## North v. South: rustbelt Ruhr hits back against Bavarian boom

The so-called *'Nord-Süd Gefälle'*, the 'descent to the south' of so much modern industry, became a major talking-point in Germany in the mid-1980s. As the older declining industries happen to be in the north, while for a range of reasons the newer go-ahead ones have mostly preferred to settle elsewhere, the image developed of a Germany split between 'sunbelt south and rustbelt north', as Rupert Cornwell put it in the *Financial Times* of June 18, 1985, adding with a touch of poetic licence: 'The southern states are exemplified by Baden-Württemberg and Bavaria which seem to consist of little else than glossy new aerospace and robotics plants nestling in pretty countryside, promoted by evocative slogans such as "come and work where others go on holiday". Meanwhile the north carries the now familiar image of closed shipyards, steelworks and oil refineries enveloped in a suitable wintry setting.'

In that period, when *Der Spiegel* ran a cover-story, 'The Great Trek to the South', the unemployment level in the five northern *Länder* was nearly 50 per cent higher than in the southern ones, and economic growth in 1970–86 had been roughly 40 per cent greater in Bavaria and Baden-Württemberg than in North-Rhine-Westphalia, Hamburg or Bremen. The drift of new industry to the south entailed also a drift of population, as in 1984 some 17,000 people, mostly young, left the Ruhr to seek jobs in the 'sunbelt'. So the Germans set about worrying over the prospect of a growing imbalance in their economic geography, with possibly serious social and political consequences.

As so often in Germany, the whole issue was exaggerated by the media, and was never as bad as it seemed. And today, only a few years later, the perspective has changed: first, Hamburg and the Ruhr are now successfully hitting back, attracting new 'high-tech' industries; secondly, the problem has been totally eclipsed by the far greater one of east German industry, and is no longer much of a talking-point. Baden-Württemberg's growth has been slowing down after its great strides in the 1970s; the decline of the old coal- and steel-based heavy industries of the Ruhr continues, but is being balanced by new modern ones. Germany in fact has not developed a north–south drift on the same scale as in Britain or, in a different way, in Italy. Hers is still a well-balanced economy, geographically, with a fairly even spread around the country not only of industry but of other activities, commercial and cultural. In fact, the *Nord-Süd Gefälle* has helped to make this so. In the old days, the imbalance was greater, to the advantage of the north.

Baden-Württemberg has possessed successful medium-sized machinery firms since the nineteenth century. But the heavy industry was all further north – the shipyards by the sea; some iron and steel in the Saar, which had ore as well as coal: and massive iron smelting and steel works in the Ruhr, where there was iron ore and plentiful coal as well as excellent transport outlets along the Rhine. Bavaria, without raw materials or such good communications, remained agricultural. But today the mines are wearing thin, steel and shipping are in crisis – and the new high-technology industries do not depend on heavy raw materials to the same extent, nor on the same kind of bulk transport, so they can settle where they like.

They have tended to choose the south for a variety of reasons. Climate, scenery and life-style certainly play a part: it is easier to woo engineers or executives to come to work near Munich than in Duisburg. Wage costs are substantially lower in the south; and the farms have long been smaller and more backward, so their modernisation has produced a steady flow of local labour; moreover, peasants generally adapt more easily to modern factory work than coal-miners do. In Baden-Württemberg, the Swabian appetite for hard work has provided another strong attraction for new investors; and the region's existing machine-tool and precision industries are better suited for conversion to the new technologies than are the cumbersome old Ruhr firms or the North Sea shipyards. For moving into micro-circuits, cuckoo-clocks provide a better background of expertise than iron girders.

Other enticements have been educational, even political. The south for historical reasons has a far better infrastructure of traditional universities, such as Heidelberg and Tübingen, and it has now supplemented these with numerous new research centres and scientific colleges, highly valuable to modern industry. In the north, there is no university older than Kiel (1665) and Göttingen (1773): strangely, the rich merchants of old Hamburg and Bremen did not feel the need to educate their sons but put them straight into trade, and those who wanted a higher education went south. In the Ruhr, moreover, it was the deliberate policy of the industrial barons such as Krupp, backed up by Bismarck and the Kaisers, to prevent the founding of universities, for they feared that these would foster a radical intellectual leadership that might stir the workers into revolt! – 'This is a region for work, not for thought,' said Kaiser Wilhelm II. Today things have changed, for the Ruhr has five new universities, and like Hamburg and other northern towns it is making efforts to develop scientific institutes – but rather late in the day, in face of the very dynamic policies of the south. Lastly, while the northern industrial *Länder* are SPD-ruled, the two big southern ones are in conservative hands – and this, for some would-be investors, is an attraction. 'Why should I go to the Ruhr, where the unions are so strong, in league with the SPD in every local council?' said the manager of one big electronics group; 'Bavaria is not only less unionised, but its leaders have a better understanding of a modern firm's needs.' Even if that last point is not really true, capitalists tend to think that way.

In Bavaria, the CSU has for years been attracting investors with its free-market, profit-orientated philosophy. Today this *Land* claims to have the largest concentration of micro-electronics factories in Europe, employing some 200,000 people, a figure that has been growing by 20,000 a year. The trail was blazed by Siemens which switched its headquarters from Berlin to Munich after the war and now employs 100,000 people (a third of its total world-wide staff) in its 25 factories and research centres scattered around Bavaria, many of them in 'high-tech' sectors. Other international firms have moved in, including Motorola, Texas Instruments and Hitachi; scores of smaller German ones have sprung up too, so today the old farming plains around Munich, and north towards Nuremberg, contain a whole web of burgeoning little Silicon Valleys.

Baden-Württemberg's rise has been less spectacular, for it was already industrialised and so has not started virtually from scratch. But today IBM has its main European plant there, with 30,000 workers, while other electronic titans are also active in the Stuttgart area, including Bosch and Standard Electric Lorenz. This *Musterländle* ('model little *Land*'), as Swabians like to call it, is intelligently exploiting its older industrial skills in the precision field – and this was very much the policy of Lothar Späth, prime minister in 1978–90, who staked his reputation on a drive to make Baden-Württemberg into a power-house of the new technologies. He believed that industry will go where the research is done, and so he set up an agency which has master-minded the creation of 30 research institutes and ten new 'science parks'. He cajoled local firms into financing institutes for data-processing, micro-electronics and molecular biology, including one at Stuttgart University costing 13 million DM. Apostle of an unusual kind of close association between universities and industry, he even encouraged professors to leave their jobs and set up their own small firms (an amazing departure for Germany), where they now take charge of the technical side and leave finance and production to hired managers. Späth urged young people to become engineers rather than unemployed teachers – and stressed the point by closing three teacher training colleges.

Impressed by this research-orientated model, the northern *Länder* have belatedly begun to imitate it. Berlin, as we have seen, has launched its own high-technology programme, while North-Rhine-Westphalia too has promoted twelve new research institutes, and Bremen has had some modest success with new aerospace and electronics ventures. But where does the funding come from? Berlin of course has received special aid from Bonn, while large federal subsidies are also given on a sector-by-sector basis to whole industries in difficulty, notably coal, steel and ship-building. But, apart from this, regional aid and planning exist only on a small scale in Germany, as compared with France. Each *Land* is left to compete on its own. And that is not so easy for North-Rhine-Westphalia and its problem region, the Ruhr.

The *Ruhrgebiet* (Ruhr district), named after a river that flows into the Rhine at Duisburg, comprises a dozen or so industrial towns with a total population of 5.4 million, in an area 55 miles wide by 40 deep. Duisburg, Essen, Bochum and Dortmund are the main ones. Today the Ruhr is not nearly as grimy and polluted as it once was, and it even contains a surprising amount of woodland and parkland. But it is still Europe's leading industrial area, producing 62 per cent of the EEC's bituminous coal and 21 per cent of its crude steel.

Until about 1850 it was rural farmland. Then its industrial development took place very rapidly, over a period of some years, and was based on the fortunate presence of coal and ore in the same area, right by the Rhine. Steel mills and engineering works were built, mainly by family firms such as Krupp and Thyssen that grew rapidly into gigantic and famous enterprises. The area soon became the stronghold of the German armaments industry, and so it continued to prosper during the First World War and again in the Nazi period. Despite heavy Allied bombing, its industrial capacity was still 80 per cent intact in 1945, but was then somewhat reduced by the Allies' dismantlement policy. This ended in 1949, so the Ruhr was able to play a central role in the 'economic miracle' of the 1950s and it became richer than ever.

By about 1960 however the first danger signs were appearing. The more easily exploitable mines were beginning to wear thin, and Ruhr coal soon found it harder to compete with cheaper sources of energy such as imported oil and gas. The first pit closure was in 1957, followed by others in steady succession over the next 25 years. Of 152 former pits, only 26 are active today; Essen, once the foremost coalmining town of Europe, saw its very last pit close in 1986, and today this city of Krupp has more white-collar workers than manual ones. With modern techniques, productivity in the mines has increased hugely, so that since the 1950s coal output has fallen by less than half, from some 120 to 61 million tons a year. But in order to remain competitive the mines have to stage massive staff reductions: over 250,000 jobs have been lost, and fewer than 100,000 miners are still at work today. The early retirements, retraining schemes and other palliatives were generously funded and were worked out in close consultation with the generally cooperative miners' union (see p. 129): as a result, there was not a single strike. But the financial cost has been great, and is borne partly by the Federal Government, which in 1969 obliged the various private mine-owners (no mines are nationalised) to merge into a big consortium, Ruhrkohle, that now receives subsidies of over 1 billion DM a year. Its major problem today is that the mines near the surface, mostly in the Ruhr valley area to the south, are now virtually used up, and it has become necessary to dig for the coal further north, around the Emscher valley, where the seams lie deeper and are therefore more expensive to exploit. This explains why Ruhr coal, once so cheap, is today undercut by imported coal; and why Germany, unlike some other countries, did not find it worthwhile to increase its coal production again after the sharp oil price rises of the 1970s.

The coal cutbacks of the 1960s at least took place during a period of general economic boom, when it was possible to find replacement jobs for many miners. Most of the other big Ruhr industries — notably chemicals and machinery — were expanding during this period, and Opel opened a larger car plant in Bochum. But the steel crisis after 1975 came at a much harder time. Germany's steel industry is much the largest in Europe and the most efficient, and over half of it is located in or near the Ruhr where Thyssen is much the largest firm, followed by Krupp and Hoesch (all are in private hands, like the coalmines). The industry was doing well until the mid-1970s, when along with the rest of Europe it began to be hit hard by world over-production and Japanese competition. In line with EC policy directives, it has now trimmed its capacity, cut back production, and moved over from ordinary steel to a higher quality product which is more saleable. But the German steelmakers resentfully complain that the British and Italian industries in particular, less efficient but more highly subsidised, are competing against them unfairly with their artificially cheaper steel. The Federal Government has been trying to persuade Thyssen, Krupp and some other firms to merge into two big groups, as a way of rationalising further and cutting costs. The merger talks failed in 1985. Even so, a fair amount of streamlining has already taken place: German steel today employs less than 200,000 people, against 420,000 in 1960. And these cuts have fallen heavily on the Ruhr steelworkers who can no longer so easily find other jobs when made redundant. Once again, there has been a remarkable absence of strikes — thanks to harmonious labour relations and to Germany's generous and successful 'social net' of welfare benefits. The Duisburg mills may be crumbling and unemployment be high: yet the Ruhr as a whole still wears a remarkable aura of prosperity.

I half expected a black and noisy inferno, and was pleasantly surprised to find that many parts of the Ruhr today are green and pastoral, especially to the south of Essen and Bochum, where the mines were closed in the 1960s. Here with true Germanic neatness the old coalpits and railtracks have been grassed over, the pitheads removed and the slagheaps planted with trees; and the river Ruhr again meanders through quiet woods and meadows, past the neat suburbs of the new commercial middle class. It is almost idyllic. Further north and west, on a line roughly from Duisburg to Reckling-hausen, the scene becomes grimier, for here there is still a good deal of heavy industrial activity — and no steel foundry can be expected to look as tidy as Herr Späth's new micro-chip factories. Though pollution has been much reduced, the river Emscher still swirls black and thick. Here the disused coalworks have not all been tidied away: but one pitwheel in the centre of Bottrop has been preserved as a kind of modern sculpture, and near Dortmund a fine old *art nouveau* colliery is being turned into a museum. Here and there between the pits, the old mansions of rural landlords survive incongruously from an earlier era, blackened by a century of non-rural soot. And, everywhere, the giant satanic mills . . . So much higgledy-piggledy industrial desolation carries, I find, a certain poetic beauty and awesome fascination. Many of the iron- and steelworks are still active, belching their smoke and flames, dirty, maybe, but heartening tokens of life. Others are closed and silent, reminders of yesterday's hard toil and today's leisured anxiety.

The Ruhr towns themselves, away from the industrial zones, are remarkably spruce and civilised places. They grew so rich in their heyday that they were able to create splendid municipal parks and fine opera houses, and today this heritage actively survives and has even been extended: Bochum is the home of one of the very best theatre companies in Germany. Housing, too, is impressive. As the industrial revolution came later to the Ruhr than to Britain, it was possible to avoid some of the British mistakes: when Krupp and others built cheap housing for their battalions of new workers, they did not imitate the cramped and squalid back-to-back dwellings that can still be found in some north of England towns, but instead they established settlements that were well-spaced and comfortable by the standards of those days. Many of these workers' *Kolonien* still exist, especially in the western parts of Essen, near Krupp's old main factory: they have been modernised, and are cosily lived in by today's well-paid workers. Often one sees a Mercedes parked outside old miners' cottages. Working-class life-styles may have been changing since the war (see p. 174), but the Ruhr, rather like industrial Yorkshire or Tyneside, remains a warm, friendly community with strong local loyalties and a greater sense of neighbourliness and caring solidarity than is usual in urban Germany. Despite unemployment, it is also a pleasanter place to live in than twenty years ago, if only because private firms and local authorities have spent huge sums on curbing industrial pollution – in response to Brandt's famous appeal in 1965, 'Let us have blue skies over the Ruhr.' Inevitably, some factories still emit smells. But smog and soot no longer cast such a pall.

Old Alfred Krupp (1812–87) founder of the Krupp empire and foremost creator of the Ruhr, was the kind of patriarchal paternalist who combined genuine benevolence with clever self-interest. Scared of the nascent trade unions, he believed that, if he treated his employees well, they would be less likely to revolt. So, as well as good housing, he provided crèches, old people's homes, and better welfare services than were usual in those days, and he tried to induce his 16,000 workers to feel that they were part of one big caring family. But he was also tough with workers striking for more pay – the grim strike rallies of those days, and the dour life of mine and mill, are vividly evoked in the photographs and souvenirs at the Folkwang museum of Ruhr history, in Essen. Krupp lived grandly, and for himself and his large family he built the extraordinary Villa Hügel, a vast neo-Renaissance monstrosity on a hill above the Ruhr valley: today it too is a museum, filled with revealing portraits of the Krupp dynasty across the years, down to their time of pro-Nazi collaboration. The family firm survived the ensuing Allied reprisals, but under poor management it later fell into a decline, and finally in 1968 it was turned into a public shareholding company. The Krupp family, defeated not by the war but by peace, today own very few shares.

After sailing triumphantly through two lost wars and other disasters, the Ruhr became so convinced of its own invincibility that its leaders failed for a long time to react to the dangers when the coal and steel crises began. They simply could not believe that the Ruhr's industrial might was seriously threatened, or that these were any more than passing setbacks. Employers and unions were united in a conservative desire to preserve the status quo: they were afraid of having to cope with new technologies, and so for a long time they failed to adapt their production or encourage new investment. This made the crisis worse than it need have been. And for a long time new investors continued to fight shy of the Ruhr, which is only now shaking off its old image of an ugly, polluted area in the grip of strong trade unions. The image is unfair, for not only has pollution declined but the unions are rather moderate.

Today the old attitudes are changing and the Ruhr seems to be entering a new and brighter era. First, some of the large traditional firms, such as Mannesmann, the steel giant, are diversifying into other products such as machinery. More important, the authorities have successfully encouraged a new wave of younger entrepreneurs, who are setting up their own small firms in high-tech fields. Some of them are not even industrialists by background, but are teachers or scientists from the Ruhr's new universities, well placed to apply their expertise in productive fields. 'The Ruhr used to rely just on its *Bodenschätze* ['earth treasures', i.e. mineral resources],' quipped one local PR man, 'but today we rely even more on our *Kopfschätze* ['head treasures', i.e. grey matter] and the lively cultural scene helps to attract the elites.' Duisburg now has the leading micro-electronic institute in Germany, while Dortmund has become a major centre for computer software. Thousands of new firms, mostly very small but of high technical quality, are now being created in the Ruhr each year. As the big coal and steel concerns are still shedding jobs, unemployment is still well above average – over 11 per cent in Essen and Dortmund, against 4.5 per cent in Bavaria and Baden-Württemberg. But the gap is narrowing, the population drift is also slowing, and the *Land*'s growth rate is now up to the federal average. Hamburg is also having success with modern industry, though in Bremen the situation is still precarious.

The Ruhr's coal and steel firms benefit from the federal subsidies for those industries, but apart from this the area does not get as much regional aid from Bonn for new investment as it thinks it should. Quite largely this is because centrally-planned regional development has long been something of a Cinderella in this decentralised free-market Germany. Not until 1965 was a Regional Planning Act passed, setting up a joint committee of the Federal Government and the *Länder* that meets annually to allocate subsidies to areas in need. Under this scheme, grants totalling up to 15 per cent of investment costs can now be obtained for new projects in parts of the Ruhr affected by steel closures. But this does not go far. The joint committee has less than 1 billion DM a year to spend overall, and the political haggling between Bonn and the *Länder* sometimes prevents the money from going where it is most needed. North-Rhine-Westphalia's specific complaint is that the fund was first conceived mainly to assist under-developed areas which had inadequate infrastructure, and this remains its raison d'être; the Ruhr, with an excellent modern transport network but other problems, is not properly catered for. Of course some other parts of Europe have similar problems with their older declining industries, and in this respect the Ruhr has been faring better than Tyneside or Clydeside, Lorraine or south Belgium. It holds strong reserves of infrastructure and expertise, which are helping it to stage its come-back against the south. This powerful spirit of competition between the *Länder*, as the rulers in Stuttgart, Düsseldorf or Bremen vie with each other dynamically to attract new investment, certainly outweighs the disadvantages of the lack of centrally-directed regional planning. And it helps to account for the striking success record of post-war German industry.

# 3

# THE 'ECONOMIC MIRACLE' AND ITS AFTER-STRAINS

Much has been written about the success of West Germany in pulling itself up from the ruins of war to build the free world's third most powerful economy, founded above all on high-quality goods and the stability of the Deutschmark. During the golden years of the so-called 'miracle', in the 1950s and 1960s, its growth rate was the fastest in Europe (averaging 8 per cent in the 1950s) and purchasing power more than trebled. Since then the growth has slowed, as in many countries, and some weaknesses in the economy have become more evident, raising doubts as to how effectively it can meet the challenge of the new high technology, and of the European single market of 1992. More recently, the burden of rescuing east Germany has begun to impose severe strains and has weakened the Deutschmark a little. But the west German economy, with its huge basic strengths, should be able to surmount this tough challenge eventually.

The post-war record has been remarkable for a country with few natural resources of its own and relatively little inherited wealth. Manufacturing output is 60 per cent greater than in Britain (for a comparable population) and the standard of living 20 per cent higher. The economy has gained added confidence from a stable currency, with the lowest inflation rate in the EC after the Netherlands (in 1986–9 it averaged 1.1 per cent, against 5.4 per cent in Britain, 3.2 per cent in France, 3.8 per cent in the United States). And exports in recent years have amounted to as much as 27 per cent of GNP, for German companies have been assiduous in exploiting foreigners' appetites for their finely made products – this applies not only to the well-known giants such as Bayer, Bosch and BMW, but also for example to some specialised family firm in a Swabian valley, turning out the world's best punching-machines or spirit levels.

The reasons for the success are not hard to enumerate. In the early post-war years, the Germans were powerfully motivated by the desire to rebuild their nation through sustained effort. And they did not have to start entirely from scratch, for despite bomb damage to many factories, industrial plant was basically intact to a surprising degree, and able to be repaired. In 1945 much less than half of German industry was in ruins; many smaller firms in out-of-the-way places were un-scathed. Then came the era of Allied dismantling, but in the Western zones this reduced plant by only 5 per cent; and, like the bombing, it was something of a blessing in disguise, for it obliged firms to reorganise with modern equipment. Germany also emerged from defeat with a pool of skilled labour and a background of expertise which the Nazi war effort had encouraged, while the refugees from the east brought the added talent and manpower that were invaluable for industry's take-off. The Germans then made energetic use of Marshall Aid and of the markets soon opened to them by the Americans. Later, from 1958 onwards, the creation of the European Community gave a further huge impetus to West Germany's export trade: in the initial period 1958–62 its sales to the rest of the Six almost trebled, and by 1984 some 47.7 of its total exports were going to other EC countries. Lastly, ever since the war the West Germans have known stable government, and despite the alternations of power they have benefited from a degree of continuity in economic policies, for in this field the divergencies between the main parties have been narrower than in France or Britain.

These factors have all played their part – and so has the positive climate of labour relations. The Allies after the war laid the foundations of a sensible trade union structure, and of a legally enforced system of consultation between unions and employers; and this has led to a stronger spirit of consensus than exists in many countries. Unions have tended to collaborate with management rather than fight it. This has favoured wage restraint, which has helped keep down inflation. It has resulted also in a very low strike level and in great advances in productivity, for seldom do German unions oppose technological change.

However, the single most important explanation of West Germany's post-war economic success may be a simple human one, hard to prove or quantify. This is the fact that Germans at all levels, from shop-floor workers to managers, just happen to be very disciplined, thorough and realistic. Their perfectionism may sometimes be a drawback, but on the

[105]

whole it has brought great economic dividends – and it does so even today, when a younger generation has become less work-obsessed. The Germans do not work such long hours as some others – their weekly rate is well below Japan's – but when they *are* at work they tend to work hard and methodically (at least in industry – less so in public offices). And that is true at all levels. On the shop-floor, an extensive and efficient apprenticeship system has produced a work-force that is far better skilled and motivated than Britain's; and managers and owners, though tending to be too cautious and routine-minded, possess a technical flair and a detailed concern for the quality of their product that have played no small part in the triumphs of the export drive.

From the late 1970s onwards the economic picture became rather less rosy, for Germany's industrial strength did not bring her any immunity from the new world conditions caused by oil price increases and the growth of Far Eastern competition. Her economic slow-down was at its worst during the final years of the Schmidt Government, 1979–82, when several big firms collapsed, including AEG-Telefunken, and the dreaded phenomenon of 'stagflation' emerged: not only were 1981 and 1982 years of nil growth, but in 1981 inflation reached 6.8 per cent, a very high figure for Germany and one that brought troubling reminders of her 1920s nightmares. The Germans had grown so used to steady growth that they did not easily adjust to the new climate; they began to panic at signs of recession, fearing worse to come, and they found little solace in the fact that many other Western countries were faring worse still. In the familiar German manner, they over-reacted.

Then the election in 1983 of a CDU-led Government under Helmut Kohl brought a renewal of business confidence and happened to coincide with an American-led economic upswing throughout the West. So the public mood soon changed. The economy became more buoyant again, registering annual growth rates of around 2.5 per cent in 1984–7. Unemployment was now much the most serious problem: it had hit Germany later than most Western countries but then rose more sharply, from a modest 3.3 per cent in 1983 to a peak of 9 per cent in 1985 (well over 2 million). However, as industry picked up, so new jobs were created, and in the later 1980s the unemployment level fell back, to around 7 per cent. Throughout this period, thanks to the German prowess in exports, the annual trade surpluses remained very high: they averaged 113 billion DM a year in 1985–9, reaching a record 135 billion for 1989. This, and the low inflation rate, accounted for the power of the Deutschmark, much the strongest currency in Europe. Growth had improved, too, spurting to 4 per cent for 1989.

It was highly fortunate that the economy was in this strongly expansive phase when in 1990 it had to face the challenge of rescuing east Germany. The mild recession affecting the United States and Britain had hardly yet touched west Germany, save to slow down its exports a little. It was therefore well placed to devote its energies eastwards: but soon it became clear that the task was much greater than had been expected (see pp. 448–65), and the burden fell heavily on the west German economy. In some ways, the new markets and building projects in the east provided a boost, so that growth actually rose to 4.6 per cent for 1990, and unemployment in the west continued to fall gently (in sharp contrast to the east). But the expense of subsidising the east's shattered economy increased the public sector deficit by 50 per cent, to an expected 150 billion DM for 1991 or 5 per cent of GNP. And the necessity to raise taxes began to slow growth, which was expected to drop to some 2.5 per cent for 1991. The west Germans could afford all this, but not so easily. And this worrying situation, which inevitably put pressure on the Deutschmark, gave ammunition to the lobby led by the Bundesbank that was pressing for a slow-down in moves towards EC monetary union (see p. 573).

By the summer of 1991 the mounting crisis in east Germany was the greatest and most immediate challenge facing the economy, but not the only one. Some other factors had for several years been causing disquiet even to the most detached and non-over-reacting observers. The Germans had shown themselves supreme at the great traditional post-war industries such as automobiles and machinery, but did they possess the flexibility for making the jump into an era of new high-technology where the Japanese and Americans were well ahead? Were their banking traditions and their capital market structures ideally suited to making the required investments, alike in these fields and in the east? Were managers and entrepreneurs showing the necessary spirit of risk-taking and adaptability? Was the German economy, still highly regulated in many sectors such as insurance, road haulage and safety standards, as well prepared as it should be for the challenge of the EC single market of 1992 (whose deadline was in fact January 1993)? And finally, if a younger generation were now querying the work-ethic and materialistic appetite of their elders, might this not reduce productivity and render Germany less competitive? Could the Germans have it both ways? The qualities of the Germans are such that they may well overcome these hurdles. But it will not happen without great effort.

## Industrial splendour – but can it meet the high-tech challenge?

Germany is run on the principles of a mixed economy, with a very strong social welfare element and only a small amount of direct public ownership of industry. This has been the model in the west, which is now being applied to the east too. The degree of government intervention, though lower than in France, is high by British or American standards. This philosophy is broadly subscribed to by the main Parties, though with nuances: the SPD puts a greater accent on social spending, on the 'social market economy', while the CDU stresses the 'free market economy' and favours cuts in public spending (more in theory than in practice).

As compared with France and its five-year plans, there is not much forward economic planning at a federal level in Germany. Nor, as we have seen, does Bonn play any great role in regional development. However, federal governments have accepted the need to shore up certain sectors with large public funds: Bonn gives huge sums of money to agriculture, and to service industries such as the state railways, and in recent years it has stepped up its subsidies to declining industries, mainly coal, steel, shipbuilding and even textiles. Total subsidy of all kinds, excluding that to east Germany, now stands at over 120 billion DM a year. The 'free market' Kohl Government is opposed doctrinally to such spending and would like to reduce it, but has not found this easy politically. Cash subsidies with direct effect on market prices rose from 1.8 per cent of GNP in 1982 to 2.2 per cent in 1989, whereas both in Britain and France they were reduced in that period.

The role of public ownership in Germany is a complex matter. In the financial field, the governments of the *Länder* each own big banks and are able to utilise these for their local economic policies. But nationwide the main commercial banks such as the Deutsche Bank are all in private hands. Thus the federal government has little direct control over the financing of the private sector – in contrast with France, where since the war most banking has been in State hands. However, the railways and the postal and telecommunications services are federally owned;

the vast Bundespost has now been split into three parts and opened up to some outside competition, but it has not been privatised. The government also hold large industrial assets, in some 80 companies, but in a rather peculiar way: it does not own big firms outright, as is the case in France and Britain, but it does part-own quite a number – in many instances (one example being the Salzgitter steel corporation) these holdings are legacies inherited from the Third Reich. Seeing that even SPD governments have shown little desire to increase this kind of ownership, nationalisation has never proved the same kind of stormy issue in Germany as it has in Britain or indeed in France. The Kohl Government has even been privatising, though not as fast as it had promised when it came to power in 1983. Since then it has sold off its 20 per cent share of Volkswagen, and its big stake in the huge Veba energy conglomerate. It has also slimmed down its former 80 per cent control of Lufthansa, though it retains a majority holding.

West German economic strength depends above all on industry, which plays a larger role than in other advanced countries. According to the OECD, manufacturing industry (including energy, oil, mining and building) represents 40.3 per cent of GDP, compared with 39 per cent in Japan, 36.7 per cent in Britain, 31.5 per cent in France and 28.5 per cent in the United States (the British figure would be much lower, were it not for oil). German industrialists, even many of the small ones, are unusually export-minded. Helped by the low level of strikes, they are scrupulous about meeting delivery dates; and they employ talented salesmen who speak foreign languages and try to come to terms with foreign habits and cultures. All this presents an object lesson to the British. And it helps to explain why Germany has nearly always produced a large external trade surplus. This in turn helps to account for the Deutschmark's strength.

The very big firms like Siemens and Daimler-Benz may have led the way: but much of the success has been due also to smaller or medium-sized concerns, many of them still family-owned and -run. This can be observed especially in an area such as Swabia, around Stuttgart, whose industrial rise has been an exceptional saga. In the mid-nineteenth century this was still no more than a poor agricultural region of small farms, much of it stony and unfertile, and often there were famines. Many farmers emigrated; but others turned to clock- and watchmaking as the best way of topping up their incomes and avoiding starvation. They mysteriously possessed some innate flair for precision work and innovation – and this has grown. Here Gottlieb Daimler, a local engineer, invented the automobile in the mid-1880s. Others in Stuttgart created the electric drill, and even the telephone (at the same time as Bell), while Messerschmitt, a pioneer of the aircraft industry, was a Swabian too. Little specialist firms of many kinds grew up, in textiles, woodwork, watchmaking, machine-tools and other branches of precision machinery. Each patiently developed its own pool of skilled labour: and this diversification, plus the stress on quality rather than size, has helped Swabia through the periods of recession. Bosch and Daimler-Benz may have grown into giants; but most others have preferred to stay in the smaller-scale league and to base their success on intelligent specialisation: one thriving family concern exports its liquid level indicators around the world, yet has a staff of no more than 200.

The typical Swabian factory is still likely to be owned and actively run by a self-made man, or the son of one. He may earn 300,000 DM a year, but he lives very simply, probably works a 70-hour week, knows exactly how to turn a lathe or adjust an engine, and will readily go to the shop-floor and discuss technical details with his workers. He has a close and benevolent contact with them, usually knowing them all by name: and he is anxious to avoid his firm becoming too large for his personal supervision and thus less efficient. His manner tends to be genial but uncouth; for all his creative intelligence, he can rarely express himself eloquently; and he has a blithe disregard for showy public relations, believing that sheer quality will win through – as usually it does. One such rough diamond is Hugo Kunze, whose factory in industrial Stuttgart-Feuerbach, a stone's throw from Bosch and Porsche, is one of the world's most successful producers of stirring, kneading and shredding machines. He explained to me in his song-song Swabian drawl: 'My father, who was an engineer, founded this firm in 1929 and invented ice-cream-making machines. After the war he sold them to the US Army. Now, we've expanded into kneading machines for dough, and we make the world's best. I too am an engineer, and I'm continually inventing new machines and product. That's how we stay ahead. Some 56 per cent of our product goes for export, much of it to Arab countries. My staff is only 130, and I have not expanded for 15 years: if we grew too big, we'd become vulnerable.' He showed me round his tidy, highly computerised factory. His manner with his staff struck me as a mixture of diffident shyness and quiet authoritarianism.

Appropriately, Stuttgart today is the home of two of Germany's three most prestigious producers of luxury cars and of Europe's leading manufacturer of electronic car components. The automobile industry remains the brightest jewel in the crown of the German economy, the premier showcase of its talents of precision engineering and of its concern for quality and reliability. It is much the largest car industry in Europe, with 4.3 million vehicles produced in 1988; and, with over 60 per cent of its output sold abroad, it is Germany's leading exporter. What is more, it has recently fared better than its main Western competitors in adjusting to a period of saturation of mass markets and of growing Japanese competition: while the American, British, French and Italian car industries have all been laying off workers in large numbers, the German industry actually increased its workforce from 740,000 in 1974 to 800,000 in 1986, despite a growth in automation.

The principal explanation is that Germany specialises in the kind of expensive high-performance car – very fast and comfortable, full of the latest gadgets – that the Japanese do not yet make, and it therefore has a surer market than for the ordinary family vehicle. Opel and Volkswagen may have many foreign peers, but BMW, Porsche and Daimler-Benz have few. And all around the globe there is a definable and steadily growing minority clientele for this kind of up-market automobile – whether it be companies buying stately Mercedes for their executives, or jet-setters wanting a snappy Porsche for private use. These cars, and BMWs too, have durability and a high resale value, and so they are often seen as a sound investment. They also appeal, as one BMW official suggested to me, 'to people who want a car as a kind of toy or status-symbol, as a life-style concept rather than mere transport equipment. They may not use all the gadgets, but they like them to be there. And they like to know that their car *could* do 250 kph if it tried even if their country's speed limits prevent them in practice from driving at more than a hundred and twenty! Silly, but there it is.' So why has Germany come to concentrate on this luxury market? – the same official went on: 'Partly it is a matter of tradition: Daimler was making cars for kings and presidents before 1914. Partly it derives from German skills in precision engineering. And partly it's because wage costs in this country are so high that we need to make a product with a big sales value. And if we produce such fast cars, well, remember that 40 per cent of our buyers are Germans, and this is the one country in the world with virtually no speed limits on motorways. We at BMW regard the *Autobahn* network as one non-stop test track.' A point that a visitor like myself, in a mere Renault 20, soon discovers to his peril.

Consistently the most successful of the German automobile firms, and the one with the strongest mystique, is Daimler-Benz, maker of

Mercedes. Its origins have acquired the quality of legend. In the mid-1880s, while Daimler was inventing the petrol engine in his garden shed at Stuttgart, by a coincidence Karl Benz was pioneering his own engines at Mannheim, 80 miles away. The two men later associated, though their firms did not fully merge until 1960. In the second war, they were making aircraft for the Nazis. Today no members of the Daimler or Benz families are directly involved in the firm, which in 1991 was owned by the Deutsche Bank (28 per cent), the Government of poor old Kuwait, and various holding companies and small shareholders (the Flick group sold its shares in 1986). Daimler-Benz has recently diversified and expanded into the defence and aerospace fields, by taking over the MBB and Dornier aircraft companies (see p. 116) and the AEG electrical giant, and today it is *the* largest of all German corporations, well ahead of Volkswagen and Siemens. So who on earth was Mercedes? Answer: when in 1899 Daimler built a new car, his leading salesman, Emil Jellinek, named it after his daughter, Mercedes. Today, all the firm's vehicles bear this name.

Besides its overseas factories, Daimler-Benz today employs some 155,000 workers in Germany, mostly in the Stuttgart area and at a big new plant in Bremen. It is the world's leading producer of heavy trucks, but is better known for its solidly-built saloon cars, probably now the most esteemed in the world in their class: recent clients include the Pope. Rolls-Royces may be even grander, but their output is much smaller. After the outbreak of the first energy crisis, Daimler-Benz was the only car firm in the world to increase its sales in 1974, and it since has expanded steadily, with demand nearly always exceeding supply: in 1986 its output of cars rose well above 500,000, half of them going for export. The management put this progress down to the fact that motorists now seek a durable car that will last at least ten years. But Daimler-Benz has also moved with the times by extending its range into smaller luxury cars, such as the compact 190 whose sporty elegance marks a break with the firm's previous rather staid image and is presenting BMW with a tough challenge. The firm's record is certainly awe-inspiring – and the directors and publicity staff never miss a chance to rub it in. Their sublime arrogance takes a lot of beating: to be conducted round the Stuttgart plant by a PR man is like being shown Buckingham Palace by the Queen's lady-in-waiting. Other firms are regarded as non-existent: when I asked an executive what he thought of the latest Audi model, he claimed not to have heard of it, and after I was seen driving away in my muddy, scratched Renault 20, I was not invited again. This kind of smooth conceit is untypical of Swabia, but then few of the directors or senior staff today are Swabians. It should be added that in its own lofty way the firm is an excellent employer, offering its staff an extensive range of welfare and profit-sharing schemes (see p. 125).

Porsche, also a Stuttgart firm, was founded in 1931 by an Austrian professor, Ferdinand Porsche, and is still largely in the hands of the family. Its bullet-like sports cars, with the look of racing-cars, are especially popular in the United States where Porsche now sells 50 per cent of its select output of some 50,000 vehicles a year. Its appeal is very different from that of Daimler-Benz, as I was assured by the firm's current chairman, Peter Schutz, a Berlin-born American: 'In a word, our surveys show that people buy a Mercedes to look ten or twenty years older, and a Porsche to look ten or twenty years younger. Mercedes appeals to the rising young executive in a neat suit, who wants to show that he has status, that he has "arrived" (even if he has not). Porsches are for those who definitely have arrived and are not trying to prove anything except how young and fit they are. Our average client is a slim, relaxed man in his fifties, in a jersey or anorak, maybe a film-director or champion golfer with a young blonde on the seat beside him.' Good sales talk, and maybe not too wide of the mark.

The appeal of BMW probably lies somewhere between those two. The Bayerische Motoren Werke, of Munich, began life in the First World War as a maker of aircraft engines, then moved into producing motorcycles, and then into sports and racing cars. These played a dominant role in European motor rallies and races, in the 1930s and again after the second war. But by the late 1950s the firm was facing bankruptcy, for it had over-extended its range. It was taken over by the wealthy Quandt family, who are still the main shareholders, and they hugely restored its fortunes: since 1970, annual output has risen from 160,000 cars to some 450,000, 60 per cent of them exported. BMW's head office in northern Munich is an extraordinary modern building, in the shape of four tall cylinders. Some cars are made here, and others at a large factory in the small Bavarian town of Dingolfing, where many workers are ex-peasants or part-time farmers (see p. 162). A new plant at Regensburg, which opened in 1986, is employing staff of a similar kind, and has enabled production to rise – demand tends to exceed supply, as at Daimler-Benz. Sixty per cent of output consists of the medium-sized 3-series cars, which outwardly may look no more exciting than a family Ford or Fiat but inside are packed with wizardry, allowing for remarkable speed and road-holding. The range extends to the luxurious 7-series, selling for up to 80,000 DM and rivalling the larger Mercedes. A BMW is more fun to drive than a Mercedes, more flexible and responsive and it has a stronger appeal to the kind of people who are really interested in cars.

The market for smaller models and ordinary family cars is represented in Germany by two American-owned firms (Ford, with a plant in Cologne, and Opel, part of General Motors) and of course by the mighty Volkswagen, which like Daimler-Benz is something of a modern German legend. Its gigantic factory at Wolfsburg in Lower Saxony, a few miles from the former GDR border, was founded by Hitler in 1938 to produce the 'people's car'. After the war it was commandeered by the British, and there was some talk of transferring the works to Britain by way of reparations. But British car makers considered that its main product, the famous 'Beetle', was too ugly and noisy to be worthwhile, so the factory stayed where it was. Soon VW was allowed to resume its own production, under a very dynamic manager, Heinz Nordhoff, who set about catering for the rocketing demand for cheap cars as the German economy got on the move. So VW expanded phenomenally, playing no small part in the *Wirtschaftswunder* of the 1950s. Being one of the State-owned legacies of the Third Reich, it remained fully nationalised until 1961: then the Government sold off 60 per cent of it to a million and a half small shareholders, and in 1988 it sold off the rest.

In the days before many people could afford Mercedes, the ungainly but robust little Beetle not only dominated the German market but spread across Europe and into America, becoming the world's most popular car, by far. But Nordhoff made the mistake of failing to develop any other model, and as buyers' wallets fattened and their tastes in cars widened, so VW's sales began to slip in the later 1960s. It went through a difficult period, which was not resolved until the development of the Golf and other new models in the 1970s. Today, thanks in part to robots, it is again doing well (and the faithful old Beetle, its global sales now beyond the 20 million mark, is still being produced in Mexico, by the VW subsidiary there). Of the group's eight factories in Germany, much the largest is the original one at Wolfsburg, which today employs 63,000 people in a town of 130,000, built for and by Volkswagen — a true 'company town'. Here, ahead of any other car firm in the world, Volkswagen in the early 1970s began to develop industrial robots, and it put them into mass operation in

1980. These strange orange creatures swirl and twist their limbs in precise balletic movements, like birds of prey, as they assemble wheels and engines, brakes and batteries, onto Golfs and Jettas moving along the assembly lines. Officials explain that 25 per cent of the final assembly on Golfs is now automised and robotised, leading to a saving of a thousand jobs, yet there have been no redundancies: as modern cars with their multiple gadgets grow ever more complex, they require more overall work, so the same labour force is needed. The unions have therefore not opposed automation.

Volkswagen also owns Audi, a smaller firm making larger, smarter cars, such as the sporty Quattro and the sleek 100. Recently Audi has done well by moving up-market as a high-performance challenger to BMW and Mercedes, and has become the third largest European importer into the United States in the luxury category, behind Volvo and Mercedes but ahead of BMW. The Volkswagen group as a whole continues to have its ups and downs, making losses in 1982–3 but then a profit in 1984–6. Its success still centres around the Golf, the most popular small car in Europe (862,000 of them sold in 1986). And in 1985–6, when most of the other European giants were reporting losses, VW remained in the black, actually nosing ahead of Fiat and Ford to become Europe's largest group in terms of numbers of cars sold, with 13.1 per cent of the total market. More than other German car firms, it is now investing heavily in east Germany (see p. 453).

So the German car industry would appear to be better placed than any other in Europe for coping with the uncertain times ahead. It cannot produce cars as cheaply as the Japanese, but it still has the edge over Japan in modernisation and applied technology – not only VW's robots, but the range of electronic equipment being developed by Bosch, including anti-skid and fuel-injection systems. Indeed, the visual array of electronic devices on and around the dashboards of some new Bosch-fitted BMW models gives the driver, in the words of one motoring writer, 'the sense of being an airline pilot in a cockpit'. However, Germany's car makers do have some anxieties. They face the problems of European over-capacity and growing market saturation, and of the Japanese challenge. All Europe is in the same boat here: Germany, though more strongly placed than most, is by no means exempt. At present Japanese imports do not amount to more than about 10 per cent of the German market: but this leaves unsolved the threat of Japanese inroads into Germany's own export fields elsewhere. So the less upmarket firms, Volkswagen, Opel and Ford, could begin to suffer.

A quick look at other leading traditional industries reveals some similar strengths. The aircraft industry made a very slow recovery after the war, partly because of the Allied ban on German development of sophisticated armaments. But today it has built itself a secure niche in European aerospace, albeit in a secondary role to the French. The biggest firm, Messerschmitt-Bölkow-Blohm, was formed from a merger of various Bavarian and Hamburg interests and no longer has much connection with the Messerschmitt family. It has its headquarters outside Munich and big factories there and in Hamburg and Bremen, which devote themselves above all to doing the fuselage work for the European Airbus, in which it has a 38.5 per cent stake. It makes the Transall military transport aircraft in partnership with Aérospatiale of France, and together with the British and Italians it builds the Tornado combat fighter that distinguished itself in the Gulf War. It also makes helicopters and missiles (it sold some military equipment to Saddam's Iraq, and is busy trying to live this down), and it shares in the French-led European space programme for the Ariane rockets. MBB with its 36,000 employees is a very successful firm, and has fared better than its smaller competitor, Dornier, at Friedrichshafen on Lake Constance, which was racked by family feuds after the death in 1969 of old Claude Dornier, the founder and pre-war creator of its famous flying-boats. In the late 1980s Daimler-Benz acquired the whole of MBB and a majority share in Dornier, thus giving it near total control of the German aerospace industry and some 60 per cent of the Defence Ministry's arms procurement spending. These moves have been criticised on monopoly grounds; it is also asked whether DB has been wise to put so many of its eggs in the defence basket, in a time of disarmament.

The chemical industry is also a post-war success story. In the 1930s, the chemical group IG Farben was by far the largest of all German firms. In a bid to prevent it from becoming again so powerful, the Western Allies then split it into three parts: Bayer, of Leverkusen; BASF, at Ludwigshafen: and Höchst, near Frankfurt. Today all three have grown bigger than the old IG Farben: after ICI, they are the leading chemical firms in Europe and they export more than half of their product. They all now have projects for investing in east Germany. As for the textile industry, like some others in Europe it went through a serious crisis in the 1960s and was often regarded as a dead duck: but, after shedding three-quarters of its workforce and installing modern machinery, it has since made a remarkable comeback and now exports nearly 40 per cent of its output.

*

The picture in these traditional industries may seem fairly bright, as it is throughout the mechanical engineering field. But many other sectors are less well placed. It is thus not easy to give any balanced assessment — and today there are plenty of Jeremiahs who predict that, quite apart from the problems of east Germany, industry in the west too may run into some trouble unless it can succeed in making certain adjustments. The OECD, in its 1984 report on the West German economy, identified three main problems: the need to shift to higher technology products; the difficulties in raising risk capital; and the low profitability of industrial firms. Certainly it is true that even in periods of rapid expansion German companies have generally tended to show only modest profits. Managers lay the blame in large part on the high wage levels and very high social charges, whereby on top of its basic wage-bill a firm must pay out a further 80 per cent on social security and various fringe benefits. They complain also about the heavy taxation in Germany, which reaches 60 per cent on the major part of a company's profits. The Kohl Government committed itself to reducing this burden with a series of large-scale across-the-board tax cuts, and this it did, though rather more gradually than many experts had advised. By 1990 the level of cuts had reached 50 billion DM a year, or 2.5 per cent of GNP. But in 1991 it seemed that some of the cuts would have to be reimposed, maybe in other forms, in order to pay for the cost of rescuing the east's economy. Yet tax relief for industry remains much needed, for although in the boom years the level of industrial investment in Germany was around 25 per cent of net profit, ahead of the rest of Western Europe, it has since fallen back to about 21 per cent — and this has been affecting the ability of firms to modernise their equipment and so face up to the new challenges from the United States and Japan.

Apart from the mammoth new east German problem, the main challenge facing German industry today is the dual one of (a) coping with Japanese competition in nearly every sector, old and new alike, and (b) adapting to the new technologies. Already in a number of traditional fields that used to be among their specialities — cameras, motor-cycles, clocks and watches — the Germans have lost ground heavily to Japan and other Far Eastern producers. Now the Japanese are starting to make inroads into the German machine-tool market, too, and are threatening the optics industry. But it is over the technologies of the future, especially micro-electronics, that the main battle is now being fought. Here for some time the Germans were curiously slow to wake up to the challenge – 'Maybe we had it too easy in the boom years,' suggests one computer expert today, 'and we basked too complacently in our progress in the classic industries.' The Germans are indeed now bestirring themselves: but like the British and French they find that others, Japanese and Americans, have moved ahead. In the 1970s the Government poured money into trying to develop a world-class national computer industry: but this failed, and today the German computer market is dominated by the Americans, though Nixdorf under its new owners, Siemens, is now doing well. More recently the German consumer electronics industry has run into trouble, and two of its household names have moved into foreign hands in order to survive: Grundig has passed under the control of Philips, and AEG has sold Telefunken to Thomson of France – a victory for European integration, but not for German pride. It is true that, as consumers, Germany's offices and factories are equipping themselves fast with the new micro-chip equipment (Germany is Europe's foremost user of semiconductors, just ahead of Britain). But, as manufacturers, German firms' share of world high-technology markets has fallen since 1972 from 26 to 17 per cent, as the Japanese surge ahead.

Some critics lay the blame on German firms' reluctance to take risks and to innovate. Others suggest that the true causes may lie deeper, in German education, culture and basic attitudes. The Germans may have industrial flair, but their education system remains stubbornly conservative: fewer schools than in Britain have yet acquired computers or made children literate in how to use them. And, for all the Germans' affluence and modernism, remarkably few individuals have yet bought personal mini-computers; one sees fewer high-street 'chip shops' than in Britain. Maybe this relates to the rise of a less materialistic younger generation, and to the influence of the Greens and of their campaign against industrial growth and the allegedly dehumanising effects of modern technology – according to one much-quoted set of opinion polls, the number of Germans regarding technology as a 'blessing' dropped from 72 per cent in 1966 to a mere 30 per cent in 1981. Maybe such figures should not be taken too literally: but the trend has worried the Kohl Government, whose Foreign Minister, Hans-Dietrich Genscher, caused quite a national stir in December 1983 when he stated dramatically: 'Whoever visits Japan finds a country in which state and society face the future full with vigour. Whoever visits the United States finds . . . a vision of a high-technology society opening up undreamed-of possibilities. Whoever returns home is struck by the whining cultural pessimism in Germany. Green ideologists and those who think like them preach fear of life, fear of technology and fear of the future.'

It was around this time, in a mood bordering on panic, that the Government decided to take stronger action. In March 1984 it approved a programme for allocating 2.9 billion DM over the next four years to the promotion of research and development in the high-technology industries, notably in data-processing and micro-electronics — a remarkable sum for a government doctrinally committed to non-intervention and lower spending. And in 1985 Kohl readily lent his backing to France's new Eureka project for European joint ventures in advanced fields. These new Government moves went to support those already being made by Baden-Württemberg and other *Länder* to promote the new technologies. So it has all added up to quite a buzz of new activity, although sometimes the complaint is voiced that the federal system makes it hard for Bonn and the *Länder* to coordinate the research projects adequately.

A number of individual firms are now making greater efforts to meet the new challenges. While Bosch is progressing with electronic car equipment, Siemens and its Nixdorf subsidiary have been expanding fast in data-processing and telecommunications. Inevitably, much will depend on the results achieved by the Siemens colossus, which employs a staff of 30,000 on research and development and devotes 3.5 billion DM a year to it — an effort without equal in Europe. In 1984–9 Siemens joined with Philips of Holland in a 2.2 billion DM 'Megaproject' for moving into the next generation of micro-chip technology, and today Siemens is taking the lead in the 20-nation 'Jessi' project. 'We are at last catching up with the Japanese in data-processing,' a Siemens executive claimed to me in 1991. All this indicates that, after their slow start, German and other European firms have now truly girded their loins. The Germans still have plenty of energy and flair; and, if they choose to apply these qualities, they may yet be able to make the Japanese tremble.

But German industry still carries some handicaps too — and one of these, much talked about, is the inadequate supply of venture capital for starting new businesses. This hardly matters for a big established firm like Siemens, which can easily find the money it needs. But it does make life harder for the smaller entrepreneur, whose contribution is also needed in this age of micro-technology. The reasons for this situation lie in the somewhat unusual nature of banking, in a Germany where the banks play so powerful a role in industry. In the continental manner,

German banks are of the full-service kind, covering a wide range of operations, including acting as stockbroker and investor. Many of the larger banks are regional ones in public hands operated by the *Länder*: but, nationwide, the scene is dominated by three big private commercial bodies, Deutsche Bank, Dresdner Bank and Commerz Bank. In the nineteenth century, private banks of this kind played an important part in financing the new industries, and thus they acquired part ownership of them. This tradition continued in the darker days of the 1920s, when banks injected capital into many firms in order to shore them up; then again after 1945 the banks provided much of the finance for the great industrial revival. Deutsche Bank in particular did well from this by investing astutely, and under its legendary former chairman, Dr Hermann Abs, it built itself a considerable empire. Today in terms of assets it is only the fourteenth largest bank in the world, and the seventh in Europe: but from its gleaming new 24-storey headquarters in Frankfurt it controls many of the levers of Germany industry, and is part-owner of many leading firms, including Bayer, Bosch, Siemens and Volkswagen.

Deutsche Bank however has become a byword for caution, investing only in enterprises with sound credentials and an existing record of success. Other big banks are scarcely less prudent – and so the saying goes, 'In Germany you can easily obtain credits, so long as you don't need them.' So to whom is the smaller, newer firm to turn? Risk capital has long been hard to find, for reasons that may be in part connected with Germany's past. One private financier suggested to me that rich family trusts which had twice seen their fortunes eroded by inflation, in the 1920s and 1940s, were still hesitant to provide backing for uncertain projects. It is also true that most risk financing used to be done by Jewish bankers, who then left after 1933; and, though Oppenheim and Warburg since returned, most others including the venerable Rothschild have not. Since the war, some German entrepreneurs have tended to seek their venture capital in London or New York, where the market for it is more highly developed. But this is not always convenient. At last, within the past ten years, the Germans have taken stock of the problem and some banks have begun to make venture capital more easily available: by 1985 some 30 funding outfits for it had been set up, with a total of 700 million DM for investment. So the finance itself is now more forthcoming: but the banks have yet to develop a tradition of being able to provide a small firm with back-up advice on how to make best use of it.

Another potential industrial handicap, much discussed nowadays, is that the Germans have ceased to be in the forefront of innovation science. This is not for want of effort; their spending on R&D has been consistently high, averaging some 2.5 per cent of GNP in the past fifteen years, half of it financed by industry. But Germans working in Germany have won few Nobel prizes since the war: they do well if they emigrate, maybe to the USA, but at home they seem to have become more successful at adapting other people's inventions than producing their own – a change since Daimler's day. Various reasons have been adduced for this. One, as in banking, is the loss of Jewish talent since the 1930s. Another, the trend in school education towards egalitarianism and non-specialisation (see p. 240): this, so it is alleged, may well have brought social and cultural advantages but it handicaps the bright up-and-coming science student. A third factor, perhaps the most important, is the climate of rigidity and orthodoxy in a great many academic research institutes, as was stressed to me by one expert British observer of the German scientific scene: 'The absurdly elevated status of German professors makes them almost godlike in their students' eyes. So it may be more than his career is worth for a young researcher to question the opinion of his professor who may well be in his seventies – with a few honourable exceptions, German research tends to be dictated by a cadre of rather elderly men. And the traditional jealousy between professors leads to a narrow tribalism where cross-fertilisation and the multi-disciplinary approach cannot easily flourish. All this leads to a situation where mediocre "safety-at-all-costs" research may be the order of the day.' Strong words.

If the German industrial record nonetheless remains so positive – and who are the British to be critical of *that*? – in part this is because firms do so much applied research of their own. But they do need the universities too – and research collaboration between the two is still less highly developed than in Britain, let alone the United States. Companies grant large contracts to universities for specific jobs: but rarer are the cases of academic scientists leaving their ivory towers to take part in the 'real world' of industry or to help smaller firms. This is something that Lothar Späth tried to change in Baden-Württemberg, and so has the new innovation centre in Berlin, BIG, whose coordinator, Hans Fiedler, told me: 'One of our member firms developed a new machine, but it was too noisy. So I found them a professor who had worked in this field, and I took him along to the company. After five hours at the drawing-board with them, he discovered a solution. That's our day-to-day work: to be brokers between small firms and the university. It sounds obvious, doesn't it? – but it's quite a novelty in Germany.'

German managements today are certainly taking research seriously. They are usually excellent too at the technical side of production, and at personnel relations: but their broader commercial and financial expertise is more often open to question. And this brings us to another of today's major talking-points: are German firms too cautious? Here, as in scientific research, it can be a matter of generation. The older breed of family owners and managers, who performed so brilliantly in the post-war decades, are now growing tired and conservative, wary of adapting to new techniques, and in many cases they have made the mistake of holding on too long, rather than finding a successor. Go to an average chamber of commerce meeting, and it is noticeable how many heads of firms are greybeards. And yet, the Germans are a people who still depend very much on dynamic individual leadership, as opposed to group work. Many of the family bosses have allowed their firms to become too big, therefore bureaucratised and hierarchical, so that the younger middle management may feel frustrated and unable to put its ideas across. Older Germans are not good at delegating responsibility to subordinates: so if for example a senior man is away, his junior will be wary of taking decisions and will let papers pile up on his desk. It all adds up, in many firms, to a certain inflexibility and a spirit of overprudence. Younger executives may be more open and group-minded: but they are also less industrious and dynamic. There are fewer successful young whizz-kids around in German than in French industry, even though for other reasons French industrial performance is less good.

This may add up to a harsh picture. German managers do have many qualities too, which should equally be stressed. They are adept at handling their staff firmly but kindly, and they tend to have a stronger social ethic than British or American ones, believing that only a happy firm can be a profitable one. They are perfectionist almost to the point of neurosis, but this does carry advantages. It makes them punctilious over delivering goods on time, and over checking and re-checking the tiniest technical details to ensure that no flawed product goes through – no wonder German cars have so fine a record of reliability. But managers, like other Germans, also have a mania for security. They feel the urgent need to reduce uncertainties, to prepare careful safety margins and fall-back positions, and to do all they can to avoid crisis, for they are not very good at handling these. So long as they are working to a set routine they do fine: but, if something unexpected happens, they are not so good at improvising. As an example, I was quoted the case of strikes: if a few key workers strike in a factory, French and British managers show much more initiative in swiftly altering work schedules so as to keep the plant going, whereas Germans will simply close it down (but then, it could be argued that the British and French have had rather more practice at coping with strikes!).

One especially negative aspect of this caution is that few younger executives in Germany have been prepared to risk leaving the security of a larger firm to set up on their own. It is true that this pattern is at last changing, and today there are some 50,000 more new firms starting up each year than old ones going bust – an amazing figure: mammoth organisations have become less popular with younger recruits who feel that 'small is beautiful'; and the old pioneering spirit of enterprise and risk-taking, that used to be common in Germany in the time of Krupp or Daimler, is starting to be seen again in the micro-technology field. But it remains rarer than in France or the United States. One deterrent factor could be the lack of venture capital: or the typically German fear of the stigma of failure, in a nation that does not readily condone weakness; or even the softening effects of affluence and the Welfare State. All these are cited as reasons. And another explanation certainly is that German colleges and universities provide very little training in business administration and entrepreneurship.

Traditionally Germany has no business schools, either public or private, of the kind so dominant in America and recently copied in Britain, France and elsewhere. Nor is there any equivalent of the French elitist Grandes Ecoles that turn out top engineers and administrators. All the training is done in the ordinary universities, which increasingly have become similar to each other and non-specialised (see p. 253). It is true that a number of Germans go to attend INSEAD (in France), or Harvard, or other foreign graduate business schools: but, when they return to Germany, they tend to go into management consultancy rather than industry. This lack of elitist education has sometimes worried Germans, especially those on the Right, and in 1967 Chancellor Kiesinger tried to set up a German version of France's prestigious Ecole Nationale d'Administration. His cabinet approved, but the project was then vetoed by a committee of civil servants. After all, education is a *Land* matter, and if a college of this kind were put in one *Land*, then the others would want them too and chaos would ensue – or so the argument ran.

So how do companies select their future senior staff? Answer: direct from the universities. The recruiting officer of a big firm will make it his duty to keep in touch with a few key professors in certain universities, who are doing specialist work of interest to the firm, and he will ask them to recommend their best students. He may know that Professor X at Heidelberg is the best for precision engineering, or Professor Y at Aachen, and so he will go head-hunting there, in rivalry with other firms. It is an *ad hoc* kind of elitism in a way, on an old-boy basis, not especially democratic. Moreover, the bright young stars thus recruited tend to have had an engineering or other technical education, rather than one in the skills of management. The bigger firms then conduct their own in-service training of graduate staff, in a range of skills including finance and administration, and this they do extremely well: Siemens in particular has a high reputation. Its senior recruiting officer, Peter Thust, explained to me: 'In the United States, management is a separate profession in itself. Here, it is not. In Germany, a manager will have the technical background of whatever his firm deals with: thus, in a bank, a manager will probably have studied economics at college; and here, at Siemens, engineering. Our sales manager is an engineer, our R&D manager a physicist; on our main board of eleven directors, only two are non-technical. This has many advantages, for it means that directors understand a firm's product. We're quite happy with the present university system, and anyway we have no means of changing it. We do not need business schools.'

Others are less sure. They argue that the system may suit a giant like Siemens which has the means to do its own training, but that it is failing to supply the wider industrial world, especially smaller firms and new ventures, with a new business breed that has the required entrepreneurial flair and modern managerial skills. Germany here is falling behind its competitors. A young man trained by Siemens to be a cog in their big machine, who then leaves to strike out on his own, may feel a little inadequate. A further argument, which I heard from several German INSEAD alumni, is that the growth of student numbers and the decline in university standards have made business schools far more necessary than they used to be. It was this thinking that in 1984 led a group of industrialists to found Germany's first private university for business administration, in Koblenz. Financed by industry and the payment of fees, it is unashamedly elitist – and it marks a new departure for Germany.

Daimler-Benz is a firm quite as traditionalist as Siemens. But there I was given a different slant on the problem, by the sales director of its Untertürkheim factory, Hans-Wolfgang Hirschbrunn: 'The universities are just not giving us the highly-qualified people that we need. Germany today is as weak at university education as it is strong on the training of shopfloor apprentices. On the other hand, my shopfloor and office staff here work very well and I have excellent relations with the works council. The ongoing success of German industry derives more than anything from its good labour relations.'

## A paradise of labour harmony – but what of the waning work-ethic?

Over brandy and cigars in their comfortable oak-panelled office, I discussed German labour affairs one day with a group of smartly dressed trade union executives in Stuttgart. One of them had a doctorate in economics; another was on the supervisory board of Robert Bosch; nearly all spoke perfect English. They could have been company directors in a board-room. One of them said: 'It is true that relations have become a little more conflictual nowadays, owing to lower growth and higher unemployment. But basically we still believe that it is by cooperating with management, rather than fighting it, that we stand the best chance of securing better pay and working conditions – and the results prove it. What is more, as we see it our moral obligation is not just to our own members or other workers, but to German society as a whole, where we must play an active role in upholding democracy and the rule of law. So, if you like, we're part of the establishment and proud of it. We're certainly not revolutionaries: we do not want to overthrow capitalism but to reform it from inside, in a more "social" direction, within the social market economy. We have moved beyond the class-war phase where so many French and British unionists are still bogged down; and we believe that workers have an interest in helping their firms to remain profitable. Not that we have illusions about German employers. Some of them, it is true, in being generous to their staff and cooperative with the unions are genuinely sincere and even idealistic. But others behave well because they have no other choice: you see, they are bound hand and foot by a powerful set of labour laws, among the world's best.'

That seemed to me an eloquent summary of the various interrelating factors that underly Germany's envied industrial harmony. This can even be traced back to the nineteenth century, for the industrial revolution arrived later than in Britain, so workers did not have to struggle for so long to achieve tolerable conditions. Bismarck in the 1880s, in an effort to avoid class conflict, was ahead of the rest of Europe in promoting welfare legislation and in sanctioning factory councils. This did not prevent all confrontation: but it did help to imbue German workers with some sense of cooperation and involvement in their firms. However by the early 1930s, though strong in overall membership (6.5 million), German unions lay fragmented in some 200 separate bodies, divided on religious and ideological lines, Catholic and Protestant, Communist, Socialist and so on – and this was to prove a fatal weakness, for it made them incapable of forming a united front against the Nazis, who thus found it easier to get their hands on German industry and to abolish the unions and imprison many of their leaders.

The survivors emerged from the war with a carefully thought-out resolve to build a stronger and more unified union structure, better able to stand as a bulwark of democracy. Some of them had fled to Britain, where TUC colleagues gave them friendly support. And so it was, after 1945, that Vic Feather and other British union leaders actively helped the Germans to set up the kind of sensible, logical framework that they would dearly have liked to see installed on the chaotic British labour scene, too! This was one of the manifold ways in which Germany by being able to make a clean start, actually benefited from losing the war.

The system thus created still exists today, and it is exemplary. While Britain has some 400 unions, often at loggerheads, the German federation, the Deutscher Gewerkschaftsbund (DGB), comprises just seventeen; and they are organised in such a way that, within one factory, all the manual and technical staff tend to belong to the same union, whereas in Britain there may be a dozen or more, split up on craft lines. Thus, for example, if you work for Bosch you are in the metalworkers' union, whether you are employed as mechanic, electrician or computer programmer. So there are no demarcation disputes. Nor is the German labour movement divided politically, as in France or Italy where the big national unions pursue their destructive rivalries within each firm. Moreover, the closed shop is illegal, and so are political strikes. This rational structure lends strength to the unions, and it greatly simplifies collective bargaining and other dealings with employers. It is certainly one of the main elements making for harmony on the German labour scene.

The seventeen unions federated into the DGB have a total membership of some 7.6 million in its west German sections; the biggest of them, IG Metall, for the metalworkers, claims to be the free world's largest trade union, with 2.6 million members in the west. There are also three other unions outside the DGB, including one for salaried staffs, and another for civil servants, who are not allowed to strike and therefore under DGB rules cannot qualify to make up a union. With rising unemployment, overall union membership has been tending to fall slightly, but less so than in most Western countries: it still stands at some 38 per cent of all employees. The figure is as much as 85 or 90 per cent in the steel and mining industries, but only 28 per cent in banking and commerce. All in all, the DGB with its headquarters in Düsseldorf is a rich and powerful organisation, and it is not ashamed to try its hand at capitalism in order to add to its resources: it owns a number of commercial enterprises with a total staff of 100,000 including one of Germany's largest banks (useful for funding strikes, when needed), the second largest insurance company, a travel agency, and shops and printing firms, and until 1986 owned the mammoth house-building firm, Neue Heimat (see p. 516). The DGB also stages arts festivals and has its own economic institute. Since 1990 the DGB has been extending itself into east Germany (see p. 459) by building up new unions there on the western model, to replace the old ones run by the Communist Party. This expensive task is taking up much of the DGB's time, energy and resources, and for the moment is preventing it from pursuing new projects in the west.

Probably the biggest single reason for the success of German labour relations is that they are governed by a strong legal framework — and in Germany you can never get very far without a good law behind you. In the first place, important federal laws provide for employee delegates to share in the process of decision-making in larger firms, while others oblige managements to consult with their staff, and seek their approval on a whole range of matters, through the works councils. Other laws lay down the rules for job security, working conditions, welfare and fringe benefits, collective wage bargaining, and so on. Of course this kind of machinery exists in other countries too: but in Germany it is particularly extensive and precise, and is strongly weighted in favour of the employee, sometimes in a manner that is almost comic (in the civil service in Baden-Württemberg, there is a rule that the head of an office *must* send a bouquet of flowers to a member of staff who has been away sick for six weeks). This battery of legislation more or less forces a German firm to be a good employer and to take labour relations in a positive spirit: benevolent paternalism is possible, but not union-bashing. And, as the Germans are a cooperative and law-abiding people, both sides in the labour partnership tend to desire actively to work together, so as to make the laws work fairly and fully.

What is more, strikes in Germany are illegal except under certain conditions. Under the labour laws, each annual wage agreement becomes a kind of 'peace treaty': unions are committed to refraining from wildcat or other strikes while the agreement is in force, and when it expires at the end of a year they can strike only in pursuit of a genuine grievance, after all means of arbitration have been exhausted. Remarkably, these restrictions were not imposed on the unions against their will by a right-wing government, but were actually elaborated by the DGB itself as guidelines for strike action, back in 1949. The DGB laid down that a strike should be called only as a last resort and not without the backing of a union's national headquarters, and only if a secret ballot of members concerned had thrown up a 75 per cent majority in favour of it: in Baden-Württemberg in 1982, a planned strike by the public employees' union was called off because the vote for it was only 74.3 per cent! In defiance of the DGB, the left-wing printers' union in 1983 changed its rules to allow its executive to call a strike without a ballot, but it is the only one to have done so.

These laws and guidelines are generally observed, and this goes a long way to explain the low strike level in Germany which in 1985, for example, involved only 90,000 workers and led to the loss of 35,000 working days, compared with 727,000 days lost in France, 6,402,000 in Britain, 3,831,000 in Italy and 7,079,000 in the United States. It is true that matters have been changing a little recently, with the rise of a more militant breed of union leader: but even IG Metall's strategic seven-week strike in the south-west in 1984, something of a new departure in Germany, was voted for with some reluctance by the rank and file. Being not only law-abiding but by nature work-motivated, German employees tend to have the gut-feeling that a strike is a sign of failure, an irritating symptom of disorder, a break in the decent business of getting on with the job – not always the British attitude: Scargill's year-long miners' strike in 1984–5 would, in Germany, have been not only illegal but psychologically impossible. Not however that all is totally serene within factories — as we can see by looking next at collective bargaining, worker participation and the works councils.

The collective bargaining is conducted on a regional and sector-by-sector basis: in every *Land* the employers' association of each branch of industry meets annually with its union counterpart to thrash out a deal on rates of pay, hours of work, holidays and other conditions. The agreement is then legally binding. As a result, governments have never found it necessary to impose a wage or price freeze, or to create a legal minimum wage as there is in France. Unions have generally concentrated on the battle for better conditions, while on wages they have shown restraint. Maybe this derives from the deep-rooted German fear of inflation, in a land still haunted by the trauma of the 1920s.

Worker participation in management (*Mitbestimmung*) began soon after the war in the coal, iron and steel sectors; it was an initiative of the victorious British, who chose it as a way of punishing the private owners of these firms for the support they had given to Hitler. The system then spread to the US zone; it became federal law, and is still in force today. Each coal and steel firm has a supervisory board (*Aufsichtsrat*), half of whose members are appointed by management and the other half elected by the staff. The board then chooses a neutral chairman from outside the firm, and he has the decisive vote. This system has generally worked smoothly and is appreciated both by owners and unions. The board of management retains the last word on policy matters, but it does pay attention to the *Aufsichtsrat*, which can use its influence quite powerfully. And this partnership is often cited to explain the absence of serious conflict during the periods of major lay-offs in coal and steel, when the unions were able to use the *Aufsichtsrat* and the works council to negotiate a 'social plan' of phased redundancies, high pensions and retraining schemes, generously funded by Bonn.

Since 1952, all limited and joint stock companies in Germany with a staff of over 500 have had supervisory boards with one-third worker representation. Then in 1976 a controversial law was passed, bringing this quota of staff delegates up to 50 per cent in all firms with a personnel of more than 2,000. But their position is not as strong as in the coal and steel industries, for their numbers must include the senior employee of the firm, and he tends to side with management; and, instead of a neutral chairman, the board is chaired by a shareholder who has an extra casting vote. This weights the *Aufsichtsrat* towards the owners — and the unions are none too pleased. Nor are employers either so happy with this *Mitbestimmung*. They opposed its introduction in 1976, and especially they object to the clause whereby it is the *Aufsichtsrat* that elects the company's own board of directors. However, many managers do find virtues in the system: 'It has proved a useful instrument for controlling the workforce and has helped to create a social consensus,' said a senior Daimler-Benz executive. But unions do not see it that way. At the Blohm & Voss shipyards in Hamburg, a militant IG Metall official told me: 'As members of the *Aufsichtsrat* we can exercise a personal influence: but management can always get a majority and we cannot block its decisions. Our economic influence is zero.' The DGB view is that *Mitbestimmung* in these firms may be better than nothing, for it at least allows the staff to give their views, but it is no real co-determination. The unions would like to see the coal and steel system applied more widely, but they see little hope of this. In the meantime, the real influence of unions and workers within a firm is exercised much less through these boards than through the works councils. These are highly prized by the unions, and along with collective bargaining they are much the most significant feature of German labour relations.

In every enterprise employing five people or more, the management must agree to the setting up of a works council (*Betriebsrat*) if the staff ask for it — and this they nearly always do, except in very tiny firms. Many a smallish company may contain no union members at all, but will still have a *Betriebsrat*. The council is elected by the staff in secret ballot, from independent and/or union-sponsored candidates. It has an office on the premises, and in a firm of any size its senior members will work full-time on their council duties while still being fully salaried by the company. The council enjoys considerable scope, with a consultative voice in economic matters and real powers of co-determination in welfare, personnel and working life. In the economic field, the law says that every three months the management must inform the council of its investment projects and financial plans and must seek its views, though it need not act on them. Over a whole range of matters that affect the daily life of the staff, including safety regulations, the installation and use of new equipment, the canteen, working hours and holiday schedules, management must seek the approval of the council making changes. The council can object, if it can argue that the measures contravene a law or wage agreement or would disadvantage employees. If no solution is found, then the matter is sent to be decided by a labour court (these generally favour the employees).

In the vast majority of firms, these procedures tend in practice to work quite smoothly – and the unions and employers alike speak much more warmly of the works council system than of the *Aufsichtsrat*. However, there have recently been growing frictions over such matters as dismissals, flexible working time, and the introduction of new technologies. These last had up till now been accepted fairly easily by unions and workers (as in the case of the robots at Volkswagen) and most employers had smoothed the way by carefully phasing the redundancies caused by automation. However, with productivity still rising steadily, some unions have grown more restive in the past two or three years. There have been cases of works councils taking employers to court over their right to introduce Computer Aided Design or electronic devices for controlling work rhythms.

The issue of recruitment and dismissals has been causing worse tensions. A works council has the right to be consulted about all new appointments, even to read the candidates' applications: the management makes the final choice, but must state its reasons. If it wants to make the lay-offs on economic grounds, then it must also give reasons: but usually it will get its way, if it can present a strong case. It may however have more difficulty if it wants to dismiss an individual for incompetence or indiscipline, or even to transfer someone to another department. Here the council can insist on full-scale negotiations, which may drag on for weeks: at one Stuttgart factory, the personnel director told me, 'We had a woman clerk who became hysterical and disruptive, but it was hard to get the *Betriebsrat* to agree to our sacking her. By law, we do have the last word in such a case. But we have to weigh this against the need to keep on good terms with the works council and our staff. Naturally, the *Betriebsrat* sees itself as the defender of labour, and on principal it is against sackings of any kind. If we dismiss someone against the council's wishes, then we usually find ourselves taken to court.'

Relations between management and councils are variable in nature, usually smoothest in the older family-run paternalist firms and not easy in larger ones where a militant union is strong. There are no shop-stewards in Germany, and a union is not institutionally represented inside the firm as it is in Britain, so it must exert its influence via the works council. And this today can cause problems. At Bosch, a group with an excellent record of benevolent staff policies, the personnel manager nonetheless expressed anxieties to me: 'Formally the unions deal with firms collectively, not individually, through the annual bargaining system. They would like to make more impact inside firms, but they can do this only through their members on the works councils. So, in the Bosch group, our works councils are becoming more politicised, owing to the presence of little handfuls of youngish IG Metall militants. They go off on trade union courses in the firm's time, and they come back breathing their dogma – so *we* are paying for them to be indoctrinated against us! With the councils as a whole our relations are excellent: it is just a few troublemakers here and there that provoke us.' I heard the same story in some other firms: 'The works council is starting to throw its weight around too much, even rebuking the managing director for parking his car in the wrong place,' or, 'The council took down the photo of our revered Founder from the wall in their office, and put up one of the union leader instead.' Such are the problems caused by the rise of a new breed of union activist ready to exploit the tensions caused today by unemployment.

The rise in unemployment since the late 1970s has shown that German unions are more concerned about jobs than wage stagnation. The years 1981–3 actually saw an overall drop of 3.5 per cent in real earnings (according to union estimates): but there was very little unrest, and unions repeatedly put their signatures to annual wage increases below the rate of inflation. This could be seen as a triumph for the collective bargaining system. It may also have been related to the fact that the Social Democrats were in power until October 1982 – and, although the DGB has no organic link with the SPD (unlike the TUC with the Labour Party), nonetheless there is much in the way of close informal links and sympathy, and a general desire by unions not to make things too difficult for an SPD government. But after the CDU came to power the picture changed. Not only did the unions dislike the Kohl regime as such, but they saw that its 'liberal' policies were unlikely to do much for employment. Kohl, it is true, produced some extra money for job creation schemes: but he refused any reflation that might stem the rise of unemployment, which in 1985 was averaging over 9 per cent. It has since been falling, as in other countries, and by the spring of 1991 it was little more than 7 per cent in west Germany (of course it is far higher in the east, see p. 457). Despite this improvement, how to deal with unemployment remains a major political issue. Kohl and his Labour Minister, Norbert Blüm, have favoured early retirement and have provided special funding for it. This palliative is also popular with a number of the unions, led by those in heavy manual sectors – construction, mining, railways – where workers soon get physically worn out. But others have preferred to go along with EC proposals for shorter working hours, even though Germans for long have been working fewer hours than in most advanced countries.

The campaign for a 35-hour week was taken up in earnest by IG Metall in 1984. This union had just acquired new and more dynamic leaders, who were anxious to rally their rank-and-file and to refute criticism that it was being too cosily chummy with employers. So they decided to make a test case of the issue, and they produced figures to support their claim that a phased reduction from 40 to 35 hours could yield 1.4 million extra jobs within two years. The employers retorted that this was dangerous nonsense: if, as the unions demanded, there were no cuts in pay, then costs might rise by up to 16 per cent, leading to a serious drop in German competitiveness — 'Yes, the 35-hour week would create more jobs — in the Far East,' read the car-stickers. Most independent economic analysts leaned towards the employers' view, and so did the Kohl Government, very vocally: whereas federal governments since the war have usually taken care to keep neutral in labour disputes, this time Kohl rather tactlessly put his weight behind the metal industry bosses — and this further inflamed IG Metall, who began to see their projected strike as a political challenge to Bonn. It was an unusual departure in post-war German labour relations. 'This is an issue that could well decide a new balance of power within European society!' proclaimed Franz Steinkühler, the aggressive and acid-tongued new deputy leader of IG Metall (he is also on the *Aufsichtsrat* of Daimler-Benz).

Since the employers refused to negotiate, the union felt that it had a legal case for industrial action. As is common in Germany, rather than stage an expensive nationwide strike it preferred to select regional target areas — in this case, the wealthy automotive industries of Baden-Württemberg and Hessen, where the employees were highly paid and secure in their jobs, and thus were prepared to risk and to fund a long-drawn-out stoppage. Here the much-publicised strike began in May: 60,000 workers were called out, the employers replied with lock-outs, and soon 300,000 were idle, some of them as far afield as Wolfsburg and Munich, where VW and BMW factories were forced to close too because of lack of spare parts from Bosch and others in the south-west. The world's Press screamed their banner headlines: 'Is this the end of Germany's vaunted labour consensus? — is Scargillism finally on the march in *Wirtschaftswunderland*?' In fact, it was not. For all Herr Steinkühler's sharp words, the strike was conducted in a fairly gentlemanly way by both sides, without violence. Most workers took part out of union loyalty rather than real enthusiasm: reporters found them apathetic, and one opinion poll indicated that only 31 per cent of IG Metall members were in favour of a 35-hour week. After dragging on for seven weeks, the strike finally ended in a negotiated compromise, on the basis of a 38½-hour week, without cuts in pay, for all workers in Germany's metal industries. Neither side seemed to have won, the union least of all, though it put a brave face on things, claiming that this was but a first step. The employers had made concessions, but were glad that the 1½-hour cut was to be applied flexibly so that in some factories, for example, key skilled workers could remain on 40 hours, while less important manual ones could go down to 37. Above all, by re-organising and taking up slack, employers found it necessary to take on no more than 70,000 or so extra staff. There have been no more serious strikes since then.

By 1990 various factors had caused a large fall in the unemployment level, despite the mass arrival of emigrants from the former GDR and eastern Europe (see p. 294). First, west Germany had been sharing fully in the economic boom of the Western world in the later 1980s which had reduced unemployment everywhere. Secondly, the decline in the German birth-rate in the early 1970s, from a much higher level in the 1960s, was by 1990 starting to make its impact on the labour market: the number of 16-year-olds fell from around 1 million in 1982 to 650,000 in 1990. Germany's slumping population, in other respects disturbing (see p. 200), was thus in this respect a kind of blessing. It even led to labour shortages in some sectors. This also helps to explain why west Germany has been able to absorb so many new refugees, without being obliged to repatriate foreign 'guest workers'. At all events, after 1984 the unions continued to press for the 35-hour week, and the employers eventually agreed, on the condition that it be applied gradually. It is due to come fully into force by 1995.

In recent years, various other *ad hoc* remedies for high unemployment have been tried out. Some firms offer reduced hours in the years before retirement, with little loss of pay; or half-time work at half-pay for ex-apprentices, which amounts to job-sharing; or fluctuating hours in line with demand for product; or extra freedom. But they are resisted by some unions, such as IG Metall, who find that the flexibility makes it harder for them to maintain a unified control over their members or to negotiate coherently with employers. In a large number of firms, however, staff have readily gone along with plans for early retirement.

The federal employment agency has also given pump-priming money to cities and *Länder* for local job creations of a minor nature, such as tidying public parks – better than nothing. More important, in 1985 the Government pushed through a bill making it much easier for firms to hire staff on short-term contracts of up to 18 months: previously many employers were reluctant to take on more than the bare minimum they needed, because of the difficulties with dismissals.

The unions have been angry at Chancellor Kohl's welfare spending cuts, which have not spared unemployment benefits. In Germany these are scaled according to previous earnings, rather than being paid at flat rates as in more egalitarian Britain; and they average 63 per cent of previous pay, for people without children, and for the first year without a job. Even so, the benefits remain fairly generous by most Western standards, and they are remarkably easy to obtain, if you try. The story is told of Peter Milz, a contractor at Siegburg, near Bonn, who fired a lady employee in order to give a job to a girl apprentice. The dismissed woman drew over 15,000 DM in benefits in one year, before it was discovered that she was Herr Milz's wife and the apprentice was his daughter. What is more, Milz was a CDU member of the *Bundestag*. His party made him promise to pay back his wife's indemnities – but he found that he couldn't. All had been entirely legal, and the state employment office refused his money. He had to give it to charity.

A question discussed today is how far Germany's vaunted labour harmony can survive, in a new period of job insecurity, declining work-ethic and disruptive technological innovation. Certainly the old values are being challenged for times have changed. In the early post-war years, union leaders easily found common cause with employers in their mutual desire to forge a democratic society and rebuild the country by sustained hard work: but today's new leaders, now taking over the reins as the old ones retire, no longer have such priorities. Many of them were students in the 1968 period. Very few are Greens; in fact they show a contempt for the Greens' 'alternative economy' ideas. But they have radical ideas and are much less ready than their elders to come to terms with capitalism. And this worries some employers, as the owner of one family firm in Bavaria told me: 'The old union leaders had come up from the shopfloor, they were close to the workers and understood realities. The new ones are university theorists, trying to impose dogmatic solutions.' But from a 38-year-old union chief in Stuttgart I heard the view: 'Our generation is certainly more dynamic and alert than the old one: we bargain more toughly, for we have to, in today's hard times. But very few of us are Marxist. We do *not* want to overthrow the system.' It may be hard to generalise about so fluid a situation: but the overall picture would seem to be that the new union leaders remain quite moderate by most British or French standards. Some unions may have moved leftwards, but they are still open to realistic compromise: the printers' union for example has become rather militant, but after a rearguard fight against planned redundancies it did finally accept the new computer technologies – as has not exactly happened in Fleet Street.

Above all, the legal framework still holds strong, adhered to by both sides and enabling most disputes to find an acceptable solution. Younger union activists in some firms may be adopting more aggressive tactics; but workers as a whole remain cooperative, industrious, and not anticapitalist. In the older family firm of the Swabian type, they still respond happily to benevolent paternalism – the kind of firm where the boss may take his foreman to a pub lunch on a Sunday to discuss his financial policies, or where a working family may feel proud to have served the same employer for three or four generations. If less so than thirty years ago, German employees still display quite a degree of company loyalty – and this may be one of the fruits of the excellent apprenticeship system.

Germany is recognised as the leader of Europe in youth vocational training. Its apprenticeships go back centuries, to the guilds of the middle ages, and today the system is highly extensive and elaborate: arguably it is one of the most impressive features of modern Germany, bringing massive advantages both to the economy as a whole and to the young individuals concerned. The rules for the scheme are laid down by the *Bund*, but it is operated and largely paid for by the firms themselves, great and small – and nearly every German employer, from Siemens down to the village butcher, will at one time or another have taken on an '*Azubi*' (*Auszubildende* – trainee). Apprenticeship places are thus provided each year for the vast majority of school leavers: in 1988, some 650,000 youngsters took them up.

The *Azubi* is given a contract for a two- or three-year course, on a 'dual training' basis, whereby he or she spends roughly three and a half days of the week in a firm, learning a particular job, and one and a half days at a *Berufsschule* (state-run vocational centre), continuing general education and acquiring a variety of skills. Formal training is offered in over 300 different vocations, among the most popular being car mechanic, bank clerk and hairdresser. The apprentice receives a small wage from the firm, some 600 to 700 DM a month, which is usually topped up by parental support. If he went straight from school into unskilled work, he might start at 1,500 to 2,000 DM: on the other hand, once qualified, he can soon be earning over 2,500 DM, so the apprenticeship is a good investment.

Some 60 per cent of apprentices then get salaried jobs in the same firm: the figure would be higher, if employers could provide more posts. Others have to look elsewhere for work, which of course has become harder to find: even so, about nine out of 10 apprentices do find jobs somewhere. This goes to explain the low level of youth unemployment in Germany, only 5 per cent in the 16-to-20 age group, the lowest figure in the EC. So it is not surprising that the apprentice-ship scheme is widely popular both with young people and with the unions. As well as school leavers of 16, an increasing number of places are now being taken up by those who stay on to get their *Abitur* at 19 or 20 but then feel that a trainee qualification offers better prospects than a university degree (see p. 249). With demand in this way outstripping supply, the Kohl Government has managed to coax more firms into offering places, with the result that all but about 30,000 applicants a year now find them. However, one growing problem is that especially in rural areas it may be far from easy for a youngster to secure an outlet in the kind of trade that interests him: cases are reported, for instance, of farmers' sons wanting to train as factory mechanics but being obliged to settle for *Azubi* posts in the local bakery or butcher's shop, in their anxiety to avoid the dole. This is frequent, and it has brought the apprenticeship system under some criticism.

In other respects, by heightening the skills of the workforce the scheme has been of immense benefit to German industry and is one of the main factors behind its post-war success. Leaving aside higher education, nearly 70 per cent of Germans are occupationally qualified, compared with only 30 per cent in Britain. And according to one international survey,[1] the higher standard of technical expertise among shopfloor workers is the principal reason for Germany's much greater level of productivity. A study of several firms making simple metal products such as coil springs found that German output per employee is 50 per cent higher than in Britain. The secret lies with the apprentice

1. Quoted in the *Financial Times*, February 22, 1985.

system, especially in the big firms with their extensive training work-shops.

Robert Bosch, the very archetype of a kindly paternalistic Swabian firm, has retained its original philanthropic spirit even though it has now expanded into a worldwide group, and it has a good personnel record too. It created its own apprenticeship scheme in 1913. At its main factory in Stuttgart, I talked to the head of training, Horst Bohne: 'I myself began as an *Azubi* here, aged seventeen. Later I went to a technical college and became an engineer. One member of the Bosch board of directors is an ex-apprentice, as are several of the supervisory board. Today we have thirty applicants for every place we can offer, we take on 950 a year, and 80 per cent of them then stay with us – a very high record.' I visited the workshop, where a group of lively Swabian girls were doing metal-work; boys in neat blue overalls, several of them Greek and Turkish immigrants, were working at micro-processors or making useful implements such as torches or electric drills. Later I went to a local *Berufsschule* (these are not run by the firms, but are part of the *Land* education system). Here, intent-looking teenagers were being taught a range of skills, from beauty treatment and tiling bathrooms to engine assembly and using word-processors. Those doing machinery in their firms study carpentry at the *Berufsschule*, or vice versa.

Bohne said: 'The dual system provides the ideal transition from school to work life for the less academically-minded youngster. Our apprentices appear to be grateful to us for training them, so they develop a loyalty to the firm and become more motivated.' Though not all employers are as enlightened as Bosch, I heard Bohne's view echoed by a secondary-school teacher in a working-class district of Karlsruhe: 'Kids who at fifteen were bored, rebellious and awkward in school seem to change completely when they become apprentices. I meet them a year later, and they are polite, enthusiastic and self-confident.' So does this mean that they still feel the incentive to work hard, as their parents' generation did?

There has been much public debate recently about the alleged decline of the work ethic, in this nation that traditionally has not only been industrious by temperament but has also believed religiously in hard work as a primary virtue. Are the old attitudes changing, as the sociologists claim? According to Allensbach surveys, in 1962 only 33 per cent of Germans would admit to preferring leisure to work time, but this figure has risen to 42 per cent by 1990; and when an international enquiry in 1983 asked for comments on the statement, 'I often give more to my job than is demanded of me, it's so important to me that I sacrifice a lot to it,' only 43 per cent of the Germans agreed, compared with 68 per cent Americans and 66 per cent of the supposedly lazy British. It might be naive to interpret such findings too literally: but they do correspond to a shift that is noted by employers, teachers and anyone who talks to young people. Work used to be an end in itself: now it is smart to find it less so. Many observers see this as a healthy trend, a sign that the all-work-and-no-play Germans are at last learning to relax and enjoy life. But for others it is a symptom of the decline of the old moral values and a threat to the economy. And so the Germans have been thrown into a frenzy of self-analysis and self-doubt on the issue. Are we, they ask, swinging from workaholism to the other extreme? 'Nein!' yelled a *Bild Zeitung* headline, 'Wir sind NICHT faul!' (significantly, 'faul' means not only 'lazy' but also 'foul, rotten, putrid', whereas 'lazy' in English is less pejorative). And so the debate goes on. Certainly attitudes to work have become more relaxed, less moralistic: but does this mean that those Germans with jobs are actually working less hard in practice?

The issue has to be seen in a post-war perspective. After the war the Germans worked demoniacally hard, not only in order to rebuild their country and find a new prosperity, but also as a kind of instinctive act of expiation for the evil of the war and of Nazism, and a means of regaining dignity and respect among nations. Then this motivation gradually waned. Already the rising generation of the late 1960s was beginning to question the work ethic, and this mood was to spread during the 1970s as older people, exhausted by the earning of their wealth, wanted more time to enjoy it, while younger ones grew up with less materialistic attitudes. These trends pre-dated the arrival of the Greens. They also had little to do with the rise in unemployment in the early 1980s.

So the Germans are becoming less neurotically workaholic, more normal and more like other nations. They have discovered the leisure ethic, but without really losing the work ethic. As one manager put it, 'After the war we made superhuman efforts. Now we have slowed down, but not become lazy.' And because the Germans still tend to work thoroughly and methodically, with care and concentration, they can get through a great deal of effective work without having to devote as much time to it as those who loll about on the job, with endless tea-breaks, like the British. After the Belgians, German employees have the shortest working year in the West: in 1986, it was an annual 1,708 hours, compared with 1,763 in France, 1,778 in Britain, 1,912 in the United States, 2,166 in Japan. Most German employers grant five to six weeks' paid leave: this, with public holidays added, means that the German today has an average of 39 days' holiday a year, against 34 in France, 33 in Britain, only 23 in the United States.

The work ethic today varies with class and age-group, and tends to survive most powerfully among middle-aged people in the middle classes, where often it is a matter of pride and social status, of keeping up with the Müllers. To lose your job, even if it is not your own fault, is a matter of dishonour, to be hidden if possible from the neighbours. And so there are stories of jobless clerks and executives who continue to leave the house each day in their office clothes, and return in the evening. Sometimes the ex-breadwinner will even seek to hide his shame from his own family – and his kids on their way back from school may be startled to come across *Vati* not at his desk but feeding the pigeons in the park.

Such behaviour is much less likely among working-class people, who have always shown more solidarity and less petty amour-propre in face of common problems such as unemployment. Nor in the middle-class would it be found so often amongst the young. This generation is not so much lazy and work-shy as more critical and demanding than its elders in its attitude to work: 'My father,' said an engineer of 30, 'would never admit that he doesn't enjoy his job. If mine doesn't satisfy me, I say so. Yet in practice I work almost as hard as he does. If he found that he couldn't spare the time for a holiday, he'd feel proud of that: but I and my friends, we take pride just as much in finding better ways of spending our leisure.' So the accent today is on trying to avoid jobs that are boring, rather than on merely looking for higher pay. In Allensbach surveys, when people wanting to change their job were asked their reasons for doing so, those answering 'Because I want a more interesting one' rose from 26 to 44 per cent between 1953 and 1979, while in 1986 some 76 per cent cited a pleasant office climate and good colleagues as the most important reason for their liking their job. The advent of automation and modern technology has left some young employees with a sense of bewilderment in face of new impersonal work routines, and this may help to explain another Allensbach finding: in answer to the question 'Do you feel free in your job?', 49 per cent said 'yes' in 1973, but only 36 per cent ten years later. Either the work has been growing less attractive: or, more probably, expectations of job satisfaction have been rising. So this new generation rejects work for work's sake and demands better quality of work. This is in line with their drive for better quality of life, better environment and less pollution.

## *The great environmental debate: nuclear power, car exhaust and death of the beloved forests*

The great German debate on the environment today centres on the pollution disaster in the eastern *Länder* (see p. 462), which for the time being has pushed out of the headlines the emotional issue of car exhaust and its likely responsibility for the grave sickness affecting Germany's forests. Public concern now also embraces the 'greenhouse effect', as well as the unresolved question of the future of nuclear power. To set this in its context, we should first look at the overall energy situation. Western Germany has substantial reserves of coal and lignite, some natural gas but very little oil, and has had to rely on imports for over half of its total energy needs, against an EC average of 46 per cent. This dependence on imports is now likely to be aggravated by the incorporation of east Germany, two-thirds of whose energy has come from locally-mined lignite so pollutant that its use will now have to be scaled right down and some imported alternatives found.

In West Germany, imports of cheap oil rose rapidly during the heady years of industrial growth: but the pattern changed after 1973 when oil became much dearer, and since then the aim has been to reduce dependence on it, through energy conservation measures and some switching to other fuels. This has been fairly successful. Between 1973 and 1984 the role of imports fell from 55.7 to 50.6 per cent, largely because oil purchases were reduced from 145 to 103 million tons; in the same period, energy-saving enabled overall consumption to be cut by some 6 per cent. Today Britain is by far the major supplier of oil to Germany, with Nigeria and Libya second and third, and relatively little coming from the Middle East. Germany produces a modest 4 million tons a year of its own oil, mostly in Lower Saxony: but the reserves are not believed to be great, and it has been unlucky in its own segment of the North Sea. Germany does much refining of imported crude oil, but unlike Britain, France and Holland it does not possess any big international oil companies operating abroad.

Hard coal, the main domestic energy asset, is seen as a crucial national resource. Therefore, although the industry is no longer so economically viable (as we have seen in the Ruhr), the Government helps the private companies to maintain it in working order, so that it could be expanded again in an emergency if imported energy supplies were to be cut off. Despite the wearing thin of many seams, output has been cut back only gently since 1973, from 103 to 79 million tons a year. Extractable hard coal reserves are still enormous, estimated at some 25,000 million tons. In addition, west Germany is the world's third largest producer of lignite (brown coal) after the Soviet Union and east Germany, and this is still being mined profitably (some 130 million tons a year), although it does cause some pollution. As for natural gas, Germany's own reserves cover about one-third of its needs, and the rest it imports mainly from Holland and the Soviet Union. In the early 1980s the gas companies joined with other European interests in promoting the construction of a huge new pipeline from Russia that has since led to a big increase in gas supplies from that source. Some voices on the Right had joined with the Americans in opposing the project on strategic grounds: but the Schmidt Government decided that there was little risk of becoming too dependent on energy imports from Russia, so long as the general trade balance remained favourable. Moreover, for Bonn to have intervened to prevent the gas companies from sharing in the scheme would have been an unprecedented step requiring special legislation, for Germany is the only EC country where energy strategy is not dictated by the Government (save in the case of coal) but is left to the free play of the market. The main gas, electricity and nuclear companies are in private hands (with *Land* involvement too in some cases).

The Federal Government has however been providing incentives for energy conservation. It has spent over 5 billion DM since 1973 on subsidies to house occupants to introduce double-glazing or other insulation, and this has led to a reduction of 30 per cent in the use of domestic heating oil, while industry by moving over to other forms of energy has cut its fuel oil consumption by 60 per cent. However, Germany has made less progress than many other countries in developing the 'new' energies – biomass, photovoltaic and geothermal power, or indeed solar heating for which hot sunlight *is* rather lacking. Nor does Germany possess many possibilities for hydraulic power, so its electricity comes mainly from conventional and nuclear sources. The share-out of primary energy sources since 1963 is as follows:

| Total energy used (millions of tons of coal equivalent): | 1963 | 1973 | 1983 | 1985 | 1988 |
|---|---|---|---|---|---|
| | 249 | 379 | 358 | 380 | 390 |
| shares (in percentages): | | | | | |
| Coal | 51 | 22 | 21.4 | 20.4 | 19 |
| Lignite | 13 | 8.7 | 10.5 | 9.3 | 8 |
| Oil | 32.4 | 55.2 | 43.5 | 41.5 | 42 |
| Gas | 0.8 | 10.2 | 15.5 | 15.5 | 16 |
| Nuclear | 0 | 1.0 | 5.9 | 10.6 | 12 |
| Other | 2.8 | 2.9 | 3.2 | 2.7 | 2 |

After a fairly slow start, Germany in the 1980s was pressing ahead with nuclear energy. By 1991 there were 21 nuclear power plants in operation, providing some 40 per cent of the nation's electricity, a higher figure than in Britain, though less than in France. While Kraftwerk Union, a Siemens subsidiary, has been selling nuclear stations abroad, the Germans have also been preparing their own fast-breeder reactor and taking part in France's Super-Phénix project. Even before Chernobyl all this nuclear development was running into a good deal of opposition, as in other countries – and more so than in most owing to the influence of the Greens and Germans' special sensitivity over the environment, as well as to fears that even a civil programme might have military applications. Just as war guilt has lent a special strength to the Peace Movement in Germany (see p. 566), so the hatred of nuclear arms has spilled over into a general mistrust of anything nuclear. The Greens have found some popular sympathy for their complaints that German-made plutonium, if exported, could be used elsewhere for bombs, and this would flatly contravene the Allies' interdiction on German nuclear weapons.

It is hardly surprising that the Chernobyl disaster should have caused a greater furore in Germany than almost anywhere else in western Europe. As levels of radio-activity rose, for some weeks a great deal of farm produce was banned from sale and destroyed on Government orders, and the farmers angrily demanded compensation. Greens and others redoubled their anti-nuclear demonstrations all over the country. At a congress in Hanover just after Chernobyl, the Green party demanded the immediate closure of all nuclear plants and voted to withdraw from its coalition with the ruling SPD in Hessen if the Social Democrats would not agree to the closure of the nuclear plants in that *Land* by the end of the year. Partly in response to this, the SPD at its annual conference in August voted to phase out all nuclear power stations within ten years, should it one day be returned to power. But the Kohl Government's reaction was to declare that for its part the nuclear programme would not be given up. Aware that this stance might cost the CDU many votes, Kohl tried to allay public fears by pointing out that the Chernobyl plant would never have been licensed in West Germany, where safety standards were far higher than in the Soviet Union.

For some years, since long before Chernobyl, one main issue as in other countries has been that of nuclear waste. The Greens and other 'anti-nukes' have succeeded in alerting public opinion, or large parts of it, and in arousing local opposition to new ventures, so that a familiar scenario has often been repeated. A power plant project would be announced, at first the local population might take it calmly, but then Green activists would arrive and explain the dangers, there would be demonstrations, and maybe the local council would take fright and get the project postponed. The final decision to license a new plant lies with the *Land* government. But first the scheme must run the gauntlet of an archi-complex process of court appeals and hearings on the safety and waste disposal issues, and by skilfully exploiting this it has been possible to slow down a number of projects by years. Political factors play a part too. As the SPD has always been more divided and uneasy about nuclear energy than the CDU, most of the plants have been built in CDU-run *Länder*.

The best-known and longest-drawn-out case has been that of the Brockdorf plant, in CDU-run Schleswig-Holstein, not far from SPD-run Hamburg. The decision to build it was taken in 1973. Then in 1976, when construction started, 30,000 demonstrators clashed one day with the police and many people were hurt. Opponents of the scheme managed to get work on it halted under a court ruling. Then a crisis broke out in Hamburg, which was to be the main client: the Senate, split on the project, kept changing its mind and finally voted against using it, whereupon the city's electricity company, private and commercial, threatened to take it to court. Building work began again in 1982 and was finally completed in 1986, when the Senate and the company agreed on a compromise. There have been similar if less spectacular disputes in other places. In Baden-Württemberg, the unorthodox and strong-minded Lothar Späth showed remarkable political courage for a CDU leader by actually siding with the environmentalists – partly out of genuine conviction and partly in order to outflank the Greens, very strong in his *Land*. Announcing that energy needs had been over-estimated, in 1984 he clamped an indefinite postponement order on a projected nuclear plant at Whyl, on the Rhine near Freiburg, which had been much besieged by both German and French sit-ins. There was also a lengthy public campaign against a nuclear reprocessing plant being built at Wackersdorf in Bavaria: the project was finally abandoned in 1989, but less because of these protests than on commercial grounds, because the complex safety requirements were judged to have rendered it uneconomic.

Since Chernobyl, Kohl has put a moratorium on plans for new power plants, under pressure from public opinion and from some *Land* Governments. The existing reactors will last until the mid-1990s, when some will have grown old and will need replacing. But a decision on nuclear power's future might have to be taken even sooner, because of the situation in east Germany: there the few nuclear plants, Soviet-built, are so far below Western safety standards that they have now been closed down, and this plus the lignite pollution problem could induce the Government to give a new green light to the nuclear programme. What's more, the main thrust of public anxiety has now switched to the 'greenhouse effect', and everyone knows that this is caused by oil or coal-fired power plants, not by nuclear ones. So this too could favour the building of new nuclear reactors. In meeting their energy needs, the Germans like others face a cruel dilemma: are they to risk a nuclear accident, or risk damaging the climate through the build-up of carbon dioxide in the atmosphere? All-round energy saving can provide only part of the answer.

The nuclear debate is just one aspect of a nationwide obsession with environmental problems that immediately strikes any visitor to Germany. When asked what is their top priority for increased public spending, 86 per cent of Germans mention the environment, according to an opinion survey conducted for the *Süddeutsche Zeitung* in January 1991. The obsession has developed momentously over the past twenty years, and embraces everything from sulphuric factory fumes to non-returnable milk-bottles. Health hazards, over-use of resources, soil pollution, noise, aesthetic damage to the landscape, threats to flora and fauna – all such ills are argued about and worried over endlessly, and campaigned against not only by Germans but by governments and local councils of every political shade. Go on a duckshoot with a party of bland businessmen and they may well spend the time fretting about soil erosion or tree sickness. And once, when I went to dinner with friends in Munich, my middle-aged hostess, certainly no Green, said to me without a trace of irony, 'Don't eat the skins on those potatoes. They might have been planted near a motorway.'

The Germans recycle 42 per cent of waste paper, reprocess 70 per cent of old tyres, and dutifully place 50 per cent of glass bottles in special coloured bins on the pavements. Concern about cancer hazards from asbestos is such that many buildings with a high level of asbestos have been closed, including 366 classrooms in 47 schools in Hamburg (not to mention the GDR's grandiose Palast der Republik in Berlin). According to one estimate, 6.7 per cent of GNP is spent on environmental schemes. But why this greater concern than in any other European country? Possibly it is related to the German passion for order and tidiness, or to their sense of claustrophobia that comes from being cooped up in a fairly small, thickly populated and highly industrialised country where space is precious. And certainly the environmental craze is being pursued with typical German obsessiveness: once they discover a cause, then they go for it twice as hard as anyone else. Might there not be a lurking subconscious element of guilt about the past, too? – like Lady Macbeth's 'Will these hands ne'er be clean?'

The Greens loudly led the way into the campaign in the later 1970s, abusively haranguing chemical firms to reduce their toxic pollution, or local councils to suspend some motorway project or improve their garbage system – 'It's a real religion war, this,' said one industrialist, 'like in the middle ages.' The Greens struck a chord of wide popular feeling; and, though some of their ideas may have been far-fetched, others did alert the established parties to some real dangers. And so the Greens have successfully made a clean environment into the new piety to which all parties must subscribe. Every German politician is now at least a little bit green, and actively so: at every level, *Bund, Land* and local council, authorities have been pouring money into helping the environment (Bonn earmarked 1.7 billion DM for it in 1984) with a mix of motives, part sincere, part electoralist.

Some German reactions may appear hysterical and out of proportion. But their practical efforts to deal with the problems are often impressive. West of Cologne, I went to look at the open-cast lignite mining that has been going on there for many decades on a huge scale. Whole areas must be cleared, and in some cases villages and townlets destroyed, before the giant holes can be dug in the ground, many kilometres long and up to 370 metres deep. The farmers and villagers are handsomely compensated, and few of the locals seem to object very much, even in this ecological age, for the Rhinelanders are realistic people and they know that the mines bring thousands of jobs. And the private mining company, Rheinbraun, is obliged by the *Land* to respect the environment as far as possible. The hills of loose earth dug out from each hole are neatly planted with trees; and, when a mine is exhausted, it is given back to nature and to human pleasure. One string of old mines has been turned into a vast recreation zone, with forty new lakes amid woodlands, where the Kölner now have better scope for fishing, surfing, sailing and swimming than the city's vicinity ever offered them before. Contrast that with the way the GDR dealt with lignite mining.

Later I visited the Ruhr soon after a smog alert during a cold, foggy spell. The Ruhr, battling with its grimy image, is the only area of Germany to have instituted this kind of alert system, and this was the first time it was used. A grade-three 'maximum alert' was sounded, leading to a 24-hour closure of all factories and ban on all private cars, while doctors advised people to stay indoors. Whether all this was strictly necessary is uncertain. The local CDU accused the SPD-led *Land* Government of over-reacting, while the Greens charged it with not doing enough.

Industrial pollution, leading to smog and worse ills, is now one of the major environmental issues. The chemical companies have come under pressure to reduce their poisonous fumes and other harmful waste matter. In 1984 a campaign by environmentalists in Hamburg led to a court ruling that obliged one local family firm, Böhringer, to close down its pesticide plant after lethal dioxin had been found on a rubbish dump. This was the first court case of its kind in Germany. Hopefully it was an isolated incident, for the chemical industry spends some 10 per cent of its total investment on fighting pollution and is subject to some of the world's strictest safety regulations that, so it claims, would make impossible in Germany any tragedy such as those at Soveso in Italy or Bhopal in India.

Sulphurous emissions from coal and oil-fired power plants present a much wider problem, and one that is international in nature because of prevailing winds. It is reckoned that west Germany 'exports' some 637,000 tons of these emissions a year, and 'imports' another 762,000, most of it from the east. The Federal Republic has also been trying hard to put its own house in order. In 1976 the Schmidt Government imposed some fairly strict measures on the power stations, and these were further strengthened by a law passed when Kohl came to power in 1983. So, in marked contrast to Britain, Germany's power industry now has the toughest clean air standards in the world, along with Japan's: and in order to meet them the electricity firms are currently having to spend between 10 and 15 billion DM on reducing sulphur emissions at the older coal-burning power plants, while a new station may well have to spend over 20 per cent of its capital costs on meeting the requirements. As a result, sulphur dioxide emission was reduced from 1.6 million to 1.1 million tons between 1983 and 1988, and the figure was due to drop to 500,000 tonnes by 1995. The power industry has reluctantly accepted the necessity for these measures, and is passing on much of the cost to the public. But the issue can also lead to the dilemma of cleaner air versus more jobs. In 1984 a much-publicised row blew up over the decision of the Lower Saxony Government to allow a new coal-fired plant at Buschhaus to start operation three years before its sulphur scrubbers had been installed. The decision was legal. With an eye on the next *Land* elections, the CDU was all too aware that the plant would create over 1,000 jobs.

In Stuttgart, I found Lothar Späth in characteristically philosophic mood about pollution: 'After the war we spent our money on non-environmental goodies like cars and TV sets. Now it is the turn of environment. We are a rich enough society to be able to spend far more on it than we do – and people accept this. So we shall have dearer electricity – and why not? Industry will go along with this, so long as there are laws that force it to do so.' Not only does Stuttgart produce Germany's fastest and therefore most pollutant cars, but the wooded *Land* of which it is the capital, comprising all the Black Forest, bears the heaviest toll of Germany's tragically dying trees. Späth was truly in the hot seat.

'*O Wald, O Waldeseinsamkeit, wie gleichst du dem deutschen Gemüt,*' wrote the poet Julius Hammer in 1851 ('O forest, O solitude of the forest, how similar thou art to the German soul'). Germany's woodlands have always lain close to the heart of the German psyche, a constant theme of popular songs and nursery tales, and of opera and literature from Wagner and Goethe to Brecht and the Brothers Grimm. Much of this feeling is purely romantic and cerebral, the fancy of wan city-dwellers who could hardly tell an oak from a beech (see below). But much of it too is real and practical. Germany's forests, covering 30 per cent of its territory, are an important national resource and they play a big part in modern leisure and tourism. With rucksacks and strong shoes, and maybe in lederhosen too, parties of Germans young and old go hiking and camping in the wide woodlands, where you never see a 'Keep Out' sign, for by law even privately-owned forests are freely open to all.

So the tree epidemic has upset Germans badly. Some reactions may have been too hysterical: but the overall mood of panic is understandable, for this *Waldsterben* is a true catastrophe – it is distressing to walk along the heights of the Black Forest, called 'black' because of the velvety opaque panorama of its pines, and to see so many trees with thinning crowns, yellowing needles and peeling bark. According to the experts, the growth-rings show that the inner sickness began 20 to 30 years ago: but it was not really noticed until about 1980. Then the first cries of alarm by a few sylvan Cassandras were dismissed as nonsense. But in 1982–3 the disease began to spread fast and the nation suddenly woke up to the peril – maybe too late. In 1982 an official report had declared that only 8 per cent of all trees were afflicted: but a year later the figure was put at 34 per cent, and by 1986 the federal Ministry of Agriculture was saying that 54 per cent of trees were dead or sick. The epidemic has since stabilised at around that figure. It had first attacked firs and spruce, and then spread to deciduous trees such as oak and beech. It is not a pretty sight. In the case of firs, first the needles turn yellow and start to drop off, then the branches droop wearily, pus weeps down the bark, roots begin to warp and shrink, insects colonise the trunks, and fresh twigs sprout bizarrely as the tree seems to be trying to compensate for its starvation. It is not merely sentimental to feel that the tree is somehow in pain, crying out for help like an animal.

But how can they be helped? By 1984 the campaign for action had become a national crusade, uniting all classes and parties, linking dreamy Greens with hard-nosed businessman who value their Sunday rambles, and city workers with the potent lobby of the timber industry. Edward Steen in the *Sunday Telegraph* (May 12, 1985) wrote of the trees: 'They stab at the national conscience, images of unthinking industrial progress, an economic miracle that has lost its magic. The trees provide both a post-war guilt complex (neurotic luxury of the prosperous) and a national cause.' One opinion poll late in 1983 found the Germans more concerned about their forests than about the topical issue of whether to accept Pershing-2 and Cruise missiles in Germany. Some critics felt that this was a little excessive: but there were many excellent reasons for the alarm. Scientists pointed out that a decline of forests could upset Germany's entire ecological balance, leading to soil erosion, death of wildlife and severe damage to agriculture. By 1984–5 the tourist industry in the south was reporting a serious fall-off in business, for many of its regular clients no longer fancied a holiday amid sick trees. And timber and related industries, on whom 800,000 jobs depend, were claiming to be losing over 1 billion DM a year.

As the precise causes of the epidemic were then far from certain, no one was quite clear what should be done. Some forest-owners tried the expensive palliative of spraying the trees with lime. More important, a vast diversified research effort began, with some 200 different programmes, many identical: the Baden-Württemberg Government was soon spending 20 million DM a year on research. And so a cacophony of bickering scientists came up with many scores of rival theories. Some thought that a plant virus might be responsible; others laid the blame on drought. The fact that there had been at least four previous forest epidemics, over the past 200 years, seemed to lend some credence to the 'climatic' or 'virus' theories. But this time the disease was on a far worse scale than before. Moreover, it was noted that the trees in the GDR and Czechoslovakia were now suffering just as badly as West German ones, whereas France, Britain and Scandinavia, with their very different prevailing winds, were hardly affected at all. This lent strong support to the view of the majority of German tree experts that the ailment was caused by 'acid rain', which forms when sulphur dioxide from factories or power plants, or nitrogen oxide from vehicle exhaust, mixes with moisture and oxygen to form sulphuric or nitric acid in the atmosphere. This can be carried by the wind a very long way, thus explaining why the trees worst affected are often on high ground and not at all close to any industrial area or motorway. What is more, experts have found that the growth-rings on many trees started to narrow in the late 1950s and 1960s: this is when the disease probably began, just at the time of the first big post-war boom in industry and car-driving.

This view today is received wisdom, and has been endorsed by Federal Government reports. It is pooh-poohed in some quarters, especially by the British who do not like to be told accusingly that the westerly winds have been blowing their own nasty acids away from healthy British forests and onto German ones. But Bonn, under pressure from the Greens and others, and needing to do something urgently, decided to act on the 'acid rain' theory. This was one of the main reasons for the new controls imposed on power stations and on car exhaust systems. Today, perhaps thanks to these measures, or to a few wettish summers, or to more mysterious cyclic factors, the spread of the disease seems to have been checked, though it is very far from cured. But the media, ever fickle, have lost interest in the subject, largely because there is little new to say about it. And the public, also fickle in its obsessions, has turned to worrying about other things, such as east Germany. But the tree epidemic has left its impact on Europe's car industry, for it led directly in 1984–5 to the furore over catalytic converters.

Even before this issue arose, technical improvements to reduce exhaust emissions had already been in progress for about 15 years throughout the world's motor industry, and with some success, for they had cut nitrogen oxide discharge by up to 50 per cent on some models. However, when the forest panic spread, the newly-elected Kohl Government decided that more drastic action was needed, for political reasons: and so in 1983 it suddenly set the very early target date of January 1986 for the obligatory fitting of a catalytic converter onto all new cars sold except very small ones. This gadget, which goes underneath the car, removes most but not all of the noxious element from carbon monoxide and nitrogen oxide; but it costs about 1,500 DM, and it requires lead-free petrol. The German car industry at first moaned a little but fairly soon it accepted the need for converters and rallied to the Government in a disciplined way. As it had already been fitting converters onto its cars exported to Japan and the United States (where the gadgets had been in force for some time), it had no lack of expertise or equipment. And the German motoring public, anxious about the trees, also demurred very little.

But Germany's EC partners were furious. Jacques Calvet, chairman of Peugeot, claimed that a 'bunch of hysterics' in Bonn was putting Europe's motor industry in peril. The EC governments, supporting their car firms, did not want Bonn to go it alone with the new controls, for this would sabotage their own imports to Germany (they even talked of 'an underhand act of disguised protectionism'): but nor were they keen to join in the scheme themselves, for they had no forest problem at home and no public pressure, and their car industries were most unwilling to start installing converters. In particular they argued that, as the cost of a converter is the same for any size of vehicle, the measure would unfairly prejudice the sales of smaller medium-sized and smallish cars, such as Fiats and Renaults, that make up a much larger part of French and Italian than of German output. The British went further than this, claiming that the catalytic converter was a cumbersome and outmoded piece of technology that would soon be superseded by the much cheaper and simpler system that *they* were working on, the 'lean burn engine': but the Germans retorted that it could not be in mass production before the early 1990s, and this would be too late.

Finally in 1985 a compromise was reached in Brussels that amounted to a greater climb-down by the other EC countries than by Germany. Bonn merely agreed to delay its timetable, so that the others could catch up; but they rallied basically to the German thesis, by deciding on a new European exhaust emission standard that would be at least as stringent as that of the United States. The new measures, due to come into force in the EC in January 1993, with the rest of the 1992 package, make 3-way converters compulsory on all new cars except for a few very small models which do not really need them. This rule had already been in force in Germany since 1986, and by 1991 some 35 per cent of all German cars were fitted with converters, many more than in other EC countries.

In 1985 the Government had also introduced a series of tax incentives, to encourage motorists to move ahead of the legal deadlines by voluntarily buying new converter-fitted cars right away, or getting their existing ones adapted. The virtuous would benefit from a reduced motor tax; others would have to pay extra. But the response was slow. One deterrent factor at first was the shortage of service stations with lead-free petrol. These have now become far more widespread, and by 1989 lead-free petrol had captured 56 per cent of the German market. Every service station now sells it. But German tourists abroad still have trouble finding it in some EC countries.

It has long been suggested that surely there exists another method, far more cheap and simple, and above all more rapid, of securing results from reduced exhaust levels – and that is to impose a speed limit. Germany is the only country in Europe without one, at least on motorways. The Greens produced scientific surveys to show that a limit of 100 kph on the *Autobahnen* would in a flash cut nitric oxide emissions by 18 per cent: the car-makers retorted that, according to their own tests, the saving would be only 3 per cent. And so a debate rich in passion developed, for if most Germans love their trees, a potent minority of them love their fast cars even more. The average German driver is highly disciplined and prudent in town, keeping carefully to the traffic-lanes, and braking at lights even when there is no pedestrian in sight: but behind a wheel on an open *Autobahn*, where there are no speed laws to hold him back, he becomes a creature possessed, especially if he is in a fast car, tearing down the outside lane, lights flashing, at 200 kph or more. Psychologists can put this down to a pent-up masculine aggression that finds little other outlet in today's peaceful, orderly republic; or else to German competitiveness; or to the German tendency to obey laws by the letter rather than apply common sense. Whatever the reasons, the practice can be unnerving for a visiting foreign motorist. In 1974, after the first oil crisis, attempts were made to impose speed limits so as to save fuel: but they were soon dropped, under pressure from an angry motorists' lobby which coined the slogan, '*Freie Fahrt für freie Bürger*' (roughly, 'a free people should have free right of way'). And this battle-cry is again being used today, for the Germans still seem to regard unlimited speed as a constitutional right, an article of faith.

Caught in what one writer called 'an emotional clash between speed freaks and tree lovers', the Kohl Government hesitated, especially since the opinion polls were conflicting. Some of these indicated that most motorists were opposed to any *Autobahn* speed limits; others, that a majority of citizens might favour them, if it could be proved that this would help the trees. Finally in 1985 the Government did embark on an experiment on the Hamburg–Bremen and Nuremberg–Ingolstadt motorways: speed was limited to 100 kph, with fines of up to 400 DM, and special test cars patrolled the routes at varying speeds, fast and slow, checking and comparing emission levels. For Germany, this was quite a bold move. But, when I myself travelled those roads in the summer of 1985, few drivers seemed to be keeping to the limit, nor did I, and none of us was stopped by the police as far as I saw. A blow for my own theory that the law-abiding Germans would instinctively obey limits if told to do so? Today, in the early 1990s, about 10 per cent of the motorway network does have a 100 kph speed limit, while the same limit is 'recommended' on some other stretches.

Curiously this whole debate about speed has centred on the issue of air pollution, and damage to trees, with very little even said about the role that fast driving may play in Germany's high road accident rate. This has led some unkind critics to suggest that the Germans seem to care more about trees than people. But the real issue is more complex.

First, through the introduction of compulsory seat-belts, better-built cars, and various other safety measures, it had been possible to reduce the annual toll of road deaths from 19,000 in 1970 to some 8,200 in 1988 – but that is still alarmingly high. Secondly, and more to the point, Germany's 7,000 km of motorways are among its safest roads, for they carry 25 per cent of traffic but account for only 6 per cent of fatal accidents. This lends some support to the arguments of the car industry and the motoring clubs, that Germany's fast cars are still very safe when driven at high speeds, that German fast drivers are not the maniacs they may appear but are skilled and responsible, and that a speed limit would probably reduce the accident rate hardly at all. Deaths are caused mainly by less experienced drivers on country roads. So the car-makers, while accepting converters, remain firmly opposed to other restrictions on the high-speed performance of their prized products. But it may take many years to discover whether converters can really do anything to save the dying trees.

## The ignored rural world and its grumbling peasantry

It is rare for a rural problem such as forestry to become a major national issue in Germany, for in this urbanised and industry-focused society the world of farming usually gets overlooked. Most city-dwellers have only a hazy idea of what modern country life is really like, and this was certainly one reason for the extraordinary impact of *Heimat*, Edgar Reitz's celebrated 16-hour film portrait of a village near Koblenz, which burst upon German cinema and TV viewers in 1984 like the revelation of an unknown world. This ignorance is curious in a way, for German farmers historically have never constituted a society apart to the same degree as the French peasantry. Today most of them live in neat modern villas, they have much the same leisure interests and home equipment as city folk, and many do office or factory jobs at the same time. They are not isolated from the community, however misunderstood they may sometimes feel.

This is one of a number of paradoxes in the world of west German farming today, where the gulf between rich and poor is at least as great as in France. The wheat barons of the north drive around in Mercedes and take holidays in the Caribbean; many Bavarian dairy farmers struggle to make a living with a herd of ten cows and 20 acres – 'the

Cinderellas of the economic miracle', they have been called. These
smallholders are not as violent as the French in pursuit of their
grievances: they do not block the roads with their tractors, nor set fire
to lorryloads of imported produce. But in their way they have now
become just as recalcitrant, and they have won a bad reputation in
EC circles for being backward, inefficient, and unwilling to pull their
weight in the campaign to reduce surpluses. Much small-scale farming
in Germany is, to be sure, curiously inefficient for so modern a
nation. And yet, viewed from another angle, German agriculture
shows an impressive record of post-war modernisation. Paradoxes,
indeed.

After the war the Federal Republic comprised only 40 per cent of the
farming land of pre-war Germany: the rest, including all the great
livestock and grain-producing estates of Prussia, lay in the territories
lost to Communist rule, in the GDR, Poland and Russia. So a cramped
West Germany then faced an urgent challenge – that of developing its
agriculture to meet the needs of a hungry people, including the millions
of refugees. Concerted efforts were made, and the success was considerable, as the figures show. By the 1980s productivity had risen sevenfold
since 1950; and thanks to huge increases in the output of meat, dairy
products, wheat, sugarbeet and wine, West Germany on balance was
meeting over 85 per cent of its own needs in food and drink. The rest
it bought from abroad, and had become the world's second largest food
importer, after Japan (mostly of fruit and vegetables, feed grains, eggs
and fish products). But, more surprisingly for so thickly populated a
country, West Germany has also become the world's fourth leading
exporter of food and drink, after the United States, France and Holland.
Its principal sales are in meat and meat products, and dairy produce
including cheese. All this points to an extensive two-way trade, two-
thirds of it being with the rest of the EC. As in other countries, the
progress has been achieved through intensive modernisation, much of
it in the form of mechanisation. The ox-drawn plough is almost
everywhere a thing of the past. It is not uncommon today to find big
grain farms with only two or three hired labourers where there used to
be 30 or 40: the total of paid workers has dropped to a mere 100,000
or so. Millions of people have moved off the land, and the decline in
agriculture's share of the active population, from 20 per cent in 1950 to
just 5 per cent today, has been almost as striking as in France: it is still
falling today, though more slowly, and may level off at about 4.5 per
cent. As farmers move away or retire, their properties are usually sold

to neighbours, so that farms have become larger: their overall number fell from 1,600,000 in 1950 to 650,000 in 1989.

These have been familiar trends in much of Western Europe. It would be wrong however to deduce that west Germany today is a land of highly effective medium-sized or large farms, like Britain. The pattern of rationalisation has been extremely uneven, with big regional variations. In a word, the north is rich and the south rather poor. The farms of the northern plains, in Schleswig-Holstein, Lower Saxony and Westphalia, are many of them large and prosperous, and so are some in Bavaria: but southern farms have always been on average much smaller than those in the north, and so they remain. As a result, the average size of a German farm is a mere 46 acres, compared with 70 in France, 173 in Britain. France is often regarded, wrongly, as a patchwork of tiny holdings: but the image better fits Germany, whose farms are on average the smallest of any non-Mediterranean country of the EC. And the problem lies especially with the dairy farms, which account for over half the total: the average herd in Germany is 30 cows, compared with 60 in Britain.

There are clear historical reasons for this state of affairs. The most important is the equal inheritance law that was introduced under Napoleon into most areas of what are now Baden-Württemberg, Hessen and Rhineland-Palatinate, and some parts of Bavaria. Here a farmer's land was divided between all his sons on his death, and this led to growing parcelisation. Today, though the system still has some legal force, it is seldom applied as such, for under modern conditions it is rare that more than one son will want to inherit land, so the division of property is usually done on a cash basis. But the law has left a heavy mark on farm structures. In the north, and in much of Bavaria, primogeniture has always been the rule: hence the greater size of farms there. And, if so many Bavarian holdings are small, it is more often due to the terrain.

A second major historical factor is that since the mid-nineteenth century German agriculture has been cosseted by protectionism, with strong tariff barriers and prices fixed fairly high. This was the policy of Bismarck and then of Weimar, and it was intensified by the Nazis who gave generous subsidies to farmers (and thus derived much of their support from rural areas). So, right up until recent times, farmers could survive with smallish properties and they had little incentive to enlarge them. Equally, the smallholders failed to develop a dynamic sense of marketing. The protectionist policy was somewhat modified after

1945, but it has since been taken over by the EC within a wider European context.

During Germany's boom years of the 1950s and 1960s, small farmers were carried along by the general national progress and most of them easily became more prosperous. Then the arrival of the EC's Common Agriculture Policy (CAP) helped the dairy producers in particular by opening up new export outlets to Italy. But, since the mid-1970s, the tide has turned against them. Costs of fuel and fertiliser have been rising much faster than prices, so that farm incomes have been falling. And now, since the early 1980s, the CAP's expensive pile-up of surpluses has reached the point where all EC farmers have been asked to make sacrifices, notably through quotas for milk production and cuts in cereals prices. German farmers, being on balance among the smallest and least efficient in these fields, feel themselves to be hit the hardest and have been squealing the loudest. They have a powerful political lobby which repeatedly has put pressure on Bonn to resist the CAP reforms (see p. 162). So Germany, as the British at least tend to see it, has become the 'arch defender' of the CAP's major abuses and a main obstacle to improvement. It is a strange reversal from the early days of the Community when it was the Germans who feared that France's backward peasant farming would be the Community's principal handicap.

Federal and *Land* governments have certainly made great efforts since the war to rationalise farming structures. Small farmers have been encouraged to organise themselves into cooperatives, for marketing and for the sharing of modern equipment; and they have been given subsidies to help them regroup scattered parcels of land into more viable units. This has borne results. Most farms now are well-equipped, within their means; and the old polyculture has given way to greater specialisation. Even quite small farms can often be profitable if they specialise in particular products, such as fruit, or poultry. But at the same time governments have always backed the smallish family farm as the basic unit. And their earlier post-war policy of encouraging farms to merge, and so increase in size, has now been modified at a time of rising urban unemployment, for other jobs are no longer available for those who leave the land. Social needs are thus being put ahead of economic efficiency. Hence also the continued official support for part-time farming.

One of the most unusual and controversial features of German agriculture is that 40 per cent of all farms, and the majority of really small ones, are worked on a part-time basis by people who have other jobs too. They account for 13 per cent of total farm area, and 10 to 12 per cent of all produce. This kind of dual activity has obvious advantages for those who do it: but it is criticised by many modern-minded experts for creating a 'black' economy and other distortions. It dates from the nineteenth century, when many small farmers were so poor that they clutched eagerly at the new work outlets offered by the factories springing up in nearby towns. Especially was this so in Swabia, with its small-scale precision industries in semi-rural settings; but even in the Ruhr a number of coal-miners and steelworkers have always been part-time farmers too. And the practice persists, especially in the south where many a Daimler-Benz welder will hurry home to tend his vines, or a Siemens worker to milk his cows. Generally the factory or office job provides by far the greater part of such a family's income: but the smallholding is kept on, maybe as a kind of hobby, or for sentimental reasons, or as a useful extra source of revenue or a prudent insurance against unemployment. Usually the wife does most of the work, and the husband helps out in his free time.

Industrial Stuttgart sprawls out widely, with dozens of village-like suburbs and hundreds of little farms within its borders. One of those I visited, at Plieningen near the airport, was quite extraordinary. Its friendly and hospitable owner worked as a clerk in a nearby milk control office, but still kept his ten dairy cows and a few acres for feed. His parlour, where we drank *Obstler*, was quite spruce: but the cowshed behind was positively mediaeval, with one sick cow, piles of stinking straw, peasanty little wife and cretinous brother, and no hint of modernisation. This, in Europe's richest city. 'We've owned this farm for many generations,' said my host, 'and I just can't bear to give it up, for farming is still in my blood — even though it brings in little money and involves a lot of hard work and getting up at 5.30 a.m. But my son, who's an electrician, sees no future in it, so when I retire in ten years or so, we'll probably sell it.' He spoke of Stuttgart, *'Die Grossstadt'*, as if it were another civilisation. I felt I was witnessing the end of an era, the twilight of a certain way of life. Like this one, many part-time farms today mark a transitional phase and are run by families who are on their way out of agriculture: often the sons have wives who refuse to do the work. However there is now a small but growing counter-trend, *into* agriculture, led by young ecologists and others with city jobs who buy a small farm as a weekend or holiday activity. Teachers or civil servants sometimes do this. So part-time farming, though it may wane, is not likely to die out fast.

Various arguments are advanced in favour of it. Perhaps the most valid is that it has served the social purpose of maintaining closer links between town and country, and this may be one reason why the German peasantry has felt less isolated than in France. In some areas, part-time farming may also be helping to save the countryside from over-depopulation. Also, so it is suggested, it adds a certain flexibility to employment, for a factory can more easily put workers onto shorter hours when times are hard, and a smallholder conversely is less vulnerable to the usual ups and downs of farming. But the counter-argument, advanced cogently by many economists, is that part-time farming acts as a drag on the efficiency and modernisation of agriculture; as one agronomist said to me: 'These part-timers don't take the job seriously, they run their holdings in an amateurish and unproductive way. They undercut the professionals. And, above all, they are simply adding to the EC's surpluses. At the taxpayer's expense, they draw subsidies that they do not really need, and they make life harder for the full-timers who do need them. It's a black economy.' And the full-time farmers themselves feel resentful of the others, for the same reasons. So the European Commission is opposed to part-time farming and has been trying to get it reduced, in all member countries. But, in Germany, federal and *Land* governments – especially the more conservative ones – continue to support it. After all, it helps to bolster many farmers' incomes and thus to contain their grievances. And it serves a political purpose too: factory workers are much less likely to be militant left-wing unionists if they also own little farms and have roots in the soil. This could well be one of the reasons for the harmony of labour relations in an area such as Swabia.

In the more remote rural areas the picture is entirely different, for here the scope for finding alternative jobs is far less great than near a town; small farmers have no other source of income, and if their soil is poor they face bleak prospects today, in a time of rising costs and EC production squeezes. Their expectations have risen since the war, they want some degree of modern comforts, and quite rightly they are not prepared to accept the drudgery and simple poverty that their parents and grandparents endured.

One such area is the northern strip of Bavaria along the former

GDR border, between Coburg and Hof. Here for over forty years the division of Germany separated farmers from some of their traditional markets. But although this problem is now solved, a more insoluble one remains: the terrain. This windy, hilly Franconian plateau with its thin soil and bitter winters has been known as the 'Bavarian Siberia' – and the allusion is purely physical, not political. Farmers have been drifting away to the towns and some land is now derelict, for buyers are hard to find. One small village I visited, Neuengrün, looked neat and prosperous in the usual German manner, with newish white-and-grey houses in a tidy circle round a wide grassy square, and pastures and grainfields rolling to far horizons: but the farmers I talked to were universally pessimistic. The Grebners, for example, farm 125 acres, with 45 head of cattle, quite a lot for south Germany; and they live in a modern house with colour TV, washing machine, and a new garden patio with smart white benches – all rather different from the rural squalor one still so often finds in, say, the French Massif Central. But Frau Grebner seemed sad and depressed, a handsome woman of about 40, old before her time: 'Farming used to be a pleasant way of life round here, but now it's *kaputt*. The soil is too stony for cereals: we get only 3 tons of barley per hectare, against 5 or 6 in a good area. Dairy farming's okay, but now the CAP milk quotas have hit our income – so what's the use of the expensive investments we made ten years ago, on a new cowshed and milking equipment? It's a waste. Our three sons are going to factory jobs elsewhere and they don't want the farm. We'd like to sell it, but we can't find a buyer.'

I heard the same lament at other nearby villages – '*kaputt!*' But were things any better in earlier days? At one upland farm I met a white-haired, rosy-cheeked peasant lady of 76, Frau Kraus, who showed me the family's neat house built in 1960 and its big barn full of modern machinery. 'In pre-war days we had no running water, electricity or tractors. Often we worked an 80-hour week, and in winter we'd get up at five to break the ice in the pails for washing, before we milked the cows. Today the family works less hard and has more comforts, but we've 20,000 DM of debts still to pay off on our investments. But why shouldn't we enjoy some of the same advantages of modern life as city people? Times have changed. I've never been farther than Bamberg in my life, 80 kilometres away: but my son is now in New Guinea. If we were prepared to live and drudge as in the old days, maybe this farm would still be viable. But we're not. Brewer's barley, wheat, potatoes, a few milk cows and bullocks – this kind of mixed farming doesn't seem to make sense any more. . . .'

Maybe the answer is that poorer districts of this kind should not be used for agriculture any more. After all, the surplus-ridden EC hardly needs their produce. But what other future might they find? Nearly all ecologists and rural experts agree that it would be wrong to let them depopulate to the point of becoming a wasteland. Some of the more attractive areas, with lakes, woods or hills, could well be turned into nature parks or tourist and recreation centres, as has been happening in many places around the Eifel, the Black Forest and the lower Alps: here farmers could stay in their villages and derive income from looking after tourists, or else become salaried 'guardians of nature' (a concept pioneered in France and now being proposed by the EC Commission). But the north Bavarian plateaux, though plentifully forested, are too dull and desolate to appeal to many holidaymakers. The thin soil may not be suited for grain crops or dairy pastures, but it might still find a future in large-scale sheep farming, of the kind so common in similar upland areas of France: but the problem first would be to convert the German consumer to the habit of eating lamb and mutton, and the farmer to the techniques of sheepbreeding.[1]

So for these lonelier rural areas there remains the possible solution of bringing the mountain to Mohammed, that is, not of expecting the farmer to migrate to the town, but of bringing modern industrial jobs to the countryside. This already has been taking place on quite a large scale, more so in Germany than in most countries. Everywhere in small towns and even in villages one finds little factories of all kinds. Some of them are traditional and relate to soil deposits or other local conditions, such as the pottery firms of northern Bavaria (e.g. Rosenthal at Selb) or the clockmakers of the Black Forest. But others are fairly new products of the 'economic miracle' years. Many have been created by ex-farmers themselves or by other local people – witness the fictional but credible example of the clever young peasant in Reitz's *Heimat* who in the 1950s founded a successful optics factory in the desolate Hunsrück. In other cases, big well-known companies have developed new plant in or

1. The British eat 50 times as much sheepmeat as the Germans, and produce 23 times as much of it, while the Germans produce and eat three times as much pork and pig products as the British. One explanation given to me is that German farms, being so small, are better suited to breeding pigs, which require less space than sheep.

near the countryside as the best way of finding the labour they need. The star case is that of BMW which in 1966 took over a small ailing independent car-making firm in the little town of Dingolfing, 100 kilometres north-east of Munich, and has since built it up into the largest of all its factories, with 16,000 employees. Nearly all of them live in the villages and farms around, and every morning a fleet of several hundred BMW buses brings them in to work from a radius up to 100 kilometres. 'Most firms find, as we do,' one BMW executive told me, 'that country people of this kind make better skilled mechanical workers than, say, ex-miners or ex-dockers do. Many still keep their little farms, and this gives them a sense of freedom and dignity – of not being slaves to factory work.' Such operations are the basis of the success of part-time farming in Germany, which will thus survive for a long time. The problem of rural unemployment and rural emigration is thus less acute than, say, in France. But, in today's economic climate, it is not easy to find new little firms for the lonelier areas where farming is doomed to decline further. The plateaux of northern Bavaria have no easy solution for their plight.

Here, as in many other areas, rising costs above all are blamed for the fact that a small farm can no longer be made viable. In a fertile spot near Stuttgart, one smallholder in his seventies, producing cabbages for *Sauerkraut* and wheat, told me: 'D'you know, in the 1930s fifty kilos of wheat would buy me two pairs of shoes: now they buy just half a shoe. Yes, productivity's gone up too, but not that much. It is costs, of fuel and so on, that are the problem. Fifteen hectares used to be enough round here for a decent living: now you need twice as many. And that dreadful Common Market is making matters worse.' Of course, farmers the world over are notorious for grousing endlessly and exaggerating their woes. Their present dilemma may be to quite an extent their own fault. But the mad logic of Community economics does give the smaller ones some cause to be upset.

The mechanism of the CAP is highly complex. Briefly summarised, it consists of a Community levy on agriculture imports into member countries from outside the EC, redistributed to farmers in the form of price supports and export subsidies (the supports cover, essentially, sugar, beef and pigmeat, dairy products, most cereals, table wines, some fruit and vegetables). This protectionist system aims to encourage EC self-sufficiency, and certainly it has done so. But it has proved expensive for national budgets, since the supports and subsidies have been allowed far to exceed the size of levy, thus leading to heavy annual deficits. This is because the EC, yielding to pressure from various farming lobbies, originally fixed the prices for most products around the level of the highest then obtaining and not the average. For instance, as wheat was cheapest in France and dearest in Germany, it was the German price that was chosen for the CAP. This simply encouraged farmers to overproduce in many sectors, knowing that their surpluses would be bought anyway and then sometimes dumped on world markets. The 'butter mountains' of the 1970s and '80s, with the cheap sale of surplus butter to Russia, caused a scandal; the EC also built up gigantic surplus stocks of beef, cereals, wine and some other products. Political horse-trading too has falsified the price policies – for example, with Paris yielding to Bonn's demands for high wheat prices in return for favours elsewhere. What is more, as the subsidies are paid on quantity of produce, inevitably the system benefits most the big farmers who need it least, and this is the major injustice of the CAP. Alike in Germany as in France, the large farms of the north with their high productivity have done handsomely, while smallholders gain relatively little: clearly the CAP's unified price system is unfairly suited to a Europe where farming is so diversified. The cost of the supports falls heavily on the EC taxpayer: but British opinion is wrong to suppose, as it often does, that 'it's all the fault of the French'. Rich British farmers, too, have benefited excessively; and German farmers' lobbies have been as much to blame as any for the insistence on high prices. Today the system is at last under reform.

German farmers' attitudes to the EC are highly ambivalent. The CAP so dominates their working lives that they have become the most Europe-conscious of all Germans: for them, the Common Market is no distant abstraction but a daily reality. The more senior or export-minded ones are constantly travelling to meetings in Brussels, or going on sales or study tours to other EC countries; and even a humble stay-at-home smallholder will discourse knowledgeably about British cattle-breeding techniques or the impact of Danish barley prices. But how far they approve of the EC is another matter. Most of them still express a general faith in the European ideal: but they have grown sceptical as to whether the CAP as such is a benefit to them. This is a recent development. Most German farmers were initially wary of the CAP, which they feared would mainly help the French: but then during its first decade or so of operation, roughly until the mid-1970s, they were surprised to find it much more advantageous than they had expected. It served to boost their exports and in particular to provide huge new Italian outlets for Bavarian milk and dairy products, thus belatedly compensating for the loss since 1945 of the East European markets on which Bavarian dairy farmers had once depended.

German farm incomes were rising on average by about 7 per cent a year in real terms until 1975; then they began to fall, by a total of some 15 per cent between 1975 and 1983, and they have continued to fall since, with some ups and downs. Various factors have been responsible for this change of fortune, one of them being American export policies and the vicissitudes of the dollar. But partly to blame also has been the CAP with its new policies of tighter pricing and campaigns against surpluses – or at least the German farmers have felt it was to blame. Not that all of these farmers are unreasonable. Most have not been blind to the CAP's injustices and wastages, and have been prepared to help in making sacrifices, especially the prosperous ones in the north. But they feel that the cuts are being unfairly applied – and, much worse, that governments over the years have misled them. One farmer expressed to me a very widely felt sentiment: 'For many years, up until recently, governments in Bonn and officials in Brussels encouraged us to produce more and more, to modernise and invest, promising that the CAP would always foot the bill. Josef Ertl[1] in particular did this. So we've invested expensively in new equipment, we've piled up big debts on the loans for it – and now, all of a sudden, we're told to cut production and accept lower prices. The politicians have been plainly irresponsible. We've been duped. Nay, swindled.' German farmers, like others, may be in many ways pigheaded: they should have seen the writing on the wall much sooner, and have cooperated earlier with CAP reform plans. Nonetheless one cannot avoid a certain sympathy for their feelings of having been led up the garden path.

Of the various CAP economy measures introduced in 1984–5, the quotas for milk production especially annoyed the German farmers. All agreed in theory that dairy surpluses must be reduced: but Brussels had left each member government free to adopt its own system of quotas, and the one chosen by Bonn was universally condemned on the farms. The small dairy producers claimed that *they* were being penalised, since they could least afford the cutbacks; the big ones retorted that, no, *they* were the ones to suffer most, as the system was unfairly exonerating

1. A Bavarian, member of the FDP, and Federal Minister of Agriculture, 1969–83. The most influential figure in post-war German farming.

the little men. 'What's more,' said one producer, quoting a common view, 'we Germans are being penalised by our own honesty. The Italians and French aren't applying their quotas properly, they let their farmers cheat. We, being German, stick to the rules – and we pay for it.' There's the European spirit for you. As for cereals, when in 1985 Brussels decided on a 3.5 per cent cut in prices, the German farm lobby showed its strength by successfully pressuring Bonn into blocking the measure. So, for the first time in EC history, Germany used its veto in the Council of Ministers ('to defend a vital national interest') – and on this occasion it stood alone. Later, it is true, a compromise was reached.

Ignaz Kiechle, Ertl's successor as Federal Minister, is also a Bavarian, but CSU, not FDP. After 1983 he tried loyally to help the rest of the EEC to reduce costs and surpluses. But this won him the wrath of Bavarian farmers (90 per cent of them CSU voters): they turned for support to Strauss, and not in vain, for the 'emperor' of Bavaria, knowing the importance of their vote, waged a campaign against his CSU colleague and won some concessions. It caused quite a rumpus. In short, Germany's farmers may be down to 5 per cent of the population, but they seem able to wield much more than 5 per cent of the political influence. Since 1990, unification has opened up new markets in the east for west German farmers. But this is of benefit mainly to the larger estates of the north: by contrast, the small farmers of the south are today afraid that the huge cooperatives of the former GDR (see pp. 460–62), once they have reorganised themselves and become efficient, will pose a serious new threat and make their survival even harder.

Not all the pressures against change have come from southern smallholders: the big landowners of the north hold even more of the power on the main farmers' union. This is the 'other face' of German agriculture, and its farms are rather different from those I have described so far. They are run not by *Bauern* (peasants) but by *Landwirten* (educated yeoman farmers), or in some cases by aristocrats or gentlemen farmers; and they do very well. An elder son is usually keen to stay on the land and to take over when his father retires; if a farm is to be sold, there is no shortage of applicants to buy it. On the flat plain of the Ems, near the Dutch border, an area where farming used to be very poor, I visited one medium-sized cattle-breeder, mayor of his village, a tall, rather cocky man with an assertive handshake: 'I've kept my farm to its same modest 125 acres, but by careful breed selection and intensive cultivation I've become quite rich. My parents never took a holiday: but now my wife and I go annually to Tenerife. Agriculture round here has completed its modernisation, it's as efficient as can be.' Heavy vulgar repro furniture in the big modern lounge; two Mercedes in the drive; a manicured lawn the like of which I've never seen on any French farm.

Up in Schleswig-Holstein, I visited big grain and livestock farms of the kind one sees in eastern England and the Paris basin. One was quite bizarre. It lay beside the North Sea coast, on a *Koog* (polder) reclaimed from the sea in the 1920s and protected by a high dyke; on the seaward side was newer reclaimed land where, to my surprise, sheep were grazing. A strong chill wind blew incessantly (it was May). The owners, a charming and sophisticated young couple, Peter Rabe and his wife, he a graduate of Kiel university, lived in a strange mansion, rather elegant, with a huge Hollywood-style stairway curving down into the big parlour: I half expected Liz Taylor to appear at the top, in a ball-gown and a tantrum. The house, like all others on the polder, had a flat green tin roof. Rabe explained, as we drove in his Mercedes along the top of the dyke: 'When my father created this *Koog*, in 1926, it was terribly poor and isolated, with no mains water, so the flat roofs were put there to collect rainwater. Today we breed sheep and export the meat to the French who – unlike the silly Germans – know how to appreciate its delicious *pré salé* taste that comes from these sea-meadows. We grow cereals, too, on this rich soil. And we have pigs – or we did, but our big new piggery burned down in the night last winter and the 200 pigs suffocated in their sleep. We found just their charred carcasses.' The odd sense of drama thickened as he went on: 'We love it here, my wife and I, we work 70 hours a week in summer but don't miss city pleasure or social life. But the Friesland peasants on the *Koog* seem not so happy. They're a weird lot, these Frieslanders, laconic, almost speechless, and mental retardment is rife. It's lonely round here, and the cold wind whines constantly through the long dark winters, fraying nerves and causing depressions. The *Koog* has a high rate of alcoholism, incest, divorce and suicide.' Peter Rabe's elderly, crippled father told me that he lived on his own. Was he widowed, I asked? 'No, my wife went away.' Maybe she couldn't stand *Koog* life. Definitely Ibsen territory, I felt.

Not far away, near Flensburg, I went to see a stud farm that collects sperm from bulls for artificial insemination. The earnest young geneticist in charge explained to me that this is international big business: he travels to America in search of the right breeds. The key to the operation is a wooden 'phantom cow', looking rather like a 'horse' in a gym. This somehow excites the bull, who mounts it and ejaculates into a rubber vagina, manned by a technician. The other bulls, standing by, who have probably never seen a real cow since they left their mother's side, get contagiously excited too and start to mount each other. Beate Uhse's sex domain (see pp. 197–9) is just a few miles away.

The post-war changes in German rural society, and more especially in city-dwellers' attitudes to it, are rather curious and reveal a good deal about modern Germany. As in other Western countries, the agricultural revolution has greatly reduced the old poverty and changed farmers' life-styles, but at some cost to warm traditional values – as Edgar Reitz showed in *Heimat*. Reitz himself was born in 1932 in the little town of Morbach on the Hunsrück plateau, between the Rhine and Moselle valleys, then an isolated and poor region of peasant mixed farming. At the age of 20 he left for Munich where he later directed a number of feature films: but he always cherished the idea of one day returning to make a film study of his own *Heimat* (homeland). This he finally achieved in 1980–84, when he spent a total of some three years in the small village of Woppenroth, east of Morbach, researching, scripting and then filming his masterpiece, made initially as an 11-part television series.[1] It was a labour of love, an intensely personal work. It details the changing fortunes of three families, related by marriage, from 1919 to 1982 – from the old days of poverty, through war and Nazism to the 'economic miracle' years and beyond, when the eldest son of the Simon family becomes a prosperous local factory owner. It shows how, after the war, its fictional Hunsrück village of 'Schabbach' (based on Woppenroth and some other places around) changed gradually from a narrow, enclosed peasant community into a kind of semi-urban suburb in the middle of nowhere; and how the old caring solidarity bred of hard times gave place to a new ambitious acquisitive society, far more mobile and open to the world, but in danger of losing its roots.

Reitz, a gentle, thoughtful person, most impressive to meet, talked to me about *Heimat* and the Hunsrück in his office in Munich's Schwabing: 'I made the film in order to tell people in the cities what village life is like. When I was a boy, in a place like Woppenroth there were fifty farmers, and now there are four. People were so poor that each winter it was doubtful whether all the members of a family would survive. But then in the 1950s people for the first time could get good jobs, buy cars and travel. Most of the young ones left; farmers sold their land,

---

1. For more details of Reitz and *Heimat*, see pp. 343–51.

and the four that remain now live quite well. Some villagers rent flats to tourists, or they commute daily to jobs as far off as Mainz. Some elderly people come to the Hunsrück to retire. But its tradition is dead: today's industrial agriculture has nothing to do with the traditional farming life. There's still a kind of village solidarity, it's true, and old people feel less isolated than in the cities. But the relationship of people to their village has changed. They live with the thought, "We don't know how long we shall stay here, or whether it will be a worthwhile place for our children" – so they invest the minimum in it, both materially and emotionally. They're no longer interested in making the place look attractive, so it isn't. As they've no long-term view, they accept any old eyesores and the pulling down of nice old houses.' These were sad words. Reitz did however agree with me that the human warmth and solidarity of those days hardly justified the poverty and hardship: they were in fact a reaction against it.

In some other parts of Germany, matters are not so different. On the dull Ems plain, near Holland, I stayed in a once-poor village that had also become semi-urbanised, with several small factories: it had far less character than the Hunsrück, and was curiously lacking in any sense of tradition. When the peasants became prosperous after the war, their first reaction was to knock down their handsome brick farm-houses and build new, ugly, almost identical villas; even the church, dating from the 1860s, was torn down because it was judged too old, and a new one put up. The villagers, it seems, had wanted to obliterate the traces not only of their poverty but of Germany's recent tragic past as a whole: so all tradition, good or bad, was banished. Only in the past five years had they begun to found an association for local history and even to plan a museum: but much of the damage had by then been done. Today many German villages, with their modern houses, well-stocked shops, maybe banks too, and other tokens of affluence, have come to resemble miniature townlets; only in a few areas, mainly in the south, does one still find really picturesque old places with half-timbered cottages and flower-filled balconies. And, whereas country people used to dress distinctively, today they look just the same as city folk. They play tennis, go to local discos, and of course watch TV, the great leveller. So many little factories and offices have set up in rural areas that a great many villagers have been able to embrace modern life without shifting their habitat – an advantage, socially, in many cases. Emigration to the towns has therefore been much less extensive than in France: on the other hand, French villages have remained much more village-like, and so indeed have many in Britain, where the tear-it-all-down-and-modernise craze has been far less rife than in Germany. Fortunately, in the past few years German country people have become less insensitive: they are now taking far more trouble to restore old buildings and generally to cultivate their past (see p. 205). But in many cases it is too late. No one would want to deny them their new prosperity: but it could have been achieved less destructively.

While the villages have become submerged by urban values, the reverse trend – the seeking out of the countryside and of rural values by people from the cities – is much less pronounced than in some other modern countries. It is true that the Germans claim to love their forests and like to hike in the hills, while the Greens profess an ecological concern for nature. But in some ways this is all very superficial and even unrealistic. Middle-class town-dwellers very seldom choose to go and *live* in the countryside, or really get to know country people, as they do much more frequently in France or Britain. And this has always been the case in Germany, where city people have either ignored the country or used it merely as a romantic backdrop for their own feelings – witness so much of classic German literature. German poetry, even more than English, is full of the love and longing for nature: trees, rivers and meadows are personified, almost mystically. But this is rarely accompanied by any sense of a tough daily local life; poets visit nature to explore their own souls and to discuss philosophy. The German novel, equally, has seldom treated themes of rural life. Theodor Storm wrote about Schleswig, while Fontane set some of his books among the gentlefolk of the Prussian estates; but there have been few equivalents of, say, Hardy or Giono, local writers identifying themselves with the peasant pleasures and hardships of their homelands.

Those who did try, in their way, to elevate rural and agricultural values were the Nazis. They promoted the nationalistic ideals of *Heimat* and of '*Blut und Boden*' (blood and soil), and within this context the farmer and his wife, true blond Germanic types honestly tilling the land, were given pride of place; farmers were granted special financial help, and were encouraged to feel that as guarantors of national self-sufficiency in food – and as guardians of honest Aryan virtues – they had an important role in the Nazi scheme of things. But after the war this reputation simply rebounded against them, and in the public mind the average farmer came to be seen, rightly or wrongly, as a clumsy peasant, old-fashioned, primitive and politically reactionary. This image may have been frequently unfair: but it carried some credibility, seeing that in the 1960s the extreme-Right NPD won its highest level of support in rural Schleswig-Holstein and in northern Bavaria. And, of the many thousands of young people who migrated from the rural milieu in the post-war years, some of them who later became writers or journalists gave highly critical portraits of its narrowness and intolerance, rather than sympathetic ones of its warmth and poverty. Kroetz's savage little plays about Bavarian peasant life (see p. 317), or films like Fleischmann's *Hunting Scenes in Upper Bavaria*, were hardly calculated to dispel urban prejudices against country life.

Today the reality of that life may have changed, but its reputation does so more slowly. This may help to explain why relatively so few middle-class Germans – writers or artists, retired people, or commuters near to a town – will choose to make their home in a village. Another reason is more or less the reverse: they know that the villages are no longer picturesque but dull and pseudo-urban, so for a pleasant social life they would do better to stay in town: 'My dear, one just *can't* live in Unterwaldheim, there'd be *no one* to talk to!' In Suffolk and the Cotswolds, in Provence and the Dordogne, and in many other parts of Britain and France, you find countless villages colonised by sophisticated people from the cities who have a full social life there: and they are not present merely as tourists or outsiders, for in a great many cases they integrate into village life and play an active role. It is the multiplier effect, which in Germany has hardly begun. My wife has a close English friend who, after early retirement from his job as an Army officer in Singapore, chose to settle in a small Wiltshire village where he and his wife ran the local shop and rapidly made many friends of all sorts; that, says Katinka, would be inconceivable in Germany. Of course it is true that many well-to-do Germans today have secondary homes in the country for holidays or weekends, especially in scenic spots in the south: but they go there for rest and seldom take much interest in the village life around them. The Germans may claim that they do not want it that way: according to Allensbach polls, the number of people saying that, if they could choose freely, they would ideally like to live 'in the country' has risen from 25 per cent in 1950 to 33 per cent in 1990, while the numbers of those opting for 'a large city' have declined in that period from 27 to 15 per cent. But how many of them think of 'country' as anything other than the old poets' world of sylvan glades and burbling streams? In practice, as several farmers told me, the city commuters and weekenders in their villages have tended to lodge complaints, German-style, against the smell of manure and even the crowing of cocks and mooing of cows in the early morning. Farms offend against the profound Teutonic need for silence.

It is true that in recent years quite a number of young Greens or other ecologists, full of good intentions, have come from the towns to settle in the countryside. Some have tried their hand at organic farming, or at nature preservation schemes (see p. 557). But in many cases they have simply irritated the local farmers, who do not like being lectured by city amateurs on how to sow their crops or plant their hedges. 'Some of these Greens are sensible and have done their homework,' said one Schleswig wheatgrower, 'and they understand about things like soil erosion. But others are dotty dogmatic idealists. They tell us to go back to primitive farming with hand-tools, and they just don't realise that we'd starve that way. And they seem to think that every bird or insect they come across is a tragically endangered species.' On the whole the movement has not been a success – as Reitz suggested to me: 'A lot of these "alternatives" and ecologists went with romantic ideas of the countryside and then they all came back. They found that the reality was more tough and humdrum than they thought, and they were disappointed. So they left, because it's more convenient to live in a town.'

So the villages today are caught in something of a vicious circle – once ignored and despised for being remote and primitive, now disdained as being too ordinary and predictable. And many small farmers seem likely to continue as the poor relations of the *Wirtschaftswunder* society.

# 4

# DAILY LIFE: A MODERNISED SOCIETY
# RE-EXAMINES ITS TRADITIONS

The tidy and affluent post-war west Germany appears in many ways as a very modern and rational society where the old tensions have been eased and individuals can live in considerable freedom. The centuries-old hatreds and prejudices between Catholics and Protestants have waned away and the two faiths now co-exist in amity. Class barriers have been dismantled far more radically than in Britain, France or many other parts of Western Europe and a new-rich semi-classless society has been emerging. Women have stepped out of their old *Kinder*, *Kirche*, *Küche* role into a broad emancipation, and along with this has come a high degree of sexual permissiveness, including the legalising of abortion. The old authoritarian spirit in school education has also greatly diminished.

These changes would seem to be mainly for the better. But do they imply that valued tradition has been thrown out of the window too? The Germans have a particular difficulty with their national traditions, because of the way that the Nazis exploited and debauched so many of them. Therefore after the war many of them reacted by turning their backs on their whole past and embracing modernism perhaps a little too crudely and thoughtlessly; architecture, such of it as had survived the bombing, was a notable casualty. Today there are signs that this trend is ending. Germans have been warily turning back to their past, and this can be seen in their new concern for restoring old houses rather than pulling them down, and in their growing love for the old local festivals and carnivals. But there are some other traditions, or rooted modes of behaviour, that perhaps still need to be modified but are proving more resistant to change. Women, for example, though they now have an easier time in social life, are still much under-represented in politics. The stiffness and formality of a great deal of social contact, and the unneighbourliness of the Germans, still strike an Anglo-Saxon as curiously inhibiting — though there are signs of an easing-up under the impact of a new generation. The old traditions of liberal university education have still not been adapted to the very different needs of a mass age. And, though the two Churches may now be at peace with each other, a new war between radicals and diehards has been simmering within Protestant ranks, suggesting that Germany's old tensions may have not so much disappeared as shifted their ground to emerge in a new form. These are some of the paradoxes to be explored in this chapter.

## *The social snobberies of a semi-classless society*

Germany today is much less of a class-divided society than it was in former times. One reason is that the war and the Nazi period destroyed much of the old order and removed many long-standing privileges, both economic and social. The war and then the 1948 currency reform knocked the bottom out of many acquired fortunes, forcing people to make a clean start. What is more, so many families have had something from the Nazi past to keep quiet about that since the war an upper-class structure based on family elitism has largely disappeared: people are wary of looking too deeply into each other's families or of asserting their own. So they depend more on themselves and their contacts than on their pedigree. After the war, the new Germany made a fresh start with an ethos of democratic equality enshrined in the Constitution. Of course this has since been modified in practice by consumer affluence and the uneven sharing of newly acquired wealth: even so, Germany today is a land of fluidity and freedom of opportunity, rather than of inherited privilege. It is something of a *nouveau riche* society, closer in some ways to the United States than to the old European order; less class-obsessed than Britain, less class-divided than France.

Factory workers, major beneficiaries of the 'economic miracle' in the boom years, have been adopting bourgeois life-styles and losing much of their class identity and former resentment of the middle classes. In Germany there was never so strong a working-class culture and tradition as in Britain, where the industrial revolution had come earlier and hit the workers more harshly; the Ruhr developed later along gentler and more paternalistic lines (see p. 101). Today western Germany has extremely little in the way of specially working-class life and leisure pursuits; what there was has largely vanished. In the Ruhr, the miners used to get so tired from physical work that they found it relaxing to breed rabbits and racing-pigeons; today their work is automated, they sit cooped up in metal cabins all day, so they prefer to play tennis and squash like the bourgeoisie. And, as most of the dirty menial jobs in Germany are now done by immigrant labour, the German workers have upgraded themselves. They earn higher wages than the majority of office and shop employees; they are as well housed as the lower middle classes, they go to the same restaurants and places of amusement, and they dress and look so much the same that you can hardly tell them apart – especially the young ones. All this is more markedly so than in Britain or France.

The class struggle, still a motif of strong sections of the Left in those two countries, has almost disappeared from Germany's political vocabulary; it is not used by the SPD, and only seldom by the unions. Of course more workers vote SPD than CDU/CSU: but few working-class bastions remain, and there is not much class bitterness, and no basic class rift in society as there is in Britain. The battle between conservatism and radicalism is fought less on class than on generation lines. And, if a gulf exists in western Germany today – as indeed it does – between the haves and the have-nots, this has been due mainly to rising unemployment. It is the gulf that separates those with steady jobs from those who fail to find them and so become marginalised. Or in some cases they drop out deliberately and marginalise themselves. For those in regular employment, the inequalities of income are lower than in many Western countries (leaving aside the fringe of wealthy people who have done well in business or the arts, or in some key professions such as law or medicine).

The table below, prepared by P-E International management consult-

|  | Germany | Britain | France | Italy |
|---|---|---|---|---|
| Managing director | 60,270 (5.8) | 55,840 (6.5) | 59,950 (7.5) | 63,590 (7.6) |
| Middle management | 27,590 (2.7) | 19,825 (2.3) | 32.295 (4.0) | 21,840 (2.6) |
| Skilled worker | 16,560 (1.6) | 14,520 (1.7) | 11,200 (1.4) | 11,580 (1.4) |
| Unskilled worker | 10,390 (1.0) | 8,530 (1.0) | 7,980 (1.0) | 8,390 (1.0) |

ants, gives average annual net earnings (in £ sterling) in 1990. The figures in brackets show the differentials of net pay.

In other words, German workers and technicians are much better off than others; middle managers earn far more in Germany than in Britain or Italy but senior managers do almost equally well in all four countries. For these reasons the differentials between top and bottom levels are lowest in Germany.

Of course, social differences and class distinctions do still exist in Germany, resulting partly from education. Most children first attend the same kind of state primary schools: but then at eleven they are streamed, either into grammar-schools (*Gymnasien*) which prepare for university, or into junior secondary schools (see pp. 237–8). In theory opportunities are equal – and certainly the number of working-class youngsters entering *Gymnasien* has greatly increased. But many working-class families still feel inhibited about sending their children, however bright, into this more cultured milieu; one reason is that they find it hard to help them with their homework (an essential task of the German parent). So they tend to prefer schools that will lead straight to jobs or apprenticeship. Hence only about 15 per cent of university students are from working-class homes.

These divisions continue to affect life-styles, values and interests in later life. In Frankfurt, I heard an interesting view from a psychologist, Carmen Lakashus: 'The classes may have moved together, and except for the top ten per cent of the middle class their income levels may be fairly similar: in clothes, cars and modern equipment, there's little difference. And yet you can still recognise the working class by its vocabulary, gestures, and above all its tastes. Workers clutter their homes with all kinds of heavy, ugly furniture; middle-class houses are more sparely equipped with light furniture. One class spends its money on Schnaps, the other on books. The middle classes wear casual clothes for leisure, even for parties; workers and farmers, when they've finished their messy jobs, want to put on smarter clothes afterwards, even to go shopping. Middle-class people like to be outdoors whenever possible, even if it's just to sit and read or chat in their gardens and patios; it hardly occurs to workers to go outdoors, except for organised sport. On excursions and on holiday, middle-class people like to be alone, to find empty forests and beaches; workers are ill-at-ease except in a crowd of their own kind. When abroad, the bourgeois make for the museums and cathedrals, and they like to explore local life and local food; the workers want a big hotel where they can stay around the bar and pool and hear German spoken.' This clever analysis I thought a little too schematic and I can think of plenty of exceptions, especially as regards clothing (surely the bourgeoisie too likes to dress up for parties? – see p. 185). But Frau Lakashus summed up acutely: 'The biggest difference of all is that bourgeois are far more aware of these differences than workers. The new-rich working class thinks that affluence has made it just the same as the old bourgeoisie: but the latter, at least the more cultivated ones, are all too aware of the gulf of taste dividing them from the uncouth workers.'

It follows that the classes do not entertain each other much in their homes. However there is plenty of free-and-easy mixing in the context of *Vereine* (associations), sports clubs and other get-togethers, especially in smaller towns and villages. And, amid today's upward social mobility, quite a number of skilled workers do in fact acquire the culture and tastes of the bourgeoisie – for example, taking their children to the theatre and opera, or playing Bach at home on their expensive hi-fi. A journalist in Stuttgart, aristocratic by origin, told me: 'Our new house in the suburbs was put up by a local building worker in his spare time. When he'd finished, we invited him and his wife to dinner as our first guests. They chatted easily and confidently, about their holidays in Greece and Paris, and the football and TV that interested us both. A generation ago, they'd have been far less at ease.' This may not be very typical: but it is becoming less and less *un*typical, in a land where workers are much less chip-on-shoulder and aggressive than in Britain. Nor can a person's class background be assessed by his accent as easily as in Britain. Swabians' range of vocabulary may vary with their class and education, but they all talk Swabian in much the same voice – in a Germany where regional differences have always been as pronounced as class ones. And, above all, the younger generations are remarkably un-classconscious. Children of all kinds become friends at school, with little concern for what their fathers' professions or incomes are. So a doctor's son may bring a bricklayer's son home to play – and the parents, too, will mind far less than once they might have done. These trends are bound to influence the future.

I have written so far about the middle and working classes without mentioning the stratifications within the middle class that play so crucial a role in British and French social snobberies. In Germany, these differences are less clear and less important. Today Germany has no real 'Establishment', of the kind traditionally fostered in Britain by the public schools and Oxford and Cambridge, or in France by the Grandes

Ecoles and a few top Paris lycées. One explanation is that the old German power establishments, formed by the aristocracy, the army and a small caste of senior administrators, were dismantled by the ending of the monarchies and by defeat in two wars and the Nazi catastrophes. Also, in this federal decentralised country, power is inevitably dispersed. A third factor is that, unlike Britain and France or indeed the United States, Germany has no elitist pinnacles in her education system. The sprawling universities today are all roughly equal in calibre; the *Gymnasien* too are much on a par, while the handful of small private boarding schools have little influence.

It could even be argued that the prevailing ethos in German public life today is lower-middle-class, or *nouveau riche* middle-middle class. And a great many political leaders have come from such backgrounds. That rough diamond the late Franz Josef Strauss, intellectually brilliant, was the son of a butcher; Helmut Kohl's father worked in a local finance office; Lothar Späth, who never went to university, was the son of a bank employee. This relatively open and egalitarian state of affairs has much to be said for it. And yet, there are quite a few Germans today who look a little enviously at the elitism of Britain and France that can produce leaders of a more patrician stamp; they lament the lack of class and style in public life, the prevailing mediocrity, provincialism and *Kleinbürgerlichkeit*. When a leader from a different mould does come along, he is often welcomed. One of the reasons for the huge current popularity of Richard von Weizsäcker – certainly the most admired federal president since the war – is that with his patrician background he does possess those rare old-fashioned qualities of dignity, breeding and cultured thoughtfulness.

It is thus significant, if at first sight paradoxical, that in this new semi-classless society the one class that does survive most distinctively is the old aristocracy. Today it has no formal status: but it still uses its titles, and it is quite widely respected and not solely out of snobbery. Aristocrats as a whole were less contaminated by Nazism than the business and professional classes; most of them served quietly in the armed forces during the war, they provided the leadership of the July 20 plot against Hitler, and so they emerged with some honour left. Today they tend to behave discreetly, even usefully, and are seen as a link with tradition. The aristocracy no longer exerts power as a class: but many individuals are in positions of public influence.

The most striking example is the heir to the Wittelsbach dynasty in

Munich, the Duke of Bavaria, who is still treated with ceremony there as a kind of unofficial head of state. In all Europe, this must certainly be the dethroned monarchy still enjoying the best privileges and honours in its homeland – and there are good reasons for it. Having ruled so benignly across the centuries, the Wittelsbachs were expropriated in a very gentle manner after Ludwig III's abdication in 1918: their principal castles and art treasures passed to the Bavarian state, but they were allowed to keep a fair amount of property and sources of revenue, as well as the right to throw parties in Schloss Nymphenburg and to reside in a wing of it for part of the year. Later they resisted Hitler rather bravely. One Wittelsbach ran an anti-Nazi paper in Munich in the 1930s, some others were put in concentration camps, including Ludwig III's son, the Duke. This helps to explain the family's prestige today. The elderly present Duke, Ludwig's grandson lives in retirement in his *Schloss* at Berg on the Starnbergersee. But his son, Prinz Franz, an art-collector well known internationally, represents him on formal occasions and plays a ubiquitous role in Bavarian life: he is on cordial terms with Bavaria's rulers and is invited to all sorts of official social functions where he is solemnly addressed as 'your Royal Highness'. The family have a free box at the opera, where they are seen regularly. Foreign consuls call on them to pay respects. Their parties at Nymphenburg are the highlights of Munich's glittering social season.

There is more to this veneration than Munich society snobbery: the family is widely popular with ordinary Bavarians too, because of its record. And most important, in this very special *Land* with its exceptional heritage and sense of identity, the Wittelsbachs are seen as the emblem and guarantors of that tradition, helping Bavaria to remain its proud self. In no other *Land* would this be possible to the same degree: The Duke of Württemberg, though also courted for his royal lineage, plays a lesser role. And the Wittelsbachs take their duties very seriously, believing that they still have a moral obligation to serve Bavaria as best they can. Just as there is no Bavarian separatist movement, so there is absolutely no local demand to restore the monarchy: both are seen as unrealistic aims. And yet, many Bavarians still look nostalgically at their royal past, and even secretly envy the British and others for their reigning sovereigns.

Germany's 50,000 or so other aristocrats are hardly in this same pampered class, not even the Kaiser's family, the Hohenzollerns. However, a fair sprinkling of noble families still retain their landed wealth and their great castles set so romantically on hilltops, mainly in the south. The Fürst von Thurn und Taxis in northern Bavaria, who died in 1990, was said to own 250,000 acres. A great many other aristocrats, including nearly all the Prussian barons, arrived as refugees from the east after 1945, abandoning their fortunes and their local servitors, and with nothing left but their breeding, their social contacts and their name. But most have shown great resilience and powers of adaption. Like most other titled people today, they have moved quietly into business or other jobs, and they live ordinary bourgeois lives. You find them everywhere, in banks, running shops or art galleries, even in Ministries: sometimes they still use their titles, sometimes they drop the prefix but not the 'von'. Some of those who emigrated from the former GDR are now seeking to reclaim their estates there, and may go back to live on them (see p. 447).

In southern Germany some of the less wealthy noblemen have converted their castles into hotels in order to keep them going. Though integrated into society, many aristocrats tend to stick together in their own social circles, calling each other by peculiar nicknames such as 'Mopsi', 'Putzi' or 'Pong'. Each year they stage exclusive 'nobility balls' evoking past grandeurs. Some of the richer ones hold boar-hunts on their estates.

However, German aristocrats seldom resemble the familiar English or Scottish stereotypes of the barbarian backwoods peer or debs' dopey delight. More usually they are cultured, urbane and serious-minded – the kind of German that an older generation of foreigners most admires (one thinks of the officer portrayed by von Stroheim in Renoir's *La Grande Illusion*). Some do charity work, many retain a real sense of public service. The dapper young Rupert Graf Strachwitz, former manager of the Wittelsbach estates, gave me a democratic beery lunch in the public garden-café at Nymphenburg: after telling me that his forebears had been Silesian landowners, he went on, 'My family feels that it owes something to society for the privileges and position that we've enjoyed for so long. So we want to serve. That's why my father became a diplomat. We also feel that Germany today has a need for this kind of benevolent aristocratic tradition, which is not at all incompatible with a modern democracy.' But of course there is more to it than this. In a society with so strong a respect for titles, the nobility are appreciated for the magic of their names as well as for their real virtues: and many a big company or public institute is only too eager to put a lord on its board. Mainrad Prince von Hohenzollern, of the Swabian and not the Prussian branch of the family, who lives during the week in a smallish flat in Stuttgart, told me of his voluntary work for cancer research and other charities: 'I'm besieged by requests to serve in this way. I do it gladly, for I feel that my family still bears a duty to Germany and to Europe, and if my name can help to promote this or that worthy cause, that's fine.'

Aristocrats may consort together, but they are seldom aloof or cliquey; most are accessible, easy, democratic. It is true that the nobility in former days had some reputation for arrogant feudalism: but this related mainly to the great landed barons of Prussia – the ones who were then exiled and dispersed. In the south, by contrast, with its mass of tiny principalities and baronies, the rural aristocracy was always much closer to the people, benignly paternalistic, and respected. They are typified by the Hohenlohe of northern Württemberg, a sprawling tribal family who still own a dozen or so castles in the lovely rolling Hohenlohe farming countryside. One of these, on a low hilltop, visible far across the plain, is the compact brown *Schloss* of Friedrich Fürst zu Hohenlohe-Waldenburg, a tall, mild, civilised man in his fifties. He and his pretty wife gave me tea and sticky cakes in their modern sitting-room: 'During the war, this castle was occupied by the *Wehrmacht* and we lived in the outhouses. Later we renovated it. Today, if I'm liked and trusted by the villagers, as I think I am, it's above all because they see me as a hard-working professional man doing a serious job. I went to forestry school, and now I farm my 5,000 acres, mostly forest, and run a farm machinery business. Yes, I have landed wealth: but my income is no more than that of an average company director. I keep out of politics, but I work for Catholic charities. I chat to the villagers in pubs and generally try to be as un-seigneurial as possible, while my sister has a full-time salaried job as probation officer for ex-criminals in Munich. A lot of people round here try to suck up to me, that's inevitable, but no one attacks me for being an aristocrat. In France, where we have good friends with châteaux in Burgundy, the landed aristocracy tends to be far more feudal. They spend much of their time away in Paris and keep aloof from village life. We here in Germany have much more of the common touch, and that's why I believe we shall survive.'

He explained that he took the title of '*Fürst*' (prince) after his father died; but, owing to the peculiar juridical status of noble titles today, he could not accede automatically as in the old days – 'I had to persuade my friendly local *Landrat*[1] to sign papers allowing me to call myself

1. The head of administration in a *Landkreis*, see page 92.

"Fürst", and I paid him a fee.' The rules are bizarre and somewhat hypocritical. Whereas in Austria noble titles have been abolished, in Germany they can still be used, but they are a legal part of the surname and are supposed to be unalterable – you cannot succeed to a higher rank. In former days, the elder son of a *Herzog* (duke) or *Fürst* took over the title on his father's death; but since 1918 the offspring must remain '*Prinz*' or '*Prinzessin*' (oddly, a fairly low rank in Germany), so the higher titles will gradually die out. Hohenlohe got round this by changing his name by deed poll and paying maybe 3,000 DM: but it was a bit of a legal fiddle, and was possible only because the *Landrat* was fond of the family and respected its tradition. In Lower Saxony, in a similar case, a *Prinz* appealed to a court to be allowed to upgrade himself, but was refused. Nor is it easy to get rid of your title: there you are all your life with '*Prinz*' or '*Baron*' on your identity card or other papers. And the same applies lower down the scale, where all the children of a *Graf* (count), Baron or *Freiherr* inherit those names. So the titles will proliferate and devalue: this was precisely the aim of the democratic legislators of 1918. Even so, it seems probable that the aristocracy will long continue to flourish and be honoured – in a Germany today eager to renew contact with the less tainted aspects of its old traditions.

If a *Graf* is revered for his title, so in a different way is a *Herr Professor*, an *Oberkirchenrat*, an *Oberregierungspräsident*, or even a simple *Herr Doktor*. This abiding German fondness for titles may at first sight seem strange in this somewhat *nouveau riche* society with its lower-middle-class ethos. But probably there is a logical connection: just because they are slightly disorientated by the new class fluidity, so the German cling to the outward forms of the old hierarchies, and to their need for categorising people which bring the security of *Ordnung*.[1] Though it may be changing with the younger generation, this remains a rather formal society, preferring formal modes of address and judging by appearances. And so anyone with a university doctorate (and there are plenty of them everywhere) will exploit the respect he can win from using his title 'Dr' – many people are even quite touchy about it, and will take offence if addressed as plain 'Herr' on an envelope or in conversation. What is more, a wife and indeed a widow takes her husband's title and expects to be called, say, 'Frau Professor'. I know

1. For the German respect for authority, and how far it is waning, see p. 523.

one woman, who years after her husband's death, is still addressed by all and sundry as *'Frau Justizrat'* (Mrs Legal Administrator).

It is true that younger people are showing less concern for titles. Many students no longer call their teachers 'Herr Professor' but just 'Herr X'; and some radio and TV interviewers dare to drop the 'Herr Doktor', unimaginable even 20 years ago. But the more deferential ranks of society – junior officials, shop assistants, domestic servants – still seem to be overawed by titles and by people judged 'important'. A Swabian friend told me, 'I get better service in the shops now that I've got my doctorate,' while an English businessman's wife in Stuttgart said of her charlady: 'This good working-class *Putzfrau* is always fuming against the *Gastarbeiter*, but she adores the rich and famous. When I told her that my husband was a partner in his firm, her eyes glowed with joy: *"Ihr Mann ist Direktor! Wunderbar! Ich habe nur prominente Leute!"* ["I work only for prominent people"].' Once on the *Autobahn* near Stuttgart I was stopped for speeding, and when the policeman found my driving licence had expired he threatened to arrest me. 'Can I ring the British consul-general?' I asked, and added forcefully, *'Er ist mein Freund'* (which happened to be true). He quickly handed back my papers and shooed me on.

It is thus no surprise that, in some big German cities, rich businessmen vie with each other to acquire honorary consulships from small Third World countries. Sometimes they even buy them, for 50,000 DM or more – a cynical arrangement that suits both sides. The title of *'Herr Konsul'*, however empty in itself and however footling the work that the post demands, provides a ready passport to a new world of social prestige. And so in some *Land* capitals there exists a fantasy diplomatic life – in Munich, Düsseldorf and Stuttgart, though not in serious Hamburg which looks down on such follies. Of the forty-one consuls in Stuttgart, only five are foreign career diplomats; the rest are local Germans with 'honorary' status. Some of these have a serious and worthwhile job to do. Others work for countries as tiny and remote as Haiti and Chad, which have virtually no contact with Baden-Württemberg, and I would guess that a third or more have bought their titles. A businessman never admits to having done this, yet he will probably feel that the large sum has been well spent. He gets no diplomatic immunity, but has perks of other kinds. He may be a small garage owner, or a maker of underwear, so the status of 'consul' lifts him out of his narrow rut onto the social Olympus. He gets invited *ex officio* to the *Land* President's annual party; he can throw a posh party himself on his country's national day. The 'CC' plaque on his car helps him with the police – needless to say. And his wife too enjoys her kudos as '*Frau Konsul*'. There is a touch of the absurd about two minor Swabian tycoons solemnly calling each other, '*Ja, Herr Konsul*', '*Nein, Herr Konsul*' – but that's Germany. Of one of these wealthy local worthies representing a small banana republic, a colleague said, 'Being a consul does actually help his business – he goes to a score of diplomatic parties a year, and these bring new contacts. He adores putting the national emblem on his firm's gate.' The consul of another tiny state told me that he had barely heard of it before his appointment, nor were there any citizens of it living locally, yet he threw a consular party each year for 200 guests in a leading hotel. Rich Germans of this kind have no doctorates and no other title, and they feel inadequate. So they create this fantasy world. It is like Genet's *Le Balcon*, where people parade as something they are not. Everyone knows the titles are void of meaning, yet they still pay extravagant respect to them. No one tries to call society's bluff.

In the 1960s and 1970s this craving for consulships was cunningly exploited by the notorious Hans Hermann Weyer of Munich, playboy, ladykiller, braggart and practical joker, one of post-war Germany's most flamboyant characters. He set up a brokerage to put rich Germans in touch with small far-off countries, taking a fat cut on each deal; and in his heyday he claimed that about one-third of Germany's 300 honorary consulships had been arranged by him. The vendor nations were contravening the Vienna Convention of 1963, which forbade the sale of these posts, and so Bonn tried its best to stamp out the traffic. But it was not easy, for Weyer did his work in secrecy. He also sold aristocratic titles, honorary degrees, and even professorships, so that thanks, say, to the University of Tegucigalpa, some Bavarian grocer who had left school at 15 could flaunt his academic distinction (but this was too unsubtle and usually got found out). Weyer himself was Bolivian consul in Munich: he called himself '*der schöne Konsul*', he grew very rich and lived in a grand jet-setting style. The Gatsbyesque parties at his villa on the Starnbergersee were frequented by princesses and millionaires from Munich's high society, who thought it a great lark to share his weird fantasy and accepted him as an amusing joker in their snobby pack. His trade may have been odious, but at least he treated it as one big giggle: 'I like turning values upside down and poking fun at society,' he told me; 'it gives me a nice sense of power, and of the absurd, when mighty magnates come fawning humbly to beg titles from me. My father was a close friend of Hermann Göring. Ever since the time when, as a small boy, I saw those rows of medals shining on his chest, I've never looked back.' Weyer was later charged with tax fraud. So he left Germany for Paraguay, one of his client countries, where today he is still sometimes featured by German magazines, living it up by his pool, with champagne, gorgeous girls, and a big grin on his face.

Munich is the one city with a genuine café-society on any scale. This is the trendy world of media stars, fashion designers, sons and daughters of rich industrialists, and exiled or local nobility such as 'Prinz Poldi', younger brother of Prince Franz of Bavaria. They throw parties in their homes, or on big rafts on the Isar with Dixie bands, and they congregate in such haunts as the Käfer café restaurant or St-Emmerans-mühle beer-garden. To be accepted in this set, you need to have a name and some money, and above all to dress very well and be stylishly self-confident. You can wear either the latest fashions or elegantly-styled Bavarian *Tracht* – for this milieu fully merits its nickname of the *'Lodenmantelschickeria'* (see page 66). Its studied Bavarian folksiness is part of the cult, and its parochialism is partly deliberate. A leading Munich beauty surgeon said to me: 'My wife takes these cocktail parties seriously and likes to meet the "right" people and appear in the gossip-columns. I go just for a bit of amusing distraction after a hard day's work. Compared to Paris or London, where the smart set is far more diverse and international, here it really is very provincial.' The daily doings of the *Schickeria* are chronicled in the *'Leute'* column of the Munich boulevard paper, *Abendzeitung*, which reports who was wearing what and where. 'Gräfin X, in *Loden* with a Cardin leather collar, was sitting in Käfer with her poodle when along came Baron Y in his new Savile Row suit. She said "hello"; he said "hello" and passed on' (an actual item) is roughly the intellectual level. Some society ladies telephone the *Abendzeitung* to tell what parties they are going to and ask that a photographer be sent; some even pay to be written about.

In more ordinary middle-class circles, in Munich and in other cities, social life is less pretentious than this; but by Anglo-Saxon standards it is still rather stiff and conformist (except between close friends and family). Peter Frei, a radio journalist now back in Germany after spending some years in London, observed to me: 'Suddenly all the parties seem to be serving slices of kiwi-fruit, or an expensive variety of smoked meat, or whatever the latest trend may be. Some society hostess will have set the fad, then it's publicised by big-selling magazines such as *Bunte Illustrierte*; and the new-rich lower middle classes slavishly take it up. The same is true for clothes, both for men and women. Even the intelligentsia here I find to be markedly more competitive, snobbish and conformist than their equivalents that I knew in Britain. This is a symptom of our German provincialism, of being a series of big villages. At parties, people are also extremely conscious of each other's positions. When you meet someone new, he will first ask what you do, not so much out of polite interest as to try to size up your importance in your job so as to see whether you are worth talking to.'

At the opera in Munich, bejewelled elderly women in chic black dresses, with modish touches of pink in their hair, can be seen parading up and down in the intervals, their hawk-eyes fixed on their rivals' attire. But this old-style conventionality is today giving way in certain circles to a new individualism, equally mannered — as Carmen Lakashus explained: 'The same person has cheap rag-like clothes *and* elegant expensive ones, and she wants to wear both — and so long as it's individualistic and doesn't look plain, that's fine. People try *not* to look just like each other: that's new, and it's running through all ages and classes.' In Schwabing I saw a girl with a very smart hair-do, in stained dungarees torn to shreds — frightfully chic. But, whereas in Britain casualness is widespread and purely casual, in Germany it is calculated for effect. You can dress any old how, but you'll be summed up for it; in Britain, people often just don't notice. And this varies from city to city. In Munich, anything goes, but in the Stuttgart bourgeoisie conventions are more old-fashioned: one francophile lady there told me that in Lyons she had found some excitingly modernistic ear-rings — 'I was longing to buy them, but I knew that I could never wear them here, as I might anywhere in France. People would have been genuinely shocked, and I'd never have lived it down.' And the wife of an English businessman in Stuttgart said: 'We get invited to parties because of my husband's position and I must dress smartly but inconspicuously. The ideal is to be *"dezent"* (discreet). My conversation, too, must not stand out. If I were to break these rules, I would be bitched at behind my back. Everyone, too, has the same kind of smart car, usually a Mercedes, and you are classified by the size of your car as well as by your job status. Even these Swabians, though they think it bad taste to show off their wealth in public, still judge each other by it in private.' In the more ostentatious towns, Munich or Düsseldorf, wealth is lavishly flaunted — but this must be done with style and assurance, not any old how.

This may seem a severe picture. But I should add that Germany is also a scrupulously polite society, in its formal way. People may flare into sudden rudeness if you inadvertently offend them, or break a rule: but mostly they are courtesy itself, even the young shaggy ones. '*Auf Wiedersehen*' is said on every conceivable occasion, even when total strangers have done no more than share a lift for two floors in a public office; similarly, if you silently share a table with a stranger in a pub, he wishes you '*Guten Appetit*', and then '*Wiedersehen*' when he leaves. But social occasions are still marked by a good deal of stiffness and ceremony. English friends told me of a Stuttgart dinner-party in the home of a rich lawyer: 'There were lots of servants and our hostess seemed tense, anxious that all should be just so. We went into dinner in pairs on each other's arms. Later the men made formal speeches with toasts — yet this was only a private party for ten.' This admittedly is an extreme, untypical example. Even so, the Germans' idea of a party is often to sit round in a neat circle of ten or twelve, and to have just one conversation going, dominated by two or three people: they are less used to the Anglo-American fluid stand-up style. However, matters have been easing recently among some of the younger generation. Some Greens and *Alternative* have even gone to opposite extremes of informality: but they too have their own social codes and categories (see pp. 558–9).

It is true also that in very small towns and villages, where the community is tighter, among all classes there is much more casual matiness and relaxed informal interchange than in the cities: but this may in turn lead to intolerance, jealousy and intrigue. The stiff formality is at its most severe in the bourgeois districts of cities, and one of its most obvious aspects is the lack of easy chumminess between neighbours. Fear of neighbours is an old German tradition: 'See what your neighbour is like, before you build your house: if he's a scoundrel, you'll be building yourself a tomb,' wrote Friedrich Rückert in 1837. Today the commonest attitude to neighbours is that with just a very few you make close friends, and with all the others you have as little contact as possible: the in-between casual acquaintanceship so normal in Britain or America is unpopular since it might lead to loss of privacy, if the Müllers next door were continually popping round uninvited. This has also something to do with habitual German reserve about making new friends. People may ask a neighbour for strictly practical help on minor matters, such as leaving keys or taking in a parcel, but that's about all. If the neighbour does something really absolutely frightful, like playing the violin after 10 p.m., or failing to sweep the snow from his share of the pavement, then lawyers' letters may be quick to ensue (see page 520). And as the German, paradoxically, not only relishes his own privacy but is also keen to mind his neighbour's business for him, life-styles may get criticised even if they are causing no active harm at all. One girl I know who worked late, and then slept till noon with the curtains drawn, had neighbours shouting at her, 'Only lazy people work at night!' Oddity of behaviour offends against the desire of the German soul for social tidiness. Once again, however, an improvement can be detected amongst younger people. Allensbach surveys of all Germany (not just of middle-class urban areas) report that the number of people inviting neighbours to their home increased from 14 to 35 per cent between 1953 and 1979.

Just as striking as unneighbourliness is the gulf in Germany between office and private life. The pattern here is much the same as in France, of which I wrote in *France Today*, 'Except at senior executive level, office colleagues do not often try to meet each other socially, and casual friendship is rare between staff of differing grades. Thus the social ambience of the traditional French office is less chummy and relaxed than in Britain.' In Germany, there may be more chumminess, but the unwritten convention remains that office colleagues are one thing, social friends are quite another; junior staff may share a friendly lunch-break for years, without it occurring to any of them to meet at the weekend. This is not so in factories, where workers play football and then drink beer together: but office life is austerely asocial. And this can make life lonely for anyone who arrives to work in a new town without existing friends. I think of poor Katharina Blum, in Böll's novel, going for long car-drives on her own, because she had so few friends. And the head of an office in Hamburg told me that, when a seemingly cheerful clerical assistant suddenly killed herself, not a person in the firm knew anything at all about her life, or had had any social contact with her, although she had been there for three years.

A major aspect of this reserve is the German non-use of Christian names. This frequently startles a British or American visitor – and it can reach comic proportions. Young typists sharing an office, of the same age and background and on cordial terms, will go on calling each other '*Fräulein*': business colleagues will remain on '*Herr*' terms. An American woman journalist, working for a US Army paper in Stuttgart, told me that she once wrote a story about a senior German official and, following American practice, needed to include his Christian name. So she rang his secretary to ask for it. 'Sorry. I don't know.' 'Oh, have you only just started to work for him?' 'No, I've been here four years. But he signs his letters with his initials. I've never heard him use his first name.' This kind of thing happens all the time. It is true that in the media and fashion worlds there is more informality: but even the open-minded *Die Zeit* remains surprisingly stiff, or so I was told by one journalist there who said that for his first five years on the paper he had remained '*Herr*' to all his colleagues. The art in Germany is to know at what point you can start saying 'Hans' without being snubbed. Generally, between males, it is wisest to leave the older or more senior man to make the first move; between a man and a woman, leave it to the woman.

Maybe the British and Americans have debased the Christian name coinage into virtual meaninglessness. But in Germany this whole situation – including the barrier between '*du*' and '*Sie*' – seems to me to perpetuate an artificial barrier between friendship and acquaintanceship, making passage from one to the other an edgy and embarrassing business, and adding to the general uptightness of public social life. In France, where the use of Christian names has increased far more than in Germany, it is common today to call someone 'Jacques' or 'Françoise' while remaining on '*vous*' terms: I have a score of French friends in that category. But in Germany it is much more usual for the moves to Christian-name terms, and to '*du*' from the formal '*Sie*', to go together. In the middle classes, the more intimate address is still largely restricted to family and close friends. But it is far commoner between workers, and in SPD party circles it is a ritual tradition (a junior party worker can call Brandt, '*du, Willy*'). For many years it has also been universal among students, and since 1968 it has been gaining ground between Greens and other younger radicals. So a thaw is in progress which may eventually permeate the upper age groups. And anyway, what's in a name? I am on warmer terms with some Germans who still call me 'Herr Ardagh' than with many Britons who call me 'John' at first sight.

It would indeed be wrong to infer from the formality that Germans are cold with each other. The positive side of their relationships is that they are very warm and caring between true friends – more than the British. Friendship for them is an emotional business. After a due period of time, when trust has taken root, a man will suggest to his new friend that they move to '*du*' and to '*Hans*': they will then drink on it and embrace, in a kind of ritual. And the friendship is for life. The Germans draw a far sharper distinction than the British between true friends and the rest; they take great trouble with their friends, keeping in touch, sending cards and presents on their birthdays, and enquiring after their problems; they depend more than the British on possessing a circle of good friends whom they see regularly. But one crucial question remains: do the Germans need these friends so much, just because their society is somewhat stiff and uncaring, and sometimes hostile? – or, conversely, do they benefit so much from their friendships, and from the smooth organisation of public life, that they have less need for the more open and pally Anglo-Saxon style of society? Maybe, the answer is, a little bit of both – but quite a lot of the former, I do suspect. And this may not be the best of situations. It could be said that the complicated Germans have two very distinct sides to their nature. On the one hand, they are powerfully drawn to the rich interior life, to the world of emotion, idealism, privacy, depth and sensitivity – and friendship belongs to this. On the other, they are very practical and ambitious, admirers of efficiency, order and authority. The two do not easily fit together – and the result is a certain hiatus in German social life. Is a younger generation, with different values, working towards a better synthesis? – a theme to be explored towards the end of this book.

## Women, sex and children: a few crusades yet to be won

'The image of the German *Frau* has changed. Because women today have a far better diet than in former days, and do more sport and gymnastics, so we are now much slimmer. And that makes it easier to be more elegant too. This in turn has helped German fashion to advance on the European scene. For example, my own firm today sells widely in Italy and holds successful shows in Milan – something unthinkable till quite recently. What! – Italians buying German clothes?'

The fashion designer Jil Sander, herself extremely slim and pretty, was talking to me in her cool white Hamburg studio – and I readily agreed with her. Personally I have always found German women much more attractive than French ones, and in their own way just as chic and glamorous. Socially and psychologically too, no less than physically, there is today something entirely out-of-date about one's old picture of the typical *Hausfrau* (if indeed it were ever true), buxom and a bit frumpish, forever baking cakes and breeding flaxen-haired children. Following upon the *Wirtschaftswunder*, the late 1950s and early 1960s was the era of the so-called *Fräuleinwunder*, with the emergence of a seemingly new breed of young women, more prosperous and self-confident, more slender and well-dressed, more set on full emancipation. German women today may still tend to be ultra-house-proud and tidiness-prone, but then so are German men, so this is not a sex characteristic. In most other respects, women have freed themselves from the heavier constraints of the old *Kinder, Kirche, Küche* ideal, once so widely preached – and accepted – as the female role. As in other Western countries, they have moved quite a way since the war towards legal equality and social and sexual freedom, in a country that now is as permissive as most and that legalised abortion in 1974. Women have edged away, too, from the desire for motherhood – indeed, rather too much so, in the eyes of those who are now so alarmed about the declining population of this nation with one of the world's lowest birth-rates.

This is not a Latin country, and even in Catholic Bavaria there are few fathers who feel it a point of honour to protect a daughter's virginity, as many still do in parts of France and Italy. Teenage girls are free to do much as they please. And, in social life, women of all ages and classes mix easily and equally with men. Sometimes, it is true, men prefer to gather on their own round a *Stammtisch* in a pub: but on the whole Germans enjoy the company of women, and in this respect there is less *machismo* than in the clublands of upper-class London or working-class Tyneside, let alone in southern Italy. Why, then, do most German women feel that they still lack real equality? – why has the recent fight for equal rights been fiercer than in most other European countries? It may be something to do with the perfectionism of a nation where demands and expectations are always pitched high. But, more to the point, there does still exist a very potent *machismo*, not in social or private life but in politics and the professions, where men have fought to keep their hold on the senior positions. This is today's great problem – and it has a long history.

In nineteenth-century Germany, women in middle-class society were subordinated even more harshly than in Victorian England – as was shown so movingly in the novels of Theodor Fontane, whose master-piece *Effi Briest* (1895) tells of a young wife abandoned by husband, parents and friends after a brief and transient affair with another man. Finally she wastes and dies. Flaubert's Emma, Ibsen's Nora and Hardy's Tess were never treated quite so inhumanely. After this, determined campaigning by women's rights leaders did achieve some progress — but later than in Britain. Not till the 1914–18 war were women admitted to the universities. They won the vote in 1918, and under Weimar they at last began to make their way in the professions and to gain a little more emancipation and social life. But then the Nazi period set the clock back. Hitler's idealisation of home and family at first appealed strongly to women's conservatism, and they provided a large part of his popular vote in 1930 and 1933. But then in the interests of baby-breeding he ousted women en masse from the professions and the universities and sent them back home — to *Küche* and *Kinder* if not *Kirche*. Abortion was made a capital offence. However, as the war wore on, with so many men away fighting, the Nazis were obliged to modify this women-at-the-hearth policy: they came back into jobs such as teaching, and in some sectors such as farming and small businesses it was they who virtually kept the country going. Then after 1945, when so many millions of men came home morally or physically broken, or had been killed, the women of Germany emerged strongly placed to play an important role in the post-war renewal. From a feminist viewpoint, this was perhaps the one bonus from this tragic time.

But the struggle was by no means ended. The Constitution of 1949 stated, 'Men and women have equal rights': but the juridical implementation of this broad ideal did not happen overnight. Only in 1957 did a new law grant equality to women in marriage property rights. And up until 1977 the Civil Code contained an astonishing clause that gave the wife sole responsibility for the household and permitted her to take a job only if her husband agreed and if it were compatible with her domestic duties! This was abolished by the 1977 Marriage Law which declared that such matters should be settled by joint agreement. It also removed the guilt factor in divorce cases, which had often prevented a wife found 'guilty' from obtaining her fair share of alimony — this was in line with similar reforms in other countries at that time. So today a woman does at last have virtual equality, in the private sphere. But in employment, and in public life in general, women still feel badly discriminated against — not in law, but in practice — by a male-dominated society that battles harder than in most modern countries to retain its entrenched positions in the professions. And it still feels superior. When in 1972 the first woman newscaster appeared on television, one leading TV presenter, Karl-Heinz Köpke, commented, 'The news has to be read with detachment: women are too emotional,' and another, Werner Höfer, added, 'Of course I was thinking about her bosom, so I didn't listen properly.' The film director Margarethe von Trotta, a moderate feminist, gave me her view on this: 'Men are very self-protective, they don't like talented women coming up to rival them. If I'd been a man, I'd probably have made my first film ten years sooner. In my generation, women were not trusted by society, so they did not trust themselves. But this is now changing.'

In politics, women have tended to be fewer in top positions than in Britain or France, let alone the United States. They have also, until very recently, been poorly represented in parliament: in 1980 only 7 per cent of deputies in the *Bundestag* were women. It was not so much that women were unpolitically-minded, as that the local party associations selecting the candidates were heavily male-dominated and they put women low down the lists. It required great efforts for women to break through this. But they have finally been rewarded, for in 1987 the figure in the *Bundestag* rose to 15.4 per cent, thanks mainly to the Greens (25 deputies) and the SPD (31); then in December 1990 for all Germany the figure reached 20.6 per cent, the proportion in the west alone being 22.6. This increase was remarkable, seeing that the Greens, that female bastion, had now been virtually wiped out in parliament, and it was in the older parties that women's numbers rose dramatically: the SPD now had 65 female deputies, the CDU/CSU 44 and the FDP 16. Today the male politicians of all these parties, and especially the younger ones, are at last accepting women in their ranks much more easily, as the old prejudices die away. Women themselves have become much more politically aware, and certainly they no longer vote just the way their husbands tell them: a few towns now even have all-female councils – a real sex-war!

In government too there has been some progress, but slow. Cabinets in Bonn and the *Länder* since the war have tended each to contain just one or two 'token' women, usually in ministries such as family affairs and health, and no woman has yet been a *Land* prime minister. However, since 1983 the SPD has put a number of women into its shadow cabinet in Bonn, while Rita Süssmuth (CDU) has frequently been cited in the opinion polls as *the* most popular of German politicians. In 1991 Kohl included four women in his new 20-member cabinet, but they were still confined to the family-type portfolios.

In the professions and in industry, women are still disadvantaged. The proportion of women university students has risen since 1957 from 22 to 41 per cent: but women still account for only 5 per cent of full professors, 5 per cent of lawyers, 3.4 per cent of senior civil servants. The percentage of female doctors has quadrupled since 1933, to reach 20 per cent; in 1989 there were four women ambassadors; and the Protestant Churches now admit women as priests (which is more than can be said for the Church of England). But there are no women in the armed forces except as medical assistants. And even in the media, though women can do well in freelance jobs, they still find it hard to secure promotion in staff executive positions, simply because men bar the way: Marion von Dönhoff, co-editor of *Die Zeit*, is a rare exception. The same applies in the trade unions, where Monika Wulf-Mathies broke new ground in 1982 by being elected head of the large Transport and Public Services Union, the first woman in such a post. In banking, business and industry, it is reckoned that only 2 per cent of all top positions are held by women. Here male chauvinism is especially strong, and a woman can rarely succeed in climbing up through the hierarchy. When she does sit at a chairperson's desk, nearly always it is either because she has inherited from a husband or father or − quite often − because she has had the courage to start her own business. This frequently pays off − as in Jil Sander's case ('Starting my own firm I saw as my only hope, if I were to get my ideas across'), or that of the redoubtable Professor Elisabeth Noelle-Neumann, head of the Allensbach public opinion institute.

At the more ordinary job level, women today account for 37.4 per cent of the total workforce, slightly less than in Britain or France. By law, they get equal pay for equal work, but in practice men are often paid more, under the pretext that they are expected to do the heavier chores or work at night when needed: men's gross hourly wages in industry in 1986 averaged 18.05 DM, against 13.22 DM for women. Women can appeal to the courts over this or other discrimination, but the legislation is vague and there are no sanctions: Germany lacks a proper Sex Discrimination Act, as exists in Britain and America. When a job is vacant, the employer will frequently prefer a man, who after all is not going to get pregnant and then take the statutory six months' paid maternity leave. Girls also find it harder than boys to secure apprenticeships, and some two-thirds of today's youth unemployed are female. Recently, with rising unemployment, this whole situation has tended to get worse, or at least is perceived as having done so: according to Allensbach, the number of people thinking that women have equal professional opportunities has declined since 1967 from 40 to 17 per cent. Furthermore, the Kohl Government since 1983 has been accused by women's rights leaders of trying to 'push married women back into the home' with the dual aim of easing pressure on the labour market and of stimulating the birth-rate. The Government has denied any such thing. However, right-wing politicians rarely manage to conceal their old-fashioned sexist image. In the 1983 election campaign, Kohl crassly wooed the female vote with the phrase, 'Our pretty women are one of Germany's natural resources.' Feminists and others hooted with indignation.

A strongly militant feminist movement developed in Germany in the late 1960s and early 1970s, much as it had done in the United States. It at least had the merit of dragging the problem of sex discrimination into the limelight and forcing a public debate. But the movement rapidly displayed a humourless stridency and fanaticism, of a kind not uncommon in German radical politics, and before long it had fragmented into numerous rival factions, divided over aims and tactics. Some feminists allied their cause to the violent extremist Left,[1] believing that only in a revolutionary new world could women gain equality. Others, far from fighting for equal rights within society, staged a retreat into their own all-female circles, breathing lewd slogans of hatred against all males, and preaching lesbianism as their ideal. Some opened bookshops and cafés from which men were barred. Such extremism probably did little good to the female cause, for it gave feminism a bad name and alienated the sympathy of most ordinary German women. However, since those heady days matters have now quietened down. The more fanatical viragoes are isolated, and others have mellowed. Angelika Sirtl, a pragmatic 'moderate' feminist on the woman's magazine *Brigitte* in Hamburg, gave me the picture as she saw it: 'Twenty years ago you could tell a feminist from her looks and dress, all greyish and no make-up. But now they've discovered that feminism need not exclude femininity, and that you can enjoy looking pretty and sexy and well-dressed, to please yourself as well as men. Those old arch-feminists may have been too aggressive, and some still are: but we all learned a lot from them. And a society needs fighters. Even some staunch conservative CSU women leaders have publicly declared their gratitude to the feminists for what they have achieved.' Yet there remains a divergence in the women's movement, between those seeking fuller

1. In German post-war politics, many of the most extreme radicals have tended to be women, without being primarily feminist. This is true of some Green leaders today, as it was of Ulrike Meinhof, Gudrun Esslin and others in the terrorist movements of the 1970s.

equality within the present social system, and those like the 'fundamentalist' Greens who want society itself to be changed first.

Many of the more militant feminists today concentrate their efforts on trying to help other women who, as they see it, are 'victims' of a *macho* society. In particular they set up and run *Frauenhäuser*, which are refuge hostels for women battered or otherwise maltreated by their menfolk. Inspired by the English model, these homes today exist in over 100 German towns; most are run as private initiatives, but some are municipally funded too. Hamburg has four, one of them for St-Pauli prostitutes who are trying to leave their profession but are terrorised by their pimps. The addresses of the homes are kept strictly secret, for there has been more than one case of an angry pimp or husband turning up with a gun, and women have been shot dead. I was not myself allowed to visit a *Frauenhaus*, naturally: but the social workers at one of them consented to meet me in a Hamburg café, where they brought with them two desperately pathetic inmates. Both had been raped – one by her father, repeatedly, as a teenager. Both struck me as badly in need of medical help. But the severe-faced social workers said: 'These are normal, healthy women. They are simply the victims of men, and of a sick society. On principle, we allow no doctors or psychiatrists to visit the homes.' Their argument is that women in this situation tend to be frightened of the welfare authorities: they have too often suffered from the clumsy, officious attempts of doctors and others to get them back into society ('We'll help you to make a new start with your husband') and they just want to be left alone. But for adopting this stance the *Frauenhäuser* have been much criticised. In some towns it has cost them their municipal financing.

As in other countries, the past 30 years have seen great changes in attitudes to sexual morality and in man/woman relations. The annual total of weddings reached a peak of 530,000 in 1962, but by 1978 had fallen to 328,000, while according to Allensbach surveys the proportion of people considering marriage 'a necessary institution, not out-of-date' fell from 89 to 64 per cent between 1949 and 1985. However, by 1989 the annual tally had moved back up to 397,000, so marriage may be coming back into favour a little. Even so, the practice of living together unmarried, once so frowned on, is now judged acceptable by 80 per cent of Germans, according to another poll; and some 40 per cent of couples in the 18 to 35 age-group live in just this way. But often they retain two separate flats, out of prudence, seeing that relationships tend to be more fragile than property leases. Today the vast majority of young couples live together for a while before getting married and often they leave the wedding until the girl is about to have a child. Divorce now terminates about one marriage in three, as in Britain. Women especially are now more demanding of their partner; marriages have become more honest, so that a couple who are basically incompatible will split up rather than make each other's lives a misery: and the laws have been eased, so that divorce by mutual consent is now quite easy after a year's separation. All these are reasons for the rise in the rate of divorce, which no longer carries any social stigma.

There has been a general rise in tolerance, too. Even twenty years ago, an unmarried mother had a hard time of it in society: today she is easily accepted, except maybe in some rural areas. And she has proper legal status; a child born out of wedlock, too, enjoys the same welfare and inheritance rights as any other. There are reckoned to be about 500,000 women who live on their own with their children and have never married; some young feminists prefer this style, using a man simply to sire their child. Homosexuality too has become more readily tolerated, both by law and by opinion; as in Britain, it is now legally permitted between consenting adults in private. A gay English teacher who has lived in Germany for twenty years told me: 'In my university circles there is absolutely no problem, though of course in schools a master has to be very careful. I'd say that, in private and social life, homosexuals are as free here as in Britain. The only difference is that here it's more hidden behind a façade of decency. You don't get all those camp jokes on television. But that's partly due to the prudishness of German TV.' A homosexual in a senior official position may still be in difficulty, especially in the armed forces.

In general, if a German politician has an 'unorthodox' private life (homosexuality, mistresses, prostitutes, multiple divorces, or whatever), he may not emerge quite as unscathed as in France, but he is less likely to have his career damaged or destroyed by it than in hypocritical Britain. There has been no post-war German equivalent of the Profumo or Thorpe affairs. And a politician who shows himself to be one for the girls may even win a certain kudos for it, as in France – and oddly enough this seems especially so in Catholic Bavaria. There is a true story that the late Franz Josef Strauss, on a visit to New York some years ago, lost his wallet and passport when on a spree with whores; and another story, less authentic, that on the same trip he slept with Marilyn Monroe. Both tales gleefully went the rounds of the Bavarian beerhalls, and Strauss's popularity went shooting up.

The 1960s and early 1970s saw a sharp rise in promiscuity among young people. Allensbach again has revealing statistics: the percentage of single girls claiming to have lost their virginity before the age of 19 went up from 31 to 73 per cent between 1963 and 1978! Since then, as in other countries, there has been a swing back, not to chastity, but towards seriousness, fidelity and the steady teenage couple. This is a trend that was evident even before the arrival of AIDS in Germany (1,224 people had died from this by 1989), and now it is even more marked. Carmen Lakashus (see p. 175) said to me, 'Sex in the sixties was very much a body thing, but now it's more emotional and romantic. The young can have sex whenever they want, so they no longer have to prove it. It's now a full rich sexuality, much more than for the sixties generation.' But I am less sure myself about the romantic aspect. The Germans may have the reputation of being a romantic people, as regards nature, poetry, music, Wagnerian heroes and all that. But the younger ones today seem practical and down-to-earth in relationships – especially the men, who are definitely *not* Latin lovers full of erotic charm. 'All these shaggy types, they're so gentle and kind and serious,' said one pretty German girl I know, 'but they're far more ready to ask your views on nuclear missiles or the next *Land* election than to hold your hand and say how lovely your eyes are.' Among this generation there has been a marked decline in the old gallantries; many young people think that opening a door for a woman is just silly. Yet there are plenty of girls who regret the change. Their scope for using their charm is more limited. The climate of gentle flirtatiousness, of pleasurable sexual tension, that still infuses social life in France or Italy, is much less present in Germany, which has probably become even less romantic than Britain or America.

After the arrival of the pill, the 1960s were the breakthrough era in popular sex education. Oswalt Kolle scored a wide success with his sex-instruction books and films such as *Deine Frau, das unbekannte Wesen* ('Your Wife, the Unknown Being'), all very explicit, serious and helpful. This was followed by the age of liberation of pornography, linked to the extraordinary phenomenon of Beate Uhse and her commercial empire of sex shops and hard-porno movies. This God-Mother of German sex – and grandmother of nine children – is Germany's supreme example of a businesswoman who started her own firm and then fought her way to supremacy in her chosen field. She began, like Kolle, as a sex adviser, but has ended up somewhat differently. I went to see her one day in her smart head office at Flensburg, by the Danish border – a slim, wiry, rather manic little lady in her sixties, grimacing, gesticulating, very quirky and appealing. I had supposed that she based herself in Flensburg because it is the nearest German town to sexy Copenhagen, but she gave me the true reason: 'I am from East Prussia. I was a transport pilot in the Luftwaffe during the war, in Berlin, and just before the Russians arrived I managed to take a small plane and escape with my baby son to Schleswig-Holstein. I had lost my husband and parents in the war, and I've stayed here ever since. I found that the wives on the local farms were fearfully ignorant and worried about sex, so I decided to try to help them. As my mother had been a doctor, I had some background. I began to print and distribute leaflets explaining the Knaus-Ogino method, and steadily this developed into a large mail-order business, selling sex-advice pamphlets and contraceptives. Of course I had to face plenty of opposition in those days, and some lawsuits, but I won through – and today the climate has changed right round and has vindicated me. I am convinced that I did a lot of good. I helped to make the Germans less repressed. Repression led to Nazism.'

So successful was Frau Uhse that later she moved into a wider and more contestable field, marketing sexual aids and stimulants of all sorts, and producing and selling her own hard-porn magazines and films. She opened her first high-street sex shop in 1962, and now has 30 of them all over Germany, patronised in part by couples wanting to improve their sex lives but also, inevitably, by the lonely mackintosh brigade. In the hygienic ambience of a superior chemist's shop, they offer vibrators, erection creams, and much else. The fourteen Beate Uhse Blue Movie cinemas show the films, few of them exactly educational, that her firm produces or sponsors. 'I don't pretend to be Jesus Christ, I'm a normal businesswoman,' she told me; 'since 1975 pornography has in most respects been legal in Germany – and I'm simply catering to a market as the law allows me to. Germany today is one of the most liberal countries in this field. And the Germans are a very sexually liberated people – more than the Americans, who are somewhat inhibited except for some groups in California.'

After a canteen lunch she showed me round her new open-plan headquarters, all as neat and antiseptic as a doctor's surgery. The demure-looking staff, in white medical jackets, were packaging plastic penises. It was the birthday of one girl clerk, who proudly showed me her gift from Beate: a small ivory penis as a brooch. Frau Uhse then pointed to the big photo of herself with Willy Brandt and the mayor of

Flensburg at a local party – 'As the model employer of an expanding industry, I'm very popular here. At the golf club, I'm the colourful bird they love.' Back in Hamburg, however, I found women's leaders more sceptical. Eva Rühmkorf, head of the Senate's Office for Equal Rights for Women, said: 'Beate Uhse began usefully. Now she's merely serving the interests of men who want to use women as sex objects.' The majority of Germans, men as well as women, would probably agree with this. However, Germany is a free country; and no one is compelled to enter a sex-shop or porn cinema (the street advertising of such films anyway has to be discreet). It would seem to me that it is better to permit pornography than to suppress it into more devious channels.

Rather more important, the new liberal era has led also to the legalising of abortion. The reform was enacted in 1974, about the same time as in Britain and France; and, though opposed by the Catholic Church, it was supported by a large part of the Catholic laity, who knew the anguish that women had suffered. The richer ones used to go to private doctors in Holland, while the poor resorted to back-street abortionists (*Engel-macher* – angel-makers) who often did the job badly. But now abortion is free on the health service during the first three months of pregnancy, so long as the woman can convince a panel of doctors and social workers that she has a case. She must satisfy at least one of four conditions: that the child would be handicapped or deformed; that her own life would be in danger; that she was a rape victim; or, the case most commonly and controversially used, that she would be 'socially' unsuited to having a child, e.g. if she is out of work, or has no husband or parental support, or is in a depressive state.

This complex legislation still confronts women with all kinds of obstacles and is being applied varyingly from *Land* to *Land*. In most parts of north Germany, abortion is now fairly easy to obtain. But, in the rural Catholic areas of the south, not only do the medical panels tend to be stricter, but a great many doctors and hospitals refuse on conscience grounds to perform the operation. So a woman must look for another doctor in another town, and for the less educated or resourceful ones this is quite a stiff challenge. In one small Catholic town in Württemberg, I was told by a local doctor, herself Catholic but in favour of the reform: 'The Catholic villages round here are incredibly conservative, and the pressures of the social environment weigh heavily on any woman thinking of an abortion. Seldom does she have the courage to go through with it, for she'd be putting herself outside her social context and would feel guilty.'

The old-style Catholics in Germany have not given up the fight, and have been trying to get the reform repealed. In 1983 an extraordinary article by a priest appeared in a Catholic paper in Munster, *Kirche und Leben*: 'The Nazi extermination of the Jews was a horrible crime, but I'm not sure it was the cruellest ever. The Nazis at least had an ideology, but abortion is cold-hearted egoism. And the Nazis attacked adults who could defend themselves, not the innocent unborn.' The Church itself would hardly back such a view. But through its allies in the CDU and CSU it has been putting pressure on the Government to tighten the laws. Then in 1990 unification brought a new crisis, for east German women strongly opposed giving up their much more liberal abortion laws, and the Catholics in the west also refused to compromise. So the debate was shelved, and each part of Germany was allowed to keep its own laws for a transitional period (see p. 441).

After reaching a peak of 62.1 million in 1973, the population of West Germany began falling gently and by 1987 was a bare 61 million. The drop would have been greater, were it not for the high birth-rate amongst immigrant workers, Turks especially. Among west German nationals the birth-rate has been among the lowest in the world since the mid-1970s, with six births for every seven deaths, and on average only 1.3 children per marriage. If the overall population suddenly swelled in 1988–90, to reach 62.6 million by the time of unification, this was due to the mass arrival of German refugees and resettlers from the east, and of political asylum-seekers. More significantly, however, the west Germans' own birth-rate at last began to rise slightly again in the later 1980s, with births equalling deaths. Was this due to some recovery of confidence among younger people, after the *Angst*-ridden mid-eighties? And if so, what were the reasons for the previous disturbing decline? It was often supposed that one major cause was the so-called 'cultural pessimism' of many younger Germans – their lack of faith in the future, their fear of nuclear war, of unemployment or ecological disaster, or their general reluctance to bring children into a world that had lost its sure values. Such feeling may well have played some part, at least among Greens and other young radicals. But the wider reasons for the decline have probably been more practical: notably, the difficulties of combining a job with motherhood, in an age when so many women either actively desire to pursue a career or else do not want to reduce their living standards, or both. Paid maternity leave and family allowances are today fairly generous (see below): but these inducements to child-bearing are seldom decisive. Other factors weigh as much as the financial ones — for example, couples with children have more trouble in finding a flat. And as one woman journalist suggested to me, 'The whole structure of everyday life in Germany is weighted against the working mother.' Children come back from school at 1 p.m. expecting to be fed; the little ones too must be collected from kindergarten well before most office jobs end; the shops close at 6.30 p.m.; and most German husbands are still reluctant to help with the chores. So a mother needs some ingenuity, and endless hard effort, to keep both a home and a job going. What is more, many young professional couples prefer to remain childless rather than sacrifice their nice life-style of theatres, late-night parties and foreign holidays. These tend to be bourgeois people spoilt by affluence: at the other end of the scale are the Greens and radicals, more generous-hearted and unselfish, maybe, but pessimistic about the future. Both these two important contrasting categories are reluctant to rush into parenthood. And so, if the Germans today tend to be *either* more materially ambitious than most nations, *or* more gloomy and apprehensive, this could go some way to explain their recent low birth-rate.

Of course it can be argued: in an over-populated world, and in a densely-populated country such as Germany, does a slightly declining population really matter? This is a complicated issue, much debated alike for its economic, psychological and even military ramifications (see p. 564). Most of the experts do believe that a low birth-rate is related to national decadence. Be that as it may, the Kohl Government after 1983 grew worried, partly for practical reasons, fearing that the armed forces would increasingly lack manpower and the rising proportions of retired people would put a strain on social security budgets. So in 1984–5 Bonn launched a new programme of incentives. This included the setting up of a 'Mother and Child Foundation', offering financial aid to young hard-up mothers-to-be who might otherwise have turned to abortion. Maternity benefits were also improved: by law, an employer must now keep a working mother's job open for up to a year, and her leave during this time is subsidised partly by the state. Monthly child allowances run at about 50 DM for the first child, 100 DM for the second, 220 DM for each one thereafter. Calling for a target of '200,000 extra babies a year', Chancellor Kohl in 1984 appealed to German patriotism: 'We must change this back into a child-loving country.' But his tone hardly pleased those feminists who habitually resent any move to 'push women back into the home'. So this problem of the birth-rate is not an easy one. Probably it will not be solved by cash incentives but only by change of attitude. One sociologist, Uli Schmetzer, has suggested that German thoroughness might finally tip the scales: 'Just as German women went over to the pill more thoroughly than others, so, if they could but be convinced that baby-making is fun, they might again set themselves to it wholeheartedly.'

Matters might also improve if society as a whole could become more tolerant and understanding of children – or so is often argued, by Germans who will readily admit that there is some truth in the nation's long-standing reputation for *Kinderfeindlichkeit* (hostility to children). This goes back into history and includes a failure to comprehend a child's imaginative world: were the Grimms' fairy tales and the *Struwelpeter* stories not only violent and cruel but too symbolic to relate properly to children? And, today, child abuse is well above the European average. According to the German Children's Aid Society, some 30,000 children each year are maltreated and some 100 commit suicide, most of them as a result of parental brutality or neglect. But it would be wrong to get the problem out of proportion. In this family-minded country, the vast majority of parents are in fact loving and kind to their children. Probably they do treat them with rather more discipline and authority than is common today in the West; but this has been getting less so, and anyway might it not basically be more caring than the opposite American tendency of so many parents to let their children run amok?

As so often in Germany, this problem of *Kinderfeindlichkeit* lies much less with private than with public attitudes. Society does not like children in public places because they are noisy and restless, they make a mess, they tread on the flowers or put finger-marks on tidy new paint – in short, because they behave like children. If a small child cries in a restaurant, or even in a supermarket, people make an angry fuss. Whereas Latins drool over their neighbours' children, Germans are constantly lodging complaints about their noise – and so it is little surprise that many young families find it hard to rent flats and must resort to buying houses at a cost they can barely afford. Today there are plenty of toyshops and clothes boutiques for children, but few town councils bother to provide adequate playgrounds for them. Yet politicians often warn against the hostility, and the public itself seems to be aware of it: when Allensbach asked, 'Do you agree that the Germans are not fond of children?', almost as many (42 per cent) said 'yes' as 'no' (46 per cent).

The most hopeful sign is that the younger generation is behaving differently. Many young parents are exemplary, especially Greens, often organising voluntary crèches to help working mothers. Most remarkable of all is the new attitude of German fathers, who used to leave the minding of small children to their wives but now take an eager and active part. Everywhere you see young men wheeling prams, or clutching babies in shops; they would certainly breast-feed too, if they could! Emotionally they are far closer to their children than before, and even officialdom is recognising this: in divorce cases, the number of fathers being granted custody of the children has doubled in ten years. Since 1986, a new law has decreed that the twelve months' subsidised vacation after childbirth can be taken by the father rather than the mother, if it is the wife who wants to continue working – and employers are obliged to agree. This paternity leave is already quite popular, and many young couples are accepting that it is the wife who should remain the breadwinner. When I asked the young leader of the Greens in Munich what his job had been before he entered the city council, he said proudly, *'Hausmann.'* Might not this trend in the long run provide some solution, alike to the problem of *Kinderfeindlichkeit* and to that of women's equality in the professions?

## *A spick and span suburbia where the shops shut early*

The post-war rehousing of the Germans was one of the more striking aspects of the 'economic miracle'. In 1945, in the area that is now west Germany, more than 8 million people were homeless. But soon the authorities embarked on a subsidised crash programme to make good the losses, and with typical German energy this went racing ahead: in the 1950s, Germany was completing new dwellings at a rate of over 500,000 a year, more than in Britain and far more than in France. Today over 75 per cent of German homes were built since the war. Not all this new housing is beautiful, by any means: but it is better equipped and more sturdily constructed than the European average, and the Germans are now certainly the best-housed people in Europe after the Scandinavians. Quality has been improving steadily: the average floor space of homes built today (over 100 square metres) is twice what it was in 1952, and for some years now all new dwellings have been provided with bathrooms and central heating. Nearly all the old slum areas have been cleared away, and today the average worker lives in a comfortable, well-lit flat or small house, either rented or owned. The percentage of flats that are owner-occupied has risen from 44 to 62 per cent since 1970.

By the mid-1970s it was officially claimed that the housing shortage had been solved. But then in 1988–90 the massive influx of new refugees from the east (see p. 294) produced a new crisis: many of the newcomers had to be housed temporarily in makeshift camps, hostels or disused buildings, while a new crash programme was started. Today, many young people and not only immigrants go to squat in derelict tenements – not by choice, but because good cheapish flats are still too few. Partly this is because of the steep rise in land prices in cities. In Germany, subsidised 'social' housing for lower-income groups is built mostly by semi-public agencies and cooperatives, and the rents are controlled by the *Länder*. But in recent years land prices have reached such a high level, and the required quality of housing has risen so high too, that most agencies have begun to find it too expensive to build in central city areas. So since 1965 the Federal Government has operated a system of rent-topping grants paid direct to poorer tenants on a means-test basis: some 1.8 million families benefit. But this has not in itself solved the shortage of suitable cheaper 'social' housing inside cities. Today the monthly rent including heating for a 3-room 80-square-metre city flat is around 900 DM, or about 20 per cent of an average worker's earnings.

Middle-class people generally prefer to own rather than rent, and for them the problem of land and building costs has become quite acute. Land prices per square metre may be only 200 to 400 DM in a residential part of Bremen or Hanover, but they rise to between 1,000 and 1,500 DM in Munich and Stuttgart, Germany's most expensive cities, where a five-room flat may cost up to 1 million DM and a family house in a good area 1.5 million or more. And, as building societies usually require a minimum 30 to 40 per cent down-payment for a mortgage, the vast majority of young couples must first spend some years in rented accommodation unless their parents can provide a substantial amount of capital. But rents too are very high, and in the private sector they are not controlled. My wife when I first met her was living in a pleasant one-room studio flat in central Stuttgart for 300 DM a month (unfurnished) and her widowed mother was paying 450 DM for a good two-room flat in a pleasant suburb of Munich, but both had secured bargains: over 1,000 DM a month for a 3-room unfurnished flat in Stuttgart is nearer the norm. These prices may seem low by the extortionate standards of *furnished* accommodation in London: but London families, if not eligible for council housing, will generally buy property, and house prices are a good deal lower than in Germany and mortgage terms more generous. When they can afford it, the Germans too will usually prefer to buy. Especially in Swabia the ideal is still *schaffa, spara, Häusle baua* (work, save and build your little house: see page 69), and many a Swabian father starts putting money into a savings bank for his son at birth, so that by the time he is 30 the young man may have enough credit to meet the mortgage conditions. And preferably it must be a real '*Häusle*' in its own garden, not a semi-detached or a flat. Look down on any townlet around Stuttgart, and you see an undulating sea of little red roofs. But this is not the dreary ribbon-development of Britain, for each house is separately conceived; nor is it the anarchy of the pre-war Paris suburbs, for individualism is tightly checked and you must build to harmonise with your neighbours.

Most spruce little German houses of this kind were either built fairly recently or have been newly modernised, inside and out. Older dwellings of character are far less common than in Britain or France. Not only were many of them destroyed by bombing, but Germans in the post-war decades actually tended to *prefer* modern surroundings. After the war they wanted, as I have said, to make a clean start, rejecting anything that reminded them of the awful past – and this led to some travesties of taste. Much perfectly pleasant old-fashioned housing that had survived the bombing was torn down hurriedly and thoughtlessly, when it could have been kept and modernised. Villagers pulled down their nice old farmhouses and built stereotyped new ones, more comfortable, with central heating; often they covered over half-timbered façades with fancy new walls of aluminium or plastic, considered more chic and practical – Edgar Reitz's film *Heimat* (see p. 339) gives a sharp picture of a local contractor cleverly exploiting this craze. And much the same happened in the towns. All became new and suburban; the only visible link with tradition was provided by the little painted ceramic gnomes, fawns and other animals that were – and are – still used by workers and petit-bourgeois to adorn their gardens and allotments (kitsch dies hard). However, since the mid-1970s there has been a radical change in attitudes. The traumas of war have been digested; the new ecological era has brought a new concern for the past and for traditional values. So the old is back in favour. Half-timbered houses – such of them as survive – are now being carefully restored rather than pulled down or disguised; and people are again looking for old homes of character. But there are not many of these left. In the wake of the Allied bombers, the ravages of peacetime bad taste have taken another heavy toll.

The living-rooms of the professional classes are nearly always smart and well-decorated, with each expensive object neatly in its place and none of the casual untidiness or unkemptness that one often finds in equivalent homes in Britain. This is evidence alike of the higher German living standards and of the Germans' passion for order and neatness. And there is even more to it than this – as Anthony Sampson astutely observed in his book *The New Europeans:*[1] 'The special relationship of a German family to their house or flat is unmistakable. A visitor is shown around the house as soon as he comes in; the objects, furniture and gadgets are laid out as if in a contemporary shop-window. . . . The completed stage leaves little room for development or disruption, and it helps to give that frozen look to German homes. There are no old sofas, junk or messy corners: and in this formal stage, people move uneasily, and the objects seem to acquire a power of their own.' I share that impression – and I would say that it goes for all social classes. Though less than formerly, many working-class families still retain the custom of '*kalte Pracht*' (cold splendour), a front parlour used only on special occasions and normally kept unheated, its formal furniture covered in dustsheets. In middle-class homes, even a lived-in sitting-room often has an oddly unlived-in feel, its books all within glass-front cupboards lest they attract dust. Once I visited an extreme example of this, a Munich home where the television set was hidden inside a Bavarian chest, and the books too were invisible behind cupboard doors; the furniture was heavy repro and the atmosphere funereal. But the average home, though as tidy as this, is rarely so gloomy. Twenty years ago the middle-class vogue was for modern Scandinavian furniture; today, in line with the new eco-nostalgic trend, German-style repro is preferred – or real antiques if they can be found or afforded.

Today, however, there has been yet another U-turn of home living styles – among some people. Young Greens and others will frequently flaunt their contempt for bourgeois values by deliberately making their

1. Hodder & Stoughton, London, 1968, p. 224.

living-rooms and kitchens as messy and cluttered as possible. I have visited the homes of teachers and writers where the chairs and sofas were covered with books and papers, cupboard doors were hanging open, dirty boots were strewn on old newspaper in the parlour, and the dirty plates and half-eaten food on the dining-table was making some ideological statement. Who says the Germans do not still fly to extremes?

When it comes to the possession of consumer durables, even Greens have their homes equipped with fridges and dish-washers, and maybe video-recorders too. In this prosperous western Germany, 18 per cent of families now have more than one car, and even the three-car family is not unusual. West Germans tend to have more of the various modern appliances than other European nations, as the table below shows (source: EC):

| Percentage of homes equipped with: | Germany | Britain | France | Italy |
| --- | --- | --- | --- | --- |
| Passenger car | 61 | 58 | 67 | 66 |
| Refrigerator | 96 | 92 | 95 | 93 |
| Deep-freeze | 56 | 28 | 25 | 25 |
| Dishwasher | 15 | 3 | 13 | 14 |
| Washing machine | 81 | 76 | 73 | 80 |
| TV set, colour or b. & w. (*figures include homes with more than one set*) | 108 | 96 | 93 | 100 |
| Telephone | 90 | 67 | 69 | 54 |

Patterns of spending have been changing in much the same ways as in other Western countries. Expenditure on food and drink has continued to rise in real money terms, but not nearly as fast as in other sectors such as travel, homes and leisure. As a percentage of the average family budget, food, drink and tobacco declined from 41 to 16.6 per cent between 1964 and 1987, while housing rose in the same period from 11 to 19 per cent, and transport and telephones from 9 to 15 per cent. Consumer attitudes have been changing, too. In the first years after the war, when money was still tight, consumers were very price-conscious, always looking for bargains. Then, from about the mid-1950s, they paid more attention to quality: they wanted goods to be expensively made, and in the shops the dearer lines would often sell out more quickly than the cheap ones. This remains so today, save that a new 'quality of life' trend has also appeared, as ecology-minded people look for healthier food and more 'environment-friendly' leisure equipment.

Large shopping-centres and hypermarkets have sprung up on the edge of towns, pushing out of business many small traditional shops such as dairies and groceries. However, in the past few years this trend towards bigger stores has been halted, as a result of opposition not so much from the small traders' lobby as from civic activists who have pointed to the human hardships that the trend can cause. A hypermarket may be ideal for those with a car; but closure of small local shops has been hard on sick or elderly people who may now have to make a long walk to find basic essentials like bread or milk. So in 1977 the Schmidt Government produced a law allowing communes to refuse licences for new hypermarkets of over 1,500 sq. metres selling space (these are unpopular with ecologists too). But this has not led to any great increase in the numbers of little general stores. Their places have been taken by new specialist shops and boutiques, selling fancy foods, unusual clothes and the like.

Under one of Germany's most controversial laws, virtually all shops of any kind must close at 6.30 p.m. sharp on weekdays, all day on Sunday, and on Saturday by 2 p.m. (it is 6 p.m. on the first Saturday of each month). This today is one of the tightest laws of its kind, in a Europe that on the whole has been relaxing the rules for shopping hours – and it surprises and annoys many visitors to Germany. It is also much debated and criticised by the Germans themselves; but efforts to get it reformed have not made much progress. This *Laden-schlussgesetz* (Shop Closure Law) was passed in 1956 under joint pressure from the unions and retailers. The unions, notably the *Gewerk-schaft Handel, Banken und Versicherungen* that covers shop assistants, wanted to prevent staff from being exploited by long hours; the retail associations wanted to protec. the little local shops (*Tante Emma Läden* – Auntie Emma shops – they are nicknamed) from too much competition from the rising new supermarkets. The legislators also had the motive of protecting small shopkeepers from themselves, in a nation then in the throes of manic workaholism. So this law was well-intentioned – but silly. It was much contested at the time, by Erhard and others, and has remained unpopular, for it causes massive inconvenience to millions, including trade union members. A working mother has to hurry out of the office to fit in some rapid shopping; buying aspirins in the evening for a headache is not easy; impromptu weekend dinner-parties are unfeasible; and so on. No wonder that Germany leads the world in automat selling-machines and in the mail-order business.

Just a few exceptions are allowed. Bakeries can trade on Sundays from 11 a.m. to 3 p.m. Chemists stay open at weekends on a rota basis. Florists – oh, compassionate lawgivers! – can trade then too if they are within 300 metres of a cemetery or hospital. And shops in the foyers of airports or main railway stations can stay open till late and at weekends 'in the interests of bona fide travellers'. You are supposed to be able to produce a travel ticket, if asked, but checks of this kind are rare: the Feinkost grocery at Stuttgart station, mercifully only eight minutes' walk from our flat, several times saved us from near-starvation. However, in other ways the law does tend to be rigidly applied, German-style. A petrol station can sell a can of beer at night to a motorist as 'journey necessity', but not to a local resident. I heard a tale of a man who walked into one service station in Hamburg at 6.45 p.m. and asked for a crate of beer; the kindly attendant, taking a chance, handed him one – whereupon the visitor whipped out his police card and booked him for a fine! A great many little local shops do gently break the law by allowing regular customers to knock on the back door at night for some item of grocery: but they have to be careful, and will not sell to a stranger. The ambience of subterfuge recalls America under Prohibition!

Britain too has had its disputes over Sunday trading: but the law that restricts it is often more honoured in the breach than the observance, at least in London. The trouble with the Germans is that, if they have a law, they tend to keep it. And this one has proved hard to reform, even though opinion polls have stressed its unpopularity. Recently a few bold efforts have been made, often with municipal support, to circum-vent it and show up its idiocy. Notably, in Stuttgart, twenty-seven small stores of all kinds in a new underground arcade beside the station stayed open till 10 p.m. on weekdays, under a concerted experiment that lasted ten years, from 1976 to 1986. Mayor Rommel lent his weight to the scheme, which according to one poll found favour with 96 per cent of Stuttgarters. The shops in the arcade, too, were pleased, for it increased their turnover by 25 per cent; and it created 100 part-time jobs. But the German Retailers' Association fought it tooth and nail as 'dangerous precedent'; and finally they won a protracted court battle. So it seemed that the project would fail, like others before it. In

Bremen in 1985, the small shops in one street had staged their own revolt, staying open till 11 p.m.: they were fined twice, then threatened with prison sentences, so they stopped. However, in 1986, the Bundestag finally accepted Government proposals for a modest change in the law, to allow some shops in the vicinity of airports and main railway stations in towns of over 200,000 people to stay open till 10 or 11 p.m. Thus the Stuttgart scheme was legalised and it has survived. Another recent modification is that on Thursdays all shops are now allowed to stay open till 8.30 p.m.

But any wider change in the law would seem to remain out of the question, for there is still an unholy alliance of unions' and retailers' interests in favour of the status quo. The unions remain opposed on principle to any reform that would run counter to their campaign for a shorter working week — even though their argument here is very weak, for shop assistants' hours could easily be staggered and no one expects them to work longer. 'The real truth,' said one observer, 'is that the unions see this law as one of their last remaining bastions. They dare not to give in.' And the retail lobby still wants to protect its smaller and weaker members from further competition and higher overheads. But this too could be regulated. In 1984 the Green party put forward a sensible compromise proposal, whereby the law should still apply to larger stores, but smaller family-run ones should be allowed to stay open later and at weekends if they wished, so long as the owners were themselves working. The SPD and unions rejected the idea — because it came from the Greens. And the Kohl Government was wary of any reform that would antagonise the unions. So the Germans remain saddled with a law that few members of the public want. It is a typical German example of a well-meaning piece of legislation that in practice does more harm than good.

## *From* Wurst *and dumplings to fancy French and food fads*

The Germans are often seen as being almost as barbaric as the British in matters gastronomic. Their cuisine, with its sauerkraut and dumplings, its fat pink *Wurst* and steaming knuckles of pork, is regarded as wholesome and tasty maybe, but coarse and monotonous. But is this image an accurate one? Of course it is true that German cooking lacks the exceptional variety and finesse of the French, or even the Italians; just as the French are less musical than the Germans, so the Germans do not imbibe gastronomy with their mothers' milk as the French still do. They do not possess the same heritage. As in Britain, the industrial revolution separated the new urban population from the old peasant tradition of inventive cooking (never very strong, anyway, compared with France), with the result that regions such as Hessen, Rhine/Ruhr and Lower Saxony are today almost as denuded of good local specialities as the British provinces.

And yet, over the country as a whole, there is much more variety and subtlety to be found than may at first be apparent. Germany produces some 200 different kinds of bread, and almost as many sorts of *Wurst*. In Baden, with its long French affinities, people have a real concern for good eating; and to some degree the same is true of Württemberg and the Moselle valley, of Franconia and some other parts of Bavaria – in fact, wherever wine is produced except, strangely, for the Rhineland. In pubs and restaurants, cooking tends to be excellent in its own way when it sticks to the simple traditional dishes; when it tries to experiment with more sophisticated ideas, or to copy French styles, then it is usually phoney and tasteless, as is so often the case in big hotels and smarter restaurants. But if a visitor learns how to avoid these pitfalls, he can find remarkable value-for-money in pleasant, inexpensive *Gaststätten* nearly everywhere, even in the north. And, even if the cooking is somewhat bland and predictable, at least the helpings are generous and the service and the presentation uniformly excellent, in line with the usual German efficiency and attention to detail. I have had dull meals in their country, but very few really bad ones, sloppily cooked or served, of the kind all too common in Britain.

It is true that one meets plenty of people with absolutely no feeling for food. Kindly hosts have sometimes taken me to nice-looking restaurants where their conversation has shone but they have passed no comment on what we have eaten: not out of stinginess, I am sure, they have maybe proposed taking a dull set menu of unseasoned cream-of-vegetable soup, a slice of beef with cabbage, a tasteless custard flan and one glass of white wine. But such barbarism is growing less common. Among much of the middle class, the past thirty years have seen quite an upsurge of interest in gastronomy, prompted by foreign holidays, by the presence of so many restaurants run by foreign immigrants, and by the new prosperity. Food is 'in'.

\*

For centuries the Germans were famous for their hefty appetites – and their waistlines proved the point. The fat-faced, beer-bellied Bavarian, two-litre tankard in hand before a plate piled high with *Wurst* or dumplings, was a stock cartoon character and not far from reality. In pre-war days, poverty often dictated diets, and potatoes, bread and cakes were staple items of nutrition. In the 1950s, this pattern changed dramatically, as sheer greed steadily replaced subsistence eating: The *Wirtschaftswunder* period was equally that of the notorious '*Fresswelle*' ('wave of guzzling'), when a new-rich nation reacted against the deprivations of wartime by tucking in more avidly than ever before – and this time to a far richer diet. This continued until about the early 1970s, when alarming medical statistics appeared suggesting that 10 million Germans were overweight, including 25 per cent of children (spas began to offer cures for fat children). As *Time-Life*'s book *Germany* has commented wittily, 'The news that the Germans' new-won prosperity was indirectly harming them was just the sort of bloomy paradox that their social history had taught them to appreciate.'[1] So, reacting to the warnings with their usual thoroughness, they began to move over to healthier foods and physical fitness campaigns.

These changes in diet have some parallels in other countries too, but are especially remarkable in Germany. Before the war, the Germans consumed nearly three times as many potatoes as the British, per capita: now they eat 30 per cent less. Before the war, they ate less fruit than the British; now they eat well over twice as much. Between 1953 and 1987, annual per capita consumption of potatoes dropped from 163 to 82 kilos; of cereal products and rice, from 96 to 78 kilos. In the same period, consumption of vegetables rose from 46 to 77 kilos, and of fruit from 69 to 109 kilos. Meat-eating went up from 63 to 103 kilos per head between 1961 and 1987.[2] This is not to say that Bavarians do not still enjoy their flour dumplings, or Swabians their *Spätzle* noodles, or Germans anywhere their thick slices of brown bread with ham, *Wurst* or cheese. They are still the world's heaviest beer drinkers, too, after the Belgians. And at least among the older generation there are still plenty of bulky, beefy figures around to bear this out. But young women, as I mentioned earlier, are far slimmer than their mothers and grandmothers were at the same age; they are eating fewer of those sticky *Torte* with cream. And many Greens and younger people have

1. p. 128 (Amsterdam, 1984).
2. Sources: EC and West German Food Ministry

gone over to a diet that is low on starch, high on organically-grown rice and vegetables, and quite often vegetarian.

Unlike the French, the Germans do not stick rigidly to two big meals a day at set times. They prefer various little snacks at odd hours, often including a *zweites Frühstück* taken in the office at 10 or 11 a.m., a cake for tea, or a late-night nibble. But, rather like the French (see my *France Today*, p. 389), their food habits have been tending to polarise. Day-to-day eating has become more perfunctory, with greater use of convenience foods and less real home cooking; on the other hand, as in France, and more so than in Britain, there has been a striking increase of interest in really good food for the once-or-twice-a-week occasion, whether it be restaurant dining-out or the dinner-party at home. For ordinary daily home eating, lunch is still the main meal of the day for most families; this is when the kids come back from school, and they need something hot. Today it may well be something easy from a tin or packet, though quite often it is still a home-cooked stew or *Schnitzel*, or a local meat dish with dumplings and sauerkraut. And father at work will have a hot meal in the canteen or pub. In the evening, the traditional meal all over Germany is *Abendbrot* − as its name suggests, a cold supper of bread with sliced meats, cheese and pickles, maybe some salad and fruit, and perhaps preceded by a warm soup. In working-class families, this is often taken at 5.30 or 6.0 p.m., when father is back from work; in the middle-classes, it is more usually at 7.0 p.m. or so. *Abendbrot* goes well with TV-watching and is still popular. But in some bourgeois circles it is being replaced by a hot cooked meal.

In the home, the new interest in gastronomy is reserved for the special occasion, which might be a family reunion or a little dinner-party for friends. Here cooking has become a modish hobby, and often it is the husband who is at the stove, trying out new recipes and using quality ingredients. Food magazines proliferate, and in the 1970s one 'Dr Oetker' cookbook was the biggest seller of any title except the Bible. Hosts will sometimes produce an 'exotic' dish discovered on a foreign holiday, such as *paella* or *moussaka* (the *Gastarbeiter* stalls in downtown covered markets are much patronised by Germans who come to buy fresh herbs and spices, peppers, black olives, feta cheese). Or they will offer a *fondue bourguignonne* or in summer a barbecue. Or they might attempt one of the old German peasant recipes now being adapted by the food writers for use with more expensive ingredients. But many couples still prefer to offer their guests an *Abendbrot*. This can sometimes be quite lavish and sophisticated; a Daimler-Benz executive's wife piled high the meat-platter with smoked salmon and rare Finnish reindeer meat; in the Ruhr, I was given a delicious supper of fruit soup, local Westphalian ham and dandelion salad with mustard dressing. But just as often this cold dinner-party fare can be rather basic – especially in Swabia, where despite their interesting local cuisine the people have an all-too-justified reputation for mean frugality. One Swabian lady who had spent some years in France told me she found this shaming: 'A company director and his wife asked my husband and me to dinner. They gave us cold meat and cheese, and sardines left in their tin. I retaliated by inviting them to a slap-up four-course French meal, which the husband devoured greedily while his wife commented sourly, "*Liebling*, you're never as hungry as that at home."'

For dining out, the major trend over the past twenty-five years has been for 'exotic' foreign restaurants, ranging from the genuine simple ethnic to the pretentious pseudo-French. In the upper *Schickeria* bracket, *nouvelle cuisine* has inevitably caught on, with its usual attendance of minuscule helpings, astronomic prices, and segments of vegetable arranged artistically on the plate like Oriental flower-decorations. French chefs in France often cook brilliantly in the *nouvelle* manner: but German chefs manage far less well with this alien imported style, and the results can be embarrassing – in one smart place, I failed to appreciate duck with rhubarb, though the glossy diners around me seemed to be enjoying it. It is true that *Michelin* in 1991 awarded its top three-star rating to three restaurants in Germany, all more-or-less *nouvelle cuisine*, two in Munich, one in Düsseldorf. But Paul Bocuse has been less impressed: 'The Germans are superb at making Mercedes. But they didn't invent cooking, even though some of them think they did.'

Social climbers may be eager to be seen dining at Aubergine or Tantris in Munich; but ordinary middle-class Germans will settle modestly for the much cheaper but tasty cuisine of Italy, Spain, Greece, Yugoslavia and Turkey. These happen to be the countries providing almost all the *Gastarbeiter* (see pp. 273–90), who in their thousands have set up restaurants on German soil, as have the Chinese too. Variety is seldom matched by quality, but at least the choice is there; and in many city centres the foreign restaurants easily outnumber indigenous ones, just as in Britain. In Hamburg the range extends to West African, Argentinian, Indian, Japanese, Portuguese, Swedish, Syrian, Thai and Tunisian. The latest vogue is for multiple eateries, where cuisines co-habit: a German may open a big pub, say, and lease out the catering, with a trattoria in one room, a Greek taverna in another, a Chinese take-away in a third. Many of the simpler immigrant-run places serve mainly their own nationals, but other visitors are welcome too – so you can eat *donerkebabs* among Turks in Berlin's Kreuzberg, or squeeze between parties of Spaniards to enjoy *zarzuela*, or join Bosnian factory-workers with their *djuveč* or *čevapčiči*. Other restaurants cater for a mainly German clientele of diners-out, but with variable results, for the food is often Germanised to suit a local taste which alas still prefers its own mushy salads to a true *horiatiki*. Nor do I personally find it appetising to read a Greek menu in German: who fancies *moussaka* when it is called *Exotisches Gericht mit geschnetzelten Schweinsfiletspitzen überbacken*?

Seduced by this foreign invasion, the Germans during the 1960s and 1970s had been tending to spurn their own national restaurants, especially in the central and northern *Länder* which have little gastronomic tradition. But today there is a move back. The true German *Gaststätte* has become fashionable again, sometimes in a new and trendy style, with candlelight maybe, and pretty waitresses in *Tracht* – and in a northern city such as Hanover or Düsseldorf, an 'Altes Nürnberg' or 'Sieben Schwaben' restaurant migrated from the south appears almost as exotic and 'ethnic' as one from Naples or Piraeus! In a less contrived genre than this, too, all over Germany solid traditional eating-houses keep up reliable standards of German cooking – places like big *Ratskeller* to be found in the basement of many a town hall, or the wood-panelled *Stube* where locals gather to drink or play cards as well as to eat. Here it is possible to find inexpensive regional dishes which, if not very refined, are at least interesting – even in the north. Hamburg has its remarkable eel-plum-and-vegetable soup, its various ways with fresh herring, and also *Labskaus*, a sailors' dish eaten at sea, which is a mush of pickled corned beef, herring, potato, beetroot and fried egg – a taste acquired only slowly, I felt. In Berlin, surprisingly, you still find old rustic dishes such as *Hoppelpoppel*, a kind of *omelette paysanne* with potato and ham. In the Frankfurt area, an intriguing snack is *Handkäs mit Musik* – a soft and smelly local cheese, doused in white wine with chopped onions (these later produce the *Musik*, i.e. tummy-rumblings). And in the south the variety is considerable. Bavarians still go for hearty dishes such as suckling pig, roast knuckle of pork and spicy Nuremberg sausages, while in Swabia the cuisine is more subtle. Just as Bologna is the world capital of *pasta*, so Stuttgart calls itself *Spätzlemetropol*, homeland of those crinkly flour noodles that accompany so many Swabian meat dishes and are delicious when properly *hand-*

*gemacht*. Also ubiquitous in this region is *Maultaschen* ('mouth-pockets'), a kind of spinach-filled ravioli eaten usually in soup. I was told of one Stuttgart firm that exports both *Maultaschen* and *Spätzle* to France, of all places.

One particularly convenient feature of German taverns, pubs and restaurants is that almost all of them will serve you either a full meal, or just a snack or a drink, as you wish. Most pubs and wine-taverns provide a number of hot dishes; and only a very smart and fashionable restaurant will refuse a customer who wants just an hors d'oeuvre and a beer. This is common in central Europe, and it is related to the fact that the vast majority of the pleasanter German restaurants are accessible middle-price places, clean and efficient; the lower end of the market is not nearly as squalid as in class-divided Britain. Go to some local beauty spot, beside a lake or a river, or on a panoramic hilltop: in France, you will probably find a luxury restaurant, and in Britain either that or the other extreme, a cheap and squalid 'caff' for trippers, but in Germany it is much more likely to be something between the two – a comfortable democratic *Stube* with an outdoor terrace, where you can admire the view and eat a heavy meal or just a snack, in assorted company that might range from directors to dustmen, from genteel old dears in flower-hats to rough types with motorbikes. A professor and his *Putzfrau* use the same haunts. It is one of the most positive aspects of the new semi-classlessness of German society.

This democracy is equally evident in the beer-gardens, wine-taverns and *Kneipen* – but less so in the big Munich beer-cellars, which are mainly the preserve of workers and tourists, and have too high a decibel level for professors or flower-hatted oldies. Cologne has lively, quirky *Kneipen* where all classes rub shoulders (see p. 74), so does Berlin. In Munich, some of the beer-gardens are frequented by the *Schickeria*, but not exclusively so, and prices are the same as elsewhere; at others, such as the vast Chinesischer Turm in the Englischer Garten you see people of every kind, who come to flirt or debate, to listen to the brass bands, to enjoy elaborate picnics which they bring in hampers and spread out on the trestle tables.

In and around Stuttgart, the winter months are the season of the delightful *Besenwirtschaften* (broom-pubs): by old custom, vinegrowers in the area put a broom outside their houses in November, to signify that their new wine is ready, and until March or so they are permitted to use their premises as an impromptu pub, selling this vintage and no other drink. The practice has become somewhat commercialised, and many of the 150 or so *Besenwirtschaften* today seem little different from a normal tavern: but in some smaller ones you really do sit in rough farm buildings, in a matey ambience, drinking giant glasses of sweetish half-fermented wine at well below pub prices. At the Zaiss wine-farm in Untertürkheim, less than a mile from Daimler-Benz, we shared a table one Sunday afternoon with a boisterous quartet of artisans and their wives; at the table behind us, a well-dressed party from the Stuttgart *Schickeria* (such as it is) were celebrating a birthday.

German drinking habits have been changing since the war, owing to various factors that include rising affluence, concern for health, and stricter driving laws. Wine consumption has nearly quadrupled, from an annual 7 litres per head in 1960 to some 26 litres today: but the French and Italians both drink four times as much, and west Germany's wine production is only one-seventh of France's. Wine in Germany is not taxed, and in the shops it is cheap, with a bottle of simple table wine costing less than orange juice: you can buy some German *ordinaires* for 3 to 4 DM a litre in supermarkets. So why is wine consumption not greater? One explanation is that mark-ups in pubs and restaurants are very high. Also, the Germans tend to drink wine less heavily during a meal than the French, though they do go on sipping it afterwards. Their style of light and fruity white wines, Rieslings and Sylvaners, lends itself to this. So do the pale and sweetish reds of the Ahr and Neckar which I came to enjoy (the French think them barbarous).

Consumption of beer remains static at 143 litres per head per year. Just behind the Belgians, the Germans are the world's second leading beer drinkers in terms of per capita consumption – and they also drink it noisily and assertively. Dortmund is the world's second leading brewery town, and Munich the third: first, believe it or not, comes Milwaukee. Consumption of soft drinks has been increasing steadily, as might be expected, especially among young people (mineral water sales have more than trebled since 1972), while hard liquor drinking has declined slightly. Gin and Scotch whisky, drunk in moderation, are the smart drinks to offer guests in bourgeois homes. But by far the most popular alcoholic spirit in Germany is still Schnaps in its various forms, especially with the working-classes, and among farmers who brew it themselves on a large scale. It is the principal cause of alcoholism. If the drinking of this and other fire-waters is now pursued less recklessly, it is quite largely because the drink-and-drive rules have been tightened. Any motorist whose breathalyser test reveals more than 0.8 per cent of alcohol in the blood is likely to be found guilty and will lose his licence for a longish period. The laws are strictly applied and – with occasional exceptions – the Germans take care to respect them. At social functions, I found that those planning to drive home were noticeably more abstemious than in Britain.

## Assiduous tourists and crazy Cologne carnivalers

The Germans today are the world's greatest tourists – or so it would seem, if the statistics are any guide. Like the French, they have made the annual departure on holiday into a major obsession, to be looked forward to all the year and talked about incessantly. This restlessness is not new – after all, the German word *Wanderlust* has passed into the English language – but it has much increased with the new affluence. It may also mark a reaction against new urban tensions, and certainly it is a facet of the decline of the old German work-ethic and the rise of a new leisure ethic (see pp. 138–41).

All employees now have a legal right to at least three weeks' paid holiday a year, rising to five or even six weeks as they grow older. The proportion of all Germans taking an annual holiday away from home climbed from 24 per cent in 1954 to 56 per cent in 1985. This figure is slightly below those for the British (59 per cent) and the French (57 per cent), but it does not include the millions of spa-cure visitors, many of whom are really taking a disguised holiday (see pp. 233–6). Of those who stay at home, many are elderly people, especially widows, while others include the chronically sick and handicapped, the really poor, the unemployed, and a great many farmers. Also some quite well-to-do people today prefer to save up for a more expensive foreign trip every two or three years: 'This year,' the saying goes, 'we're taking our holiday *nicht auf dem Balkan sondern auf unserem Balkon*' (not in the Balkans but on our own balcony).

Among those Germans who do leave home on holiday, the most striking feature is that they travel to foreign countries in greater numbers than any other nation. The proportion of holidays spent abroad has risen from 15 per cent in 1954 to 66 per cent today, and this is the world record, eclipsing Britain's 39 per cent and Holland's 50 per cent. Since 1976, Germany has overtaken the United States (with four times the population) in its annual total of citizens travelling abroad as tourists. The Germans go above all to neighbouring Austria and to the Mediterranean, where Italy and Spain are the favoured venues, followed by France, Yugoslavia and Greece. Germans account for 70 per cent of all foreign tourists in Austria, and 43 per cent in Italy.

The reasons for this annual migration are not hard to identify, the main one being climatic and geographical. Germany is a smallish and rather densely populated industrial country, with a short coastline and other nations on every side: and this induces a slight feeling, if not of claustrophobia, at least of being hemmed in. There are some pleasant tourist areas in Germany, but little spectacular scenery; the climate is central European and the beaches all northerly. So no wonder the Germans look to the sunny south. There may also be an element of desiring an annual escape from a land of unhappy memories that is still rather disciplined and conformist. And another factor is that holidays have now become a kind of status-symbol, like dressing elegantly or owing a smart car, at least in the bourgeoisie and the new-rich working-classes. Neighbours and new acquaintances will categorise you by the kind of holiday you take. To stay in Germany is to be thought very provincial (unless maybe you go to the island of Sylt, see p. 222). To go each year to the same little house in Tuscany or Sweden is to be judged sympathetic, individual, but maybe boring. If you go to the Bahamas, or on a Kenya safari, you are interesting, but pretentious.

Two distinct trends in foreign holidays have been developing: the gregarious, typified by the Mediterranean package tour, and the individual and adventurous. Most Germans may be sheepish in their holiday habits. But by contrast a growing minority are much more spontaneous, non-conformist and enterprising, ready to seek out remote or far-flung corners on their own. They include not just the rich who jet off to Nepal or Yucatán, but all kinds of student types or young ecologists who will camp and hitch-hike or drive old jeeps up mountain tracks. These are the new German globe-trotters, more numerous than in any other European nation, and you find them everywhere — exploring the upper reaches of the Nile, following the reindeer tracks of Lapps near the Arctic Circle, or camping beside a lonely Greek mountain temple to watch the dawn break. They are serious, civilised and curious, anxious to come to terms with foreign cultures.

In between this and the other extreme, there are still a fair number of older, more conventional culture-tourists, the kind who dutifully go around Burgos cathedral, Baedeker in hand. But the great majority of Germans go abroad to relax, to sunbathe, and to have fun, and they show little curiosity about the country they are visiting. This is partly a matter of social class (see p. 175). These gregarious people, many of them working-class, prefer to stay in big groups – and preferably German groups, not so much out of national feeling as because they want to feel secure and understood, and to carry a familiar environment with them to a strange land. So the package-tour, in a hotel geared to German needs, suits them ideally. Or even if they travel on their own, in a car with a caravan, they will still make for the camping-sites where they can find plenty of other 'D' plates. In the big resorts along the Mediterranean, led by Rimini, Benidorm and Palma, a whole mass industry has grown up to cater for the German package-tourist: here you find whole streets full of cheap restaurants with menus in German, offering *Bratwurst, Eisbein* and other such comforting dishes; and bars and *Stuben* run by Willi und Heidi, providing *Echte deutsche Stimmung* for the cohorts of other Willis and Heidis from Würzburg or Wuppertal.

These are the holidaymakers who in the 1950s and 1960s began to give Germans abroad so bad a reputation. They came to be seen as *more* rude, nude, lewd and crude than any others, and noisier too, with their boisterous singing in the streets at night and their brash disregard for local habits and susceptibilities. The very same Germans who at home were so mild and orderly seemed, once on foreign soil, to become creatures possessed. Maybe it was a normal holiday reaction against so much discipline; or, as one social analyst in Munich suggested to me: 'The German abroad believes that with his package-tour fee he has also bought himself the right to behave as he likes; and if the Latins or Greeks are untidy, loud and disorganised, why shouldn't he be so too? Being released from the laws and regulations and neighbours' intolerances that keep him so orderly at home, he feels himself to be on holiday from social responsibility. So he runs wild.' But German politicians and opinion-makers became worried at this national image: one writer, Gerhard Nebel, described southern beaches as 'an inferno of brown-baked, probably drunken, entangled flesh, fat buttocks and floppy breasts'. And for a few years the Federal Government even issued 'Golden Rules' for good behaviour with all new passports. Those leaflets included the advice: 'Don't deny the fact that your parentage is German, but see to it that the foreigner is pleased and surprised by it. If you are of the foolish opinion that everything outside Germany is worse, stay at home.' Whether or not these pompous admonitions had any effect, the situation does seem to have improved since the 1970s. Ordinary Germans have become more used to the unsettling novelty of foreign venues and have grown more at ease there. Whether or not foreign holidays of this kind really reduce chauvinism and promote mutual understanding remains a moot point. But if Greeks, Spaniards and other southern *Gastarbeiter* are today finding social acceptance more easily in Germany than 20 years ago (see p. 277), it may be partly because so many Germans have now visited their homelands and seen that they are not simply barbarians.

Middle-class Germans of the more conventional kind, if they go farther afield in a group, or on one of the club-holidays now so popular, will always expect good German comforts. Hence the success of the Frankfurt-based Club Robinson, which operates twenty quite luxurious club-hotels around the Mediterranean and as far afield as Brazil and Sri Lanka, catering for an 85 per cent German and Austrian clientèle. Johann-Friedrich Engel, the lawyer who runs this somewhat uninspired organisation, told me that it is *not* a copy of the Club Méditerranée, even if it has taken over a few of Le Club's best-known features such as bead-necklaces for money and shared dining-tables of eight. Club Robinson lacks the inventive flair and zany nonchalance of the wonderful and unique French club (see my *France Today*, pp. 404–15): it is more sedate, for that is what the guests expect, and more conformist and cliquey. At Club Med, everyone mixes freely at the tables of eight and a solitary newcomer is made welcome; at Robinson, a group appropriates a table and spurns strangers. The Germans do frequent the Club Méditerranée itself, in some numbers, where according to my own experience they keep a discreetly low profile, probably overawed by those exuberant Gallic types. The main complaint against them is that, sedulously *sportif*, they get up earlier than the French and others and monopolise all the best windsurfers, tennis-courts and other equipment.

Unlike the French, the Germans since the war have not innovated and pioneered with new holiday formulae. One invention of a sort however is the so-called 'coffin-bus', devised by a Bavarian firm, Rotel Tours. These giant touring caravans are trailers affixed to trucks, and they sleep 50 people, slotted in like sardines with just a few free inches above their heads. They have communal cooking and washing facilities aboard, and they tour as far as India or Morocco, taking German tinned food with them. Bar hitch-hiking, it is much the cheapest way of visiting these distant lands; and the tours are popular even with octogenarians, who find the cramped conditions quite cosy and chummy in their way. There has been a fair boom in other types of organised adventure travel too, for those who want unusual forms of travel to exotic destinations without having to fend for themselves. Firms offer jeep treks to the Sahara; safaris in Kenya; sleighing in Lapland; romantic trots round Ireland in gipsy caravans; or, a speciality for the jaded businessman, in-depth visits to the sex-haunts of Bangkok that may yield the added bonus of finding a Thai wife to bring back home. One sociologist assured me: 'The monotony and lack of challenge in German daily life make all these outlets popular.' Especially the last.

A holiday inside Germany earns less prestige, save at one or two of the Bavarian alpine resorts in winter, or on Sylt in summer. This long, flat island off the north-west coast, near Denmark, has a windy but highly invigorating climate and has been a fashionable resort since the last century; Thomas Mann and Marlene Dietrich used to holiday here. Today much of it is quite down-market, full of camping-sites. But in the 1960s the area round the village of Kampen became 'the St-Tropez of the North', a showy rendezvous for the *Schickeria* of fashion, business and the media. Playboy sons of tycoons came in Porsches with blonde starlets, they danced on the tables after midnight, the young Günther Sachs was much in evidence, and the champagne frothed higher even than the waves on the wind-torn beaches. Today much of that glamour has gone, for times have changed and the movie stars and the titled jet-set prefer warmer southern climes. But Kampen is still chic in its self-conscious way, full of fancy night-clubs and boutiques bearing such names as Cartier and Cardin. In a more sedate genre, Sylt is also the summer holiday venue of many senior and highly-respected German politicians, bankers and journalists, among them President von Weiz-säcker, Bertholdt Beitz the chairman of Krupp, and Rudolf Augstein the publisher of *Spiegel*. In this nation with no single major capital city (even today), Sylt in a way has provided a national focus where top people could meet and talk privately in a relaxed setting (and who wants to meet in Bonn, if he can help it?). Maybe Sylt has played the role, sometimes claimed also by Frankfurt and Munich, of being Germany's 'secret capital'. It is famous, too, for its nudist beaches.

More ordinary folk go to other north coast beaches and islands (the Baltic resorts of the former GDR, such as Warnemünde and Hiddensee, are set to become popular again with Berliners and westerners); or they hike in the Black Forest or the Alpine foothills; or they bathe and boat at the Bodensee or other lakes. The resorts of hilly south Germany are crammed with elderly keep-fit walkers, firm or frail, and here tourism blends with the spa-cure trade. Though most Germans may just want to relax and enjoy life, a sizeable minority also seek a holiday that does you good; hence the development of active and creative holidays. You can go on summer courses in villages to learn handicrafts or painting, harp-playing or calligraphy. Or you can stay on a farm: many farmers have converted their outhouses or disused cottages into holiday villas for tourists, who if they wish can lend a hand at the milking or haymaking, or can learn how to make cheese or keep bees. The vogue for these farm holidays is growing, but it is less pronounced than in France where rural traditions are much stronger.

Or of course you can go on a sporting holiday – as many do. Outdoor exercise has become something of a cult, and energetic sports with a keep-fit rationale have increased in popularity: a near-static game like *boules* or cricket would be less likely to interest the Germans. Today one citizen in three belongs to a sports club: the football federation has 4.3 million members, followed by gymnastics (3.1 million) and tennis (1.2 million). Once the preserve of the upper classes, tennis-playing has now spread widely, and it was given an added boost in 1985 when Boris Becker, the 17-year-old wonder from Leimen, near Heidelberg, became the first German ever to win the men's singles at Wimbledon. The young Steffi Graff and Michael Stich have since won equal glory. But, if the Germans love their sporting heroes, even more they love their peace and quiet, and one tennis hazard is that the ping and pong of balls in residential areas can provoke that most frightening of German phenomena, the wrath of intolerant neighbours. Some tennis-clubs have even been sued for breaking the peace: in Berlin, one resident sued a club of which he was himself a member! So it may be safer to play an indoor game like squash, today popular even with the Ruhr miners. Some 65 per cent of Germans go swimming, while 14 per cent make for the ski-slopes, mainly in the Alps. Horse-riding has come into vogue too – so much so that horses are again being bred in some numbers. In the 1950s, during the period of rapid farm mechanisation, the equine population was starting to decline: but now it is back to above its pre-1939 level.

In the 1960s and 1970s, federal, *Land* and local governments poured large sums into providing new leisure amenities, so that today nearly every little town has its public swimming-pool and sports centre. There is still rather little organised sport in state schools: but children and young people find plenty of scope for it in their leisure time. In the West, young Germans were never pressured into sports training as they were in the East (see p. 378), and this explains why the Federal

Republic's record in international competitions was less spectacular than that of the GDR. None the less, it has done well. When the Olympic Games were held on its own home ground, in Munich in 1972, it came fourth in the medal table, with thirteen golds, and then again fourth at Montreal in 1976, with ten golds. Los Angeles in 1984, when the Russians and East Germans were not competing, it came third, with seventeen golds. And in Seoul in 1988 it came fifth with eleven golds. West Germany has also shone at football, and its team's record over the past twenty years has been the best of any European country: it won the World Cup twice (in Munich in 1974, then in Rome in 1990;) it reached the final at Wembley in 1966 (defeated by England), in Madrid in 1982 (defeated by Italy) and again in Mexico in 1986 (defeated by Argentina). Football is by far the most popular competitive sport in Germany, alike for spectators and participants, and star players past and present such as Franz Beckenbauer have become major national idols. Idolatry has also engulfed champion boxers and athletes: and it reached a high tide of frenzy when the media turned the floodlights on young Becker after his Wimbledon victory, causing the moralistic *Die Zeit* to ask worriedly whether the Germans were not in danger of rediscovering a Führer-style cult of personality. This of course is nonsense. In any country, sport provides a focus for national feeling, sometimes hysterical and excessive but at least better than making war; and in Germany today it offers a fairly harmless channel for the tentative rediscovery of a national spirit and a sense of identity. At least German football fans abroad do not go lethally berserk.

As with sport, so Germany's innumerable festivals and pageants, religious and secular, and its rich life of traditional clubs and associations, are also playing some role in helping to heal the psychological wounds of the Nazi period – not so much by promoting national feeling as through a strengthening of local patriotism and a reaffirming of old innocent traditions not soured by politics. Especially this is noticeable in the pre-Lenten carnivals. But first a word about the *Vereine* (clubs and associations), which play so important a role in local social life and in many cases have deep historical roots. Germany has 14,500 choral societies, with over 1.5 million members, as well as clubs for every kind of hobby such as rabbit-breeding or pigeon-racing. Everywhere in small towns and rural areas you find *Schützenvereine* (rifle clubs), often centuries old, each with its own banners, badges, uniforms, and ceremonial meetings that preserve something of the atmosphere of a medieval guild. As the *Time-Life* book on Germany puts it, 'There is no doubt that members spend more time lifting their beer-glasses than their rifles' – but they do manage to hold an annual shooting tournament too. In Bavaria, each town and village has its *Trachtenverein*, devoted to the wearing of local traditional costumes: its annual festival is often held in a big beer-tent where the Catholic Church plays a key part: there is beer drinking, then a religious service in the same tent, then more beer, and folk-dancing.

The German fondness for keeping up the old family customs and rituals shows itself at the time of the major Christian festivals. The warmly emotional family Christmas has long been a German forte,[1] and today the Germans still make much more fuss of Christmas than the British or French – even if a commercial spirit is sometimes more apparent than a truly religious one. Various little ceremonies mark the Christmas period, starting with the Advent Wreath of decorated fir branches that bears four red or gold candles, one of them lit for each Sunday of Advent. Most families still place this wreath in their homes every Advent, and a great many offices, shops and hotels display one too. Then at Christmas itself, whether or not a family has children, it is much more likely than in Britain to deck out its home with holly, tinsel, stars and candles, a Christmas tree and maybe a crib: the big outdoor *Christkindlmarkt* (Christmas-present market), held in the squares of many towns, give an idea of the vast range of kitschy trinkets on sale for the occasion. Then during the year there are other rituals too, some purely secular. If you build a house, when the roof is put on you must be sure to hold a *Richtfest* (roof-topping ceremony), which means a party for friends, neighbours and above all the building workers, and the affixing of a little tree to the summit.

The main public festivals tend to centre round wine-making and the brewing of beer. More than enough has already been written by others about the world's greatest beer festival, Munich's *Oktoberfest*, which dates from 1810 and is held every year in tents on the Theresien meadow at the foot of a 60-foot statue of the goddess Bavaria. During its sixteen days, locals and tourists consume some 40 spit-roast oxen and 500,000 barbecued chickens, and they down 4.5 million litres of beer, brought to them by the famous beer-hall waitresses trained to carry up to eight litre tankards at a time. Even Münchner who feign to

1. An Allensbach survey that put the question, 'What in life is most sacred to you?' found that 'Christmas in the family' came top of all the answers, ahead even of such things as 'Being able to live in a free society'.

scorn the *Oktoberfest* nonetheless go along as a matter of ritual. And many adore it. I knew one modest landlady who would save up for it each year, then go on her own every single day, make chums at the trestle-tables, and come home roaring drunk each night.

Some other towns have their own more muted versions of this kind of festival. Staid Stuttgart puts on its Volksfest, also local in origin, founded in 1840 by the King of Württemberg as a kind of harvest festival. Here the prudent Swabians keep their end up against Munich by consuming a respectable 1.5 million litres of local beer and 300,000 chickens; they sing the usual German songs swaying to and fro with arms linked, they visit the scores of garish side-shows, and spend more money on fun than they would dare to do in the rest of the year. But they have had to sink their pride and borrow from the Bavarians the accoutrements of jollity and folksiness, for lack of suitable ones of their own. The men, from Mayor Rommel downwards, wear pointed green Bavarian hats with feathers and grey Bavarian tunics; the waitresses are in Bavarian dirndls and high-busted white puffy bodices; the musicians of the beer-tent orchestras, clad of course in lederhosen, are mostly imported from Bavaria for the occasion.

German organised merriment finds its keenest expression in the big pre-Lenten carnivals, known as *Karneval* in the Rhineland, *Fastnacht* or *Fasnet* in south-west Germany, and *Fasching* in Bavaria. These carnivals are believed to have originated as pre-Christian pagan fertility rites, heralding the return of spring. Later they became more or less Christianised, in the sense that the Church sanctioned them as safety-valves of naughtiness before the serious business of Lent. Today they are pagan again — that is, rather commercialised, though the spirit of fun is very real. They are confined mainly to the Catholic parts of Germany. In the Rhine area, the main carnivals are at Mainz, Aachen, Bonn, Düsseldorf — and of course Cologne, the biggest and zaniest. (In 1991, when the Gulf War broke out, the main Rhineland carnival festivities were all cancelled, partly because of the danger of terrorist attacks on the huge milling crowds, also because it was thought such wild jollity would be in bad taste.)

'He's got the loveliest legs in Cologne, hasn't he?' said the Socialist Lord Mayor, presenting to the crowds *'Seine Tollität'* (His Craziness) the Carnival Prince, Karl-Josef Kappes, a grinning, rather camp figure in red-white-and-gold doublet-and-hose, in real life a choirmaster. Beside him on the podium stood the two other 'Stars' who rule the city during

*Karneval* – the Peasant (Reiner Toller, owner of a refuse-collecting firm) in a tall white hat with peacock plumes; and the Virgin (Fritz Voss, car varnisher), a 66-year-old in blond plaits. The Carnival Virgin has always been a man – save for a while under the Nazis, who hated transvestism.

The 'Three Stars' are elected each October from among the members of Cologne's 105 historic carnival associations. Mostly they are small businessmen – and competition to be a Star is intense, for the honour and publicity are considered good for trade, even though a Star must devote ten full weeks to his duties and dig deep into his own pocket; he pays for his costume, for the tons of toffees he hurls at the crowd during the Rose-Monday parade, and for gifts for the mayor: the Stars of 1985 gave him three grizzly bears for the city zoo, as the *Karneval* theme of the year was 'Going to the Zoo'.

The city council itself also spends some million DM on *Karneval* – to the growing fury of some intellectuals who call it a waste of public funds in a time of high unemployment (14 per cent locally) and say the money should go to job creation schemes. But their outcry makes little impact, for Kölner in their mass, young and old, still adore their carnival and treat its zany jollity with true Germanic seriousness and thoroughness. 'Whoever is not foolish at *Karneval* is foolish for the rest of the year,' is a local saying. The carnival's two elements fuse together: there is the official organised *Karneval* of parades and ceremonies, very much a local Establishment affair; and also the big popular booze-up-love-in-and-laugh-in, a true mass-participation event, closer in spirit to Notting Hill than to over-commercialised Nice. It is a pre-Lent explosion of street-parties and pub-parties, of affable crowds in mad costumes and painted clown-faces. Even the dogs wear carnival cloaks and hats.

The Kölner's intense self-loving city-patriotism (see p. 74), the equal of any in Italy, finds its supreme expression in *Karneval*. And so does their peculiar spirit of jokey whimsy. This goes on all the year: but as Lent approaches it reaches fever-pitch, as the local radio blares out non-stop the *Karneval* songs in Cologne dialect that every citizen knows – for example, '*Mer losse d'r Dom en Kölle*' (i.e., 'let's leave the Cathedral in Cologne and not exchange it for the Eiffel Tower or the Pentagon'). So much of the fun-making is in local dialect, with local in-references, that a visitor to 'Kölle' is bound to miss much of the point – and be spared a thousand bad puns.

The fun starts on the Elfte Elfte Elfte Elfte, i.e. 11.11 a.m. on

November 11. It continues in lower key for three months, to reach its climax in the *Tolle Tage* ('Crazy Days') before Lent. Thursday is *Weiberfastnacht* or women's day, when the fair sex, long excluded from *Karneval* in the nineteenth century, take control and exact revenge by cutting off the tie of any male within reach (very Freudian?). Then on Sunday there is a big informal procession by school and suburban groups usually including topical anti-Government floats; and on Monday comes the main procession with a million lining the route. There is much pelting with cheap horrid toffees, bought in bulk in eastern Germany (and singing of toffee songs); pirouetting by the acrobatic Mariechen (sort of majorettes); and comic uniforms. The Prince's royal bodyguard, in early nineteenth-century soldiers' uniforms, symbolise Cologne's anti-militarist tradition by sticking flowers in their rifle-barrels and carefully disobeying orders, e.g. turning left when ordered right. These anti-Prussian antics date from 1823 when the modern *Karneval* was created: Germany's more recent history gives them an added ironic twist today.

The entire carnival seemed to me revealing of present-day Germans' ambivalent attitudes to wearing uniforms. At the big parades and costume-balls there were citizens in every kind of attire – Attila-the-Hun groups in hairy hides and horned helmets; charming pierrots and harlequins; people dressed as animals, or as fruit; clowns clad in coloured woolly balls; a few Turks and sheikhs, even a British policeman – but not a single twentieth-century German uniform. The Germans still adore dressing up en masse, but they remain wary – thank God! – of putting on anything modern and military.

The best carnival parties are private. But the big costume-balls are open to the public and not too costly. We went to one in the Gürzenich, a vast Renaissance civic building holding some 5,000 people, with five live orchestras in different halls. It was all very good-humoured and traditional, relatively tasteful and undrunken, with less rowdy vulgarity than you often find at such an event in Britain. It seemed to me a harmless outlet for the German passion for songful togetherness, and a safety-valve antidote to hard work and *Ordnung* during the rest of the year. All those neat, serious bank-clerks go wild in motley for a few days, then on Ash Wednesday are back at their desks, bleary-eyed but neat and serious again. 'Love me for Three Crazy Days' is one old carnival song – and is it not true that adultery during *Karneval* has never been grounds for divorce?

It is much the same in other Catholic areas with other carnival traditions. In Munich, *Fasching* is presided over not by three middle-aged tradesmen but by a good-looking younger couple, 'Prinz' and 'Prinzessin', chosen usually from the wealthy bourgeoisie. Munich's carnival is more stylish and sophisticated, less rowdy and facetious than Cologne's, and less overwhelmingly unavoidable: you can even stay quietly at home, or walk out in ordinary clothes, without being thought quite stupidly sane. At Elzach in the Black Forest, masked fools dressed in red with large decorated hats run through the town beating people with blown-up hog's bladders. At nearby Rottweil, rival groups of fools jump through the town's Black Gate at 8 a.m. At Wolfach, fools stroll around in nightgowns and night-caps; at Überlingen on the Bodensee they crack long whips.

The entire razzle-dazzle of *Karneval/Fastnacht/Fasching* is a ritual today sedulously and lovingly kept up by this anxious nation seeking its identity and concerned to restore its broken links with past tradition. These traditions are variegated and local, rather than national, and they have little to do with 'Germany' as such, so this makes carnival rather different from, say, the Quatorze Juillet or even Guy Fawkes' night. One advantage of it, surely, is that in its very mindlessness and silliness it has not been tainted by politics, nationalism or ideology. So it has survived intact the national nightmare. After all, the Nazis never approved of it: first they banned it for a while, then censored it.

## *The spa romance – by courtesy of a lavish health insurance system*

West Germany's social security system is one of the oldest of its kind in the world and has long been one of the most progressive too. It was founded by Bismarck, in 1881, to meet the needs of workers at a time of rapid industrialisation; and since then it has been developed steadily, especially in the years after 1945. Today it looks impressive. It is lavishly funded by obligatory contributions – too lavishly, some right-wing critics argue, though this does enable hospitals and surgeries to be very well equipped and staffed. The medical services thus work far better than under the penny-pinching British system. The prosperous Germans get excellent free health care – but indirectly it costs them a lot.

Health insurance is compulsory for all employed and self-employed people and their dependants. Under this system, you must belong to one of a range of statutory but semi-autonomous insurance agencies (*Krankenkassen*), or in some cases you can opt for a private one. By law each employee gives his agency 6.3 per cent of his income, and his employer adds a similar amount. The system is socially fairer than in Britain, for contributions are related to earnings; the poor pay less, but they get the same service. A patient is treated entirely free of charge (save that he pays 2 DM per prescription, and sometimes for 'extras' such as new spectacles), and the doctor or hospital then invoices the agency, under a fixed scale of charges. So in Germany there is national insurance but not really a national health service, for the doctors – and many hospitals – function free of any central control. Their position is more like that of a private garage which is paid direct by an insurance firm for car repairs after an accident. It does involve a great deal of form-filling.

Some 85 per cent of hospitals are run by the cities and *Länder*, while 14 per cent belong to the Churches (see p. 264) and other non-profit-making bodies. They charge the agencies per diem for each insured patient's stay, under an agreed scale that varies according to their level of equipment and averages 350 to 400 DM per day. So the hospitals have an incentive to advise convalescents to stay on as long as possible – so unlike the situation in Britain, where the overcrowded and under-funded hospitals will often bundle a patient back home before he is really well. Until the early 1970s, some German hospitals too were over-filled and often there were waiting-lists for operations. But this has since been remedied by a handsome increase in federal grants. The satisfactory record of German hospitals has been borne out by an Allensbach poll in 1987 that found 53 per cent of its respondents regarding them as 'good', while only 4 per cent felt them to be 'poor'.

General practitioners, dentists, and other doctors not on hospital staffs work as an entirely free profession, like lawyers or architects. A patient can choose his GP freely, so the doctors are in open competition for custom and the bad ones simply go out of business. Doctors charge the agencies for each consultation, including the use of their surgery equipment and supply of medicines, and occasionally this has led to abuses: a team of young GPs in the Ruhr were prosecuted for sending fake invoices to the agencies, and this led two of them to commit suicide. But mostly the system is honestly applied; and so generous is the permitted scale of fees that a good doctor can always earn a lot of money, especially a surgeon or other specialist. These '*Götter in Weiss*' (gods in white) are among the wealthiest members of the post-war German plutocracy.

Medicine has therefore become a very popular profession. It has begun to attract young careerists greedy for money, the kind who might otherwise go into business or banking, rather than old-style hippocratic idealists with a true sense of vocation — and this trend dismays many older doctors. Students flocked into the medical faculties during the boom years; and Germany has now one of the world's highest doctor/population ratios, 3 per 1,000 people compared with 1.7 in Britain and 1.8 in the United States (but 3.6 in Italy). It is true that German doctors are still too few in some remoter rural areas, where Turkish, Indian or other Asian GPs often make up the numbers; but, in the cities, doctors crowd thickly and Munich is said to have the world's highest density of paediatricians. This increase in competition has alarmed the profession, and in the late 1960s was one of the main factors that led it to induce the Government to set up a *numerus clausus* for entry to medical faculties.[1] This has since helped to slow the flood of recruits; but it did nothing to assuage the growing public feeling that doctors were *too* well paid. Then in the early 1980s a campaign by the media cast a spotlight on the huge incomes being amassed by surgeons and other specialists, who for relatively little work were able to charge the insurance agencies extravagant sums for the use of their modern equipment. Under this pressure, the medical profession finally agreed to accept some cutbacks in their scale of consultancy fees. Even so, they still do very nicely.

As in some other European countries, the social security system as a whole has recently come under growing criticism, for being too expensive and comprehensive. The Germans, more than most, have since the war built up their Welfare State into a vast protective blanket that anti-Socialists now feel has become too costly a luxury as well as a threat to the spirit of individual self-reliance. Until recently, overall spending on social security was rising much faster than national revenue: whereas in 1960 it had amounted to only 16 per cent of GNP, by 1982 the figure had risen to 32 per cent. About one-third of this sum now goes on health and the rest on other benefits, mainly old-age pensions, which are unusually generous. The health legislation guarantees an employee six weeks' sick leave a year on full pay; after

1. Pressure on laboratory space was the other factor: see page 250.

this, he or she can claim sickness benefits from health insurance for up to 78 weeks. The Germans readily make use of these and other advantages. According to one estimate, the number of pills prescribed by doctors has risen ninefold since 1968.

In line with its overall drive to limit public spending, the Government has made a few modest cuts in welfare budgets since 1982. Unemployment benefits have been reduced and the rate of pension increases slowed – but only very gently. Though the Kohl Government has been ideologically in favour of budgetary economies, the CDU and CSU both have a strong tradition of social action, espoused by influential party pressure-groups, and this has deterred Kohl and his monetarist hawks from taking any drastic steps to dismantle the welfare state. Nonetheless, a body of opinion on the right of those parties has been arguing, with some indignation, first that the high social charges are an obstacle to German industry's international competitiveness, and secondly that too much cosseting by welfare services (notably under Social Democrats in the 1970s) has been tending to make the Germans grow soft, over-dependent, and less ready to take risks or work hard. This lobby points to the ease with which anyone with the slightest physical handicap or sickness record can get himself registered as 'disabled' and thus receive special benefits. It is a familiar debate: is it good for people to be mollycoddled by the State in this way, as happened so blatantly under Communism in the GDR?

That humorist, Manfred Rommel, Lord Mayor of Stuttgart, gave me his own account of how he personally had dealt with the overcosseting of one special section of society: tramps. 'In the early 1980s, this city was the German capital of tramps. We attracted them from all over the country because of our positive welfare policy: we believed that the tramp problem would not be solved by neglecting them, so we gave them money each day, and free meals and flats. Stuttgart became a tramps' paradise. We hoped that other towns would follow our noble example: but all they did was export their tramps to us. Police in other *Länder* even dumped them on us. We had up to 3,000 at a time, and our lovely Schlossgarten was full of them – not a pretty sight. When the EC Heads of Government held their summit here at the Neues Schloss in 1983, I was so afraid of the bad impression the tramps would cause that I had them taken in buses thirty kilometres out of the city – and they had to walk back. Later, I finally decided to clamp down on the tramps. But this brought me into conflict with my left-wing social workers, who were trying to motivate them politically. They tried to get them to demonstrate against me, but the poor creatures were mostly too drunk to cooperate. The following winter, we transferred the tramps from flats to wooden huts and we reduced the quality of their free meals. They were so angry at this that many of them left the city; word then soon got around the tramp world that Stuttgart had ceased to be utopia, so others stopped coming. Today we have fewer tramps, but we still try to re-socialise those that remain. Many of them are young drop-outs who can't stand the competition of jobs — tragic cases.'

The recent cuts in public health spending have fallen especially on the German passion for spa-going, thus spelling trouble for scores of resorts. The Germans are the world's most inveterate spa-cure addicts. It is an old tradition, dating back long before the days when Goethe took the waters at Marienbad in Bohemia; and, whereas in those times it was the privilege of an elite, today the practice has spread down to all classes. By 1981, over six million Germans a year were attending spas, many of them on social security; and they accounted for more than half of the domestic tourist trade. It has all become very big business. The hilly parts of central and southern Germany are fertile in mineral waters and allegedly therapeutic mud; and here over 200 resorts are officially designated as health spas, ranging from regal Baden-Baden to obscure villages. Nearly all of them add the prefix *'Bad'* to their name. Here *eine Kur* is taken by people of all kinds, most of them middle-aged or elderly, who come in search of rejuvenation, or the relief of some ailment, or just for a free rest and holiday in the *Kurort* (spa). These *Kurgäste* (they are never called patients) are put under the care of a *Kurarzt* (doctor) who prescribes their *Kurtherapie* and *Kurdiät*; they take walks in the neatly landscaped *Kurpark*, and in the evenings maybe they attend a *Kurkonzert* arranged by the *Kurverwaltung* (spa authorities) or even go dancing in the *Kurhaus* and perhaps enjoy a *Kurschatten* (spa romance).

Why is the spa habit so widespread in Germany? Maybe it is related to the new perfectionist keep-fit vogue, an antidote to post-war heavy eating; or to the fact that so many spas lie amid pleasant holiday scenery, such as the Black Forest, and not on a dullish plain like Vichy or Cheltenham. But the massive post-war growth of spa-going has above all been stimulated by an indulgent health insurance system; and Germany's new semi-classless society has readily seized this chance to behave like the monarchs of old. Until 1982, when the cuts began, it was all so easy. You went to your local GP, complaining, say, of rheumatism, or catarrh, or bad circulation, and he would send a recommendation to your insurance agency, whose own doctor would then inspect you and authorise the cure: the agency would then select the date and the place. Cures were granted very readily, often on the scantest medical evidence, so that many people were in effect getting a free holiday of three or four weeks – and employers were not always too pleased. There were frequent abuses. I heard of a Munich postman, always healthy and sport-loving, whose status as civil servant entitled him to a free cure every two years, once he was past fifty. And he took it. But his wife, a hard-working charlady, had no such rights and was not allowed to accompany him. She died of cancer.

The mounting deficits of the insurance agencies led to pressure on Bonn to take action; and the Schmidt Government, though itself very welfare-minded, finally did so in 1982. Under the law it enacted, subsidised cures are now allowed only every three years, except for the really ill, and *Kurgäste* must themselves contribute 10 DM a day. Doctors are now stricter about proposing cures. As a result, trade slumped badly in the more down-market spas that depend mainly on paid-for clients. Bad Soden, a big popular place near Frankfurt where 95 per cent of the beds were in agency hands, lost over half of its guests. Some spas have tried to compensate by jazzing up their image, in a bid to attract other kinds of visitors too: they have laid on discos and pop concerts and distributed sexy posters, 'Come to fun-packed Bad Mergentheim'. This has not worked too well, for a younger clientèle would rather have fun on an Italian beach than in a sodden Bad Soden still noticeably geriatric. Some spas today have had to reduce their facilities and lay off staff; others still manage to do well, by appealing to the congress trade, or by persuading their regular clients to fork out of their own pockets. In this they seem to have succeeded for, after its initial 1982–83 slump, by 1984 the annual total of *Kurgäste* was again over the 6 million mark, even if they were now staying on average only 13.9 days instead of 15.5. The Germans still believe that a spa cure is something they cannot forgo.

But what is the real value of the treatment? The war-weary Roman legions were the first to use it, and they found it soothing. Today, most British and American doctors pour scorn on the myth of a spa's healing waters, and claim that you can get the same benefit by staying at home in a warm bath. I have met plenty of German doctors who share this view, though they put it in better perspective – as did one GP I talked to in Bonn: 'In the old days, the waters were certainly valuable in the treatment of many diseases, through bathing, drinking and inhaling. But modern drugs have rendered this completely out of date, in the case of kidney ailments, arthritis and many other complaints, even rheumatism. So why use the spas? Well, the installations are there: and most people *believe* that the treatment does them good, so probably it does. The value is 90 per cent psychological. The spas are like health farms. But the exercise in warm water probably *is* of some use.' The spa doctors themselves are naturally more enthusiastic. They praise in particular the new Japanese ice-shock treatment, and the taking of baths in hot mud made of powdered volcanic stone.

A *Kurgast* usually takes his cure very seriously and will sedulously obey the spa doctor's instructions on exactly how many glasses of local mineral water to drink per day, or how many kilometres of exercise to take. If he is on social security, he will be assigned to a hotel, or more probably to a sanatorium, most of which are owned or rented by the insurance agencies. In the older sanatoria, he or she may well have to share a room with a stranger of the same sex. The new ones have single rooms — and quite luxurious these places are too, with sun-lounges, swimming-pools, thick carpets, and none of the tawdry institutional ambience of an English public hospital. At a sanatorium in Badenweiler, I met a rheumatic sexagenarian nun who showed me her lovely room with telephone, separate bathroom and panoramic balcony, and she was paying merely her 10 DM a day. The cost to the agency, including treatment and medical charges, is generally some 1,300 to 1,600 DM a week.

The routine is quite strict. Up at 6 a.m., exercise and massage, then an hour's walk, then treatment at the baths, then after lunch a two-hour rest in bed, then more treatment, then maybe a stroll into town for shopping or coffee. This is where trouble can begin, for many a *Kurgast*'s disciplined obedience breaks down at the sight of creamy cakes or a jolly beer-parlour — and nearly all cures include a strict diet with *no* alcohol. Especially is this a problem in spas frequented by bibulous factory workers. Often a spa doctor has to write to a wayward guest, 'If you're caught at it again, you'll be sent home', and to remind him of a federal law that protects the agencies against any such abuse of their largesse. In the evenings, the scope for sinfulness is less great, since most sanatoria oblige their guests to be back home and in bed by 10 or 10.30 p.m. So most spas tend to be dull places at night; they put on a few concerts and film shows, but most attempts to start up night-clubs soon fail. Not that this worries many of the *Kurgäste*, whose average age is about 60. These veterans do however go in for a certain amount of late-flowering romance. One important rule of cures is that you must not bring your spouse with you, not so much for economic reasons as because a complete break with home surroundings is part of the treatment: a *Kurgast*'s ailment is often diagnosed as psychosomatic, induced by family tensions. So here are all these delightful not-so-young people from modest backgrounds, separated from their beloveds perhaps for the first time in decades. The *Kurschatten* (spa romance) is as common a German phenomenon as the shipboard flirtation used to be on Cunard liners. The divorce lawyers are familiar with it.

At the grander spas, most of the *Kurgäste* are private. Of Baden-Baden's 200,000 annual overnight visitors, two-thirds come for congresses or ordinary holidays and only a third for cures, and of these less than 30 per cent are paid for by social security. So this queen of health resorts has not been much affected by the cutbacks. Inevitably it has declined from its nineteenth-century heyday as the summer capital of Europe's aristocracy, when hotel beds totalled 15,000: today their number has dwindled to 4,000, and the grand old Hotel Kaiserhof has become a supermarket. But Baden-Baden still boasts a smart summer season, with Ascot-like racing events and concerts in the garden of the stately colonnaded *Kurhaus*. Yet all this is not private enterprise: as in the case of most German spas, the *Kurhaus* and the thermal establishments belong to the *Land*, which in 1985 built an expensive new Baths of Caracalla, circular in shape, with wide panoramic windows. Next door, in the cavernous marble halls of the old Friedrichsbad, *Kurgäste* and others come to enjoy the spa's unique speciality, an elaborate sauna-cum-Turkish-bath ritual, men and women in the nude together: it is known as the 'Roman-Irish bath', apparently because Roman colonists from Ireland in the time of Caracalla invented this technique of alternating hot-air and warm-water treatments.

## Schools: educating the mind, but not so much the character

In this section and the next we shall examine education in west Germany, first schools and then universities. A nation with an exceptional tradition of scholarship has been having great difficulty, more than most others in western Europe, in adapting its distinguished system to the needs of today. The primary and secondary schools, after some difficulties, are now working fairly smoothly. But for more than twenty years now the universities have been in a state of crisis and malaise, sometimes erupting into violence as in the post-1967 period, but more often – as today – characterised by apathy and mediocrity. Of all the main areas of life in west Germany today, this is the one that strikes me as being the least efficient and least self-confident.

It is not easy to generalise about school education for the situation varies considerably from *Land* to *Land*. The *Länder* do coordinate their policies to the extent that everywhere you find the same types of school and examination: but, since they are virtually sovereign in this field, they display wide differences in curriculum, length of study cycles, styles of teaching, and even pedagogic philosophy. Whereas Bavaria in particular remains traditionalist, with fairly rigorous academic standards, some of the *Länder* in SPD hands, notably Bremen, Hessen and North-Rhine-Westphalia, favour the modern free-and-easy self-expressionist approach, less academic. And these variations can be disconcerting for families moving from one *Land* to another. Hence in some border areas you will find cases, for example, of academically-minded parents in Frankfurt (Hessen) sending their children to day-school in Aschaffenburg (Bavaria), 25 miles away. Or a father who has strong views on education may choose his job accordingly: in Hessen, a CDU politician furious about local policy said to me, 'Why do the two southern *Länder* attract new industry so much more easily than we do? One reason, without any doubt, is that their schools have much higher standards, and senior staff are therefore readier to settle there.'

There are however many factors common to all *Länder* in west Germany where 95 per cent of children attend state as opposed to private schools. Everywhere they go first to a primary *Grundschule* from the age of six to ten or eleven, and are then divided into three streams on the basis of their monthly school marks and of teacher assessment and teacher/parent discussion. The brighter or more academic ones go to a *Gymnasium* (grammar school) that prepares for university entrance. The middle range go to a *Realschule*: this provides a general education till sixteen and often leads the way to a vocational college or apprenticeship (see page 136). And the least academically-gifted (about 35 per cent of the total) attend a *Hauptschule* until fifteen, where they receive a rather more practical preparation for apprenticeships or for the job market.

The strength of this system is that children are more carefully trained according to their aptitudes than in most countries: a comparative survey published in London in 1983 found that, whereas Britain is probably better than Germany at educating its elite, at the *Realschule* and *Hauptschule* levels German kids are some two years ahead of their British equivalents in such key subjects as maths and science – with ensuing advantages for the economy.[1] But, within Germany, the system has run into a good deal of criticism for its alleged divisiveness and social unfairness. According to this view, the streaming at an early age marks off an academic minority, mostly middle class, from the others: also it harms late developers, for a transfer from *Realschule* to *Gymnasium*, though possible in theory, is not easy in practice. It is a problem familiar to many countries. And so in the 1960s pressures grew for the introduction of comprehensives (*Gesamtschulen*). The Brandt Government produced enabling legislation for them in 1969, and left it to the *Länder* to introduce them at their discretion. The more left-wing ones rapidly began to do so; but the others found all sorts of pretexts for delaying the scheme, under pressure from middle-class parents as well as from teachers who feared a drop in academic standards if *Gymnasien* and junior schools were merged. Even the SPD too began to have qualms, when it realised that many well-to-do parents might simply switch their children to private schools, and this would accentuate privilege rather than reduce it (precisely as has happened in Britain, with Labour's merger of many grammar schools into comprehensives). And so by the mid-1980s the *Gesamtschule* venture had ground to a halt. Berlin today has twenty-five of them, but Bavaria only one. In most *Länder*, they are still seen as merely experimental; virtually all *Gymnasien* have survived unchanged, so *Gesamtschulen* are little more than *Hauptschulen* under another name. It is a victory for conservatism, or – as others might see it – for the realistic view that children are not equal and cannot be treated as such.

In some other respects, however, German schools have changed quite strikingly over the past twenty years. In the old pre-war days they were ruled by a rigid discipline, inspired, as one writer put it, 'not by Goethe or Socrates, but by the Prussian petty officer'. A class would rise and stand to attention as its teacher entered the room. This authoritarianism was easily exploited by the Nazis to their advantage, and so after the war it was modified. Then, as in other countries, the post-1968 reform era brought further liberalisation. The older genera-

1. *Schooling Standards in Britain and Germany*, by S. J. Prais and Karin Wagner (National Institute of Economic and Social Research).

tion of more autocratic teachers gradually retired, to be replaced by younger ones with a more informal and humane approach: and in many *Länder* they were officially directed to apply the new pedagogic principles of self-expression and group work, in place of the former heavy emphasis on learning by rote and writing long essays. And so, amid a certain amount of cheerful chaos, these changes were steadily applied. Classes became more casual, often more unruly too; it was no longer enough for teachers just to lecture the class, they now had to get the youngsters to think for themselves, and sometimes the pupils now called them by their first names. In some *Länder*, parents began to be allowed to sit in on classes if they wished. These reforms may have been for the better on the whole but they have also brought some drawbacks. The new stress on oral rather than written expression, while it may have had little impact on maths, science or crafts, has led to quite a dramatic decline in spelling, grammar and handwriting, especially in schools other than *Gymnasien* – and many employers as well as teachers have been lamenting this. The head of training at Daimler-Benz said recently that, while he was pleased with his apprentices' practical flair, 'their writing skills have reached a deplorably low level'. In some *Länder*, moves have now been made to redress this situation, for example by reintroducing the learning of poetry by rote in primary schools.

The fall in standards does seem to be confined to the mastery of the German language (absurdly over-complicated anyway), and it has not affected wider aspects of education. On the whole, German children are still taught a remarkably full range of subject matter, and more rigorously than in most countries. Most schools, even primary ones, still hold regular little class exams and written tests every few weeks, and the marks are posted up in public. This creates a spirit of intense competitiveness and in the eyes of some radicals it can lead to nasty tensions, or worse: 'The kids,' said one mother-of-four in Bavaria, 'live under the tyranny of these marks, and of what their parents will think if they do badly. Sometimes a child gets beaten up by his father and he may even run away from home. Hence the high level of teenage suicides in Germany.' These may be extreme cases. It is true that ordinary German schools, with their stress on academic achievement, are still rather inept at dealing with the backward or problem child: Bavaria in particular has been slow to come to terms with dyslexia. But, in general, German schools today are much more relaxed, humane and friendly places than they used to be.

At *Gymnasium* level, one undoubted strength of the German system is that it still lays rather more emphasis on a good general education, as opposed to early specialisation, than is the case in many countries such as Britain. A pupil is required to prepare quite a range of subjects for the *Abitur*, the major examination taken usually at 19 that is the essential passport to university. It is true that the regulations have been modified repeatedly over the past twenty years, in different ways in different *Länder* and amid much controversy. Especially in the more 'progressive' *Länder*, the *Abitur* has been made much easier, under pressure from politicians who have wanted more young people to be given the chance to go to university: the proportion of all German teenagers obtaining the *Abitur* has risen since the 1950s from 5 to 22 per cent, with consequent university overcrowding, as we shall see. Today the *Abitur*, though still on the whole a more rigorous test than its English A-level equivalent, has certainly become easier than the French *baccalauréat*. Of course this has produced a stream of complaints of falling standards, from university rectors and others – and as a result the pendulum recently has been swinging back a little. In Baden-Württemberg, the most rigorous *Land* after Bavaria, it is still possible to take sport as a 'main' subject, but only if it is balanced with something more academic such as maths or history for the other main one. In a word, Germany's educationalists have been little more successful than others in trying to decide how far the old academic grind is still important for today's age.

Despite this confusion, almost all British parents who come to live in Germany and put their children into its state schools are impressed by the quality and seriousness of the teaching and the high level of pupil motivation – at least in the *Gymnasien*. Modern languages in particular are taught very thoroughly, and the youngsters throw themselves eagerly into learning them well. And one group of English sixth-formers on an exchange visit were amazed to find that their German counterparts knew more about British history and institutions than they did themselves. The syllabus, in most subjects, has become less theoretical and old-fashioned than it was twenty years ago, and is now better geared to the modern world and modern needs. All in all, and despite the new problems I have described, German classroom teaching seems to represent a happy medium between British laxness and French encyclopaedic academicism. But what of school life outside the classroom? Here, alas, a British visitor is far less likely to be impressed.

*

The traditional German view of school education, as in many Continental countries, is that its function is to train the mind rather than to indulge in character-building or to promote civic responsibility or the full use of leisure. These matters are seen as the role of parents, or maybe of the churches or of youth bodies such as scouts or guides. Hence, by Anglo-American standards, German state schools appear utilitarian places, lacking in any warm sense of community. For one thing, a school is alive only in the morning. Almost all the classroom work is done intensively between 8 a.m. and 1 p.m.; some schools do have a few afternoon classes, or they stay open then for voluntary club or cultural activities, but mostly the kids clear off home for lunch and then devote the time to their own pursuits, including at least two or three hours of homework. So, at a time when English schools are buzzing with valuable non-academic activity, German ones are largely deserted. Since about 1970, some attempts have been made to change this by promoting *Ganztagsschulen* (all-day schools), but this has been done less for educative reasons than to keep children out of mischief when both parents have full-time jobs. The experiment has not got far. Teachers and pupils resent losing some of their free time, while parents tend to complain, 'Our children are being taken from us!' Despite official efforts, these 'all-day schools' still account for no more than 3 per cent of all pupils. In east Germany, children have always continued school in the afternoons (see p. 377), and there have been some suggestions that this model could now be copied by the west: but it is most unlikely to happen.

Many schools do have clubs for photography, chess and suchlike, as well as choirs, orchestras and drama groups, and sometimes the results are impressive: the pupils of one *Gymnasium* near Stuttgart have used a local theatre to give public performances of plays by Wilde and Albee in the original English. Activities of this kind have intended to increase since the war: but they are hampered by the lack of suitable premises in schools, and they depend upon the enthusiasm of individual teachers prepared to give up their free time: official *Land* policy offers them little encouragement. As for sport, individual skills such as gymnastics and athletics are taught in school hours as part of the curriculum: but team sports hardly figure at all, and few schools have their own playing-fields or swimming-pool. Those who want to play football, or swim, do so voluntarily in their home context by joining a local club or sports centre. Homework permitting, many children do in fact enjoy quite an intense and varied leisure life, centred around their families and peer groups – and in defence of the German system it can be argued that it is good for a child to remain part of adult life and the real world rather than be to cooped up within the artificial milieu of a school. Even so, it is surely an opportunity missed if an education system fails to make use of schools to develop a sense of loyalty, responsibility and teamwork. (If Britain in this century has had a better democratic tradition than Germany, is it not vaguely something to do with the Thomas Arnold tradition?)

As in France and Italy too, German state schools provide very little practical training in leadership or civics. Of course there are classroom lessons where the pupils are taught about the Constitution and the legal system, and how the *Bund* and *Länder* operate: but they are given little chance to rehearse democracy in practice. There is nothing to parallel the American system where a school becomes a parliament-in-embryo, nor the British one where senior pupils are in charge of discipline. This is left to the teachers: for an eighteen-year-old boy or girl to boss around junior ones would not only be illegal in Germany, but parents would never stand for it. Each class formally elects its own delegates, who can go to the staff with complaints and suggestions: and since the 1968 period each school has a kind of assembly where pupil, staff and parent representatives meet on an equal basis to discuss minor practical non-pedagogic matters such as whether smoking should be allowed in the corridors – but this is marginal. There are not even any school debating societies where political muscles can be flexed. And this whole system comes under some criticism from the Germans themselves: one liberal-minded *Gymnasium* headmaster, whose wife is English, said to me, 'Maybe school prefects in Britain have too *much* power, and this can lead to abuses. But your system does provide youngsters with real experience in taking responsibility for their community, and this we fail to do. As a result, though they are meticulously law-abiding, the Germans tend to be lacking in spontaneous concern for others, and in a sense of civic initiative.'

The focus of a pupil's loyalty is much more his classmates than the school as a whole. A class will organise weekend outings together and maybe go on visits abroad too, and they will often develop an intense camaraderie. Groups of ex-pupils will keep in touch, so that sometimes you come across silver-haired oldies banqueting round a *Stammtisch* in a pub to celebrate the fiftieth anniversary of their taking the *Abitur* together. But few of them ever return nostalgically to the old Alma Mater itself, which seldom stages alumni reunions. The reasons for this lack of community are in part logistic: many distinguished *Gymnasien* do not even have a big hall for concerts or speech days, and so the school never meets as one body. The *Land* usually refuses to pay for such an 'extra', and schools lack their own budgets for it.

In all fairness I should add that the atmosphere in all the state schools I visited was perfectly friendly and cheerful; the staff seemed kindly, and I was assured by both sides that teacher/parent cooperation was good. But the buildings were usually drab, and they lacked amenities such as good libraries for the pupils' use. This wealthy nation, whose public hospitals, sports centres, opera houses and suchlike are usually so magnificent, has never thought to devote a similar largesse to its schools. Moreover, many *Gymnasien* doubled or trebled in size during the years of the boom in *Abitur* applicants, and some even had to turn their libraries into classrooms. The effects of the low birth-rate began to reduce overcrowding a little in the 1980s: but now the influx of refugees from the east has worsened it again.

Lastly, one other major contributing factor to the somewhat soulless nature of German state schools is that they are rigidly run on bureau-cratic lines by the *Land* ministries of education. The head of a school has far less autonomy than in Britain. He (or she) cannot select his own staff, but has them foisted on him by the ministry; and, as teachers enjoy civil service status and security, it is difficult for a head to get rid of a bad one. A school must also comply with rigid and uniform *Land* regulations about punishments and marking systems, which have legal force and cannot be modified. 'If a parent thinks that I have punished his child too severely, or given him too low marks, then quite probably he will sue me: the Germans adore lawsuits,' said one headmaster; 'I merely pass the file on to the ministry to be sorted out.'

Dissatisfaction with state schools has driven a minority of families, mainly middle-class ones, to seek refuge in the private sector which is still small in Germany (5 per cent) but getting less so. Especially they move to the Waldorf (Rudolf Steiner) schools, which originated in Germany and have since expanded steadily (except during the Nazi period, when they were banned). Steiner was an Austrian scientist and humanist, founder of the anthroposophical movement (see p. 557), who set up his first school in 1919 in Stuttgart, and there it still stands and flourishes. His schools have had a worldwide influence: there are 200 around the globe, eighty of them in Germany itself. In so far as they have no prefects and few afternoon activities, these *Waldorfschulen* (as the Germans call them) are in some respects closer to *Gymnasien* than to the British system: but in many other ways they mark quite a break with German tradition, for they try to care for the creative personality in a warm, attractive environment, and they put the emphasis less on academic work than on culture, handicrafts and group activities. Boys and girls alike all learn knitting and metalwork, as well as ceramics and carpentry; much classroom time is given over to music-playing, singing and drama, including the staging of plays, a compulsory subject. There is no streaming: an age-group stays together, moving up the school as one class, with the same teacher all the time who becomes a kind of foster-parent, getting to know each pupil very closely. Another original feature is that there are no printed school-books, for these are thought to result in parrot-learning: instead, children are expected to devise their own textbooks, based on research done in groups on their own initiative. It follows that academic standards tend to be lower than at a *Gymnasium*: but they have been improving recently under pressure from parents who want more than culture and joyous liberation for their young. Only the brightest 30 per cent of pupils are encouraged to sit for the *Abitur*, and they tend to do quite well at it. One lecturer at Stuttgart university was enthusiastic about them: 'Students who have come from *Waldorfschulen*,' he told me, 'may arrive with less knowledge than the others, but they have been taught to think for themselves much more. So in the end they are the better ones at university, where a student has to learn to work on his own.'

One *Waldorfschule* teacher, a large motherly lady in her fifties, very proudly showed me around the *maison mère*, a group of handsome pink buildings on the crest of one of Stuttgart's hills. I admired the décor and architecture, all intriguingly asymmetrical, with no right-angles – 'Yes,' said my guide, 'that was Steiner's idea, to make buildings gentle and irregular, just like people. After all, our heads aren't right-angled, are they?' Inside, all was wood-panelling, sloping ceilings, pretty pastel colours in varied shades – delightfully unlike usual school classrooms. One class that I visited was doing sculpture, another was playing the flute; tots of seven were making carnival costumes; an *Abitur* class had put flowers on the teacher's desk for her birthday. There was even a big school hall where all 800 pupils can attend concerts. As at other *Waldorfschulen* in Germany, the intake is mainly middle-class: but the fees, paid on a sliding scale according to means, are fairly modest, since city and *Land* both contribute sizeable subsidies. Many German intellec-tuals and professional people admire the *Waldorfschulen* and send their children there: recent parents have included Helmut Kohl and the late Joseph Beuys, the artist. In later life the pupils tend to do well in artistic professions, but less well in more formal careers. Nearly always they are happy at school and retain an affection for it: alumni associations flourish.

The other private schools are mostly run by the Churches. Some of the older ones have quite a sense of tradition and community; often they have remained single-sex, whereas almost all state schools are now mixed. There are also eighteen *Landerziehungsheime*, private non-confessional boarding schools in rural settings, modelled partly on English public schools: the best-known is Salem, near Lake Constance, founded by the late Kurt Hahn who went on to create Gordonstoun in Scotland. Charging about 2,000 DM a month, these schools are patronised by senior German diplomats and businessmen posted abroad, or by well-to-do parents of children who do not fit into the austere *Gymnasium* world. I visited one, Schöndorf, set in parkland beside the Ammersee, west of Munich, and I found it pleasantly relaxed and convivial in spirit, but not very academic. It puts an accent on handicrafts, music and drama as well as on sport; as at English boarding schools, the boys and girls live under the supervision of housemasters and housemistresses. Alumni links are strong, and many ex-pupils look back nostalgically on the school as a kind of surrogate family. Clearly these *Landerziehungsheime* have much to commend them, but they are too few in number, and too elitist, to have any great influence on German education as a whole. They are for a privileged minority – as German universities used to be, but most definitely are no longer.

## The never-ending university malaise

It is a far cry from the green calm of the old Philosophers' Walk, above the river Neckar at Heidelberg, to the overcrowded lecture-halls of some hideous new utility campus such as Bochum or Dortmund – from the old ideal of secluded scholarship to the clamour and discontent of the modern student broiler-houses. In west Germany, as much as anywhere else in Europe, changing economic needs and the explosion in student numbers have been forcing the universities to adapt to a new role and to seek a new identity. But in trying to reconcile the requirements of mass and elite education they have not been too successful; and the resulting confusion and decline in standards have been causing some anxiety to politicians, employers and others. 'In our efficient modern Germany,' one CDU leader said to me, 'the universities shine out as *in*efficient. Why do we consistently fail to solve this problem?'

In the nineteenth century, German universities were noble centres of pure scholarship and research, devoted to the principles developed by Wilhelm von Humboldt who founded the University of Berlin in 1809. Students were a privileged and pampered few, sitting at the feet of great professors endowed with lofty public prestige. This charmed era continued until the 1930s, when it was shattered by the universities' generally craven subservience to Hitler, as a result of which some 4,000 teachers were ejected from their posts in the denazification era. The universities did manage to recover from this shame: but then they signally failed to march with the times in the new, more egalitarian Germany. Hierarchies remained rigid and routines crustily old-fashioned; the senior professors arrogantly ruled the roost, drawing fat salaries, dictating every detail of the duties of their assistants, and rejecting all calls for change. Some rectors still insisted on being called officially by the old title of '*Ihre Magnifizenz*'. The few attempts at reform – notably at the new Free University of Berlin, where in 1949 students were allowed to elect their own delegates to the Senate – proved short-lived.

During the 1960s, as the students' numbers steadily increased, so did their dissatisfaction with the status quo – and this discontent was shared by many of the junior teachers. It paved the way for the great student uprisings (see p. 535) that began in Berlin in 1967 and the next year spread to France and elsewhere. The Leftist leaders of this rebellion were cleverly exploiting the general malaise, even if relatively few students shared their more radical political objectives: the ills of the university were for them just one aspect of the rottenness of a whole society that must be abolished. Their revolt hardly succeeded in these broader revolutionary aims: but it did manage to break the university mould and in the long run to usher in a new order. In the early stage, the years after 1967 were marked by constant left-wing agitation and disruption in many universities, notably Berlin, Frankfurt and Marburg: Maoist and other groups, in fierce rivalry, roamed the faculties breaking up lectures, sometimes locking professors into their rooms or scuffling with the police, while student boycotts led to many seminars and courses being cancelled, especially in the social sciences. The agitators hardly spoke for the average student, and in the short term their disruption did a good deal of harm: but it did impel the Federal and *Land* governments into attempting some reforms that were aimed at answering the widespread desire for more democracy and less professorial autocracy.

The results have been most uneven. At first, some of the more left-wing *Länder* introduced *Drittelparität*, a bold innovation whereby the university senate and faculty boards were each to be made up in three equal parts of professors, junior teachers and assistants, and students – and so in 1969 the Free University of Berlin elected a sociology assistant as its president. This was exciting stuff for radicals: but it did lead to a good deal of muddle, squabbling and inept decision-taking, as professors were outvoted by their inexperienced and sometimes vindictive juniors. The pendulum had swung too far to the other extreme. So in 1976 the *Bund* stepped in with an outline law[1] that abolished *Drittelparität* and called on the *Länder* to apply a more moderate and coherent system. Though the *Länder* have not reacted uniformly, the overall situation today in senates and other university bodies is that the professors have an absolute majority but other categories are by law quite strongly represented too. Thus, in the senate at Tübingen, professors have twenty-one seats, junior teachers seven, other staff (including cleaning ladies) seven, and students seven: as the other groups never agree, the professors can usually secure the decisions they want. Nearly everywhere, professors have now reasserted their control after the post-1967 crisis period, but in a more discreet style than before. In the more conservative faculties such as law and medicine, they may still try to be authoritarian: but mostly they have learned their lesson and are now more open-minded and easy-going towards students and junior staff. And as the older generations retire, this becomes more so. After the wasted years of muddle and incoherence, it could be said that a reasonable balance has finally been struck.

One instructive example is the University of Bremen. This was founded by the SPD-led *Land* government in 1971, as a new-style democratic venture, and it rapidly filled up with left-wing teachers and

1. Higher education is primarily the responsibility of the *Länder*, which provide the money and decide how it should be spent, and are supposed to coordinate their policies. However, since 1969 the *Bund* has increased its own powers of coordination: it shares the financing of universities, and no *Land* can found a new one without *Bund* permission.

students, many of them refugees from Göttingen where radical rebellion had collapsed in ruins. With its young president in jeans and everyone on chummy *'du'* terms, Bremen soon won the reputation of being the most 'Red' of German universities and the one with the lowest academic standards: its graduates generally found it hard to get good jobs. But today it seems to have settled down and become more moderate, without having entirely abandoned its earlier ideals – as one of its sociology professors told me: 'We've managed to hold on to many of our innovations, some of them still unusual in Germany. For example, inter-disciplinary studies; a credit system in place of some exams, very popular with students; and organic links with local trade unions. We've even retained *Drittelparität*, in defiance of the federal law.'

This issue of democratisation is no longer the main problem facing the universities. It has been partially solved, or at least has become dormant, and has now been far outstripped in urgency by the more intractable problem of massive-scale student entry: this has led to overcrowding, under-funding, a bad student/teacher ratio, harassed staff and lonely, ill-supervised students, and a general apathy and lowering of standards, with adverse effects even on research and scholarship at the upper level. It has completely overwhelmed the old Humboldtian ideal of serene academic dedication and has led to the asking of all sorts of fundamental questions, such as 'What is the purpose of a university?' or 'Should everyone have the right to higher education?' Or should the number of graduates be limited to the nation's requirements, as it was in the GDR, where at unification in 1990 the total of students was only 130,000, per capita about 30 per cent of the West German figure? (See pp. 487–9 for the current problems of remodelling the east German universities on west German lines.)

During the years of full employment, more and more young people came to feel that a degree was worth having, and so the student numbers in higher education rose steadily, from 200,000 in 1959 to some 1.5 million by 1988. The growth was hard to control, for it is a strong tradition, even written into the Constitution, that the *Abitur* gives automatic right to university entry; moreover, universities are forbidden by law to do their own selection on merit, as they can in Britain and the United States. Until about 15 years ago, the growth in numbers was actually encouraged by governments (except in medicine) – first for political and social reasons, since the SPD in particular felt that it was desirable for the humbler ranks of society to have fuller access to higher education; and secondly for practical reasons, for in those days it was argued that a country's economic strength was related to its number of well-educated graduates, notably in the sciences. So public money was poured into the expansion of higher education: between 1959 and 1979, 20 new universities were built as well as numerous polytechnics, and academic staff increased from 19,000 to 78,000.

But the extra funding has not kept pace with rising student numbers. The major expansion of infrastructure in the 1960s was planned to cater for an expected student total of 750,000, so it has now become completely inadequate. What is more, ever since the *Abitur* has been made easier, a large number of less academically gifted people have been entering university, including – so it is widely argued – many who are just not suited for it. And this situation is made worse by the liberal German system, splendid in the old days but less realistic today, that allows a student (except in some disciplines) to study whatever he likes at university, irrespective of his *Abitur* specialisation: there are frequent cases of people taking, say, German and history as their main *Abitur* subjects and then switching to chemistry or physics. Hence many students arrive ill-prepared for their university work and are then inadequately taught owing to the pressure of numbers. Many find that they just cannot cope, and so they drop out after a year or two. Others struggle on, and achieve a low-grade degree.

In earlier days, these weaker students could generally expect to find some suitable job. But the rise in unemployment since the early 1980s has increased the number of young graduates without work: teachers and would-be teachers are the worst affected. Many are obliged to take jobs well below their qualifications. One professor told me that his best recent student was now a taxi-driver, while at a famous museum in west Berlin I found that the young man hanging up the coats in the cloakroom has just graduated from an art college – it was the nearest he could get to his beloved subject! And so, politicians constantly issue the warning that Germany is creating an overqualified academic prole-tariat that could prove more dangerously explosive than in the 1967 period. However, the new youth generation itself is now more aware that a university education may not be so useful, and an increasing number of them now look elsewhere after the *Abitur*, often to apprentice-ships. The number of *Abiturienten* going straight on to higher education, which used to be 90 per cent, has dropped down to 75 per cent since the early 1980s; I met one senior professor's daughter, with an excellent school record, who was training to be a hairdresser, unimaginable 20 years ago. The government, in an about-turn of attitude, is now pleased with this trend. And yet, the overall student population has continued to rise, simply because people have been taking longer to complete their studies.

One especially striking aspect of the liberalism of the German tradition is that you can go on studying for as long as you like. Only in a few subjects, such as law and medicine, are degree courses of fixed duration, generally five or six years; in the others, they are unlimited, and if you fail your final exams, you are allowed to take them one more time, though it must be within two years. This generous system possibly made sense in the old privileged days, when 'the eternal student', cultured, dilettante and fun-loving, was a figure of some respect: but today it is a major reason for the unwieldy size of the student population, and it also means that a great many German graduates enter their careers in their late twenties, with some of their best years behind them. What is more, fear of unemployment has today been tempting many students to postpone the evil day as long as possible, often by eking out a living with part-time jobs when their grants have expired: since the 1960s, the average length of study has risen from 11 to 14 semesters (seven years), and I met one man who was in his fifty-fourth! Despite the poor study conditions, many young people still enjoy the relative freedom and leisure of student life, and they find that the official status of 'student' brings with it many perks which they are reluctant to lose – very cheap meals in university canteens, cheap health insurance, cheap theatre and train tickets, and so on.

In the past few years, the authorities have finally been making some attempts to contain student numbers by introducing a *numerus clausus* system in certain subjects. This first began to be applied in medicine in the late 1960s – partly because there were insufficient laboratories for coping with the growing flood of students into a popular profession (see p. 231) – and it has since spread into related disciplines such as pharmacy, dentistry, psychology and biochemistry. The selection is not done by individual universities, but by a central computer in Dortmund which sifts candidates on the basis of their *Abitur* marks and other factors, and then distributes them as it pleases with typical computer caprice: the system is detested by students for its arbitrary impersonality, and by professors for its hideous complexity – 'I try not to understand it, as I fear for my sanity,' said one dean of admissions.

The computer has had some effect on numbers, though many would-be medicos find ways of sneaking in through the back gate, either as 'mature' late entrants, or else by qualifying first at some foreign university with an easy open-door policy, such as Bologna. More recently, some university departments in other subjects have been empowered to start up their own *numerus clausus* (for example, political science in Freiburg), but on a first-come-first-served basis and not one of merit, for this is still banned by law as being anti-egalitarian. All in all, selective entry is so alien to German practice that it is still viewed warily by many professors as at best a necessary evil. And the student unions are flatly opposed to it.

The vast majority of senior university teachers are in favour of sterner action, as much with a view to raising academic standards as to reducing overcrowding. Alike in private and in public, they have been proposing a number of related solutions. Most would like to see the *Abitur* made harder again, and/or limits imposed more widely on length of studies. Many suggest a weeding-out exam at the end of the first year; or (as in France) the division of the standard master's degree course into two short cycles, with a diploma exam after two years that would provide at least some qualification for weaker students, who could leave at that stage. Plenty of professors, especially those on the Right, want universities to be allowed to do their own selection, preferably on merit. And many would favour the introduction of tuition fees, arguing that this might deter quite a proportion of the less serious students from middle-class families, while it could actually help working-class ones, if it were based on a means test and coupled with higher grants.

These various measures would all seem to make sense, and many have long been common practice in countries such as Britain or the United States. But in Germany they would run up against all kinds of vested interests and rooted habits. In particular, the eleven *Länder* are so split between Left and Right on so many issues that they would never easily agree to coordinated action. Constitutionally speaking, a *Land* could probably get away with carrying through some of these reforms unilaterally: but it would cause such a political storm that in practice it might prove impossible. Meanwhile, a cloud of gloom hangs over the world of German professors. Nearly all of them complain that they are bogged down in administrative chores and have too little time for research. It is true that in many ways they are still quite a privileged class, very well paid and more highly respected by society than almost any other profession (in a Germany still so title-conscious, the magic word 'Herr Professor' can cast a spell of deference over any social gathering). Yet they are probably justified in their grouse that they are being asked to do the impossible in trying to combine scholarship with preparing a lumpen student mass for the labour market.

Another steady lament concerns the universities' lack of autonomy and the interference by *Land* bureaucrats. By law, German universities are subject to their local education ministry, which allocates their budget and decides how it should be spent – 'If I want a new word-processor,' said one teacher, 'it has to be approved by the *Landtag*'s finance committee, and that can take months.' Ministry permission is also needed for the creation of a new chair, and for changes in the curriculum, especially if money is involved. A university elects its own president (rector) and can choose its own junior teaching staff, but all new appointments of professors are decided by the Minister, on the basis of a short-list drawn up by the Senate: generally he accepts its own preference, but he need not do so. Of course this whole situation leads to running feuds between *Land* and university authorities, with the latter complaining that 'the bureaucrats do not understand our problems', and rectors being obliged to devote much of their time to political lobbying. In this struggle, the civil servants have the whip hand, for in true Germanic style they rule the universities through a vast and complex battery of formal regulations – 'Look,' said the head of administration at Tübingen University, showing me the set of fifteen fat green lawbooks behind his desk, '*this* is what we're up against!' And financial 'meddling' by the ministries has even tended to get worse recently, as universities' needs have grown more complicated while budgets have got tighter. Professors have sometimes been refused funds for travelling to seminars abroad, while the august president of Munich University had his official car's logbook scrutinised to see whether he was illicitly using it for private purposes. An Oxford don would throw up his hands in amazement and horror; even in centralised France the universities nowadays at least receive their budgets in a lump sum to spend partly as they choose. But the Germans still sweat it out under a tighter tutelage.

This all seems a far cry from the old historical image of Heidelberg, say, or Göttingen, as noble self-governing centres of learning. But times have changed – and recent decades in particular have seen a deliberate government policy of levelling down of all universities towards a dull uniformity, in the sacred name of fairness of opportunity.

It is true that Germany has never possessed an elitist superstructure in quite the manner of Oxbridge, the Ivy League or the *Grandes Ecoles*: even in the good old days, German universities were bound by a certain concept of equality, enabling a student to move freely from one to another and spend a year or two in each, in pursuit of a degree. But the universities then were relatively few in number, and students likewise. The system did also enable great professors to take root in a particular place, endowing it with a reputation in their field – as Göttingen for maths and science, and Tübingen for philosophy and theology. Today west Germany has some forty full universities (as well as seven technical and seven 'comprehensive' ones), all bound by much the same regulations, all with very similar systems of admission, study methods and per capita budget allocations. And they fall into three main types: the ancient classic universities in medium-sized towns (Heidelberg, Tübingen, Freiburg, Göttingen, Münster, Marburg); those in very big cities, founded mostly in the nineteenth century (Berlin, Munich, Hamburg, Frankfurt, etc.); and the score or so of post-war ones, some of them pleasant smallish campuses on the edge of historic towns (e.g. Konstanz, Regensburg), others large new concrete eyesores (e.g. Düsseldorf, Dortmund).

Of course they still look and feel very different from each other. Heidelberg, founded in 1386, with its romantic old student taverns and its lovely buildings in the heart of the medieval town below the great red castle, seems to inhabit another world from, say, Bochum, largest and ugliest of the new utility campuses of the Ruhr. But look more closely and you find much the same students facing much the same problems and conditions, the only major distinction being that Heidelberg is still able to attract a more distinguished kind of senior professor, simply because he will find it a pleasanter place to live in. In the same way, a few universities do still manage – if less than in the old days – to outshine the others in some particular field, owing to the presence of a few star professors. Thus, for example, Cologne is noted for economics, Aachen for engineering, and Tübingen still for theology (with Hans Küng) as well as for medicine. But that is about as far as dissimilarity goes. As a university cannot select on merit, and as the vast majority of German students go to the one nearest to their home, it follows inevitably that the average quality of students varies very little and that almost all universities have today become equally provincial – even the most world-famous. It is all rather sad.

After 1969, this trend was deliberately accentuated by the SPD-led

governments of Brandt and Schmidt, with the aim of giving all students
equal chances as far as possible, and of making degrees more directly
comparable. Their policies put pressure on the *Länder* in this direction.
But the result — in the eyes of most university leaders and all right-
wing politicians — has been a levelling down towards a general
mediocrity. Lavish research funds are now spread so evenly that there
are few concentrations of specialised excellence any more, with consequent dangers for German economic progress, especially in high technology — and this state of affairs is often blamed for Germany's poor
recent showing in the Nobel prize-lists, as compared with pre-1933
days when it was gaining more such awards than any other nation.[1]

In 1984 the president of the Technical University of Munich,
Professor Wolfgang Wild, issued a stern warning: 'The intellectual
sparks which glitter in the stimulating atmospheres of Harvard and
MIT, Tokyo or Kyoto, Oxford or Cambridge, are extinguished here in
the ashes of prevailing mediocrity. Researchers, able to achieve the
extraordinary when working at a top-class university abroad, achieve
only the ordinary on their return to German universities.' This recurrent
Cassandra-cry of 'mediocrity' has been voiced also by the Foreign
Minister, Hans-Dietrich Genscher, in a boldly-worded speech (see also
p. 118) that was to make a distinct impact: he claimed that the
equalisation process of recent years had severely damaged the
universities, with disastrous results for research, for academic excellence,
and for training the top scientists needed for Germany to make up lost
ground in high-technology.

Urged on by Genscher and others, the Kohl Government began to
do just a little to redress the balance. Genscher argued eloquently that
the only way to bring any rapid results was to loosen the state
monopoly in higher education and sanction the setting up of private
fee-paying universities, elitist in nature, which could train specialists in
certain fields. And this has begun to happen, but on a very modest
scale. In 1983 a small university, mainly for medicine, opened at Witten
in the Ruhr; another followed in 1984 at Koblenz, for training business
managers (see pp. 123–4). Both are financed by industry, and from
students' fees. The trend has been welcomed in some circles, even by
the liberal *Die Zeit* whose co-editor is Helmut Schmidt. But this radical
break with German tradition has also aroused criticism and scepticism:

1. This may have been a factor: but a far more important one was surely the
emigration of the best scientists, especially Jewish, after 1933.

Schmidt's SPD colleague Willy Brandt called Genscher's ideas 'an attack on the democratic and social foundations of the German Constitution'. Other critics have wondered whether it is indeed possible to create a truly superior university from scratch in the space of a few years, short of quite excessive funding. And some have even argued, not very convincingly, that past elitism in German society led to Nazism and must not be encouraged again in any form. By 1991 the new private universities were not yet doing very well: they inevitably lacked the endowments to provide full facilities, and it was found that in Germany not many students or the parents, even rich ones, were prepared to pay for higher education. Today the future of the new trend remains in doubt. And even if it does a little to help the economy, it will hardly solve the problem of what to do with the over-swollen state campuses.

Tübingen, just like Heidelberg, is a charming old town on the Neckar in Baden-Württemberg. Untouched by wartime bombing, its fifteenth-century gabled houses stand terraced on the steep slope above the river, all prettily painted in pastel shades of pink, blue and ochre. Here is the Protestant *Stift* where Hölderlin shared lodgings with Hegel and Schelling, and the old tower-house by the river where the poet lived in later life. The university today has spread out everywhere even into the courts of the great eleventh-century Schloss on the hilltop; and in term-time the streets are filled with idling or scurrying students, so that Tübingen certainly has the feel of a university city, 29,000 students and staff amid a total population of 75,000 – 'we have a town on our campus,' the local saying goes. But what is there of live tradition or true university life? A few student pubs and cafés; some venerable old bookshops; the literary and intellectual activity of a few select cliques, centring around brilliant figures such as Küng or the writer and critic Walter Jens; and on warm days the lively impromptu forum of the Holzmarkt where buskers perform and Greens and Leftists argue and harangue. In summer on the river, there are even student rowing-races, and girls lazing in punts, as pretty as any on the Cherwell. But of stirring ritual, or collegiate or club life, or sheer zany youthful fun, there is not much sign. No Commem balls, no dons at high tables, no Union Society debates, no degree ceremonies in full regalia. Might it not be said that Tübingen is as inferior to Oxford as Austin Rover is to Daimler-Benz?

One tradition that does still just about survive – though at Tübingen as elsewhere it has fallen mightily into disrepute – is that of the student fraternities (*Verbindungen*), many of them still addicted to the archaic pastime of sabre-duelling. These are all-male residential clubs of a sort, whose members live, study and drink beer together in handsome, crumbling old houses. In the old days, most higher-class students belonged to these bodies, which were supposed to inculcate a respect for tradition and hierarchy and a sense of honour. Today they are somewhat out of favour; but a number still exist, mainly in the older universities where sometimes you see their little cohorts parading through the streets in their bright sashes and funny caps, singing lustily. At Tübingen they hold a big annual torchlight procession where they regularly clash with left-wing students. Today not all *Verbindungen* practise duelling; but the more purist and conservative ones still do, and it endows them with an even more reactionary image than is really justified. One wintry night, a young professor took me along to a seedy Victorian mansion in a Tübingen residential street, whispering as we entered, 'Look out for the bloodstains on the cellar floor.' We didn't in fact see any – but the inmates did put on a duelling display for us, wearing eye-shields but bare-headed. The president, a law student, explained that it was compulsory for every member to duel in a tournament twice a year – 'Today many student members would like duelling to be dropped, or at least made voluntary,' he said, 'but our rules are fixed by our alumni association, and the old boys insist nostalgically on keeping up the tradition. They feel that the younger generation should not have things easier than they did. And besides,' he added lamely, 'duelling teaches physical courage and self-control, and surely that is good, isn't it? If your head is cut, you mustn't flinch.' Afterwards we drank beer in the refectory where three girl-friend visitors (innovation!) had come for dancing. I was shown the yellowing photos of past members on the walls, the collection of uniforms, sabres and other cabalistic souvenirs, and I was told of their parties and their punt, and their difficulty in recruiting new members – the club once numbered sixty, but now it was down to fifteen, seven of them living in. The place reeked with tradition, but oh so sad and moribund. My host explained that this *Verbindung*, like others of its kind, was not directly political or right-wing – 'It's just that we uphold conservative values.' He also pointed out that it was no longer socially elitist. That was clear. One of the inmates was the son of a Stuttgart baker.

The *Verbindungen*'s fortunes reached a nadir during the post-1967 period of Leftist upsurge, when they hardly dared show their faces in public. Now they have revived just a little, in line maybe with the general ideological recovery of the Right in Europe during the 1980s. Some students join them out of sheer loneliness; others because they think it will help them later to get jobs, seeing that the old-boy networks are dedicated to mutual self-help among members and many of these *alte Herren* (alumni) are now in influential positions. Some of the non-duelling *Verbindungen* have cultural and sporting activities and are quite sensible and up-to-date: but these are only a minority. Overall *Verbindung* membership even in Tübingen is now down to a mere 2.5 per cent of all students (most are in law or medicine faculties). In a university system that has no collegiate life other than dull student hostels, these fraternities are surely in principle a splendid concept — and it is sad that it has proved impossible to adapt and modernise them.

Neither the social nor the working life of the average student is any paradise. There has never been any organised tutorial system in the Oxbridge sense, and now the rise in numbers has made direct contact with senior teachers even more remote, so that the nearest a student will often get to his professor is at seminars, which in popular subjects may well be groups of 30 to 40. It is true that links with junior teachers are closer, and many professors do hold *Sprechstunde* ('consulting hours') where students can come individually to seek their advice — but many are too shy or confused to make use of this, or so the professors allege. The fault may be on both sides. Certainly nearly all students complain of a lack of guidance and supervision in their work and a sense of intellectual isolation — and it takes some ingenuity to get round this barrier, as one girl I met at Göttingen had managed to do. She was a keen linguist: but, rather than opt for the hurly-burly of the French and English departments, she chose Slavonic languages, and in Serbo-Croat found herself the *only* student in her year. So she and her professor held their 'seminars' together in a café — and she got a first-class degree. But such *ad hoc* tutorials are quite exceptional.

When teachers and students do make personal contact, relations are generally much more friendly and easy-going than in pre-1968 days: professors have become more relaxed and human, and many junior lecturers do now make efforts to get to know at least a few students personally. But there is virtually no sherry-with-the-dons social life of the British kind — and one reason is that teachers do not have this kind of chummy activity with each other. Even today, hierarchic dignity is still such that a full professor will seldom hobnob socially with a junior one. Faculties have little informal contact with each other, and even within a faculty there is rarely any kind of friendly social club. It is all a long way from the cosy Oxbridge college world where a history don's best friend may be a teacher of physics. At one modern German university, I met a British lecturer who said of his colleagues: 'If they rarely entertain each other, and if I certainly don't want to entertain *them*, it's because they're all such bores – *Fachidioten*, narrowly obsessed by their own little subjects and incapable of talking about anything else. An expert on nineteenth-century literature knows nothing of the eighteenth century, and vice versa. They lack all curiosity, and they can't cope with me at all, because I enjoy, and talk about, pop music, jazz and Rossini. This is how they've been trained – force-fed and blinkered. It's the system that makes them like this.' And of course this rubs off on students and adds to their loneliness and confusion. If one of them has a personal problem, he (or she) has no 'moral tutor' *in loco parentis* to whom he can turn – only the university welfare department, which may perhaps send him to a psychiatrist. 'The trouble with our German system,' said one sympathetic teacher, 'is that it has always assumed that students are mature adults who do not need looking after. But now the rising suicide rate has been forcing us to change.' Most professors remark that they find their students docile, passive, reticent, and doggedly studious. One positive sign is that they seem to be showing a renewed interest in their subject for its own sake, and not merely as a means of getting a degree – or so several teachers told me. My British acquaintance again: 'I've been here twenty years and I've seen three distinct waves. The restless post-'68 generation were contemptuous of their studies, or affected to be. Then in the '70s the students were cramming-minded, anxious to get good grades and not very concerned with the subject. But today's vintage seem to have swung back to a greater interest. Maybe, paradoxically, it's because they're so despondent about job prospects that they feel they might at least enjoy academic study while it lasts. Ten years ago, when I laid on a seminar on modern English poetry that was outside the syllabus and not "useful", I had no takers; this year, I have twenty.'

Since the mid-1970s, political activism has died right down and the campuses have returned to a sullen calm, apart from the occasional flare-up in Frankfurt or Berlin where the Left has always been strong. Elsewhere, the few surviving extremist groups appear completely isolated, while the mass of students concentrate on their work, on private life and values, or on ecological causes which they pursue outside the university. 'It's all rather dull and disappointing,' said one professor in Göttingen: 'I think I really preferred the old restless, troublesome days, when the students in lectures asked difficult and interesting questions. Now they're so tame.' The students do not even wax militant over matters that affect their own position. For instance, in 1983 the Federal Government presented a bill to replace the usual grants with a system of loans, to be repaid later over 20 years when the graduates had started their careers (the motives for the scheme were partly Hayekian and money-saving, and partly to deter the less serious entrants and thus reduce numbers). The students of course were opposed, and they did manage to stage a few feeble demonstrations – but not enough to prevent the law from being passed, and applied. Yet, in Britain at the same period a similar move by the Thatcher Government collapsed under student hostility! (The scheme was much criticised for deterring poorer students and thus making campuses 'a preserve of the middle classes'. It was modified in 1990, so that now only half the sum given to a student is repayable loan, the rest being a grant.)

German students have also been showing curiously little concern to make use of their new role in university co-management, through their representation on the Senate and faculty boards. In elections for these bodies, their voting turnout rarely exceeds 10 to 20 per cent, and, as most *Länder* have a quorum system, this means that they cannot take up all their seats. In Baden-Württemberg there is no quorum, but student delegates have been boycotting Senates because, as one militant girl told me in Tübingen, 'the Senate does not even listen to our views, and we feel we have absolutely no influence. If we present motions on the kind of external political issues that interest us, such as Israeli aggression, we get ruled out of court. And there's no point in raising university issues, since everything is decided by the *Land*, not the Senate.' The more radical students, usually still the ones who get elected, are also angry that since 1976 the federal student union organisation, ASTA, has been barred from political activity as such and confined to social and welfare activities. Its leaders have retaliated by refusing to cooperate with the authorities. So at this level there is a kind of cold war, even though informal and personal relations remain quite friendly.

Apart from the activities of church associations and the occasional student orchestra or drama group, there is not much organised cultural or club activity in universities. One possible exception is Heidelberg, which does have a degree of Anglo-Saxon-style animation – but maybe that is due precisely to its strong leavening of American students! Elsewhere the pattern is much as described to me by one teacher at Tübingen: 'Students today look on the university just as a facility for getting a degree, and not as a community where they can have fun and find personal enrichment. They lead their active lives outside its framework.' For some of them this is a positive choice. They do not want to be cooped up in what they see as an artificial academic ghetto, cut off from the rest of society and its problems; so they may prefer for example to join local youth or arts centres, or citizen initiative groups, where they can mix with 'real' people like workers or immigrants. It is in many ways laudable. But in the eyes of an Oxford man like myself it does leave a depressing vacuum at the heart of what should be a rich university experience.

In the big cities such as Munich or Hamburg, most students are local and live at home; they keep to little circles of friends they have known since childhood and do not readily make new ones through the university. Only Berlin remains, as it always has been, a melting-pot attracting young people from all over Germany and abroad, and there the scene is more vibrant. In big cities, it is easy for students to be part of a real metropolitan world if they choose: but at the older universities in smaller towns they have less scope – as one professor at Göttingen remarked to me: 'Today they come mostly from petit-bourgeois families in the towns around; during the week they stick with a little group of pals of their own kind, they go home every weekend and have no real university life. Students in the old days had much more sense of fun.' The old tradition of migrating from one university to another has declined – partly because of economic reasons, partly because the *numerus clausus* computer tends to allocate people near to their home, and also because today's ordinary mass-student often fears being lost and lonely if he were to move to a strange part of Germany where he would know no one. So the universities have become more local. At Tübingen, the proportion of students coming from its Baden-Württemberg catchment area has increased from 40 to 80 per cent since 1965, with 15 per cent from the rest of Germany and 5 per cent foreigners – and one professor remarked sadly, 'Most of them today are so unadventurous, so narrow in their horizons. Tübingen used to be the focus for some of Europe's greatest scholars. Today it's provincial.'

Repeatedly in Germany I have been struck by the contrasts between the dispirited, antiquated ambience of the universities and the dynamism and confidence not only of economic life but of so much of local government and the public services. Not only is the malaise doing some practical harm to the German economy (as Genscher and others have warned), but in the long run it might be damaging to the morale of society as a whole, as generations of graduates are soured by their university experiences. Possibly this danger can be exaggerated, for young people the world over habitually show astonishing resilience, and most of them seem able to surmount the handicaps of a poor education — as France and Italy have shown in recent decades. In those two thriving countries, the educational crisis is if anything worse than in Germany: but all that this proves is that western Europe as a whole has not yet worked out what the purpose of its universities should be in today's world. In Germany, serious reforms will have to come: but as one paediatric professor remarked, 'As we've seen with the crisis in the medical schools, the reforms always limp along piecemeal about ten years or more behind the needs.' Maybe the much-praised German federal system is in this respect a handicap, for the *Länder* never find it easy to achieve a common policy and the *Bund* has only limited powers of imposing its own; on the other hand, centralised France has hardly fared any better with the problems. Clearly some more effective means of controlling student numbers will have to be found. If the venture for private universities fails, some other way is needed for breaking the sterile monopoly of the *Länder* in higher education, so as to bring in at last a real spirit of competition and feeling for excellence. After all, the healthy competition between Catholic and Protestant churches has worked wonders for the liveliness of Christianity in Germany today — as we shall now see.

## Catholics and Protestants: a new amity, but new internal conflicts

On the face of it, west Germany appears to have been slowly becoming de-Christianised, like so much of the Western world: since 1950, regular church attendance has declined from some 55 to 33 per cent among the Catholic population, and from 20 to less than 10 per cent among Protestants. But such figures hardly give the full picture, at a time when many people have come to practise their religion outside the framework of church buildings. What I find more remarkable is that the Catholic and Protestant Churches do still play so lively and vital a role in the life of western Germany, certainly more than in either Britain or France, or many other countries. But how far this is for strictly moral and spiritual reasons, rather than more secular ones, remains to be examined.

The overriding secular factor is that the Churches in western Germany are very rich. They derive enormous incomes from voluntary taxes levied on some 90 per cent of Germans, and they devote much of this money to running a vast array of schools, hospitals, charities and other welfare bodies. This gives them a much stronger base in society, and a bigger voice in public affairs, than they might have if they were poor like the Catholic Church in France. Of course they have a spiritual role too. And they exert a curious influence in German politics, ranging from the conservative to the radical. On the more conservative side, this can be seen for instance in the links between the Catholic Church and the ruling CSU party in Bavaria. At the other end of the spectrum, the powerful progressive element among Protestants has actively promoted a number of radical causes – priests in cassocks have often been seen at CND rallies.

Have the Churches become *too* concerned with secular issues? The question is often asked. And this is just one of many subjects of lively debate and conflict that spill out into a wider public discussion, in the Press and on television: what the Churches think and do is often front-page news. Among a people as serious and self-questioning as the Germans, maybe it is not surprising that the moral issues raised by the Churches should find so wide an echo, or that young people should be turning back to religion in some form. I noticed this at the Protestants' *Kirchentag* in Düsseldorf in 1985, a vast biennial five-day rally that drew some 200,000 people from all over Germany, most of them young, to sing and pray together, and to debate *Angst*, nuclear weapons, and other issues. I have been impressed also by the vitality of ecumenical links today in parishes throughout Germany: the long-lasting rift provoked by Luther's Reformation seems to have healed at last, and the two confessions are now living together in an active harmony that extends even to their neat numerical balance, for western Germany today has almost exactly as many Protestants (25.2 million) as Catholics (26 million). (In the east, the vast majority of Christians are Protestant: see pp. 384–8.)

The prestige of the Churches today may seem surprising in view of their dubious role during the Nazi period; but in fact that débâcle enabled them afterwards to renovate their image. In the 1920s, and earlier, both Churches had been profoundly conservative and deferential to established power, and this hardly fitted them for the task of opposing Nazism. The Catholics' Centre Party even helped to vote Hitler to power in the Reichstag in 1933, and then stood helpless when he signed his Concordat with the Vatican. As for the Protestants, whose tradition of support for the State stemmed direct from Luther's day, they at first did nothing to counter the new regime. Then the Nazis made efforts to win control of the Protestant Churches and to unite them in a new German Christian movement, liberated from its Jewish origins: but this encountered such opposition from a number of brave pastors, led by the young Martin Niemöller, that Hitler soon dropped the scheme. After this, however, none of the official Church organisations, Protestant or Catholic, showed any boldness in speaking out against the persecution of the Jews, the shackles on the Press, the political imprisonments, or other Nazi evils.

It was left to a few courageous individuals to salvage what they could of the Churches' honour. Some priests and pastors went into underground resistance, or they took the courageous step of denouncing the regime from their pulpits, and paid for it with their lives or by imprisonment — like Pastor Niemöller, who was in a concentration camp from 1938 to 1945, and Dietrich Bonhoeffer who died in one. This movement was wide enough for the Churches after 1945, hurriedly purged of their 'collaborationist' bishops, to re-emerge with some credibility as bodies that were not totally tainted with Nazism, and to plan a new start. Many Christian leaders publicly expressed their genuine guilt at not having resisted more actively. And, in that anguished *Stunde Null* period of hardship and desolation, millions of Germans turned back to Christianity as the sole meaning in life: the churches (such as were still standing, amid the ruins) were packed every Sunday. The Churches now began to plot a new course that would make them less passively subservient to the state and more able to influence it independently and to play their part in building a new Germany. It was in this spirit that both Churches joined to support the creation of the Christian Democratic Union, which then became the ruling party of Germany, under Adenauer, a convinced Catholic. Catholics have always wielded more influence than Protestants within the CDU, and even more so in the Bavarian CSU. The SPD on the other hand (while formally a lay party) is much closer to Protestantism. Helmut Schmidt for example is an active Lutheran. Today the Churches enjoy a rather special juridical status. They are not established within the State to the same degree as the Church of England: but they are certainly not disestablished like the Catholic Church in France. Their rights and status are guaranteed under the Constitution and by separate concordats, and they have senior representatives in Bonn to protect their interests. The State pays towards the salaries of the clergy. In all State schools, religion is taught in separate confessional classes as part of the curriculum (though there are no religious services as in Britain). And the State universities contain faculties of theology where many future clergy are trained. It is a privileged situation, free of the petty feuding over *la laïcité* that still sometimes bedevils education in France.

The major feature of this entente is the right granted by the State for the Churches to derive tax from their members. This system is rare in Europe, though it does exist in a different form in Scandinavia. In Germany, it dates from the nineteenth century, when the Churches were allowed this privilege in return for being dispossessed of some of their lands. Today the tax is collected by State revenue offices on behalf of the Churches. Amounting to some 5 billion DM a year for the Catholic Church and a roughly similar sum for the Protestants, it equals about 8 per cent of an individual's income tax and is paid alike by churchgoers and non-churchgoers, but on a voluntary basis. This *Kirchensteuer* makes the Churches wealthy — as is easy to observe. Senior prelates have comfortable modernised offices and drive around in large Mercedes; ordinary parish priests live rather well; the churches themselves, and the imposing new church social centres, are noticeably better maintained than in Britain or France. Even in areas that were not bombed, a remarkable proportion of west German churches are new: and new ones are constantly being built.

Not that the Churches spend the tax just on their own affairs. They use a large slice of it to run kindergartens, old people's homes, centres for the handicapped, hospitals, schools, and so forth, and they see this as a part of their social duty. Their hospitals are often more popular than the *Land-* or city-run ones, for they tend to be cheaper and more efficient, since the nuns who work in them are on the whole more dedicated and hard-working than medical staff in the public sector. The Churches also spend part of the *Kirchensteuer* on helping their poorer colleagues in eastern Germany, as they have done for many years (see p. 476); they spend a big part of it, too, on massive aid to the Third World (such as famine relief in Ethiopia) where the German record is much the best in Europe. At one Catholic church in a small Württemberg town, I found the vestry piled high with parcels about to be sent to Africa. 'We still feel so grateful, to the Americans in particular, for their generous aid relief to the Germans just after the war, that we now have a special obligation to help others in our turn,' I was told by the head of the Protestants' *Brot für die Welt* (Bread for the World) organisation.

Well over 90 per cent of Germans are still registered as tax-paying members of their Churches, even though most of them no longer practise their religion. To cease paying the tax, you must formally leave the Church by going to sign a declaration in the *Rathaus* – and few people are willing to take this step despite the money it would save. Probably they are held back by vague feelings of guilt, loyalty and tradition, or by the thought that they might need the Church again one day. In particular, most Germans want a Christian burial and officially a priest is not allowed to provide this for a non-member (though a few can usually be found who are prepared to bend the rules for a family they know and like). Many parents also feel that they should stay in their Church for the sake of the children – one Protestant doctor in Munich summed up a fairly general view: 'My wife and I are not churchgoers, but what right have we to deprive our kids of the benefits they may later find in the Church? It's much easier for them to opt out later, if they want, than to opt in to something they have never known. What's more, I think the Churches do a very useful job with their welfare work. Their competition keeps the public welfare bodies on their toes. If they stopped, the State would have to take the work over, and we'd be paying the same tax in another way.' Another factor, in the more devoutly church-going areas, is that to opt out can carry a social stigma. Under a new Secrecy Act, the *Rathaus* is legally forbidden to divulge that a member has left the Church. But an employer knows, for the tax deduction will appear on the individual's PAYE slip, and so the news can leak out. Some employers might even take reprisals: in Bavaria, where the Education Minister is a militant Catholic, there have been cases of teachers in State schools being refused promotion if they leave their Church, and this has even deterred a number of them from doing so.

Even so, the steady trickle of Germans who go to sign off at the *Rathaus* has been increasing recently, to reach a level of some 170,000 a year: this is largely due to economic factors, in a time of high unemployment. A few others leave because they can no longer stomach their Church's political stance: especially this has been true of the Leftward Protestant trends, which caused the late Axel Springer, right-

wing Press tycoon and devout old-style Christian, to leave the Lutherans and switch to some small free church group. Many other people,
while accepting to remain members, think that the level of tax should
be reduced. As for the Church leaders themselves, in the post-war years
some of them expressed dislike of the *Kirchensteuer* system because they
felt it made them too dependent on the State: but today such complaints
are rarely heard. 'The tax enables us to play a full part in a prosperous
society,' one Protestant bishop told me; 'if we had to rely on voluntary
gifts, or on our revenue from landed property, we could not do our job
adequately.' Catholic leaders share this view.

This is one of the many questions on which the Churches today see
broadly eye to eye. Indeed, the growth of a tolerant ecumenicism has
been one of the major success-stories of post-war west German society.
It is quite an achievement in a land with so tragic a history, where the
Reformation and then the Thirty Years' War split the nation into two
warring halves, racked by a religious bitterness and intolerance which
has deeply marked the German character and from which it has only
recently freed itself. Even as late as the 1950s there were still many
tensions and prejudices to be found, such as a wide-spread hostility to
mixed marriages, and some bizarre barriers: in some villages, separate
bakeries for Catholics and Protestants; in some schools, separate
bicycle-racks for pupils of the two confessions. However, a post-war
virus of change was steadily at work, induced not only by the new
ecumenical spirit in the world but by population shifts within Germany.
Until 1945, its Catholic and Protestant areas had mostly been separate
from each other, and this bred an intolerance based on prejudice and
sheer ignorance: a Catholic breathing fire and damnation against Protestants, or vice versa, had very often hardly met one in his life. In pre-
war days, the territory later to become West Germany was two-thirds
Catholic, while most Protestants were in the east. Then, when Germany
was split in two and the refugees arrived in their millions, a surprising
number of Protestants opted to settle in Catholic areas (e.g. Bavaria),
while many Catholics from regions such as Silesia moved into the
mainly Protestant districts, such as Stuttgart. So the two populations
became much more jumbled up, and each found the other to be not so
bad after all. This was one factor in the new tolerance: others were the
painful lessons learned from Nazism and the war, and the general desire
to build a better, more democratic Germany.

Nowadays, on my recent visits to urban and rural parishes all around western Germany, I have failed to discover much trace of tension or bigotry, save in a few northern areas where the Reformed (as opposed to Lutheran) Church is still somewhat anti-papist. Elsewhere I found co-existence and even cooperation. Of course ecumenicism still has its limits: but Germany today is full of examples of partnership at local level — joint prayer and discussion meetings, joint welfare activities, the lending of churches, and even a few joint services. In many parishes, priest and pastor are close friends. And mixed marriages, once so rare and so frowned on, now account for as many as 47 per cent of all church weddings. 'It's marvellous,' said a Protestant leader in Munich, Kirchenrat Paul Rieger; 'this peaceful competition between two Churches of equal influence is extremely fruitful. It keeps both of us on our toes, and it offers the faithful a real choice' (a nice consumerist touch, I felt) 'between Catholic authority and ritual and Protestant openness and flexibility.'

This is the situation at ordinary parish level. Between the senior hierarchies, however, ecumenical relations have tended to become a little less warm since the election of Pope John Paul II. His visit in 1980, the first made to Germany by any Pope for nearly 200 years, was the occasion for some tactless public criticism of the Lutheran tradition by one or two Catholic leaders. And since then a new Catholic Archbishop in Munich has been dissuading his parish priests from consorting too closely with their Protestant colleagues. Even so, a certain amount of ecumenical work does go on discreetly at a high level. The Churches are even prepared to campaign jointly on certain issues — for instance, to protect the human rights of Muslim immigrant workers.

The two confessions have very different histories in Germany. The Reformation reduced the Catholics to a mere one-fifth of the population, and since then the predominant culture of the country has been Protestant; its great poets and philosophers have come mainly from that background. The Prussian Kaisers were Protestant, as were most of the ruling princes (but not the Wittelsbachs in Bavaria), while Catholicism was strongest among poorer people and peasants. Bismarck even sought to limit the Catholics. So inevitably the Catholic Church has long been on the defensive in Germany, and is only now emerging from this. Today it remains much more preoccupied than the Protestant Churches with its own internal problems of doctrine, discipline and liturgy. It was heavily shaken in the 1970s by the affair of Hans Küng, the Swiss theologian at Tübingen University who wrote books questioning the infallibility of the Pope and other dogmas, and was finally dismissed from his sacred offices by the Vatican. At the same time, the Church in Germany as elsewhere has been struggling to come to terms with changing attitudes to abortion (see p. 199) and to the celibacy of priests. The maintenance of the celibacy rule has contributed to the steady decline in recruitment to the clergy, with the result that the average age of priests is now over 55, and in many dioceses one priest has to look after two or three churches. This crisis is less serious than in France, but it is growing. Many priests who wanted to marry have now abandoned holy orders, while others have been permitted to resolve their private problems in an elegantly hypocritical manner – at Tübingen University, I was told that eight of the ten priests teaching at the faculty of theology co-habit openly with their common-law wives, and they are accepted in society as couples; the Church turns a blind eye. But, if they were to commit the monstrosity of legalising their liaison, they would have to give up their priesthood and their jobs. It is a charmingly Alice-through-the-looking-glass inversion of society's traditional attitude to married versus non-married couples. Of course, in a Bavarian village a priest would not be able to behave so brazenly: but Tübingen is more sophisticated.

In many Catholic parishes, tensions over moral issues today frequently exist between older traditionalist Christians and younger ones who are more critical of the Church's official teaching and more politically and socially involved. Yet the Church as a whole remains unified and disciplined and the level of attendance at Mass is fairly high, ranging from some 15 per cent in the big cities to 60 per cent or more in parts of Bavaria. In these smaller towns and villages, the Church is still the dominant local force, and regular appearance at Mass is necessary for social acceptance. Many rural parishes are still deeply conservative, but newer suburban ones less so – in the Munich commuter suburb of Baldham, I found a big bright modern church animated by a young priest who conducted his Sunday morning service in a breezy get-together style, using a mike to chat up members of the congregation like a compère in a TV talk-show.

In contrast to the Catholics, the Protestants have a low level of church-going (about 9 per cent, falling to 5 per cent in the cities) but far fewer problems of recruitment of clergy: there are twice as many good candidates as posts to be filled. Another important difference is that the Protestant Churches are a loose federation of semi-autonomous regional bodies where secular leaders play as influential a role as ecclesiastical ones. This federation, the *Evangelische Kirche in Deutschland* (EKD), is an alliance of 17 *Land* churches, of three main kinds: several Lutheran (strongest in the south and around Hanover); two Reformed (in the north-west); and eight United (in Berlin and the Rhine regions), formed of mergers between Reformed and Lutheran groups. These Churches are heirs to two traditions, Lutheran and Pietist. Just as Lutheranism began as a revolt against the corruption and worldliness of Rome, so the Pietist movement first developed in the later seventeenth century as a reaction to the Lutheran Churches which by then had become deeply conservative and wedded to the established political order. The Pietists, whose influence is still alive today in parts of north-west Germany and Swabia, laid their emphasis on the individual's spiritual life, on prayer and moral renewal, and on parish welfare activity, without any regard for politics. It was in many ways an austere and puritanical faith – but not without its inner warmth. Even today, the Germans' concern for the interior life of feeling and for the close emotional bonds of family and friendship, the value they set on celebrating birthdays and feast days and on giving little presents as tokens of affection, to a degree that some foreigners may find sentimental – all this can be related to the Pietist tradition.

It is possible also to trace some link between these earlier German anti-material'st reform movements, Lutheran and Pietist, and the more recent radical Leftist trends among Protestants – but only in the wider sense of 'protestantism', for today's Christian protesters are not exactly Lutheran in spirit. Since the war, a number of Protestant leaders and their followers have consistently sought to influence politics in a Leftist direction – with greater or lesser success. Pastor Niemöller in the 1950s argued in vain against German rearmament and entry into NATO. But then in the 1960s the Protestant Churches did play a crucial role in preparing the ground for Brandt's *Ostpolitik*, by urging reconciliation with Poland and a gentler attitude to the GDR. A few Church leaders also supported the student Left during the 1968 period, and even spoke up for justice for the Baader-Meinhof terrorists.

During the 1980s, the peace movement (see p. 566) became the main focus of attention. While the Catholic Church still officially tolerates the nuclear deterrent as the lesser of evils, the EKD has taken no formal stance on the matter, for its members have become deeply divided. Many priests and lay leaders, and some bishops too, spoke out publicly in the 1980s against the new American missile bases in West Germany, and in some cases priests scuffled with the police at peace rallies. In the years before the fall of the Berlin Wall, many radical Protestants would even argue that it was the moral duty of the Church to remain neutral in the East/West ideological struggle, for Communism with its stress of brotherhood was just as near to Christianity as capitalism was; these radicals then warmly backed Neues Forum's efforts to find a 'third way' (see pp. 427–9). During 1990, these tensions within Church ranks were then much reduced by East/West progress on disarmament, by the apparent end of the Cold War and the collapse of Communism. However, many pastors today remain pacifist and will even urge the young men in their parish not to do their military service with the *Bundeswehr*. They were also prominent in the peace rallies during the Gulf War.

Inevitably, all these issues have led to mighty arguments within the Church, and some bitterness. Older conservative Protestants have sometimes walked out of church services when radical pastors, invoking the Sermon on the Mount, have preached against the bomb from the pulpit. And, in Hamburg, the middle-of-the-road Bishop Krusche explained to me his dilemma: 'Some of my young clergy preach that it is a Christian's duty to refuse to serve with the *Bundeswehr*. I say to them, no, you can give private advice of this kind, as a friend, but you should not involve the Church as such. It's the same with priests who go in their cassocks to peace demos. We say to them: go along if you like, but not in a cassock, for that gives the public the false impression that the Church officially is against the bomb. A lot of priests disobey us on this – but what can we do? Unlike the Catholics, the Protestant Churches today are so decentralised and liberal that anyone can do what he likes.' Down in Pietist Swabia, I heard a very different slant on this issue from Erhard Eppler, a former chairman of the EKD, former SPD minister in Bonn, and the best-known lay Protestant leader in the peace movement: 'The split in our Church today is very severe. Old-style Pietism is rising up again, in a new ultra-conservative guise. These Pietists seem to be just as concerned as in the old days to steer Christianity away from politics and secular issues – and so they denounce the peace movement. But, for us, Christianity and disarmament are inseparable. It's a fundamental divergence.'

It is an ironical situation. The old pre-war conflicts *between* Catholics and Protestants have now been replaced by others almost as sharp *within* each of the Churches – Catholics against Catholics over abortion, Protestants against Protestants over the bomb, and so on.

Some idea of the mood of liberal German Protestantism can be gained from a visit to the famous *Evangelische Kirchentag*, a five-day event held every two years. This is not an official synod but a big popular rally of 200,000 or so people, organised mainly by lay leaders, and in its sheer size it is unique among Protestant gatherings in Europe: the pilgrimages to Taizé, in Burgundy, may be more fervent, but they are much smaller. I attended the 1985 *Kirchentag* held in June in the decidedly uncharismatic setting of the Düsseldorf trade exhibition centre. Its vast halls, normally full of tidy short-haired salesmen parading the latest consumer products, were this time given over to untidy long-haired radicals in charge of stalls denouncing consumerism, or promoting such causes as homosexuals' rights, help for battered wives or support for Nicaragua. There was hardly a cassock or dog-collar in sight; the priests were in mufti, and the only 'uniform' was the purple scarf of the peace movement, worn by most of the younger pilgrims. The scarves were all over town too, as the rally spilled out unofficially into the heart of this fearful city of Mammon, whose piazzas and terraces in the shadow of the big banks were filled incongruously with little groups of hymn-singers, meditators, mimes and buskers.

Each day at the *Kirchentag* one could choose from scores of bible meetings, prayer meetings, concerts, cabarets, hymn-singing sessions and talk-ins. Yet it was all curiously low-key and earnest, rather than animated, lacking either the pageant of Catholic ritual or the emotional revivalist fervour that would surely mark any such rally in the United States. A group of swaying white-robed nuns, chanting their love for Jesus, struck a rare note of true spiritual joy. By contrast, much the biggest attendances were for the lengthy talk-in sessions on serious lay topics, some of them addressed by senior politicians including President von Weizsäcker and Johannes Rau of the SPD. Here young people in their thousands sat uncomfortably on the floor for up to three hours, to hear debates on unemployment, disarmament, Third World aid, East–West relations, and so on. After one session, on 'Why are the Germans so full of *Angst*?', we were split up into little groups of eight to discuss with strangers our own private *Angst* problems, and then our *rapporteurs* spoke from the floor. One girl announced solemnly, 'What gives me *Angst* is worrying about whether or not I ought to feel *Angst*.' No one laughed. To an outsider, the session seemed close to a self-parody of the German talent for being unblinkingly serious.

The radical bias and secular preoccupations of the *Kirchentag* have so annoyed the more conservative Protestants that in 1985 they staged a boycott and held their own rival assembly in Stuttgart, dedicated to what they saw as the true spiritual values. So this is one of today's major talking-points: is radical involvement compatible with true religious faith? – is there not a danger, amid all the discussions on nuclear missiles and unemployment, ecology and the position of homosexuals, that real devotional questions and the love of God might be overlooked? Many, such as Eppler, believe that the two go hand-in-hand: but many others, and not only the diehard Pietists, are worried that young Christians' concern with secular rather than spiritual matters may be going too far. Probably this is a question that only the individual conscience can answer. Some not very religious people may be using the Church as a forum for social attention: others, as they parade their peace placards, may be genuinely fired by the mystical love of Christ. Who can tell? Certainly it would be wrong to deduce that religious interest as a whole is declining in Germany: after a trough in the 1950s and 1960s, all the signs point to a modest revival in the past few years, alike among Catholics and Protestants. The churches may have been emptying for their formal services of worship, but the faithful have been turning to other forms of religious expression – not only to secular activism, but to all kinds of informal prayer meetings, Bible readings, charismatic groups and the like; 'The best Christians today are often not churchgoers,' said one Protestant leader. The general impression of nearly all observers is that the Germans today, and especially the young, have been turning towards Christianity in an age of uncertainty.

# 5

# TURKISH 'GUEST WORKERS' AND OTHER IMMIGRANTS: A PAINFUL PATH TOWARDS ACCEPTANCE

Ever since the 'economic miracle', rich and stable West Germany has beckoned as a promised land of opportunity and freedom for millions of immigrants, foreign or ethnic German, from less prosperous or happy countries. Many have found good jobs, and settled down well: but others have been disappointed. And their mass arrival in a thickly populated country with little multi-cultural tradition, indeed with a tragic legacy of anti-semitic racism, has provoked some social tensions.

After the initial mass influx of 14 million German fugitives from Communism in the first post-war years, four distinct categories of other immigrants have since been arriving. First in the 1960s and 1970s came the so-called 'guest workers' (*Gastarbeiter*) from Turkey and other southern countries, welcomed in by the Government to provide needed labour for the fast-growing economy. Then in the 1980s, much less welcome, came a fast-growing number of would-be political asylum-seekers (*Asylanten*) from the Third World and eastern Europe. More recently, the flow of German migrants from the east has resumed on a big scale – first, a mass of ethnic German resettlers (*Aussiedler*) from Poland, Romania and the Soviet Union and secondly the flood of emigrants from the GDR (*Übersiedler*) in its dying months of 1989–90 (see p. 422–9).

Altogether nearly 1.5 million Germans or people of German origin arrived from the east in 1989–90 alone. It says much for the booming state of the economy that West Germany has been able to absorb them without too great difficulty and that most have found homes and jobs; also that the Government has not felt obliged to conduct large-scale expulsions of the foreign 'guest workers', in order to make room for them. As most of the newcomers are still of working age, or younger, they have even done something to make up for the very low birth-rate. However, despite official efforts, the strain on housing resources, on social services and the job market has in some areas been considerable. Popular resentment against all immigrants, German or foreign, has been increasing. And this has not made life easier for the now well-established communities of over 4 million foreign *Gastarbeiter* and their families, the first and main subject of this chapter.

You can see them in their hundreds at the weekends in the vast halls of the German railway termini, which they take over as informal meeting-places and endow with the ambience of some Mediterranean town square. Here shops and stalls sell them kebabs and pizzas, or their national newspapers such as *Hurriyet* or *Gazzetta dello Sport*, while the trains coming and going from Istanbul, Athens or Naples provide nostalgic hints of home. Or you notice them in the streets of the poorer quarters, outside cafés and groceries with strange names and spicy smells – spare dark-eyed Sicilians, moustachioed Montenegrins, and dumpy Anatolian peasant women in headscarves. Including their families, these foreign workers total well over 4 million: about one-third are Turkish, with Italians, Yugoslavs, Greeks and Iberians as the next most numerous. They were invited so pressingly to Germany during the years of fast economic growth, when labour was in short supply: but, though some have now been here for decades, relatively few have integrated into German society or have felt encouraged to do so. Especially this is true of the Turks, whose culture, life-style and religion are so different. They live in run-down housing that the Germans don't want, their children swell the classes of German schools, and they smart under the resentments they arouse. It is all quite a problem. As the liberal writer Max Frisch has put it, 'We called for a labour force but we got human beings.'

Much has been written about the plight of the immigrant workers in Europe, especially in West Germany. Sometimes the newspapers carry reports of Turks committing suicide in desperation; or the slogans aerosoled on walls, '*Türken raus!*' (Turks out), bring echoes of the '*Juden raus!*' of the 1930s. So, when I myself began to explore this subject, I feared the worst. However, after much research in the main cities and talks with Turks, Germans and others, I reached the conclusion that although of course the problem exists it has tended to be exaggerated.

For there is a positive side to the picture. First, one comes across countless examples of personal friendships and good neighbourly relations, while innumerable German organisations and individuals of all kinds devote their time generously to helping the immigrants. Secondly, there is much less violence or open conflict than in a country such as Britain with a higher degree of integration; the average German's attitude is one of polite indifference, or grumbling contempt, rather than active hostility. But of course the foreigners chafe at their treatment by a society that takes their labour but does not make them feel accepted — in a Germany that, unlike the United States or the ex-colonial powers, has virtually no experience of absorbing alien cultures. And this complex problem of the *Gastarbeiter* — as they have long been called unofficially, with what today seems a touch of irony — has come to trouble the conscience of the more liberal Germans. Does it not cast a shadow over the new Germany's bright ideals of 'Europeanism' and 'internationalism'? — or even raise basic questions about just how kind and tolerant this new German society is?

In the first years after the war, the arrival from the east of some 14 million refugees, nearly all of them German, provided the reborn economy with the extra labour it needed. But by the later 1950s this supply had become inadequate (in 1961 there were some 500,000 unfilled job vacancies): so the Federal Government began to look abroad, to the poorer countries of southern Europe. And they poured in very readily, these Italians, Yugoslavs and others: most of them at that time were single men without their families, attracted by the opportunities to learn some skills and above all to earn far higher wages than was possible back home, and thus buy a house or land or start a business. The governments of the 'donor' countries happily supported the emigration too, for it eased their own unemployment, it brought in foreign currency, and it provided free training for workers who in modern factories picked up techniques that their homelands could never have given them. Therefore several nations, including Turkey in 1961, signed treaties allowing Germany to set up recruiting offices in their cities for use by German firms. The arrangement suited all sides. Some *Gastarbeiter* were even welcomed with bouquets at railway stations by grateful mayors; the millionth to arrive officially, a Portuguese, in 1964, was fêted as a hero by the German media and given a motorbike as a present. Those were the days. . . .

Around 1970, German industry was making another leap forward, and even more immigrants were needed. But by now the Spanish and Italian economies had so far improved that the supplies from those quarters were drying up, and many Spaniards and Italians were returning home. So the Bonn Government turned to the best other source available: the Turks, already present in modest numbers. Whereas many of the south European workers were by now semi-skilled or even skilled, the Turks were most of them poor peasants from Anatolia; and they have always proved quite ready to take on the more menial jobs — in the mines, on building sites, as sweepers and refuse-collectors — that the Germans spurn. They arrived intending to remain just a few years, but most have stayed on far longer — 'finding German money sweeter than Turkish honey' (as one Turk said to me), and often deterred by the acrid taste of that honey in a Turkey of high unemployment, great poverty and political severity. And yet, like most other *Gastarbeiter*, few of them have really put down roots in Germany. All foreign workers legally employed are entitled to the same pay as Germans; they have full welfare and social rights and most employers treat them fairly. But few have even applied for German citizenship. They retain their ties with home and their dream of returning to live there one day, and so in Germany they remain in a kind of limbo between two cultures. There is little of an American-style 'melting-pot'.

Ever since the first signs of world recession at the end of 1973, the Government has imposed a virtual ban on new recruitment from outside the EC. But this has had a paradoxical effect. Knowing that they might lose their work permits if they left Germany for more than three months, many hitherto itinerant *Gastarbeiter* simply decided to settle there and to get their wives and children to join them; the Turks in particular, so family-minded, were also unhappy at remaining as single men in an alien Christian culture so far from home. So the Turkish families have blossomed and bred: despite the ban, the overall Turkish population rose from 1,028,000 in 1974 to 1,581,000 in 1982, and by 1990 was over 1.6 million. Other figures are equally striking: whereas the ban did succeed in reducing the numbers of active foreign workers from 2.6 million in 1973 to 1.9 million a decade later, the overall foreign population continued to rise in this period, from 4.0 to 4.6 million (by 1990 it was 4.8 million). Family dependants today account for 60 per cent of the total, whereas in the 1960s some 90 per cent of the workers were single men — living in the sad dormitories of cramped hostels and chasing German girls (or at least, the Italians did; the Turks, whatever their other 'faults' in German eyes, are much less lecherous).

Today (1990 figures) the Turks number 1,612,000, while the other main communities are the Yugoslavs (610,000), Italians (519,000), Greeks (293,000), Spanish (126,000), Portuguese (75,000) and Moroccans (62,000), with some 150,000 others also in the *Gastarbeiter* category (such as redundant Glasgow shipyard workers). Today the general German view, alike governmental and popular, is that there are too many of these foreigners for the good either of society or of the economy. And so, with unemployment rising, resentment has been growing – ironically, just at a time when integration, especially of the non-Turks, has finally been making some progress.

One day, in the little Swabian town of Horb, I enjoyed a lunch of taramasalata and moussaka, washed down with retsina, in a big, stylish restaurant adorned with blown-up photographs of Greece, owned and run by a dapper and self-confident 35-year-old born in Salonika. His wife did the cooking, helped out by young *Gastarbeiter* from Izmir, Sarajevo and Liverpool. He said: 'Ninety per cent of my guests are German. I have no problems here, I've always got on well with the Germans and I learned good German here at school. Life is far easier for me than it was for my father when he arrived here from Greece as a manual worker, 25 years ago, speaking no German. Yes, we Greeks *are* integrating slowly, and we're far better liked than those illiterate Turks, who don't bother to pick up the language or even to learn the rules of living here. But I still want to live in Greece again one day. It's still my home.' This, with its touch of Hellenic turkophobia thrown in, is a not untypical experience. The Greeks, Yugoslavs and others still tend to be socially separate, but they have finally won a certain acceptance and respect. A great many Germans go on holiday to their countries and to Spain and Italy: thus they discover at first hand that these are civilised European societies, they often acquire a smattering of the language too (especially Italian), and they enjoy the cuisine and folklore.

Quite a few of the immigrants are middle-class educated people, or they have moved into that category (like the Greek in Horb), and quite often they open shops, restaurants (see p. 214) or other businesses. They have added greatly to Germany's cultural variety. At Hechingen, a small town not far from Horb, a colony of Italians arrived in the 1950s and soon took over the local sheep and cattle trade that used to be in Jewish hands: they made money, and as well as running the best boutiques and eating-places in town they have now acquired and beautifully restored a number of lovely old half-timbered houses damaged in the war. All in all, a triumphant neocolonisation in the footsteps of their Roman forebears who settled in the area 2,000 years previously.

Of all these nationalities, Yugoslavs tend to be the best liked, and are much appreciated by employers for their intelligence, politeness and hard work. Spaniards are popular too; but there is still some prejudice against south Italians, thought of as feckless and noisy. In one suburb, the Germans complained so much of *bambini* shouting in the playground that the police arrived with decibel measures. Working-class *Gastarbeiter* are seldom invited socially into German homes, and for their leisure they still stick to their own communities – as witness the Greek pub I visited in a poor quarter of Stuttgart, all bouzouki music and sirtaki-dancing, where old peasant grannies in black sat along one wall and I was the only non-Greek present. In this as in other suburbs, the Greeks have their own shops and cafés, bakeries and laundries. For their welfare problems, throughout Germany the Greeks are helped by a German Protestant organisation, federally subsidised, while Caritas, an international Catholic welfare body, takes care of the Spanish and Italians. Ever since the inception of the EC's free labour market, the Italians have been at liberty to live and seek work in Germany much as they please: but this has not led to any flood, for the reasons I gave earlier. The Greeks, who joined the EC in 1980, have since then been acquiring a similar freedom; and since 1986 the same is now true of Spaniards and Portuguese. But there has been no massive influx: so these nationalities are not regarded as posing any great threat – and when a German today says, 'I hate *Gastarbeiter*', he usually means, 'I hate Turks.' Some 80 per cent of all Turks in EC countries are in Germany.

If they were all from the Istanbul middle classes, there would be much less of a problem. But they have tended to come from rural Anatolia, often illiterate; and in so many ways they are so 'different' that inevitably the mutual culture shock has been far greater than in the case of the European immigrants. Reacting with blind prejudice rather than trying to understand, many ordinary Germans fear and despise the Turks for their 'alien' Muslim religion, their seclusion of their women-folk, their teeming kids, their 'dirt' and 'noise', their garlicky breath and cooking smells (not necessarily worse than those of Greeks or Sicilians) and the more bizarre of their household practices. I heard tales of sheep and goats kept tethered on tenement landings; and in one extreme case a peasant family horrified their Berlin landlord by taking three sheep up to their flat, slaughtering them in the living-room for a festival and then stuffing the remains down the toilet. Usually it is the newly-arrived ones who have behaved like this: after a while they learn to 'adapt', so today such incidents are much more rare.

It is not easy to draw a fair and balanced picture, for much of Turkish peasant custom and behaviour (concerning more serious matters than sheep-ritual) does seem genuinely shocking to the very same European liberals who plead for kinder treatment of Turks – just as it does to radical modern Turks themselves, such as the film-maker Yilmar Güney who died in exile in France in 1985: his masterpiece *Yol* gave a terrifying portrait of the feudal cruelty of a rural society where a man can torture his adulterous wife to death. In a less harsh form, such patriarchal severity can sometimes manifest itself in Germany too, where a kindly German teacher may well be horrified when a Turkish boy appears in class, pulls up his shirt to display the weals and bruises on his back, and says, 'Look what my father did to me. He was angry that you gave me such low marks – so it's *your* fault!' One German told me that he came across a Turk beating up his ten-year-old son in a park. When he tried to intercede, the Turk took the boy up to his flat nearby, opened the window and went on beating him in full view, calling out, 'You can't stop me exercising my parental duty in my own home!' Many Turks will indeed claim that this paternal discipline is a wise and just system: they point to the solidarity and security of Turkish family life, where the very old are warmly cared for, and they compare this with 'heartless' European society with its drugs, promiscuity, broken homes, dangerous freedom for young girls, and grannies left lonely in old people's homes ... it all leaves German liberals in quite a dilemma. On the one hand, they plead with their fellow-citizens to show more sympathy and humanity towards the Turks in their midst. On the other, they hope fervently that Turkey's own society will evolve and modernise, and that German education and standards (for all their shortcomings) may have some beneficial influence on Turks living here.

Like the Blacks in Britain and America, the Turks in Germany have grouped themselves into some of the seedier parts of inner cities. These get dubbed 'ghettos' by the media: but the term is hardly accurate, for generally the population remains mixed, including a few poorer Germans – even though most Germans do move out when Turks begin to settle in force in a tenement. Here they do their best to recreate their home ambience. They run shops selling Turkish books and video-cassettes, as well as Turkish rugs, strong dark coffee, lentils and spices; oriental music strains out from café doorways in the dark, slummy streets. The Turks cling to Islam and traditional ways, often converting upper shop-floors into little *ad hoc* mosques which serve also as Koranic schools for their numerous children (their high birth-rate, three times the German average, is one cause of German alarm). By law the kids must also attend German state schools all morning, boys and girls together in class (oh, Allah!) – and so they are caught in quite a culture conflict, often speaking neither language well. Hence they tend to be under-achievers at school, and few go on to *Gymnasium*. When they do secure apprenticeships, they usually do well at them: but their youth unemployment rate is far above the average and this leads to frustration and delinquency – as with young Blacks in Britain. Certainly the *Land* education authorities have been making efforts to help the children, including the training and paying for hundreds of Turks to be teachers in state schools (320 in Berlin alone), so that some classes are held in both languages. But this has not worked out easily, owing to the great differences between the Turkish and German school systems. In most areas, the Turkish pupils go into the ordinary German classes, where in some cases they account for well over half the numbers. This tends to slow down the others – and it can lead to tensions with German parents, even though between the children themselves there are seldom conflicts. At a *Hauptschule* in Karlsruhe, a most sympathetic German Jewish woman teacher told me: 'The Turks in my class very seldom get bullied or teased. The boys are high-spirited, naughty, charming – and not keen on work. The girls are terribly pretty, very intelligent, but quiet and shy: the only problem is that the German kids don't like sitting next to them because, to be honest, they do smell. The fourteen-year-olds explain to me: "We're not allowed to bath more than once a week, the Koran says it's immodest for girls to be naked." A pity – it's just the kind of silly thing that makes these silly cleanliness-obsessed German parents so racist.'

But I must again stress that many Germans of all kinds do make great efforts to help the Turks and other immigrants. Not only do the Churches run welfare centres and kindergartens, but the *Bund* and *Land* governments and city councils have social affairs departments staffed by well-meaning liberals who wield sizeable budgets and generally do their bit – as witness the city-funded local street festival I found one Sunday in Munich, where a troupe of Turkish youths and blonde local *Mädchen* gave a display of folk-dancing.

Individuals are active too: in Bavaria alone, there are some 30 German volunteer organisations who help Turkish children with their homework. The unions, in defiance of the racist element in their rank-and-file, also have a good record: *Gastarbeiter* make up 10 per cent of DGB membership, and a few have even been elected to factory works' councils. As for employers, most of the larger firms at least treat their immigrants well and will seldom dismiss a Turk if he is a good worker.[1] Some companies have even made efforts to come to terms with the Turks' religious customs: a Turkish leader in Berlin told me that he had persuaded Siemens and some other firms to instal little Islamic prayer-rooms in their factories, as well as to provide special canteens serving Oriental food. As for the old Koranic rule that even a man must not be seen washing naked, for some years this caused problems in the big communal shower-rooms of the mines and steelworks, for the Turks demanded separate cubicles, but were refused. Finally, a senior 'liberal' mullah came from Istanbul and explained to the workers (who in Germany tend to be under the sway of reactionary mullahs) that the new modernised Koran had lifted the ban on male nudity. So all ended happily.

Robert Bosch is a marvellous firm with a long philanthropic tradition and a first-class personnel record (see p. 138) and its *Stiftung* (charity foundation) has been running projects for teenage children of *Gastarbeiter* in Munich, Berlin, and its home town of Stuttgart. Here, in a large and gloomy old working-class housing-estate behind the main station, I talked to Bosch's team of young German social workers, some of whom had specially learned Turkish. The flats, mostly built in the 1920s without indoor plumbing, are used by the *Bundesbahn* and the Post Office to house their own workers and families, German and

---

1. It is true that a very different account was given by the investigative journalist Günter Wallraff, who in 1983–5 spent two and a half years disguised as a Turkish worker and took all kinds of menial jobs in order to find out how bad the experience could be. The resulting book, *Ganz unten* (*Lowest of the Low*), sold over 1.7 million copies. Wallraff produced evidence that some leading firms, including Thyssen, exploited immigrants as virtual slave labour. Much of his reporting was certainly authentic and it painted a horrific picture: but it applied only to a tiny minority of illegal immigrants who had no redress against such treatment and had to take any work they could find. His book, which secured world-wide publicity, gave a thoroughly partial and untypical portrait of the fate of the average guest worker in Germany. It was also widely claimed that he had faked many incidents in order to strengthen his story.

foreign: Turkish bronze ornaments and bright carpets were decorating many balconies. I was told that relations between Turks and Germans on the estate were satisfactory, for there is a certain worker solidarity; but each national group tends to keep on its own, socially. At one street corner, a group of Italian men were earnestly discussing football or politics, just as in any Italian town. 'But,' said my guide, 'it's through the kindergarten and the youth club that we're hoping that the next generation will start to integrate' — indeed, in the club, Italian and Spanish girls (but of course not Turks) were flirting with Yugoslav boys, and then two Turks of 14 and a Neapolitan came in from playing football together. One of the Turks, moustachioed and looking at least 17, said he wanted to be a doctor and to go back to Turkey, 'because it rains too much here.' They giggled, and laughed off my question about whether they felt there was prejudice against Turks in Germany — 'Oh well, yes, what do you expect? — we don't take it too seriously.' I was then taken to the Bosch centre, to meet some Turkish girls, and was told by the social workers: 'Their parents won't allow them here at all, and very few Turks let their daughters aged 13 or more go swimming with boys. The girls have to stay at home, helping mother.' In a room with Güney film posters on the walls, three Turkish girls of 14, lively, precocious, enchanting, all with good German, were allowed to talk to me (my greyish hair presumably put me outside the taboo age-group). One of them said her father worked on night-shift cleaning trains: 'My parents are left-wing and not very religious, so they let me go out. I've been in Stuttgart since I was six, and I feel as much German as Turkish. I want to spend my life here, for women have so much more freedom, and I'd be glad to marry a German.' Another girl, alas less untypical, said, 'My father would never let me marry a German, it's against Islam. Yes, Turkey is still my home and I want to go back one day.'

In Stuttgart, and in Munich or the Ruhr, nearly all the Turks are in more-or-less working-class jobs; likewise in Frankfurt, where tensions are much the worst and 22 per cent of the population are *Gastarbeiter*. Berlin is the one German city where the Turks, like the coloured minorities in London or New York, have their own educated elite, playing some part in local intellectual life. Here you find Turkish writers and lawyers, and exhibitions by Turkish artists, while the number of Turkish university students is far higher than elsewhere. This city with its 125,000 Turks (the biggest Turkish town outside Turkey) also has much the best municipal record of trying to help them: this was due quite largely to Richard von Weizsäcker, now

Federal President, who as CDU governing mayor in 1981 poured funds and staff into a new *Land* welfare centre for immigrants, and also plastered the city with propaganda posters of happy young Turks and Germans, hand-in-hand together.

This was not the picture 15 or 20 years ago, after the Turks and their sheep had first settled en masse in the slums of the Kreuzberg district, near the Wall, and the startled Germans had reacted angrily. This was the 'Kreuzghetto' of the tabloid headlines, where rival gangs of youths were reported to be assaulting each other nightly. But today this image of Kreuzberg is out of date. All has become fairly amicable. First, the Turks are now numerous enough (35,000, or 25 per cent) to feel reasonably secure and at home, in a 'town' of their own of some two square miles (though by no means a ghetto). Secondly, Kreuzberg since the mid-1970s has become a true Greenwich Village, filling up with middle-class Greens, Leftish intellectuals and the kind of radical-*Schickeria* who, unlike working-class Germans, actually think it smart to live in a racially-mixed area, where they can have Turks as neighbours and get friendly with them. Kreuzberg is 'in'. During the squatter period, young radicals eagerly helped Turkish families to settle in empty buildings; and nowadays the local Turks seem to be almost outnumbered by the sociologists, media Lefties and assorted do-gooders who have come to scrutinise them like some rare wild-life species. True, this idyll is sometimes shattered by the *Schlägerbanden*, gangs of young neo-Nazi skinheads, usually out of work, who bash up Turks – and some young Turks bash back. But such incidents are far rarer than they used to be. By contrast, in some tenements the Turks have finally become friends with their poor and elderly German neighbours, the original inhabitants, and mutual help has developed: the Turks haul up coal and wood for the oldies, who in turn do baby-sitting when the Turkish wives are at work.

I visited the city-funded Turkish social centre in Adalbertstrasse. It is run by and for Turks. More Güney posters on the walls, and portraits of Ataturk. There was folk-dancing, an engagement party, and a more emancipated atmosphere than in Stuttgart. Here I met Emine Altiok, a dazzling young woman from Adana who had studied at Berlin University and was now with the state *Rundfunk*, making radio programmes for local Turks: 'I'm second generation. I came here as a small girl with my father, who makes furniture. I'm married to a Turk, who is culturally "integrated", so he doesn't try to dominate me: I'd never stand for that. Most second-generation Turkish marriages split up, however, simply because the women have become emancipated in Germany, they earn their own living and won't accept the usual role of a Turkish wife.' Turning to the general position of Turks in Germany, she went on: 'In every way, things were far tougher for my father's generation: they had language problems, and the Germans were more xenophobic in those days. For us it's easier, but we have a new problem of identity. Are we Turkish or German? We cherish our own culture and religion, but we see positive things in European society especially for women. Many women who go back to Turkey just can't cope any more with the restrictions, at least not in the provinces – it's easier in Istanbul or Ankara. We, who plan to stay in Germany, intend to work out a middle way between Turkish female subservience and German excess of liberty.'

It was ironical that just when Turkish/German personal contacts seemed to be improving, and the Turks were at last starting to feel more at home, so the rise in unemployment in the 1980s increased German prejudice against them. Broadly the pattern seems to be that, on the one hand, friendliness and neighbourly good-will have increased among those who know each other personally, but at the same time there has been a growth in indiscriminate ill-feeling towards foreign workers as a whole – 'Kemal next door, he's a good chap – but what of all the other Turks?' is a common German attitude. And, since *Gastarbeiter* are supposed to be stealing jobs from Germans, the facile equation can be made, 'Two million foreign workers = two million German unemployed, so send them all home!' Sensible people realise that this is nonsense, for most out-of-work Germans are not seeking the same jobs as Turks, too often relegated to the most menial chores. And if they *were* sent home, who could be found to do this kind of work? In Düsseldorf, the SPD-led city council commissioned a study which showed that, if the 36,000 immigrant workers departed, rubbish disposal services and public transport might well collapse, and hospitals and the building industries would be seriously short of labour.

Even so, by 1982 the opinion polls were indicating that over 80 per cent of Germans thought that there were far too many foreign workers. Moreover the Turks themselves were the worst victims of unemployment: by 1983, 16.7 per cent of them were out of work, twice the federal average, and this put a burden on the social security budget. So the Kohl Government decided to take action. Large-scale forced repatriation was not an option – for political and humanitarian reasons, and also because Turkish workers do possess some rights of access to

Germany under Turkey's EEC association agreement of 1963. But for a few months in 1983–4 Bonn did try out an incentive scheme for voluntary departure, whereby any *Gastarbeiter* on short-time work or made redundant through plant closure could obtain a grant of 10,500 DM (plus 1,500 DM for each child) and a refund of his pension contributions, so long as he and all his family left promptly. It was not exactly a generous offer, but it did have some success: about 80,000 wage-earners applied for the money, and in all some 300,000 immigrants left, 80 per cent of them Turkish. But for most Turks the choice was a painful one: it was quite a wrench to leave a Germany where they were paid well and had begun to settle, and to return to their backward homeland with its 25 per cent unemployment. No longer at ease in either culture, many Turks find it very hard to readjust if they go back home. Hence, the vast majority remain in Germany.

The English sociologist and immigration expert Stephen Castles, who lives and works in Frankfurt, has analysed the subject from a Marxist viewpoint in his interesting book, *Here for Good: Western Europe's Ethnic Minorities* (Pluto Press, London, 1984). He told me: 'History shows that labour immigrations always lead to permanent settlement, unless forcibly prevented – look at the Asians and West Indians in Britain, or the Polish miners in France. German governments have failed to understand this, so they have applied only *ad hoc* short-term solutions to the problem and have not accepted that many families will remain and finally integrate. Holland, Sweden, and even France have far more intelligent policies. Today the Germans have at last woken up to the real issues, so there's quite a political debate in progress.' Mr Castles may well be proved right. But neither the Germans nor the Turks have yet fully faced up to what permanent settlement would involve. Would it lead to integration? – or assimilation? – or neither? Integration means that immigrants adapt to German standards and are accepted into German society, while retaining their own culture and, probably, citizenship; assimilation means a much fuller process of Germanisation, which very few Turks wish for. But, in the longer term, is integration possible without assimilation? And is Germany ready yet for a multi-cultural society?

Though the Turks in Germany would certainly like to feel more secure and better accepted, most of them remain wary of integration. Here they are under powerful pressure from fundamentalist Islamic forces which, strangely enough, are stronger in Germany than in Turkey itself, and are also linked with the Turkish extreme-Right

[285]

political movement, the Grey Wolves. These groups exert considerable influence over a bewildered peasant population in a strange land: they preach that integration into this 'infidel' society is wicked, and that Turks should not adopt 'decadent' European habits such as alcohol or freedom between the sexes. The mullahs in Koranic schools sometimes tell their pupils not to believe what they are taught in German classes. Here I quote a leading article in *The Times* of September 5, 1983, about the North Africans in France as well as Turks in Germany: 'In both countries, fundamentalist Islamic groups, suppressed by their home governments, are exploiting the relatively free and plural nature of West European society, as well as the alienation and disorientation felt by many of the immigrants, to try to impose on the immigrant communities a totalitarian and intolerant world view, with the result that the most well-meaning attempts by the French and Germans to assimilate, emancipate or simply educate the immigrants sometimes encounter a discouragingly hostile response.' Hence, for example, the difficulty in persuading Turkish parents to permit their teenage daughters any leisure life outside the home. And the few families who dare to step out of line and Germanise are often rejected by their own people – 'There's a growing dichotomy,' I was told by Carla Baran, a psychologist from Istanbul who works for the official Bavarian welfare service for Turks, in Munich; 'some families are growing more liberal, others more traditional. And it can be the same inside families: I get visits from girls of 14 who've run away from home, or attempted suicide, because they can't stand their parents' strictness. These tensions are worse here than back in Turkey, because of the German influence and the fears of Germanising. It's a tough situation: but I think integrating is bound to come within another generation or so. The fanatics will lose in the end.'

Within Muslim circles in Germany, as in the Islamic world at large, there is quite an ideological conflict. Moderate Turkish Muslims are disturbed that fundamentalism (in Iran and elsewhere) should be spreading so harsh and archaic an image of their religion, thus fuelling German prejudices. One day, in the 'red light' district of Frankfurt near the station, I explored the Turkish Bazaar, a large complex of shops and cafés, and here I called unannounced on the little makeshift mosque upstairs, where a charming, soft-mannered acolyte plied me with mint tea: 'If the Germans bothered to learn more about Islam, there would be fewer tensions here. We see Mary and Jesus as holy, and we are taught a lot about them – but what do Christians ever bother to find out about Mohammed and the Koran? Ours is a very kind and gentle religion at heart, and its paternalist tradition is humane. My father is 82, and I still obey his very word. That's good. But the Germans have destroyed family life, so their young people are adrift, they commit suicide, they have a hunger in the soul.' When I cautiously asked him about the video-cassettes in the shop downstairs, with their lurid covers of Turkish mediaeval warriors butchering Christian crusaders, he said, 'Yes, we regret them, of course, but we can't stop them. The fundamentalists encourage them.' These cheap imported video films, Turkish equivalent of Westerns, depict the crusaders pillaging and raping, and the Turks exacting revenge – and Turkish children sit at home by their TV sets, cheering as the hated Christians are tortured and decapitated. It is the usual problem of video-nasty violence – but especially nasty in a social context where young Turks and Germans are supposed to be learning to love one another. The reactionary mullahs bear some of the responsibility. Fortunately, the right-wing army-backed government in Turkey, whatever its faults, is anti-fundamentalist, and with the active support of Bonn it has been sending some modern-minded mullahs to Germany (like the one who persuaded miners to accept communal showers) to preach a more moderate version of Islam. So the struggle for and against integration goes on.

'Integration' is the current catchword – but what does it really involve? The German authorities claim that it is official policy for *Gastarbeiter* to integrate into German society: but the Turks say, 'This is hypocritical. If they were sincere, they would make it easier for us to stay. They do not give us enough security of residence.' Here the legal position is that a foreigner is first given a short-term permit; after a few years he can acquire a permanent one, as well as an indefinite residence permit. He does not lose his work permit if he loses his job; but if he commits a crime he is likely to forfeit his rights of residence and be expelled. A German also by law has preference over a foreigner for filling a job vacancy. German officials claim that today some 85 per cent of foreign workers have unlimited work permits, and that in the present climate it would not be politically feasible to grant them fuller rights. And yet, many Turks claim that they still feel insecure. One factor may be that anyone with a dark face is vulnerable to the frequent random identity checks by the police who are trying to hunt down the large number of illegal immigrants.

Another issue is citizenship. Many German politicians, especially in the CDU, argue that if the *Gastarbeiter* really want to stay they should take German nationality, for this would help them to integrate, it would also ease tensions and solve the problem of residence rights. So this is official policy: but the Germans do not make it so easy to acquire citizenship. As in many countries, there are various hurdles on the way: you must have been in Germany for eight years and have had a secure job and residence and no criminal record; above all you must pass a stiff language test that may even include speaking the local dialect, such as Bavarian. These are not insuperable obstacles, and most applicants do succeed if they try; what's more, in 1991 the rules were relaxed, and citizenship can now be obtained much more rapidly and cheaply, especially by foreigners born in Germany. However, the real problem is that Germany is more strictly opposed than most European countries to the granting of dual nationality, whereas Turkey is more easy-going. Many Turks would take German citizenship if they could keep their own: but for emotional as well as practical reasons they are most reluctant to make this break with their homeland. And the same is true of other *Gastarbeiter* too. As a result few apply, and Germany has one of the lowest levels of naturalisation of any Western country: of resident foreigners only about 0.5 per cent a year become German citizens, compared with 2.0 per cent in Britain, 1.2 per cent in France, and 5.2 per cent in Sweden. In France, a child born to foreign parents living there can automatically take French nationality at 18 if he wishes, but not so in Germany, and a recent opinion poll suggests that any such measure would be very unpopular with Germans. These attitudes do not exactly encourage integration. The problem was emphasized to me vividly by a gentle Turk of 25 in Munich who had studied at Mainz University and was now driving a bus: 'I get on well with the Germans and I like living here. My main problems are legal and political, for neither government makes things easy. I feel that I now belong to both cultures and I'd like to be able to move freely between the two countries. But Germany won't grant me citizenship unless I give up my Turkish passport, and Turkey won't let me take that step legally unless I first do my military service — and I hate the thought of 22 tough months in the Army under that harsh regime. So I can't even visit Turkey till I'm 32, when I would no longer be liable for service. But it's hard to find a job here as a non-EEC foreigner. I have no legal security, yet I love Germany.'

One step forward, so it is suggested, would be to allow *Gastarbeiter* to vote in municipal elections, as they now can in Sweden and Holland. This might give them a greater feeling of involvement in Germany, as well as encourage local politicians to take more account of their interests. The Churches have campaigned for the proposal, which is backed also by the Greens and most of the SPD. But the Kohl Government has said no (could it be that local CDU leaders are fearful of how most *Gastarbeiter* might vote?). In general, the CDU's local record on helping *Gastarbeiter* is patchy to say the least. In Berlin it has done well: but elsewhere many CDU-led councils have appeared reluctant to spend too much money on helping immigrants, for they fear this would lose votes. So they leave most of the work to the Churches and other bodies. In Frankfurt and some other cities where latent racism is high, CDU leaders in local election campaigns have even demagogically accused the foreigners of aggravating unemployment. This, says the Left, simply fuels xenophobia. 'And it's stupid of Bonn,' added one Marxist I met, 'to ban the Turks' own political parties from activity in Germany, for this throws Turks back on their religion, reactionary and nationalist, and so makes integration even harder.'

So, if the Turks are going to stay in Germany, what is the solution for them? They want better security, kinder acceptance by the German people, and the possibility to keep their own culture. For this to be possible, each side will have to take a few steps towards the other, and Islamic and German popular attitudes will both need to be modified. In the United States, many immigrant groups have retained their own culture and customs while at the same time becoming Americans both legally and psychologically. So it can be done: but in Europe it is much more difficult, if the immigrants want to retain their own citizenship. Moreover, the Germans have never been a major colonising people like the British, French and Dutch, and so have little experience of coming to terms with non-European races and religions. Though their conscience today is still troubled by the Nazi purge of the Jews, they cannot cope with alien cultures. 'Germany,' said Stephen Castles, 'is becoming *de facto* a multi-cultural society. But the trend still frightens people here.'

In human and cultural terms, no less than economic ones, the immigrants are surely a great asset for Germany, for they add vitality and variety to local life, just like the ethnic minorities in Britain or France. But this potential is sadly under-used. Occasionally a civic hall or theatre will offer a stage to some Latin or Balkan dance troupe; a Turkish rock group won fame in Berlin; and a Sicilian fringe theatre company based in Frankfurt tours all Germany (see page 323). But it is not so often that *Gastarbeiter* arts and folklore are given chances of this kind to emerge from their ghettos onto the wider German scene. And yet, matters have been steadily improving; and the more liberal of the immigrants' own leaders are relatively optimistic that social integration will in the long run become easier, as a new generation grows up, both Turkish and German, that has sat together on the same school benches and is more open-minded than its elders. With some exceptions, young Germans are markedly less racist than their elders. So the problems of the *Gastarbeiter* will probably ease with time. Even today, it is less acute than that of young Blacks in Britain.

Lastly, I heard a charming note of objectivity from a Japanese girl at the Trumpf factory in Stuttgart, secretary/interpreter of the sales manager. When I asked her whether there were many Turkish or other foreign workers in the firm, she replied with a smile, 'I wouldn't know. You all look the same to me, you Westerners.'

One special test of radical attitudes has been provided by the recent influx of refugees demanding political asylum, most of them from eastern Europe or Third World countries. Anxious to make amends for the Nazis' treatment of the Jews, the Federal Republic today has Europe's most liberal legislation on this matter: the Constitution itself declares that no one arriving on German soil and claiming asylum can be turned away without a fair investigation. And many people have made use of this. Germany has thus taken generous quotas of Boat People as well as many fugitives from right-wing regimes such as Chile and Iran – and indeed Turkey. But since 1981 the numbers seeking asylum have risen so rapidly that the Germans have grown alarmed. And officials have become convinced that many of the would-be refugees are not political but 'economic': enticed by tales of the good life in Germany and its generous social security, they flood in from very poor countries, using asylum as a dodge. Many of them used to fly first to East Berlin on Aeroflot or Interflug (GDR) flights, much cheaper than those of Western airlines. There they could cross easily into West Berlin. In the early 1980s, Tamils from Sri Lanka were the most numerous group. Of course, as the world knows, Tamils have genuinely been suffering persecution at home: but the Federal authorities felt certain that most of the migrants had been lured by 'fantasy' stories, put about by the airlines and other traders, of Germany as a land of easy money. Many stayed in Berlin, often taking to drug-trafficking or other crime. Bonn also grew suspicious that the GDR and the Soviet Union might be fostering the inflow deliberately in order to create political trouble. So in 1985 Bonn opened talks with the East German Government on the matter, and finally in return for a promise of commercial loans (the usual German–German barter in human beings: see page 413) it did persuade it to limit the illegal Tamil entries. Their flow slowed down: but their places were simply taken by Iranians, Indians, Ghanaians and others, and during 1986 the problem grew more serious than ever: the total number of foreigners applying for political asylum that year was 99,650, compared with 74,000 in 1985.

While his case is being heard, which can sometimes take up to three years, the asylum-seeker (*Asylant*) is put in a camp or hostel at public expense – and for the first year he is not allowed to work, though some people illegally do moonlighting. Conditions in these camps have been sharply criticised by German liberals. At one camp in Tübingen, a former French Army barracks, independent witnesses found 500 *Asylanten* cooped up in premises intended for 250: they had 'appalling' sanitation and were forbidden to do their own national cooking. Some went on hunger strike. Most were middle-class, university-educated people. Many critics believed that the CDU-led government of Baden-Württemberg, and Bavaria's too, were deliberately creating harsh conditions in the camps so that the word would get around and thus deter future asylum-seekers. Politicians tacitly admitted this. When I asked Lothar Späth about the Tübingen camp, he said, 'Yes, of course the people are poorly housed: but they'd be worse off in their own country, wouldn't they? We have the world's best liberal laws to protect genuine refugees. But if we let in the mass of phoney ones, and then devote big sums to giving them a life of ease, sooner or later there'd be a German popular backlash against *all* refugees. So I have to be severe, to protect our liberal laws.' No doubt Späth had read the opinion polls, showing that 71 per cent of Germans thought the authorities 'too generous' towards *Asylanten*, while only 4 per cent found them 'too mean'. So well-meaning politicians like Späth have clearly been in a dilemma. On the one hand, they are under popular pressure to be tougher with the flood of entrants. On the other, they are saddled with this liberal legislation that Germany, because of its black past, could not make more stringent without causing an outcry at home and abroad. Most German leaders, except for a handful on the hard Right, genuinely wish to remain liberal in these matters, and to educate the public towards more tolerant attitudes. They do not always have quite the courage of their convictions.

In December 1990, I visited a typical hostel for *Asylanten*, in Munich.

It was a disused printing works that had been fitted out with dormitories for single people and makeshift cabins for families – all rather squalid, but well-lit and well-heated, and there were little electric stoves where the refugees could at least do their own national cooking, rather than rely on the kind of alien German dishes served up at Tübingen. The smell of burnt fat was pervasive. Each *Asylant* had 260 DM a month from social assistance, and some also got food parcels from home. I talked to educated young Biafrans, Iranians and Bangladeshis who said they had genuinely left their countries for political reasons, and were waiting for things back home to improve, so that they could return; they did not wish to settle in Germany, but were obliged to appeal for asylum if they were not to be thrown out. I also met some families of Romanian gypsies: today these tend to be the most rowdy and noisy inhabitants of the hostels, and are not popular with the other refugees. The staff at the hostel I visited were mostly university students, working part-time and paid a pittance (but they found the work fascinating, especially the sociology ones). They said that the *Asylanten* kept in their national groups and showed little sympathy for each other, although their problems were often very similar. They were also convinced that the city and *Land* authorities deliberately kept the hostels squalid so as to deter future migrants – 'But it doesn't work, people still pour in, expecting paradise, and are startled when they don't automatically get given a good job and a nice flat.'

To enter the country, you need to know just one word of German, '*Asyl*': say that to a border guard, and at least you are assured of bed, board and a hearing. There have been many abuses: escaped criminals and drug-traffickers have come in from Third World countries, posing as fugitives from political persecution. The Government has tried to clamp down, for example by tightening the rules on visa entry. As far as possible, all entrants are given a fair hearing, though of course errors can occur, when the innocent suffer. Seven Sri Lankans and Pakistanis once committed suicide together, when they learned they were to be expelled. And so, notoriously, did a young left-wing Turk, Kemal Altun, in Berlin in 1983. The Turkish Government was demanding his extradition for some alleged crimes. At first he was granted asylum, but then Bonn insisted on further hearings; and, after Interior Minister Zimmermann returned from a visit to Ankara, he demanded Altun's 'immediate' extradition 'in the interests of good cooperation with Turkey'. At this, Altun threw himself from the sixth-floor window of the courtroom that was trying him. It was all too obvious that

Zimmermann had traded him for Turkish promises to try to reduce the *Gastarbeiter* flow. There was an outcry, and the Minister's resignation was called for. He refused.

The opening-up of eastern Europe has now brought massive new waves of would-be *Asylanten*, few of them genuine political refugees. Some 120,000 applicants arrived in 1989, and 193,000 in 1990. And the Third World is now in the minority: in 1990 the entrants were mainly from Romania (35,000, most of them gypsies), Yugoslavia (22,000, also substantially gypsy), Turkey (22,000), Lebanon (16,000) and Poland (9,000). In a bid to control this flood, screening has now been tightened and the legal process speeded up: most cases are now settled within three months, though some can drag on for a year or two. Only about 5 per cent of applicants are finally granted asylum (and hardly any of these are from Poland, where there is no longer political persecution, nor from Yugoslavia). The rest are supposed to leave Germany at once. But in practice the authorities turn a blind eye (or are plain inefficient), and it is estimated that an amazing 70 per cent of *Asylanten* stay on indefinitely as *de facto* clandestine refugees – some 300,000 are thought to be in this category. Everyone accepts that it's a crazy situation, which Federal and *Land* Governments seem incapable of solving.

Many politicians, especially in the CDU/CSU, are now in favour of modifying the basic right to claim asylum. The most likely solution is to introduce new EC legislation – this is now being discussed in Brussels – whereby Germany would align itself on the stricter asylum and immigration rules of the French and others, and would thus find a convenient 'Euro-alibi' for becoming less liberal! But even this would require a two-thirds majority in Parliament for changing the Constitution; and the FDP and SPD both remain wary of tightening the rules. Yet some ways will clearly have to be found of deterring the thousands of 'economic' (as opposed to genuine political) refugees. 'If our laws are being abused, it's our own fault,' I was told in 1991 by Barbara John, the humane and liberal director of Berlin's immigrant welfare office. 'We give the world the misleading impression that it's easy to find asylum in Germany, so we are falsely luring people here. It's inhuman. But the politicians seem to have no solution.' Meanwhile the ubiquitous groups of Romanian gypsies in their bright scarves and dresses, hawking their goods, begging with their babies, or camping on vacant lots, will remain a picturesque but sad sight in many German cities.

Another and much larger wave of immigrants, not foreign but ethnic

German, has also been arriving in very recent years – quite legally, but they too have been posing problems. These are the *Aussiedler* ('reset-tlers') – descendants of Germans who settled in eastern Europe usually centuries ago, and are wanting to return to their roots now that those countries have opened their frontiers and are letting them go. They are coming mostly for reasons of national sentiment or economics, not because of oppression; and if they can prove their ethnic German origin (they must get a visa to this effect before they go) the Constitution stipulates that they cannot be refused German citizenship. In 1988 some 200,000 arrived, mostly from Poland; in 1989, over 300,000; in 1990, some 400,000, of whom 150,000 were from the Soviet Union, 135,000 from Poland, 112,000 from Romania. It has been Europe's biggest mass migration since the 1940s. The Poles are mostly from Silesia, which until 1945 had been part of the German realms for 600 years, so they are not actually *re*-settling: by 1991 their exodus was slowing down, for most of those wanting to leave had done so and in 1990 the Polish Government agreed with Bonn to grant a better deal to ethnic Germans there, including the use of their own language, hitherto outlawed. But the flow from the Soviet Union, where ethnic Germans have numbered some 2 million, has continued to rise, and it is feared that unrest in those Republics could increase it further.

They are a curious lot, these *Aussiedler*. Many do not even speak German, or they speak an odd kind of archaic biblical German. Some wear old-style peasant clothes, like *babushkas*; or they arrive with idealised notions of some old pre-war Germany, and are shocked to find it all very modern and Americanised, with women in jeans! They tend to stick together in their own ghettos and do not find it easy to adapt to the Western rat-race. But officialdom at least treats them much better than the *Asylanten*. Initially they are put in special camps, then distributed among the *Länder* (each has a quota) where they are tolerably well housed, given full unemployment benefits, and German language courses and re-training if they need it, and are helped to find jobs. But their qualifications do not always suit the German market, and many do not find work easily.

Resentment against them has been building up amongst ordinary Germans, who fear for their own jobs and housing prospects: an Allensbach survey in 1989 found 58 per cent of the sample thinking that 'too much' is done officially for the *Aussiedler* and only 6 per cent thinking 'too little'. Though much less unpopular than the *Asylanten*, these immigrants are not seen as 'real Germans' – unlike those from the old GDR, who are better tolerated. And the resettlement has been costing the German taxpayer some 10 billion DM a year.

Official policy today is to try – in cooperation with the Governments concerned – to persuade the would-be resettlers to stay where they are, by making life more attractive for them and more 'German'. Bonn is sending German-language teachers and schoolbooks, setting up German cultural centres and satellites for receiving the German television channels, all with the aim of providing some modern German ambience in farthest Transylvania or Kazakhstan. Whether this will slow the exodus is not yet certain.

Finally let us return to the issue of attitudes towards the *Gastarbeiter*. The question 'Just how xenophobic are the Germans?' is not an easy one to answer. Certainly horror-stories can be quoted by the score, but these may not give a fair picture. First we must distinguish between xenophobia, i.e. dislike of all foreigners, and racism, which is more selective. The Germans today are one of the least chauvinistic of major Western countries: they positively fawn over Scandinavians, Britons or even French . . . But, when it comes to darker-skinned or more alien folk, matters are different: probably the Germans *are* on average more racist than the British, or even the French, but they are well behind the Swiss, European champions in this field. In Germany, there is little actual violence towards immigrants, as we have seen. Neo-Nazi thugs try to whip up hatred, and some have been jailed for it: but these tiny extremist groups have little popular following (see p. 505), and their slogans (e.g. 'We finished off the Jews: Turks, it's your turn next'), though nauseating, are not representative. The average German may not warm towards *Gastarbeiter*, but he shows little residue of the old Aryan super-race mentality of the Nazi creed: it is significant that the Allensbach polls, though recording plenty of xenophobia in other respects, found only 8 per cent of respondents saying 'yes', and 69 per cent saying 'no', to the crucial question, 'Are German children more intelligent than those of foreign workers?'

Guilt over the Holocaust may have exorcised this kind of feeling: and yet, the old prejudices that bred anti-semitism do linger on, in a milder form. Ordinary people may no longer feel racially superior: but they do want the *Gastarbeiter* to keep their distance and leave them alone. They dislike having them as neighbours: Turks, Blacks and others with dark faces usually have difficulty in finding lodgings. In this neighbour-prying country often this is more a matter of 'What will the

Müllers next door think?' than of personal prejudice. I know a liberal couple in a rented flat in Stuttgart who befriended a Turkish family living nearby and invited them twice to their home: at this their landlady, a typical Swabian bourgeoise, said, 'Please stop that, we don't want a Turkish commune in our house! We're not racist ourselves, mind you − but you know what people round here are like, and we have to keep on good terms . . .' If this kind of vicious circle could be broken, matters might improve. It is also true that ignorance is the main barrier. Those who do get to know Turks or others, as neighbours or at work, frequently end up on friendly terms, yet remain convinced that 'their' Turks are a special case: 'We're so lucky, *we* have such a nice family next door. But all the others . . .'

When it comes to marriage, most German parents today are perfectly happy for their daughter to wed, say, a Dane or Canadian (this used not to be so). But, if a Greek or South Italian suitor turns up, there may be trouble: and this may not always be xenophobia so much as a legitimate parental anxiety that the girl might not be happy living in a *macho* society. The girls are wary, too. When an Allensbach poll asked, 'Would you marry a Turk?', only 4 per cent said 'yes': but even for an Italian the 'yes' was a mere 10 per cent, against 14 per cent for a Yugoslav. Blacks scored 7 per cent. Generally, the lighter the hair and face, the milder the prejudice. But, as this poll indicates, Blacks tend to be better accepted than Turks − partly because they are far less numerous and usually better educated. What is more, many Blacks in Germany are American. I heard of a family who refused to let their younger daughter marry a Turkish worker she loved, so she tried to kill herself. The mother would not relent, saying, 'I'd rather she starved to death than married that wild rat!' I tell this horrific and (I hope) untypical story, simply because the elder daughter had already been cohabiting happily with a Black GI for two years, and had two kids by him. 'Oh, but he's an American,' said the mother. There are legal obstacles, too, in the path of foreigners who wed German girls and live with them in Germany. Until recently, marriage did not grant them right of residence. However, some potent campaigning has now been done by the Frankfurt-based Association of German Women Married to Foreigners. Thanks to them, foreign husbands now have better security; and a child born to a German mother and foreign father can now acquire German nationality at birth, as was previously possible only for the child of a German father.

However, in this law-ridden country, one surprising and serious lacuna remains, the absence of effective laws against racial discrimination. Small ads for job vacancies or flats to let often stipulate, '*Nur für Deutsche*' or '*Nur Europäer*'; many pubs refuse *Gastarbeiter* and one in Frankfurt even had a notice up, '*Kein Zutritt für Hunde und Türken*' (No Entry for Dogs and Turks); some public discos in Frankfurt deny entry to coloured people (except if a white man brings a coloured girl — that's quite chic). In Britain, under the Race Relations Act, all this would simply be illegal. In Germany, to pass such a law would require huge political courage; and it might take many years, for it would involve the amendment of forty existing laws.

In the meantime, could not the media and the authorities play a firmer role in trying to educate people away from prejudice? Weeklies such as *Die Zeit* and *Der Spiegel*, it is true, have an excellent record of anti-racist articles, while any average regional daily is usually quite free from xenophobia. But this positive side is counterbalanced by the pernicious influence of the mass-selling tabloid *Bild Zeitung* (see p. 365): it is not openly racist in its editorials, but with their shrieking headlines its news stories do endlessly sensationalise the 'misdoings' of Turks and others (e.g. stories about child-beating), and this whips up popular prejudice. The public television channels give a balanced news coverage: but they provide too few background programmes about the lives and problems of *Gastarbeiter*, the nature of Islamic religion, and so on. So potent a medium could certainly be playing a stronger educative role. And, as I have already suggested, the Federal and *Land* governments could do more to lead opinion and set a positive example. As all politicians know well, the treatment of immigrants remains one of the most crucial tests of the new German democratic ethos. The *Gastarbeiter*'s very presence forces the Germans to look at themselves more closely.

# 6

# ARTS AND INTELLECTUALS: LIVELY ACTIVITY, BUT LOW CREATIVITY

In Germany, as in many other Western countries, this seems to be the age of the performing arts rather than of individual creation. The theatres and museums, concert halls and opera houses draw large and enthusiastic audiences, and are backed by generous public subsidies on a scale unequalled in Europe. The cultural scene is refreshingly cosmopolitan, too. Many front-rank musicians and other performers come from abroad to live and work in western Germany, where managers and public alike are alert to the latest influences from the outside world. It is all very open and stimulating.

But where is the new creative artist? – or the great new philosopher, in this land of *Dichter und Denker* (poets and thinkers)? The novel, since the heyday of Grass and Böll, has gone into a strange hibernation; few post-war painters or sculptors have made much impact apart from the extraordinary Joseph Beuys; the cinema blossomed unexpectedly in the 1970s, but its condition is now again precarious; *und so weiter* . . . This creative malaise, in contrast to performing vitality, is not confined to Germany: it is even more noticeable today in France, and it has a number of complex causes common throughout the West. In Germany, one particular factor is that the Nazi period created a rupture with the past that cut writers and artists off from their natural traditions and left them rootless and confused, and these wounds have taken a long time to heal: the Nazis distorted German culture for their own purposes, debasing the coinage of many crucial German ideas and styles which thus could not easily be used any more. Continuity was shattered. In addition, the vast majority of worthwhile intellectuals and creative people had moved either into exile or into prison, and many of them – notably the Jews – either never returned or were exterminated. Germany's culture has been tragically impoverished by the loss of its Jews, who before the war had played so fertile a role.

Summed up in a word, German culture in the past has been marked by two major traditions – one of quiet philosophic humanism, and the other much closer to the Gothic or baroque, full of violence and fantasy, as seen in the work of Hieronymus Bosch, the Brothers Grimm or the Expressionist cinema of the 1920s. Since the war, the philosophical trend has become less abstract, and German humanism has moved closer to daily life, as is seen for example in the novels of Heinrich Böll or in Edgar Reitz's film *Heimat*. But it is the violent/fantastic tradition that has come more strongly to the fore. In an age when, in many countries, art sets out to shock or provoke, the Germans have made a speciality of it – and much of their most striking work has been in varying degrees extravagant, grotesque, frenzied, baroque, Expressionist, bizarre or downright romantic. One could trace this through the *Leitmotiv* of physical foulness in the novels of Günter Grass; the *arte povera* belligerence of Beuys's conceptual sculptures; Peter Zadek's provocative stage reworkings of Shakespeare or Schiller; the violent Expressionism of Pina Bausch's dance theatre; the extravagant romanticism of the films of Werner Herzog; and even in the despairing stylised brutality of the work of Fassbinder or the tender cruelties of the plays of Franz Xaver Kroetz. All these possess essentially German imaginations and are products of the German psyche, moulded also by the *Angst* of modern times.

## *The novel: waiting for successors to Böll and Grass*

West German literature since 1945 can be said to fall into three main periods. First was the time of the so-called 'literature of the ruins', when writers were painfully struggling to come to terms with their experiences of the war and of Nazism and were groping towards new values. This was followed by the left-wing political commitment of the 1960s, a period of angry disillusion with Germany's materialistic and conformist new society. Then since the early 1970s writers have been retreating again from public and social themes into their private worlds of individual feeling, nostalgia and *Innerlichkeit* (inwardness). The first two of these periods produced at least two novelists of major world rank, Heinrich Böll and Günter Grass, as well as a number of other significant writers such as the poet and critic Hans Magnus Enzensberger, the novelists Siegfried Lenz and Martin Walser, and the playwrights Peter Weiss and Rolf Hochhuth. The third period has been much less distinguished.

After 1945 some writers returned from exile abroad and others from the 'inner emigration' of silence imposed by Nazism. They were free again to write what they wished in their own land: but amid the numbing desolation of the *Stunde Null* they had great difficulty at first in finding the words to express their feelings and experiences, and some were tempted to share the sharp judgement of the Frankfurt philosopher Theodor Adorno, who said that to go on writing lyric poetry after Auschwitz was 'barbaric'. The Nazis with their propaganda literature had so debauched the German language and values that no words were safe any more, and this induced in writers a certain verbal paralysis. But some gradually found their outlets through a kind of dazed deadpan description of what they had witnessed – the early stories of Böll, who had served on the Russian Front, are full of war-wounded youths and war-weary veterans, the muddle and futility of battle, and the shell-shocked apathy of those who will never re-adapt to normal life.

The rebirth of German literature was given a special impulse in 1947 when two left-wing authors and ex-POWs, Hans Werner Richter and Alfred Andersch, founded the famous '*Gruppe 47*'. This was an informal association of young writers from all over Germany who began to hold meetings where they would comment on each other's work. Böll and Grass, Enzensberger and Uwe Johnson were among those who joined *Gruppe '47*, which soon was exerting a good deal of influence: it mobilised petitions, fostered friendships, helped writers to find their voice again and even organised meetings abroad. It was neither a formal political movement nor politically cohesive, but most of its members were on the Left and they believed that writers should band together to play a part in shaping the new German democracy. As such, *Gruppe '47* remained a vital force for the next two decades. Many writers during this period were directly involved in political and social questions, both in their writing and in their lives – Günter Grass for example campaigned actively for the SPD – and in so doing they were making a significant break with the main tradition of German letters: though Theodor Fontane, Heinrich Mann and a few others had been exceptions, literature hitherto had generally preferred to restrict itself to philosophical, spiritual and private subjects. But writers after 1945 felt that these ivory tower attitudes had led to Nazism and should not be repeated.

Even more than Grass, the towering figure of German post-war literature was Heinrich Böll, and he remained so until his death in 1985. Son of a cabinet-maker from Cologne, he had a typical Rhinelander's sense of humour allied to a poetic eye and a sharp sense of social satire. Above all he was a humanist, defender of the underdog and critic of established society. His novels *The Clown* (1963) and *Group Portrait with Lady* (1971) both explored the theme of how a sincere and gentle outsider in society can become rejected and trampled on by the parvenue bourgeoisie. Böll publicly expressed sympathy for the student rebels of 1968 and then spoke up for a fair trial for the Baader-Meinhof terrorists and a better understanding of what had driven them to their desperate adventures. For this he was lacerated by the entire German establishment and especially the right-wing Press. He retorted with his short and brilliant polemical novel *The Lost Honour of Katharina Blum* (1974), the story of a young woman harried and destroyed by a ruthless and mendacious tabloid newspaper (similar to *Bild Zeitung*: see p. 366) because she was suspected of sheltering a terrorist. In *The Safety Net* (*Fürsorgliche Belagerung*, 1979), Böll then described the paranoia of the wealthy class in the face of a youth protest movement that it was unable to comprehend. He was a shy and retiring man whose outspokenness on such issues propelled him into a moral leadership of a kind that he had never sought; in the eyes of many liberals and radicals, he came to appear as the voice of the nation's conscience in a time of confused values. He was a practising Catholic who never ceased to criticise official Catholicism, and he was one of the earliest supporters of the Greens. In 1972 he became the first German to win the Nobel Prize for Literature since Thomas Mann in 1929.

The novels of Günter Grass dealt less often with contemporary Germany than with the war period (witness his most famous book, *The Tin Drum*, 1959): yet he too would sometimes poke a satiric finger at the insensitivity of the new-rich society around him. His dominant theme was the failure of ordinary Germans to come to terms with the Nazi past. (Grass the Socialist has always been urgently involved in public issues, and in 1990 he was campaigning vociferously, though with no success, against German reunification which he saw as a sell-out to big-business values.) The novelist Martin Walser also wrote satirically about the bourgeoisie, focusing on the competitive status-conscious world of Swabia and Lake Constance, where he lived. One strength of all these writers, and of some others too, was that they gave vivid and realistic portrayals of precise settings that they knew well – Walser's Bodensee, Böll's Cologne district, and the pre-war Danzig of *The Tin Drum*. The poet and essayist Hans Magnus Enzensberger, two years younger than Grass, was an even more vitriolic critic of the new society of the 'economic miracle' and in 1967–8 he sided with the student rebels and urged Marxist revolution in the streets; but later he was to become much more moderate. A number of playwrights such as Rolf Hochhuth and Peter Weiss (see pp. 315–16) were also turning to political themes during this period.

From the late 1950s much of the best German writing was coming not from the West but from the GDR (see p. 398). Uwe Johnson, born in what is now Poland, lived in East Germany until 1959 when with some regret he moved to West Berlin in order to have the freedom to publish his novels: *Speculation about Jakob* and *The Third Book about Achim* were two honest and thoughtful critiques of GDR-style socialism, written from a left-wing viewpoint. Some others later took the same route to the West, including the poet and singer Wolf Biermann: but several good writers chose to remain in the GDR, where sometimes they would resort to allegory or coded references in order to express their thoughts on society. It appeared that the difficulties of living under a restrictive regime, far from stifling these writers, in some cases acted as a creative stimulus.

In western Germany, by contrast, the permissiveness and normalcy of daily life today seems to have been depriving writers of inspiration. The anti-bourgeois indignation of the 1950s and '60s has played itself out; subjectivity has come back into fashion and novelists have again been dealing with the age-old subjects of love and family, childhood, nostalgia and private sensibility. These are no bad themes for literature, but in Germany today they have certainly produced no Prousts. All the critics lament a decline in the novel that is even more acute than in France – and it is hard to think of any significant names that have emerged in the past ten or twenty years. Perhaps one could mention Christoph Ransmayr, Herta Müller (a German-speaking immigrant from Romania), Patrick Süskind whose clever historical novel *Perfume* (1985) was a major best-seller, and Botho Strauss who is both novelist and trendy playwright.

What are the reasons for the current decline of literature? In Tübingen I visited the left-wing critic Walter Jens, a doyen of German letters and one of the early members of *Gruppe '47*, and he said: 'The crisis of the novel is common to all the West. In Germany, writers today find it hard to identify with any political line, there are no dreams any more, no causes to espouse like Dubček or Allende, and in literature no *maîtres-à-penser*. The Greens and young "alternatives" are anti-literature, they prefer the visual — Wim Wenders and Werner Herzog are the kind of people they look to, so writing is not "in". A *Gruppe '47* would be inconceivable today.' And in Munich I heard a perceptive and fascinating explanation from another *Gruppe '47* veteran, Hans Magnus Enzensberger, who has mellowed a lot since his Angry Young Man days: in his airy flat in Schwabing we talked for two hours over a whole range of subjects, and of all the hundreds of conversations I had for this book, I would single out this as the most stimulating, and Enzensberger as the most interesting individual I met in modern Germany. Of the plight of the writer he said: 'Intellectuals in the 1960s felt strongly about the injustices and rigidities in German society, and we fought hard against them — with some success. We made an impact in those days. Thanks in part to the student revolt of the 1968 period, certain barriers have been broken and Germany has become a more open, tolerant and informal society, more so than ever before in its history, and an easier place to live in. But in the process the edges have been blurred and it's also become a duller place, a sort of porridge. And it's not easy to write about a porridge. So there is a price to pay for normalcy.

'Another problem for the writer,' he went on, 'is that he's too cosseted today. All these subsidies for literature and culture don't necessarily make for high creativity. If you invest a billion dollars in the car industry, you probably get some interesting new models; but that doesn't hold good for artistic creation. A young man publishes his first novel, maybe something about his childhood, the kind of book that anyone has it in him to write: this let us say has a certain success, and so he becomes "a writer" and thinks of himself as such, and he embarks on a phoney career. He gets interviewed and lionised, he wins a scholarship or little prize and maybe his home town does something for him. So he finds it easy to do lecturing, or to go round Germany giving readings of his work, which pays very well, and to do radio as well — we have eight cultural radio networks in this country, and they all pay good money, better than the BBC. So there are all sorts of fundings and semi-fundings for the writer, it's much easier than in Britain. But what is our young chap to write about next? He lacks experience of real life. So you find writers writing about writers who want to write a book — so depressing! Or you come across this tame little novel about living in the communal flat and going to the peace demo. People have such narrow horizons. Admittedly, in the past, writers would often produce great art out of solitary confined experiences – but somehow there was more intensity in those days and the writer's fight was much harder, the oppression was greater. Today it's all too easy. And there's a simple lack of talent, too – hard to explain.'

Another factor is that, rather as in France, a great gulf exists between 'literature' and mere popular entertainment. The kind of robustly readable but basically serious fiction of the John Fowles or Graham Greene type that so solidly fills the middle ground in Britain is hardly present in Germany, where the critics expect a new novel either to be avantgarde in a self-conscious 'literary' way or else to deal solemnly with philosophical or moral themes; 'Once a book is entertaining,' said one publisher, 'then it ceases to be culture.' This inhibits many a young novelist, who has to choose between being pretentiously highbrow or merely commercial. Yet at the same time the prestige of intellectuals is much *less* great than in France, and so is their impact on public life. They may, as Enzensberger remarked, have been able to play a part in changing society in the 1968 period: but their own world of verbal polemic and clashing ideas does not fascinate a wider public as it does in France where Sartre and Barthes, Foucault and the *nouveaux philosophes* have in their time been popular stars like athletes or singers. Possibly one reason is that the French enjoy novelty and exhibitionism, and they like to be startled by ideas they do not necessarily share: the German public, much less secure, more anxious and conformist, does not. So the parading on television of a view generally thought 'shocking' will not provoke hoots of outraged delight (as in France) or tolerant smiles (as in Britain) but a solemn outcry that few network chiefs will want to risk. And German politicians, at least those on the Right, have always disliked intellectuals (who are nearly all somewhere on the Left or centre-Left): Adenauer despised them, Erhard once called them *Pinscher* (pipsqueaks), and Chancellor Kohl, who has taken pride in identifying himself with the no-nonsense man-in-the-street, has enjoyed relations of mutual hostility with them. The cultured de Gaulle would never have adopted such a stance: nor would Giscard, who once invited Sartre to the Elysée.

Another difficulty facing the intellectuals is that they suffer more than most Germans from the lack of a true capital city. Munich, Berlin, Frankfurt and some other towns each has its little milieu of writers and thinkers: but they are somewhat separate and there is no national focus of the kind provided by Paris, London or New York. This makes German intellectual life more provincial, and its impact less great, both at home and abroad. *Gruppe '47* marked an attempt to overcome this handicap, by summoning writers from all over Germany to its sessions: but it imposed a strain on their time and their budgets, and ultimately it failed. The influence of the literary magazines such as *Neue Rundschau* has also waned: today the main impact comes from the literary pages of the weekly *Die Zeit* in Hamburg, of the *Süddeutsche Zeitung*, and of the *Frankfurter Allgemeine Zeitung* whose literary editor, the renowned and feared Marcel Reich-Ranicki, remains the pope of German letters, able to make or break a new book's sales with a few strokes of his caustic pen.

Although these papers do provide some interchange of ideas, most intellectuals tend to live in narrow little circles, separated from each other not only by city but by profession: academics, journalists and creative writers do not have much communication across their self-imposed barriers. The university world in Germany is notoriously closed (see p. 258), and it is less common than in Britain or the United States, or even France, for academics to appear on TV debates or write newspaper articles (except on their own special subjects). Modern German philosophy has been highly distinguished in its way: of the older pre-war generation who survived into the 1960s and '70s, mention should be made of Karl Jaspers, Ernst Bloch and Martin Heidegger, as well as of the so-called 'Frankfurt school' led by Max Horkheimer, Theodor Adorno and the much younger Jürgen Habermas who is still in his fifties. But the trouble with many of these wise men is that they wrote so obscurely as to be almost unintelligible even to specialists. Honourable exception should be made of those great humanists Bloch and Jaspers, who wrote with admirable lucidity on a range of topics. But Habermas is extremely hard to comprehend, and so is Adorno, whose ideas on 'the authoritarian personality' would appear to be so interesting and pertinent. There is a story from the 1968 period that when a student said to Adorno, 'Your theory just does not equate with reality,' the sage replied, 'Then we must change reality.' And this is the trouble with much German intellectual discussion: it is either extremely practical, i.e. about nuclear power or dying forests, or else it is maddeningly over-theoretical, and never the twain do meet. Philosophical writing can also seem wilfully obscure, as witness this example by Reiner Wiehl, quoted in English in *The Times Literary Supplement* of May 4, 1984 (I do not have the original German, but it probably sounds even worse): 'Particularity is no rational datum that comprises within itself or beneath itself in the mode of a highest concretion a given simplicity and universality. Also, particularity is no third independent datum of equal concretion and reality as given singularity and universality.' Quite so.

Professors cling together socially, and more than in most countries they tend to look with disdain on any outsider, such as a mere journalist who trespasses on their speciality. To me they were unfailingly courteous: but sometimes they failed to hide their astonishment that I should be writing a serious book on Germany without, like them, holding a university post. That is a normal reaction: more curious maybe is the gulf that exists between the academic world and that of creative writing. Few German novelists come from a university milieu – Böll and Grass had no higher education at all – and rarely would a professor dare to do anything so frivolous as write detective stories or children's books in his spare time (as Oxford dons have been doing since Lewis Carroll's day). That would make him lose credibility with his colleagues as a serious thinker. Creative writers in their turn tend to lead secluded lives, and sometimes they complain of feeling isolated and ignored. But this may be unfair, and is probably due more to their own social reticence than to any hostility against them: for while a writer may not enjoy the same public prestige as in France, he nonetheless tends to be better treated by publishers and reading public than in Britain, another land with a strong literary tradition. Writers are frequently invited to give public readings of their works – by bookshops, adult education institutes, literary societies and so on – and for these they can expect audiences and good fees.

The novel may be in creative decline, yet the Germans still read and buy books as much as ever, and the statistics show that they are greater book readers than either the British or the French. Television and video have not made such inroads as might have been feared, at least not with more educated people: Allensbach surveys found that the numbers of those claiming to read a book 'at least once a week' rose from 42 to 44 per cent between 1967 and 1980. Municipal lending libraries have been improving and are far better than in France, though less impressive than in Britain: Munich's big new central library and its 27 branches report a total of some 7.5 million borrowings a year, roughly six books per head. Bookshop sales of all kinds have also held up well. Travel and practical books and light fiction are of course the most popular, but there is still a heavy demand for the classics and for serious modern books. Again according to Allensbach, the proportion of families with at least 100 bound or paperback books in their home rose from 26 to 34 per cent between 1967 and 1978 – but admittedly, as one publisher put it, 'many of these house-proud Germans buy series of handsomely-bound books as part of the furniture and maybe never read them.' For these and other reasons, the German publishing industry is still in rather good shape, though of course it complains of crisis just as in other countries. After the war it had to come to terms with the loss of its markets in the former eastern parts of Germany, and then with the decline of the German language to the benefit of English in areas such as Scandinavia. None the less it manages to produce some 60,000 titles a year, far more than France, and much more too than Britain with its infinitely wider world market. Munich, Frankfurt and Stuttgart are the main publishing centres: Bertelsmann, based on the modest town Gütersloh, is the largest publishing group in Europe. And, notoriously, Germany plays host to the world's leading annual book trade fair. Before the war this was held in Leipzig, and in 1949 it moved west to Frankfurt where every autumn it now attracts some 5,700 publishing houses from about 80 countries, exhibiting some 300,000 books. The general bedlam tends to horrify the average Briton or American who visits the fair only because professionally he must. But in Germany its doings are always front page news. It may be concerned more with commerce than literature: but it remains a symbol of how seriously books are still taken by a nation that has always liked to call itself *'das Land der Dichter und Denker'*.

## The State's role as Maecenas: taking culture out of the 'temples'

The exceptionally generous scale of public patronage of the arts in Germany derives from a tradition dating back to the eighteenth-century and earlier, when each royal court, dukedom or free city would maintain its own opera house, theatre and museums. Today that responsibility has been inherited not by the Federal Government but by the individual *Länder* and city councils, and they feel a sense of duty and of local pride in keeping up the tradition. Add to this the prosperity of the Germans and their formal respect for *Kultur*, and maybe it is not so surprising that public spending on the arts should be the most lavish in the free world – per capita it is roughly four times the British level, and even higher than in France with its parallel but more centralised system of largesse. In western Germany today, some 50 opera houses and 70 orchestras, over 100 theatres and nearly 1,300 museums, receive subsidy. All the opera houses and nearly all the main German theatres are publicly owned either by *Land* or city, or in some cases by the two in partnership. And some leading private theatres – such as the celebrated Schaubühne in Berlin – have become so dependent on subsidy that in practice they are similar to the public ones.

One advantage of this structure is that it provides a fairly even spread of activity around the country. Even quite a small town will often possess a good civic theatre and concert hall, while the metropolitan culture found in London or Paris is in Germany shared between several cities, and a big place like Frankfurt or Cologne will offer a much better quality and range of artistic performance than its British or French equivalents, say Manchester or Marseille. Municipal councillors, and their electors too, regard culture as an important element in their city's overall prestige and so are ready to devote large sums to it. They may even see it as a valid economic investment too, a means of attracting new industry and commerce, as the arts officer of Stuttgart suggested to me: 'Without the culture that we sponsor, this would be a boring place and many dynamic citizens would move away. Besides, we have a duty to cater for Stuttgarters' spiritual needs.'

Cities are constantly in competition with each other, to see which of them can lure the most distinguished talent and which in the eyes of the critics has the finest opera, ballet or theatre companies: as many observers have noted, it is rather like a football league. As in football, much depends on the general manager, the highly-paid *Intendant* who is hired by the authorities to run the theatres or opera houses, or sometimes the two combined. Once appointed, he is then allowed artistic freedom: but, as in football, if his teams do badly he may be the scapegoat and get the sack. And cities' rival fortunes tend to rise and fall with their *Intendanten*: Stuttgart for example in the 1960s enjoyed a golden age under Walter Erich Schäfer when its ballet was the best in Germany and its theatre and opera among the three or four best, but it has since declined. Cities tend to specialise. Summed up in a few words, the form in the early 1990s was that Hamburg had the best ballet under John Neumeier, with Stuttgart perhaps still second; Hamburg and Munich vied for first place in classical opera; the best theatre companies were at Hamburg, Munich, Berlin and Bochum in the Ruhr; the finest symphony orchestra was still the Berlin Philharmonic; Cologne excelled in modern music and modern art; the best classical art museums were in Munich and Berlin, the best modern ones in Frankfurt, Stuttgart and Düsseldorf – and so on. Many critics might query these placings, but they would probably agree that Munich's forte is conventional classical culture, while Berlin holds the blue riband for the modern and experimental, with a strong international flavour. Now that it is reunited and again formally the capital, Berlin is certain to pull ahead of its rivals as *the* major cultural city of Germany: but it will never achieve the same near-monopoly as Paris does in France, and other big towns will continue to challenge it. In this federal country, Munich will never dwindle into a mere Manchester or Marseille.

These inter-city rivalries undoubtedly are healthy in many ways – but not in all. Leading managers and producers travel around Germany to scrutinise each other's work, as do the critics, though with a certain *parti pris* of local patriotism: when, say, the music critic of the *Süddeutsche Zeitung* goes to Hamburg to review a new Wagner production, he may be hoping fervently that he will be able to report that it is not as good as Munich's – and who can say if judgements are thus not sometimes clouded? But only a tiny proportion of the total audience travels in this way. As nearly all productions are home-produced, and as there is very little touring by national companies as in Britain or France, this means that the average culture-goer in say, Stuttgart, will see little all year except his own city's opera and theatre performances and he may thus form an exaggerated opinion of their merits. Berlin is the only city that regularly holds pan-German and international festivals with visiting companies of high quality. Elsewhere, the lack of opportunities for comparison may encourage a certain provincialism of taste and outlook – a drawback to the federal system that I referred to earlier and will return to later.

A few statistics will give some idea of the size of the sums officially devoted to culture. In Munich, *Land* and city each spends about 250 million DM a year; the town has also built itself a big new multi-purpose arts centre, the Gasteig, at a cost of 350 millions. In Frankfurt, 11 per cent of the city's overall budget goes on the arts. Several German opera companies have much larger subsidies than Covent Garden, while the average public theatre expects to need to derive only 15 to 20 per cent of its income from box office, even though houses are often full or nearly full: this allows for more money for productions, and tickets are a little cheaper than in Britain. This scale of public spending would in Britain not only have given Mrs Thatcher a heart attack but also would soon spark off a ratepayers' revolt. In Germany it is considered normal. One reason certainly is that the citizens tend to share the council's views about prestige and local patriotism. In Dortmund, a town with a mediocre opera company and 17 per cent unemployment, there was some talk recently of closing down the opera to save money: but local people, *including some of the unemployed*, retorted with protests in the streets, arguing that such a terrible step would spotlight the city's decline and thus be counter-productive. Exactly the same happened in Bremen, and in both cases the operas were saved. In many towns, to attend the opera or ballet is a way of showing loyalty to the city – yes, it *is* a bit like going to cheer one's local football team. In Stuttgart, when the great John Cranko was running the ballet under Schäfer, this company's biggest ever ovation was for its first performance after returning from a triumphal American tour – and Cranko and his dancers were a bit put out, fearing that they were being applauded less for their own merits than for having waved the local flag in New York.

Another factor that goes to explain the support for high subsidies is the traditional German veneration for culture, still very strong at least among the older middle-class generation. The average consumer of this kind tends to be more self-consciously 'cultured' than his English or even French counterpart; and he may well hold to a very Germanic concept of *Kultur* as an immutable value system that you learn to receive – like taking Communion – with a view to self-improvement. Culture is not just entertainment but a means of permanent education, both moral and spiritual. Such a person may even feel a sense of duty to himself in being able to speak about music and theatre and keeping in touch with what is offered locally. And of course, in many bourgeois circles, this ties in with a good deal of social convention and keeping-up-with-the-Müllers: people want to be seen at the right cultural events and to be able to talk about them with friends and neighbours, and much more than in Britain they like to dress up for the occasion. Most of them take out an *Abonnement* (lower-price season ticket) that commits them to seeing a certain number of shows each year. Nor is this dutifulness confined to the middle-classes: the trade unions have a system of block bookings at low rates, and these are very fully patronised (especially for the more popular classics) by an important minority of skilled workers, technicians and clerks. So, all in all, there is no lack of takers for the vast amount of officially-sponsored culture available. In Munich, for example, the distinguished Kammerspieltheater plays to over 90 per cent capacity, while the opera and ballet tend to be booked out months ahead: at the start of an opera booking season, it is not uncommon for devotees to queue all night for tickets. And in Stuttgart I was told that nearly twice as many people each year go to drama, ballet and opera at the Staatstheater as to football matches in the city stadium.

It is of course the established classics – alike of music and drama – that tend to draw the biggest and most regular audiences. But there is also a somewhat different but sizeable clientèle for 'difficult' or provocative modern plays, and another for modern music. So an *Intendant* can skilfully appeal to various sections of the community. In the German manner, however, whether classical or contemporary, his offerings will almost all be serious and 'cultural'. As we shall see, commercial comedies or new musicals of the *Cats* kind are seldom considered worthy of the subsidised houses and will not find their way there – until maybe they have acquired through time the status of minor classics, like *My Fair Lady* which was staged recently by the Hamburg State Opera.

This formal and often highbrow programming has in recent years come under frequent criticism from the new radical generations – Left-wingers, Greens and others – who have claimed that it is too elitist and out of touch with the taste of most ordinary people. It is not that they are demanding more commercial mass-entertainment, for this they equate with the Americanisation that they detest most of all. What they do want however is more 'participation' and spontaneity, and less of the well-intentioned official spoon-feeding by paternalists who think that they know best what is good for the public – the kind of spoon-feeding that the older German audiences have long accepted with happy docility. 'I'm opposed to this sterile "temple" culture, a feudal legacy from the royal days,' said one Stuttgart radical, Klaus Hübner; 'we must take culture out of the museums and opera houses and into the streets. I'd like to see a big outdoor leisure zone in the city centre, with music and "happenings" and café-theatres. But the bourgeoisie are always scared that if something spontaneous occurs the police will turn up. As no doubt they would.'

So all over Germany the call went out for more street festivals and suchlike. As in other countries, worthy efforts were also made to 'bring culture to the workers', to the philistine masses who enjoy *Bild* and the comic-strips and would never join the elites of the union block bookings. Several major directors led this movement, including Peter Zadek, then in charge of the famous Bochum theatre, who would put on little plays in pubs and factories and try to woo workers to his own stage with simple popular works and soup served in the interval. Experiments of this kind have borne some fruit in populist Britain: but in Germany with its different traditions they were not a great success and were abandoned. As the deputy manager of the Bochum theatre said to me: 'We are not workers, our interests are different from theirs and it's pointless to try to reconcile them. The way to woo the working-class is through the next generation, by inviting teachers to bring school groups here so that *they* can get used to what a theatre is all about. This we do.'

Meanwhile, in the past ten years or so many cities have given some positive responses to the kind of anti-elitist challenge formulated by Hübner and others. Culture has at last been widened out and some of it made less formal. The programming of the 'temples' themselves has scarcely been altered, nor their budgets reduced: but city councils have begun to put money into street festivals and 'happenings', now much in vogue. They have also sponsored new small-scale arts centres in the suburbs where modest professional events of all kinds are held from time to time – recitals, art shows, etc. – and where amateur groups can operate too. This is routine in any Western country today: but for German official policy it marks quite a bold departure, an enlarging of the classic concept of *Kultur*. Even in these centres there is still quite a dosage of municipal spoon-feeding: but spontaneity and participation are present too, linked to the recent blossoming of 'citizens' initiative' units so much favoured by the Greens (see p. 548). Little groups will sometimes write and act their own playlets about local history and folklore – all a little too parochial and inward-looking maybe, but very much in tune with the current anti-consumerist, small-is-beautiful, love-your-local-*Heimat* trends. Councils are also giving some money to the professional 'fringe' theatre, but less than in many European countries (see below).

In their overall patronage policies since the war, most cities and *Länder* have shown themselves remarkably liberal and have often supported theatre or art that is provocatively modernistic or highly critical of society. Of course the pattern varies. Some smaller towns in right-wing hands have been reactionary. But in the big cities like Munich or Frankfurt, so much in the limelight, so intensely in rivalry, and with sizeable and demanding 'egghead' audiences, even CDU or CSU rulers have not felt it prudent to oppose the new cultural trends too openly. Councillors who admit to hating modern art will often vote public money for avant-garde exhibitions, or for buying works by Beuys and others, so that their city can keep up with its peers in this field. And in some cases a strong and liberal-minded CDU mayor has been able to override his more conservative colleagues and give backing to progressive local arts managers.

This has been the case in Frankfurt under Walter Wallmann, and also under Manfred Rommel in Stuttgart, a city that provides a good illustration of the various culture conflicts. The local Swabians with their pious and cautious temperament are not exactly the most obvious patrons of the avant-garde, and they have fought battles against both *Land* and city schemes. In 1971 the *Land* Government, wanting to do its bit for modern art, spent 50,000 DM on a reclining figure by Henry Moore, whom they knew to be a big, acceptable name. But there was an outcry, many burghers denounced as 'ill-minded' this harmless sculpture of a draped female – and for 13 years it remained hidden away behind bushes. 'Typical,' was one liberal's comment; 'these Swabian culture-snobs, they want to buy the best, then don't like it.' Finally in 1984 the Moore was reprieved and now stands very conspicuously just across the motorway, at the entrance to the no less controversial new extension to the Staatsgalerie, the town's main art museum, owned by the *Land*. Designed by Britain's James Stirling (see p. 70), this striking and unusual building also came in initially for its share of local abuse: but, when the world's architectural critics proclaimed it a masterpiece, the Swabians soon started to feel proud of it. The Moore, too, now causes hardly a murmur. So there has been a certain progress.

The theatre in Stuttgart has faced somewhat similar problems. The main civic theatre is owned by the *Land*, with city participation; and in 1963 *Generalintendant* Schäfer chose as its director the already well-known Peter Palitzsch, a Marxist and former pupil of Brecht in East Berlin. In picking such a firebrand for so prudent a town, Schäfer wanted to bring in new ideas and put Stuttgart on Germany's theatrical map. He succeeded – at a cost. Palitzsch gave a Marxist twist to Shakespeare's histories; he introduced Stuttgart to Brecht and to Brechtian methods, and he drew round him a new regular audience in beards and duffle-coats, very different from the conventional opera-goers. But increasingly he fell foul of the *Land* Government. The *Theaterbeirat*, a *Land*-cum-city advisory board, did not have the right to veto his plays directly, but they could and did put pressure on Schäfer, complaining that his productions were too Leftist *and* too erotic. Ultimately Palitzsch wearied of the feuding and moved off to Frankfurt. It was a saga typical of that politicised era. He was succeeded in 1974 by Claus Peymann, equally celebrated but less political, and for a while he did well. But he too fell out with the *Land*, especially when in 1976 he posted up in the theatre an appeal for funds to help pay the dentist's bills of Gudrun Ensslin, the terrorist leader then in prison outside the city. Lothar Späth's patience snapped and Peymann was eased out and went to Bochum. After this, radical theatre in Stuttgart went through a lean period, but finally Rommel himself came to the rescue. Werner Schretzmeier, a young left-wing producer who had been running an 'alternative' arts centre in a town nearby, was invited by Rommel to take over a disused factory in the city and turn it into a similar kind of informal multi-purpose complex, with a 300,000 DM annual subsidy. This duly started up, with a mixed fare of jazz, political cabaret, talk-ins and the like. Some councillors were indignant, but Rommel got his way. 'There are two cultures in this big city, official and alternative,' he told me, 'and it is only fair to cater for both. Schretzmeier is a political opponent of mine, yes, but one would never find a right-wing person suitable for such a venture.' In short, this city of Pietist tradition will still fight its rearguard battles and will sometimes win them, for a while. But finally it has accepted the need to march with the times.

## *Theatre: morally serious, wilfully provocative*

Since the war, the London theatre and the German theatre have both of them frequently been described as 'the best in the world'. But so different are they that it is hard to judge their rival merits. The British theatre is much more commercial: not only are fewer companies subsidised but its attitudes and those of its public are very different from those in Germany. When Schiller in the eighteenth century described theatre as a 'moral institution', its role being to instruct and not simply to entertain, he carried out this precept in his own plays, and so did others who came after him, including Büchner, Wedekind and Brecht, all of them writing dramas that were quite often didactic and political. And, since the war, Hochhuth, Weiss, Dorst and others have done likewise.

Today, theatre managers may not necessarily want plays to be directly political, but at least they expect them to be serious, to shed light on social or philosophical problems, and not to appear too frivolous — and that is what their public expects too. So, just as in the novel, there exists a far greater gulf than in Britain between this 'moral' theatre and mere commercial entertainment. The Anglo-American genre of sophisticated comedy, above all witty and amusing but also casting a satirical eye on the human condition — this hardly exists in Germany, where the commercial 'boulevard' theatre is of low prestige and generally low quality, devoting itself mostly to humdrum farce and sit-com. And this poses a problem for anyone trying to import good new British plays into Germany. Where are they to fit in? The state and civic theatres usually turn up their noses at Frayn, Ayckbourn and Neil Simon as being much too light; sometimes they will produce Pinter or Stoppard, but with a slightly guilty conscience; and even Shaffer they and the critics fail to take quite seriously. *Amadeus*, treated as such a cultural event at London's National Theatre, was performed apologetically by some of the big German companies rather in the way that an opera company will sometimes lower its sights to stage an operetta. After all, did Shaffer not treat the plight of our great and wonderful Mozart rather too . . . *flippantly?*

Because theatre has so long held this moral role in Germany and is so central to the nation's intellectual life, it was encouraged to play a part in the reforging of German democracy after 1945. By September 1944 the Nazis had closed down all theatres in Germany and Austria, and by May 1945 most of their buildings lay gutted or in ruins. The Allied occupiers then actively helped them to make a new start, and during the next decades over 100 theatres were restored or rebuilt, some quite sumptuously. In the early years, the companies eagerly set about playing the many works — by Brecht and many others — that had been banned under the Nazis and were still largely unknown to German audiences. Then in the early 1960s the new German political playwrights arrived upon the scene, prompting the radical British critic Kenneth Tynan (amongst others) to call the modern German theatre the finest on earth. These new plays were of various kinds. Some dealt in a forceful semi-documentary style with major themes of guilt and responsibility for the war and the Holocaust — for example, Rolf Hochhuth's *The Deputy* (1963), about the failure of Pope Pius XII to condemn the Nazi crimes against the Jews; the same author's *Soldiers* (1967), which questioned Churchill's role in the war; and *The Investigation*

(1965), a meditation on Auschwitz by Peter Weiss, who had lived in Sweden since 1939. A few other political plays were on post-war themes, such as Grass's *The Plebeians Rehearse the Uprising* (1966), which criticised Brecht's failure to support the East German workers' revolt in 1953. Others again took historical subjects and hinted at their contemporary relevance: among them, Weiss's *Marat/Sade* (1964), the shorter title of his masterpiece about the murder of Marat, and Tankred Dorst's *Toller* (1968), a study of the left-wing insurrection in Munich in 1919. These and other such plays were enthusiastically performed all over Germany in the 1960s and early 1970s, and so were the works of the great Swiss dramatists, Max Frisch and Friedrich Dürrenmatt, and (a little later) the Austrians, Peter Handke and Thomas Bernhard. (Rather as the British will sometimes appropriate Synge or O'Casey, German theatres and critics have a habit of annexing these German-speaking Swiss and Austrian writers and regarding them as part of German drama – a cultural *Anschluss* that seems to me questionable.)

Just as in literature, political theatre has gone largely out of fashion since the mid-1970s, yielding place to plays on more personal and reflective themes.[1] This shift has mirrored basic changes in the mood of the times: but in part it was also a reaction against the political turmoil that affected theatres in the 1968 period, when young actors and staff sometimes tried to unseat or demote the *Intendant*, to bring in collective leadership and fill their stages with agit-prop activity. That phase has

1. There has also been a decline in the excellent German tradition of political satiric cabaret, whose brilliant heyday was in pre-Nazi Berlin. It made a modest comeback in the 1950s and 1960s, but has since suffered from the impact of television, and more especially from the fact that German society has become more open and placid, so that cabaret lacks effective targets – as Heidi Zerning of the *Kommödchen* cabaret in Düsseldorf told Richard Mayne in a BBC interview in 1984: 'Twenty years ago people had the feeling that cabaret was very daring and courageous, but today it is no longer necessary to be so bold, for democratic freedom has become established.' Some cabarets do still survive – the best, along with the *Kommödchen*, are probably *Die Stachelschweine* in Berlin and the *Lach und Schiess Gesellschaft* in Munich – and they play to full houses of neatly-dressed bourgeois groups enjoying the cosy jibes about the neatly-dressed bourgeoisie. But the bite and the wrath are not there. Mild satire of this kind has now spread out into full-scale productions in the big civic theatres, and these can be very successful – as witness *München Leuchtet* (see p. 65) and a lively revue, *Unsere Republik*, devised and performed by the Bochum company. Until 1989, true satiric cabaret as an outlet for political frustration could at least be found in the GDR: but, now that it can say what it likes, it too has lost much of its sharpness (see p. 481).

now long since ended: as in the universities, the old guard has discreetly reasserted itself. Meanwhile, the new writers of the 1970s and '80s have not turned their backs on moral and social questions, but they treat them in a more oblique and philosophical manner. Plays dwell on the isolation of the individual, the pressures of modern society, the contradictions and absurdities of life, illusion versus reality, and the artifice of theatre itself; or they indulge in low-life social realism.

The most talented and prolific member of this new wave is the Bavarian arch-realist Franz Xaver Kroetz, whose forty or so plays have been translated and performed in over thirty countries. Kroetz has at various times held jobs as lorry-driver, male-nurse and casual labourer: he has a keen empathy with the joys and miseries — mostly miseries — of the peasantry and working-class, and he depicts them with a savage candour that some audiences find hard to take. Actors swear foully, masturbate on stage, and so on. Mental retardment, peasant primitivism, divorce, unemployment, the corroding effects of capitalism — these are among Kroetz's themes, and his characters indulge in incest, rape, murder and even crucifixion. Yet he is not just seeking shock effect: he writes with great sincerity of feeling and appears to be a genuine poetic misanthrope and pessimist, a little like the French film-maker Maurice Pailat. *Stallerhof* is the compassionate study of a Bavarian farm-worker's love for the mentally-defective daughter of a brutish farmer who cruelly puts an end to the affair; *Through the Leaves*, which I saw beautifully performed by Scottish actors at London's Bush Theatre, charts the hopeless liaison between an affectionate middle-aged woman and an emotionally-deprived worker who can express his feelings only through abuse and rejection. More recently, Kroetz has turned away from this kind of lyrical realism towards didactic social analysis (*Furcht und Hoffnung der BRD*) or portentous fantasy (*Bauernsterben*), and some critics feel that he has begun to lose his touch. *Bauernsterben*, a study of young peasants destroyed by city life, was presented in 1985 by Munich's Kammerspieltheater, complete with pissing and copulation on stage, and was then prosecuted for obscenity (unsuccessfully) by a Catholic institute.

Even more fashionable today than Kroetz, though less interesting a writer in my own view, is Botho Strauss of Berlin, whose plays deal in various ways with lack of human communication, the yearning to find a meaning in life, and other modish themes. In 1984 his five-hour *Der Park* enjoyed a huge cult success throughout Germany, where it was staged by as many as twenty different theatres: a free updating of *A Midsummer Night's Dream*, it showed Oberon and Titania coming to the earth in search of true feeling, but finding only selfishness and triviality. Some critics felt that with this clever-clever self-indulgent work Strauss had fallen into his own trap and was himself showing a lack of feeling. Some talented young women playwrights have recently emerged, among them Elfriede Jellinek and Kerstin Specht, who explore imaginary poetic worlds of their own.

These and other modern writers — including Heine Müller of east Berlin, and the Austrians and Swiss — appear from time to time in the repertory programmes. So do the German classics, and far more frequently: Schiller and Brecht (now a classic) are in the lead, followed by Goethe, Lessing and Kleist. The subsidised theatres have a statutory duty to perform these considerable authors, who apart from Brecht are too little known in Britain. Happily, this ignorance is not reciprocated. The Germans may pooh-pooh modern British drama: but they adore Shakespeare, who in the fine nineteenth-century translations of Schlegel and Tieck (and sometimes in modern ones too) is much the most widely performed of *any* playwright. Shaw and Molière, Ibsen and Chekhov are popular too.

Major productions of these classics are quite often flamboyantly experimental, and this has led to heated controversy. Almost as much as in the France of Chéreau and Planchon, the German stage today has become a director's theatre: led in the 1970s and 1980s by Peter Zadek, Peter Stein and Claus Peymann, a new kind of virtuoso director has come to the forefront, and he more than the actors or the author becomes the play's real superstar. For better or worse, he imposes his personality on the text, not necessarily changing its words but often restaging so as to alter their significance. It is a theatre of gesture, movement and elaborate lighting effects. Sometimes, in the right hands, the results are brilliant and they bring out new subtleties in the play — witness Stein's *Three Sisters* in Berlin — but in other cases a showy director has been over-experimental and this has shocked the older generation. 'No one has a right to object to new interpretations of old plays,' Gordon Craig wrote in *The Germans* (p. 225); '. . . on the other hand, one is entitled to expect of new versions a decent fidelity to the author's purpose and his text, or so one would think. In the West German theatre this was not always a sound expectation. What often took place there was nothing less than an unashamed manipulation of the classics. Schiller was so often the object of this kind of treatment that one was almost persuaded that directors were revenging them-selves upon their schoolmaster for having made them memorize pas-sages from *Maria Stuart* or *Don Carlos.*'

More to the point, these gifted directors were bored with the prospect of mounting yet another loyal presentation of some play that had been done hundreds of times, and they wanted to add their own creative bit. Freed by their subsidies from the usual box-office restraints they were keen to impress the critics with their originality – and sometimes they went too far. Professor Craig instances Zadek's *Othello* at Hamburg in 1976, with Desdemona as a prostitute in a bikini; Alfred Kirchner's *The Tempest* in Berlin (1978) that made Caliban, not Prospero, the true hero; and similar liberties taken by Stein with Goethe's *Tasso* and Hansgünter Heyme with Schiller's *Wilhelm Tell.* Other examples include a *Hamlet* staged in Munich by Maximilian Schell who wrote a modern translation, to have the Prince declaiming to Ophelia, 'Go to a brothel, go!' In one *Maria Stuart* production, the queens Mary and Elizabeth appeared on roller-skates; in another, done by Heyme in Stuttgart, these two royal enemies became friends and lesbians united in a feminist cause, dancing together and combing each other's hair. Audiences would tend to walk out from such oddities – leading one Stuttgart cloakroom attendant to complain to my wife, 'It's infuriating! In the old days, once I'd taken people's coats I could settle down to a quiet three hours knitting jerseys for my grandchildren. Now I'm continually interrupted.'

It would be wrong however to give the impression that all the innovative productions by star directors have been of this kind. Many have preserved the authentic spirit of the original play while exploring it from new angles – this has been true of much of the work of the Schaubühne in Berlin which during the 1970s and 1980s was generally regarded as the best theatre company in Germany. It was founded in the early 1960s on a collective basis by a group of ex-students, and today it is still privately run, though it receives a large subsidy from the city. It inhabited a modest theatre building in Kreuzberg until 1981, when it moved to a splendid and expensive new one on the Ku'damm: here it has much better scope for elaborate staging, though some critics feel that the move has dampened the exuberance of its spirit. Up until 1985 its presiding genius and co-manager was Peter Stein, a gentle but intense individual, who himself directed many of its finest productions – for example, Chekhov's *The Three Sisters*, ecstatically praised. Michael Ratcliffe wrote in the *Observer* of March 17, 1985: 'Few non-German speakers could fail to be moved at the very start by the clamour of birdsong, the distant bells in the town and the brilliant spring sunshine flooding the deep-set windows ... The virtuoso second act is lit almost entirely by candlelight and spoken in the low voices of evening ... The wind rises in soft moans about the house, as though lifting it a little above the earth ... Most graphic of all are the little gestures of arm and hand ...' Stein had in the 1960s played his part in the let's-bring-theatre-to-the-workers movement: but by the 1980s his and the Schaubühne's concerns had become much less social than aesthetic, and he was on record as saying, 'Theatre and the politics of direct action do not mix. Theatre is an irrational, undoctrinaire medium.' In 1985, feeling that he had been with the company long enough, he left Berlin to freelance and was soon in Cardiff, directing Verdi's *Otello* for the Welsh National Opera. He remains a guest director for the Schaubühne. But the theatre's quality today has much declined.

Peter Zadek, much more the extrovert maverick than Stein, is given to making highly quotable remarks such as, 'We Germans are surely the only people on earth who enjoy a bad conscience more than a beautiful woman.' The 'we' should perhaps be qualified, for Zadek having fled Germany with his parents to avoid Hitler, then spent twenty-five years in London where his theatre work began: his staging there of *Le Balcon* led him into a famous row with Genet. Zadek later was one of the relatively small number of Jews who chose to return to Germany to pursue artistic careers, and in the 1970s he was *Intendant* of the Bochum Schauspielhaus which he built up into one of the three or four best in the country. He then revived the fortunes of Hamburg's famous Schauspielhaus, where his blood-and-gore *Duchess of Malfi* raised some eyebrows. 'Theatre,' he says, 'must be free from all taboos.' Hence his deliberate shock treatment of the classics – an Othello in tails with black paint running down his face, hanging the dead Desdemona nude over a clothes-line. Zadek has now left Hamburg and is in semi-retirement.

It is clear that this German system of highly-subsidised non-commercial theatre has both strengths and drawbacks. The free rein that it gives to innovations of the Zadek kind may lead to some excesses, but it can also stimulate a degree of creativity that would be harder to achieve in the commercial theatre. It makes for handsome productions on good modern stages, with large companies of well-paid actors used to working together. Freed from the constraints of needing to pander to the star system, they can stick to the German tradition of ensemble acting: big names are seldom invited from outside, and the repertory cast take it in turns with parts large and small. But the other side of this coin is that the theatres with their big public budgets tend to get weighed down with bureaucracy and civil service regulations; the actors, most of them on permanent contract, cannot easily be dismissed if their work deteriorates, and this makes for a static situation that can affect quality. Even the high level of subsidy can in some ways be a handicap, as Zadek once told the BBC: 'Of course it's marvellous for someone working in the theatre, but it's also a killer – after a while you stop thinking realistically about your audience, as the play is going to run anyway.' Moreover, even though a theatre does not live under the tyranny of the box-office, there are other masters it must take account of – the politicians who supply its budget and the voters on whom they in turn depend. Individual productions cannot be interfered with, but if a manager's or producer's policy becomes too unpopular, he can face heavy pressures or even dismissal, as we have seen in Stuttgart. During a local election campaign in Berlin in 1970, the CDU charged the Schaubühne with 'subversive indoctrination' because of its production of a Brecht adaptation of Gorki's *The Mother* – whereupon, soon before polling day, the SPD-led city council cravenly reduced the theatre's subsidy. Fortunately, this kind of direct political victimisation happens only rarely.

Nonetheless, the dependence on local subsidy does tend to influence an *Intendant*'s policy in one of two contrasting ways. Either a theatre will seek to demonstrate its independence by staging productions that are artistically or politically provocative. Or else more frequently, at least in the smaller cities, it will prefer to play safe and follow the latest fashions set elsewhere. After all, it may not depend commercially on large audiences but it may still want to show its sponsors that it knows how to please the public. In their choice of new plays, these smaller theatres generally prefer to cash in quick on some modish trend coming from Munich or Berlin, rather than try out some little-known author they have found themselves: for example, Botho Strauss wrote *Der Park* under the aegis of his friend and mentor Stein, and in 1984 the Schaubühne was one of the first to stage it, whereupon twenty other theatres around Germany applied to do so too, since Strauss is so à la mode. This state of affairs was strongly criticised to me by Christof-Johannes Vitali, a Swiss cultural manager working in Frankfurt: 'New plays tend to be given these very spectacular, highly-financed productions, and then they just disappear. Every theatre today feels obliged to do the new Strauss: but I bet his agent will have trouble selling that play in five years' time. It's a feverish, unnatural situation, less healthy in my view than the one in Britain or America where a new play has a more continuing life. Plays there may need to be more accessible and amusing: but with all the varied commercial theatres they really find it easier to win an outlet.' A few established figures like Strauss and Kroetz do very well: the rest find it hard to gain recognition. It may well be that very few good new plays are being written: one manager told me that he and his staff read 150 new texts a year and only about five are at all worth considering. But it is probable that many young would-be playwrights feel deterred from writing for the theatre, not only by the lack of interest, but, as in France, by the star directors' obsession with their own *mise-en-scène* that distorts or ignores the text. Many authors prefer to write for radio or TV, where they get more money and quicker recognition. Or else, for lack of scope in the big theatres, they fall back on the 'fringe'.

This fringe – the so-called 'free theatre groups' and others – has developed later and less effectively than in many neighbouring countries and today it is not as flourishing as in Holland, Britain, Italy or even France. One reason generally given is that the authorities in those countries grant much less subsidy to the public theatres and so are readier to help the fringe, which in Germany is starved: in Munich the city council allots 25 million DM a year to its Kammerspieltheater but only about 1.5 million DM to the 30 or so fringe groups put together, and this pattern is much the same elsewhere. There are some German drama critics who argue that this is as it should be, for the quality of the fringe is mostly poor – this is true – and there is no point in wasting public money on it. Others retort – perhaps more fairly – that the fringe does at least contain latent talent, and if it were encouraged it could improve and make a real contribution which at present lies wasted.

Berlin unsurprisingly has the liveliest fringe scene in Germany, followed by Frankfurt and then Munich. Of the more than forty theatres and theatre groups in Munich – a lot, for a city of that size – three are public, five or six are 'boulevard', and the rest are fringe in one way or another: only about half these groups have their own theatre and the rest are itinerant and ephemeral, using improvised premises such as rooms at the back of beer-halls. As Munich is Germany's film capital and the site of Germany's main drama academy, there are always plenty of young actors looking for work, and some of them turn to forming fringe groups, with varying success. Some of them put on modest but respectable productions of, say, Sartre or Stoppard. Others, the more radical or 'alternative' ones, prefer to write or improvise their own little plays about their own little lives and problems (being ill or out of work, going on peace demos, sharing a flat), such as the tediously wordy non-drama about unemployment that I saw in Hamburg at an improvised theatre complex in a disused factory. Other groups prefer the avant-garde: at the aptly-named little Black Box Theatre in Munich's new Gasteig complex, I attended a 'happening' devised by a local luminary of the high fantastic Alexis Sagerer, who looks as seedy as Fassbinder and is said to have been influenced by Beuys. Helped no doubt by this pedigree, he mounted a satire on the Munich composer Carl Orff that included making music with saucepans, saws and squeaky toys, against a flickering backdrop of thirty banked-up video screens showing old films, while a girl combed five live and rather smelly pink pigs. In the intervals of nodding off, I fell to reflecting that the fringe and avant-garde in Germany, like so much else, have suffered from the lack of a big capital city that could set a standard and thus separate the sheep from the goats – or pigs. Sagerer is well known in Munich, but not in the rest of Germany. Inevitably his shock tactics smack of provincialism.

Frankfurt has a remarkably active fringe, whose various groups often play to full audiences and include an English company that on my last visit were doing *The Mousetrap* – not quite Sagerer's style. Much the most impressive fringe venture in Frankfurt, indeed in all Germany, is the Gallustheater, operating from a very crummy hall in an industrial-cum-working-class district. In the wake of the ideas of 1968, it was founded by a handful of Leftist people, as an amateur-drama-cum-youth-and-social-centre and a 'forum for research into cultural conflict and integration'. A few years later its liveliest habitués were some Italian *Gastarbeiter* teenagers, mostly born in Sicily or Apulia, then brought up in Germany and feeling adrift between two cultures. So good was their amateur acting that the Gallus *animateurs* formed them into a semi-professional group which still flourishes today and has won quite a success. In a mix of German and Italian they improvise their own plays on the problems of immigrants' integration, and they tour Germany and other countries, including their own south Italy. It is probably the most striking single contribution that *Gastarbeiter* have made to the German cultural scene (see p. 289). 'They are young factory workers who've become real professional actors,' I was told by

[323]

Brian Michaels, an English theatre producer living in Frankfurt who took the lead in creating the group. 'But,' he went on, 'the city gives us only 50,000 DM a year in subsidy, compared with 19 million for its civic theatre – disgraceful. All over Germany, there's far too great a gulf between the official theatre and the fringe, which gets pushed aside. Yet the big theatres *need* the fringe as a breeding-ground of new ideas and talent.'

Some others would disagree. One leading critic, Peter Iden of the *Frankfurter Rundschau*, told me that he felt the established theatres did a perfectly adequate job in spotting fringe talent or nurturing their own. But the more general view in Germany today is that the theatre, after some brilliant periods in the 1960s and 1970s, is marking time and resting on its laurels. The structure is impressive and the potential is there. But the whole operation has grown top-heavy and lacking in new inspiration. Rather as in the university world, the big public theatres with their near-monopoly of talent could probably do with a little competition not only from the fringe but from the despised commercial sector – and here Germany may even have something to learn from Britain, where the National and the RSC may set the pace but are usefully kept on their toes by Shaftesbury Avenue. Probably, above all, the serious Germans need to be able to forget Schiller's dictum and to laugh and relax a little more in the theatre. That is why I was cheered by seeing *Unsere Republik* at Bochum, a lively and light-hearted ensemble revue, home-produced by the company. It had serious overtones, but it also wittily poked fun at many of the foibles of post-war Germany. It was truthful yet *entertaining*. Such torch-bearers of the old flame of satiric cabaret are most welcome – but still rare.

Music in Germany today, despite the inevitable rivalries between devotees of classical and modern, is much less controversial a matter than theatre – but it is even more omnipresent and well patronised. Any visitor is at once impressed by the richness and variety of the musical life of this nation that still has music in its blood and lovingly cultivates its marvellous heritage – and this applies not only to professional performance but to amateur activity. Many people eagerly join choirs or chamber groups in their leisure time. And the attractive old tradition of family *Hausmusik*, which had been in decline during the hectic *Wirtschaftswunder* period, is now blossoming again in an age that puts more stress on quality of life and personal values. At a middle-class social evening, it is not unusual for the host and hostess and their teenage children to perform quartets for their guests. Maybe the daughter is a gifted pianist and the son plays the flute. It is endearing, and like something out of Jane Austen.

As music by its nature is less 'ideological' than the other arts, it suffered less from the Nazis' distortions of German culture – apart from Hitler's appropriation of Wagner – and so after 1945 it was more easily able to regain its position. The Germans turned to it thankfully as one of the least desecrated of their traditions, a valued link with the older past. Today there are some seventy subsidised symphony orchestras: the best is probably still the Berlin Philharmonic, which for thirty-four years until his death in 1989 had the great Herbert von Karajan as its chief conductor. Claudio Abbado has now taken over from him. Stuttgart has no less than five symphony orchestras, whereas an equivalent British city might have just one; and its main concert hall is always filled in advance with block-bookings, at least when the better-known classics are being played. But all over the country the interest in modern music is quite strong too, and in this field Germany has played an important role, attracting a number of leading composers. Pierre Boulez for some years made Germany his home base, before he was finally welcomed home by his native France; Mauricio Kagel, born in Argentina but now a German citizen, settled in Germany in the early 1960s because, he said, he found it the most stimulating country for modern music. The electronic studios of the radio station in Cologne were at that time the most advanced of their kind in the world, while the Darmstadt summer school also played a major role as a meeting-place for the post-war avant-garde. Its regular attendants included Germany's two most influential modern composers, Hans Werner Henze who lives in Italy and in Munich, and Karl Heinz Stockhausen who still lives in Cologne.

The tradition of classical opera is alive and well. Some fifty subsidised houses have regular companies, and they attract varied audiences: though a Munich first night or the Wagner season in Bayreuth may be diamond-studded high-society affairs, many a simple typist or technician will happily pay 50 DM to see *Figaro* in Kiel or Karlsruhe. Hamburg's opera, which plays to 98 per cent capacity houses and gets a 70 million DM annual subsidy, is today probably Germany's best. Its prowess was built up by the great Swiss, Rolf Liebermann, who was *Intendant* in 1963–73 and then returned to the post in 1984–8 after a brilliant period at the Paris Opera. A tall, relaxed figure in his late seventies, he received me with warmth and charm: 'I'm here in the front row of the stalls every night – the audience expect it of me. It's like running a restaurant. My main problem here is the shortage today of really good European singers, plus the fact that my permanent ensemble of chorus and orchestra cannot be sacked and many are simply too old.' When I asked him which was today the best opera in Europe, he answered pat, 'Geneva.'

All over Germany, opera-goers tend to prefer the classical repertoire: but Liebermann, Schäfer and a few others have made serious efforts to woo them to modern or even to specially-commissioned works. 'In my view,' said Liebermann, 'an opera house only justifies its vast subsidy if it puts on at least some new works, and thus helps living composers. Why should the taxpayer give us large sums to stage *Tosca* for a moneyed minority?' This policy has borne some fruit, but not as much as was hoped. Instead, in the recent years the emphasis has switched to new interpretations of traditional operas – sometimes experimental, though seldom as iconoclastic as in the case of drama. Patrice Chéreau's inventive productions of the *Ring* at Bayreuth marked the high point of this movement, and they delighted even German Wagnerians. In the 1980s the principal regular testing-ground of this kind of new creativity was the Frankfurt Opera, which under the *Intendant*-ship of the conductor Michael Gielen become 'Europe's most radical and controversial centre of music theatre', in the words of Peter Heyworth of the *Observer*. Gielen sponsored productions that sought to return to what the composer really had in mind and to free the work from later accretions – while also making use of some accretions of his own in the form of startling modern decor and lighting. The results frequently split the local public, so that the opera lost part of its old audience but gained a new one. Gradually Gielen wooed many Frankfurters to his ideas: and he was consistently backed by Mayor Wallmann and his council who may not have relished this style of opera themselves but were glad of the fame and prestige that it brought the city, in a country that thrives on operatic controversy. Since Gielen's departure, Frankfurt opera has returned to a more conventional style.

As much as opera is a great German tradition, classical ballet is not. Dance training has always been neglected. Times however are changing and Germany since the war has finally built up several world-class ballet companies, albeit that this has been achieved mostly by hiring outside talent: some 85 per cent of dancers are foreign, and the two best ensembles have been raised to their present quality respectively by an American, John Neumeier, now in charge at Hamburg, and by a

South African, the late John Cranko, who after some years as a choreographer at Covent Garden ran the wonderful Stuttgart Ballet from 1960 until his sudden death in 1973 at the age of only 47. It is ironic that Cranko should have needed to come to Germany to find the scope and recognition that had eluded him in London. He told me soon before his death: 'I've had opportunities here that I'd never have found at the Garden. We do about eighty evenings of ballet a year in this opera house, and we can stage three new programmes a year. This is a better deal than the ballet gets anywhere in Britain.' How did it happen? Schäfer, believing in Cranko, persuaded the *Landtag* to vote the money needed to build the company – 'It had to be explained to them,' I was told, 'that a dancer needs more than one pair of new shoes a month.' Cranko then set about creating a regular audience, in a town that had virtually forgotten ballet. His genius lay essentially in the reworking of classical ballets in new forms, and this suited local taste: but he also created some memorable modern pieces, such as *Poème de l'Ecstase* written for Fonteyn. He helped Marcia Haydee, his Brazilian prima ballerina, to become one of the world's great dancers, and he was able to spot young local talent and create soloists from it. He became a hero in Stuttgart even with the people with no taste for ballet. After a period under Glen Tetley, the American choreographer, the company was then taken over by Haydee herself. Still in charge today, she has retained most of Cranko's repertoire and has built up his ballet school into the foremost in Germany. Though still excellent, the company has inevitably been tending to mark time, and in most critics' view it has now been overtaken by Hamburg.

It is in the area of modern as opposed to classical dance that Germany's own home-grown talent has made its more distinctive contribution – thanks above all to the celebrated Pina Bausch and her Tanztheater in the Ruhr town of Wuppertal. It might seem an unlikely setting – but this is decentralised Germany. Bausch was born in 1940 in nearby Solingen and, after training and working in New York with the New American Ballet and the Metropolitan Opera, she decided to return to her roots to form her own company; and here she won subsidies from city and *Land* as well as the right to use the Wuppertal opera house as her base. She draws big audiences from the Ruhr and Rhine towns, as well as frequently touring abroad. Local people were hostile at first to her strange and provocative work – it harks back in some ways to earlier German Expressionism – but, typically, they soon accepted it when the world's critics acclaimed it. Yet it is not for all tastes, this highly emotional mix of mime and dance, theatre and circus, acrobatics and incantation that has been described, less than kindly, as 'a collective therapy session'. Children's games or scenes of great stillness alternate with bouts of frenzy as actors hurl themselves against walls or mime sexual couplings, while the stage is sometimes covered with turf, earth or water that impedes their movements. Bausch refuses to see her work as therapy: but dance for her certainly signifies release of feeling and expression of personality – 'I am interested,' she says, 'not in how people move but in what moves them.' Her concern, she has said, is to project the emotions that classical dance tends to cloak or stylise.

In the world of the visual arts, Germany in the first post-war decades went through a somewhat barren period as far as new creative work is concerned, with the exception of the efforts of the late and much-contested Joseph Beuys. Whereas the First World War had led to a remarkable flowering in the 1920s, with the work of Beckmann, Dix, Ernst, Grosz and many others, this was not repeated after 1945. Most of the best artists had emigrated to escape the Nazis' persecution of 'degenerate' modern art, and those who stayed or then returned did not seem inspired by the experiences of war and post-war to the same degree as the novelists and poets of that time. A few sombre works evoked the ruins and desolation, but they were not especially memorable; and the 1950s and '60s were a humdrum period when it was hard to pick out any new painter of great worth and only the Düsseldorf abstract 'Zero' group made much impact. In the past 20 or so years however the scene has become more lively and a number of new talents have emerged, most notable among them being Baselitz, Pench, Hodicke and Anselm Kiefer. Their paintings mark a certain return to figurative art and to traditional German themes and techniques. Berlin in particular has become very lively: most notably it has nurtured the so-called '*Junge Wilde*' (young savages) group, who use bright, bold colours and vivid subject-matter. More artists today live in Berlin than anywhere else, but the art-dealing and exhibiting scene is concentrated primarily in Cologne, followed by Düsseldorf, Munich and Berlin, and it is very active: many Germans and visitors to Germany are prepared to spend lavishly on new works. New York may still hold the lead: but most experts would agree that the interest in modern art is far more intense and widespread in Germany today than in either London or Paris. Whether this is any indication of the quality of the work being produced is another matter.

High prices are still being paid for the 'action sculptures' of the conceptual artist Josef Beuys, who lived in Düsseldorf where for some years he was a professor of sculpture. Beuys always arouses strong feelings. Like many people, I myself am no great lover of his work, but I am intrigued and attracted by his personality and what he stood for, and I recognise that he had a far greater influence on post-war German art than anyone else. When he died in 1986, aged 64, Waldemar Januszczak wrote of him in the *Guardian* (January 25), 'He was the most radical, charismatic and evocative artist of his times', and another critic called him 'the father of the avant-garde'. But many other art-lovers have sneered at his 'creations' – as when, for example, he filled a piano with washing-powder or painted frankfurters with brown shoe polish. He adored rough materials and would make sculptures out of bits of wood and steel, old newspapers, discarded junk and refuse – and especially felt and fat. These last two were his private symbols of rebirth, for in the war he had been a bomber pilot, and when his aircraft crashed in the Crimea he was saved from death by some Tartars who wrapped him in felt and rubbed fat into his skin. To protect an old war wound, he would also always wear a felt hat. But he was not simply a pretentious poseur, nor was he 'sending up' modern art. He had a generous belief in the potential of every individual for creating art; he also liked to involve himself in public issues and was a founder member of the Greens. With his craving for absolutes, his poetic extremism and his gift for abstract ideas, many critics have seen him as a quaint, essentially Germanic artist. Whether he was also a great one, time will tell. But he certainly helped German artists to recover their identity and self-confidence after the bleak post-war years.

Ours may not be the age of the solitary creative artist, but it is certainly that of the big public museum and the large brilliantly-mounted exhibition: from Beaubourg to Guggenheim this is a world-wide trend, and in Germany the results are as striking as anywhere. Generously funded, imaginatively set out and quite often 'socially relevant', German museums are far from being the dead fusty places that the term so often evokes – and the public responds to them: it is claimed that more people visit museums and exhibitions than go to football matches. Of Germany's 1,500 or so museums, some 86 per cent are publicly subsidised, while many of the others receive funds from private foundations, churches, and commerce and industry. Somewhat later than in the United States, many leading firms such as BMW have now begun to support modern art on a big scale by giving money to museums, galleries and exhibitions, thus supplementing the funds that come traditionally from the cities and *Länder*. Thanks to this varied patronage, new museums of all kinds are being built all over the place: seven devoted to modern art were opened in 1983 alone. In Frankfurt, the council has recently created or refurbished six museums along the banks of the Main. One of these, for handicrafts and applied art, is in a lovely bright shimmering new building designed by the New York architect Richard Meier; another, a museum of local history, follows the 'culture for all' philosophy of the city's famous former culture manager, the socialist Hilmar Hoffmann, and tries to relate history to the daily life of working people. The superb Folkwang Museum in Essen does the same for the industrial history of the Ruhr.

Remarkable new art museums, or major extensions to existing ones, have been opened recently in Mönchen-Gladbach and Düsseldorf, and in Stuttgart where the excitement over Stirling's new wing to the Staatsgalerie has resuscitated interest in the contents of the museum as a whole: in the extension's first year of operation, 1984–5, annual entrances went up five-fold from 210,000 to over 1,300,000. This is encouraging, for the old and new parts of the Staatsgalerie between them house the best twentieth-century art collection in Germany outside Düsseldorf. Stuttgart is not otherwise so noted for the visual arts: but it benefits from a most enlightened policy of the Baden-Württemberg Government which since the 1950s has been devoting a major part of the profits of the state lottery to the acquisition of new works for the various *Land* museums. Currently this runs to 3 million DM a year, ten times the Staatsgalerie's own purchasing budget. This does of course lead to disputes over choice. When the museum wanted to buy a Beuys for 500,000 DM, the *Landtag* raised its horrified Swabian eyebrows very high: but the *Land* Minister of Culture had the last word, and he backed the idea. So there this great debris-like sculpture now sits, filling one entire hall in all its Beuysterous glory, and it is almost the first work you see as you enter across Stirling's green rubber floor and mount in his glass-walled lift. Beuys, Kroetz, Schretzmeier, Zadek, Bausch, even Achternbusch . . . there is no doubt that Germany's official patrons are on balance liberal in accepting modern culture that they do not much care for themselves. Or at least they do not want to appear to be fuddy-duddies.

Museums will from time to time stage special exhibitions of a documentary nature than can shock the older generation. In Stuttgart in 1984, one small municipal museum mounted a remarkably frank survey of life in the city under the Nazis (see p. 501). And in Munich the Stadtmuseum under a left-wing curator has on several occasions angered the CSU establishment – for example, with its critical survey of the *Oktoberfest* (see p. 67). In 1984 it held a brilliant and astonishing exhibition on the theme of Bavarian attitudes to death – room after macabre room filled with coffins, skeletons, and sculptures and paintings of deathbed scenes, operations, torture, and Death visiting the dying. 'Munich,' wrote one paper, 'has broken Vienna's monopoly of the death cult.' And the curator, Christoph Stölzl (now in Berlin), told me: 'Our policy here is to provoke, to look critically at society, to present new values, not bourgeois ones. And Munich is so self-confident that it feels prepared to be tolerant towards its *enfants terribles*. It's a city where culture loves to be provocative. Look at me. Look at Kroetz, Achternbusch, Sagerer. Look at Fassbinder!' Indeed: let us next look at Fassbinder.

## *Fassbinder, Herzog and Reitz's* Heimat*: the brief golden age of the 'New German Cinema'*

Suddenly in the late 1960s and 1970s the moribund German film industry produced out of nowhere a wonderful flowering of highly original work by gifted young directors – Fassbinder, Herzog, Schlöndorff, Wenders and others – and this 'New German Cinema', though in no sense forming a 'movement', soon came to be recognised as one of the most fertile developments in West European film since the war, exceeded only by the Italian Neo-Realists and the French *nouvelle vague*. Today, decline seems to have set in, with Fassbinder dead so young and other directors running short of inspiration or financial backing, or preferring to work abroad: but the appearance as recently as 1984 of the best film of the lot, Reitz's masterly *Heimat*, shows that the German cinema may yet be capable of surprising us again.

The renaissance of the 1960s was especially remarkable in its context, seeing that Germany was, and still is, a country with very little film culture – unlike France or the United States – and its previous cinema record had been extremely patchy. There had been a distinguished period in the 1920s, with the work of Lang, Lubitsch, Murnau, von Sternberg and others: but even before the rise of Hitler many of the leading directors had succumbed to the lure of Hollywood, and then the Nazis yoked the cinema to their own propaganda machine even more thoroughly than in the case of the other arts. After the war, an effective new start proved much more difficult than in the theatre or literature, for the tradition was not there. Just a few good films were made on anti-war or anti-Nazi themes – one could cite Helmut Käutner's *The Devil's General*, based on the play by Carl Zuckmayer, and *The Bridge* by the Swiss-born Bernhard Wicki – but apart from this the output consisted of banal down-market comedies and thrillers, or equally escapist *Heimatfilme* that gave droolingly sentimental portraits of rural life. In those days before the impact of television, the German cinema was prosperous commercially: but it included virtually no counterpart of the kind of personal film of quality then being made in France or Italy, or even sometimes in Britain. Unlike the theatre, cinema in Germany was not taken seriously by intellectuals as a cultural medium; audiences of all social classes simply wanted to be entertained.

By the early 1960s, however, new talent was impatiently looking for outlets. The event that is often regarded as marking the origin of the New German Cinema was the signing of the 'Oberhausen Manifesto' in 1962: at the festival of short films held annually in the Ruhr town of Oberhausen, twenty-six directors working in short films and documentaries came together and drew up a document proclaiming 'the old cinema is dead' and demanding 'new freedoms' for 'the creation of the new German feature film'. These young radicals were inspired by the recent successes of the *nouvelle vague* in France, and they even took over a number of its ideas and slogans. Only two of them, Kluge and Reitz, went on to achieve prominence as directors (and Reitz was to wait 20 years for this): but the impact of their manifesto was immediate. It focused attention on the mediocrity of the film industry, and within a very few years it had prompted the Federal Government to start granting regular subsidies for film-making. This funding has not been ideally organised, as we shall see; but it did prepare the ground for the major directors who soon appeared. Without the backing they gained from the state, and later on from co-productions with television, they could never have found the money for their unusual and 'difficult' films.

The breakthrough began in 1966 when Kluge's first feature, *Yesterday's Girl (Abschied von Gestern)*, won the Silver Lion at the Venice Festival and Schlöndorff's *Young Törless* was well received at Cannes. Soon afterwards Fassbinder embarked on his prodigious output of two or three films a year, though it was not until 1974 that he began to attract world-wide attention when *Fear Eats the Soul* won a top prize at

Cannes. Within a year or two critics on both sides of the Atlantic were describing this new cinema as 'the liveliest in Europe'. Then in 1979, with the great commercial success of Schlöndorff's *The Tin Drum* and Fassbinder's *The Marriage of Maria Braun*, a film wave that at first had been confined to the art-houses began to achieve wider audiences. The new directors were so diverse in their styles and outlook that they never constituted a 'school': but they nearly all lived in Munich, the German film capital, and many were friends. Like the French *nouvelle vague*, they worked at first on the margins of the main commercial film industry, making low-budget movies with their own little production companies – and again like the French they were true *auteurs*, in the sense that each film bore the personal stamp of its director who often doubled as producer and scriptwriter too. Many of them preferred to work regularly with the same well-tried actors (Herzog with Klaus Kinski, Wenders with Rüdiger Vogler, Fassbinder with Hanna Schygulla and others) who in those early years were not yet stars. And some of the *cinéastes* – notably Schlöndorff, but not Fassbinder – preferred to adapt novels rather than use original screenplays, partly because of the lack of any tradition of good scriptwriting in Germany. But the vast majority of their films, whether based on some Grass or Böll best-seller or springing from the director's own imagination, were dealing with essentially German themes or looking squarely at German society; or at least, as in the case of Herzog or Syberberg, they were giving expression to the German soul and character. And that is why this New German Cinema is so intensely interesting, and so relevant to a book such as mine. So let us take a look at the work of some of the main film-makers.

Alexander Kluge, born in 1932 near Magdeburg, is the oldest of them and the most political. Right from the start at Oberhausen he established himself as the group's chief ideologue and in some ways its spokesman; and just as he himself had been influenced by Brecht, so in turn he influenced some of those who followed in his wake. *Yesterday's Girl*, his first feature and still to date his best, was based on a real-life case: it is the story of a Jewish girl, Anita, who arrives penniless from the GDR and then drifts through a series of casual encounters and disappointments in West Germany, sometimes exploited by others, sometimes herself committing petty crime, to end up as an unmarried mother in a penitentiary. The film's original German title, *Abschied von Gestern* (Farewell to Yesterday), was more ironically meaningful than its English one, for Kluge showed how Anita's attempts to make a clean new start in the West were constantly thwarted by her own and the collective German past. Himself a lawyer by training, he satirised the clumsy and sententious efforts of the legal and reformatory authorities to help Anita in her predicament, as she moved against a backdrop of the glossy greed of the *Wirtschaftwunder*, an isolated drop-out in that pre-1968 era, before such misfits had found any kind of solidarity or identity, as they have today. In the main role Kluge cast his own sister, Alexandra, who had never acted before but gave a mesmeric performance; and this he backed up with a shooting and editing style that was deliberately elliptical and staccato, full of jump-cuts and sudden shifts from reality to fantasy, leading all the critics to compare him with the early Godard of *Vivre sa Vie* (1962). But, while Godard was the more original lyricist, Kluge was the sharper social analyst. After this promising start, the best-known of his subsequent films, *Artists atop the Big Top: Disorientated* (1967) and *Occasional Work of a Female Slave* (1973), dealt more obliquely with the moral dilemmas of the individual in society; and then, though he stayed in the limelight as an intellectual and polemicist, in his films he seemed to have little more to say. Much of his later work appears pretentious and over-fragmented.

Volker Schlöndorff, like Kluge, is a man of the Left who has made films critical of society: but his approach is far less cerebral and rarefied. His work is smooth and entertaining, for he believes in putting across his message to a wide audience and has stated that only as a popular medium can cinema be justified. Born in Wiesbaden in 1939, he trained in France where he worked as assistant to Malle and Resnais. His first feature, *Young Törless* (1966), was based on a novel by Musil set in a boarding-school at the turn of the century. There followed a number of full-length films on contemporary social themes, often feminist, before in 1975 he made his first big public impact with a version of Böll's celebrated novella, *The Lost Honour of Katharina Blum*, published the previous year (see p. 301). This was something close to polemical film journalism, for Schlöndorff took Böll's bitter tale of an innocent hounded by the gutter Press and pointed up the political moral for all it was worth, casting the police in a more pernicious light than the book had done and stridently satirising the *Zeitung* and its owners (a barely-concealed attack on *Bild* and Springer). Some critics felt that the subtlety of the original had been sidestepped: but this vigorous film was a huge popular success, largely deserved.

Four years later Schlöndorff turned to Germany's other great post-war novelist by taking his cameras on location to Danzig for *The Tin Drum*: though it cut short the finale, in other respects his film was remarkably faithful to Grass, physical grotesquery and all, and throughout its assured two-and-a-half hours it packed a terrific punch, helped by a fine performance from the diminutive 12-year-old David Bennent as the child Oskar who refuses to grow bigger. After this Schlöndorff made *Circle of Deceit*, a decent liberal film also drawn from a recent novel, about the dilemmas of journalists in war-torn Lebanon. And then, to the surprise of many of his admirers, he deserted modern political issues for the high-society salons of pre-1914 Paris, by returning to his beloved France to take up a challenge that Visconti, Losey and others had toyed with but declined: the filming of Proust. But, though he sensibly confined himself to just one section of the enormous novel, his *Swann in Love* was little more than a distinguished failure, handsomely mounted, superbly acted by Jeremy Irons and others, but ultimately a hybrid that did not penetrate beneath Proust's wafer-thin skin. Enlisting a galaxy of talent, with British, French and Italian stars, music by Hans Werner Henze, Sven Nykvist of Sweden as cameraman, and script by Peter Brook and Jean-Claude Carrière, it seemed to be just the kind of expensive international prestige production that the New German Cinema had initially set out to oppose; and it left some critics wondering whether Schlöndorff in his search for major commercial success had not somehow lost his way and deserted his German inspiration — especially as his next project, in America, was a version of Arthur Miller's *Death of a Salesman*, with Dustin Hoffman. He has since made other films in America, none of much distinction. He is a very fluent and talented director, and his fondness for distinguished literary material is perfectly valid in its way: but his exploitation of trendy subjects has come to seem more than a little glib.

Schlöndorff's former wife, Margarethe von Trotta, collaborated with him on several films, acting as co-director of *Katharina Blum*: and then she went on to make her own features and to become Germany's best-known woman director. As well as being also on the Left, she has decided feminist views (see p. 192) and nearly all her films have been about the struggles of women in German society. Most notably, *The German Sisters (Die Bleierne Zeit*: 1980), a study of the terrorist Gudrun Esslin and her relationship with her sister, gave a moving and perceptive account of the pressures that can drive a gentle and educated girl to violent extremism. It deservedly won the Golden Lion at Venice. Then in 1985, with *The Patience of Rosa L.*, von Trotta chose another subject well suited to her: a portrait of the German pre-1919 left-wing leader Rosa Luxemburg. It won the 'best actress' prize at Cannes in 1986 for its star, Barbara Sukowa.

Wim Wenders, for all his recent obsession with America, remains every bit as Germanic at heart as Kluge or von Trotta. His films have a brooding, restless quality: they deal with footloose wanderers searching for home, and they exemplify a certain forlorn German romanticism. Born in Düsseldorf in 1945, Wenders attended film school in Munich and then first attracted attention in 1971 with *The Goalkeeper's Fear of the Penalty*, based on Handke's short existentialist novel, set in Austria: the solitary hero committing the perfect gratuitous murder, in the book a typically cerebral Handke creation, became in the film a typical Wenders romantic. There followed three celebrated 'road movies', all set in Germany, all quests or journeys both emotional and practical, all revealing of modern Germany as Wenders saw it. *Alice in the Cities* (1973), for my money the most attractive of all his films, had a journalist and a girl of nine meeting by chance in New York and travelling back to Wuppertal together in search of the child's family: here Wenders for the first time revealed his love-hate attitude to America and his feeling that Germany, warts and all, might be the more gentle and homely place. *Wrong Movement* (1974), a modernised version, scripted by Handke, of Goethe's *Wilhelm Meister's Apprenticeship*, was altogether more bleak, however: like the novel of 1795, it traced a young man's educational journey across Germany in search of self-realisation, meeting various strange characters on the way. But, whereas Goethe's book was fairly optimistic, Wenders and Handke showed a modern Germany that amidst all its affluence was a melancholy place. The bleakness continued in *Kings of the Road* (*Im Lauf der Zeit* – in the course of time: 1976), about two laconic and wistful young men who travel in a van across a dreary strip of territory beside the GDR border, repairing projectors in small run-down cinemas. The mood of desolation is not as metaphysical or as contrived as, for instance, in Antonioni: in fact, the film has a gentle human warmth about it, as the two men strike up a kind of comradeship. But it hardly paints a very rosy picture of life.

'The Yanks have colonised even our subconscious,' says one of the men in *Kings of the Road*. By now Wenders was not only fascinated by America but also disturbed by what he saw as the damage that it had done to European culture – and this was a theme of *The American Friend* (1977), a thriller set in Hamburg but filmed mainly in English.

The 'friend' of the title is shown as a broken, sad drifter, far removed from the confident 'colonisers' of the early post-war period. Then, to explore more closely this tarnishing of the American dream, Wenders moved to the United States itself where he made his next four films. The best-known of them, *Paris, Texas*, won the Grand Prix at Cannes in 1984. Its story of a man with his child on a quest for his estranged wife took up, in a sense, the theme of *Alice in the Cities*, and then developed it much further; again, as in many of Wenders' earlier films, the desolate landscapes and cityscapes enhanced a mood of bleakness redeemed by gentle humanism − but touched this time by sentimentality in its improbable, over-dramatic ending. Some critics saw the film as a marvellous European vision of a certain America: I found it slow and portentous compared with *Alice*, and it seemed that Wenders' search for the American dream might have landed him, like his hero, on a Texan railtrack leading to nowhere. He sensed this too, for since 1985 he has filmed not in the USA but in places such as Japan and Australia. In a very German way, he is a man with the *Wanderlust* spirit, carrying his German obsessions with him across the globe. But he also brings them back home to his adored Berlin, where he now lives. Here in 1987 he set his much-admired *Himmel über Berlin* (*Wings of Desire*), a meditation on the human condition that was also a hymn of love to the city. In 1991 he was at work on a sequel to it, set during the fall of the Wall.

The *Wanderlust* spirit also marks out the work of Werner Herzog, who along with Fassbinder − and now Reitz too − must be reckoned the most important of the post-war directors. He is also much the most eccentric and visionary. He likes to film in extraordinary locations − not only the Peruvian jungles of *Aguirre, Wrath of God* and *Fitzcarraldo* but, for example, the Sahara where he contracted bilharzia while shooting one of his early films, *Fata Morgana*. And for one sequence of *Heart of Glass* he took his team in open boats through rough seas to the remote and rocky Skellig isles off Ireland. Above all, Herzog's heroes are just as fanatic and visionary as he is − extraordinary, haunted people, operating at the end of their tether or pursuing bizarre dreams. Fitzcarraldo pulling his great ship over a hill in upper Amazonia, and Aguirre on his mad journey into that same jungle, are the best fictional examples: but Herzog will also seek out real-life people just as tormented, as in his documentary about the high-level ski-jumper Walter Steiner, giddily testing himself to the human limits. He will sometimes do astonishing things to his actors, as when he put the whole cast of *Heart of Glass* under hypnosis; or he will seek out unusual performers for his films, such as the Berlin lavatory attendant and former mental home inmate whom he picked to play *Kaspar Hauser*, or the scores of dwarfs who made up the cast of *Even Dwarfs Started Small*.

It follows that Herzog's films are hardly about modern Germany in the manner, say, of Kluge or Fassbinder: most of them are set abroad, or in Germany's past like *Kaspar Hauser*, or in some fantasy realm. Yet he firmly denies that his films are not on German themes – as when I met him at his office in Munich: 'All my work is about what the Germans are feeling inside themselves. They have these poetic images and urges which they suppress, and I help them to bring them out, by showing them Kaspar's dreams. I'm a Bavarian, and my films are in that tradition, they show the crazed Bavarian pursuit of the useless – mad King Ludwig was just like Fitzcarraldo.' I found Herzog a mild, soft-voiced, poetic man, not looking as if he were about to eat his boot or hike from Munich to Paris (two of his better-known exploits). He has often spoken of his belief in the validity of the irrational, of seeking 'planets that do not exist and landscapes that have only been dreamed'. He is a true genius, and his best films are venerated by cinemanes around the globe. But in Germany he is not too popular: most filmgoers find his work outrageous, even disgusting, and his box-office takings are low.

Born in Munich in 1942, Herzog grew up on a remote Bavarian farm: his work certainly has the baroque, heavily romantic quality associated with Bavaria. *Aguirre, Wrath of God* (1972), his first film of wide appeal, traced the fortunes of a crazed conquistador in the Amazonian jungle, who in the final mesmeric sequence is alone on a raft with his dead daughter and a swarm of monkeys, the last survivor of his lunatic expedition. Much of the film's bizarre effect was due to the presence in the title role of the mad-eyed, skull-faced Klaus Kinski, an actor who has often played with Herzog and whose manic temperament perfectly suits the director's style. Next came *The Enigma of Kaspar Hauser* (*Jeder für sich und Gott gegen alle* – each for himself and God against all: 1974), Herzog's most distinguished film and arguably Germany's post-war best until the arrival of *Heimat*. This was his own version of the true and oft-told story of the young man, brought up apart from all human contact, who was found in the main square of Nuremberg one day in 1828, and was then kindly cared for and taught to speak and behave like a 'normal' person, until five years later he was mysteriously murdered. It was the most warm, humane *and* humorous of Herzog's films, a parable of innocent purity in face of the follies of the world. Then in *Stroszek* (1977) he strayed into Wenders territory with a tale of a trio of German émigrés facing the sour reality of American life. Some other films of this period, such as *Nosferatu* and *Heart of Glass*, were less successful. But two further Kinski vehicles were brilliant: *Woyzeck*, adapted from Büchner's grim story of betrayal, and the astonishing *Fitzcarraldo*, another epic fantasy of mad ambition in the upper Amazon. After this Herzog was off on his travels again, filming in Australia, the Himalayas and Nicaragua. It is impossible to sum him up. He pursues his own luminous vision and has compromised very little with the commercial cinema. Perhaps only a German could make films like his. Sometimes his work topples over into the ludicrous: but it is saved from Germanic gloom or solemnity by his coruscating visual imagination.

Herzog's fellow-Bavarian, the late Rainer Werner Fassbinder, might also be loosely described as 'typically German' or 'typically Bavarian' – he had a sentimental streak tinged with cruelty, a generous but aggressive temperament, and a fondness for excess. Like Herzog he was driven by some inner demon: but his life-style and approach to filming were utterly different. He travelled rarely. Of his prodigious output of forty or so feature films in the space of thirteen years, only one was made abroad. With all the rest, he chose intensely German settings for propagating his own curious brand of provocative yet compassionate pessimism. He had many admirers, who warmed to his patent candour and originality: but there were fierce detractors too, who found his films trite, over-melodramatic and given to maudlin self-pity. I count myself categorically among the admirers.

More than with most artists, the key to his work lies in his life, for his own restless bisexual bohemianism as well as the bitter tears of his films were both of them products of his chronically disturbed psyche – leading to his death at 36. He was born in 1946 in south-west Bavaria, son of a doctor, and his childhood was scarred by his parents' vociferously unhappy marriage. He attended drama school, then in 1968 in Munich he created his famous *'anti-theater'* with some friends, including his star-to-be, Hanna Schygulla. This was a new kind of spontaneous theatre with improvised scripts, performed in derelict cinemas or rooms behind pubs. Next he began shooting low-budget films: one of the first, *Katzelmacher* (1969) – about a Greek *Gastarbeiter* lynched by young Bavarians because his sexuality excited their girls – impressed the critics and won a prize. Throughout his career he always worked very fast, with amazing fluency: he could shoot a film in ten days or write a whole play on a train journey. Both in theatre and cinema, he also liked to use his own little team of regular actors, who tended to idolise him and would tolerate his capriciously alternating bouts of generosity and callousness.

By keeping generally to low budgets, he secured the backing from television and other sources to maintain a steady output. While his films touched upon a wide range of subjects, the more important of them nearly always turned upon the themes – very personal to him – of love rejected or trust betrayed. The archetype, *The Bitter Tears of Petra von Kant* (1972), was drawn from his own stage play about an hysterical fashion designer who has a lesbian affair with a younger woman and is then exploited and deserted by her. This was a deliberately theatrical and hyper-stylised film. But in *The Merchant of Four Seasons* (1971), the study of a middle-class man bullied and rejected by wife and friends and driven to suicide, Fassbinder was able to treat the same theme in a low-keyed naturalistic style; it was a gentle and compassionate film, even though spiced with barbs against bourgeois self-seeking. *Fox* (*Faustrecht der Freiheit* – right fist of freedom: 1975) returned to the motif of homosexuals exploiting one another, this time with Fassbinder himself in the part of the doomed working-class hero. Like much of his work, it was open to the charge of being too fatalistic, with the dice too systematically loaded against its main character.

Unlike Schlöndorff or von Trotta, Fassbinder seldom made films on directly political or topical subjects. But his somewhat simplistic para-Marxist philosophy saw the individual as the victim of 'our phoney society that corrupts all human contact', and this theme constantly recurred – as in the film that first won him international fame, *Fear Eats the Soul* (1973), about a scandalised society's destruction of the love-match between an elderly Munich charlady and a much younger Moroccan *Gastarbeiter*. Generally, as in this case, Fassbinder preferred to write scripts based on his own stories: but, when he found a classic that fitted his *Weltanschauung*, he was able to make a sensitive adaption, as with his version of *Effi Briest* (1974), Fontane's nineteenth-century story of an innocent woman victimised by family and society – a truly Fassbinderian heroine, finely portrayed by Schygulla. He found an equal affinity with a contemporary writer, none other than his fellow-Bavarian Franz Xaver Kroetz: they worked together on the film of *Wild Game* (1972), one of Kroetz's bitter little studies of peasant ignorance and brutality.

After this spate of small-scale and frequently excellent films in the 1970s, with *The Marriage of Maria Braun* (1978) Fassbinder moved on to a work that had a much bigger budget and broader canvas and dealt far more directly with post-war German society — the story of a woman (Schygulla again) who becomes tough and cynical in her efforts to survive and prosper amid the rapacity of the 'Economic Miracle'. The film was untypical also in the way that the main character this time is not crushed by those around her but outwits them and wins through, though at great cost to her own soul — hardly an upbeat ending. *Maria Braun* was much the most successful commercially of all Fassbinder's work. The previous year he had already forayed into the international field with his first film in English, and with an English star, Dirk Bogarde: this was *Despair*, based on a novel by Vladimir Nabokov set in 1920s Germany. The foreign dialogue clashed uneasily with the German milieu and characters; Fassbinder was clearly not in his element and the film was no great success. After this, he kept again to real German films. In an odd way he had always been fascinated by Hollywood, and he received plenty of offers from it after *Maria Braun*. Wisely, he never let himself be lured. In that ruthless dream-factory, so wayward a rebel would surely have come to the same kind of sticky end as his heroes. But his later work in Germany was very uneven, culminating in a somewhat overblown television series based on *Berlin Alexanderplatz*, Alfred Döblin's picaresque novel of pre-war Berlin.

I interviewed Fassbinder in 1976. I had heard so much about his turbulent personality that I was surprised to find such a mild, shy-seeming, defensive young man, with an ugly urchin face, smoking nervously and smiling little during our long talk. 'My father was chaotic,' he said, 'and I still bear those scars so deeply that I could never settle in a stable home. The terrible quarrels of my parents have warped me for ever. I'm a behaviourist: I believe that if the parents are playing false roles, then the child copies these mechanisms and is distorted. No authentic relationship is possible. The answer? — abolish marriage and all society based on property and desire for possessions, the root of our ills.' A facile and unoriginal view, maybe, but sincere. Fassbinder did genuinely suffer. This lent him his creativity, but also made him hard to work with. Peter Zadek, for whom he once produced a play in Bochum, told me: 'Rainer's a little shit, but one can't help liking him. He can be so generous, yet feels this need to work in a permanent state of quarrel.' And a film critic added, 'Behind his façade of Hollywood tough-guy, with his black leather jackets and lower-class slang, he's pathetically vulnerable, sensitive, sentimental.' He was always generous towards the spongers who surrounded him: his flat, dirty and disorderly, was full of these parasites making cooking smells and sleeping on the floor. He hated smart clothes or nice homes and was frank about his sex life — 'When I was young I preferred older men, substitutes for the father I hardly knew. Then I had a woman phase and now it's both.' Drugs entered into it too. His death in 1982 from a mixture of cocaine and sleeping-pills may or may not have been suicide.

So how lasting will his *oeuvre* prove to be? His films were always a mixture of realism and stylisation, sometimes veering from one to the other within the same sequence, and this disconcerted many critics. But there was remarkable visual elegance and fluency, even in a minor and rather contrived film such as *Veronica Voss*. His plots and treatment were frequently melodramatic — hence his admiration for Hollywood — and this too disturbed the critics. But he claimed that life itself *was* melodrama; and through his genuine compassion he was able to give true emotional force to a trite situation. The sentimentality, the heart-on-sleeve pessimism, were all part of the package. He was not really a political animal. 'In the sense that I hate capitalist society, yes, I'm on the Left,' he told me; 'but I see no remedy and I detest all "isms" and movements.' The German far-left detested him in return. There are plenty of critics who regard him as a cryptofascist and believe that he would have been quite happy under Hitler. This to my mind is plain nonsense. He was no more than a shallow thinker and his reactions were those of the gut not the head: but he had real strength of feeling, and real pity for the underdog, not just for himself. His life was a minor tragedy, but it produced triumphant art.

These are some of the main directors of the New German Cinema. In their diverse galaxy, a few other names are worth mentioning too. Reinhard Hauff, for example, an associate of Schlöndorff and von Trotta, has made some good political films: his *Stammheim* (1985) was a worthy dramatisation of the Baader-Meinhof trials. Helma Sanders-Brahms, another radical, is Germany's best woman director after von Trotta: her *Germany Pale Mother* (1979) was a highly sensitive portrait of a young woman traumatised by the war and unable to adjust to the world of peacetime. Themes of German guilt and the burden of German history have been evoked also in the weird films of Hans Jürgen Syberberg, most notably in his 'German Trilogy' of biographical studies of Hitler, 'mad' King Ludwig of Bavaria and the popular novelist Karl May. Syberberg, an eccentric outsider in German cinema, has some affinities with Herzog – just as there are echoes of Fassbinder in the films of the engagingly provocative Rosa von Praunheim, (see p. 44). He ('Rosa' is a pseudonym) has recently returned to Berlin after some years in New York, to continue his vivaciously anarchic studies of his demi-monde of gays and beatniks: *City of Lost Souls* (1982) he described to me as 'a report on the lives of American drag artists living in Berlin. I like to let it all hang out, to show life as it is, dirty, messy and real.'

By 1984 this New German Cinema appeared to be running badly out of steam. Fassbinder was dead; Herzog, Schlöndorff and Wenders had deserted Germany: they and other directors seemed to be repeating themselves and lacking new ideas; very little new talent was emerging; tighter financing was making it harder to find backing for new projects. The situation seemed even graver than in France where the *nouvelle vague* and its successors were similarly jaded and frustrated. And then through the gathering clouds there unexpectedly broke the brightest, most life-giving sun. In the summer of that year, Edgar Reitz's *Heimat* was shown in Munich, then at the Venice Festival and around the world, to an intensity of critical applause that surely has had no equal in European cinema since the early work of Godard, Truffaut and Resnais.

Ironically, this was no 'new talent' but the work of a veteran director in his fifties who had been around for longer than any of them except Kluge. Ironically, too, this $15\frac{1}{2}$-hour masterpiece was conceived and made as an 11-part series for television and only because of its great acclaim was it also shown in cinemas. But, although *Heimat* is most unlike the average small-screen soap-opera, it is the sheer length allowed to a TV series (by cinema standards) that has helped to give this film its special strength, by enabling it to achieve a scale, depth and resonance, and a leisurely sense of detail, that have led many critics to liken it to some classic nineteenth-century novel. Its story, in a nutshell, is that of three related families between 1919 and 1982, in a farming village on the plateau of the Hunsrück between the Rhine and Moselle rivers, south of Koblenz: and the history of Germany in our time is followed through the lives of these ordinary people, from the poverty and isolation of the 1920s, through the first happy acceptance of Nazism and the weariness and disillusion of the war and its aftermath, to the massive transformation of rural life wrought by the *Wirtschaftswunder*. Though many other German films had dealt with wartime and Nazi themes, this was the first to look quite so honestly at the impact of these events on the 'little people' of Germany; and it was certainly the first to give so detailed and realistic a picture of the too-often-ignored world of rural Germany and its changes (see p. 167). In its mood and human approach too, *Heimat* marked a break with previous German films: here was none of the gloom of Wenders or Fassbinder, nor the rhetoric and symbolism of many of the new directors, but a straightforward and affectionate humanism, critical but ultimately optimistic. Reitz's work appears closer in spirit to Olmi, Satyajit Ray or Renoir than to the German cinema's own tradition. His long and uneven film may have its faults: but it could well be regarded as the most significant single artistic achievement of post-war Germany.

It differs from the usual TV drama series in being an intensely personal work, a true labour of love, with some autobiographical elements. Reitz is a quiet and thoughtful man, with a grizzled beard and gentle eyes, and when I talked with him in his office in Munich in 1985 he seemed quite untouched by the sudden fame that had engulfed him. Son of a watchmaker, he was born in 1932 in the small Hunsrück town of Morbach where his mother and brother, who carries on the family trade, still live. He was the first member of his family to have any academic education, and at the age of 19 he left Morbach for Munich where he took a degree in art, history and theatre. Then he began making documentaries and in 1962 was one of the Oberhausen signatories; along with Kluge, a close friend, he came to be regarded as one of the more intellectual of the new film-makers. His first feature, *Mahlzeiten* (1966), the story of a tragic marriage, won a prize at Venice. But his subsequent films were somehow too unassuming to make any wide impact, though several were of some quality: *Stunde Null* (1976), foreshadowing some of the themes of *Heimat* and most recognisably by the same hand, was a witty and endearing portrait of a group of villagers near Leipzig in July 1945, awaiting their future in a strange limbo between the departing GIs who had just 'liberated' them and the Red Army yet to arrive.

Then came the making of *Heimat* — itself a remarkable saga. 'In 1978,' Reitz told me, 'I made a fairly expensive historical film, *Der Schneider von Ulm*, that was a critical and commercial flop and I was 250,000 DM in debt. I felt I would never film again and I was terribly depressed. I went to stay with friends on the island of Sylt, and there through a long snowbound Christmas I found myself watching the

[344]

American *Holocaust* series on TV. I was horrified at this cheap sentimental rot being taken seriously by German intellectuals as a treatment of our national guilt, and it made my depression even worse. So I began writing. I wrote pages and pages of notes, trying to explain to myself how I felt about these things, about my childhood memories of the war and the Hunsrück, and then about why I left home at nineteen. I wrote about my mother, my family, my first love, all the idyllic escapades – and gradually I found that fictional elements were entering in, and soon I had part of a kind of film-script. So you could say that *Heimat* grew out of a reaction against *Holocaust*. I took my draft to my friend Joachim von Mengershausen at the WDR TV station in Cologne, and he said: make me a film. I asked the scriptwriter Peter Steinbach to help, and with him I went back to the Hunsrück where I was upset to see the destruction caused by modernisation and how the place had changed. We visited various villages and in one of them, Woppenroth, we found a hut in someone's back-garden that we could rent cheaply, and there we spent 13 months, writing hard; in the evenings we'd talk to the villagers in pubs, about their memories, so the story filled out and finally we had 2,000 pages of script.'

With a contract from WDR and Sender Freies Berlin, Reitz then took eighteen months to shoot his film, in Woppenroth and four nearby villages. It was mostly done chronologically, so the villages were first disguised to look like the 1920s and then gradually brought back to their present neat but ugly state. Reitz used 28 professional players, none of them stars, plus a host of amateurs (the old blacksmith in the film was a real local blacksmith) and some 5,000 extras. 'The Hunsrückers were sceptical at first,' Reitz told me, 'for they felt that as filming is artificial it was bound to be all lies. But steadily they came to trust us. And now this film is more real to them than their own lives, and in their minds its characters still live there with them. It's quite eerie.' At the end of the film is a wonderful sequence – one of its rare departures from realism – where all the people who have died during the 63-year story come back to visit the central character, Maria. This was not Reitz's idea: the actors requested it, for they could not bear the story to end without them. A cinema or TV audience too becomes willingly involved in the story and characters, nearly all of them so real and warm. I myself have seen the full $15\frac{1}{2}$ hours three times; and though I grew more aware of the film's flaws I was never for one moment bored and would happily sit through it all three more times.

The story revolves around the Simon family in the fictional village of Schabbach. Young Paul Simon returns from the First War in a restless mood, not too keen on settling back to help his father with his smithy and little farm. He marries Maria Wiegand, daughter of a richer neighbouring farmer and they have two sons. But Paul is still dreaming of faraway places and one day he goes out for a beer – and disappears. Later he writes from America, where in time he becomes a successful factory owner. Meanwhile life in the village goes on, Maria stoically survives, and Paul's sickly brother Eduard goes to Berlin where (somewhat implausibly) he marries a brothel *madame*, the ambitious Lucy, and brings her back to the Hunsrück. Then the Nazi regime arrives and is greeted with a shrug by most of the villagers and quite eagerly by some of them: Maria's younger brother joins the local SS. Schabbach grows patently more prosperous, as cars replace carts in its main street. Maria has a love-affair with a visiting engineer and bears him a son, Hermann. Then comes the war which is patiently endured, as families split up, Maria's lover is killed and her two elder boys go off to fight. In 1945 the gum-chewing GIs turn up on the heels of the Nazis and they too are accepted quite naturally; Paul himself, now rich and self-confident, pays a return visit from Detroit and finds himself welcomed by all the family with a fond passivity as though he had scarcely been away. But they do not need his help, for next comes the Economic Miracle which brings greater transformation to the Hunsrück than all the preceding world events. Anton, the eldest son, builds up a prosperous optics factory in Schabbach and acquires a large yellow Mercedes; Hermann, Maria's love-child, has a love-affair that ends cruelly, then leaves for Munich where he becomes a successful modern composer. Meanwhile the wise and gentle Maria grows old with dignity, puzzled but unruffled by the changes around her, just as Paul's splendid old mother had been before ('Six times in my life there's been a "new era" – they don't stop coming'). Finally, the whole clan gathers at Maria's funeral. With her, a world and a way of life had died.

Reitz passes no moral judgement on these events or characters. Only the SS boy is treated rather too superficially, as something of a stage villain. Despite a few improbable twists in the plot, the supreme quality of the film is its evocative realism: it gives a wonderful sense of place, in this village of stone and timbered cottages amid the copses and rolling cornfields, while the texture of daily life is conveyed in hundreds of little scenes and incidents, some pathetic, some droll, some deliberately humdrum – picnics and birthdays, harvesting and cake-making, bike-rides and family tiffs. Reitz has shot in luminous black-and-white, but with occasional splashes of colour which, he says, 'I used intuitively, to point up an emotion or stress a change of scene, rather than according to any strategy'. This adds to the lyrical quality. But, if the film itself is black and white, the characters are not: apart from the SS boy, there are few stereotypes, and even the saint-like Maria is seen to be capable of acts of meanness, while the most harsh or staid character can show sudden humour or generosity. In particular, in the post-war scenes, Reitz cleverly allows our sympathy to shift from one to the other of the elder Simon sons: Anton, at first an insensitive bigot in the way he stamps out poor Hermann's love-affair, is seen later as an honourable and benevolent employer, while his weak brother Ernst, much kinder towards Hermann, emerges as a drifter and a spoiler of Hunsrück traditional values. And the acting throughout is magnificent – not only from the professionals, led by Marita Breuer, a young actress from Cologne who specially learned the difficult Hunsrück dialect for her role as Maria and who across the 63 years ages miraculously in voice, walk and gesture. The amateurs too are inspired, some of them local farmers, teachers or schoolkids, and one pastor. Glasisch, the village simpleton who acts as a kind of Greek chorus, introducing and linking each episode, is played by a musician and student; and a local amateur theatre group member took the part of Paul's mother, the wise old peasant matriarch who recalls Maxim Gorki's *babuschka* or Ma Joad in *The Grapes of Wrath*.

In this long and imaginative work, Reitz has allowed his material to dictate the form, so that the episodes are of varying lengths and styles and do not slot into each other smoothly as in a studio-made TV soap-opera. This is no matter: but there are some elements of loose editing and even of self-indulgence in this sprawling film, where a few sequences seem irrelevant or drag on too long – the later war scenes, for instance. Also, in his concern maybe to appeal to a wide audience, Reitz in a few instances has sacrificed naturalism to comedy, albeit very good comedy – notably in the case of Lucy, the irrepressible opportunist from Berlin who improbably settles for Hunsrück domesticity. And, as several critics have felt, Reitz does lose his sureness of touch in the one directly (and avowedly) autobiographical episode, the lengthy story of the 15-year-old Hermann's affair with a girl eleven years his senior. One could cavil, too, at the almost total absence of any references to the role of the Churches, in a mixed Catholic/Protestant area where there were certainly conflicts.

A more fundamental criticism is that possibly the film is *too* cosy and

generous in its portrait of an enclosed pre-war peasant community that
– like any other in Europe in those days – must surely have had its full
share of ignorance, prejudice, intolerance and feuding. Such tensions
emerge in a few episodes, but mostly they are glossed over or played
for their more humorous side. As with Renoir or Truffaut, has Reitz's
warm humanism not led him to portray people as just a little nicer than
they are? To this, he replied to me: 'I think you are wrong. In those
days, the villagers lived so much on top of each other, and needed each
other so much, that they were forced into a solidarity that surmounted
the tensions. Certainly, a rebel or non-conformist was victimised merci-
lessly – but he or she then had to accept exile from the community, as
happened in the first episode to Apollonia, the girl who has an
illegitimate child by a French soldier. Today, all that has changed. An
Apollonia would be accepted: but the old warm solidarity has gone.'

This indeed is one of the film's most central themes: the transfer from
an old traditional way of life, safe but restricting, to a new more fluid
one of greater personal freedom but greater uncertainty, too, and the
tensions that this can cause. The old Schabbach that Maria loved was
comforting but, for Paul at least, impossibly claustrophobic: is the new
wider world, that has opened out for their sons, any improvement? Reitz
seems to have his doubts. And linked to this dilemma is the film's
recurring *motif* of departure and homecoming, of being at home and
feeling for home – all bound up with the great theme enshrined in the
film's much analysed and heavily meaningful title, 'HEIMAT'. The
word translates as something much more than 'home' or 'homeland'. For
Germans, it is also a state of mind. Ernst Bloch described it as 'an
abundance of desires and longings, wishes and yearnings, the great
storehouse of customs not yet domesticated and desires yet to be
fulfilled'; and Reitz himself has said, '*Heimat* means nostalgic memories,
and wanting to go back to where you were happy as a child.' This very
human desire for belonging has always held a strong appeal for the
German imagination. So the Nazis, in their bid for popularity, made
concerted propaganda use of the term '*Heimat*' as a sentimental patriotic
ideal. Then after the war it was ideologised in a different way, by right-
wing exiles from Silesia and other lost territories who formed *Heimatverbände* (homeland associations), demanding the recovery of those areas.
Around the same period, the cinema was flooded with the commercial
banality of the *Heimatfilme*. So '*Heimat*' was trebly discredited, a word
used only sneeringly by German liberals – and it took some courage on
Reitz's part to choose it as his title and thus restore it to its proper place.

More than this, one of the reasons for the great success of his film in Germany is that Reitz has helped to bring audiences back in touch with traditional values, not only by portraying the country life of the past – and here his contribution is unique – but also, perhaps better than other post-war artists, by focusing on the Nazi period in a way that has helped to cure the collective blackout caused by that cataclysm. Reitz has said, 'We Germans have a hard time with our stories. Our own history is in the way. The year 1945, the *Stunde Null*, wiped out a lot, creating a gap in people's ability to remember. Our film consists of these suppressed or forgotten little memories. It is an attempt of sorts to revive memories.' And the English film-maker Chris Petit has written perceptively in *Time Out* (February 1985): 'This inability to remember – which is also the impossibility of forgetting – is *the* recurring subject of recent German cinema. It is most often identified as a spiritual homesickness: one sees it in Wenders' restless characters "at home nowhere"; in Herzog's exiled megalomaniacs; and in Fassbinder's pressure-cooked domestic dramas. *Heimat* is a most ambitious attempt to overcome the rupture, to return home in a sense, by trying to restore continuity to those frozen years. As such it is the most patient and painstaking recuperative exercise in German cinema.'

To achieve this, Reitz had to find a way of dealing with the Nazi and wartime periods, which occupy over a third of the film. He shows that these self-absorbed Hunsrückers, people no better or worse than anyone else, easily accepted Nazism for a number of reasons – they had no idea what it was really like, there were no Jews in the village who might trouble their conscience, Hitler specifically gave financial aid to small farmers, and family loyalty was such that Maria's SS brother, though not approved of, was gently tolerated. All this is perfectly convincing. But I do feel that in the later wartime sequences Reitz has failed to illustrate how the villagers really feel about the prospect of defeat – are they resigned, or upset? – have they yet lost faith in the Führer? Nor, after May 1945, does he show properly how they reacted when they finally learned the truth about Nazism. Is he suggesting that so remote was it from their own daily lives that they felt very little? He does seem to have avoided the issue just a little. And so the film leaves the impression, I am sure unintended, of erring more on the side of justifying the ordinary German's acceptance of Nazism than of condemning it. A number of American critics made the same point, and forcibly – 'soft on Nazism, not enough guilt,' wrote the *New Yorker*. But in Germany itself the film ran into a certain hostility for the opposite reason – from older people who did not want to be reminded of their guilt.

These however were only minority voices amid the general enthusiasm. When *Heimat* was first shown on German TV, audience ratings rose from 26 per cent at the start to 36 per cent by the eleventh episode, which gives some idea of its impact; since then, cinemas all over the country have held frequent weekend screenings of the film in its entirety. And Reitz himself has suggested that, in this video age, maybe the classic 100-minute cinema feature film has become an outmoded form, whereas the television series with its far greater length can provide the serious *film d'auteur* with a new and vaster scope – this leads us back to the notion of *Heimat* as successor to the classic Balzacian novel. Here again, the film could mark a watershed. It does not yet seem to have inspired other directors. But in 1985–91 Reitz himself was at work on a mammoth sequel, *Die Zweite Heimat*, that was planned to be even longer – twenty-six hours, to be shown on German TV in thirteen parts. This film, due to be premiered at the Venice film festival in 1992, does not return to the Hunsrück but follows the fortunes of *Heimat*'s young Herman among a group of artistic and intellectual friends in Munich in the 1960s and 1970s. 'It is going to be as great a film as *Heimat*,' wrote Carole Angier in *Sight & Sound* in 1991 after seeing some parts of it.

Abroad, *Heimat* has by now been shown in some thirty countries, on the big and small screen. As a result, the dull little village of Woppenroth has become a kind of tourist centre, a mini-Stratford-upon-Avon – and the proud and canny villagers are cashing in on the boom. One local teacher conducts guided tours of the spots where the film was made: the local publican, Rudi Molz, offers a *Schabbacherplatte* of cold meats and sells bottles of *Hermännchen* Schnaps; the mayor has changed the placard at the entry to the village to 'Woppenroth/Schabbach' (echoes of Proust's town, now officially Illiers/Combray). And some of the cohorts of visiting tourists are convinced that the story was real. One Dutch family turned up asking to see 'Maria's grave'. So Molz, saying it was too dark to see anything, put them up for the night, sold them breakfast too, and meanwhile got some pals to mock up a slab in the cemetery. The Dutch went away happy. I had the same feeling myself when Molz showed me the cottage used for the exteriors of the Simon house, with the nailmarks still on the door from one scene where Anton tries to board it up. I caught myself thinking, 'how fascinating, *that* is where it happened' – before I remembered that it was just a bit

of filming. When fiction is as powerful as this, we cannot bear it not to
be true.

Above all, *Heimat* has proved a marvellous ambassador for modern
Germany around the globe. Perhaps it has done more in one stroke
than many years of patient work by the Goethe Institut or Inter
Nationes. Its warmly sympathetic and wryly engaging portrait of life
on this windy plateau above the Rhine valley has dealt a head-on blow
to many foreign clichés about the Germans – above all, that they are
stiff and pompous and have no sense of humour. As the *Observer* wrote
of Reitz in its profile of him (May 4, 1986), 'he has helped to restore to
our consciousness the great tradition of German humanism that was
obliterated by the blood and ashes of the 1940s.'

This New German Cinema, as my survey will have shown, has proved
an excellent barometer of the shifting moods and preoccupations of
post-war Germany – immeasurably more so than the *nouvelle vague* in
the case of France, where so many of those lovely poetic movies were
pure escapism. A high proportion of the better German films have
either sought to look realistically at society (whether in the manner of
*Heimat* or of *Katharina Blum* or *Maria Braun*), or else more obliquely
they have mirrored certain German dilemmas (*vide* Wenders' loners), or
as in the case of Syberberg they have tried to lay the ghosts of a
troubled past. Many films by a whole range of directors have dealt
with the effects of the war, or with terrorism, or with the position of
women or old people in Germany, or with farmers or *Gastarbeiter*. One
could mention Werner Schroeter's *Palermo oder Wolfsburg* (1980), an
interesting but overblown study of the travails of a young Sicilian
working at Volkswagen; or Peter Fleischmann's *Hunting Scenes from
Lower Bavaria* (1969), a bitter caricature of the cruelty of a rural society,
itself a kind of early anti-*Heimatfilm* albeit in an opposite manner from
*Heimat*.[1] More recently, Michael Verhoeven's *Das Schreckliche Mädchen*
(*The Nasty Girl*; 1989) was a lively satire based on the true story of a
bold young woman who dared to investigate the Nazi past of esteemed
burghers in the Bavarian town of Passau.

However, German society has seldom reciprocated this interest by
flocking to these various films in any great numbers. The early

1. Most of the slushy *Heimatfilme* were also set in Bavaria, clearly the place that
most often evokes extremes of sentimentality or savagery in portraits of rural life
(NB also Kroetz): to find moderation on this subject, one must look north.

productions, Kluge's for example, tended to be elitist and 'difficult'. Since then, from Schlöndorff to Reitz, some of the best work while remaining serious has also become much more commercial and accessible: but many other directors have remained too moralistic, didactic and hyper-critical, or too plain fanciful, to attract a general audience.[1] This is a land without a strong film culture where even a high proportion of educated people refuse to take cinema seriously in the way they take theatre or music, and so it is little surprise that the new directors have won a far better response abroad than at home: von Trotta told me that her *The German Sisters* had a cinema audience of 2 million in Italy but only 600,000 in Germany despite its topical German subject. It is true that some 120 towns now have subsidised municipal cinemas which give one-off showings of serious films, mostly old ones: but of Germany's 3,250 commercial cinemas only about 150 specialise in the more demanding kind of 'art movie'. Since audiences are predominantly teenage and want easy entertainment, few distributors will take risks. This attitude also effects imported films, which in Germany are virtually always dubbed rather than sub-titled. This may hardly matter for *Star Wars*: but Kurosawa's samurai, Nashville's songsters, and Liverpool's Shirley Valentine, all also talk nothing but German – with ludicrous effect. One reason for this barbarism is that the German dubbing industry is large and powerful enough to exercise a near-veto on sub-titling. It employs top actors and pays them well, and the results are technically superb – John Wayne once said, 'My German voice is better than my own.' But culturally it is a travesty. Non-dubbed versions *are* available, for Switzerland frequently puts German sub-titles on its imports: but these versions do not reach the Federal Republic. And, in this land of cinematic philistines, the popular demand for authentic films is not vocal enough to break the dubbers' grip.

In this disastrous film climate it is remarkable that the New Cinema was able to get as far as it did. This was thanks to public financing. Since the late 1960s the German film industry has received subsidies,

---

1. Some intellectuals too dislike the new films. Walter Laqueur, an American of German origin, wrote in his *Germany Today* (1984; pp. 115–20) that the new directors 'were devoid of compassion and a sense of humour', their treatment was 'heavy-handed', they 'knew only grotesque grimaces of the margins of society', and 'in the last resort these movies tell us very little about Germany in the 1970s'. A view with which I could not agree less.

from federal and *Land* sources, on a more generous scale than in Britain. They were initiated in response to the Oberhausen appeal, with the aim of helping young directors: but matters have since grown much more difficult, for the old guard has hit back successfully, with the result that most of the cash is now allocated to routine projects on criteria that are more commercial than artistic. A few grants are also awarded annually on a quality basis for promising new scripts; but the jury that decides them is under the aegis of the Minister of the Interior, of all unsuitable people, and he has the last word — 'This is typical of the way the cinema is regarded in Germany,' said one director. The minister in the later 1980s, Friedrich Zimmermann, was not exactly a paragon of liberalism, as we have noted earlier, and several times he used his powers to nip in the bud projects that he disliked — including a script by the avant-garde Bavarian director Herbert Achternbusch that was judged 'blasphemous'.

Extremely few really good new films have been made in Germany by German directors since the mid-1980s. Serious film-makers have been finding it harder and harder to get the backing they need. When they do succeed, it is usually thanks to co-productions with television. A federal law of 1974 obliges the TV stations to spend certain sums each year on sponsoring productions by independent film companies which the networks themselves cannot then screen until two, three or five years later (depending on contract), after the film has exhausted its main cinema potential. This system works fairly well, and Fassbinder was one of those who benefited from it regularly. But as in other countries television is also the main enemy, the prime cause of the decline in cinema attendances which in Germany fell from 16 cinema visits per head in 1956 to 1.8 visits in 1988, the lowest figure in the EC. And, in today's video age, matters are growing worse. With the exception of Bavaria Film in Munich, which is highly commercial, there are no big production companies in Germany, and most of the serious directors prefer to have their own little independent outfits. This gives them more freedom, but they need to rely on outside backing, and today nearly all of them complain that this is getting harder and harder to find: 'Even the TV networks,' said one, 'now want tame, obvious subjects, not those with any strong critical element.' Some directors have opted for the big commercial subject with international appeal — notably Wolfgang Petersen, who made the massively profitable *The Boat* and *The Never-Ending Story*. Others have gone abroad, and not only because — like Wenders or Herzog — they are genuinely fascinated by foreign subjects: the reason may equally be that the backing is easier to find in America, or that they are dispirited by Germany's lack of good scriptwriters with new ideas. Percy Adlon, who went to America to make *Baghdad Café*, is a good example. All in all, the kind of heavy commercial/cultural pressures from Hollywood that have long bedevilled the British cinema, and that the French have so cleverly withstood, are today almost as powerfully omnipresent in Germany as in Britain – and this despite the fact that Germany shares with France the *cordon sanitaire* of a language barrier. But *does* she? – many of the biggest German commercial films, such as *The Never-Ending Story*, are now being made in English. As in other areas of modern life, the Germans have only themselves to blame if they let themselves become so Americanised.

After a period of great brilliance, the future of the New German Cinema today looks uncertain. *Heimat* may offer new hope, not only through its own virtues, but because of the prospect it offers of a new kind of television outlet for the personal film of artistic worth that can also tell a good story. But this will depend on the continuing courage and enlightenment of television sponsors such as *Westdeutsche Rundfunk*. And today, in the new age of the satellite, the oddly-structured German television system itself faces new challenges. These might usefully invigorate it, but equally they could be harmful to serious feature film-making.

## *Television becomes less tame, but* Bild *stays barbarous*

If the BBC, ITV and Channel 4 constitute 'the least worst television in the world' (in Milton Shulman's phrase), then the west German networks might just about be regarded as the second least worst in Europe. It is no great claim. German television is very competent, very worthy, but generally dull and timid because it is straitjacketed by a well-intentioned balance of political interests. This derives from a bid by the Occupying Powers after 1945 to prevent the new German broadcasting from becoming too dependent on a central government and thus again a potential tool of state propaganda, as it was under Hitler. So radio and TV were decentralised and placed under the aegis of the *Länder*, but in such a way that each regional station should enjoy some autonomy and freedom from direct interference – a little like the BBC. This was the theory. In practice it has not worked out well, for television has tended to fall victim to the rivalries of those set to guarantee its balanced objectivity.

Private commercial television made its debut in Germany only in 1988, in the form of four new channels (see below). As yet these do not have very large audiences, and have not had much impact on the existing structure, which is a complex and unusual one – neither state-controlled on the former French model, nor purely private as in the United States, but something more like a mixture between BBC and ITV. The first network is run by the ARD (very short for *Arbeitsgemein-schaft der öffentlich-rechtlichen Rundfunkanstalten der Bundesrepublik Deutsch-land*), a federation composed of eight separate regional corporations which roughly follow the *Land* divisions save that Hamburg, Schleswig-Holstein and Lower-Saxony have clubbed together to form *Norddeutscher Rundfunk*, while *Südwestfunk* in Baden-Baden bestrides Baden and Rhineland-Palatinate. These eight bodies each produce some programmes for local consumption and the rest for the network, rather like ITV, so that an evening's viewing can hop, say, from Cologne to Munich to Hamburg. Each station is responsible to a *Rundfunkrat* (broadcasting council) made up of delegates from the local political parties and from trade unions, the Churches and other such 'social groups'. This *Rat* is a watchdog which can conduct post-mortems on programmes but is not supposed to interfere in their planning or production: it does however appoint the station's senior executives, notably the *Intendant*, who in theory has editorial freedom together with a statutory duty to be objective and to give a fair voice to all main currents of opinion. The nightly news programme the *Tageschau*, is run from the NDR's Hamburg studios under the joint aegis of all the corporations – a little like the relationship between ITN and ITV.

ARD operates a radio network as well as television. Its TV rival, the *Zweites Deutsches Fernsehen* (ZDF), is a television-only station based in Mainz and run as a consortium by all the *Länder*, under much the same kind of public supervision as ARD. Today, ARD and ZDF are broadly similar in their programming and appeal: but ARD also operates a Third Channel which is much more regional in its content and a little more cultural and educational. (The television and radio networks of the former GDR were in 1991 being remodelled and integrated into the western system: see p. 486). The networks derive the major part of their financing from the licence fees (currently some 200 DM a year for a colour set) which they collect directly from viewers and share between them. They are also allowed to show advertising, which yields some 20 per cent of ARD's income and 40 per cent of ZDF's. But this is even more tightly controlled than in Britain. Not only is direct sponsorship of programmes forbidden, but advertisements are limited to twenty minutes a day and can be shown only between 6 and 8 pm, which is the period also reserved for local programmes on ARD. For the rest of the evening, Persil and Pepsi must not disturb the smooth high-mindedness of the German soul at debate with itself on the silver screen.

This broadcasting structure is all very well meant and rational in its neat German way. And it does lead to a number of very good programmes, especially cultural and documentary, while the sponsoring of feature film series can sometimes yield superb results, as we have seen. But it has become cramped by politics in ways that were never intended, and this has a harmful effect on the news and current affairs output. Firstly, in each ARD corporation, since the political parties are represented in the *Rundfunkrat* in proportion to their strength in the local *Landtag*, it follows that the majority party can nearly always secure the appointment of an *Intendant* of its own colour. He may have a supposed duty to be impartial, but he is also a political nominee. And, in order to correct bias of this sort, it is the custom that other senior posts in the station should be shared out between the parties also in proportion to their local strength. Thus, if the head of some department is CDU, his deputy will generally be SPD, and this so-called *Proporz* system has spread down through the echelons so that technical staff and even programme assistants are paired off. Across the years this has become intensified – 'At this rate, we'll soon be getting *Putzfrauen* with party cards,' jested one frustrated producer. Ironically, while the *Proporzsystem* does indeed help to achieve political balance, it also introduces political tensions at a level where they are hardly relevant. It can lead to stalemates harmful to lively broadcasting, for a programme may be shorn of its controversial content in order to balance the rival views of those making it.

In just a few cases, whole programmes are paired off. On ZDF, for example, of the two main current affairs magazines *Kennzeichen D* is permitted to have a left-of-centre producer giving a radical slant, in order to balance *Studio I*. This kind of solution at least makes for hard-hitting opinionated programmes, but not exactly for dispassionate seeking-after-the-truth, since each editor strives to counter the other. When there is no such pairing, then balance must be found within the programme and this can lead to worse problems: to cite an example, one producer prepared a report on the Italian Communist Party, only to be told that he must pare it down in order to give equal screen time to the Italian Right and their view of the PCI. This made the item look absurd. In this climate, journalists and producers who prove too rebellious or outspoken tend to get shunted off the political programmes onto some safe sideline such as science or sport (they cannot be sacked, for once on the staff they have public-service security of tenure). And the ones promoted to executive level are usually the yes-men who will play their roles quietly and cautiously. This makes for unexciting television, especially as the job security makes it hard to shift a mediocre man from a top job. What is more, many of the party nominees under the *Proporz* even take pride in their political function and dual loyalty: 'A key part of my job at this *Funk*,' said one head of department in Hamburg, 'is to ensure that CDU views are fairly represented in its programmes.'

The degree to which local politicians exert pressures on television varies very much from *Land* to *Land*. In Bavaria the CSU is so powerful that it dominates the *Rat* and fills most of the *Proporz* posts, so any pretence of balance is lost. So in the *Bayerische Rundfunk* liberal producers have a hard time of it and controversially radical programmes seldom get accepted. But in the other *Länder* things are easier, especially in Baden-Württemberg where an open-minded CDU regime deliberately leaves the local station alone and tolerates criticism. At the *Norddeutscher Rundfunk* however the *Rat* is so evenly balanced between the SPD and CDU that there is constant tension and in-fighting: I heard of various cases of TV staff executives, alike CDU and SPD, suppressing items disliked by their own party. Here and elsewhere, though the role of the *Rat* was originally conceived as one of protecting the stations from political interference, in practice it does not always work that way – and one main reason is that German politicians in the past few years have woken up to the huge influence that television can wield electorally, as borne out by all the opinion polls, and so they seek to shape it themselves. And the senior TV executives generally feel the need to be pleasing and subservient to the various delegates on the *Rat*, on whose goodwill they depend for their posts – hence the inordinate amount of air and screen time, on news bulletins or similar programmes, that is devoted to interviews with spokesmen of the various groups represented on the *Rat*, not only the parties but organisations representing women, sport, culture, farming, the Press, as well as unions, chambers of commerce and the Churches. If, say, a local farmers' union is holding some routine meeting to be addressed by a *Land* minister, it will ring up the *Tageschau* to ask for coverage and probably will get it, whatever the news value. The BBC or ITN would be far more selective. 'It's all very fair and democratic, but it's just not newsy and it makes for dull viewing,' said one jaded producer, weighed down by years of this kind of work; 'my bosses just daren't say no, so the bulletins are filled nightly with these boring pronouncements by official representatives. In Germany, we do not have a genuine public service television but one of multiple interest groups, each wanting its slice of the cake.' Many Germans have long lamented this situation. But it has proved hard to change, for the harmony of German society depends on this kind of delicate balancing of rival forces, and it was feared that to weaken it might let in the kind of disorder that the Germans fear most. The arrival of commercial channels, which are not subject to the same degree of restriction, has now slightly modified the picture.

Outside the more sensitive areas of topical subject matter, a fair number of good programmes are none the less screened, for there is plenty of talent in German television, and once a programme idea has been accepted a producer is generally left to get ahead with it in some freedom. Excellent documentaries are made quite frequently on historical subjects (including the war and Nazi period) and on foreign countries: alike in its news and general coverage, German television is far less parochial and more international-minded than BBC or ITV. But, when dealing with Germany's own society today, its documentaries tend to be much less bold and probing. Studio discussions and political interviews are formal and wordy in the German manner; interviewers are deferential especially to people of importance, and they will seldom interrupt or question toughly *à la* Robin Day. Far less effort is made than in Britain to go out and canvas off-the-cuff *vox pop* views in the street, for it is thought safer to stick to the 'official' reactions of spokesmen invited to the studio. And a news magazine will seldom include off-beat human-interest items, funny or endearing, of the kind so beloved of British TV, for these it considers trivial: it keeps to issues of 'serious public interest', not only political but economic, technical or environmental. In fact, just as in the theatre or the novel, so in television a gulf exists between the 'serious' and the 'merely entertaining', and the two genres must not be mixed up. So a studio discussion or magazine item on a basically serious topic is not made lively or amusing; most producers would consider this a betrayal of their duty to the public, and they leave such levity to the variety shows and quizzes (which are usually feeble). It is the opposite extreme from Britain, where jokey casualness and matey frivolity creep into every kind of programme − *ad nauseam*, one sometimes feels. A sitcom satire about the Church, or a cartoon send-up of the Chancellor and his ministers (to allude to two recent British parallels) would be inconceivable. And though there are good programmes on art and music, and some good feature films and series, sophisticated modern TV comedy is rare. So different in fact are the British and German styles, and the French too, that it is not easy to see what an EC satellite channel of international appeal − the dream of many dedicated 'Europeans' − could possibly be like.

In any event, the arrival of the satellite age has now spawned some private commercial channels, thus modifying the structure of German television. Already in 1981 the Federal Constitutional Court had ended the public monopoly by ruling that private broadcasting was admissible so long as free opinion was assured. Then in 1984 transmission by cable began in a few selected areas, and major publishing groups such as Springer and Bertelsmann began to create consortia for operating commercial networks; in 1985 one pioneer channel, SAT−1, began broadcasting by cable and satellite to some 250,000 subscribers. But for the next three years wider transmission was blocked by disagreements between the *Länder*. While the CDU and CSU were in favour of private commercial television, the SPD were mainly hostile, for obvious political reasons and for cultural ones too: they feared a lowering of standards, and who could blame them? Finally in 1987 the SPD-led *Länder* agreed to sanction a new system, but on condition that balance should prevail: they did not want the new networks to be the creatures of the big right-wing publishers.

Today four private commercial channels are operating − by cable for subscribers, by satellite for those with dishes, and in some areas also by public land-based transmitters which so far cover only about half the west German territory. Springer and the Italian TV magnate Silvio Berlusconi each have a 15 per cent share in SAT−1; its main rival, RTL-plus, is owned 46 per cent by Radio-Télé Luxembourg and 39 per cent by Bertelsmann; the two other channels are much smaller. Although the public transmitters can reach only half the population, the new channels already have a 30 per cent share of the total audience, as compared with 31.5 per cent for ARD 1, 29 for ZDF, 9 for ARD 3.

But among homes that are cabled the new channels' share is over 50 per cent; and the older networks are afraid that this could become the figure overall, once the public transmitters cover the whole country. Although the new channels all lost money at first, by 1991 SAT–1 had broken even, with RTL-plus set to follow: so their future looks fairly assured, short of a major recession. And the battle for ratings has become intense.

The new channels have been spending lavishly on top-level celebrity performers, and on buying the exclusive rights to some major sporting events: to the fury of the public networks, RTL-plus secured the German rights of the Wimbledon tennis championships. Besides a diet of sport, variety shows and feature films, the new networks also offer provocative quizzes and TV games of a kind that the staid public channels would never show – for example, *Tutti Frutti*, a quiz where the losers must gradually strip naked. RTL-plus even has a late-night soft-porn show for women viewers, full of pretty men. But alongside these frivolities are some serious hard-hitting news magazine programmes, some of them presented by newspapers such as *Spiegel* and the august *Frankfurter Allgemeine Zeitung*. By law there must be 'balance' of views, but these can be within the station's overall output, not within each programme. So the tone can be quite outspoken, and interviewing of politicians is far less tamely deferential than on the old networks. Presenters are emerging of a kind entirely new in Germany: one is a punk lesbian.

It is thus hard to say whether the new private channels have lowered the cultural standard of German television, as many had feared, or on the contrary have provided a welcome new liveliness. A bit of both, it seems. Certainly there is less 'serious' cultural content on the new channels than the old ones. On the other hand, they have brought in a new sense of daring and a breath of fresh air, and are much readier to allow discussion of difficult subjects such as abortion. So far, perhaps surprisingly, they have not made any great impact on the style or content of the public networks, which show little inclination to imitate them, in the search for ratings. Maybe some older programmes, such as ARD's nightly *Tagesthema* news magazine, have been prodded into becoming a little more slick and outspoken; and on the other hand, the output of serious drama has declined, in favour of 'soap' series such as the popular new *Lindenstrasse*, a kind of *Coronation Street* set in Munich that can be quite daring (a man dies of AIDS in it). So German television today is on the move. It is becoming a little less hidebound, more exciting. But, as the private channels grow in strength and the tussle for ratings intensifies, will it simply descend towards an Italian or French-style trivial mediocrity? Or will it take a step towards the British model of fertile competition, not to trivialising, between public and commercial networks? In any event, as many critics ask, is it healthy that Germany's already powerful Press groups, such as the much-contested Springer, should be allowed to extend their empires into another media in this way?

The Press in Germany is strong, flourishing and free of state control. There are no fewer than 356 dailies, and they have stood up well to the rise of television, actually increasing their total sales from 13 million in 1954 to 24.3 million in 1990. But it is a measure of German decentralisation that virtually all these papers are regional rather than national. Apart from the mass-selling *Bild* and its more sedate Springer stablemate *Die Welt*, only the *Frankfurter Allgemeine Zeitung*, the business-men's favourite, has a truly nationwide readership; the left-of-centre *Frankfurter Rundschau* also sells quite well in other cities and so does the *Süddeutsche Zeitung* of Munich, widely regarded as Germany's best daily, but even this great paper relies on Bavaria for two-thirds of its 373,000 sales. People turn first to their local or regional paper. And so, in Cologne, Hanover, Stuttgart and many other towns one finds these immensely solid and respectable dailies, each full of long serious articles and page upon page of local, national and international news: their foreign coverage is often excellent, and many have their own staff correspondent abroad. It is rather as if Britain had nothing but the *Sun* and the *Financial Times* and then lots of superior *Yorkshire Post*s all looking like *Le Monde*. Apart from *Bild* none of these dailies has a sale exceeding 700,000, but many of them are very rich, packed with advertising (the *Süddeutsche* on a Saturday runs to 150 pages); and they coped far earlier and more successfully than Fleet Street with the task of persuading the unions to accept the new technology. Their coverage is full and thorough, but not always very newsy: an obvious official declaration may get greater prominence than some more exciting item, buried down page. Nor do they very often indulge in sharp investiga-tive reporting (the *Süddeutsche* and the *Rundschau* can be honourable exceptions) or in the kind of crusading that might inflame local passions: 'We fought the *Rathaus* over its snow-clearance and forced it to act!' I was told proudly at the *Stuttgarter Zeitung* as an example of its radicalism.

Investigative journalism is left mainly to *Der Spiegel*, the weekly news-magazine edited in Hamburg that is the foremost of its kind in Europe and holds a dominant position in the German Press. *Spiegel* was founded under British auspices just after the war by a brilliant young intellectual, Rudolf Augstein, who is still its publisher today; and it was modelled on *Time*. But its style today is far more racy than *Time*'s: for a foreigner it is not easy reading, for its writers make a sport of using the most unusual words possible in the enormous German vocabulary and they create neologisms too (such as *videot*: video-viewing zombie). More important, *Spiegel* is also a far more relentless ferreter-out of unpleasant truths than its American counterparts. Across the years it has proved bolder than the parliamentary opposition in exposing the faults and abuses of government ('*Spiegel* really runs this country,' someone said) and on occasions ministers have hit back. In the famous '*Spiegel* Affair' of 1962, after the magazine had published a well-researched critique of federal defence policy, Franz Josef Strauss, then Minister of Defence, suddenly lost his head and had the police raid *Spiegel*'s offices and arrest Augstein and some other editors. There was a flaming crisis, as many observers both German and foreign anxiously suggested that such Gestapo-like behaviour by a minister in peacetime did not bode well for the new German democracy, then still on probation. Finally Strauss was pressured into resigning and Augstein had clearly scored a great moral victory. Today *Spiegel* is still prolific with its scoops and exposures: but it always does its homework very carefully and it seldom exaggerates unduly or gets things radically wrong. It is a non-party paper, just as happy to unearth an SPD or trade union scandal (e.g. the Neue Heimat affair, see p. 516) as a CDU one such as the Barschel affair (see p. 517). But it is not a moral crusader, working to create a cleaner society: Augstein and his staff are motivated mainly by professional pride in doing a brilliant job, and by the commercial drive to keep up their sales of almost one million copies.

Of the other serious weeklies, by far the most important is *Die Zeit* (circulation, 450,000), a striking contrast to *Spiegel*. This conscience of the German liberal intelligentsia has no news columns but a large number of thoughtful and wordy articles on political, cultural and other topics: it is a little like a much fuller and better *Spectator* or *New Statesman*, plus the *Observer* shorn of its news pages, and it does something to make up for the virtual absence in Germany of serious Sunday papers. The infamous *Stern* magazine used to make efforts to rival *Spiegel* at in-depth reporting: but in 1983 it made a big fool of itself when, like the *Sunday Times*, it published the 'Hitler diaries' believing them to be genuine, and since then it has retreated down-market into sex-and-drug cover-stories and other sensations, though still with a semblance of seriousness. If its circulation has dropped since 1983 from 1.6 to 1.4 million, this could be due not only to the Hitler fraud fiasco but to growing competition from even more trivial and gossipy rivals in the weekly illustrated Press, such as *Quick* and *Bunte*. But there are some good respectable women's periodicals too, such as *Brigitte*, a little bit like *Elle*. All in all, the weekly magazine market is far stronger in Germany than elsewhere in Europe or America. This could be in part a reflection of German affluence: but probably the main reason is that German television is so tame, whereas these papers are able to be far more lively and uninhibited.

With one or two glaring exceptions (see below), the German Press today is fair and responsible, and it forms a valued component of the new German democracy; the Constitution specifically protects it against censorship. The principal dailies constitute a reasonable political balance. On the Right, the *Frankfurter Allgemeine* is conservative but intelligently so and it fairly reflects the attitudes of the business world; Springer's *Die Welt* is far more rabid, but has been losing influence and now sells less than 200,000. These papers are balanced on the left-of-centre by the very honest and liberal *Süddeutsche Zeitung* and the somewhat more radical and *Guardian*-like *Frankfurter Rundschau* which is sympathetic to the ideas of the Greens. The majority of the better regional dailies such as the *Kölner Stadt-Anzeiger* and the *Stuttgarter Zeitung* are reasonably open-minded and middle-of-the-road: they may not be very zealous at sniffing out injustices themselves, but once *Der Spiegel* or someone else has done so, then they will decently bring pressure to bear until the guilty politician resigns or makes amends. There may even be some truth – though I wonder how much? – in the point made to me by Christoph Bertram, political editor of *Die Zeit*, that Germany's system of government is so open that the need for investigative journalism is less great than in some countries. There are however some dangers in the present Press situation, and one is the growth of local monopolies due to mergers or ententes made for economic reasons. Many local papers have either come under the control of larger ones or they have grouped and pooled their resources, and this destroys competition and variety: Stuttgart's two dailies, for instance, are jointly owned and both editorially very bland, so this *de facto* monopoly means there is no local outlet for radical journalism.

A far worse threat – or so a great many Germans believe – comes from the excessive power wielded nationwide by one stridently right-wing megagroup: Springer. The late Axel Springer himself was the most spectacular of German post-war tycoons, a very rich man who married five times, owned five houses, collected Kokoschkas, and was propelled by an almost mystical Protestant faith and an equally fervent anti-Communism. Like Augstein, he was first given his chance just after the war by the British, who let him start a radio programme guide, *Hör Zu*, and then a Hamburg evening paper. After launching his tabloid *Bild Zeitung* in 1952 he steadily built up a newspaper, periodical and publishing empire that today is the largest in Europe: Springer dailies are read at home by one German in three, and they account for 20 per cent of all newspaper sales.

To be fair, there were some quite attractive things about Springer. He was a generous employer, strong on welfare, and so he was grudgingly liked by the unions. He repaid his debt to the British by remaining warmly anglophile. And he made reconciliations and reparations towards Israel into a personal crusade, pouring money from his own fortune into Jewish causes and obliging his papers to take Israel's side against the Arabs. But his cold-warrior stance, acceptable in the aftermath of the Berlin airlift and the Berlin Wall, made him look increasingly isolated as *détente* developed. In 1959, as a calculated act of defiance, he built his new Springer group headquarters right beside the Wall in Kreuzberg, a nineteen-storey block with a neon sign beaming out 'Berlin bleibt frei' from its roof. He fought hard against *Ostpolitik*, and this led him into a permanent vendetta against Brandt, instructing *Bild* to remind its readers that their Chancellor was born illegitimate and had returned to post-war Germany in Allied uniform. In the 1968 period he campaigned for harsh law-and-order measures against student rioters and terrorists: when *Bild* urged its readers to take the law into their own hands and one of them shot Rudi Dutschke, it was as if Springer had himself pulled the trigger. From then on, he was the number one enemy of the German student Left. He died in 1985, but the group has since continued much as before, in other hands. Springer claimed that his papers, *Bild* especially, spoke for the true feelings of the mass of ordinary Germans and he challenged the right of intellectuals to behave as the nation's conscience. This populism might have been creditable were it not that *Bild* plays upon the darker side of

German popular prejudice – racism, intolerance of non-conformity, and the rest.

*Bild Zeitung* is a German phenomenon. Published in several cities simultaneously, it is Europe's biggest-selling tabloid (4.3 million circulation), and in Germany it has no rival save for a few small local rags, none of them so strident. As there are no big papers of the *Daily Mail* type to fill the middle ground, it polarises the German Press. Its garish red-black-and-white front page has giant headlines screaming of rape, torture, incest or the intimate vices of the great and famous – and curiously enough it is actually bought and read by a good many such VIPs, and others. They do so not out of voyeurism or a desire for titillation but because, stranger still, *Bild* in its laconic way does include some sharp political reporting. With its massive staff and resources it is able frequently to secure scoops – it was the first, for example, to announce the cancellation of Honecker's visit to Bonn in 1984 – and in its way it is very well informed. So in trains and smart restaurants you will see senior executives quietly reading their *Bild*, though they may not bring it home to their families. The headlines such as 'Sweetheart Beheaded, Cooked and Tinned in thirty-nine Pieces' (front-page lead, December 9, 1985) they glance at with a wry smirk.

*Bild* is not necessarily more vulgar or sensational than the Murdoch gutter-Press. But it is more ruthless at grabbing or inventing its stories, and at intruding into private grief. When two brothers committed suicide, *Bild* carried a big photograph of the young men swinging on ropes from a tree, next to one of the anguished mother learning the news: photo-reporters were somehow able to follow the police on their way to tell her of the tragedy, and they snapped her at that very moment. On another famous occasion, under a headline 'German Pupil Drank Blood of Girl', *Bild* told how a former butcher's apprentice had brought girls to his flat, taken their blood and drunk it mixed with tea or sherry. The boy was then arrested, and *Bild* ransacked his flat, taking photos and private papers. But at his trial he was fully acquitted: it was found that he had carried out chemical experiments, no more. The *Bild* reporters pleaded guilty of fabrication and were sentenced to eight months' prison, plus a 15,000 DM fine which the paper cheerfully paid. This public verdict at least spotlighted *Bild*'s use of criminal methods. But there have been many other cases that have not come to trial, where a probably innocent victim has had his or her reputation destroyed. *Bild* will sometimes break into people's flats; and if it cannot get the story it wants, then it will invent, for its sales depend on a steady stream of these horror-stories.

That German society tolerates this as much as it does seems to me worrying. Of course there have been protests. After *Bild* had verbally tormented the 'Red terrorist' Heinrich Böll, he retorted with his splendid *The Lost Honour of Katharina Blum* (see above). And in 1977 the famous investigative journalist Günter Wallraff had the clever idea of joining *Bild*'s reporting staff for a few months, under a pseudonym, with the aim of writing an exposé of it. He succeeded, and his book *Der Aufmacher* caused a sensation. As in his more recent book about Turkish workers (see p. 281), he may perhaps have done his own share of inventing: but much of what he wrote rang true. Next Wallraff founded an anti-*Bild* association, to rally and support its former victims, and soon he had gathered 4,500 names as well as lawyers prepared to help in the fight. This seemed to have some effect for *Bild* did then tone down its excesses a little, and a senior Springer executive admitted to me that in the past there had been 'irresponsible reporting'. The paper is today a little milder. But the problem is that most of *Bild*'s victims are very ordinary people who do not have the initiative or funds for a lawsuit, while the rich Springer group can readily lavish money on brilliant defence lawyers.

Clearly *Bild* hides too easily behind the post-war German insistence on absolute freedom of the Press; and clearly there is a case for tightening the German libel laws, lax as in other Continental countries. But probably more is needed. In 1980 a number of leading radical intellectuals – including Böll, Grass, Habermas, Schlöndorff and Jens – signed a public declaration that they would never write for the Springer group. But when I asked senior liberal journalists on *Die Zeit* and the *Frankfurter Rundschau* how they felt about *Bild*, I was startled to find them shrugging it off – 'No one takes it seriously, and it doesn't really do much harm,' said one of them; 'besides, in order to remain free we have to accept a certain misuse of freedom.' He was alluding to the fact that the German newspaper world is still so haunted by the Nazis' murder of Press freedom that it is utterly determined that nothing, repeat nothing, should be done to put limits on its present liberty. This is understandable. But clever German lawyers ought surely to be able to devise some ways of curbing *Bild*'s excesses without harming basic freedoms. That there has not been more effective public action against *Bild* seems to me worryingly symptomatic of the Germans' relative lack of concern for the weaker members of their society, and of the failure of most individuals to take the initiative in tackling public abuses or standing up to established power. *Bild*'s sheer cultural bad taste is of little consequence: its affront to human rights, in this of all Western democracies, seems to me more serious. So in the final chapter, we shall look at the biggest question of all: how deep and secure is German democracy? Could Nazism ever happen again? But first the 'Other Germany'.

# 7

## THE OLD GDR; DAILY LIFE UNDER GERMAN-STYLE COMMUNISM

When my wife and I were researching the previous edition of this book, in 1985–6, we were allowed to spend only a short time in the German Democratic Republic, and of course we were far less free than in the West to travel and to meet people. I had applied to the GDR Embassy in London, where I was told that they did not like the idea of a book about both German States within one cover, as this was contrary to their basic policy. Could I not write two separate books? I explained that in publishing terms this was impossible. Finally, thanks to a bit of subterfuge, by pretending that we were really going there to research newspaper articles, Katinka and I did win permission to visit the GDR, under supervision. We were allotted a pleasant and helpful young guide, who showed us around and was present at interviews. But we also had time free to meet a good many private contacts, unescorted, and they spoke frankly; we also talked to scores of people in the West who had recently left the GDR and knew it well. Thus we were able to build up what I think was a fairly accurate and balanced picture, for a chapter of some seventy pages.

I have now shortened that chapter a little and put it into the past tense, for the fifty pages that follow. Apart from this, I have not altered it with hindsight, as I might have done – save for a short passage at the end about the GDR's economy, which before 1989 had seemed stronger than it really was to nearly all Western observers. The chapter still has some historical validity, as an account of what life was like in the mid-1980s for the 17 million inhabitants of the *Deutsche Demokratische Republik* (DDR). Nearly four million had emigrated to the West since the war. Of those who stayed, the great majority had come to terms with their destiny; they found life under Socialism grey and frustrating, but perfectly liveable and even with some advantages. So the regime had a degree of passive public acceptance — but not nearly enough to save it, when the moment of truth came in 1989.

A brief historical survey of the GDR could well start with the fact that initially neither Stalin nor the Western Allies intended the division of the country to be formalised: but gradually the logic of the cold war made this inevitable. Under Russian tutelage, the German Communist leaders began to take some control in the eastern zone from 1945 onwards. Many of them had been in Nazi concentration camps, or they had spent years in exile in Moscow — like Walter Ulbricht, who from 1945 was the Party's effective leader. With Russian backing, these men swiftly set about punishing the Nazis and their 'bourgeois' accomplices. Full-scale communisation was to take place more gradually, and initially some multi-party pluralism was permitted. But as early as April 1946 the Communists forced the Socialists to merge with them into the Communist-dominated Socialist Unity Party (SED) that was to remain the country's ruling force until 1989. When the Federal Republic was set up in Bonn in 1949, the Russians retorted by taking steps to balance it with a new state of their own: and so, after elections with a single list of candidates, the birth of the Deutsche Demokratische Republik was proclaimed on October 7, 1949. Next the SED moved to consolidate its power. It set up a National Front to supervise society at local level, and it purged from public positions thousands of people suspected of being pro-Western; in 1951 Soviet-style collective agreements were introduced into factories, and a year later the collectivisation of agriculture was intensified. All this provoked a growing exodus to the West of middle-class people, farmers and others: at this time the border was still open and departure was easy.

After the first seven or eight years, even those who might expect to benefit from the regime, such as factory workers, were becoming disgruntled. The weight of Soviet reparations, and the disruptions caused by massive nationalisation, were putting severe strains on an economy still struggling to recover from the war; and the Government's reaction was to ask workers to accept even higher work loads, despite the fact that living standards were still pitifully low. Finally on June 17, 1953, the building workers in East Berlin moved spontaneously into revolt: they stopped work and called for a general strike, and quickly their movement spread to other big towns. When some of the demonstrators began to make political demands, for free elections and the restoration of unions, Ulbricht called for Russian help and the tanks of the Red Army garrisons were sent into action. The revolt then quickly subsided, but not before twenty-one people had been killed. The regime alleged that some of the strike instigators were rabid anti-Communists such as former pro-Nazi teachers who had been drafted into manual labour after 1945. There may have been some truth in this. But the historic 'June 17 Revolt' was largely a movement of popular grievance. And its aftermath of punishment and reprisals led to widespread disillusion among many who had hitherto been sympathetic to the SED regime.

A period of modest liberalisation followed the death of Stalin, but was killed by events in Hungary in 1956. After this, gloom again descended on those who hoped for a less rigid kind of socialism, and the exodus to the West increased. It averaged 230,000 a year in 1949–60, rising to 30,000 a month in the first part of 1961. Half of all those who left were under 25, while the older ones included thousands of engineers, doctors and other specialists vital to the GDR. The country was bleeding to death; and it was this brain-drain above all that in August 1961 led Ulbricht, with Moscow's backing, to build the Wall and so block the easy escape route to the West. It was an ignominious confession of failure by the GDR to prove its worth, as Ulbricht is said to have admitted in private. But, he said, he had no alternative. And the Wall did produce the desired result of stopping the exodus; it even gave the GDR some new lease of life. East Germans at first reacted with despair and fury at being trapped: but gradually this mood gave way to one of sullen acquiescence, an awareness that they had better make the best of it. And Ulbricht was able to build on this, as he tried to inculcate some sense of national pride into the people of this artificial little state.

But relations with the Federal Republic remained remote and icy, because of the Wall and other East–West tensions. This was the period of the 'Hallstein doctrine', initiated in the late 1950s by Walter Hallstein, then a junior minister in Bonn – a deliberate West German policy of seeking to boycott and undermine a GDR regime seen as illegitimate and not wanted by its own people. Bonn threatened to cut off aid and sever diplomatic ties with any state recognising East Germany; it also waged direct economic campaigns against the GDR and in some cases used sabotage. The policy had some effect. But it was smartly dropped when in 1969 Willy Brandt and the SDP came to power and began to develop their *Ostpolitik*. Brandt broke new ground in 1970 by travelling to Erfurt for a meeting with Willi Stoph, the GDR Prime Minister. A year later, Ulbricht was eased out of power by Moscow, for he was judged too rigid and hostile towards a détente that the Russians too now wanted. He was replaced as First Secretary by Erich Honecker, a younger, more flexible and open-minded figure, less tainted by the Stalinist era. He and Brandt established relations of a sort between the two Germanies, leading to the exchange of permanent missions and a big increase in trade and in visits to the GDR by West Germans. They also laid the basis for new guarantees for West Berlin (see p. 35). During the 1970s Honecker also eased the regime's domestic severity a little. The viewing of West German television was sanctioned; a deal with the Protestant Church gave it a degree of independence. By the standards of East European leadership, Honecker remained a tolerably successful and respected father figure, right up until the later 1980s. But behind the scenes the police state remained rigidly intact.

One much-noted achievement of the GDR in those years was its economic progress. This occurred within the protected East European market, and once it was fully exposed to the rich capitalist West in 1990, its fragility became all too clear. But until then the GDR remained economically and industrially much the strongest country in the Soviet bloc, with living standards an estimated 50 per cent higher than in Russia; by 1970 it had become the world's eleventh largest industrial power. This could be attributed above all to the innate German qualities of thoroughness, technical flair and so on, and to an old industrial tradition, almost as strong in Saxony as in the Ruhr. Even so, the achievement was remarkable when set in the context of the enormous handicaps that the GDR had to face at the outset, the heaviest being Soviet reparations. In contrast to the modest amount of dismantling carried out by the Allies in the West, and soon outweighed by Marshall Aid, the Soviet Union after 1945 set about exacting revenge on a vast scale. Its dismantling reduced East Germany's industrial capacity by some 40 per cent, equal to twice the damage done by the war. The Russians transplanted whole factories to their own country, or they expropriated East German output without compensation, and this pillage amounted to an average of 25 per cent of GNP until 1953. Then the Soviet Union changed its policy. Within the context of Comecon, the eastern bloc's new economic planning system, it decided to oblige each member state to specialise; and the GDR was allotted the role of supplying precision instruments, machine tools and other sophisticated goods, also some chemical products. And this remained the position until 1989. There were no more reparations, but the GDR was still penalised, for the Soviet Union, its main trading partner, did not always give a fair deal. The GDR depended on Russia for 80 per cent of its oil and gas supplies, which it had to take at inflated prices; in return the USSR paid poorly for GDR exports.

The GDR faced other economic handicaps too. It inherited a part of Germany that had few mineral resources, apart from lignite and potash. And East Germans had foisted on them the Soviet system of state centralised planning and bureaucratic management; and although they coped with this more rationally than, say, the Poles, or the Russians themselves, it did not always lead to efficiency, to say the least. In the early post-war years some 10,000 businesses were nationalised. Some thousands of small private concerns were still allowed (see p. 390), mostly in the service and crafts sector, but they remained marginal to the economy, The main factories were regrouped into some 300 combines (*Kombinate*), each of which had its production levels, its prices and its distribution outlets fixed for it in advance by various State planning bodies. This kind of coordination and target-setting can sometimes bring advantages, for example in France: but in the GDR the absence of a free market led to rigidities, bottlenecks and shortages. In 1963 the much-heralded 'New Economic System' gave the combines a shade more autonomy and put more stress on managerial skills. This brought some results and was a factor behind the economic progress of the mid-1960s. But then came a shift back to centralisation, partly in reaction against the 'dangerous' liberal ideas of the Prague Spring. And so life continued, following a cyclical pattern common in the Soviet bloc. One East Berlin engineer expressed to me his frustrations: 'If only we could manage things our own way, and if so many of our ablest people had not fled to the West, how brilliantly we could do!' The GDR's annual growth rate averaged 5 per cent in the period 1963–73. But after this it failed disastrously to keep up with the West's advance in modern high technology.

Collectivised agriculture, like industry, was much more efficient than in most other Soviet bloc countries. Just after the war all holdings of more than 250 acres were confiscated without compensation from the wealthy land-owning *Junker* class, and most of this land was redistributed to farm workers, peasants and refugees. Massive collectivisation followed later. At first it was disastrous, for many farmers were hostile and the Party bureaucrats put in to run the new cooperatives had little idea of farming realities. Many of the most competent farmers left for the West. Gradually, however, things settled down. Some 95 per cent of the land was farmed by cooperatives, on a large industrial scale, well mechanised. Productivity was lower than on larger farms in the West: but it compared well with the Federal Republic's many small family farms. According to Bonn sources, wheat yields per acre were only about 15 per cent lower than in West Germany. Above all, the Party collectivisers sensibly allowed members of cooperatives to retain private ownership of enough livestock and farmland (1.2 acres) for their own needs, and farmers thus came grudgingly to accept the system. It was a good example of how the regime tried to balance the requirements of Socialism and of individual privacy – a theme to be explored next.

## *Private values amid public collectivism*

'This society may be far from perfect: but at least we have eliminated real poverty, and that's more than you have done in the West,' said an idealistic old-style Communist whom I met in Berlin in 1985. The wide-ranging welfare system, the full employment and job security, the reasonable standard of living for all thanks to a policy of very cheap subsidised basic goods – it could be argued that the regime should be given some credit for these social achievements, even if in other ways it supervised and restricted its citizens so unpleasantly, especially those who failed to toe the line.

Prices for many of the basic necessities of life, pegged very low, had in many cases not risen since the 1960s. Rents accounted for only 4 to 5 per cent of a family's income; a tram or S-Bahn ticket in Berlin cost 20 Pfennigs for a journey of any length, the same as in the 1940s; theatres, concerts and restaurants too were amazingly cheap. Much basic food, such as bread, milk and *Wurst*, was also heavily subsidised, but only the lower-quality *Wurst*: if you wanted a good one, you had to pay maybe four times the price and probably go to a special quality shop. The artificial gulf between the 'luxury' and 'basic' ranges was huge: at a bar we paid 4.80 Marks for a glass of *Sekt* and 40 Pfg for some horrid GDR cola, whereas in the West the difference might have been only two to one. Some 40 per cent of the State budget went on these subsidies, which covered some 80 per cent of consumer goods and utilities. Certainly this helped to banish poverty, for anyone on a basic income could live tolerably. But the system, introduced for ideological and social reasons, caused economic distortions; and it prevented money from being spent on the modernisation of industry and infrastructure.

The regime also sought to narrow the gulf in incomes and life-styles. Of course senior Party officials and their families enjoyed many perks and privileges (and some were seriously corrupt, as emerged later, see p. 437). But among lesser mortals, wage differentials were modest. The average worker might earn 800 to 1,000 Marks[1] a month, but an engineer or teacher no more than 1,100 to 1,600, while even a factory manager or senior doctor might not get beyond 2,000 or so. Apart from the top Party figures, the most affluent people in society were the star musicians, actors and athletes; also some independent craftsmen, artisans and tradesmen in the tolerated private sector. But their prosperity was still modest by Western standards.

Under the Constitution every citizen had the duty as well as the right to work (a basic tenet of Marxism). The full employment was a matter of official pride, mixed with scorn for the West, and it was achieved by careful control. Numbers at university and technical colleges were fixed according to the needs of the economy and society, so that a student on entry was more or less assured of a job later; school leavers were treated similarly. In the 1950s there was much forced direction of labour: but by the 1980s it was generally possible to choose one type of job, though it was harder to change later. Firms each had their quota of staff fixed by the national plans, and they could not easily make dismissals: in practice, in most firms and other bodies, there was overmanning by about 40 per cent compared with the West, often more, and many people were obliged to work below their qualifications. So unemployment was disguised through under-employment and mis-employment.

Somewhat paradoxically, it was also official policy to urge mothers with young families to take jobs, in the interests of boosting the economy. And the State helped them by providing plenty of crèches and kindergartens. Some 85 per cent of women of working age were said to have a job outside the home, and most young couples welcomed this second income. Although in politics women in senior posts were as rare as in West Germany, they accounted for well over half of the nation's teachers. Yet the regime also provided strong incentives for young people to marry and breed several children. Newly-weds under

1. At the official rate, a GDR Mark equalled exactly 1 DM, but on the black market one DM could fetch up to four GDR Marks.

26 could obtain an interest-free 5,000-Mark loan for furnishing their homes, and its repayment was progressively waived as children were born. Family allowances became very generous for couples with three children or more; a working mother could get six months' maternity leave on full pay for a first child, then a year's paid leave at home for each subsequent one; and large families had top priority on the long waiting lists for flats.

This dual policy, of sending women to work while also encouraging them to breed, did have some success. The birth-rate was falling until 1973, but then it began rising sooner than West Germany's, and for some years the population was stabilised, despite emigration. This was remarkable seeing that since 1972 both abortion and the pill had been freely available to all women over 16. But a great deal was expected of GDR women and they felt the strain: it was not so easy to combine a full-time job and running a family in a cramped flat, as shopping required endless queuing. All this, and the fact that most couples married very young, helped to explain a high divorce rate that ended two marriages in three – twice the West German figure.

The health services and hospitals, though mostly short of modern equipment, were usually efficient and considerate. Yet the GDR's prized welfare state did contain some notable inadequacies. Elderly people were well cared for in a human sense, and young people were encouraged to come and look after the old at 'solidarity centres'. But pensions remained low, barely half an average worker's income (was it that old people were not so useful for the nation's future?). Housing too was mostly of poor quality. In the 1950s the GDR was so busy trying to strengthen its industrial base that it neglected to create new homes to make good war damage, and its building rate *per capita* was only one-fifth of West Germany's. Later the programme was speeded up, but more in terms of quality than quantity, and by 1986 only 36 per cent of homes had central heating, and only 68 per cent had bath or shower. Rents were low, yes: but as a result the housing authorities lacked the money for repairs. Hence the crumbling façades that still today strike any Western visitor – plus a less visible but worse hazard, leaking roofs. Yet if you went to the city housing office to report a leak, you would be met with a helpless shrug or at best be lent a bucket. So tenants would try to do the repairs themselves: but it was hard to obtain tiles as most of the GDR's output was exported. Such were the hazards of life.

The long neglect of house-repairing was due also to shortages of paint and other materials, and to an official view that neatness and elegance were decadent bourgeois qualities. Public buildings were as much affected as housing. But the policy may have been counter-productive, psychologically. One East Berlin writer suggested to me in 1985: 'People have grown so used to the drabness that they hardly notice it. But I'm sure it's one reason why they are not more cheerful. If only there were a bit more fresh paint in the GDR, more fun and fantasy too, probably fewer people would want to emigrate.' Housing was also in very short supply: newly-weds had to wait two years on average to get a flat of their own, while a childless couple might have to make do with one room. The shortage could often make it hard to accept a better job in another town − unless you could find someone wanting to swap. The regime did begin encouraging people to build their own little bungalows (in fact about a quarter of homes were privately owned), but this was hardly a real solution.

Education, by contrast, was never stinted to the same degree, for the regime saw it as a crucial investment: there were more teachers per head than in West Germany, and a larger share of GNP was spent on schooling. The State assumed a kind of para-parental role, seeking to win the hearts and minds of its young citizens from their earliest years, and it permitted no private schools. First, children in their crèches and kindergartens were taught to get used to collective living, and were primed in the elements of Socialism and 'the anti-fascist struggle'. Then from 6 to 16 all attended the same kind of ten-year comprehensive 'polytechnic schools', where history and literature were taught the Marxist-Leninist way; everyone learned Russian, and a few later learned English or French too. But the main emphasis was on mathematics and science. The vocational element was very strong, noticeable in the most distinctive feature of the GDR school system which was its special link with adult work. Each school was 'adopted' by a nearby factory or farm cooperative, and here from the age of 13 all classes went to spend a full day once a fortnight, where they did some practical work and received instruction. The aim of the scheme was to 'bring the classroom closer to real life' and to make for an easier transition later from school to working life; also, to reduce some of the bias against manual labour that still existed even under Socialism. This admirable system had its critics, but it worked quite well: the philosophy was that all young people, however intellectual, should acquire some basic technical skill. Thus I met a young historian who had been trained to repair tractors. And one top Communist, Gregor Gysi, Party chairman after 1989, had learned to milk cows, and was proud of it. Many of those leaving school at 15 or 16 went into an apprenticeship system not so different from West Germany's.

Another arguably positive aspect of the GDR system was its provision of scope for hobbies, crafts, sport, debating and other extra-class activities: in this respect it was closer to the British than the West German model, where the school day tends to end at 1 p.m. In the GDR, where children were seldom left to their own devices, they stayed on at school during the afternoon for these supervised pursuits, which were ideologically flavoured. Many took place within the frame-work of the Pioneer organisation, which was the junior branch of the ubiquitous *Freie Deutsche Jugend,* the Party's youth movement. Member-ship of the Pioneers was voluntary, but to opt out was not easy, and in practice some 90 per cent of children belonged. At 14 they joined the FDJ itself, and prepared for the *Jugendweihe* ('youth consecration'), an initiation ceremony devised to replace Christian confirmation: here they had to affirm their Socialist faith in public. The *Jugendweihe* likewise was not compulsory, but few youngsters felt bold enough to refuse it. The smart red-and-navy-blue uniforms of the FDJ were much in evidence at public rallies; the FDJ also had branches in schools and universities which organised discos, carnivals and regular political discussions. In summer Pioneers and FDJ-ists went to holiday camps where they lustily sang Socialist songs. It was rather like Scouts and Guides but more political. No other youth movements were allowed.

I was taken to visit one model comprehensive in Erfurt where the atmosphere seemed humane and caring, not too regimented. There were anti-NATO and anti-Reagan posters on the walls, but also one of Luther. Some senior pupils were presented to me for interview. One very bright 15-year-old daughter of a policeman declared proudly that her aim was 'to identify with the State and serve its interests' (I wonder what she is doing today). Others denounced the 'class struggle' in the West and told me of the leisure time they spent caring for the sick and elderly. Clearly the FDJ and Pioneers did provide some outlet for the social idealism of many young people; or, as one Western observer suggested to me, 'The Party survives in power not only through Soviet guns but because it still gets enough genuine support from a young idealistic minority in each new emerging generation.'

Competition for university was fierce, for places were few. Students were selected not just on merit, but on such things as their parents' political record and whether they had been zealous in the FDJ at school. In the 1950s children of workers and peasants were given a high priority: later this waned, but some bias remained against bourgeois families and practising Catholics or known non-Communists. University courses were rather utilitarian, geared to the market's needs. From his first day, a student knew what kind of job he would get at the end. The absence of graduate unemployment eased youthful anxiety, but it made life a bit boring; and all the students that I met, even in Berlin's famous Humboldt University, seemed innocently docile, more like schoolkids than adults. Students were invited to help their teachers administratively, not in pedagogic matters but by help in selecting their fellow-students for bonuses, job vacancies, etc. In other words, under their teachers' tight supervision, these young people were set to watch and assess each other, in a way that hardly encouraged creative non-conformity.

Sport, that crucial GDR speciality, was exploited as a focus for national idealism, and was compulsory even at university level. Sometimes, from the age of 7 or 8 children showing great athletic promise were transferred to one of twenty special sport schools, to be rigorously trained as future champions. It was Ulbricht who initiated the policy of using sport as an instrument for winning international prestige and for boosting domestic patriotic morale. The State spent an estimated 2 per cent of GNP on sport, and in a sense this paid off: the GDR was better known abroad for its sporting victories than for anything else. It first established its supremacy at the 1976 Montreal Olympics, where it won more gold medals than any country except the Soviet Union; it did the same again at Seoul in 1988, winning thirty-seven gold medals, one more than the United States. The GDR also did very well at the Winter Olympics – remarkable for a country with few good ski-slopes. As for swimming, in the 1983 European championships its women competitors won every single title. The nation's star athletes received many privileges, including large apartments, cars without the usual long wait, and free seaside holidays in Cuba. But ordinary recreational facilities for a wider public won a lower priority, and many local sports centres were badly run-down. However, the huge biennial Spartakiad youth games and sports festival in Leipzig drew 70,000 participants; and the regime did partly succeed in imbuing its people with an enthusiasm for sport and a veneration for its top athletes.

Throughout their lives, the regime strove to inculcate into its citizens a sense of identification with the Socialist State. For some Party officials, mostly the older ones, the motives were idealistic: to develop a warm and brotherly community where all could feel secure and wanted. Others were more concerned with channelling energies so that the Party could retain its grip on power. Witness the way that factories and other work-places were given a highly assertive role in people's lives, extending to welfare services, social activity and politics. The SED and its affiliate bodies were omnipresent in the work-places, where they held propagandist rallies among the staff. And a doctor who had just escaped to the West told me: 'If you are in a position of responsibility, it is not easy to avoid having to make public declarations, praising the gallant struggle of the workers, extolling Party resolutions or other such Marxist crap. In my hospital, some people did this sincerely and most others followed suit out of opportunism. I couldn't bear the shamming any longer.' All citizens had to belong to a 'collective of socialist labour' attached to their work-place or their village. If you were by nature a loner, or a sceptic, you were regarded as an odd fish, and before long the Stasi might be making enquiries.

Worker delegates in factories sat on 'production councils' whose job was to advise management. But it was the plant's director and its Party secretary, and the bureaucrats above them, who took all the decisions: so this GDR version of *Mitbestimmung* had even less influence than the West German kind. Workers tended to feel apathetic about the factory and alienated from the remote men of power at the top. The trade unions were run by the Party, so that union officials and factory managers were both on the same side, and union members' influence was minimal. Strikes were forbidden. On the other hand, the social and welfare roles of the work-places were popular: workers expected their factories to find them a flat, run holiday camps for them and provide crèches. And it was the unions that ran a firm's holiday centres and hospitals and spent money on sport and leisure. A union thus was management's welfare agency, not its bargaining adversary.

Another curious example of the all-embracing role of the work-place concerned the handling of minor delinquency and petty offences. These were not referred to outside courts but were dealt with inside the factory by 'conflict commissions' made up of elected employees: so his work collective was supposed to be the best able to provide an offender with discipline, help and re-education. To quote an instance I was given, a lorry-driver might be hauled up before his colleagues for stealing vodka from the canteen. If found guilty, the offender had to apologise in public, repair the damage done and maybe pay a fine. More serious cases, possibly involving a prison sentence, were given to a regular court. These conflict commissions worked quite well in their way. They were just one aspect of the earnest school-like moralistic atmosphere that pervaded so much of public life in the GDR, alike in factories and offices, State shops and colleges, even TV studios. All were run in much the same way. Only amid the privacy of family and close friends could an individual easily escape the nanny-like supervision of the State.

Popular attitudes to the regime were of course impossible to quantify: but it was usually estimated that about 15 to 20 per cent of people were sincere supporters (that is, about the same number as the 2 million or so members of the SED). They included, first, a sizeable section of the older working class, the ones who had perhaps benefited most from socialism. Next came the battalions of small Party officials and local bureaucrats, some of them sincere, more of them opportunists enjoying their perks and petty power — 'Because I'm in the Party', said one civic employee with ingenuous candour, 'I was able to obtain some scarce building materials for making myself this nice little house. This is a lovely society!' Third came the idealists, some of them very young, like my policeman's daughter, but more of them found among the old guard, those who had fought for their faith during the hard Nazi years and then helped create the regime — like one elderly Jewish lady I know, who reflected sadly that too many of her friends and neighbours had lost much of the original caring community spirit: 'They've grown selfish and consumerist, they think it a disaster if they can't get their deep-freeze quickly.'

So much for the supporters. Of the other 80 per cent or so, just a few were true dissidents who tried to find ways of emigrating (many did so). The rest, the majority, simply acquiesced and tried as best they could to enjoy their private lives.

'The initials "DDR" stand for *"Der doofe Rest"'* (the dopey dregs), ran a familiar joke. Certainly it was the more bright and resourceful ones who tended to leave for the West, in the days when they could, and the less ambitious who stayed, at least among professional people and technicians. So, much more than Poland or even Hungary, the GDR lost much of its enterprising elites. This was damaging to the regime, but maybe it also made it easier to control society. Those left behind after the building of the Wall, at first despondent, later developed a certain resignation and came to terms with a situation they could not change. They even found that life became more tolerable as living standards rose, consumer goods became more plentiful, and visits to the West a little easier. It could even be said that Honecker reached a tacit agreement with his people, whereby he allowed them some privacy and a decent living, in return for them not rocking the boat too much. 'The regime treats people just like domestic pets – protected, but not free', was one comment. It just about worked – until Gorbachev set eastern Europe in ferment and even the dopey dregs wanted to emulate the Poles.

Many people came to identify with the GDR and see it as their home, especially those who had never known the days before the Wall. They resented being patronised by wealthy visitors from the West who told them how unfortunate they were. They were proud of their country's sporting successes, of its apparent economic progress in face of such odds, and of some cultural achievements. Some of them, without necessarily liking the regime, saw the GDR as a society less violent, permissive and over-competitive than the West, a better preserver of some old German values.

These values were essentially private ones. But if they were being preserved, it was less by virtue of the regime than in defence against it – a point I cannot stress too strongly. To compensate for the irksome official pressures, the boring collectivism and the generally grey surface of life, most citizens retreated into private pleasures and the gentleness and trust of their circle of family and close friends. Almost everyone who knew both Germanies well would stress that wherever this trust existed, human relations tended to be closer, warmer and more genuinely caring in the GDR than in the Federal Republic, where families were more geographically dispersed and many people were to a degree tainted by the consumerist, careerist rat-race. In the GDR, because officialdom was not to be trusted and you never knew which neighbours might be Stasi informers, individuals depended on each other emotionally much more; because daily life with its queues and shortages was not easy, so people relied much more on close friends and relatives for practical help; and because the pace of life was less hectic than in the West, so they had more time for each other and were readier to look after dependants. One emigrant I met in Hamburg said, 'My elderly widowed mother would be allowed to come and live with me here, but I've dissuaded her. I work all day, and she would never adapt to the solitude.' Boredom and frustration were common in the GDR, but loneliness much less so. However, if a mildly oppressive State served for the wrong reasons to make people nicer, that hardly helped to justify the regime. The supreme irony was that the warm human community advocated by Socialism was then created *against* Socialism, within the little groups.

The people I have met privately in the GDR have always struck me as noticeably less assertive or sophisticated than West Germans, more gentle but more subdued too, with an oddly tentative manner. Before 1989, they did not chat readily in public or talk to strangers in queues. In crowded East Berlin cafeterias you could have heard a pin drop, whereas in the West those same clerks and typists would have been laughing and gossiping. When couples met for the first time in the home of mutual friends, initially they were wary of talking to each other. This appeared to be more than just an instilled fear of informers; it was also a cowed spiritlessness after decades of being told what not to say. One popular joke was about a GDR dog meeting a Polish dog on the frontier, each on his way to the other's country. 'But why on earth are you going to the GDR?' 'I simply must eat. And you, why go to Poland?' 'I simply must bark.'

Günter Gaus, the distinguished liberal journalist who served in East Berlin in 1974–81 as the first head of the West German mission there, wrote a book describing the GDR as a *'Nischengesellschaft'*, or society of little niches. 'It's a police state, yes, but not an arbitrary one', he told me in 1985, 'and that's an important distinction. The rules are clear, and so long as you stick to them, nothing awful will happen to you. So, apart from the tragedy of the dissidents, anyone can live quite privately in his little niche and not be disturbed. That is the State's tacit deal with the citizens'. Another leading West German journalist formerly in East Berlin, Robert Röntgen, described it to me as 'not only a niche society but a group society. Many people form into exclusive little groups of some twenty to thirty, where they cling together for discussion and friendship, and for mutual help in coping with officialdom, material shortages and so on. The groups therefore tend to be multi-professional, so as to maximise skills and contacts: I know one that includes an actress, a doctor and a factory technician. People depend on such friends far more than they would in the West. The groups are non-political and not actively dissident: but the regime does not like them much, since they tend to shift the focus of loyalty away from State collectivism. There's a lot of petty corruption in the GDR, and officials often need to be bribed. But within a group people never cheat each other.'

It was noticeable too that professional people tended to be much less career-minded than in the West. The State might try to woo workers to greater efforts: but, as it also offered job security, most people felt little incentive to work hard and would conserve their energies for their leisure or for moonlighting. As wage differentials were small, it was often thought pointless to strive to get a better job that would involve more work and invidious responsibility for little more pay; apart from a number of SED loyalists, the only people working really hard in the GDR were the few thousands in the private sector – a free-lance window-cleaner could earn more money than many an engineer. To climb a hierarchy inside a firm, you had to appear as a devotee of the regime; plenty were prepared to do this, but they often lost their true friends. So, in this non-risk-taking society, many talented people settled for a junior position and a quiet life. On the other hand, to opt out and live on your wits, as some young bohemian people might be tempted to do, was not easy. To live modestly as an independent artisan, for example making pottery, you needed a permit and a tax number, which were not always given. Without them, you could be arrested and punished.

One feature of the 'niche society' was that more and more people were building their own little villas or bungalows, on the edge of towns. This was a bid to circumvent the housing shortage, or to escape the collectivist constraints of life in blocks of flats, or to enjoy gardening, or all of these at once. What is more, the State in the 1980s increasingly encouraged this trend. It leased the land without charge, and it provided access to building materials and loans for authorised types of house design. Those following this scheme usually built these simple little homes themselves, with the help of friends. Some 20 per cent of new dwellings were in this category.

If the State supported this kind of private ownership, it was partly because of the housing shortage. But there was another and more significant reason, too, that lay at the heart of the odd paradox of the regime's collectivist-versus-privacy attitudes by the mid-1980s. It still pursued collectivism through the youth movements and so on: but it had come reluctantly to accept that these could not alone satisfy people, and that it must find other ways of answering their consumerist urges and desires for a private life. And so the regime – not unlike Tory Governments in Britain! – began promoting owner-occupation as a means of securing a more stable and contented society, one with a stake in the status quo and thus less likely to be tempted into Polish-style unrest. For a few years the policy worked. And everyone knew about it. One left-wing writer, critical of the regime but not totally hostile, suggested to me: 'Although it will never dare say so, this deeply conservative government wants its citizens to be conservative too. And so it is creating just the kind of selfish consumerist petit-bourgeois society that decent Socialists are supposed to hate. Party leaders are fully aware of these dangers, but one can't discuss them in public.' The dilemma was not new. In 1975 the 'reformist' Marxist, Robert Havemann, published an article in Hamburg complaining that the GDR was entering into competition with the West for all the wrong materialistic things: instead of liberalising towards true democracy under Socialism, it was selling out to consumerism. For uttering such home truths, Havemann was put under house arrest.

## Dilemmas for the Church, wooed but wary

The policy of relaxing the reins in private matters (while keeping tight overall political control) was applied especially to religion and to watching West German television — two vital areas of life in the GDR. Until the 1970s to view Western TV was forbidden: many people surreptitiously did so but were sometimes punished for it. However, with the coming of détente and the milder Honecker line, the 'crime' became sanctioned in 1973. It had never been technically possible to jam Western TV; and as many Party leaders watched it, the hypocrisy became untenable. By the 1980s, in the territory covered by Western transmitters, some 95 per cent of GDR citizens viewed it regularly. Above all they watched the news and current affairs documentaries, where the GDR's own coverage was predictably biased and boring. So the East Germans tended to be well informed about the world, even though Western newspapers remained banned. Television was their link with outside reality. Nor was the regime really so displeased, for since Western programmes were filled with news of unemployment, crime, *Angst*, demonstrations and so on, it felt that this TV fare might make its own people less keen to emigrate. It also knew that watching Western TV assuaged the claustrophobia caused by the travel restrictions: the West could at least be enjoyed vicariously. In fact it was noted that applications to emigrate were always highest in the Dresden area, which for reasons of terrain was the main region unable to pick up West German stations — either this made the people there feel more isolated and discontented, or else they alone were not sharing the nightly spectacle of the West's miseries, or maybe a bit of both.

The State also greatly improved its relations with the Protestant Church, which came to enjoy a more privileged position than any other in eastern Europe, even the Catholic Church in Poland. Honecker came to accept that he needed the cooperation of an influential Church that still had millions of registered members. Regular churchgoers were few – for example, only 7 per cent of East Berliners – but this was no true measure of its real support, in a country where the Churches offered the only organised public alternative to the official value-system, and thus attracted many people not otherwise very religious. The Catholic Church, in this traditionally Lutheran part of Germany, had only 1.2 million members; it kept a lower profile, and was wary of reaching any active accommodation with the State.

After the war, the anti-Nazi resistance record of many Protestant leaders, as well as their egalitarian ideals, won them a certain respect from the new Communist rulers, some of whom had even shared prison cells with them. This may explain why the Church was not victimised as severely as in some East European countries at that time. There was however much harassment in the 1950s and 1960s, as the State sought to restrict a rival ideology. A few priests were jailed; church literature was burned; student Christian groups were outlawed. The regime was above all angry that the Evangelical Churches of East and West Germany remained closely united within a single body, and it thus tended to see the GDR churches as agents of the West. Later, under State pressure, the GDR churches split off from the Western ones, to form their own federation, and this eased the situation. But they managed to retain close spiritual links with their partners in the West, and they relied on them heavily for financial aid.

In the 1970s the Party steadily modified its hostility. In 1976 it formally guaranteed freedom of religion and belief. And talks in 1978 between Honecker and the Lutheran leaders produced a *modus vivendi* whereby the regime offered various privileges and rights to Christians, in return for a Church commitment not to meddle in politics. Honecker probably had various motives. He saw that the Church could be of practical use through its welfare work with the sick and handicapped; and at a time of growing restive disillusion among young people, he hoped that the Church might act as a moderating force, helping to channel the dissidence. The Church with misgivings tacitly accepted this role.

Its principal moral and political gain from the deal was that the State now largely ceased making propaganda against it. In the words of one priest, 'The regime now accepts that besides our spiritual role (which of course it thinks is nonsense), we also have an ethical and social part to play, in helping to improve people's lives.' The *quid pro quo* was that the Church stopped fighting against the State: this still caused heartache among some priests, but the more virulently anti-Communist of them had by now left for the West. One tolerant pastor even suggested to me, 'You know, I don't think old Honecker is entirely atheistic, he considers it normal and right that each village should have its little church. For our part, Lutherans in Germany have a long tradition of accepting the established political order — for good or ill.' (A tradition, you would have thought, that the wiser of them would have learned to forget, since the Nazi period.)

After the 1978 agreement, the Protestant Church found it easier to secure sites for new churches, financed from the West; and it won increased time for programmes of its own on State radio and television, including a religious service each Sunday. Six State universities had departments of theology, where some 600 students were studying to be priests. And the GDR was one of the few Warsaw Pact countries to tolerate conscientious objection, at least to the extent that Christian and other objectors — though their careers might suffer for it later — were permitted to do their military service in non-combatant army units. The Church was still forbidden to have its own schools or youth movement, but it carried out much social and welfare work. Helped by State subsidies, the Protestant and Catholic Churches between them ran eighty-two hospitals and did most of the work for the mentally handicapped in the GDR. The State was glad of this help — just as it seemed to be appreciative, even envious, of the Church's disciplined hand over young people. Its rallies were noticeably less affected by unruly behaviour than those of the Party.

The most amazing episode in the regime's bid to move closer to the Church came in 1983, the year of the 500th anniversary of the birth of Martin Luther in a town near Leipzig. Nearly all the main events in his life had taken place on what was now GDR territory — at Wittenberg, Wartburg and Erfurt. But in the first post-war decades he was officially regarded as 'an enemy of the people and traitor to the peasants', and schoolbooks were still teaching this in the mid-1970s. Then all began to change. Luther became 'a precursor of Marx, as John the Baptist was of Christ' and 'the man who mobilised the progressive forces in Germany against the Papal exploiters'. So the history books were rewritten, to the confusion of many loyal Marxist teachers. It soon became clear that the turnabout was partly by way of preparation for the anniversary, when the State staged giant celebrations that led some Western critics to pour scorn on this 'ungainly effort to appropriate Luther as an ideological forebear of Communism' (as one writer put it). Honecker chaired the organising committee, State television gave live coverage of the opening ceremony at Wartburg castle, and East Berlin's Opera House was lent to the Church for a festival where Honecker and the Archbishop of Canterbury were among the guests of honour, while millions of Protestants poured into the GDR from all over the globe. Once again, the State had various motives. It was happy to be earning the hard currency from so much tourism: but the rehabilitation of Luther was also clearly a part of the new policy of seeking to strengthen GDR citizens' sense of national identity by reinstating great figures from the German past (see pp. 418–19).

Church leaders, fearing that Honecker was trying to upstage them, remained wary. And they had reason to be so: despite the entente, the State in the 1980s still pursued subtle or not-so-subtle discrimination against many lay Christians. If less than in former days, their children still found it harder than others to be accepted for university. Practising Christians were barred from almost all teaching posts, and from political ones such as being a senior civil servant, so they often found it hard to win promotion. The only exceptions were the members of the Christian Democratic Union (CDU), which bore no relation to its West German homonym but was a satellite party under the aegis of the SED, made up of 'socialist citizens of the Christian faith'. The State used it as a means of pressing talented Christians into its service if it really needed them: for example, if some brilliant individual who happened to be a Christian was required to fill some key post as surgeon or professor, then he would be invited to join the CDU first. And some did so. But Church leaders kept their distance from this party, and looked on it with scorn.

The issue of what the role of a Christian should be in an atheistic State – how far should he collaborate? – was constantly exercising priests and their congregations, and not all saw alike. The regime, for its part, kept up its wooing: 'Surely we have a common struggle,' Party members would tell Christians; 'like you, we desire peace and brotherly love. Was Marx's teaching so different from the Sermon on the Mount? Join us in building a more equal society!' And some priests reacted positively: believing that the Communist regime was here to stay, and even admiring its social achievements, they were prepared to join in some of its activities and in trying to liberalise it further. Others were more reticent: but they too mostly believed that it was quite possible to lead the Christian life in the GDR and that the Church needed the strength of its supporters. So they continually urged their faithful not to try to emigrate.

Inevitably the Church became a magnet for all kinds of outsiders, many not Christians at all, including homosexuals, punks, Oriental sects, and others frowned on as 'unsocialist' who sought its protection. This put the Church in a dilemma. Naturally it wanted to help those in trouble with the regime: but it did not wish to prejudice its good relations with the State. A similar problem arose over the Peace Movement, which struggled along somehow in the GDR despite official hostility. The anti-missile campaign of 1982–3 in West Germany spawned a modest counterpart in the east, where in Dresden young people wearing CND badges held candlelight vigils in a ruined church, and soon the badges were seen all over the GDR. At this the authorities' patience snapped: arrests were made, peace marches in Berlin were banned, and leaders of a big rally in Jena were put in prison. The official reason given for the clampdown was that 'dissident elements' were joining the rallies and 'counter-revolutionary ideas' were in danger of taking over. In reality, Honecker was at one with Moscow in opposing protests against Soviet nuclear arms.

The conflict put the Church in a difficult position. In the West, the Churches were split on the nuclear weapons issue. But in the GDR virtually all Christians favoured the peace movement, for *none* of them wanted to be defended by Soviet missiles. So the Church could hardly disown the demonstrators. Prudently it avoided campaigning too openly on the nuclear issue, and devoted its main peace efforts to opposing the growth of military training in schools (see p. 396). But it did hold discussions on peace on church premises, for it was aware of its parishioners' passionate interest. Ironically, in 1989 it was these meetings which generated the great demonstrations that finally toppled the regime (see p. 422). The Church did not itself lead these protests, but it gave them crucial support and cover. So the regime's policy of wooing and indulging the Church had, in the end, savagely rebounded against it.

## *The watchful grip of the one-party State*

The curbs on freedom of expression – over disarmament and so many other issues – certainly infuriated an important minority of people, those who in Western societies would be opinion-makers or social critics. But these curbs were seldom what average citizens found most irksome about life in the GDR. They had grown used to the system; and most of them had no direct experience of Western democracy (after all, the last free elections had been in 1933). Their concerns were more practical and material. If asked what annoyed them most, they would probably cite first the ban on travel to the West, then might add the distortions and omissions of the State Press and media, which they could compare with Western TV. But most would put in second place the unpredictable shortages in the shops and the difficulty of getting the simplest repairs done. 'If Communism were less plain inefficient, we would accept it more easily,' said one housewife. The shortages – no advertisement for the centralised planning system – contrasted oddly with the decent overall level of prosperity: some 99 per cent of homes had refrigerators, 87 per cent had television sets, 91 per cent washing machines (but only 22 per cent had telephones); and homes with private cars rose since 1970 from 16 to 42 per cent, comparing well with Russia's 13 per cent. But, unless they had special Party contacts, people still had to wait between six and ten years for a new car, and then all they were likely to get was an ungainly little two-cylinder Trabant or Wartburg, made in the GDR and sold at an artificially high price. It was the shortage of imported materials, and the absolute priority given to exports, that made cars in such short supply.

The recurrent capricious shortages of smaller everyday items were due in part to these same factors, as well as to the clumsy distribution system and the inflexibility of an industrial planning process that would fix a factory's targets with scant regard to consumer needs. Suddenly nails would completely disappear from the shops, or wallpaper, or underpants – or they would re-emerge in bulk but all the same colour. A supermarket might be out of orange juice but have piles of rhubarb juice. And even in summer the selection of fresh fruit and vegetables was appalling. Hence the queues, and the frustrations of daily shopping. Much of the best of the GDR's output – of fresh flowers, clothing, furnishings and so on – was sold to the West for hard currency, so that only the second-rate remained. If some key item was suddenly unobtainable, it might be that it was being used to exploit some new export opportunity, as when Volkswagen placed a mass order for car tyres. But these sensible commercial deals were never reported in the media, which would never explain *why* some shortage was occurring. Many older Party loyalists cited this privately to me as one of their main criticisms of the regime. And the ordinary citizen felt treated like a child. He had money, but not much choice to spend it on, unless via contacts in the West he had access to Deutschmarks, with which he could buy luxury imported goods at special 'Inter' shops that took hard currency only.

In the ordinary shops, people kept on the alert for something unusual or attractive to appear – say, good linen or Meissen porcelain – and then seized their chance to buy up a large stock, so as to be able to give most of it to friends in return for other items bought in the same way. 'Life has reverted to barter as in pre-money days,' said one man; 'when I wanted to build a *dacha*, I couldn't get concrete anywhere. Finally I swapped some for a lorryload of sand.' Or else people resorted to subterfuge. I heard of a man who was trying the join the Party, so he needed to be very discreet about his Western contacts, especially as he had a brother in West Berlin. His washing-machine kept breaking down, and spare parts were unobtainable: so the brother was telephoned and came over with the spares, tactfully parking his car two blocks away. People regarded such deviousness as normal routine. Similarly, as services and repairs had been much neglected by the planners, the State sector included extremely few garages, cobblers, plumbers and the like. So the gap was left to be filled by private entrepreneurs, to whom the State even gave loans.

As in other Communist countries, private business on a small scale was permitted: as well as the service and repair firms, a good many craftsmen, artisans, small shops and restaurants fell into this category. They tended to be family-run, but were allowed up to ten employees each. Most of the better bistros, bakeries and boutiques were privately owned, and they had a more personal touch, and a far better sense of quality and service, than the bureaucratic State concerns. Such families worked hard, and were often among the most prosperous in the GDR – for example, a boutique-owner I met in Dresden who had his own pleasure-boat on the Elbe. But they were careful not to flaunt their modest wealth as they might in the West, for this was still ideologically *mal vu* and it could invite close tax scrutiny or other reprisals. So the status-symbol society was here turned on its head. Most small restaurants, while perhaps neat and cosy inside, looked deliberately down-at-heel from the outside, as if they were even trying to deter custom. This added to the GDR's general drabness.

Although some commercial ventures were arbitrarily refused licences, on the whole the regime seemed to accept and even encourage the private sector, for it needed it. So one might have expected these little firms to be on the increase, seeing that they offered some scope for independence and initiative amid the collectivist wasteland. But curiously the total of full-time ones had actually declined from 250,000 to 80,000 between 1955 and the late 1980s. One main reason was that in this passive niche society few people were prepared to accept the risk and hard work involved (this same lack of initiative was to hamper the process of privatising the economy after 1989, see p. 455). Often they found it difficult to raise the initial capital, or a restaurateur might be scared of having to depend on the vagaries of state food supplies; or they feared that the regime might suddenly change its policy. On the other hand, the 1980s saw a marked increase in part-time enterprise in the form of moonlighting by people with full-time state jobs: for here much less risk and commitment was involved. After his factory work, a man in the evenings or weekends might turn his hand to house-building, car-repairing or suchlike: he could get away with charging three or four times the official rates for these jobs, and could always find customers. It took hard work, yes, but was more flexible and less worrying than running a proper business.

The failure to report or explain the consumer shortages was just one aspect of a general suppression of information and ultra-selectivity of news in the State-controlled newspapers, radio and television. Any event at home or abroad that embarrassed the regime or went against its policy was passed over in silence or relegated to an inside paragraph. Thus in 1980 the major crisis over Solidarity in nearby Poland was barely mentioned, even though people knew all about it from West German TV; and when in the 1960s a senior GDR minister committed suicide under political pressure and a storm broke out in the Party, it was not reported at all, and the news only spread later by word of mouth. News priorities were entirely different from those in the West, and this was not just a matter of expected political bias but of a different philosophy of the role of the media. As Lenin laid down, the task of newspapers was not merely to report events but to 'join in building socialism' by stimulating morale and defining objectives: so they had to be systematically optimistic about developments in the GDR and the Soviet Union, and had to produce daily evidence of the decline of capitalism in the West. But, because the distortions were so obvious, this educative campaign tended to defeat its own ends when directed at educated people with their own television window on the West.

The most important daily was *Neues Deutschland*, the GDR's equivalent of *Pravda*, with sales of about a million. It was the organ of the SED and like the Party's many other publications was controlled by its Department of Agitation and Propaganda. Its main headlines and news stories were often planned weeks in advance, for they tended to relate to anniversaries, Party congresses or economic progress reports, and they were repetitive and predictable, in the genre of 'Delegates Unanimously Praise Workers' Collectives'. Foreign events were given little coverage unless they could be given an anti-capitalist twist. All the SED-controlled newspapers gave extensive space to sport and culture, but little to crime or human interest stories; local weeklies were sometimes able to touch on real local problems, such as pollution or vandalism, but these papers were not seen outside their own areas. The Churches were allowed their own weeklies and magazines, which were distributed privately among their own members and had to be careful to keep off politics.

As for the State radio and TV networks, they often produced cultural and entertainment programmes of some quality (I saw an excellent one about D. H. Lawrence), but their documentaries and home-grown serials tended to be of the earnest socialism-building kind (e.g. how a young divorcee makes a new life thanks to the support of her factory comrades), while the news programmes were in much the same style as *Neues Deutschland*. So citizens turned for their information to the West German networks, with which the GDR ones hardly tried to compete: editors privately tended to take the defeatist line, 'We know the West will cover this story better than we can, so let's not mention it.' The only retort that GDR TV did make to Western competition was to run a programme called *Der Schwarze Kanal* (black channel) that sought to show up the week's 'lies' and 'distortions' on West German TV. Its editors claimed that Western networks deliberately beamed propaganda to the GDR, just as the CIA-backed Radio Free Europe did from Munich. But this was not so: West German stations covered GDR events as fully as they could because their own audiences were interested, and no programmes were made specifically to influence GDR viewers.

I found that East Germans were more indignant about the shortcomings of the media than any other aspect of GDR life except the travel restrictions and consumer shortages – and the grumblers included many Party supporters. 'The failure to mention events like the Prague embassy sit-in' (see p. 411), said one elderly Communist, 'makes the media a laughing-stock, so that people ask, "If they lie about this, what else might they be hiding?"' And one leading writer, basically in favour of the regime, said to me: 'Why this policy? I don't think it's purely a rigorous line coming from the top of the Party. Editors could get away with much more open and critical reporting if they tried: but over the years they have grown timid and lazy, they can't be bothered to cope with controversy, so they practise self-censorship more than they need. It's appalling.'

It would be wrong, however, to conclude that in the GDR there was no public opinion, nor any debate on public issues. Debate did take place, but not in public. It went on within the two-million-strong ranks of the SED, where village and factory cells could express their views: these were then filtered up to the hierarchy, where at least they were listened to, though usually not acted upon. This was about as far as 'public opinion' had any organised forum. The Party rulers would also listen to the views of a kind of institutionalised counter-elite, made up of scientists, academics, managers and senior economic officials who could express their opinions on specialist matters, but must then dutifully execute Politbüro policies. So the rulers did consult the ruled, or some of them. But of course they retained the last word, and there was no means of ousting them through elections.

As elsewhere in the Soviet bloc, the Party and State apparatus operated in parallel, down through a double hierarchy from summit to local level. At the very top, controlling both of these channels, was the all-powerful Politbüro, a non-elected self-perpetuating body made up of some twenty-five senior SED officials, ministers and military men. It alone decided all policy. Below it, on the Party side of the structure, came the policy-executing Secretariat whose general secretary (Honecker 1971–89) was also the Politbüro's leader; and below this was the Central Committee, whose members were elected by the Party Congress. Seldom did either of these bodies defy the wishes of the leadership. Further down the SED hierarchy were the regional bodies and local cells.

On the State side of the structure, below the Politbüro came the Council of Ministers (a cabinet) and junior ministers. They in practice took their orders from the Politbüro, but constitutionally they were also responsible to the Volkskammer (people's chamber), a parliament made up of the SED and eight other parties and mass organisations, all nine forming a coalition known as the National Front. In this 500-member chamber, the SED itself had only 127 seats, while each of the other four parties had fifty-two and the trade union federation sixty-eight; three other bodies representing culture, women and youth (FDJ) were also present. But this semblance of pluralism was little more than a façade. Although the other parties did in theory speak for distinct interest groups – one was the Democratic Farmers' Party – it was the SED that effectively controlled the National Front, and its dominant role was even written into the GDR's Constitution which declared the State to be 'led by the working-class and its Marxist-Leninist Party'. And the Volkskammer was little more than a rubber-stamp assembly. It met for only four or five days each year, its votes were generally unanimous, and it was elected from a single list of candidates selected by the National Front.

Even left-wing foreign observers largely sympathetic to the GDR's other achievements had few illusions about its democracy. Jonathan Steele of the *Guardian* wrote in 1977 of the SED's mass membership:

> It certainly does not ensure genuine influence from the bottom upwards. On the contrary the Politbüro still follows the tight-lipped conspiratorial traditions of its days in opposition and the underground. All decisions are taken at the top and there is minimal public or press discussion of them. Under the principle of democratic centralism decisions are passed down the line to the central committee and local party organisations for implementa-tion. Top party politicians still live in suburban seclusion in a guarded residential area at Wandlitz outside Berlin. They probably have less contact with ordinary people than most West European politicians do ... There is no chance of voters exerting any influence against SED policy.

How far the average citizen felt irked by the lack of freedom of expression was not easy to assess. One West German diplomat in East Berlin suggested to me that it was not felt as the worst of deprivations: 'Remember that there has been no democracy here since before 1933, so even the older generation has no clear idea of what it is like. Sometimes people ask me, "Why on earth do you permit those Leftist demos, or the neo-Fascist meetings? It's shocking," and I try to explain that democracy must mean giving freedom of speech to those you disapprove of. They do not always get the point.' Those better attuned to Western ideas certainly did feel cramped by the curbs on free speech and political choice. As officialdom became a shade more tolerant, so they grew a little more relaxed about talking freely in public or to strangers: but they still set limits on what they said. They knew that you could now get away with airing grievances about daily inconveniences or bureaucratic slip-ups: but if you voiced basic dissent about Socialism, or Honecker, or the Soviet ally, you could well be in trouble if an informer or Stasi agent overheard you. 'Twenty years ago they'd send you to prison,' said a student I met; 'today you merely lose your job, or get banished to some remote place or have to emigrate. An improvement, I suppose.'

While criticism remained taboo in the mass media, it was sanctioned within limits in satiric cabaret, where it reached smaller audiences and was less 'dangerous'. Cabaret of this kind has a potent tradition in Germany, especially in Berlin. Today it no longer has much function in the west: but in the GDR it provided a rare if modest outlet for national self-mockery and the release of frustrations, and so it flourished – and was accepted by the regime as court jesters might be. The venerable State-run *Distel* (*Thistle*), in East Berlin, much frequented by Western tourists and even by local FDJ groups and GDR soldiers in uniform, was very much an establishment affair, but lively. In its cramped theatre, clever performers went through the nightly ritual of lampooning GDR life as best they dared, with scripts vetted in advance. In the show I attended, a sales-girl looks at the dead flies in a State shop-window and says, 'I'd like to clear them away but it's not my job, so I daren't.' In a football stadium, workers are erecting a big poster advertising an Italian fruit juice, and one says, 'That's how we sell our principles, to earn hard currency.' Not really very hard-hitting stuff.

Other sketches poked fun at bureaucracy and consumer shortages. Cabaret in Berlin was able to satirise people's failure to live up to the challenges of Socialism, or even (more daringly) to chide the regime for compromising its own ideals. But it could not safely question the system itself, or the leadership, or make jokes about foreign policy or the Russians. In the provinces, some of the small intellectual cabarets were able to be a little more outspoken, as they were less in the limelight. At the *Akademixer* in Leipzig, I sat in a lively studenty atmosphere to hear a talented young cast making clever word-play about Party hypocrisies. The audience was tense and expectant, as at a sporting contest, which in a sense it was: in the GDR people went to a satiric cabaret for the thrill of seeing just how far the actors and writers would dare go. Even in these little places, scripts had to be vetted. But there was also some improvisation – and this, if the secret police were sitting in the hall, could be quite a game of Russian roulette for the producers and cast.

The GDR's secret police, the notorious Stasi (see p. 439), had become less oppressive than in Ulbricht's day: but behind the smooth façade it still kept a watchful grip, and people did their best to keep clear of it. In Schwerin a drunken policeman had an argument with three men in the street and fired shots at them: none of the onlookers would lift a finger to help, for they did not want to get involved with the police. The men were left lying in the road and two later died. This was the kind of story one heard. Uniformed police were far more prevalent than in the West, and though generally polite they would quickly turn to rough-handling any citizen who dared answer back. One loyal Communist told me: 'Our kindly police have a secondary *de facto* role as social workers. They keep a close watch on families, and if, say, they notice that a father is maltreating his children, they'll report him.' This may well have helped to check child abuse: but the prying certainly had another, more political function too. Any citizen, however blameless, had a police dossier, where reports from school and workplace were included, and where any small or unorthodox things that he might have said or done were entered down, and might be quoted against him years later. This may all sound sinister and *1984*-ish, but except in rare cases the police system was no longer used arbitrarily. So long as he stuck to the rules and did nothing wrong 'politically' (not always so easy), a citizen could expect to be treated fairly by the law, in a police State that was highly legalistic in the true German manner and anxious to be seen to be behaving legally. Citizens were often too ignorant or submissive to make proper use of their legal rights: but if they did, they would generally get justice.

The army, like the police, was much in evidence, and was closely meshed into the life of a country that was decidedly more militaristic than the Federal Republic. The National People's Army, with 115,000 men, plus 50,000 border guards and 52,000 in the navy and air force, was highly modern and efficiently armed. Some 55 per cent of its strength was made up of conscripts who did eighteen months' service. On enlistment they were first taken to Buchenwald concentration camp to swear their oath, and were then carefully indoctrinated in the 'anti-imperialist struggle', for one day they might have to fight fellow-Germans. Controversially, their pre-military training had started some years earlier: children of 12 or 13 were encouraged to attend 'defence education' classes in school where they were taught about the role of the army. Then para-military training, including marksmanship, was compulsory for boys of 15 and 16; and those of 17 and 18 were obliged to attend summer camps where they took part in field manoeuvres and shooting exercises. At Defence Spartakiads, girls as well as boys could be seen stripping machine-guns. The aim of this early training was two-fold: to prepare conscripts for their national service; and to imbue them with national and military feeling at an age when they were still malleable. As Roger Boyes of *The Times* commented wittily, 'The ideologists have to get in quickly before *Dallas* poisons combat morale' (from West German TV). This martial indoctrination of the very young angered many parents, and the Church took up their cause, with repeated protests — but to little effect.

The GDR also kept a large part-time militia of some 400,000 men. Each factory and office of any size had its own militia unit, comprising some 20 per cent of its male work-force: they were volunteers, led by SED activists, and at weekends you could see them out in the countryside doing field training. This militia was set up after the strikes of 1953, with the aim of providing cadres to forestall any future workers' uprisings, and this internal security role remained its main purpose. Few other features of the GDR system struck me as more unpleasant. 'If only the Poles in 1980 had possessed a militia like ours,' one SED man told me unblinkingly, 'they might have spared themselves all that trouble with the Solidarity counter-revolutionaries.'

## Brecht to Biermann: dealing with the intellectual dissidents

Party watchdogs were equally on the alert against rumbles of dissidence in the cultural field, where over the years quite a number of artists and intellectuals were harassed, censored, denied publication, expelled from the country or in a few cases put in prison. But the regime's policy was oddly erratic, even capricious: in some periods quite a degree of open criticism was allowed, in others the clamp-down was heavy. The GDR's overall record was about average for Eastern Europe — more oppressive than Poland or Hungary, less so than Romania or post-1968 Czechoslovakia. The writers who were expelled, or left of their own accord, tended to accept exile much more easily than, say, Poles or Hungarians, for the obvious reason that if they went to West Germany they remained within their own culture and language. Some writers the regime was glad to be rid of, but for prestige reasons it did not want to lose too many. It was proud of the GDR's literary record, which indeed included some of the best post-war German writing. As in the case of South Africa or Latin America, the challenge of a harsh regime will often bring out the best in a writer – or drive him out.

In the initial post-war years the movement was in the other direction. Several committed left-wing writers, many of them Jewish, chose to settle in East rather than West Germany when they returned from exile, eager to join in creating the Socialist society of their ideals. They included the novelists Anna Seghers and Stefan Heym, the poet Stephan Hermlin, the philosopher Ernst Bloch, and most notably the poet-playwright Bertolt Brecht. But many soon became disillusioned. By 1951 the new regime was actively imposing the cultural doctrine of Andrey Zhdanov, Stalin's son-in-law, which laid down that style, formalism and aesthetics were to be rejected since the role of art and literature was to express Socialist Realism and to educate the workers in the spirit of Socialism. Many writers, but few of the best, agreed to toe this line, so they dutifully churned out their tales of the gallant struggles for higher production norms in farm and factory – and were well rewarded. Others took refuge in novels about the horrors of the Nazi period, where it was often easier to write sincerely without displeasing the Party. But the more individualistic spirits began to chafe, or even to dare a few criticisms, and before long they were paying the penalty. Brecht, the GDR's brightest cultural star, fell into some disfavour (see p.402). The Marxist philosopher Wolfgang Harich was in 1957 sentenced to ten years' hard labour for advocating intellectual liberty and a Yugoslav-style democracy. His fellow Marxist thinker, the great Ernst Bloch, began to attack the GDR's 'petrified dogmatism' in his lectures at Leipzig University: after 1956 he left for West Germany. The novelist Uwe Johnson also emigrated at this time.

The Party was now becoming worried by this disaffection, and so at a conference at Bitterfeld in 1959 it launched a new initiative to try to regain writers' loyalty. Under the slogan, *Greif zur Feder, Kumpel* (seize your pen, mate), it urged writers to move closer to the workers, decreeing that each of them should spend some time working in factories or on farms, not as manual labourers but for example running the works' library or editing its news journal. This was in some ways an excellent idea, and along with the inevitable stream of hack novels it did produce a few good ones: Christa Wolf's *Der geteilte Himmel* (*The Divided Heaven*, 1963) was partly inspired by her time spent at the railway works at Halle. Wolf was perhaps the most talented of the new authors emerging in the GDR in the 1960s, who managed to write with some honesty and realism, without falling into disgrace. This was a period of reduced Party pressures, which continued after Honecker took over in 1971. At first he declared that so long as the works were 'rooted in socialism' there need be no taboos in art and literature, and in some respects he fulfilled his promise. In 1972 the provocative play *Die Neuen Leiden des Jungen W.* (*The New Sorrows of Young W.*), by Ulrich Plenzdorf, was allowed to be publicly staged and then published as a novel. It is the story of an outspoken young drop-out, long-haired, bejeaned, crazy about rock music, who escapes from the harsh atmosphere of his factory to live in a shack outside Berlin. Plenzdorf seemed to be making a plea for a more tolerant official attitude towards youth, and his play was a big success and caused a stir. Probably it was officially tolerated because it showed the hero's gesture as finally pointless and self-destructive; it implied that the energies of youth could in fact be harnessed to Socialism, if only more understanding were shown them.

Soon after this the climate again worsened, as Party hard-liners infiltrated the Writers' Union, using it as a base for vendettas against non-conformists. Their most celebrated victim was Wolf Biermann, the satirical poet and singer. He had been brought up in Hamburg, but was drawn by his Communist sympathies to move to the GDR in 1953. His immensely popular poems and songs were always pro-Socialist, but they included gibes against the Wall, the Stasi and so on: from 1962 he began to be in trouble with the regime, which banned his works from being printed and for a while would not let him perform in public. But he was published in the West, where his witty, passionate lyricism and his bold anger won him a big reputation; and the regime, perversely proud of its rebel genius, even allowed him to make concert tours abroad. It was after a concert in Hamburg in 1976 that the regime finally broke with him, depriving him of his citizenship for 'publicly slandering our socialist State'. So he regretfully settled back in his native city, where his creativity waned.

His expulsion caused a furore both at home and abroad. It was denounced by such left-wing luminaries as Jean-Paul Sartre, Joan Baez and Rudi Dutschke, while within the GDR twelve top writers including Christa Wolf and the normally loyalist Stephan Hermlin signed an open letter to the Party begging it to reconsider the move. But the regime refused to budge and even exacted reprisals: Wolf was expelled from the SED. And there followed a further tightening up. The eminent economist Rudolf Bahro, who had produced a reasoned Marxist critique of the regime's shortcomings, was arrested on fake charges of espionage and imprisoned; and several other well-known writers, including the poets Günter Kunert and Reiner Kunze, were either expelled or else harassed so much that they opted for exile. Why was the Politburo clamping down like this, at a time when it was liberalising in other fields, such as relations with the Church? Clearly it held the view that disaffected intellectuals were dangerous: given an inch they might take an ell, and their influence could spread.

Günter Kunert left of his own choice in 1979, to settle in rural Holstein where I went to see him. 'I have always been on the Left and at first I welcomed the regime,' he told me;

> but my poems are on private themes, and I just could not turn out the kind of ideological 'public' poetry expected of me; also, one theme of mine is the dehumanising effect of modern techno-logy, and Marxism does not tolerate this kind of pessimism. The Party finally refused to publish me. But my books were being well received in West Germany, partly *because* people knew that I was in trouble in the GDR. And the authorities continued to let me travel, for lecture tours and so on. So like Biermann I benefited from a paradox: oppression at home led to notoriety in the West, which then provided a refuge from the oppression! My break with GDR-style Socialism was painful, and I still think the regime has many virtues — but not for an artist. However, I'm still a GDR citizen, I can pay return visits when I wish.

By the 1980s the situation had calmed down, and the hostile writers still remaining in the GDR had become more discreet — but not all. The veteran Stefan Heym, born in 1913, was tolerated as a kind of licensed dissident, too old and venerable to be openly victimised. Heym, who is Jewish, was born in Chemnitz, and later fled to the United States where he became an American citizen and served in the US Army. As a Communist he was persecuted in the McCarthy era, and in 1952 he returned to his native East Germany: but soon he was following the familiar path of disillusion. He wrote a number of critical novels, including *Five Days in June* (1975), a dramatised account of the June 1953 uprising that stood somewhere between the Western and GDR versions of it. Soon he was being refused publication at home: but he continued to publish in the West, although he was once fined

9,000 Marks for doing so without permission. I visited him in East Berlin in 1985 – a large, humorous man with a puckish grin and a mock-arrogance that made a charming contrast to the usual GDR solemnity. 'I am the greatest and the only Social Realist, for I alone describe the truth and know that true socialism will one day come to pass on earth. People smuggle in copies of my new books from the West, so I'm read quite widely here. This is a very mild, scared little dictatorship today. Their image took such a world-wide punishing over the Biermann affair that never again will they expel or imprison a writer, I'm sure. But they keep close tabs on me. They'll know that you've come to see me.'

Christa Wolf on the other hand was one of a small number of writers officially permitted to publish in West Germany. This modest, withdrawn person has always been more concerned with personal than public themes (see p. 483), and has tended to couch her criticisms somewhat obliquely, as in her famous novel *The Quest for Christa T* (1968); even so, this book was denounced at the time for its failure to laud collectivism. Other such nonconformist books appeared from time to time, for example Volker Braun's satirical *Hinz und Kunz* (*Every Tom, Dick and Harry*, 1985). But critical books of this kind were generally given very limited print runs, so they sold out rapidly in the shops and then circulated from hand to hand like rare editions: the best-seller system was turned on its head. There was an acute paper shortage in the GDR, and the officials who decided these things saw no reason to squander the precious supplies on such renegade novelists. On the other hand, those who wrote the kind of books officially in favour were assured of large sales and in many cases given State salaries and other privileges. But the 1980s did see an easing up in the publication of some classic authors previously taboo. Freud, once the major class enemy, became permitted; likewise Kafka, Joyce and Proust. Finally the ban was also lifted on *The Tin Drum* by Günter Grass, whose outspoken anti-Communism had long outlawed him (unlike Böll, whose works had long been more acceptable). But under pressure from Moscow the Party still drew the line at Solzhenitsyn – 'And quite right too,' one SED lady told me. 'Why should we waste our paper on that CIA-inspired rubbish? Who would want to read him anyway?'

In the other arts, life for painters and musicians was generally easier than for writers, since they dealt less with ideas and facts. A few good artists, such as Roger Loewig, were harassed and driven into exile: but it did gradually become more possible to create and exhibit the kinds of modern art that lie outside the canons of Socialist Realism. In music, the GDR was proud of its record, and had some excellent opera houses and orchestras, in the German tradition; its leading performers were allowed to tour abroad on the usual circuits. The East German cinema produced a number of worthy films on social themes; it was under the same kind of State ownership as television, and unorthodox scripts were seldom accepted (see p. 481).

Theatres, like opera houses, were nearly always full, for thanks to lavish subsidies the tickets were very cheap; also, people had fewer other outlets for their leisure than in the West. Theatre fare consisted mainly of the classics, from Shakespeare and Schiller to Brecht, plus routine 'Socialist Realist' offerings and some approved imports, many from Russia. But there were few good new East German plays on modern themes. The GDR's best-known playwright since Brecht, Heiner Müller, a critical Communist, stuck mainly to historical subjects such as Frederick the Great: one of his few forays into the present day, *Der Bau* (*The Building*), *a frank study of cynical wheeler-dealing by* Party bureaucrats in industry, won him odium in the 1960s and was never staged. In this climate, many of the best directors and actors inevitably emigrated to the West, where they could gain more money as well as more freedom. Worried by this brain-drain, the regime latterly allowed many of them to move to and fro between the Germanies without losing their GDR citizenship or domicile.

Bertolt Brecht's plays were always widely performed in the GDR, even though he himself had clashed with the regime. He founded his famous Berliner Ensemble theatre in 1949, with the aim of its becoming the main focus for acting and playwriting in the German-speaking world, but the division of Germany made this impossible. Though he tried to remain loyal to the GDR, his epic style and his concept of alienation brought him into trouble with the prevailing Zhdanovite orthodoxy and his work was variously attacked as defeatist or lacking in realism. Two of his plays were withdrawn after the first night. Brecht wanted his audiences to view his characters and the world in a critical spirit, but that is just what the Party wanted to avoid. To his credit, in his own work he never seriously betrayed his artistic principles, even though publicly he made obeisance to the regime. After his death, his position remained ambiguous: he was still officially venerated by the GDR as its major post-war author, yet his work also remained an inspiration to free-thinking writers.

After his death, control of his theatre company was taken over by his widow, Helene Weigel, and then by their daughter Barbara and her husband Ekkehard Schall, the GDR's leading actor. So highly did the Party rate its Brechtian heritage that the family was granted a privileged status, including the ability to travel freely to the West and a grand flat with servants. The theatre continued faithfully to present a repertoire of the master's works, to local audiences and bevies of Western tourists: but most Western critics felt that the productions had tended to become jaded and mechanical. The *Dreigroschenoper* which I saw in 1985 was truly dreadful. Far better Brecht was to be seen over in the West – but that was then a different world.

## Travel to the West: harshest of the curbs on freedom

The notorious division of the German nation before 1989 was marked physically on the GDR side by a fortification of great complexity that wound for 870 miles from the Baltic to Czechoslovakia. In the first years after the war this remained an open border between the Soviet and Western occupation zones, lightly patrolled and easily crossed, for it was then not intended to split Germany permanently. But by 1952 the GDR regime had grown so alarmed by the refugee exodus that it set up what it called a 'protective strip', with armed guards and barbed wire, backed by a five-kilometre-deep 'forbidden zone' where only those with a special pass could go. The building of the 'Iron Curtain' – a term made famous by Churchill – had begun. Then in 1961, when it built the Berlin Wall, the GDR also massively strengthened its defences along its whole western border – the first time in world history that so huge a forticiation had been erected not so much to hold up invaders as to prevent escape, as from a prison. It had minefields, shrapnel-scattering trap guns, parallel steel fences, lethal guard dogs and sinister watchtowers on stilts.

By the 1980s there were nine regular access routes by road across the border and four by rail. The division of Germany had severed about 160 other roads and twenty-five railway lines, and had separated communities that had lived together for centuries; in at least four cases, the barrier went through the heart of a village or between adjacent ones so that former neighbours could meet only by making a long detour. West Germans living within about fifty kilometres of the border were allowed, by a special GDR dispensation, to make up to thirty-six day trips a year to visit friends or relatives on the other side. But, as the crossings were few, this was not always easy. And as entry to the 'forbidden zone' was banned, the meetings in many cases had to take place somewhere else. Many inhabitants were evicted from this border zone, where farming went on under tight military supervision.

On the Western side, the sealing of the border was greeted at first with sheer disbelief, then with fury. But gradually people grew used to it, and tensions waned as détente set in. 'It's like living beside a cliff or deep river, we hardly notice the border any more, and we've stopped wondering about life on the other side,' said one Bavarian peasant. At Lübeck, the only big Western town very near the border, middle-class suburban villas were built within 200 metres of it in the 1970s, and amazingly the land and house prices there were little lower than elsewhere. At Lübeck and in some other spots – in the Harz mountains or in Bavaria – the border even became a tourist attraction for sightseers, while parties of schoolchildren were dutifully taken to inspect what had happened to the *Vaterland*. They gazed at the ever-silent GDR sentinels, and they read the signs on the Western side: 'AUCH DRÜBEN IST DEUTSCHLAND' (over there it's also Germany). The Federal border police erected placards that gave full illustrated details – as in any well-run tourist venue – of the deadly arsenal of the GDR defences and how they exterminated escapers. But while most of the border area became normally prosperous, some poorer upland areas, or salients half-enclosed within GDR territory, suffered badly from the loss of their hinterland. Within a belt some forty kilometres deep from the border, farms and other businesses received Federal subsidies to compensate for their difficulties, but these were not always adequate.

The border was patrolled by the Federal frontier police, the green-uniformed *Bundesgrenzschutz*. One senior officer took me for a tour near Lübeck, showing me the fifty-metre empty strip on GDR soil between the actual border with its white posts and the first steel fence. 'Some local kids like to play cat-and-mouse with the GDR guards by hopping into this strip, but they know what they're doing. Tourists tend to be more unwary, especially in wooded areas where they don't notice the white posts, and they may get arrested. There's a senior-level joint border commission for serious incidents.' Over 3,000 East German guards had defected across the border since 1952, so they were now made to patrol in pairs or groups and were carefully screened for political reliability. 'It's a rum business,' my guide went on, 'they hide in the bushes and peer at us through their field-glasses, but they are forbidden to smile or respond to a wave, let alone utter a word. Here we all are, fellow-Germans in uniform, playing deaf-mute with each other across the years – crazy!'

Along the seventy-five-mile Wall around Berlin, the system of controls was much the same. So how did the GDR leaders explain away this monstrosity? Everyone knew why the Wall was built, and as most Party loyalists tended to be embarrassed about it, they talked about it as little as possible. But sometimes they had to try to justify this 'Anti-Fascist Protection Wall', as it was called officially. As recently as 1985 one East Berlin newspaper wrote that the building of it had been 'vital to head off Western invasion plans. The soldiers on guard watch that no one from the West comes to hinder the building of our Socialist state.' Yet thousands of Westerners were daily entering the GDR quite freely! A more sophisticated justification, much nearer the truth, was: 'We have expensively trained many key people who are wooed by the West with higher salaries, and until we are stronger we cannot afford to lose them.'

During the difficult 1960s after the building of the Wall, it was not only near-impossible to get out of the GDR but also hard to get into it, for only those West Germans with close relatives there could obtain visas. But after the 1971–2 agreements matters were greatly eased, and almost any West German became free to enter the GDR for up to thirty days a year. By the mid-1980s the number of annual visits was averaging about 3.5 million from the Federal Republic plus another 3 million from West Berlin. Some 90 per cent of these visitors were estimated to have relatives or close friends in the GDR, and in many cases they stayed in their homes. So, after forty years of division, the cross-border contacts were still numerous and close, even though inevitably the kinship ties were weakening, as near relatives died and the links became more often between cousins than brothers and sisters.

Some other people travelled to the GDR on business or for pure tourism, while just a few went with a sense of moral duty to keep in touch with fellow-Germans deprived of their freedom. A middle-aged civil servant in Hamburg told me that he went at least once a year in this spirit and GDR citizens were now amongst his best friends. Indeed, East Germans would frequently stress to their Western friends and relatives, '*Please* don't leave us isolated, come and see us as often as you can, we're so grateful for it!' But usually they would ask not to be contacted via their place of work: those known to have too many

Western contacts could still find their children denied higher education, or be prevented from visiting the West on official delegations. Above all, anyone in any kind of official position in the GDR was formally classified as a *'Geheimnisträger'* (bearer of secrets) and was forbidden to have any dealings with the West, on pain of losing his job. This applied even to teachers and municipal employees. One senior journalist in Hamburg, originally from East Berlin, told me that his aged mother was still living there, also his brother, an executive in a State firm: 'He of course is a *Geheimnisträger* and mustn't see me: in fact his promotion has been blocked because of my very existence. When I go to stay with my mother, he parks his car two blocks away and comes to meet me there. He is sure that the Stasi are tailing him, but they don't seem to mind so long as he's discreet. That's the GDR for you.'

Restrictions on talking to foreigners were even tightened in 1979, under a law that made it illegal for anyone to pass information 'judged to be damaging to the Socialist State'. This hardly affected discreet conversations in private, but it did greatly limit the scope of Western journalists and television teams. And the reason for the new law was simple. Until 1979, West German TV and radio reporters would regularly do *vox pop* street interviews, and found that many people were prepared to take the risk of talking critically. So GDR screens tuned to the West were nightly full of citizens airing their grievances, thus making nonsense of the official line; moreover, people could see that their own complaints were widely shared. It is hardly surprising that the regime finally felt obliged to act. So life became harder for visiting journalists, and for the permanent correspondents whom most West German papers and networks kept in East Berlin. Officially they had to apply in advance to do any interview, however non-political: but the more canny ones dodged the rules by talking off-the-record in private with their own trusted contacts.

Another well-known hazard of travel in the GDR – the border controls at entry and departure – became less burdensome during the 1980s. The first time you entered at one of the *Autobahn* checkpoints it all looked pretty sinister – the guards with their sub-machine-guns, the successive barriers to be negotiated, the long queues of cars, the steely-faced *Beamte* scrutinising every passport. But after a second or third visit it began to seem routine. The officials were given orders to be courteous and would sometimes even smile; occasionally they would inexplicably search through your wallet, or scour the car from boot to bonnet, or ask probing questions about your trip and whom you planned to see, but this became rare. And the list of forbidden imports, headed by West German books and magazines, became more identifiable. But there could still be bureaucratic traps over visas, as Katinka and I discovered on more than one occasion: since my passport was British and hers West German, we faced different sets of rules. When in 1985 we wanted to extend our visa by one night, our East Berlin hotel fixed this for *me* on the spot, but told Katinka that *she* would have to leave for West Berlin by midnight and then re-enter. So I drove her to the Friedrichstrasse Bahnhof and then waited for what seemed like an eternity, suddenly loathing this police state with all my guts, while she went through the ludicrous process of checking out through one set of controls, walking across to the incoming platform, and then checking in through the other set where she managed to explain the situation, show her hotel booking, and get a new visa. These she achieved just in time, before midnight struck and the frontier closed for the night. The operation would have been far more hazardous, indeed impossible, a few years earlier: but by the 1980s GDR officialdom had at least become more reasonable in helping visitors to find a way through the maze of its bizarre rules. Nevertheless the little incident did give both of us, however irrationally, a Kafkaesque frisson of fear and hatred.

Travel possibilities from east to west were not improved at all for the average GDR citizen under the 1971–2 agreements, and people came to yearn for this freedom more keenly than for any other of the rights denied them. The right to leave the GDR was explicitly removed from the 1968 Constitution and was then graciously allowed only to certain categories. The most important was retired people (women over 60, men over 65), who were allowed to leave for up to sixty days a year: by 1985 some 1.5 million such visits were being made annually. So the GDR, as the joke went, was a rare country where you could look forward to growing old. Few of these travellers elected to stay in the West: if they did, the regime cared little for they had ceased to be useful. Every night at the Friedrichstrasse you could see them returning by the late trains from their day trips, clutching their bags of goodies given them by friends or relatives in West Berlin.

Younger people could get special permission to visit close relatives in the West for weddings, funerals and some other 'urgent family reasons'. But a married couple could not both go at the same time, and single men under 26 were generally barred. The other category allowed out was the trusted ones sent on official delegations – senior Party members, privileged businessmen and unionists, some youth groups, as well as sports teams, singers and other star performers who earned prestige and hard currency for the GDR. They were generally screened for their reliability. Party leaders' wives could go too, for shopping. In West Berlin, you sometimes saw their chauffeur-driven Volga limousines parked near the KaDeWe's luxury foodstore. Those debarred from such delights could go on holiday to other Soviet bloc countries – to the Black Sea, or to Hungary or Czechoslovakia (Poland became virtually out of bounds after Solidarity's rise). But most people took their annual holiday within the narrow confines of the GDR: some would rent a modest rural *dacha*, while the majority went to a hotel, camp or hostel organised by their workplace, on the Baltic or in the Harz or Thuringian hills. Often they had little choice where they were sent, for facilities were limited.

Poles, Hungarians and even Czechs were all much freer than East Germans to visit the West. The reasons were obvious: the GDR was the only Soviet bloc country with a sister nation along its border, sharing the same language, culture and history, and where some 30 per cent of its citizens still had relatives. And in the eyes of GDR rulers, West Germany exploited this kinship to exert 'intolerable pressures'. For domestic political reasons as well as sincere moral ones, successive governments in Bonn had not only refused to recognise the legitimacy of the East's regime, but had claimed to be the only rightful rulers of all Germany – to the extent that any GDR citizen would automatically be treated on arrival as a West German citizen, if he or she wished. A GDR émigré could obtain a passport within minutes of entering a police station, and would straightway be granted the full rights *and* duties of citizenship. What is more, there were no border controls of any kind on the Western side.

The GDR leaders were furious at this 'suborning' by a richer power. And they seemed to believe that, if the travel ban were lifted, it would lead to a new mass exodus. But Western journalists and others who questioned large numbers of GDR citizens gained the impression that only about one in ten would leave permanently for the West if they could: most realised that unemployment there was high. The main reason for wanting to travel – from this smallish country with few scenic wonders – was simply to take a look, say at Paris or the Alps, and then come back. Few could afford this: but even a visit to an aunt in Karlsruhe, and then a trip round the Black Forest, was better than nothing.

Finally in the mid-1980s, under pressure from inside and outside the

Party, the Politbüro did relax the ban further by granting permits more easily for visits for family occasions. It need no longer be a sister's funeral; an uncle's seventieth birthday would do. Whereas until 1985 only about 70,000 such trips were being made a year, by those under retirement age, in 1986 the figure rose dramatically to about 500,000, and was nearly a million in 1987. But the permits were still carefully controlled. A traveller could take only 15 Marks out of the country with him, so was entirely dependent on the largesse of his Western contacts. Young single people were generally refused permission. Husbands and wives were still not allowed to travel together, nor to bring their small children with them: this was to lessen the chances of defection. And the cleaner your political record the better. The regime seemed to be trying to use the visits as a means of rewarding those who worked hard and did not dissent. And the policy seemed to work to the extent that, until 1989, fewer than 0.5 per cent of those allowed out failed to return. Others were tempted, but were doubtless aware of the harm their defection would have caused to their families back home, and to the whole experiment – one young engineer had been told by his factory manager, 'If just one of those I approve for exit fails to return, I shall refuse permission for all employees.'

For the majority without relatives in the West, there were no such breaks. And the ban on travel became a cause of moans and complaints even within SED ranks. 'The leaders should trust the people more,' one senior loyalist told me; 'the claustrophobia leads to a national psychosis, affecting even workers and others who might not normally want to go abroad: but because they can't, they resent it.' And so, as memories of pre-Wall days receded, the GDR's population became steadily more isolated and provincial, more cut off from the world outside. Even educated people often struck me as being oddly naive, unable to make normal comparisons; and whenever I did meet someone fortunate enough to have travelled to the West, his relative sophistication and liveliness of mind made a bracing contrast. The others were merely wistful. I dined with a scientist whose requests to attend conferences in the West had always been turned down because he had a sister in Frankfurt. As we gazed down from our East Berlin rooftop restaurant, at the lights of the West a million miles away, he asked sadly, 'Is Frankfurt as bright as that?'

Some people took the desperate step of trying to escape physically across the border: but they were few, for the risk of death or capture was high. In 1970 about 1,000 succeeded, but by 1985 the annual figure was down to 160, of whom only six got away over the Berlin Wall. Estimates of failures varied, but some seventy people were thought to have been shot while trying to climb over the Wall, while those found moving towards the 'forbidden zone' along the West German border were generally arrested, tried and imprisoned. Some successful escapes across this border were made by swimming the Elbe, by hiding in barges, and in many other ways: in 1979 two families each with two children made their get-away by flying for twenty-five miles in a home-made hot-air balloon.

Less hazardous than a bolt across the border was the practice of escape via a third country, when on holiday or with some visiting delegation. Some 3,000 a year managed this with success. In Cologne I met a couple in their forties, both doctors, who had gone on holiday to Hungary with their son. There they found a West German lorry-driver prepared to stow them away with his goods, and he took them into Yugoslavia: but there the lorry was searched and they were arrested. Such incidents occurred often and the Yugoslav authorities were basically helpful: that is, they would send the refugees on to West Germany rather than back home to face imprisonment. But it could take time. The family I met spent three weeks in separate cells while their case was being sorted out, and were then allowed to travel to Cologne where they had friends and soon found suitable jobs. They had left the GDR, they said, 'because as known churchgoers our hospital careers were blocked and so was our son's education.'

In Karlsruhe I heard a remarkable saga from a young teacher:

As a schoolboy in Leipzig, I asked awkward questions in class, I even proclaimed my sympathy for Dubček, and so I fell into disgrace. I wanted to be an engineer, but instead they sent me to a teacher training college, where they hoped to stamp the nonsense out of me. By now I was toying with the idea of escape. So I kept quiet politically for a couple of years, and they thought they *had* converted me! I was musical, so I joined a folk-group as a guitarist, for I knew this might offer chances of foreign travel. My break came when the group was sent to sing political songs at a big left-wing rally in Milan. Of the ten of us, two were Stasi and they wouldn't let us out of their sight for an instant. But when I went to the loo I crawled through the back window, then made my way to the West German consulate which paid for me to join my sister in Karlsruhe, and here I've got a job as a teacher. The GDR authorities' reprisal was to remove my father from his job as manager of a factory and set him to be its night-watchman. But he doesn't blame me. He even admires my courage.

In 1984 a sudden vogue emerged for another attempted means of exit via third countries: sit-ins at West German embassies. The demonstrators hoped that they could thus cajole the Federal Government into granting them asylum and citizenship. In fact it is against international law for an embassy to abet this kind of venture: but as under West German law these refugees were its own citizens, Bonn felt obliged to help them, even at the risk of upsetting its new improved relations with Honecker. To the embarrassment of both sides, one of the first East Germans to try it on was none other than the niece of Willi Stoph, the GDR Prime Minister: in February 1984 she took refuge with her husband and two children in the embassy in Prague. After frantic behind-the-scenes negotiations, the family finally went back to East Berlin with a promise that they would be granted exit visas: this was honoured, and they left for Hamburg. But their success encouraged a flood of other attempts. During the next year over 200 East Germans 'occupied' Bonn's embassies in Prague, Warsaw, Budapest and Bucharest, and other groups did the same at the American embassy and the West German mission in East Berlin. Again there was much secret bargaining, and finally most of the asylum-seekers went back home with promises of visas for the West, granted by the GDR in return for large credits from Bonn – a typical example of the familiar German/German barter in human freedom against hard currency (see below). However, after one three-month squat by over 150 East Germans in the embassy in Prague, Bonn warned the GDR population via radio and television that it would no longer tolerate these sit-ins. They then ceased until 1989.

By the mid-1980s, authorised emigration by those who applied for an exit visa and finally got one had become much the commonest form of departure: five to ten times more people left that way than by illegal escape. The regime still refused to release those whom it considered valuable, such as scientists and key technicians: but, as we have seen in the case of some writers, it became readier to say goodbye to restive critics and malcontents whose presence disturbed morale. However, it did not want to encourage too many visa applications, so it harassed and even penalised those who dared to show ingratitude to the Socialist fatherland by asking to leave it. In many cases, the applicant would rapidly lose his job and possibly also be restricted to one part of the country, while his children would be discriminated against at school. Especially this happened if another member of the family had already left illegally for the West. Applicants might have to wait around for years in this state of disgrace, not knowing whether their visas would ever be granted: so only the really determined ever applied. Even so, the waiting-list rose to an estimated 500,000. About 15,000 to 20,000 a year were being let out: so, if the visas were granted in turn, the average delay would have been nearly fifty years and it would be more sensible to wait to become a pensioner and then go freely! But the system was more capricious than this. Many applications were shelved indefinitely, with no reasons given and no means of finding out the prospects. Others were accepted within a year or two.

During 1984 the gates were suddenly opened more widely, leading to a total exodus for the year of nearly 35,000. Had Honecker been smitten with the spirit of generosity? Probably not, for the flow later dropped back to nearer its normal level. Was he trying to get rid of more trouble-makers than usual? Unlikely. Soon, however, the most probable explanation emerged. The GDR in 1983 had successfully negotiated a 1 billion DM bank credit from the Kohl Government, and the unwritten *quid pro quo* was this 'special delivery' of emigrants. It was the largest of a number of secret deals of this kind in the 1980s, whereby the GDR traded these human concessions for the hard currency loans that it badly needed. Bonn would never admit publicly to these transactions: but the news leaked out, and the average 'ransom' was believed to be around 10,000 DM a head, with the tacit agreement on both sides that the trade would continue.

When the emigrants first arrived in the West they were usually delighted by their freedom, and amazed by a society where the shops were so full, the buildings so well cared for, and public debate so open. Many of them, the more resourceful or those with good qualifications or friends to help them, managed to adapt fairly easily. But others did not. Either they failed to find a suitable job or in other ways they became steadily disillusioned. Used to being cocooned, spoon-fed and herded together, they could not cope with having to fend for themselves, with the competitiveness and faster pace of life, with the sheer indifference of most people. A woman from Leipzig who had settled in Munich said to me, 'Here, if you paint yourself red, blue or green all over, no one will care or even notice. In the GDR you must first think carefully how red, blue or green would be interpreted.' And in Hamburg a lady running a charitable agency for émigrés commented: 'Some of them have been spoilt by Western TV and come with false ideas of our society. They expect to be supplied with a big flat, a regular job and plenty of money, and they have no idea how to freelance or fight for themselves to obtain these things. So they get disappointed.' Often they found that they were not always greeted with open arms by their fellow-Germans, who in a time of high unemployment had come to treat the newcomers warily – if not as resentfully as they treated Turks. An Allensbach poll in 1984 found 48 per cent of West Germans saying, 'They are also Germans and we should welcome them,' but 38 per cent thought they would only cause difficulties. Of course, some of the worst misfits were the kind who would be unhappy anywhere; a few turned to drugs or petty crime, especially in West Berlin. And each year some 1,500 went back to the GDR. This involved some risk, for they were likely to be put in some menial job, or to face worse penalties: far from welcoming these prodigal sons, or exploiting their return for propaganda, the regime preferred to punish them for their betrayal, so as to deter others from seeking to leave.

If the GDR rulers became resigned to a certain exodus of their citizens, at least they tried to strike a hard bargain over it: this was true especially of the notorious traffic in political prisoners, whose freedom was bought individually for cash, as with slaves in ancient days. In 1963 the GDR first suggested to the Federal Republic that it was prepared to sell prisoners: Bonn accepted, thus embarking on a trade that it discreetly labelled 'special humanitarian activities'. According to Amnesty International, in the later 1980s there were about 5,000 'political prisoners' in the GDR, some 70 per cent of whom had been arrested while trying to escape. Since 1963 they had been released to West Germany at the rate of about 1,000 a year, sometimes more, and Bonn was believed to have paid over 3 billion DM for them. The price for each was fixed individually, and the money had to be paid two weeks in advance into an East German account in Frankfurt. Then the ransomed convicts came out in buses, mostly from a prison at Karl-Marx-Stadt, and were taken to a camp at Giessen in Hessen to be de-briefed. The fees were kept secret: but it was believed that an artisan would cost about 30,000 DM, a junior teacher 50,000 DM, and a doctor or professor 200,000 or more, while 2.5 million DM is said to have been asked for one senior academic. And so keen was the regime on winning these funds that – or so Bonn officials said privately – it made efforts to ensure that its prisons were kept well stocked. At least, the number of political prisoners rose in the 1980s.

On the GDR side, the barter was conducted by the infamous Wolfgang Vogel, an urbane and cosmopolitan private lawyer in East Berlin whose Mercedes could sometimes be seen parked outside the Federal Government's office in West Berlin. It was he who also negotiated many of the high-level Soviet/American 'spy swaps'. He stated that by 1989 he had sold some 33,000 political prisoners, at an average price of 95,000 DM. When asked to justify this trade, he would advance the official GDR view that the money was needed, firstly to compensate the State for the 'damage' done to Socialism by their political actions, and secondly (the excuse given for the trade in ordinary emigrants too) to repay the money invested in their education. Meanwhile, the Federal Government too sometimes came in for criticism in the West for sharing in this traffic. Was it justified morally, some people asked, in lending itself as an accomplice to the GDR's breach of human rights? And ought it to encourage the export of the very people whose critical presence might help to liberalise the regime, if they stayed? Whatever the validity of these arguments, almost any Bonn politician would reply – correctly, in my view – that the cause of helping victimised fellow-Germans must come first.

## Inter-German relations: détente, but silly games with protocol

Despite these and other fundamental differences between the two regimes, the links between them grew steadily closer after the 1971–2 agreements, leading to a highly equivocal situation in the years before the Wall fell. These two halves of one nation, divided by a barrier of steel, did not formally recognise each other diplomatically, yet they negotiated constantly and traded intensively in all kinds of commerce; they were sworn ideological foes, yet despite the close frontier their human contacts and exchanges were closer, warmer and more numerous than between almost any other neighbouring states in Europe. How did they learn to live with these paradoxes?

West Germany, for its part, had long abandoned the Hallstein doctrine of the 1960s and had tacitly accepted that the GDR might be there to stay, so that a *modus vivendi* had better be reached. The East

German regime, on its side, had by now greatly modified the policy of *Abgrenzung*, or distancing itself from Bonn, which in response to Hallstein it had long pursued. After the arrival of *Ostpolitik*, it found that *Abgrenzung* no longer really worked, nor was it so necessary: so it decided to take the risk of rapprochement and to exploit this for its benefits, which were above all economic. Each side accepted that it needed each other, and at official level the contacts multiplied. Since Bonn still refused to accept the GDR's sovereignty, there could be no exchange of embassies: but after 1974 each state maintained a *Vertretung* (permanent mission) in the other's capital, staffed much like an embassy. And the diplomats and other officials enjoyed fairly affable relations, including discreet little lunches where they teased each other about the protocol absurdities dividing them. In Bonn, Chancellor Kohl had a grey telephone in his office with a direct line to Honecker. And although GDR leaders seldom visited West Germany, the traffic in the other direction grew remarkably. Franz Josef Strauss paid two private visits to Honecker in 1983–4, and from these was able to claim the political kudos for negotiating the loans that led to an increase in emigration.

The growth of economic links was illustrated by the fact that the level of trade between the two Germanies more than trebled from 1974 to 1989, to reach a total of 28 billion DM a year. West Germany supplied large quantities of half-finished goods and spare parts, and through a special credit system the GDR was able to avoid having to pay for them in hard currency. In turn it sold its neighbour a wide range of consumer goods such as clothing, shoes, toys, porcelain and electric motors. It also gained special free access to EC markets, for since Bonn refused to treat the border as a true frontier, it persuaded its eleven partners to affix a protocol to the Treaty of Rome, whereby its imports from the GDR escaped the normal EC tariffs. East Germany sought industrial investment and expertise from the West, and found several big firms ready to cooperate, including Siemens and Krupp. Above all, Volkswagen signed a contract for setting up a plant at Zwickau in Saxony that would make Polo cars, and Polo engines for GDR cars. The Soviet Union exerted pressure to avert the deal, for it did not want the GDR to become too dependent on Western technology. But this was one of the occasions where Honecker successfully defied Moscow.

West Germany became the GDR's biggest trading partner, after the Soviet Union. There were many reasons why its leaders came to set such store by the various economic links. They helped to reduce the GDR's large external debt and to modify its dependence on Comecon; above all they made it easier for Honecker to maintain a decent living standard for his people and thus limit restiveness. This was crucial for him. The Federal Republic, on the other hand, gained little from the exchanges in strictly economic terms. It saw them rather as a key weapon in its moral and humanitarian strategy – a means of exerting leverage over the GDR. Trading cash for human concessions was the name of the game: the secret *quid pro quo* for the 1983–4 loans included not only the release of more emigrants but an easing of travel formalities for pensioners and the dismantling of thousands of the deadly scatter guns along the border. All this was done.

So there was a fundamental gulf between the two sides' motives in seeking rapprochement. One Bonn official put it to me neatly: 'Each side propagates its separate fictions – the one, that Germany is really a single country, the other, that it is two distinct sovereign states, unconnected save by proximity. The GDR's central aim in rapprochement is to have this *status quo* recognised and confirmed; the Federal Republic's aim is to encourage a more fluid situation that might lead eventually, if not to reunification, at least to a kind of federalism based on a more liberal regime in the GDR. But the two paths are irreconcilable.'

The GDR's strategy was to thus manoeuvre Bonn into a *de facto* political recognition, and to make it be seen publicly to be treating it as an equal partner. This seemed to be making some progress. Meanwhile Bonn's attitude was highly equivocal, a kind of double act. Although it still held to the moral principle that the GDR regime had no legality, it also accepted pragmatically that the best way of helping the East Germans was by treating with the hated non-State across the border and wheedling concessions out of it. 'A more self-confident GDR Government, stronger both politically and economically, is in our interests,' said one Bonn official, 'for it will feel more secure and be readier to give its citizens more liberty' – a *volte face* from the Hallstein doctrine. This was roughly the Brandt and Schmidt approach and was followed by Kohl who in his own way made quite a contribution to *Ostpolitik*. But there were plenty of right-wingers who still thought it immoral to parley in a friendly way with a totalitarian regime that had been imposed on Germans against their will. And the majority of West Germans, while not going as far as this, none the less still believed that it would be wrong to extend full recognition to the regime. All

Allensbach polls of the pre-1989 period consistently showed between 70 and 76 per cent of the sample agreeing that the following clause should be retained in the Constitution: 'The entire German people are called upon to achieve in free self-determination the unity and freedom of Germany.' So these were the political realities of domestic opinion that guided the Federal Government in its difficult balancing-act. It infuriated the GDR rulers and was one cause of its tough stance on travel. And even in the West some felt it was time to recognise the GDR as a separate state.

Meanwhile both sides played absurd verbal games with each other, in the battles over protocol and status. While the GDR used its foreign ministry for dealing with West Germany, the latter conducted affairs through a special 'ministry for internal' (*not* 'inter') 'German relations'. Maps and atlases printed in West Germany showed the country as one, with the internal border hardly visible; weather reports on TV gave the same details about rain or shine in Dresden as in Stuttgart; and signposts in Hessen gave the distances to Eisenach or Leipzig. The GDR hit back in its own way. Its maps of East Berlin showed the western zone as a blank space, while bedside telephone listings in luxury hotels would tell you how to dial Oslo or Belgrade but not Frankfurt or Hamburg! The sharpest wrangle was over Berlin: the Allies with legal right on their side still refused to recognise East Berlin as the GDR's capital, so the regime retorted by downgrading West Berlin as much as it could. On the transit *Autobahnen* from the West to the big city, large signs gave the distance to 'Berlin, Hauptstadt der DDR', with just a small side-mention of 'Westberlin' (all one word). It would all have seemed terribly childish, were it not also so terribly significant.

Erich Honecker was keen to score the diplomatic triumph of an official visit to Bonn. He was born in Saarland, and no doubt was filled with an old man's desire to revisit the places of his youth; but the political motives were far stronger. Under pressure from Moscow, a planned visit in 1984 was abandoned. But he finally made it in September 1987, and was given a red-carpet welcome in Bonn, only a little below that normally reserved for Heads of State (he had thus more or less won the protocol battle surrounding his visit). He and Kohl agreed to cooperate more closely over technology and the environment, to develop youth exchanges and further ease travel, and to give their blessing to the town-twinnings (e.g. Rostock and Bremen) that had begun to emerge. Honecker at one point spoke of the need for a more friendly border'. But in another breath he stated publicly that

'Socialism and capitalism cannot any more be united than fire and water'. In other words, his basic position had not changed.

Right up until 1989, reunification of Germany still seemed out of the question. There had been much talk about it in the years before the building of the Wall, and even after this the goal of a reunited Germany remained a kind of official myth in the Federal Republic. But it was believed that the Soviet Union would never allow it, while the Western Allies did not want it either: everyone remembered François Mauriac's often-quoted remark of the 1950s, 'I love Germany so much that I am glad there are two of them.' Even in West Germany, people were losing interest. When the Allensbach institute asked, 'What do you think is the most important problem facing Germany today?, in 1959 far more of the sample (45 per cent) quoted reunification than any other topic. By 1980 those figures had changed dramatically: the economy came first with 86 per cent, peace and détente second with 33 per cent, while *less than one per cent* cited reunification. A few people still believed that it might happen slowly by osmosis: but many more expected that it would steadily become less likely, as the ties of kinship loosened and each state went its separate way. It was older rather than younger people who went to visit relatives in the East: newer generations felt much less personal concern.

And so matters might have remained, for many more years, had not Gorbachev begun to promote *glasnost* and *perestroika* in the Soviet Union, and had not the Poles and Hungarians taken this as their cue for moves towards democracy. Honecker grew alarmed. The East German leaders had always held up the Soviet Union as a model, to their own people, and they depended on it: but now it was proving subversive. So they even banned the sale of some German-language editions of Soviet publications. Honecker refused to follow Gorbachev's *perestroika* policy: when asked about this in public, he explained that East Germany with its successful economy did not have the same problems as the Soviet Union, thus implying that it did not require the same treatment.

Meanwhile, during the 1980s, the leaders continued their policy of trying to build up a real GDR national identity, with the dual aim of impressing world opinion and of creating a focus of loyalty for their own people. For this they utilised culture and history, as well as sport. By teaching the great German classics in schools, by expensively restoring some historic buildings, they sought to encourage citizens to feel proud of belonging to this heritage – and fairly so, for towns such as Leipzig and Weimar, so closely linked with Bach, Goethe and others, lay in the heartland of German culture. As for history, Party ideologists sought to stress that the GDR emanated from the age-old peasant and worker traditions of the German nation, with its roots in the peasant revolts of the Middle Ages, the 1848 uprisings, and of course the teachings of Marx and Engels. More surprisingly, the Party even began to rehabilitate aspects of the old Prussian past that had no such leftish credentials. The statue of Frederick the Great was restored to its old place on the Unter den Linden in Berlin, after having been removed and hidden by Ulbricht; and Luther came back into favour, as we have seen. And whereas Frederick the Great and Bismarck had for years been officially denounced as 'forerunners of Hitler', in 1985 the GDR published an intelligent biography of the Iron Chancellor, written by a Marxist historian, that stressed his 'progressive historical role' and his work in founding Germany's social welfare system.

How far the regime succeeded in imbuing its citizens with any sense of national pride and identity was not easy to assess. They remained very aware of their Germanness, and they sedulously kept up many of the old customs and traditions – for example, the custom of providing a child on his first day in school with the comforting gift of a *Schultüte*, a decorated conical bag filled with sweets and toys. They lived in a land where, despite political revolution, life-styles remained in some ways closer to the old leisurely Germany of the 1920s than they did in West Germany, far more touched by modernism. Their isolation tended to reinforce this provincial, old-fashioned flavour of life. But whether they took pride in belonging to the GDR as a nation was less certain. Through nightly television, through their yearnings and curiosity about a world forbidden them, they remained far more aware of West Germany, and of their national affinity with it, than West Germans felt with regard to them.

In their basic strategy of holding on to power at all costs, the GDR leaders saw the strengthening of the economy as a crucial element. It was important for the country's world position, also for keeping up living standards and thus reducing the risks of unrest. And for twenty-five years the economy had outwardly done rather well, in East European terms. Helped by German industrial flair, it had a good record of engineering exports to the rest of the Soviet bloc, a healthy trade balance, and a farming system that was fairly efficient. The figures looked quite good, and citizens had a tolerable standard of living, if the consumer shortages were discounted. But there were serious underlying weaknesses. The system only worked because of its captive eastern market, the high level of tacit aid from West Germany, and the massive level of artificial subsidies; and progress was only achieved by severe neglect of investment in some key sectors – infrastructure, environment, housing, telephones, and so on.

More important, the industrial base was becoming increasingly fragile, for the leaders had not had either the hard currency or the wisdom to invest adequately in the new technologies, or to renew outdated equipment. And this was beginning to tell. From the 1960s, like the rest of Eastern Europe, the GDR had failed to follow the capitalist West in the big leap forward into a new high-tech era, and so it was living on borrowed time. It was hampered, it is true, by the US-led Cocom ban on the export to the East of certain 'strategic' materials, and by the lack of money for buying Western know-how: but it was also severely held back by its own managerial attitudes. Factory managers were aware of the situation, but they lacked the courage or initiative to explain it to their political bosses and get them to act; the planning bureaucracy was too inert and heavy to be able to cope with the vast shake-up that would be needed, to introduce the new technologies into the production process. One expert suggested to me: 'The structure is just not geared to the kind of risk-taking and incentive motivation that these new innovative industries need. The top jobs are held down by mediocre Party apparatchiks who fear they would be shown up as inadequate, maybe replaced, if the system were changed. So they favour the *status quo*, and they have the numbers and influence to ensure that it is kept.'

Thus, after November 1989, once its subsidies and protected markets had been removed, the GDR's industry just crumbled – more rapidly and completely than even the experts had expected. The GDR's vaunted 'economic miracle' was revealed as a bit of a sham. And, once the borders were opened, the political apparatus of the regime collapsed even more quickly. It had been held together by the secret police, by a core of Party devotees and time-servers, by public acquiescence – and by the threat, now removed, of Soviet armed intervention. Once true unrest began, the Party lacked the moral resources even to put up a fight. Forty years of artificial nationhood went down the drain.

# 8

## THE NEW EAST GERMANY, FREE BUT ANXIOUS

The period of gentle revolution that the Germans discreetly call *die Wende* ('the change') lasted from autumn 1989 until the first free elections of March 1990. While Poland and Hungary were steadily throwing off Communism, East Germany remained outwardly unchanged until the late summer of 1989: it was still an orthodox Leninist state, unwilling to flirt with Gorbachev's reformist ideas. Within the Party, some debate was at last developing, as younger activists and intellectuals began to contest the rigid Honecker line: but this was never reflected in public, and there was still no organised political opposition, of the kind that had played so powerful a role in Poland. Most ordinary people remained passively acquiescent, enjoying in private their modest prosperity, still obeying their tacit pact with the regime not to rock the boat. They could see from television what was happening in Poland and Hungary: but they stayed quiet, and the informers of the secret police were still ubiquitous, as everyone knew.

Those who could not stand the regime any longer preferred to vote with their feet, by moving to the West. They applied to emigrate legally, or they escaped illegally via a third country, or they got themselves deported as 'troublemakers'. Sometimes a demonstrator arrested by the police would be offered the choice between a prison sentence and immediate exile, and of course he took the latter. Many of those leaving had lost hope of the regime's improving: some in industrial jobs knew how grave the economic situation really was. The exodus increased greatly during the late summer, and it was this pressure which set in motion the downfall of the regime — more than the street protests, which came later.

The earlier easing of travel restrictions had simply whetted appetites, for more people had now seen for themselves what the west had to offer. In May, the liberal Hungarian government partly dismantled its fortified border with Austria, so a number of East Germans smartly marked down Hungary for their summer holiday, and by the end of August some 6,000 had made their escape that way. At the same time the sit-ins outside West German embassies began again, on a large scale, in Budapest, Bucharest, Prague and Warsaw. Then in September Hungary fully opened its Austrian border and allowed East Germans to cross it freely without visas, in breach of its treaty obligations with the GDR. The West German, Hungarian and Austrian governments concerted their help for the refugees, by setting up special transit camps; and so the columns of Trabis and Wartburgs, full of mainly young families, nervously exuberant, trundled down the Danube valley to Bavaria and freedom. Some 25,000 people, who had come to Hungary on holiday, left that way. The GDR government protested sharply to Budapest, but in vain. It banned further travel to Hungary, but this was too late. And it seemed almost paralysed by the trend of events. Curiously, it even increased the granting of legal emigration permits during 1989, as if by letting the malcontents go it could ease the situation. Of the 130,000 people who left in the first nine months of 1989, far more than in any previous year since 1961, about half went legally.

The Bonn government, too, was concerned at the scale of the exodus. 'We don't want reunification happening on West German soil, by the whole GDR population moving here,' said one senior official with a touch of hyperbole. Bonn was worried about the likely impact on housing and social services, and on a public opinion already restive about the mass arrival of other newcomers. It was not so concerned about the effect on unemployment, for the economy was now booming, there were even shortages of skilled labour, and nearly all of these GDR refugees would find jobs. Many who left illegally were technicians, skilled workers, managers and doctors, just the people the GDR could ill afford to lose (some hospitals were becoming severely understaffed).

As the restiveness grew, and as the regime seemed to be weakening, so in late September the street demonstrations began. One or two small opposition groups had just been formed — notably Neues Forum, led by the painter Bärbel Bohley and Professor Jens Reich, a biologist, who said, 'We have been silent and tolerant for too long.' These groups were made up quite largely of intellectuals, including many pastors – people with left-of-centre views who did not want to destroy the GDR but to push it to reform, and to create a better kind of socialism. They began to hold weekly discussion meetings in churches, where they were relatively safe from the police. At first they were reluctant to take the risk of letting the meetings spill out into the streets. But, pushed on by their swiftly growing crowds of supporters, they became bolder. And so, after one regular Monday meeting in the Thomaskirche in Leipzig, on September 25, some 8,000 people, most of them young, marched through the streets chanting 'We shall overcome' and holding lighted candles as symbols of non-violence. Thus Leipzig became the foyer of the 'revolution'. Its inhabitants had been especially incensed by the blatant rigging of the local elections in May, and by the way that the regime had long neglected this great city, in favour of East Berlin.

The demonstrations rapidly grew in size, in several cities. The protesters saw that non-Communist governments were being formed in Poland and Hungary, and the Soviet Union was not intervening. This made them bolder. Many pinned their hopes on Gorbachev who – ironically – visited East Berlin on October 7 as a guest at the GDR's official birthday celebrations. The crowds that were dutifully lined up to cheer Honecker began joyously chanting 'Gorby! Gorby!' instead. That night, thousands of demonstrators took to the streets of the capital, and the police beat some of them up and made arrests; there were clashes in other towns, too. In a remarkable statement made public by his own press officer, Gorbachev that day warned Honecker: 'Those who delay are punished by life itself.' But the GDR's leader was too old, and too sick, to be able to adapt to the new situation, which it seems he barely comprehended. He and the rest of the Politbüro, most of them also elderly, lived and worked in the seclusion of their compound outside Berlin, and were largely isolated from the real mood of the country: unpleasant truths were hidden from them by frightened officials. Honecker seemed like a King Canute telling the east European tide to flow back.

Now that the Soviet Union would no longer help him, Honecker could hardly crush the unrest by taking violent and forceful measures, as he might have liked. But at one point he came within an inch of staging a crackdown. Just before the Monday rally of October 9 in Leipzig, the city was filled with rumours – later proved true – that Honecker had given orders for force to be used, and that the army and police had been issued with live ammunition and the hospitals told to expect casualties. But at the last minute local Party leaders, and Leipzig's renowned conductor, Kurt Masur, pleaded with the officers to use restraint and the orders were not carried through. In the event, the huge demonstration of 100,000 people passed off peacefully. Thus narrowly the GDR was spared a massacre that would certainly have had appalling consequences.

This incident marked a turning point. As word of it spread around the GDR, the protesters took heart in many cities, and their rallies grew even bigger. They were calling for a radical reform of the system, and the resignation of the old guard. And the refugee exodus continued, too. Barred now from Hungary, the fugitives turned to Czechoslovakia, and to Poland which some of them reached by swimming across the Oder. The Czech Communist authorities were less helpful to them than the Hungarians had been, and soon the GDR closed that border too. But this did not prevent thousands from besieging Bonn's embassies, demanding safe passage to the West. By mid-October some 4,500 were squatting in the grounds of the West German embassy in Prague, a handsome eighteenth-century palace turned refugee camp, and another 1,400 were in Warsaw. The GDR regime felt it had no alternative but to arrange with the Czech, Polish and West German governments for their transfer; special sealed trains were laid on, which carried some 12,000 of them to the West. It was an amazing episode.

In face of a rapidly worsening situation, many senior people in the Party were now pressing for reforms to be made, and for a change of leadership at the top. Finally on October 18 the Politbüro voted for Honecker's resignation, and he went. He was replaced by the devious Egon Krenz, who had hitherto been a hardliner but now at least had the realism to see that the promise of reform was necessary. He began talks with Neues Forum and Church leaders, he purged a few elderly Stalinists from the Politbüro, and he went to Moscow where he publicly pledged support for *perestroika*. But the people remained unconvinced by Krenz's change of tactic, and their demonstrations grew yet larger and their slogans more radical. They knew that they held the initiative. Some 500,000 marched in Leipzig on October 30, and again on November 6, amid cries of 'free elections!' Another half million were demonstrating in East Berlin itself.

Events now moved fast, as Czechoslovakia opened its borders to the West and 30,000 East Germans there poured out. The GDR government was in panic. On November 6 it announced a further easing of travel restrictions: all would now have a right to go abroad for thirty days each year, but they would still need exit visas and these could still be denied, for such reasons as 'public security'. Then on November 7 the Government of Willi Stoph resigned, and he was succeeded as prime minister by Hans Modrow, an SED leader of known liberal views who had been waiting in the wings. But his arrival was too late to save the regime. At this point, the use of force to crush the unrest was again narrowly averted. On November 7 the Politbüro had rejected by one vote a proposal to put the army on the streets: but the next day some senior officers with hardline views put troops and tanks on full alert and issued live ammunition. The coup was only called off because the officers were not sure that the conscripts would obey orders. On November 8 the Politbüro was reshuffled, and a spokesman said that it was 'working on electoral reform' that could theoretically lead to the Party losing power. The protesters now had the full initiative, and it seemed that they only had to demand a concession for it to be granted.

Then on the evening of Thursday, November 9 there occurred the single most spectacular event in post-war European history. Almost casually, at the end of a press conference, the Politbüro's propaganda chief, Günther Schabowski, announced that all citizens were from now on free to travel across any border checkpoints. The Iron Curtain was in effect no more.

At first people could hardly believe it. But that same night some thousands began to visit West Berlin, where they were greeted joyously amid scenes of high emotion (see p. 49). They were supposed still to need exit visas, now obtainable on demand at any police station: but that night they were just waved through by the dazed border guards, who joked cheerfully with those they would have had to shoot a few hours earlier. That first weekend, some four million East Germans went on visits to the West – not only to Berlin but across all the western border, to nearby towns like Hamburg and Kassel, and to smaller places which they packed out with their little cars and special bus-loads. They did some modest shopping, they visited friends and relatives, or they simply savoured the new sensation of being no longer cooped up. And almost all of them came straight back. So at first the regime thought that its gamble in opening the border had paid off, and that people would no longer try to emigrate, if they saw that they could now come and go as they wished. But this hope was short-lived, for the real emigration went on at the same rate as before, mainly now for economic reasons. By now some 200,000 had left during 1989, about half of them illegally.

The Modrow Government and the new, reformed Politbüro now promised sweeping reforms. Schabowski spoke of free elections and 'pluralism'; promises were made to disband the Stasi; Krenz pledged that reports of corruption by the old guard would be investigated; some senior hardliners were expelled from the Party while others resigned from their posts, all over the GDR. The opening of the borders had altered still further the balance of power between the people and the regime; and now, with democracy clearly on the way, all officialdom suddenly began talking a different language. The State media had already grown more outspoken in October (see p. 485), and now it became more so. This official ADN news agency spoke not of 'fascist provocation' but of 'a revolutionary people's movement . . . the GDR is awakening'. Party functionaries, senior bureaucrats, academics and others declared openly that they welcomed the changes, and talked as if they had been true democrats at heart all along. Some were probably sincere, having been forced to lie or keep silent for so long; others simply turned their coats as quickly as they could. 'They have seen the writing on the Wall,' joked one sceptic.

It has to be asked how it was that the best-organised regime in the Communist bloc, the most tightly policed outside Romania, and one that seemed economically to be doing quite well, should have crumbled so suddenly, almost without a fight. It was victim in part of its artificiality, being not a real state like Poland, but just an ideology held up by Soviet arms; bred of the Cold War, it would now perish with the Cold War. Moreover, some senior Party people were aware of the real dire state of the economy, and of how hard the future was going to be. Morale was low. As one still bemused opposition leader remarked in December to Mark Frankland of the *Observer*, 'Was it really because citizens took peacefully to the streets, and lit rows of tiny candles, that the regime collapsed? Had we known that its moral disintegration was so far advanced, we would have done it sooner.'

That was the heart of the matter. The regime by now was cynical and corrupt, and had lost sight of its original vision; it was fatally weakened from within. A core of idealists still believed in socialism, but few of them believed in the Party or Government that were supposed to be carrying it out: yet they did not have the power or courage to change things. Honecker had only partly understood the people's real needs and was not capable himself of making democratic reform: he did not believe in it. By the time others took his place, the regime was beyond saving. By a miracle it had been a very gentle revolution, the first non-violent one in German history, achieved virtually without leaders. With hindsight, one can now see why it was all so easy.

The SED now tried to salvage what it could. In early December, Krenz was forced to resign as Party leader and head of state. The SED held an emergency congress, purged many of its hardliners, changed its name to the Partei des Demokratischen Sozialismus (PDS), and elected a new leader, Gregor Gysi, aged only 41, a clever and charming lawyer of liberal views who had previously defended several dissidents. The Party also formally gave up its constitutional right to a monopoly of power. But these moves to remodel itself did not prevent a steady erosion of its membership, from 2.3 million down to about 500,000. Also in December, under Modrow's impetus, Honecker was arrested on corruption charges, the militia groups were abolished, and the slower process of disbanding the Stasi went ahead. 'Round table' talks began between the PDS, its 'front' parties, and the new opposition groups such as Neues Forum, with a view to preparing free elections, at first scheduled for May.

The public's initial euphoria, in the first weeks after the fall of the Berlin Wall, changed before long to a mood of anger and bitterness against the old regime, and even against themselves for having put up with it. 'Why were we lied to for so long?' 'Why have we wasted all these years?' were remarks often heard. And this feeling increased as details came out of the extent of the pollution, the true state of industry, the Stasi brutalities, and the corruption of Honecker and his clique — all worse than had been thought. The liberated state television showed pictures of the former leaders' luxurious hideouts and Honecker's smart hunting-lodge (see p. 437). And the Stasi operation, with 85,000 full-time staff, was shown to be on a much larger scale than supposed (see p. 437). Citizen groups broke into Stasi offices and tried to seize files. Some physical attacks were made on Stasi officers or other known hardliners, and this raised fears that mob justice and revenge might develop. But happily this kind of violence remained limited.

A more important change in the public mood in December, and one that was to have a huge impact on the future of all Germany, was that the main thrust of the demonstrators' demands, in the big rallies that still continued, shifted from reforming the GDR to getting rid of it altogether, via unification. The masses now took over from the intellectuals. The initial leaders of these rallies had been mainly middle-class people, educated and thoughtful, who rather than try to emigrate had stayed on in the GDR in the hope of helping to create a better Socialism; they believed in a 'third way' between Communism and capitalism, they felt that some GDR values were worth preserving, and they certainly did not want unification with the West. But they were not very representative. And gradually a gulf developed between these intellectuals and the mass of ordinary people, who wanted Western life-styles and quick. The rallies became more working-class. By early December, the protesters' initial stirring battlecry of '*Wir sind DAS Volk*' ('we are *the* people') began to change, significantly, to '*Wir sind EIN Volk*' ('we are *one* people'), as banners and slogans proclaimed '*Ein Vaterland!*' Chancellor Kohl himself played up to this new mood, when he paid his first visit to the GDR on December 19, and told a huge crowd in Dresden: 'My goal remains the unity of our nation . . . God bless our German fatherland.' He was answered with wild cheers, cries of '*Deutschland, ein Vaterland!*' and a sea of West German flags.

There were those, notably foreign observers, who saw in the cries of '*ein Volk*' a sinister echo of pre-war Nazi rallies. But this was not a real parallel. It is true that some extreme-right elements from the West had by now infiltrated the rallies, and were becoming highly vocal. But ordinary East Germans were impelled far less by crude nationalism than by simple materialism. They had now been to the West, they had seen for themselves its glowing prosperity, its neat efficiency — and they wanted the same. Nor did they trust Modrow's restyled PDS, or Neues Forum's 'third way', to give it to them. 'Socialism has not delivered what it promised, and nor will this "new socialism",' proclaimed one worker at a Leipzig rally; 'we are not guinea pigs.' And an elderly man said, 'This experiment has failed, we don't want to be experimented with again. Why this insistence that we should go our own special way, and not the normal way?'[1] Most people believed that only unification could bring them the life-styles that they wanted; they were Germans, keen to have their share of the new successful Germany. But they were not prompted solely by materialism. They wanted also to share in West Germany's democracy, its free press, its rule of law, its federal system — everything that worked well there.

The Neues Forum supporters were somewhat bitter. 'Of course we feel betrayed,' said one of their leaders; 'we were out there demonstrating, risking arrest or even being shot, and now we are shouted down

---

1. Remarks reported at the time by Timothy Garton Ash, and by Mark Frankland of the *Observer*.

for suggesting that quick unification might not be the best solution. People imagine it will be the answer to all their dreams, but of course it won't.' This feeling was understandable. The crowds now safely clamouring for unity were those who had passively acquiesced in the regime all those years, not the ones who had dared to criticise. But this was not the first time that a revolution had devoured its own children. The leaders of Neues Forum lacked political experience, inevitably, and they were out of touch with popular feeling. However generous their ideas of a 'third way', they proposed only the vaguest of economic blueprints. The videos and BMWs of the West seemed to offer a much more plausible path to paradise.

By February the polls were showing 75 per cent in favour of swift unification. The much-respected Hans Modrow had now formed a coalition Government, and was doing as good a job as he could: but he had no real mandate, and the old administration had virtually collapsed. The SED still held all the trappings of power, but had lost its authority: so there was a power vacuum. Meanwhile the economic situation was worsening, as protected markets were lost and the exodus of key personnel continued faster than ever. Despite the drastic changes, many professional people still had little faith in the GDR's uncertain future, and they saw that an economically grim period lay ahead. So they left. While a total of 350,000 had emigrated in 1989, now in early 1990 the rate was even faster, some 2,000 a day. Between October and February, nearly 9,000 doctors and nurses had left, and some hospital departments were having to close; many factories were in a similar state. It was clear that only a democratically elected government had a chance of stopping the rot and creating confidence; and Bonn, while ready to start pumping in aid, refused to do so until free elections were held. So, in face of this crisis, the election date was advanced to March 18.

With the exception of the PDS and small local groups such as Neues Forum, all the main parties contesting these elections were carbon copies of their Western counterparts. A social democratic party had been formed just before the *Wende*, and it now merged completely with the West's SPD. Much the same happened with the FDP. For the Christian Democrats matters were more complicated, since the East's CDU had been a 'front' party of the SED and was thoroughly tainted. But it now managed to revamp itself and bring in new leaders, notably Lothar de Mazière, a liberal lawyer; it allied itself closely with Kohl's CDU, but without yet merging totally. The election campaign, as it got under way, was totally orchestrated by the Western parties. The star speakers at the election rallies were Kohl, Brandt and Genscher, not de Mazière or other local leaders; and this led to the first taunts, in some circles, of a 'Western takeover'. But what else could have been expected? These were the first free elections in this part of Germany since 1933, and only a few greybeards had any experience of democracy. Inevitably people turned to the West.

The campaign passed off smoothly and fairly. At first the SPD seemed likely to win, according to the opinion polls; it too favoured unification, but at a gentler rate than the CDU was proposing. In the event, the CDU and its allies won easily, with 48.1 per cent of the votes, while the SPD took only 21.8 per cent and the FPD 5.2 per cent. Voters had been impressed by Kohl's promises of swift and easy unity, and clearly they felt that his party, so closely allied to the big banks and industry, was the best placed to help them economically. The PDS scored 16.3 per cent, creditable in the circumstances; its vote reached 30 per cent in East Berlin, where huge numbers of civil servants feared that unification would cost them their jobs. Bündnis 90 (Alliance 90), comprising Neues Forum and some similar groups, won less than 3 per cent.

With de Mazière as prime minister, the CDU now formed a coalition Government. Its defence minister, Rainer Eppelmann, was a pastor and pacifist who had been imprisoned under the old regime for opposing Soviet nuclear missiles: now he was in charge of the armed forces of a country still in the Warsaw Pact! Another irony: the main task of de Mazière's government would be to prepare for its own disappearance, for the election results had given a clear mandate for the two Germanies to negotiate unification, with each other and with the four Allied Powers. This they began to do. The task of renewing the East's economy, and of privatising its industry, also now went ahead in earnest, and was masterminded from Bonn, with de Mazière as little more than a puppet obeying orders. One of the most urgent priorities was to stem the emigration, which had reached 144,000 since January 1. Since these migrants were now moving west for purely economic reasons, and not political ones, Bonn decided to abolish the special social benefits and subsidies that had always been granted to refugees from the GDR. This step, plus the election results, did have some effect, and the exodus slowed down.

In May, municipal elections were held and the CDU again did well, though the SPD won in East Berlin and Leipzig. Most of the new mayors were local people, but some were brought in from the west –

for example in Leipzig, where the mayor had held a senior post in the *Rathaus* of its twin-town, Hanover.

The next hurdle was to create currency union between the two Germanies, which Bonn argued was essential as a basis for economic recovery. Kohl promised publicly – and rashly, as it later turned out – that 'no one will be worse off' as a result of this union. All Ostmarks were now to be turned into Deutschmarks – but at what rate? Kohl proposed 1–1, which was generous to the East, seeing that the black market rate was 5–1 or more. The prudent Bundesbank argued that 1–1 might be inflationary, and wanted 2–1; it stressed that while 1–1 would be nice for individuals in the East, it might hamper outside investment as firms would become overpriced. But Kohl had the last word. And so on July 1 the Deutschmark took over in the East and the feeble Ostmark disappeared, its flimsy aluminium coins now useful only for a few slot-machines. All border controls now vanished, the Bundesbank imported 20 billion DM in notes and coins, and parties were held for 'dancing into the Deutschmark'. It was a Sunday, and the Deutsche Bank's big new branch on the Alexanderplatz opened specially, for people to change their money: some 10,000 customers besieged the building, and thirteen were injured in the scuffle.

The shops instantly filled up with Western goods of all sorts. And people found that many of them were much cheaper, as well as better in quality, than similar GDR goods had been before. They could now buy a Western TV set for 1,000 DM, whereas a GDR one cost 6,000 Ostmarks; stylish Western shoes cost maybe as little as 80 to 100 DM, against 150 Ostmarks for an inferior GDR pair; and while a new Trabant was 10,000 Ostmark, you could pick up a far superior second-hand BMW for as little as 4,000 DM. Of course this was damaging to the East's factories, whose sales quickly slumped. Many people splashed out on Western second-hand cars, new videos or furniture. But the initial spending spree soon subsided and was not as great as feared. For one thing, only the first 4,000 Marks of each individual's savings could be exchanged at 1–1, while for the rest it was 2–1.

For a number of reasons both political and economic, Kohl was anxious to press ahead with full unification as fast as possible. First a Treaty of Unity was drawn up between the two German Governments, and the formal approval of the four Allied Powers was obtained. Then lastly the East German Parliament voted to accede to the Federal Republic, under Article 23 of the latter's constitution. It all went smoothly, and the two Germanies were formally united at midnight on

October 2/3, when President von Weizsäcker and Chancellor Kohl came to Berlin for a great celebratory party at the Brandenburg Gate. But not everyone took part in the nationwide rejoicing. Many pastors in the east refused to join in the ringing of church bells. And all over Germany people on the left were annoyed that Kohl seemed to be exploiting unification as his own personal triumph, for electoral purposes.

On October 14 the voters in the east were called to the polls for the third time in seven months, for *Land* elections. The GDR regime had abolished the old *Länder*, but these were now reconstituted – five in number, with the new united Berlin forming a sixth – and each was to have a semi-autonomous government, as in the west. Again the CDU did well, scoring 42 per cent, against 27 for the SDP and 12 for the PDS. But Kohl no longer had such an easy ride. Unemployment was now rising fast, as the east's antiquated factories began to close, and the earlier mood of delight at unification was turning to one of anxiety. Kohl was heckled at some meetings, and was obliged to warn the people of sacrifices ahead. But basically he was still trusted to carry through his promises of economic recovery. According to an opinion survey at that time, 67 per cent of people blamed their present troubles on the legacy of forty years of communism, and only 5 per cent put the blame on the Federal Government.

The first pan-German elections for the Bundestag were held on December 2. The CDU and its coalition partners, CSU and FDP, scored a fairly easy victory, doing even better in the east than in the west. The percentage results are shown in the table (in brackets, the figures for 1987 in the west, for March 1990 in the east):

|                   | National % | (seats) | West %      | East %      |
|-------------------|------------|---------|-------------|-------------|
| CDU               | 36.7       | 268     | 35.9 (37.0) | 43.4 (42.7) |
| CSU (DSU in east) | 7.1        | 51      | 9.1 (9.8)   | 1.0 (6.6)   |
| FDP               | 11.0       | 79      | 10.6 (9.1)  | 13.4 (5.6)  |
| SPD               | 33.5       | 239     | 35.9 (37.0) | 23.6 (20.8) |
| PDS               | 2.4        | 17      | 0.3 (–)     | 9.9 (16.3)  |
| Alliance 90/Greens| 1.2        | 8       | –           | 5.9 (2.9)   |
| Greens            | 3.9        | –       | 4.7 (8.3)   | –           |
| Republicans       | 2.1        |         | 2.3 (–)     | 1.3 (–)     |

Several points emerged from these results in the east. First, the continued erosion of the PDS vote. Second, the very poor showing of the Republikaner, which allayed fears of an extreme-right resurgence. Third, the improved score for Neues Forum's alliance, thanks largely to its electoral entente with the Greens. Fourth, the sharp rise of the FDP. This was due in part to the popularity of Hans Dietrich Genscher, who was seen as a prime architect of unification: he had been born at Halle in Saxony-Anhalt, where the FDP vote reached 19.7 per cent. And some people, women especially, voted FDP because they hoped that its more liberal stance on certain social matters, notably abortion, might exert influence on the CDU. Fifth and last, the turnout in the east was only 74 per cent, compared with a remarkable 93 per cent in March. Perhaps this reflected a fatigue at having to vote for the fourth time in 1990. Or even, in some cases, a certain disillusion with the democratic process, which was slow in producing the hoped-for economic results.

During the winter the mood grew worse and unrest began. By mid-January unemployment had reached 27 per cent (including the euphemistically styled 'nil-hours short-time work', see p. 457), and this in a land where people had no experience of being out of work. The renewal of the economy was proving much harder and slower than expected. The factories had now lost their old state subsidies and their guaranteed east European markets, and were finding it hard to sell their second-rate goods within the new open German market; many were unable to find buyers, and were being closed down by the official agency now in charge of privatisation, the Treuhandanstalt. And new investment from the west was coming in much slower than anticipated, deterred by the claims on property and other factors (see pp. 451–3).

'Many people had naively expected wealth to flow automatically after currency union, and now they're disillusioned,' said one observer. They had voted again for Kohl in December because he still seemed to offer the best hope, and in their mass they did not regret unification: but they were worried about the turn it was taking. And so in March the demonstrations began again, this time not *for* Kohl as a year or so earlier, but *against* him. Some 60,000 marched in Leipzig on March 21, and 80,000 a week later. The protesters demanded better retraining and job creation schemes, more favourable conditions for investors, an end to the policy of factory closures. People's anxieties were understandable. But in some ways they seemed to be over-reacting, for in fact their standard of living had not yet suffered. Although wages were still only one-third to one-half of western levels, people had benefited from the

1–1 conversion rate, and rents and some other basic necessities were still far cheaper than in the west. Those out of work received fairly generous benefits, paid for by Bonn. But they were aware that these gigantic sums of money could have been better spent on investment and job creation.

'Bonn does not understand our problems', 'Bonn is not doing enough to help us', became common complaints. This was not quite fair, for Bonn was doing a lot, and at great expense. But clearly the Government had seriously miscalculated the difficulties and the cost of renewing the east's economy. Kohl's promises in the spring of 1990, that no one would be made worse off by unification, now rang hollow. Why had he made them? Was it a reckless election pledge that he knew he could not honour? Or had he been misadvised by his experts who had underestimated the problems? Probably mainly the latter, but a bit of the former too. And yet, the arguments for going ahead fast with unification, rather than slower, still held good. No other policy had been possible, and the traumas that went with it were inevitable. The task of converting a rickety command economy to a dynamic free market system was bound to be horrendous. But all this should have been foreseen more clearly, and explained in advance more frankly.

The practical economic problems were compounded by the psychological difficulties of east Germans in coming to terms with their past and adapting to Western ways and Western values. This too was inevitable, and as much as the economic crisis it coloured the mood in the east during 1990–91.

## A traumatic adaptation to the West

After the initial euphoria had passed, the mood in the east during 1990 was one of bewilderment and conflicting emotions. 'The old regime collapsed so quickly, and the West has now moved in so totally, that we are all left confused,' said a pastor I met in Leipzig. Many people felt, on the one hand, a vague generalised sense of guilt at having condoned the regime or been party to it; and on the other, a vague resentment of the West, a sense of inferiority, a doubt as to whether they could learn to compete with it. They were torn between a post-mortem on the past and anxiety for the future. And inevitably, in some cases, this became tinged with self-pity. Few people had any special desire to retain a 'GDR identity' (that much-discussed term): yet they felt deeply coloured by a common experience that marked them off from West Germans; and, as they entered a new highly competitive world, they even felt fearful of losing some of the slow, gentle, compassionate values that had been bred of having to survive under the old regime. Notably for older people, there was also the sense of waste, of having spent forty years as guinea-pigs of a Socialist experiment that failed.

For those who had sincerely believed in Socialism and had served the regime loyally (while maybe turning a blind eye to its faults), the moral disarray was especially great. They were having to rethink their value system, or to ask themselves if they should feel any share in the guilt. A journalist aged 40 on *Neues Deutschland*, a decent, kindly man, gave me this patently sincere account of his agonising:

> I was brought up and educated by that regime, I never knew anything else, I truly believed it was right. I trusted 'my' Party and 'my' Government, and I genuinely thought that the Stasi were doing a good job to protect society – until two or three years ago, when stories of their brutalities began to leak out, but at first I just didn't believe them. I became critical of some economic policies, and I aired my views in Party meetings, seriously believing that they would be passed up to the leadership and listened to. But now I see how badly we were misled: centralism didn't work like that. I always refused to watch Western TV, and I never visited the West until 1988 when I went to a trade meeting in Hanover. It was a great shock. I had believed that the West was full of poverty, strikes, unrest and drugs, and I found Hanover horribly peaceful, orderly, prosperous – it made me so *angry*! I suppose that my doubts about our system dated from then. Now I feel bereft. Yet I still believe in the socialist ideal.

Some others spoke to me just as ingenuously about what they reluctantly admit was a certain naivety. 'I joined the Party, not only for my career,' said a woman teacher in Dresden, 'but also because I had Socialist beliefs, I saw the regime's good aspects, I wanted to join in trying to improve it from within. Then after the *Wende* we found out that it had all been far worse than we'd feared – the corruption, the Stasi, the killings at the border. It upset me so much that it has taken me a year to recover.'

Among the more senior Party people, a few felt a more direct sense of guilt, and some even turned to the Church, their old enemy, to help them to come to terms with the past and find a new value system. In east Berlin I met a senior Protestant pastor who told me how he and his wife, a psychologist, were doing this work of rehabilitation:

These SED leaders know that the Church behaved honourably under the old regime, it told the truth: and so they trust us now and some of them seek our guidance, after their whole world has collapsed. Our first task is to help them to accept their guilt — not easy for Communists, who lack the Christian moral concept of sin. I went to see Egon Krenz himself on Christmas night and we talked about guilt; he was very afraid of going to prison. Then his wife asked my wife to visit her, and showed her the stone which some angry people had thrown through her window. This had shocked her. But my wife said, 'As a senior teacher, you had been in charge of indoctrinating young minds, instilling passive obedience. So you too, in effect, threw stones at people. First you must accept this in your heart.' We find that we *can* help younger or middle-aged people to make a new start. But with the Honecker generation, it's too late.

A few SED leaders and Stasi officers committed suicide — for example, Helmut Mieth, the Party chief in Bautzen, Saxony, who broke down totally when the town turned against him, in October 1989. Others, having been pushed out of their jobs, just sat gloomily at home all day. But some, mainly younger ones, showed much more resilience. In a residential suburb outside Berlin, I met a clever couple in their thirties who lived in a chic modernised villa and had clearly done well out of the old regime: he had a senior position with the Interflug state airline, she was an SED official in a local factory. Now both had lost their jobs. But, making use of their expertise, they had smartly set about creating two small private firms, both in the transport sector — the kind of resourceful initiative still very rare in east Germany. These charming 'Commie yuppies' impressed me with their pragmatism — call it opportunism if you will. The husband said:

We were both eager SED members since we were eighteen. But Socialism made too many mistakes here, especially with the economy: so it has lost the battle, and capitalism has won. A pity, but never mind: now we shall both put all our efforts into becoming really successful capitalists! And it's one or the other —

I don't think the middle way of social democracy has any meaning. Socialism remains for me the right ideal, but the world isn't ready for it yet.

This at least was a frank, practical approach. But plenty of others turned their coats rather less honestly, Vicar-of-Bray-wise, as they sought to cling on to their posts under new masters. 'Of course I was always a reformer at heart . . . I'd have pushed for change, had it only been possible . . . they were bad, those times, but there was nothing we could do . . . yes, I'm basically in favour of the *Wende*', were the kind of remarks heard on every side, from former SED loyalists. Maybe they were often sincere: but it was just too easy to say this now, rather than sooner. This species was dubbed the *Wendehals* (wryneck), the name of a small bird that can turn its neck right round – and the prime example was Krenz himself, who turned overnight from hardliner to reformer, though it didn't enable him to last long. Others were to be found running factories, or in the universities, hospitals or local administration: some quickly lost their posts, but others were kept on if their skills were needed, or if their record was not too black, and all in public posts were to be subjected to screening in due course (see p. 474).

It was a time of great moral confusion, as in Germany after 1945, and it was hard to tell who should be blamed and penalised, and who not. Of those who had worked for the omnipresent State, many were simply time-servers who had maybe tried do something useful for society in a non-political way; and they were now less criticised than those who had played an active political role but were now pretending to have been liberals at heart. Factory managers, nearly all former SED members and some hard-line, were kept in their posts until privatisation because their experience was needed (see p. 455) and this caused resentment among staff. Others, like the couple I quoted above, turned to setting up their own little firms, using their skills and contacts. It was often the most able and resourceful, having already done well under the old system, who now proved the most adept at changing to a new one, and picking up the tricks of the free market.

If the public were vaguely disturbed about all this, they were much more indignant at the slowness of official moves to prosecute the really guilty – the clique around Honecker, and the Stasi leaders. People had been genuinely incensed by the details of corruption which had come out in December 1989: Honecker's hunting-lodge with its staff of twenty-two, his holiday island on the Baltic, his wife's monthly trips to

Paris for a hair-cut, and the luxurious compound for the Party elite at Wandlitz, in the woods outside Berlin, where the shops were full of Western goods denied to ordinary citizens. Worse, evidence emerged of illicit arms sales to Third World countries, and of some 200 million Marks having been smuggled out of the country into Swiss banks, by the alleged arch-embezzler Alexander Schalk-Golodkowski, former senior foreign trade official. The luxurious living was not excessive by the standards of the Western world, where many political leaders and tycoons live in similar style: but it was considered scandalous for a regime that had always preached equality and proletarian simplicity.

Pressure grew for trials of the guilty, not only for these abuses but for political crimes, such as ordering the border guards to shoot escapees, and Stasi harassment of dissidents. However, these unpleasant actions had not in fact been illegal under GDR law and Bonn knew that it would therefore be very hard to prosecute, since West German law could not easily be applied retrospectively to acts committed in another State. What is more, much of the written evidence had been quietly destroyed by the old regime during its dying days. So the Federal Government decided, perhaps wisely, not to stage any political trials after unification; instead, it was left to the independent judiciary in Berlin to proceed with some cases where prosecution was feasible, notably those involving corruption, which had certainly been a crime in the GDR. Several SED leaders had been held for months on these charges, including Erich Mielke, the hated former boss of the Stasi. But the first corruption trial in 1991, that of Harry Tisch, the former trade union leader, did not succeed; the charges against him were not proven, and he was freed. As for Honecker himself, he had now been under house arrest for over a year; but as he was very ill from cancer, probably too ill to stand trial, he had managed to get himself transferred to a Soviet military hospital in east Germany, whence the Russians spirited him away to a hospital in Moscow in March 1991. Bonn feigned indignation, but was in some ways quite glad to have been relieved of a prisoner whose trial would have stirred up a legal and political hornets' nest.

Honecker, Mielke and some others were in fact charged not only with corruption, but with the manslaughter of 190 people shot trying to flee the GDR: investigators had unearthed more than 400 files linking them to the shoot-to-kill orders. For this, and for other actions such as the Stasi torture methods allegedly authorised by Mielke, the Federal Government could possibly have overridden GDR law and used the 'crimes against humanity' charge employed at Nuremberg in 1945–6. But it was not an easy choice. On the one hand, political and moral justice seemed to demand that some leaders at least should be brought to trial for their worst abuses; and the public on the whole wanted this. On the other hand, to enter this legal minefield, and to stage anything resembling a show trial, might aggravate the paranoid tensions among east Germans already confused about their share in the general guilt. It was an invidious situation. Many of the top leaders, including Honecker and Mielke, were now aged, and maybe it was wiser to leave them to disappear quietly. 'After 1945, the issues were more clear-cut and the crimes far greater,' one Western lawyer told me; 'and it was the Allies who staged the trials. That made it easier. Now it is Germans judging fellow-Germans.'

And what should be done with the Stasi, the hated police of the *Staatssicherheit* (state security)? At the end of 1989, public fury had erupted against them, too: in Berlin and elsewhere, their offices were stormed and files seized, though they managed to hide or destroy many others. People were angered to learn of the sheer size of the Stasi operation – some 85,000 full-time staff, up to half a million paid informers, secret files on about one citizen in three. And a vast budget, that could have been spent on improving the economy! The Stasi had even aided and abetted the extreme-left RAF terrorist movement in West Germany (see p. 538). 'They were everywhere, creating fear and mistrust,' said one pastor; 'maybe my closest friend informed on me, how was I to know? They were a poison in the blood of our society.'

The Stasi were progressively disbanded early in 1990; some of them were sent to work in the lignite mines. A debate then developed as to whether a few at least should be prosecuted. But their actions too had been legal under GDR law, and so proceedings were dropped; it was felt also that any generalised witch-hunt against them might stir up a bitter atmosphere, since so many people had been implicated as informers. However, some ex-Stasi officers were able to use the size of this informer network to attempt a kind of revenge: it was easy for them to allege that almost anyone in public life once had Stasi links, and so they set about spreading rumours. One of those implicated in this way was Lothar de Mazière himself, who in December 1990 felt obliged to resign from Kohl's Government until he could clear himself. He admitted that as a lawyer in the GDR he of course had dealings with the Stasi, in order to defend his clients: but he denied that he had ever worked for them or been paid by them, and he was later able to prove it. This and other such incidents left a nasty taste. They indeed showed how far East German society had been poisoned; and it might take years to clear up this legacy of fear and suspicion that affected millions of people. '*They* are still around, below the surface, *they* are still watching us, I'm sure,' said a farmer's wife I met in Thuringia in October 1990.

By this date, just after unification, the people of east Germany were in a curious world of transition. Although the GDR was no more, their GDR identity was still clinging to them; and few of them yet felt '*Vollbundi*',[1] even though they now had full *Bund* citizenship. Nearly all were glad to be rid of the old regime, or at least they knew that the *Wende* had been necessary: but now they faced new anxieties, as their jobs vanished and they had to adapt to the Western system. For the young, this might not be so difficult; but for older people it was going to be harder, however much they welcomed the change. Some people seemed to want to have their cake and eat it – to embrace what the West had to offer, without losing the incidental good aspects of the old regime, such as job security, cheap food and rents, advantages for working mothers, abortion on demand.

And so during 1990 many people asked themselves: were there any aspects of the old 'GDR identity', or of life in the GDR, that were worth trying to preserve? Were there some values or life-styles, developed either *by* the regime or in defence *against* it, that should be cherished and might even influence the west? What of the group solidarity, the personal warmth, the slower, more thoughtful tempo of life? Had the east anything to teach the west, or was it all to be one-way? 'Not all was bad in that regime,' said one newly-elected CDU mayor. 'People were modest in a nice way, the difficulties brought them closer together, some of them learned moral courage. Now they'll become more pushy and egotistic. The solidarity groups are already breaking up.' Moral qualities developed against the regime seemed likely to perish with it. There were pious hopes at first that the west might learn from them, but it did not seem in practice very probable.

Of the GDR regime's own concrete social achievements, how much would survive? It had created quite a good welfare service and social net, of which it was proud. But West Germany's own welfare system,

1. '*Bundi*', i.e. citizen of the *Bundesrepublik*, is what West Berliners used to call West Germans. After unification, everyone was really a *Bundi* but, to quote a new catchphrase, the east Germans yet had to feel so fully (*voll*).

now taking over, was in many ways better, and far more lavishly funded. The west had better hospitals, better pensions, better social housing. The big loss for the east Germans was job security: but this in time would be compensated by much greater freedom of choice, and higher incomes. The easterners would also be losing their leisurely pace of working life: but this had been due mainly to over-staffing, lack of materials, and bureaucratic inertia. They would now have to learn to work harder, but would be rewarded for it.

It was not easy to draw a fair balance-sheet. Certainly there were some aspects of the GDR system which liberals in both Germanies thought might be worth trying to keep or even extend to the west. In education, there were the links with working life, the afternoon sport and cultural activities, and arguably the university selection: shorn of their political distortions, might not these features still have something of value? The newly-created eastern *Länder*, now in charge of education, were pondering the question: but it seemed most likely that they would choose to rebuild the system entirely on the western model (see p. 491). Then there were the advantages for working mothers, especially the free kindergartens. But here too there had been political motivation. And the new *Länder*, so severely short of money, seemed in little mood for such expensive social luxuries. Finally, there was the stormy question of abortion, less a matter of cash or politics than of religious principle. In the GDR, abortion was free on demand until the thirteenth week of pregnancy; in west Germany, it was much harder to obtain it legally (see p. 200). And east German women, backed by liberal opinion in the west, campaigned strenuously to prevent this aspect of GDR society from being 'westernised'. They won a reprieve. After a long debate in Bonn, with the CDU/CSU on one side and the SPD and FDP on the other, it was agreed that for a two-year transition period each part of Germany would keep its own rules, pending the drafting of a new law that would try to reach some compromise.

With one or two exceptions such as this, it seemed that very little specific to the old regime would survive — neither in the legal system, nor in education, welfare, local government or the economy. 'The western takeover will sweep it all away, the good with the bad,' was a remark heard commonly. And with it would go, in time, the so-called 'GDR identity'. Some regretted this. But what in fact was this identity, aside from the artificially-created State which no longer existed? This, too, was a question much debated. The Honecker regime had tried to stimulate a patriotic pride in the GDR, for example through the sporting achievements. Few citizens responded very eagerly. And yet, after the borders were thrown open, they did grow more sharply aware of how differently from west Germans they had been moulded by their separate experience. And this gave them a kind of identity, perforce. They even spoke the German language differently, using old pre-war formal phrases that had slipped out of parlance in the west, plus a dosage of Socialist bureaucratic jargon.

Many people wanted to forget the nasty past and adapt to the west as quickly as possible. But others, the more thoughtful ones, and not only in PDS or Neues Forum circles, were aware that it would be wrong to try to blot out forty years just like that. 'What matters for us now is *not* to forget our past, what we believed or thought we believed, even the lies we were told,' the actress Johanna Schall (Brecht's granddaughter) suggested to me; 'it is dangerous for a people to lose its memory — as the west Germans have done, sweeping the Nazi period under the carpet.' And a Protestant friend of mine in east Berlin, who had suffered under the regime, said: 'Even if there are no good things worth preserving, we still should not just forget. I think that many of us did our best in difficult circumstances, so we need not feel ashamed of those forty years. They taught us something.'

Whatever their views on that past, and however glad to be part of a new united Germany, east Germans were now in need of a new focus of identity and loyalty — beyond that of the *Bundesrepublik* which for many of them was a bit daunting and distant. Could a worker in Chemnitz be expected to identify easily with a Badener by the Swiss border? Hence the great importance of the five new eastern *Länder* (see p. 472), all of them corresponding to former kingdoms, dukedoms or provinces with their roots deep in history. Saxony, like Bavaria, had been a kingdom until 1918; Thuringia and Mecklenburg-Pommern, too, had their own potent traditions, Brandenburg and Saxony-Anhalt perhaps a bit less so. The pre-war *Länder* had been abolished by the centralised GDR regime, which taught very little in schools about their history or culture. But now they could come into their own again, with their own governments. By the autumn of 1990, the flags of Saxony and Mecklenburg were to be seen flying again on many a building. And if the *Länder* in West Germany, after the war, had played so vital a part in providing a defeated people with a new focus of loyalty, an alternative to nationalism, could not the same happen now in the east? Here the east Germans could find a new regional home for their sense of identity, and allow their 'GDR identity' decent burial.

'East Germans are now outwardly very free, but they are not yet internally free, the Wall is still inside their minds,' said a psychotherapist I met. After being isolated from the world for so long, cooped up, supervised, watched by the police, told how to behave, some of them now gave vent to a pent-up emotion and frustration, even to long-repressed feelings of violence. Some young people reacted badly to their new freedom, thinking that democracy meant you could do what you like. There was a sharp increase in petty crime, notably by east Berliners who went burgling or shoplifting in the west, or raided the cars of visitors. And there were outbursts of hooliganism, some of it with a neo-Nazi tint. Groups of skinheads and neo-Nazis, some come over from the west, others formed locally, would meet on the Alexander-platz at weekends, and would go off hurling abuse at Poles, Turks and Blacks, or even beating up left-wing squatters. Football rowdiness was another Western import, and the east German police had no experience at handling it. At a match at Leipzig in November 1990, as some 500 skinheads surged through the ground yelling 'Heil Hitler!', the 200 police panicked and opened fire: one youth was shot dead. At Dresden next March, battles between rival fans forced the abandonment of a European Cup match between the local team and Red Star Belgrade. These were new experiences for the east, where football matches had always been so peaceful.

Some commentators saw in these events a sinister political portent – the rise of a new extreme-right in eastern Germany. They pointed out that, just as mass unemployment had fuelled the rise of Hitler, so now a similar insecurity was prompting the new hooliganism. Their alarm was understandable, but maybe excessive: after all, as in west Germany (see p. 505), the actual neo-Nazi groups were a tiny fringe minority, without influence and almost completely leaderless. In the December 1990 elections the Republikaner, not neo-Nazi but certainly far to the right, had polled a mere 1.3 per cent in the east, little more than half the 2.3 per cent it scored in the west. East German youth, or part of it, might be restless, angry, even sometimes violent: but as yet there was not much sign of its being politically motivated, any more than the football hooliganism of the British.

More serious, or at least more widespread, was the rise of xenophobia in the new east Germany: it took the form of sharp insults, even physical attacks, against anyone Asian or African, or identifiably Polish. The old regime had preached 'brotherly solidarity' with the Third World, but in practice it had kept its officially-invited 'guest workers' tightly segregated. East Germans were not used to living with foreigners in their midst, and their enclosed society encouraged conformism rather than acceptance of diversity. So, suddenly free, they felt a bewildered mix of emotions. They feared that foreigners would take their jobs; or, looked down on by west Germans, they showed a typical 'poor white' contempt for anyone whom in turn they could treat as inferior; or some were even reacting against the old regime's sham philosophy of friendship — 'At last we can now openly express our racism,' was one ingenuous remark. All in all, the feelings were stronger than in west Germany, where people had at least grown used to the *Gastarbeiter*. So was this xenophobia a temporary problem of adaptation, that would disappear with time? Or, as some observers feared, did it herald the rise of a new German intolerance that might spread to infect the west?

By 1989 there were some 85,000 'guest workers' in the GDR, all from Communist countries, Vietnam, Mozambique, Angola and Cuba, invited by the regime as a gesture of Socialist amity. They came on four- or five-year contracts, mostly to do menial jobs. And they were housed apart in special hostels and blocks of flats, so that they did not meet East Germans outside their work-place. Mainly this was to avoid the kind of tensions so common in West Germany. But it was also to prevent citizens from becoming exposed to more exuberant life-styles that might increase their restless claustrophobia: when some jovial, songful Cubans managed to escape the *apartheid* and became popular with East German students, they were promptly sent home — especially as they had also begun to spread the truth about Castro's paradise.

After the *Wende*, all these visitors were free to fraternise as they wished and while liberals welcomed them warmly, others were more hostile. Gangs of youths would sometimes beat up Asians or Africans in the street, or on housing estates, and the police no longer had the influence to prevent it. There were also cases of attacks on visiting Vietnamese professors and students. I met a Palestinian student living in west Berlin, who said that after his first brief visit to the east he would never dare to go back: he was shouted at repeatedly, 'Go home, you bastard, you're taking our jobs! We'll kill you if you don't get out quick!' So from August 1990 the de Mazière government, with the backing of Bonn, began to repatriate the *Gastarbeiter*, partly for their own safety. By October some 2,000 were leaving each week. They were given 3,000 DM each and a free flight home; and although in theory they could stay till the end of their contracts, few chose to do so. Some had already escaped into west Germany.

There were also some cases of friction between the Turks in west Berlin and visiting easterners. Many Turks were much better off than the average east German and had more secure jobs, so this could cause resentment. And yet, the bold Turks who began to set up mobile snack-bars or street-stalls in the east were very rarely molested: on the whole, Turks were seen as a settled part of west German society, therefore in a superior category to the east's own short-term 'guests'. In fact, it was Poles much more than Turks who were targets of the new xenophobia. Partly this was due to traditional German scorn for Poles, seen as poor, feckless and undisciplined; and many of the Polish traders who now passed through the east, on their way to the rich west, did behave in a somewhat boorish, untidy manner. So, the east Germans tended to vent on the 'backward' Poles their annoyance at being treated as 'backward' by smooth westerners. At its nastiest, this xenophobia became sheer brigandry, as armed gangs attacked laden Polish cars entering Germany on the *Autobahn* to Berlin; and by spring 1991 there was talk of sending federal troops to protect this route.

If I have painted a harsh picture, it should not be thought that all east Germans were infected by the xenophobia. Many were appalled by it: when a Mozambican worker was killed by a neo-Nazi in Dresden in April 1991, five thousand citizens attended his funeral. Some of the violence was deliberately fomented by racist agents who had infiltrated from the west. And the Press often treated the whole problem too sensationally. It could hardly compare with the generalised anti-Jewish witch-hunts of the 1930s – and this time all the authorities were totally opposed to it. In fact, there was reason to hope that it might prove a transitional phenomenon. 'You have to remember', I was told by an official in Bonn, 'that for the past forty years West Germans have been civilised by a close involvement with their European neighbours, and are even learning tolerance towards coloured minorities, too. The enclosed East Germans still remain in a pre-war mould of suspicion and hostility, that's inevitable. They now have to get used to being part of an international community.'

These were noble sentiments, if put rather smugly. But they glossed over another problem of adaptation that went deeper, was even more widespread and intractable, and was partly of west Germans' own making. This was the mutual resentment between east and west Germans – 'Ossis' and 'Wessis' as they dubbed each other – that developed during 1990. At first in 1989 they had embraced each other warmly as long-lost brothers: but soon frictions and misunderstandings appeared. These, like the xenophobia, tended to get exaggerated by the press and media: but they certainly did exist, and the causes lay on both sides — insensitive, contemptuous Wessis and jealous, grasping Ossis. Now that they could travel and talk freely, many easterners gave vent to an envy that they had kept bottled up for years. 'You've had the good life for forty years, now we want it too, and quick!' — 'Yes, but we had to work hard for it' — 'Lucky you, that you had the chance', was a typical exchange. And stories were told of Ossis in shops in west Berlin, barging to the head of the queue with the words, 'We had to wait patiently in line all these years, now it's our turn to be served first!' Even within families, relations sometimes deteriorated after the *Wende*. I know a lady in Hamburg who over the years had devotedly kept in touch with her relatives in Magdeburg, had brought them money and gifts on her visits, and all this had been gracefully, gratefully accepted: but now they turned on her accusingly for being too privileged. Perhaps these were the inevitable teething-troubles of adaptation, as Ossis vented on Wessis their sense of injustice at having been the 'unlucky' Germans. And some Wessis in turn became irritated by what they saw as a whining, ill-mannered self-pity.

As they surged over to the west on their shopping sprees, in their polluting little cars, many of the less well-behaved Ossis displayed just the same kind of naive, grasping materialism that west Germans had shown during the get-rich days of the economic miracle, in the 1950s and 1960s. They invaded the streets and supermarkets of border towns such as Hof, in northern Bavaria, and made themselves much disliked. Everywhere, westerners tended to scorn their hapless compatriots for being poorly-dressed, slow and uncouth. Their sallow skins, awkward gait and old-fashioned shoes, and the women's frizzy hair-dos, instantly picked them out. At petrol stations and in shops, they tended to hold up the queues, by fiddling with their cars or fussing over their purchases — time, in the GDR, had been on quite a different scale from in the brisk, urgent west. And Ossis in turn regarded Wessis as brusque, impatient and patronising, which often they were. Westerners on visits would sometimes show their anger at the slow, listless service in the east: at a hotel in Potsdam, just after currency union, I heard a well-heeled Wessi remark to his wife, 'When we paid in their silly mickey-mouse money and it was all so cheap, I could tolerate this appalling service. But now we are expected to pay in *our* good Deutschmarks, at our prices!' The waitress heard too, and scowled.

Then there were the private property claims, a ripe source of mutual ill-feeling. An estimated half-a-million west Germans were now making claims to recover their former homes in the east, which they had abandoned as emigrants during the post-war years. In many cases the houses had been appropriated by the GDR authorities, then resold to east Germans, so there was now a clash between two rightful owners. In some residential suburbs of east Berlin, and around Potsdam, as much as 70 or 80 per cent of housing was in this category. Sometimes a west German would turn up out of the blue at the weekend, and start haranguing the unsuspecting occupants – 'This is *my* house, my father built it, and I lived here till 1950 – why have you let it get in this mess? I'm now going to court to get you evicted.' In such cases, where the property had been resold, the legal position was highly uncertain, for clearly both sides had a legitimate claim: legal tussles followed, and the judge had to decide each case on its merits, with the unsuccessful party receiving state compensation. In other instances, where the GDR State had held on to the property and turned it into rented flats or an institution, matters were easier: but here, too, tenants could face eviction if the former owner wanted to live in it again. This was the case with some stately country homes now being claimed back by *Junkers* who had fled west in 1945 to escape the Russians. All in all, these property disputes did not help Ossi–Wessi good relations.

Tensions were above all created by the mass arrival of Western experts to help rebuild the east's economy and administration. They came in their thousands, as civil servants or lawyers, as investors or prospective investors, or as members of the Treuhandanstalt agency charged with the programme of privatisation (see pp. 448–57). And they did not always behave very tactfully. Their job was to bring in Western expertise, to align the east on Western standards, and of course they thought they knew best: some of them went around high-handedly telling the Ossis how to do it all. This was resented, and this kind of Wessi was dubbed 'Besserwessi' (*Besserwisser* is German for 'know-all' or 'smart-aleck'). A Leipziger I met, who had joined the local branch of a Western computer firm, told me that his colleagues made him feel inferior, by stressing how much more they knew about the job than he did. And an east Berlin journalist said: 'We may be glad of unification on the whole: but at the same time we feel overwhelmed, not only by the sheer speed of the process, but by the pressure of domination from the west. We have the sense of being shunted aside, taken over. It's humiliating.'

Once again, the faults were shared. In many sectors, the Westerners did indeed know best, and their skills were crucially needed: this was true throughout the legal field, for West German law had replaced that of the GDR, at unification. And in factories and businesses, Westerners were often irritated by east German slowness, lack of initiative, or what they tended to regard as 'laziness'. But this was not quite justified: on the production line or at building sites, the slowness of the work tempo had been due largely to the erratic supply of materials, while it was the centralised command structure which had sapped the spirit of initiative and decision-taking. There was no reason to believe that Ossis could not pick up Western work methods in time. But what the Wessi visitors often lacked was the patience, or the readiness to understand their psychology.

There was quite a common feeling in the east that the west's takeover had been too sudden and too total, and that neither Kohl's Government nor de Mazière's had taken the trouble to see what might be worth preserving. This was felt especially by the Neues Forum tendency, one of whose leaders, Michael Hamburger, told me: 'It's been a humiliating policy of colonisation. The West has ruthlessly implanted its structures and values, and does not want anything from the GDR to survive. It does not believe that there was anything good here.' Psychologically, there may have been some truth in this charge. Although Easterners had three times voted for unification, and in their majority wanted it quickly, there is little doubt that the West could have applied it more tactfully, at a day-to-day human level. On the other hand, if the East's ailing economy was to be rescued, there seemed little alternative to a swift and massive takeover.

## *Privatisation, pollution and property*

The State-run industry bequeathed by the old GDR regime was a sorry spectacle. Much of it was handicapped by old-fashioned equipment, outdated technologies, rampant pollution or chronic overstaffing, and productivity levels were about a third of those in the West. Firms had suffered from the exodus to the West of many of their best technicians and specialists. They were also losing their State subsidies and their protected markets in Eastern Europe, and would be incapable of facing Western competition in a free market.

[448]

The de Mazière and Kohl Governments decided that mass privatisation was the best answer. Western investors would be encouraged to buy up and modernise firms as fast as possible; others would be restructured first, then sold; and the more hopeless cases that could never find a buyer, perhaps a third of the total, would be closed down. This would lead inevitably to extensive unemployment, which Bonn would pay for. To handle this vast operation a special body, the Treuhandanstalt (trust agency), was set up in the spring of 1990, and it started work in a big, ugly office block on the Alexanderplatz in East Berlin. This much-to-be-contested 'Treuhand' became the central pivot of the huge task of renewing east Germany's economy, and it had some 8,000 former State firms under its control.

At first it made mistakes. It connived at the policy which the Modrow Government had previously initiated, of allowing big West German firms to carve up between them certain service sectors, in a manner that went against anti-cartel principles. Thus the Allianz insurance group, the West's biggest, was permitted to take majority control of the GDR's main State insurance system; two or three large Western electricity companies bought up much of the energy industry; and the same process began in the retail sector, as the supermarket chains moved in. All this may have been useful in strictly economic terms, but it ran into criticism on monopoly grounds. Yet, before unification, the West's anti-cartel watchdogs had little power to prevent it.

Later, as the Federal Republic absorbed the east, the Treuhand improved. It acquired a capable new chief executive from the West, Detlev Rohwedder,[1] who quickly vetoed plans for the lump sale to the Steigenberg hotel group of the GDR's state hotel chain, Interhotels. He also decentralised the Treuhand, making it better able to deal with local investment; and he removed from his staff most of the old SED apparatchiks who had little idea of capitalism save when it involved selling off little firms to their cronies. Even so, the agency remained harassed and understaffed, still working out by trial and error how to cope with the entirely novel task, unique in history, of privatising a whole economy – improvisation, as I have said, was never the Germans' *forte*. When I visited the Berlin head office in 1991, I found an

1. In April 1991 Rohwedder was murdered at his home in Düsseldorf by terrorists of the Red Army Faction, as part of their campaign against 'greater German imperialism'.

atmosphere of cheerful chaos in the drab corridors, as visitors were kept waiting hours for their appointments.

The gravest problem, only partly the Treuhand's own fault, was that the privatisation was going much slower than had been expected. By spring 1991 only about 600 firms had been sold, out of some 8,000 in the Treuhand's charge. And as many others went bankrupt and closed, or virtually ceased production, unemployment including 'nil short time' (see p. 457) rose to 30 per cent of the work-force. The Treuhand, it is true, was anxious not to push sales through too hurriedly but to get the details right first, in view of the avalanche of property claims that could easily invalidate a transaction. It was also being held up by the difficulty of setting a fair price on the companies it wanted to sell: book-keeping had been minimal in the GDR, where firms were given dollops of State cash and did not bother with costs, so that no one could now tell their proper value.

For a number of reasons, most potential Western investors were acting warily. They were put off above all by the property ownership issue; also, if they were buying an existing firm, many of them feared having to help pay for clearing up the pollution damage, or being obliged to take on more staff than they needed. Many preferred to wait for the firm to go bankrupt, and for the Treuhand to then lower its price. And some investors thought that, despite the low labour costs, it might be wiser not to manufacture in east Germany but simply to use it as a new market for their existing Western products. They were alarmed by the difficulties of restructuring plant and of retraining a labour force whose capacity for hard work they often doubted. It is true that a few key firms, including Siemens and Volkswagen, had begun to invest on a big scale by early 1991; but although 50 per cent of larger German companies claimed they wanted to follow suit, only 3 per cent had started to do so. Foreign investors, including the Japanese, were being even more cautious.

Was privatisation the only answer? Rather than wait for private investors, might not the Government do better to restructure some firms at its own cost, then operate them itself for several years, with the Treuhand thus becoming a State holding company rather like IRI in Italy? In the rest, Volkswagen had remained nationalised until 1961, and had done well. Would not this solution prevent many needless closures? This cogent argument was put forward quite widely as the crisis worsened, especially by groups such as Neues Forum. Even the new CDU prime minister of Saxony, Kurt Biedenkopf, desperate to create new jobs in a *Land* verging on catastrophe, began to advance ideas of this kind. But the Government remained ideologically hostile, declaring that the free market alone should decide which companies were to survive. 'An IRI-type solution might have been possible in the early post-war years,' a Treuhand official told me, 'but not in the free-market 1990s.' Even so, the Treuhand did lend sizeable credits to help some firms to restructure.

The famous *Eigentumsfrage* (property question) was much the biggest factor deterring investors, and it raised heated debate. In the year or so after the *Wende*, more than a million claims were lodged by people whose land, firms or other property had been confiscated by the GDR regime after the war, or by their descendants; most of them now lived in the West. Some of the claims came from Jews who had been expropriated by the Nazis in the 1930s and whose property had then been bought by others before falling into GDR State hands: so there could be two or more claims to the same site. A large proportion of them related purely to farmland or to housing, which raised separate problems (see p. 447): but many others came from former owners of firms still in operation, or from former landowners whose terrain might now be suitable for industrial development. And as the deadline for most types of claim was not until March 1991, new ones kept cropping up; moreover, the notorious slowness and complexity of the German legal system, plus the shortage of trained staff to deal with the problems, meant that most of the claims were taking ages to sort out, let alone to settle. Both before and after unification, the cases were being handled by local East German courts and councils, who had little expertise in these matters and could seldom afford to hire qualified help from the West.

It was therefore small wonder that most investors were wary of acquiring a firm or a site whose former owner might suddenly turn up, demanding either compensation or right of repossession. And the Treuhand, too, became wary of selling until ownership was clearly established. Some of the claims were possibly just try-ons by Westerners who could not even identify their forebears' property. But most were clearly genuine, and in many cases the right lay clearly on both sides. I found a vivid illustration of this in the tiny town of Creuzburg, near Eisenach. Like many, it was a small-scale investment by local people, not a big one from the West. A modest and pleasant young couple, Ernst and Susanna Heinemann, had in 1990 opened an electrical shop and repairs firm, in an area badly in need of such ventures. 'We rented from the town council', they said, 'a building that had formerly been

State-owned, and we were assured that later we could buy it if we wanted. So we invested six months' hard work, and all our savings, in restoring these derelict premises that still have no running water, heating or toilet. Then last month a family turned up from Frankfurt, saying, "*We* lived here till 1950, when the Russians exiled us to Siberia, claiming we were spies. Now we want our home back!" We were stunned. We had signed a lease with the town, but now we face a long and costly legal battle with this family. Meantime we've halted our improvement work. So no heating this winter.'

Maybe the town was imprudent in granting the lease: but the Heinemanns were keen to do a job that needed doing – and who could have guessed that the other family might return? There are many such cases where both parties would seem to have a valid case: and it may take a very wise local Solomon to settle them. 'There is a lot of other new investment that we want to promote,' the mayor of Creuzburg told me, 'such as new roads, new little workshops, new shops and hotels in this touristy area. But we can't because of the property claims. It's maddening.'

A few cases have had a happier outcome, and some claimants have themselves invested rapidly and effectively. In Eisenach, the main department store once belonged to the local Schwager family: when they were expropriated in 1950, they moved west to the Hanover area, where gradually they built up five stores that today are booming. Then in 1990 they triumphantly returned: under the Treuhand's aegis they set up a joint venture with the public concern that was now running their old store. Pumping in their own Western money and know-how, they transformed it from a dreary State emporium into a bright modern palace brimming with Western goods: I attended its festive opening in September 1990, all coloured balloons and jostling crowds. For Ralf Schwager, a dynamic Western businessman amid his passive but grateful fellow-Eisenachers, it was quite an emotional homecoming. But the freehold ownership had still to be settled.

Cases such as this, where a claimant wants to operate his old firm again himself, have been relatively infrequent: most claimants to firms have simply wanted compensation, or use of the site for other purposes. But this has put severe obstacles in the way of new industrial investment. And in a bid to overcome these, the Federal Government early in 1991 decreed new rules that gave absolute priority to new investment likely to create or preserve jobs. In such instances, a claimant had only four weeks in which to prove his case and thus stop the sale. Otherwise, the investor could safely buy the property from the Treuhand: if the claimant later won his case, he could not regain his property, and would be compensated by the Treuhand, not by the investor. By spring 1991 it was not yet clear whether these new guarantees would unleash much new investment; some legal experts feared that claimants could perhaps take their cases to the Constitutional Court and win, in this land where property rights are so sacrosanct. All in all, the property question seemed likely to disrupt new investment for a long time to come.

Some big firms went quickly into action, however, on sites where there were no ownership disputes. Volkswagen had begun to manufacture at Zwickau even before the *Wende*, in a joint venture with the GDR firm making Trabants; and in May 1990 its first Polos rolled off the production line there. Then it agreed to take over the entire Trabant operation in Zwickau, Chemnitz and Mosel, closing some factories and building new ones, to form a giant new company, Volkswagen Sachsen: this would mass-produce Golfs and Polos (they were East Germans' dream cars, according to market research), while the dread 'Trabi' would be phased out. Siemens, for its part, was investing 1 billion DM in twenty different projects, due to create 30,000 jobs by 1993, and was buying up several firms via the Treuhand. 'Some of these GDR companies were crazily diverse,' a group executive told me, 'you'd find bicycles, umbrellas and microchips all being made in the same factory. So we have to restructure, to put it mildly!'

Daimler-Benz, Bosch and AEG were active, too, together with a few foreign firms such as GKN and Toshiba. And so was General Motors, via its German subsidiary, Opel, whose take-over of the Wartburg plant at Eisenach provided a vivid case-study of the hazards of rescuing East German industry. The car factory in the town centre was one of the world's oldest, dating from 1896 – and it looked it. Until 1945 it was part of BMW. Then the State took it over, calling the firm Automobilwerk Eisenach (AWE); and here in 1990 a staff of 8,800 were producing the Wartburg (named after the famous castle on the hill above), a slightly less ugly and pollutant little car than the Trabi. Not only was the plant so antiquated and overmanned that productivity was very low, but east Germans were now preferring to buy Western cars, so the Wartburg was being made only for export, mainly to Eastern Europe. But after currency union this market too collapsed. Production was cut back, and many workers stayed at home on 'zero short-time', i.e. unemployment with 85 per cent of wages.

So who would rescue this dinosaur? A Paderborn firm took on the modern steel-pressing plant, but this preserved only 250 jobs. Opel agreed to create an assembly line for its Vektras, in a joint venture with AWE, and this was opened in October: but again only 250 workers were involved. What of the rest? Opel came under heavy pressure from the Treuhand to invest in a much larger new manufacturing plant: but General Motors, facing other world-wide problems, acted coy. The American chairman of Opel, Louis R. Hughes, stated bluntly that he was not prepared to take on AWE's staff if it involved paying Western-level wages – cheap labour, for GM, was the name of the game. GM also seemed to be waiting for AWE's plight to worsen and its price to drop, which would enable it also to call the tune on the number of staff it retained: AWE had 800 people in administration alone, and experts reckoned that the work could easily be done by 200.

Finally in January 1991 a compromise was reached. Opel agreed to buy AWE for 30 million DM (very cheap) and to invest one billion in a new modern plant outside the town, where 2,600 workers would produce some 150,000 Cadett and Corsa models a year. The old factory would be scrapped, and Opel would spend 100,000 million DM on clearing up the environmental mess it had caused – *ten* times the cost of buying it! Many workers faced dismissal. And there was no provision for Opel to continue making the Wartburg car – to the fury of Dr Wolfram Liedtke, the clever Communist who was still in place as AWE's managing director. He had urged that the Wartburg be kept in production at least until its centenary in 1996. And he knew that his own days with the firm were now numbered. At the signing ceremony with Opel he blew his top, accusing Rohwedder of perfidy.

The famous Zeiss optical works, of Jena, failed to find a private buyer, and was saved only *in extremis* when the *Land* government of Thuringia agreed to take it over. Some other well-known firms collapsed completely, and closed without finding a buyer. For example, Pentacon of Dresden whose Praktica cameras were known around the world for their quality: three-quarters of them were sold to the West, and in Britain they held 25 per cent of the single-lens reflex market. Because of its hard-currency earnings the old regime gave Pentacon heavy subsidies, which disguised its high production costs and overmanning. Once the subsidies ended in 1990, the firm began to make losses of up to 500,000 DM a day, and after failing to sell it the Treuhand had no option but to close it down, with a loss of 5,600 jobs. By 1991 much of the GDR's electronics industry looked like suffering a similar fate, as did the Rostock shipyards and most heavy machinery plant. Investors baulked at the cost of replacing the heavy equipment, some of it dating from the 1920s; and they were alarmed at the likely expense of environmental clean-up. This was especially true of the old chemicals firms around Leipzig, cause of much of the worst pollution. Here several factories were closing after Western firms had refused to buy them up.

Some companies in more modern sectors fared better. In a few cases, a firm's former Communist managers were able to turn it themselves into a successful new private venture, with financial help from the Treuhand but without relying on a Western take-over. For instance, the managers of the GDR's former radio and television-set-making *Kombinat* turned part of it into their own company with the aid of loans from the Treuhand: they then did a trading deal with a Finnish firm that provided technology and training, and in 1991 were producing some 500,000 TV sets a year. These capable entrepreneurs had swiftly taught themselves the new alien concepts of costing, profits and marketing, and were clearly enjoying the transition to capitalism. Some other individuals started up their own small enterprises – like the dynamic young Communist couple near Potsdam whom I quoted earlier. Both had just lost their jobs, she as Party supervisor in an electronics firm, he as a senior engineer with the State Interflug airline: so they were now creating two service firms of their own, one in road transport, one for hiring out light aircraft, both making full use of their contacts in the West. However, not many former GDR executives have had this spirit of initiative. Most firms that do well have had to rely at least on a joint venture with the West, to obtain the ideas and the enterprise, the funding and the technology.

What is more, few of the former GDR managers showed the same intelligence and dynamism as those who set up that television firm. After the old regime collapsed, in nearly every firm the same managers remained in charge, but with no State or Party to control them any more, just the vaguely supervising Treuhand. So they could behave much as they liked. Nearly all had been SED members, and some of these now tried to block the privatisation of their firm; others opportunistically switched to capitalism, hoping thus to hold on to their jobs. But few of them had much feeling or initiative for the changes that were needed. And many of them behaved high-handedly towards their staff; or they gave themselves salary increases or extra perks, as was apparent from the new BMWs and Mercedes that suddenly appeared.

All this made them unpopular with the staff, who could do little about it however. And nor really could the Treuhand, for these old *Genossen* (Party comrades) alone knew how to run the firm, and there was no one to replace them until it was privatised. A friend told me about the medical equipment factory where he worked: 'We formed a new free trade union which tried to get rid of the *Genossen*, but these old pigs just dug their heels in. The firm is about to collapse, and the *Genossen* are looking for a Western buyer: but they tell us nothing of their plans, they behave even more autocratically than when they had the Party behind them. And the Treuhand just hasn't the staff or the time to go round its thousands of firms, checking on these abuses. It would rather leave the *Genossen* in charge, and keep quiet. We're all fed up and worried, I can tell you.' This malaise was widespread, and it added to the general economic gloom in the east.

In the hotel and catering industry, too, privatisation was running into trouble. The Steigenberger group had made a bid for the Inter-hotels, the GDR's chain of large modern business hotels, efficient if dull: but the Treuhand vetoed this on monopoly grounds and was aiming to split the chain between various buyers. Of the GDR's medium-sized hotels, most were post-war utility rabbit-hutches of extreme drabness and poor design, or they were old castles badly converted: in one, the kitchens were 300 metres from the dining-room. This was hardly an enticement for the investor, especially as the staff, mostly slow and listless, would have to be retrained to Western standards of brisk cheerfulness. As for the kind of small, charming traditional *Gasthaus* so common in west Germany, there had been plenty of these in the east too, before the war: but those that survived the bombing had been turned into hostels, clinics, blocks of flats, Party clubs or even Stasi centres. Many small investors were now keen to convert them back into family-run hotels, or build new ones in similar style: but once again the property problem held up progress. So the tourist had to choose between a dull, overpriced modern hotel or bed-and-breakfast in a private home, which at least was now possible since the *Wende*.

In the case of restaurants, the issues were much the same. In Dresden, I found that the city council early in 1990 had been eager to sell off some establishments quickly to Westerners, who were keen to buy: then the Treuhand stepped in, and insisted that ownership and planning questions be settled first. So by early 1991 hardly any restaurants had yet changed hands – and the formerly State-owned ones were most of them still awful, alike in their decor, service and cooking. A buyer had to agree to retain most of the staff, then pay for their retraining and the refurbishment. Few private restaurateurs from the West were prepared to take the financial risk, so it seemed that most places would be acquired by the big impersonal chains, such as Mövenpick or the steak or burger houses – not quite worthy of historic Dresden. And anyway, amid the growing economic crisis, with few local people willing to spend money on dining out, was this the time to start a restaurant? By 1991, virtually the only new private ventures in this field, many of them just street-stalls, were by a few intrepid Chinese, Italians and Turks. When Italians from Düsseldorf opened a modest pizzeria in central Dresden, it was quite a novelty event; when Saxony's first Chinese restaurant opened in nearby Freiburg, it hit the headlines.

Fortunately, a few private locally-owned pubs and small, cosy restaurants had been allowed under the old regime, unlike in the hotel sector. In many towns these were now prospering, so long as they kept their prices down. Of the countless State eateries, most had now been turned into limited companies (GmbHs) under the Treuhand's aegis, and were operating independently, like the factories, while awaiting a buyer or closure. Some had responded well to the new consumer ethos, and had managed to improve their dreary food and to serve with a smile. In others, managers and staff saw little point; the waitresses hung around, barely reacting if a customer walked in. 'This place is bankrupt, it may well close, so the management just aren't bothering to improve things, and we're all worried for our jobs,' said one sweet girl who served us a grisly steak with mushy vegetables.

Fear of unemployment lay heavy on the land. In a country where jobs had been guaranteed for all and seldom was a worker laid off, the east Germans now found it psychologically hard to adapt to a disturbing new situation. The Government sought to cushion the blow: for firms that had to reduce staff, it introduced the option of '*Kurzarbeit null Stunden*' (nil-hours short-time work), whereby an employee stayed at home but was still on the payroll and received 85 or 90 per cent of his salary, mostly paid for by Bonn. This euphemism for unemployment maybe salvaged pride a little; and in fact about three times as many workers were on this *Kurzarbeit* as were fully on the dole, where unemployment benefits averaged 70 per cent of previous wages. Even so, by spring 1991 the total not at work had reached 3 million (33 per cent), as gloom and unrest grew – and the *Kurzarbeit* scheme was due to end in July. People hung around at home, not knowing what to do. In the old GDR, the workplace had often been the social focus of their lives; the work tempo was slow, allowing plenty of time for a friendly gossip, or for going out shopping, and all this they now missed. Heads of department faced the entirely novel problem of which of their staff to send home, and for the more kindly of them this was agonising: 'All my team are good, they all need their jobs, and I feel I'd rather sack myself – bloody capitalism!' said one senior journalist.

Even those still at work faced the added threat of a possible decline in living standards, as costs and prices rose while wages were still at one-third to one-half of Western levels. After currency union, the workers were paid in solid Deutschmarks but at their old rates, while prices were now in DM too. The powerful Western trade unions moved in to the east, taking over from the discredited Party-run unions; and it was tacitly agreed between unions, employers and Government that wages in the private sector would rise gradually, perhaps reaching parity with Western ones by about 1995. But the speed would depend on rises in productivity, and the Government hoped that the unions would not rock the boat by pressing for too rapid rises that might prejudice economc renewal. The pattern varied widely. Some of the unions, notably IG Metall, negotiated immediate pay rises in their sectors, bringing wages up from *c.* 30 to *c.* 45 or 50 per cent of Western ones; some service firms were already paying about 60 per cent, and IG Metall hoped to reach 65 per cent by the end of 1991. Workers were certainly much less well off than their Western counterparts: but the low level of house rents and most utilities made the real disparity smaller than these percentages might suggest. Even so, there were resentments, especially in border areas where the gulf was most apparent: near Eisenach I met a teacher earning 1,000 DM a month, whose sister was commuting daily to work as a salesgirl in a nearby Hessen supermarket that paid her 2,000 DM.

It was in the public sector that the disparity was greatest. Civil service wage scales in Germany are always statutory; and in the Unity Treaty it was laid down that for an indefinite period salaries in the east would be 35 per cent of those in the west. For one thing, the new *Länder* and the town councils hardly had the money to pay more. But this meant that in the same office a *Beamte* on secondment from the west would be far better off than his eastern counterpart doing the same work. In Dresden, the Saxony Government Press spokesman, Dr Michael Kinze, a local man, told me: 'We are trying to rebuild this country, but our low wages are destroying morale, and unless they are raised soon, there will be serious unrest. We are losing good people to the private sector, where my secretary could earn twice as much as here.' However, as Dr Kinze admitted, few employees' living standards had as yet actually fallen as a result of unification, even in the civil service. It was true that basic foodstuffs such as milk and bread were now much dearer, for their subsidies had been slashed: on the other hand, many imported goods had lost their luxury tax and were now much cheaper. 'A bottle of wine used to cost 11 DM, now I can get it for 4 or 5 DM,' said Kinze, 'and I can buy a good Italian refrigerator for 300 DM, whereas we formerly had to pay 1,300 DM for an inferior GDR one.' However, in 1991 housing rents began increasing sharply, as did charges for domestic heating, public transport and other utilities, all hitherto highly subsidised and very cheap. This, plus rising unemployment, was certain to make many people feel the pinch. The worst, it seemed, was yet to come.

Many workers began to grow restive. In November 1990 the railway employees of the east's Reichsbahn, now being merged into the west's federal Bundesbahn, went on strike for higher wages, and won a partial victory. It was the first of a number of strikes that in 1991 spread to postal workers, miners and others. And for Ossis this kind of action was a novel experience. The strikes were backed by the western unions of the DGB: these had moved into the east in 1990, to fill the vacuum caused by the eclipse of the old GDR unions which had been run by the Party and were never democratically representative. IG Metall soon had 800,000 members in the east, a proportionately higher figure than in the west. The DGB unions helped to set up proper elected works councils, and they poured in advisers and funds to enable the workers to establish branches on the Western model. But it was not easy. 'We're all Germans, but we just don't speak the same language,' said one IG Metall leader, who told me how hard it was to explain to employees the role of a union in a free society: 'they expect us to provide ready solutions for all situations, they have no experience of fighting their own battles. But of course they'll learn.' Meanwhile, the full panoply of the west's excellent labour relations structure, including *Mitbestimmung* and the apprenticeship scheme, was being extended to the east by the Federal Government.

Worry about jobs and wages also infected east Germany's 800,000 farmers and farm workers, most of them employees of their own cooperatives. If less so than industry, agriculture too was in economic crisis; and it needed drastic reorganisation if it was to compete within the European Community. Many cooperatives were running heavily into debt, scarcely able to pay their own staff. First, with the collapse of the old regime they had lost their guaranteed markets and most of their State subsidies; secondly, after currency union the food stores became flooded with Western produce, which Eastern shoppers assumed to be of better quality than their own. Certainly it was far better presented and packaged, especially the dairy goods. Suddenly there were twenty-five enticing varieties of yoghourt, instead of just one; and some goods bore seductive slogans, such as, 'Dr X says this makes you healthier!', which were readily believed by Ossi buyers unused to Western advertising techniques. Some Western wholesalers even played on this trend, by filling the stores they now controlled with their own imports, thus pushing local produce off the shelves. You could buy Dutch tomatoes more easily than Brandenburg ones. All this was hardly fair, for the GDR's vegetables and even much of its meat and processed foods were perfectly good: it was just that they looked less nice – and weren't Western. So the farmers found it harder to sell their produce. In addition, now that it would be sold in hard currency, they risked losing much of their East European market.

Prices for the producer began to tumble, due above all to the cuts in subsidies. A kilo of pork now fetched 2 Marks instead of 8; a litre of milk fell from 1.70 Marks to 59 Pfg. And so the cooperatives found it hard to pay their overheads. In the summer of 1990 many farmers utilised their new freedom of public protest: some 250,000 of them packed the Alexanderplatz in Berlin, pelting de Mazière's agriculture minister with eggs and tomatoes, even forcing his resignation. The Government did then grant the cooperatives special loans, to enable them to pay their wage bills: but these only made up part of the deficit. Under the old system, subsidies for farming had been at two-and-a-half times the EC level, accounting for nearly 12 per cent of the GDR state budget: this was part of the policy of making basic necessities very cheap for the population. And the farmers themselves earned good wages by GDR standards.

By the winter the crisis had subsided a little, as the novelty of buying Western produce wore off, and as cooperatives began to cut their costs by shedding staff and selling surplus livestock. But it was clear that they would need a basic overhaul, in order to face the new market conditions, and that the 800,000 people employed in farming and food-processing should be reduced by about half. Most of the 4,500 cooperatives, each covering some 10,000 hectares, were not only overstaffed but poorly managed; the bureaucratic system had too many middlemen, and in true GDR style was geared more to production targets than market needs. I heard of one cooperative near Potsdam that produced a dull-tasting but high-yield apple for East Berliners. It could thus easily fulfil its quantity targets: but once it lost its protected market, its sales inevitably dwindled away.

Under the old regime, some farmland was owned directly by the State. But most of it was in the form of cooperatives still owned in theory by their members, who had been forced to pool their land in the 1950s. And now, after the *Wende*, under a new law, they were being given the chance to buy it back and farm it again individually, if they wished. But, believe it or not, very few of them opted to do so – less than 1 per cent. This was not in fact so surprising. First, after more than thirty years most farmers had lost any sense of attachment to their own parcel of land, or had even forgotten which fields had belonged to their family; if they were to take them back, it would be for economic, not sentimental reasons. Secondly, the cooperatives were so organised that each member had his own technical speciality, and only a few dealt with marketing and accountancy: so a farmer was scared of running his own business, if he had no experience of these matters. A cowhand might know nothing about pigs or sheep. Thirdly, and most important, the work was shared out on an easy rota basis, and farmers had most weekends free. With its regular lunch breaks and short hours, it was more like an office job than the seventy-hour week and hard responsibility of a family farm – so why should members want to give up this easy life?

Near Eisenach I visited a livestock cooperative that grouped four villages. Its buildings looked quite neat and trim, with a modern social meeting-hall adorned with murals of country scenes. I was told that since the *Wende* the staff had been reduced from 110 to sixty-five: some had taken early retirement, while many of the artisans and technicians had found other work in Eisenach (like most cooperatives, this one used to have its own electricians, carpenters and so on). Some of the livestock, too, which included 120 milk cows, 2,800 pigs and 1,000 sheep, were being sold off or slaughtered, for the EC was imposing quotas on the overstocked east German farms. The cooperative's president, Helmut Zelmann, told me that he was worried about how to adapt to the EC's agricultural regulations, during the agreed five-year transition period. And the EC milk quotas made him especially excited: 'The old regime encouraged us to produce as much milk as possible, and now we're told to cut right back. But what do we do with the cows? They're not machines, we can't just switch them off. And if we sell them, we get only 1,500 DM a cow, one-quarter of the pre-1989 price.' Even so, he felt that it should now be possible to run the farm with as few as forty workers, instead of 110, 'so long as we reorganise, bring in modern methods, and replace the awful old machinery we were given. On the whole', he went on, 'I'm glad the old system has gone. It produced a certain team solidarity, but gave us no freedom. So long as we can solve the economic questions, I think we do have a bright future. But the transition to a new system is too fast and brutal.'

On this cooperative, only one member wanted to return to private farming. And who could blame the others? In France, Bavaria and elsewhere (see p. 154), the mystique of the small family farm remains strong: but often this leads the farmer into unnecessary hardship and drudgery, even inefficiency. In Europe, the way of the future could well lie either with large private estates or with well-run cooperatives whose members freely share the ownership, tasks and responsibilities. According to many experts, if those in east Germany were properly modernised and democratised, and split up into smaller units, they could well become competitive within a year or two, at least in cereals, fruit and vegetables (for livestock, it might be more difficult). Much of the farmland is good and fertile – except for the areas near factories, mines or waste dumps, so sadly polluted.

Environmental pollution in Eastern Europe, it has been said, 'could well be Communism's most enduring legacy'; and in industrial East Germany it was as bad as anywhere outside the Soviet Union. The GDR had the world's highest level per capita of sulphur dioxide emissions. From the chemical factories and power stations, from the uranium and lignite mines, and from ordinary domestic lignite-burning and car exhaust, the varied poisonous fumes poured out over town and country, ruining health, blighting forests, blackening rivers, sickening the air and in some places clouding the skies. Many people contracted asthma, bronchitis, even cancer. And the tree sickness from 'acid rain' was in many areas as bad as in West Germany, though less publicised.

The reasons for the high pollution were economic. Desperate to increase its industrial output and its exports, the old regime refused to squander money on costly environmental measures, such as air or water purification. And there were neither the funds nor the technology, nor the political will, to modernise the filthy pre-war industrial plant. What's more, the GDR had few domestic sources of energy except plentiful lignite, so this smutty fuel was exploited to the maximum, and in the cheapest way possible, so as to avoid paying for oil or gas imports that would either cost hard currency or increase dependence on the Soviet Union. It was all a matter of trade balances and national self-sufficiency.

The rulers knew about the problems, but did not tell the public. Discussion of pollution was taboo, in the Press and media, and in speeches. In some of the worst areas, local doctors gave the Health Ministry worried reports about the effect on health: but these were hushed up. Anger and anxiety grew in these places, and some of those who left for the West were 'environmental refugees' concerned for their health. Then after the *Wende* the 'national catastrophe' (as one mayor called it) became revealed in all its ghastly detail, and many east Germans were more shocked by this than any other aspect of the old regime, even the Stasi. When I asked one Party loyalist, a senior journalist, what he thought about pollution, he said, 'But here in Berlin we just didn't know about it – how could we? – no one told us. And anyway', he added ingenuously, 'it was the fault of the West with its Cocom ban on technologies for modernising our factories.'

In 1990 it was estimated that the total cost of the clean-up might be as much as 45 billion DM a year over ten years. And there would be added social costs too, for many factories were to be closed down or restructured on environmental grounds, thus adding to unemployment. Private investors were being asked to pay a part of the total bill: but the Federal Government, and thus the Western tax-payer, would have to pay the lion's share. As opinion polls were showing that 80 per cent of west Germans regarded the pollution problem as *the* top priority in the east, Bonn was hopeful that they might be prepared to contribute. For a people as environment-conscious as west Germans, the inheritance of such a disaster on their doorstep was especially horrifying: but, ironically, they had helped to cause it themselves! Since the early 1970s several West German cities, notably Berlin, had annually sold the GDR millions of tons of their rubbish for disposal, much of it toxic, and this had earned the East up to 1 billion DM a year. Few of the dumps were environmentally protected, so they added to the pollution. Now these irresponsible deals were expensively boomeranging.

Much of the acrid smell in the streets of east German towns came from the exhaust of 'Trabis' and Wartburgs: but this menace seemed likely to solve itself before too long, thanks to the Ossis' new passion for buying relatively hygienic Western cars to replace their 'little stinkers'. Far more serious was the problem of the lignite, which provided 83 per cent of the GDR's electricity and supplied 69 per cent of its total energy (most of the rest was from imported oil and gas, with nuclear power only 3 per cent). The GDR was the world's number one consumer of this 'brown coal', which lay near the surface and was mined open-cast, mainly in Saxony. Here the digging of flaky, poor-quality lignite scattered millions of tons of dust over the ravaged countryside and into people's lungs: in some areas, the giant craters, the brown, barren fields, the rickety equipment, looked like the aftermath of some holocaust. The lignite was used in factories, and for nearly all domestic heating. Modern flats had central heating, but in older homes the lignite was put raw into stoves: it was dumped in heaps outside blocks of flats, and people had to haul it themselves up flights of stairs. The smell was everywhere.

In 1990 the lignite clean-up began, with the aim that electricity, oil or gas from the west should gradually take its place. Some of the more noxious mines were closed; some would be tidied up and returned to nature, as the west Germans had done so well in the Cologne area (see p. 146). Many factories would still use lignite: but, with better technology, it could be burned more cleanly than hitherto. As for domestic heating, most towns were planning to lay on gas or oil, but this was expensive and would take time, even with the help of loans from Bonn. At a small spa in Thuringia in 1990, I found the streets full of roadworks for new gas mains. 'As we're a health resort, it's the least we can do,' said the new CDU mayor; 'otherwise, our guests will simply go elsewhere, now that they are free to choose their own holidays. This new gas will still come from the same lignite, but it will be clean heating. Crazy that it wasn't done years ago.'

The GDR's few nuclear power stations were all being closed down, for they had been built with Soviet technology, judged unsafe. And what of the uranium mines in the hills near the Czech border, far more damaging to health than the lignite mines? Uranium had been mined there for many years at Soviet insistence, to provide material for their military warheads: but the first victims were the local people, who began to suffer from lung diseases, cancer, loss of hair and other ailments caused by dust from the mines. 'There's a sense of doom about the place,' reported Nick Thorpe in the *Observer*. The Soviet-GDR mining company, Wismut, generously issued free vitamin injections, and wigs for those with no more hair! After the *Wende* the Wismut mines were closed, under strong public pressure.

The other major black-spot was the chemical industry's heartland north of Leipzig, where Bitterfeld was described by *Der Spiegel* as 'the most polluted town in Europe'. Over half of the GDR's emissions of sulphur dioxide came from this area. Giant belching chimneys and slagheaps stood right next to soot-blackened housing where pale children, prone to bronchitis and tumours, played amid the waste land; the air smelt foully of chemicals and lignite-dust; much of the factory machinery dated from the 1920s. In 1990, here and at nearby Buna and Leuna, many of the worst of the carbide furnaces and other toxic plant began to be closed down – at the price of many lost jobs – and the air became a little clearer. But a grey Los Angeles-like pall still hung over the sky at some hours of the day. And the poisons that had sunk deep into the soil might take decades to remove.

Other varied poisons had severely polluted the lovely river Elbe, as it curved gracefully through the hills of 'Saxon Switzerland' to the battered spires of Dresden. The Czechs upstream had been to blame, as much as the GDR: both had thoughtlessly poured industrial effluent into the river, while at Dresden the city's sewage went in untreated. Fish were found dead on the banks, as the water swirled black. In 1990, over 1 billion DM of Government money was earmarked for a clean-up of the Elbe: local cellulose factories were closed, and soon the improvement was noticeable. All over east Germany, some two-thirds of the rivers were polluted, and new purification plants were badly needed to improve the quality of the water supply. In the Leipzig suburbs, a river once used for bathing and boating was now seething with toxic foam. At Potsdam likewise, bathing was forbidden in its necklace of lovely lakes, fed by a polluted canal, whereas two miles upstream in west Berlin the sparkling Havel lakes were a paradise for bathers and surfers. A new water treatment plant was now due to be built.

And so, with typical thoroughness, the Germans set about cleansing the east of its pollution, after the criminal neglect of the Honecker regime. So important was the health aspect that it probably justified the huge sums to be spent, even if this meant diverting funds that might have been used for new investment and new jobs. Most of the money would come from the rich west. But the new *Länder* and town councils in the east would have to pay a part, and they could ill afford it. So next we look at the problems of local government.

## Land *and* Rathaus *renewal: keeping the old comrades?*

Travel notes on visits to Saxony and Thuringia, 1990–1:

We arrive in Dresden, capital of the old kingdom of Saxony and now the *Land* capital. It used to be one of Europe's loveliest cities, known as 'Florence on the Elbe'; Schiller felt 'lifted to heaven' by its glorious ensemble of baroque palaces and churches. But its soul has been deeply bruised, first by the Allies, then by Communism. It has never really recovered from the Anglo-American air-raid of February 1945 that killed at least 35,000 civilians; and it still wears a stunned, scorched look, even though some of its finest buildings, notably the Semper Opera and the Zwinger, were carefully restored under Honecker, using the original stone. But so fierce was the heat of the fire-bombing that much of the stone, once all golden, is now irretrievably blackened, while some palatial buildings are still gaunt ruins – a grim sight by day, but strangely beautiful at night when skilful floodlighting lends these fried façades a ghostly grandeur.

From the cathedral's lofty parapet, statues of saints look down accusingly on the havoc wrought. The city council is now restoring the giant *Schloss* next door, which will house a museum. But the famous Frauenkirche will probably be kept as an evocative ruin, like the memorial church in west Berlin: its two stunted towers rise above its own weed-covered rubble, in stark contrast to the glossy new luxury hotel beside it. Some other downtown areas have been rebuilt since the 1950s in Stalinist-concrete style: witness the once-so-elegant Pragerstrasse, now a graceless shopping mall, and the brash Palace of Culture. In fact, a walk through the city centre makes for an awesome encounter with the changing moods of history, from the majestic eighteenth century via wartime horror and Socialist drabness to today's more hopeful era, when new chic is appearing in shop windows and posters announce joyously, 'Back in Dresden, the Dresdner Bank!' (Germany's second biggest, founded here in 1872). But the sombre-looking, poorly-dressed crowds, queuing for hot-dogs or pizzas at the new makeshift stalls in the muddy main square, do not seem to feel that the new golden age has yet arrived.

At night we come out of the serene floodlit Zwinger courtyard into the Altmarkt and a scene of total contrast – a giant Munich beer-tent provided by Bavaria's right-wing CSU party, full of sozzled 'free' Saxons, noisy vulgarity and crude anti-Marxist election posters. The band in *Lederhosen* is playing the Beatles' *I Believe in Yesterday* – a sentiment shared by the 9 per cent of Dresdners who still vote PDS? But the new CDU-led city council believes in tomorrow, despite everything, and aims to turn Dresden back into a cultural and touristic metropolis that can rival Munich, centring round the Semper Opera and the marvellous paintings in the museums. For this it has to replan the whole city centre, still a drab and desolate mess, and will invite architects to compete with new ideas.

Meantime, everything remains provisional. The *Land* Government is temporarily housed in a pompous grey hulk by the Elbe that was built in 1904 by the Saxon royal rulers. The ramshackle industrial zone to the west has reduced its noxious fumes but is yet to be razed and rebuilt. And the shabby downtown *Wurst* and pizza stalls are the best that new free-enterprise catering can provide until investors get round the property problem. However, a few older private restaurants are flourishing, and they shine out amid the solemn State-created ones. We dined divertingly at Linie 6, a bistro made in part from an old tram-coach and full of comic tramway gimmicks. One of the jokey whistle-blowing waiters tells us: 'In 1989 we ran a sort-of cabaret here which was a centre of dissent, and we almost got closed down. The Stasi would sit outside in their cars and try to listen – so we invited them in for a drink.'

Leaving Dresden for the *Autobahn*, we pass a giant BP service station, just opened. It claims to be Europe's largest, with shops and café, and space for twenty-six cars to fill up at a time; and it is highly popular with Dresdners who find it an exciting contrast to the gloomy little State petrol stations. The automatic car-wash, for them a real novelty, draws long queues although it costs 12 DM. BP managed to get in quick and lease the land from the city before the Treuhand could step in; now the company plans 250 other outlets in east Germany. Its only complaint: many local motorists fill up and then drive off without paying.

We take the *Autobahn* going west. Heavy lorries hurtling towards Frankfurt. Tiny Polish cars laden with crates and bundles. A few shiny new Opels with eastern number-plates; but far more pale-green rusty Trabis and urgent western Audis. Along this and all other roads in the east we see virtually no police: yet before the *Wende* there were always swarms of them, quick to stop and fine in Deutschmarks (and possibly pocket the proceeds) any Western tourist exceeding the strict 100 kph motorway limit. Then in 1990, scared and discredited, bereft of authority, the police kept the lowest of profiles. As a result, most people drove at 120–130 kph or more – not only the visiting Mercs and BMWs but also the local Trabis and Wartburgs not built for such speeds. No wonder the east's road-accident rate rose fourfold. And today, after unification, the police are still absent and the cars still go as fast, even though the speed limits remain in force.

We come to industrial Chemnitz, which has now won back its proper name after spending forty years as Karl-Marx-Stadt. A titanic twenty-two-foot bronze head of that old bearded Leftie, the work of a Soviet sculptor, still stands in the main square. The town council wants to sell it – but who would buy? Albania? Highgate cemetery? or some nutty American collector? Nearby, we see long dismal queues outside a foodstore, next to a snazzy new shop selling saunas and jacuzzis from Bosch and Siemens – and who buys *them*, in this run-down dump of a town? We escape into the Saxon hills, and pass the one British-number-plate car that we see on the whole trip. It turns down a road signposted 'Colditz' – typical British, their minds still firmly stuck in the last war.

We pass through a number of quiet villages. As all over east Germany, the villages with their cobbled roads and old farmhouses have a quaint, timeless look, as if unchanged since the 1930s. In a way, one would wish them to remain so nostalgically unspoilt. But the broken-down telephone kiosks, the seedy grocery stores, the crumbling walls, the solemn elderly women trundling heavy handcarts, reveal the reality of long waste and neglect behind the picturesqueness. Here and there, a brand-new sign for Bosch or Coca-Cola proclaims the future now arriving. A poster in one small town announces the opening of a 'Sex-Shop'.

We reach Leipzig, a slightly bigger town than Dresden, and to my mind far more interesting and appealing. It *looks* terrible, yet is vibrantly alive, with a quirky spirit all its own. We try several hotels but all are full: so we turn to the tourist office where an engaging gay gives us the strangest sales-spiel, talking French in a thick Saxon accent: 'My dear, everything here is *foutu*. One hotel has been bought by Count Lamsdorff, the politician; and our tourist office is getting a new boss, a Westphalian count who's a cousin of a city councillor. A lot of former SED people are still in top posts, too. So the old and the new *Seilschaften* (networks) are carving the place up – and as usual it's the little people like us who suffer. We've lost most of our tourists. But the hotels are packed out with Western businessmen and officials who stay for months, as you can't get flats.' So he sends us into the suburbs, to B&B with friends of his in a tiny modern flat where they lend us their bedroom and sleep on sofas. They need the money, as they are both out of jobs. The wife, the kindest, cheeriest soul, with a droll humour, has been a *coiffeuse*, so she cuts our hair for a few Marks each – 'I'm glad to do this for our Western guests, now we can buy good Western shampoos. Ooh, it's so lovely having visitors from all over the world, after all those dark years. Yes, times are still hard, but maybe they'll get better. Never grumble, I say. Here, have a cognac – it's on the house!' She tells us that she has cancer.

Dresden was the old royal and residential city of Saxony, a bit staid, and Leipzig the commercial, musical and literary city, much more fun. In the eighteenth century it was known as 'the market-place of Europe'; its university, founded in 1409, became a major literary focus (Goethe, as a student there, learned to write erotic poetry). Bach lived and worked there 1723–50, Wagner was born there, and until 1945 Leipzig was the major publishing and printing centre of the German-speaking world, with 900 firms involved and the world's biggest book fair. The GDR regime then kept this fair going (despite the transfer of the major part to Frankfurt), as well as the big twice-yearly Trade Fair which it used as a shop-window for exporting to the West. But in other ways Honecker neglected Leipzig cruelly, depriving it of resources for the benefit of East Berlin; and the fierce local resentments help to explain why in 1989 it became the motor of the revolution.

The city never lost its spirit, which today can flourish more freely again, despite the economic crisis. The jumble of the much-bombed and much-rebuilt Altstadt, where a few old buildings survive, has a civilised ambience with touches of sophistication unusual in east German towns – due maybe to the trade-fair links with the world, to the big university right in the centre, and to the sprightly temperament of these Saxons, less severe than the Prussians to the north. There are smart boutiques and bookshops, satiric cabarets, lots of neat cafés. Out in the suburbs, the potholed roads, crumbling façades and rickety factories are as woeful as in any east German city. But even they can achieve a certain melancholy beauty, as a wan winter sun shines mistily through the haze of pollution. I even feel that this might be a city I could live in, and forge with it a passionate love-hate relationship – a place of strong local pride and creativity, now engaged in an epic struggle to regain its former role.

In a cellar in the Altstadt is Auerbach's Keller, the historic but now rather gloomy restaurant where Goethe set a scene from *Faust*. The nearby grimy hulk of the Neues Rathaus (1899), under its new lord mayor from Hanover, has already acquired a new roof of coloured patterned tiles; appropriately it is next to the new local headquarters of the Deutsche Bank, which like the other big Frankfurt banks now holds the real power in the town. Spiritual power focuses on the white-naved Nikolaikirche, whose Monday meetings spawned the revolution; and on the fifteenth-century Thomas Kirche where Bach was organist and choirmaster. Its pastors can be wittily critical on current issues. On my first visit, in 1985, I found daringly displayed inside it a quotation from Luther, 'A Christian is a free man in all things and no man's slave.' That was about as far as dissent could go, in those days. Returning now, after currency union, I find this poster replaced by one of a man blindfolded by a 100 DM banknote, with coins covering his eyes and the words, 'Man does not live by money alone.'

Another pompous blackened palace, the Reichsgericht, was the seat of the Reich's supreme judiciary from 1895 to 1945: here in 1933 the Nazis staged the Reichstag fire trial, and tried to pin the guilt on the Bulgarian Communist, Georgi Dimitroff. The GDR regime then turned the Court into a propagandist museum of the Working-Class Struggle Against Fascism. Like most GDR museums that touch on social or historical questions, it is now being ideologically revamped: some of its more blatant exhibits have been removed, but not all. We are button-holed by a manic lady in a blouse almost as deep a red as her views, who insists on showing us round. 'Today', she concludes, 'let us pursue together the democratic fight against world fascism!' I suggest that in this town the recent democratic fight has been against another 'ism'. '*Leider, ah, leider,*' she replies. In the street outside, a big framed colour photo of Honecker is lying in a dustbin. I pick it up. A girl passing on a motorbike sees it, grins at me, and makes a throat-cutting gesture. No redshirt, she.

The dilapidated Connewitz district of Leipzig shows signs of becoming a small-scale Kreuzberg. Since 1989 it has acquired a way-out art gallery, some bohemian late-night cafés, and an excellent 'alternative' bookshop where writers hold readings. Students and artists have squatted in a group of derelict tenement blocks. But, apart from occasional bashings-up between local 'redskins' (extreme-left) and skinheads (extreme-right), it is all very peaceable, with an atmosphere of innocent novelty, as if Connewitz were suddenly inventing the kind of scene that the West knew in the sixties. Some foreigners have moved in, too. A young Californian painter and his Japanese wife have opened up an arty candlelit café where she cooks sashimi; he tells me that the city gives him a small grant to run the place as a community and race-relations centre, a retort to east Germany's mounting xenophobic racism. I find Connewitz rather inspiring. All it needs is some latter-day Goethe to be writing erotic poetry.

Our next stop is Weimar, a haven of civilised serenity with more cultural history per square foot than any other town in all Germany − Goethe, Bach, Schiller, Liszt and many others all lived here. The GDR regime treated Weimar with respect, and did not try to harness its heritage for propaganda; it has also remained surprisingly well-kept and unshabby. But the tourists are now flooding in − will it go the way of Stratford and Venice?

On a hill behind the town is Buchenwald concentration camp where the Nazis killed 56,000. The GDR regime respectfully made it into a memorial for the victims, but with the accent firmly on the sufferings of German Communists and Russian soldiers, not others. And so the usual problems now arise of correcting the bias. In the museum, next to a caption abusing the bourgeoisie for abetting Nazism, is a new notice: 'Dear visitors, changes are to be made, be patient.' And at the entrance is an appeal for 'witnesses of the true facts' to come forward − I learn that this refers to the fact that in 1945–51 the Soviet Army ran the camp and filled it with thousands of Nazi suspects rounded up in the region, many probably innocent (my own mother-in-law, the least Nazi of gentle ladies, was in one such camp in Silesia, and nearly died). The Russians did their share of torture, and mass graves of the victims have been found near by. But of course all this was hushed up until very recently. Certainly the Nazis' own crimes should never be minimised. But nor should others'.

Finally, on our way to the West we visit Erfurt and Eisenach, two mediaeval Thuringian towns with a strong sense of local pride and identity. Their fine ensembles of old half-timbered houses were already partly restored before the *Wende*: much more work of this kind still needs to be done, but it is far from being the top priority. In Eisenach, right by the Hessen border, the hilltop Wartburg castle where Luther translated the Bible is now thronged with west German tourists, and so is the Bach museum (he was born in the town). This brings in money, but only a tiny fraction of what is needed for dealing with housing, roads, pollution, and a score of other urgent problems. All east German towns, and the new *Land* governments, are very seriously short of cash, and of good qualified staff. Local government has been democratised, but that is only a start.

On unification, the west German system of local government was extended fully to the east. After the war the Communist regime had abolished the old *Länder* and imposed its own highly centralised structure. It is true that in schools in Saxony, for instance, some Saxon history was still taught, but mainly in terms of the workers' and peasants' heroic struggles against royal oppression. In Thuringia, some people managed to keep the old local folklore groups alive: but these were frowned on by the authorities, who did not want any local patriotism of this kind to compete with loyalty to the Party and State. Now, in 1990, the *Länder* were re-established, on a slightly different geographical pattern from pre-war days. Saxony was the largest in population and most important, followed by Saxony-Anhalt, Thuringia, Brandenburg (the region around Berlin, which was a separate *Land*); the smallest was Mecklenburg-West-Pomerania, beside the Baltic. It was hoped that these *Länder* might help to provide people with a new sense of identity, to make up for the loss of the much-discussed 'GDR identity', and thus assuage any dislike of simply being swallowed up into west Germany. After all, if a Bavarian could feel such loyalty to his *Land*, why should not a Saxon? It might not happen all at once, after the forty-year vacuum. But there were signs that people were ready to revive these loyalties, especially in Saxony and Thuringia.

After their elections on October 14, 1990, the new *Land* parliaments and the ministries set up house where they could, often in makeshift premises. In Potsdam, Brandenburg's *Landtag* and prime minister took over a splendid Prussian château: but the environment ministry had to make do with an old dilapidated GDR institute up in the woods. These *Land* governments, and the new democratic town councils, had to set about running themselves on the exact Western model, and under West German law. And as if this were not problem enough, they found themselves even shorter of money than they had anticipated. The Federal Government and the western *Länder* had promised a global subsidy of 150 billion DM, to be shared out between them over four years. But this had presupposed that they would earn sustantial income also from their own taxation. In the event, this was much lower than expected, owing to the economic downturn which reduced their local tax revenue from companies and individuals. Saxony had hoped to draw 30 per cent of its budget from its own taxes, but found the figure was only 10 per cent. All this severely impeded the urban renewal so badly needed. Dresden had to cut its culture budget by a third.

The new local administrations badly needed good qualified staff at all levels. Naturally they did not want to take on too many of the SED apparatchiks who had served the previous regime; nor did they want to hire too many westerners, for this would be expensive and would add to charges that the east was being 'colonised'. But to find others with the right experience was not easy. At the top level, some of the east's own leaders were excellent, for example, Dr Manfred Stolpe, the Protestant churchman who became SPD prime minister of Brandenburg. But in the middle and lower ranks, the quality was poor, for the stratified GDR system had seldom offered people the right experience.

In the shorter term there was no choice but to seek help from the west, especially for learning how to adapt to Western law and administrative methods. A few Western politicians and senior officials came voluntarily to serve the new *Länder* and to settle there – either because their roots were there, or in a spirit of idealism or adventure, or because their careers had come unstuck in the west. Or a bit of all three. The star case was Professor Kurt Biedenkopf, who had been a distinguished figure in the CDU in Bonn, but had fallen out with Kohl: he now lent his talents and prestige to the Saxons, who elected him their prime minister (all the other new *Land* premiers were local men). Similarly some towns elected mayors from the west: Leipzig's had held a senior post in the Rathaus of its twin-town, Hanover. These transplants were generally successful: but sometimes the Wessi would throw his weight around tactlessly, as if he knew everything best.

The eastern *Länder* twinned themselves informally with western ones, which bilaterally gave a good deal of help at their own expense, in the early days. Thus North-Rhine-Westphalia sent 1,000 civil servants on one or two years' secondment to Brandenburg, to help mainly with accountancy, staff training, and the complex new legal problems that needed a knowledge of Western law. These 'advisers' (as they were tactfully called) had Western salaries, and often went back home at weekends. Some eastern *Länder* and cities also hired Westerners directly on longer contracts. But this was expensive, for they had to be paid at Western rates; and the volunteers were few, for not many of these experts relished eastern living conditions and life-styles ('What! – no private tennis-clubs or swimming pools?'). What is more, the new *Land* leaders realised that to pack their upper echelons with know-all Westerners might cause resentment in the middle ranks. 'For forty years we were unable to run our own affairs', said one Postdamer, 'and we don't want it to happen again in another guise.' And a talented Dresdner on Biedenkopf's staff told me: 'It is humiliating for us to find out how much we do need Westerners' expertise, so at least we expect them to be tactful. Some of those who come to work here have no understanding of our psychology or of local conditions, yet they strut around as if they had all the solutions. Bonn should realise that it's not enough just to change the laws. The human factor counts, too.'

The other alternative was to hire former SED members who had served in the old regime: but this posed greater dilemmas. Should some of these old *Genossen* (comrades) be allowed to continue in public posts, or not? It was a problem that concerned all local government, as well as schools and universities, hospitals and lawcourts; also the factories, as we have seen. And it became a subject of sore debate. On the one hand, many of these *Genossen* had the experience and ability that were now much needed; and many had not been sincere Communists but had joined the Party to further their careers, and could easily re-adapt. On the other hand, public opinion was extremely angry to see old SED loyalists still in their jobs, especially if they were thought to have had Stasi connections. So it was a tricky job to sort out the hard-liners from the others, the reconvertible from those who deserved to be cast aside. 'It's the problem that West Germany knew after 1945, but with differences,' said one CDU man; 'The Nazis were so much more evil than the SED, so the moral choice then was clearer. And the Nazi regime had lasted only twelve years, so it was easier to find people who had not been indoctrinated. Even so, far too many old Nazis were allowed to keep their jobs, and we want to avoid these mistakes. Last time, the Allies did the job for us initially, and they made many mistakes. Now we Germans must do it for ourselves, and get it right.'

But how? A vast screening process began, whereby all those in the public sector above a certain junior level were given elaborate question-naires about their past activities. Some in more delicate or politicised fields, such as judges or history teachers, were dismissed and put on a 'waiting list' at 70 per cent of full salary, until their case was cleared; others were provisionally kept in jobs, but they still had to submit to screening if they had been in the Party or held a post of any influence. And as this screening included questioning of witnesses, a nasty imbroglio of lies and distortions sometimes ensued, as some witnesses denounced the *Genossen* in a spirit of revenge, while others tried to mount cover-ups for old buddies. In this confused situation, the advice of Bonn to the *Länder* was to avoid any systematic witch-hunt, but to err on the side of strictness, for this is what the public seemed to be demanding. 'When I addressed election rallies in east Berlin in November 1990', a CDU deputy told me, 'this was the main question I kept hearing: why aren't you being tougher with those old bastards?'

For the local authorities closer to the human and practical problems involved, it was not so easy to decide whom to keep even provisionally, and whom to sack. And mistakes were certainly made in both directions. I heard the story of an excellent gynaecologist, popular with his patients, who was now unable to practise just because his senior position had obliged him to join the Party. On the other hand, *Länder* and town coucils were retaining a few hard-liners because of their expertise. In Potsdam, one liberal-minded *Land* executive told me, 'When my young assistant saw a well-known Party expert sitting on the sofa in my office, she burst into tears afterwards. "How terrible! After all the harm that skunk did to me and my family, I never thought I'd be serving him coffee as your guest."'

As far as possible, however, the criterion was to retain only those people who still had public trust, thus eliminating those who were thought to have worked directly with the Stasi. Another criterion was to retain people in junior posts more readily than in senior ones. In Eisenach, mayor Brodhun dismissed or demoted all but two of the former department heads in the Rathaus. 'But the two I kept are doing their jobs very well,' he told me. And the Potsdam executive quoted above said, 'I'm trying to give a few good people the chance to show that they *can* change and now loyally serve a different system. It's silly to call them all *Wendehals*. Many did have a genuine human sense of public service, even under the old regime.' Many senior *Genossen*, however, left of their own accord, either unwilling to serve the new regime, or knowing that they would never be accepted. Some of them, often talented people, then moved straight into the private sector, where they used their contacts and their expertise to set up their own businesses. And they did very well: 'If you can't work for Socialism any more, at least you can become a millionaire', was one jibe. For example, the *Genossen* who had organised international youth concerts for the Party now created their own agency, doing the same thing. Such clever opportunism was widely resented: but there was no legal mechanism for preventing it.

In this way, various little groups of old faithfuls, the so-called *Seilschaften* (rope-teams: a mountaineering metaphor), clung together to help each other in a new hostile society. And these rope-teams were especially active across the perilous rock-face of the legal profession. Almost all judges and state prosecutors had been dismissed before being screened, and it was thought that very few would ever get their jobs back: first, their qualifications were of little use for handling Western law, and secondly most of them had been hand-picked by the old regime as reliable Communists. But some now simply turned to private practice as solicitors, and there was nothing to prevent this: amid the deluge of property claims, they easily found clients. More serious, a number of SED lawyers were discovered to have given false affidavits about each other to their screeners, in a bid to whitewash the truths about their careers. Thus did the *Seilschaften* operate. Meanwhile, the entire apparatus of justice in the east was taken over by judges from west Germany.

A word about the changed role of the Church. Pastors had played a key part in the revolution of 1989, being drawn into political activity almost unintentionally. But now the Church was back on the sidelines, with its influence reduced and its congregations falling off. 'It's inevitable,' said one pastor; 'people now don't need our solace and support so much any more.' And the Churches were as severely short of money as ever. They were now due to adopt the west German system of voluntary church tax. But their parishioners were much poorer than in the west, and fewer: whereas some 90 per cent of west Germans paid the *Kirchensteuer* (see p. 264), in the east less than 40 per cent were registered Church members and in Berlin it was 7 per cent.

'That's what forty years of Communism have done,' said one Leipzig pastor bitterly, 'They've destroyed the broad popular base of the Church, especially in the cities, and I don't think we'll ever get it back. Only 10 per cent of people in this town have church funerals, less than 5 per cent are baptised. Kids round here ask, "Who was Jesus?" Yet it was *we* who made the revolution!' So the Churches would continue to need financial support from the rich west: but they feared that, now they were free again, this might be given less readily. However, not all the clergy were so gloomy. A senior pastor in Eisenach told me: 'The Church was the only institution to survive that regime with integrity. The people know it, and they respect us for it, even if our churches are now emptier. Christians in this town used to be publicly derided, but now we walk very proud. In November 1989, I was summoned by the Party district chief who wanted to make his resignation in front of me.

When I asked why, he said, "But in front of whom else can I decently resign?"'

Alike in *Land* goverments and in city and rural councils, the practical tasks facing the new local authorities were stupendous. 'Sometimes I fear I just can't cope, we're such a bunch of amateurs in this Rathaus, we have so much to learn,' said the 35-year-old CDU mayor of Eisenach, Hans-Peter Brodhun. A doctor of biology, in May 1990 he had left his research institute to head a CDU/SPD coalition in the Stadtrat after the local elections. Charming, energetic, manifestly liberal and humane, he had all the qualities – expert administrative experience. 'When the citizens have come to me all day with their problems, their loss of jobs, their leaking flats with no toilets, I often lie awake at night worrying. What a task we have! But if we really work hard, I think we'll catch up with the west in about ten years.'

Eisenach, like many other towns, was given some direct help by its twin in the west, the old university city of Marburg, in Hessen. The twinning had begun cautiously under the old regime in 1987. It was based on a common veneration of St Elisabeth, a renowned thirteenth-century princess who lived in Wartburg Castle, then in Marburg, and devoted herself to the poor and sick of both towns before dying of exhaustion at the age of 24 – with these credentials, even a holy royal was acceptable to the previous SED mayor of Eisenach. Then in 1990 Marburg's devotion to its poor twin included a gift of buses, a big sum for roof repairs, and training courses for officials. Hessen was also helping Thuringian hospitals, much in need of modern equipment and know-how. In Erfurt, some historic buildings were being restored by Rhineland-Palatinate, while Dresden was receiving aid from Hamburg, its twin-town at the far end of the Elbe.

Mostly, however, towns were having to finance their own renovation, with the help of loans from Bonn, from Brussels, or from the banks ('I have two people full-time looking for money,' said Brodhun). But where to begin the mammoth task of renewal? In Eisenach, the SED regime had cleared a large slum area in the town centre, and had been about to build tall concrete blocks of flats in its usual style; the new council cancelled this project, and began planning smaller-scale housing in local traditional style, with little shops and cafés. In Leipzig, where much of the city needed a drastic overhaul, it seemed likely that private developers would first begin building on vacant spaces, while the more difficult and expensive renovation of older buildings would come later. Plans for new banks, offices and department stores in the city centre were being held up, as usual, by the property question. In both Leipzig and Dresden, the city councils were anxious to prevent 'wild' redevelopment and to rebuild in harmonious style, following a new master-plan. But with money so very short, it seemed that profit-minded promoters might end up wielding much more clout than sensitive architects or conservationists.

The housing in these and other towns, much of it in shocking repair, had either been owned by the State and was thus now inherited by the municipality; or else it belonged to tenant cooperatives; or it consisted of new private bungalows (see p. 383). Most town councils now wanted the tenants to share in the cost of renewal: so they encouraged people to purchase their flats, so long as they promised to renovate. But soon a Catch 22 appeared. First, it was not clear who was the legal owner of the cooperative flats. Secondly, people who lived in the cheap, ugly post-war flats had little desire to buy, for these blocks built with inferior materials were already falling to bits and offered little resale value, as well as being no joy to live in – many inhabitants just wanted to get out as quickly as possible. The older villas and mansions that had been divided into flats offered a much better buy, but as they were liable to claims from their pre-war owners, a city dared not sell to the tenants.

In Leipzig, where the council faced 25,000 such claims on its property, I met a professor with a spacious ground-floor flat in a mansion where the roof leaked and the façade was crumbling. He and the other tenants were ready to buy and renovate, but the council could not clear the ownership issue, nor would it renovate at its own cost, for the rents were far too low. A vicious circle. Throughout the GDR, the old regime had frozen rents at a very low level, so of course there had been little money for repairs or modernisation: in Brandenburg, some 30 per cent of all homes had no bathroom or indoor toilet. Under the Unity Treaty, rents were now due to go up fast; even so, new house-building was bound to be slow. Many people for years might still have to put up with those leaking roofs, drab façades and dingy stairways, which so often were in contrast to the flats' interiors. I have found that although the furnishings are often rather drab, homes in east Germany tend to be at least comfortable in an old-fashioned way, and older ones can be remarkably spacious.

After unification, improving the public infrastructure of railways, roads and telephones became largely the responsibility of the Federal Government. It was reckoned that about 100 billion DM would be needed to bring the railway system up to Western standards: only one-third of it was electrified, and many trains crawled at a snail's pace. Another 100 billion or so would be needed for the motorways and main roads. In the country, secondary roads were fairly good, but in towns and villages the rough, uneven cobblestones and frequent pot-holes put a strain on any car's suspension. In 1990–1 there were roadworks everywhere, but work on them was still proceeding as slowly and fitfully as in the old days. Many roads were closed and the detours were badly signposted, with a typical GDR disregard for the customer. The old *Genossen*, it would seem, were still in their jobs.

As for the telephone system, this was a major cause of hysterical frustration after the *Wende*. In the GDR there was one telephone for every ten people, as against almost one for two in West Germany, and the average waiting time for a private phone was ten to fifteen years. The equipment was pre-digital, much of it dating from the 1930s. And in 1989 only 200 lines connected the two German states. This was tolerable before the *Wende*: but when the borders opened, the rickety eastern system was quite unable to cope with the extra load. Telephoning even between the two parts of Berlin became virtually impossible except in the middle of the night, and people spent hours dialling fruitlessly. Many firms resorted to hiring expensive radio-phones, while after unification some public offices installed telephones with west Berlin numbers in their east Berlin branches. Gradually, however, matters improved, as the Bundespost embarked on a crash programme, with the help of Siemens and other specialist firms. By January 1991, new phone-card call-boxes had begun to appear in the east; and it actually became possible to get through from east to west Berlin after, say, only five dialling attempts instead of fifty. The Bundespost was due to invest some 7 billion DM in 1991, on extra trunk lines and new modern equipment.

At least, when the diverse renewal is finally completed – of factories and offices, of transport and telecommunications – eastern Germany may end up with some of the best and most modern infrastructure in the world. Perhaps by the year 2000.

## *Dilemmas for writers, new values in the classroom*

For the artists and actors, musicians, filmmakers and writers of the old GDR, the *Wende* proved a mixed blessing. Many of the best-known, though no lovers of the Honecker regime, remained attached to some form of Socialism: that is why they had not tried to leave for the West. And so, while they welcomed the new freedom of creative expression, they grew disturbed at the turn taken by unification.

Their personal livelihood was now at risk, too, in many cases, for the theatres and orchestras faced big cuts in subsidies, while individual writers and artists lost the State grants which had afforded them a safe income. They were thrown on to the free market, and few had either the experience or the taste for coping with it. 'We are simply exchanging political for commercial censorship,' said the playwright Heiner Müller. He and others feared that culture would be the first casualty of unification, for its subsidies would now win a low priority: some even accused the Western 'colonisers' of seeking to stamp out east Germany's culture along with the rest of its identity. But some writers in the west replied by accusing their eastern colleagues of excessive self-pity, and of having accepted the old regime's privileges without daring to voice their criticisms of it – until now, when it had become so easy. All in all the cultural mood in the east in 1990 was one of insecurity and depression.

This malaise much affected the world of drama. In autumn 1989 several East Berlin theatres had played a part in the uprising: they held public meetings on stage, and the big staff bar of the Deutsches Theater, the leading state repertory company, became a rallying-point for dissidents of the Neues Forum kind. Productions grew more daring. Then after the *Wende* theatres were quick to present a number of GDR plays long banned, such as Ulrich Plenzdorf's *Kein Runter Kein Fern* (No going out, no telly; 1975), about a sensitive boy destroyed by his Stalinist family. The mood at first was buoyant, but soon the financial problems emerged. The Deutsches Theater kept its subsidy, but its costs doubled after currency union: so it had to start shedding part of its hugely excessive staff of 450. Many GDR actors hitherto on thirty-year contracts now faced dismissal, and it seemed that some theatres would have to close (see p. 56). In this mood, Heiner Müller in March 1990 presented the premiere of his production of *Hamlet* at the Deutsches Theater: dressed entirely in black he announced, 'This is a funeral party for the East German theatre.'

A box-office crisis worsened the situation. Although east Berlin theatres gained new audiences from the west, their regular local ones fell off badly in 1990, for several reasons. Ticket prices doubled or trebled after currency union; easterners now had other things to spend their money on, such as travel; and most important, now that the media were free, the theatre had lost its political role as purveyor of coded messages of dissent. There used to exist a close relationship between audience and actors, who in a classical play such as *Antigone* might accentuate the references to freedom and dictatorship, or even subtly alter the text, and this teasing-the-censor made theatre-going exciting. This now ceased to have significance.

It was a change that affected satiric cabaret even more directly: the famous *Distel* in east Berlin (see p. 395), along with the *Pfeffermühle* in Leipzig and others, could now say whatever they liked and it made them much less interesting. The *Distel* production that I saw in 1991 was full of slick jokes about Wessis and Ossis, about Honecker's sins and Kohl's blunders: but although the new liberty made for speed and sharpness, there was no more tension, no more waiting to see how far the actors and the script would dare to go. The *Distel* would probably still survive, but artistically it seemed set to follow the west's political cabaret into the twilight of a once-glorious Berlin tradition.

An even worse fate befell the famous DEFA film studios near Potsdam, where most of the great pre-war German classics were made. DEFA then became the GDR's main State film-making centre, with excellent facilities. But it now lost its subsidies; and the west German film companies, themselves in dire financial crisis, refused to buy up even parts of it, so it seemed likely to close. At best, some studios might still be hired occasionally for specific films. The veteran GDR director Heiner Carow, whose film about gays, *Coming Out*, won the Silver Bear at the Berlin festival in 1990, explained to me: 'Though I'm a Socialist I was very critical of that regime, and it banned several of my films and scripts. Even so, all of us at DEFA, directors and technicians, had regular State salaries and at least we *could* make films, so long as we toed the line. Now the brutal free market arrives, DEFA's entire staff of 2,200 including forty directors are being dismissed – and at sixty I have to go begging cap-in-hand to the west for finance. I'm too old to adapt. The GDR regime, for all its faults, did at least take cinema seriously as culture. In west Germany, it is just treated as commerce.'

Music fared better. All of its more prestigious institutions seemed certain to survive, including the two east Berlin opera companies, the Semper Oper in Dresden, and the Gewandhaus orchestra in Leipzig under its great conductor, Kurt Masur. But the future of several of east Berlin's eight full-time orchestras looked much less sure. As for the artistic scene, some 2,000 of the GDR's painters and sculptors used to belong to a State-supervised union that guaranteed them regular work and income, so long as they behaved; much of their more conformist work was acquired for State museums, schools and public buildings. This system too ended in 1990, and the artists were thrown on the market: the better ones found galleries in the west, others had to look for other jobs. Most GDR art was expectedly 'safe'; but in the 1980s some rebellious avant-garde artists emerged whose startling fantasies expressed their frustration and anguish. Some found ways of exhibiting clandestinely; others left for the West. Opinions on the quality of their work vary, but few critics rate it very highly. At least it is different: 'East and west German art are in total contrast,' was a view put to me by a west Berlin expert, Michael Haerdte; 'the east's is full of emotion, pathos and suffering, the west's is far more detached and ironical, as you might expect. How long will this raw feeling last?'

The members of the writers' union, like the artists, were now bereft of the assured state incomes that had enabled some five or six hundred of them to live from literature, as few writers can in the West. Some of the better known, such as Christa Wolf and Volker Braun, had publishers in the West, too, and were read there widely: but for the rest, prospects were now rather bleak. Many Eastern publishers were closing down, having lost their protected market for German books. What is more, books had risen sharply in price. And the east German public, no longer in such need of the solace of serious literature, was instead buying books on foreign travel, do-it-yourself or how capitalism works. 'It used to be exciting', said one cultured east Berliner, 'to search the bookshops for some new obliquely critical novel with a limited print-run. Books of this kind had a real value for us. Now we can buy anything, and I don't bother to look.'

Heiner Müller was this kind of writer, a life-long Communist but anti-Honecker, who was now horrified by the advent of capitalism. 'We shall be submerged by American mass culture, and true culture will suffer,' he told me in 1990. 'The GDR's old ideological kitsch, which people just ignored, will be replaced by commercial kitsch, which gets much larger and more eager audiences. That's dangerous.' I went to see Müller in his flat with a leaky ceiling, on the top floor of a hideous, decrepit block of modern utility flats in east Berlin. But he seemed impervious to these surroundings, and had just come back from being fêted in Japan as east Germany's leading playwright-director. After some of his earlier plays on social themes had been banned in the

1960s, he turned to classical subjects where he could make his points more obliquely. And he always had privileges: he could travel abroad, and his works were performed and published in the West, ensuring a steady income. So after the *Wende* he had fewer money worries than most Eastern writers. He talked to me about his dilemma of serving under a GDR regime whose tainted idealism he felt unable to redeem – and it seemed apt that he should have just directed *Hamlet*. As Michael Ignatieff wrote in the *Observer* of that production: 'The hero is the very image of the irresolute East German intellectual who acquiesced in tyranny in public and agonised in private. Some say the *Hamlet* is Müller's political self-portrait.'

Leading writers such as Müller, Christa Wolf and Stefan Heym, though very different from each other, had all remained in the GDR for much the same basic reasons. Socialism was still their ideal society; and they hoped that by staying they could perhaps do something to improve and liberalise the regime. But, a shade less honourably, they also enjoyed the privileges that it gave, which for most of them included freedom to travel and assured home sales; and so they had to be careful not to speak out publicly against the GDR when visiting the West, or they might suffer Wolf Biermann's fate (see p. 399). The regime, for its part, was happy to exploit the prestige of its star writers, and it did not want to lose them. Most of them were at first pleased by the *Wende*, seeing it as a chance at last for their kind of Socialism: Christa Wolf spoke eagerly about this at a mass rally on the Alexanderplatz in mid-November, and on November 29 she, Heym and Braun were among the writers who published an appeal for people to uphold the 'moral values' of the GDR and to create a 'new, true and genuine' Socialism. But they were soon disappointed. And then voices in the west began to reproach them for having compromised with a regime they disliked.

Hence the well-known affair of Christa Wolf and her novella *Was Bleibt* (what remains). Wolf, now in her early sixties, was a very private, withdrawn person, who wrote on themes of individual integrity. She considered that for a critical Socialist it was more courageous and 'mature' to stay in the GDR than to take the easy way out of moving to the rich West, as some writers had done. She criticised openly some aspects of the regime, its bureaucracy and conformity, while making it clear that she shared its basic ideals; and this may have helped some of her readers to come to terms with the system. But she remained a Party member until the late 1980s, and she allowed it to fête her publicly. This equivocal stance might have passed without much comment after the *Wende*, were it not that in summer 1990 she published a short novel, *Was Bleibt*, about a well-known woman writer who in 1979 is shadowed by the Stasi, and then suffers bad conscience after failing to help some young dissidents; the incident damages the heroine's integrity, as she reflects on her 'shameful need to get on with all manner of people'. In interviews, Wolf did nothing to deny that the work was autobiographical. Several papers in the west, from the conservative *Frankfurter Allgemeine* to the liberal *Die Zeit*, then pounced on her, accusing her of cheap self-pity and of trying to pass off as a crypto-dissident when in fact she had condoned the regime. If she had published the book in the West back in 1979, they said, it would have been honourable; to publish it now, as a kind of apologia, was indeed 'shameful'. Maybe these criticisms were too strong – and some writers including Günter Grass did spring to Wolf's defence. But certainly she had been tactless.

In my own view, these writers were probably right to stay in the GDR, where they could share with fellow-Germans the experience of living under Communism, and leave some literary record of this, quite apart from possibly influencing the regime. But it was always a difficult moral balancing-act, and it could be argued that Wolf went too far in letting the regime exploit her and then seeking to justify it. Some others maybe behaved with greater integrity – for example Heiner Müller who, when I asked him why he had not moved west, replied teasingly: 'I grew up under Nazism, then lived under a second dictatorship which at least was anti-Nazi, so I could accept it. I got used to breathing the air of dictatorship. I need its pressure for my writing!'

Indeed, as so often in a totalitarian regime, the GDR writers' dilemma was a source of inspiration to them, and it gave their work a piquancy that made it eagerly read for its 'coded messages'. Wolf and others were highly praised in the West, where many critics argued that the best German writing was coming from the GDR. But today some of those same critics feel that the praise was too high, and the interest had been more in the writers' predicament than in their literary quality. So younger writers in the east may now have to find new themes; or they will treat the GDR experience in a new, more historical perspective. But this may take time, as was the case with writers who needed years to digest the Nazi experience (*The Tin Drum* did not appear until 1959). Christoph Hein's excellent novel *Der Tangospieler* (The Tango Player), about an innocent victim of the regime, published in 1989 just as censorship crumbled, was maybe a foretaste of other good things to come. But neither in literature nor in other fields did the *Wende*'s new freedoms appear to unleash any sudden outburst of avant-garde creativity: it would have been naive to expect it. People were too locked in their new financial insecurity, in anxiety about adapting to the West, to have much time for free creative self-expression. Nor was there any sign of banned masterpieces being removed from cupboards to appear on publishers' desks.

If in the cultural world the revolution came to arouse mixed feelings, in the State-run Press and media, hitherto so tightly shackled, its impact was much more obviously positive – indeed, a number of bold journalists and producers had themselves helped to bring about the *Wende*. Already in September and October 1989, as the Party's grip waned, a few TV magazine programmes became more critical and adventurous, under new editors. Then after Honecker's departure on October 18, one of the Politbüro's first actions was to dismiss the hardline propaganda and media chief, Joachim Herrmann, and staff took this as their cue to become yet bolder. TV screens showed the Leipzig demonstrations, Neues Forum radicals were interviewed, and the real mood in the country was reflected on the media as would have been unthinkable three months earlier; even *Neues Deutschland* suddenly became more readable, as it began to report what was really going on in the Politbüro.

After the fall of the Wall this process gathered pace. The senior TV management resigned, newscasters were replaced. And two TV news magazines in particular, *Aktuelle Kamera* and *Elf-99*, were soon sending their cameras into Stasi headquarters and the luxury hideouts of the corrupt former leadership, or putting sharp questions to Party leaders. It was remarkable how swiftly and skilfully these young journalists picked up Western techniques of investigative reporting, as if born to it, whereas their GDR training had taught them just the opposite. Their programmes became livelier than those of Western TV, and they stole back much of its audience. In the Press, the SED-owned *Berliner Zeitung* also probed into corruption – 'We now have 120 per cent Press freedom,' claimed one of its editors, turning his neck round from having been a dutiful Party hack. Nor was the process confined to Berlin. In Leipzig, the modest radio studios there had been a mere adjunct of the State network in the capital, under the old centralised system: but already in October the staff had begun to take matters into their own hands, ousting their hardline bosses and reporting freely on the great Leipzig events. Within months they had mounted their own fully-fledged regional station, Radio Saxony, led by the stalwart Manfred Müller, a liberal journalist from Halle who had been sacked five times by the old State radio for refusing to toe the line.

For a few months there was glorious freedom in the east: but then some new constraints began to emerge, from the west. When it came to deciding on the future of the state networks, the Unity Treaty laid down that they should be remodelled, regionalised, and incorporated into the Western structure. This was to be fixed in detail by the end of 1991. Meanwhile, partly on economic grounds, one of the two GDR TV networks was closed in late 1990, while the other was merged into the Western ARD network but continued to produce some programmes of its own. At the sprawling studios in the south Berlin suburbs, where overmanning had been rife, some 2,700 staff were dismissed. The six new *Länder* including Berlin were likely to be grouped into three regional stations within the ARD structure; and to supervise this operation, Bonn appointed a tough right-wing TV chief from Bavaria, Rudolf Mühlfenzl. His high-handed approach antagonised the liberals who had made the 1989 revolution and were now quietly running what was left of their radio and TV networks. 'Of the GDR's TV output, there is nothing worth preserving,' he assured me – whereas in fact many of the cultural and entertainment programmes had been of some quality. Then I met Manfred Müller in Leipzig: 'We built up this radio station ourselves after the *Wende*, we already have loyal audiences, our own foreign correspondents, and a close liaison with the BBC. We don't want some Bavarian coming to dictate to us how to do it. But at least Mühlfenzl is an honest adversary who will listen to me, unlike those old Stalinists in Berlin. He even answers my letters.' For the time being, private commercial channels would not be allowed in the east, where television and radio seemed set to embrace all the advantages, and drawbacks, of the old west German *Land*-run system.

Newspapers, however, were now largely free to follow their own devices. 'Journalists in the GDR used to be despised as creatures of the Party, but now we find we're quite admired,' one reporter said. In Erfurt, staff of the SED daily *Das Volk* staged a virtual *Putsch* in January 1990, renamed the paper *Thüringer Allgemeine*, and ran it on liberal Western lines with the help of a Press group in the Ruhr; their circulation topped 400,000. In Berlin and elsewhere, newspapers and magazines also sought to survive through Western backing – and several of the big Press groups began eagerly to move in, including

Springer, Burda, and Gruner & Jahr, owners of *Stern*. They took over existing papers, or formed joint ventures. Springer started up new dailies in Dresden and Chemnitz. And the ubiquitous Robert Maxwell acquired a controlling interest in the lively *Berliner Zeitung*, which even in its Party-owned days had been relatively readable.

So where did that leave the Party flagship, *Neues Deutschland*? Rejecting Maxwell's blandishments, the new-style PDS decided to keep it as their mouthpiece. But its survival was not going to be easy, for by early 1991 circulation had fallen from over a million to around 100,000 and many of these readers were elderly. The paper had become more readable, but was finding it hard to get the advertising it needed. 'We never had to worry about running it as a business,' said its deputy editor, Reiner Oschmann, 'but now we have to adopt Western methods.' He and the other more open-minded PDS members of staff argued that it could only survive as an independent left-wing paper, shorn of its invidious Party links. But the PDS feared to lose it.

East Germany's education system, like its TV and radio, was now to be remodelled on Western lines. The minister until 1989 had been none other than Honecker's loyal wife Margot, which gave some indication of the centralised orthodoxy. She was in charge of a structure that sought from an early age to imbue young people with Socialist principles. In practice, however, by the mid-1980s a more liberal spirit had emerged in some schools – in one that I visited, teachers would discreetly discuss with their class the previous evening's West German TV programmes. Many teachers, whether Party members or not, were good at their job and understanding towards their pupils. In universities, critical discussion of official Marxist theories was becoming tolerated.

After the *Wende*, the first task was to remove the old political bias, then to decide which teachers should be kept and which dismissed. This was not easy. After unification, the new *Länder* took full charge of education, as in the west, and began to apply the west German model. This they did a little insensitively in some cases – or so it was felt by liberals who argued that the GDR system, despite its strong political slant, did have certain aspects that might be worth preserving, and from which the west could itself perhaps learn. They cited the links with working life, and the afternoon classes for club and cultural activities. But these suggestions did not get much of a hearing. It seemed more likely that the faults as well as the virtues of west German education would simply be extended *en bloc* to the east, alike in schools and in universities.

In the universities and institutes of higher education, early in 1990 almost all the rectors and directors were dismissed, for they had been hand-picked Party loyalists. After the March elections, all fifty of the departments of Marxism-Leninism were closed down, as well as such highly politicised bodies as the SED's *Hochschule* in Potsdam, and their teaching staff of 600 or so were sacked. These moves were inevitable: but more controversial was the decision, enshrined in the Unity Treaty, to close provisionally all university departments in such sensitive fields as law, economics, modern history, philosophy and social sciences, where the teaching and subject matter were judged to have been 'tainted' by the old regime. Some of their professors were to be allowed to go on teaching until September 1991, so as to enable students to complete the academic year and take their exams; others were pushed out right away, on 70 per cent of full salary for six months. And all would have to be screened and vetted before they could re-apply, as in the other public services (see p. 474); and few were thought likely to get their jobs back. Thanks to these and other dismissals, the teaching staff was reduced by about 25 per cent, and the *Land* authorities were pleased to have this opportunity to limit the chronic overmanning (the teacher–student ratio was 1:5, against 1:18 in the west). These 'sensitive' departments were to be restructured and reopened later, probably under deans brought in from the west: but some would possibly close for good.

All this was a little harsh. And in the winter of 1990–1 the students reacted angrily, with protest strikes and marches, notably in the east's two most prestigious centres, the Humboldt University in Berlin and the Karl-Marx University in Leipzig. The students' motives were mixed: some feared understandably that their own studies would suffer; some thought that the treatment of their teachers was arbitrary and unjust; and some disliked being co-opted on to committees to take part in the screening process, which they considered invidious.

Many professors too were indignant, needless to say, and not only those directly affected. They argued that, since the restructuring related foremost to departments and not to individuals, many of the latter were not getting their deserts – as a liberal professor of English in Leipzig explained: 'Some of the mathematicians, medicos and scientists *also* helped to shore up the regime, for example by distorting statistics or failing to speak out against pollution, so why should *they* now get off scot-free? Conversely, some people in the history or economics departments were in fact quite critical of the system, so why should *they* suffer? In many cases, it's the wrong people who are staying on, or getting pushed out, just like after 1945!' It was true that at Leipzig the departments of philosophy and economics had nurtured a critical analysis of Marxism that intellectually may even have played a tiny part in the regime's downfall. And at Humboldt I met a physics lecturer who had opposed the regime and therefore stayed at a junior level: now, instead of being promoted, he found the old SED men still in the best jobs because their qualifications were much better than his, inevitably. As in all professions, plenty of teachers were quick to be *Wendehals*, claiming that at heart they had always been against the regime and had joined the Party just out of career necessity (some 85 per cent of university staff were SED members). However, despite the various protests, the restructuring went on. Some on the Left and in Neues Forum circles talked of 'purge' and 'witch-hunt', and saw it as part of a deliberate attempt by the west to eradicate east Germany's cultural identity. But this was surely absurd. After all, this was only a transitional phase: some professors might in the end be happily reinstated after their screening, in departments cleansed and renewed.

As for the students, they had played strangely little part in the events of autumn 1989; with a few exceptions, they had not led the flag of revolt as students often do. Perhaps an explanation is that in the GDR they were a relatively privileged breed: they had been selected for political reliability, and although their conditions were poor (often four shared a room), they had assured career outlets. Even those who had become critical of the regime, and thus basically welcomed the *Wende*, remained mostly on the Left in the manner of young people, and few were lovers of capitalism. On a more practical level, many of those in the 'tainted' disciplines felt that their years of study had been wasted; and although they were promised that their diplomas would still be valid, they nearly all faced bleak job prospects if they stayed in the east. Younger ones, about to try for university, would now have the same liberal access as in the west, where the proportion of students was over three times bigger (1.5 million against 130,000). But would this simply mean that the west's malaise of overcrowding would be extended to the east?

In school education, the transition after the *Wende* went rather more smoothly. In the spring of 1990 all head teachers were obliged to resign, but could then if they wished stand for democratic election by a joint committee of staff, parents and pupils in each school. Perhaps surprisingly, only about one-third of these committees chose a new head, usually from the existing staff, while two-thirds reappointed the previous one: it may have been that many old-style teachers feared dismissal if a new liberal head was named, but more often it was simply that the old head teacher was liked and respected. The Education Ministry had the right to override the committee, if it reappointed a suspected SED hard-liner, and this sometimes happened.

Most teachers of Marxism were also dismissed, and some other teachers took early retirement, unprepared to adapt to the new regime: but the rest kept their jobs, though all had to submit to the usual questionnaires and screening. The task of suddenly confronting the pupils with a new set of values and ideas, especially in a subject such as history, and of teaching in a different, freer way, was of course enormous – a delightful challenge for the younger, more liberal teachers, harder for many older ones. At one comprehensive in the Berlin suburbs, the new headmistress, whose career had hitherto been blocked because she had refused to join the Party, told me: 'Nearly all my staff have welcomed the *Wende*, including the SED ones. The ambience in class is now much lighter, and the curriculum less rigid. The kids can discuss things freely, ask awkward questions, as they couldn't before. And the teachers are much freer in how they handle this. They can improvise, choose their own texts. Some of course can't cope.' In another Berlin school, a history teacher said: 'At the start of the new term, I had to tell my pupils honestly that I was not a liar, I had not actually sought to deceive them, I had truly believed in what I taught them. Making the change is not easy, I can promise you.' One young teacher, loyally SED, was asked by her class about the Berlin Airlift. She had never heard of it: as it was a defeat, the textbooks did not mention it.

The compulsory weekly classes in Socialist civics, a key indoctrinatory feature of the old curriculum, were abolished in spring 1990 and their teachers transferred to other subjects or dismissed (some found new jobs for example as garage hands or shop assistants). The classes were replaced by others on 'social studies', along Western lines. The teaching of history, which had put heavy emphasis on the GDR success-story, was also changed radically, and here the main problem was to get hold of new textbooks. The Bonn Government provided a 70 million DM grant which enabled Western publishers to pour in books, but many of these were ill-adapted for use in the east. 'The ones we have been given make practically no reference to east Germany, just as our old ones virtually ignored the west,' said one teacher; 'so we're having to improvise — something we're not used to doing.'

A third area where much change was needed was that of foreign languages. Hitherto Russian was compulsory for all from the age of ten, with English or French as an optional extra from twelve: but few pupils took either of these, and today it is still uncommon in the east to find any adult speaking good English, in sharp contrast to west Germany. From 1990, however, a pupil now had a choice between Russian, English and French as his compulsory first language, with a second to be added later, as in the west. Some who had got far with Russian continued with it: but the vast majority opted for English, or maybe French. And of course this led to a big surplus of Russian teachers and a shortage of the others. As many as possible of the former were hurriedly re-trained in crash courses — the British Council was asked to help with 9,000 of them — but their pronunciation left much to be desired. If English had been badly taught in the GDR, it was partly because few teachers ever had a chance to visit an English-speaking country — 'I paid my first visit to England this year', said a teacher I met in Eisenach in 1990, 'and I found it quite different from what our textbooks had taught us — less feudal, less dominated by workers' strikes. Now at last we are getting schoolbooks that give a proper picture of Britain today.'

And so, amid a certain cheerful improvisation, the changeover to a new school system went ahead. The western *Länder*, confident that they knew best, gave help with retraining and organisation — 'After their decades of isolation,' said one Bavarian bureaucrat loftily, 'their pedagogy is so out of date that they do need us badly.' So was the merger to be all one-way? Many radicals feared so: 'Our old system was a disaster, but the official Western model has its faults too,' said a Green I met in Dresden — and he therefore had helped to create a local Waldorfschule, one of seven that had sprung up in the east.

Each new *Land* was free to decide how far to copy the Western system: but all sixteen, new and old, were expected to work towards consensus, as was the federal practice, and it seemed in 1991 that they would allow few if any features of the old GDR system to survive. 'I think this would be a pity,' said a senior liberal educationalist whom I met in Bonn, Dr Hildebrandt; 'there is a lot we could learn from the east, and it would be wrong to impose our system *in toto*. But alas my view is in a minority in the *Länder*'s coordinating conference.' He was referring to the free kindergartens that were helpful to working mothers; to the sporting, cultural and club activities in afternoon classes; and to the links with working life, whereby pupils went to learn a skill in factory or farm. If shorn of their ideological orientation, and better funded and organised, these features might be of value to a west German education system that was in some ways too exclusively academic. But it seemed that there was neither the money for this, nor the will. Children in Leipzig would soon be following exactly the same pedagogic path as in Munich. And in the universities too, the constrained severity of the GDR system would soon give way to the messy free-for-all of the western campuses.

The change of regime has brought east Germans so many problems that today its very positive side is sometimes overlooked. So let me end this long chapter on an upbeat note, with the story of one village in the former 'forbidden zone' beside the old border. Lauchröden, in Thuringia, west of Eisenach, is separated by only a stream and a field from the Hessen townlet of Herleshausen, and many families are closely related. But until November 1989 it was separated, too, by the grim weaponry of twin electrified fences, mines and guard-dogs. And the high steel fences went round three sides of the village, virtually cutting it off also from its closest GDR neighbours: to get to a village two miles away, people had to make a twenty-two-mile detour. This criss-cross grille along the entire border area was intended to make escape more difficult. 'We were all in a prison,' said one farmer; 'there was a curfew at 10 pm, even to go for a walk we had to take a special permit, and it was hard for other east Germans to get permission to visit us. The Stasi were everywhere, and life was ruled by suspicion. Anyone heard criticising the regime was liable to be packed off into exile in some far part of the GDR.'

The opening of the border was followed by heady weeks of jubilation. 'Today, more than a year later, it still seems like a dream,' one housewife told me. 'I wake up each morning thinking I've dreamed it all. We never believed it could really happen.' In December 1989 the villagers set about wrecking the hideous watchtowers beside the fences, while the guards just looked on. By the summer, tourists were coming to peer inside these derelict symbols of terror, and to look at the vegetable gardens now planted in the no-man's-land where the guard-dogs prowled. The fences were being pulled down, but one or two watchtowers were to be kept as memorials – 'We should never forget that bad time,' said the village pastor; 'that is why I have placed a big piece of fence inside my church.'

The villagers eagerly resumed their former close links with Herleshausen. In these border areas of Hessen and Thuringia, the country people had been inter-related for centuries, they shared common traditions and temperament, and so there were few of the usual Ossi/Wessi frictions. The Hessen police built a bridge across the broad stream forming the border. Then at Christmas the two communities held a joint festival, which led to the first inter-village wedding in the area; on Unification Night there was another party, on the bridge, with music and fireworks. Herleshausen council began to give practical help to its poorer neighbour, and a few shops set up branches across the stream. But there was little employment in Lauchröden, so people looked for commuting jobs across the border. From this and other villages, buses took some of them each day to Frankfurt, 100 miles away, to work in a supermarket. Herleshausen, in an enclave of Hessen, had also been much affected by the division of Germany: Eisenach, only ten miles away, had formerly been its natural centre for shopping, schools, culture, hospitals. It was now set to regain this role – but only when its amenities had improved.

Daily life in Lauchröden changed radically. For 120 years the Wittig family had owned and run the Zur Krone, a simple but picturesque sixteenth-century pub, half-timbered and flower-girt in the best German style, and they had somehow kept it looking spruce, in contrast to the usual GDR shabbiness. 'Through those dark years we managed to retain ownership of the building,' said Helga Wittig, 'though we were forced to join a State consortium for our supplies and finances. Life was hard, and so *boring* – we just saw the same old faces. Now we are fully private again, we have to work far harder, but it's so much more exciting and varied. Our old village clients travel elsewhere, and instead we get others from outside, many of them tourists.' (A family from Cologne came up to give her a present.) 'We buy supplies in Hessen, and we're expanding our menu, which used to be so basic. But we don't want to go all posh, like places in the west; we'll keep this a simple pub.' I remarked on the archaic earth-closet in the backyard. 'Yes,' she said, 'we've just got a grant from the EC's regional fund, for putting in modern toilets at last.'

I heard another upbeat story from the new mayor of Lauchröden,

Günther Fey, a charming 37-year-old. 'I was born in this village, and by the age of 25 I was head of the SED's youth organisation (FDJ) for the Eisenach area. I was a fervent Communist. Later some doubts developed, and the turning-point came in 1986 when I went with a Party delegation to a village near Koblenz. To my surprise, I found a very happy, prosperous and democratic community, so I realised that all we have been told about West Germany was lies and propaganda.' He then took a handwritten slip of paper from his desk: 'In that village I made a list – here it is – of all the amenities that they enjoyed and we lacked. And I vowed that in time I'd get them for Lauchröden too, even under our GDR system. A butcher, petrol station, public phone box, central heating – practical things like that. Then the Party sent me to study for three years in Berlin, and I was glad, for I naively believed that education would give me the scope to carry out my local plan. But afterwards the Party wouldn't even listen to my project, they were sending me to Erfurt. I had a great row with those Stalinists, so they expelled me from the SED and sent me to another town as a humble worker. The Stasi were set to watch me.' (This somewhat ingenuous account was confirmed to me by other sources.) 'After November, the Party made cringing apologies, but I told them to get stuffed. I came back home, and the village pastor asked me to stand for mayor on his list. My story by now was well known here, and I was elected with a huge vote. So now here I am in this little Rathaus, at last carrying out one by one all the items on that list – but under a totally different system! Look what I've already ticked off – butcher, baker, carpenter, petrol station, phone box, heating system, removal of that terrible fence. Even a village song. Next I'll go back to that Moselle village and tell how they changed my life.'

Not so many personal stories of the *Wende* were as happy as this. And even Günther Fey was having problems with the new house he was building, for westerners had just turned up to claim the land. Throughout eastern Germany, by the summer of 1991 people were finding the transition harder than they had expected a year earlier. Few of them regretted the old regime, or 'wanted the Wall back' (as the saying went): but they felt that unification had been mishandled. Alike in east and west Germany, and in all milieux, there were plenty of people who argued that it might have been wiser to manage it more slowly, to restructure the east first before exposing it to full absorption by the west. But the more general view in political and business circles, that I for one would share, is that this might not really have been feasible, either politically or economically. Once the old regime had collapsed, leaving a weak and artificial rump of a state, Bonn had little practical choice but to take full responsibility as rapidly as possible. However, the process could certainly have been handled more shrewdly and sensitively. The Kohl Government should have been more honest about the difficulties. It should have acted faster and more effectively to sort out the property fiasco. And probably – but this was antipathetic to its free-market ideology – it should have played a larger direct part in industrial restructuring, at least in the shorter term, rather than leave the main burden to reluctant private investment.

Understandably, the ordinary east Germans were so preoccupied with their immediate problems, with losing their jobs and having to adapt to the west, that few of them could take a long-term view or see the silver linings to their clouds. But others, with a more detached vision, were aware that the longer-term prospects were bright. And this is the position as I write today, in the summer of 1991. Short of a major world recession, or some new upheaval in Europe (maybe radiating from the Soviet Union), west Germany with its massive resources *will* succeed in rebuilding the economy of the east; and east Germans *will* learn to adapt. It will take rather longer than expected, but it will happen. After all, nobody can afford for this great venture to fail: the Government, and German firms, are committed to its success. There will still be two or three tough years ahead for east Germans, but most probably by 1994–5 a new 'economic miracle' will be in progress for them. Today they may still be marked out from west Germans by forty years of a different system, but its impact will wane, and with it the present Ossi/Wessi tensions will probably wane too. After all, they are all Germans, resilient, disciplined and hard-working at heart, sharing a culture that goes back far before Honecker and Hitler. And if Saxons, say, will always be different from Swabians or Rhinelanders, that will be in the same way that west Germans too retain their diversity.

Yet it will take time, maybe a generation, to cleanse the worst of the legacy of the past – not only the pollution deep in the soil, the decrepit towns and villages, but also the psychological scars. The adaptation will be easiest for younger people, harder for older ones who lived their full lives under the old regime. Some may never adjust. But few really believe that the fall of the Wall was in vain. 'We are like a patient after a cancer operation,' said one woman I met in Dresden; 'it was necessary to save your life, but at first you feel much worse.'

And after all, the Germans in the west recovered ebulliently from a far worse situation after 1945, to build a strong economy and a sound democracy.

# 9

# CONCLUSION: HOW STABLE A DEMOCRACY?

When this new Germany has worked its way through the immediate difficulties of unification, what will its longer-term future be? In this last chapter, I shall try to draw together some of the threads that have run through this book, and to examine a few major questions. What is the influence today of the Nazi period, and what scars has it left? How stable is German democracy and how deep does it go? What is the true impact of the values of a new generation (as symbolized by the Greens and others), and how far have their ideas marked any real change? And, in the light of unification, how do Germans today perceive their position in the world, and in the defence of the West, and will unification help them to come to terms with the old problem of their national identity?

## Digesting the legacies of Nazism

What does the average German feel today about Hitler's regime? – about how and why it was able to take hold in a free society, and whether the nation should continue to bear collective guilt for events that only those now well into their sixties experienced as adults. In coming to terms with their Nazi legacy, the west Germans have had to face moral problems of horrendous proportions, and it is hard to arrive at any balanced assessment of how they have coped. On the positive side, it is clear that what is loosely known as 'neo-Nazism' is today a marginal phenomenon of little influence. What is more, the media in the past fifteen or twenty years have done an excellent job in dragging the whole subject of Nazism and German guilt into the open forum of public discussion, through a steady spate of books, articles and programmes; and this, together with the simple passage of time, has served to break the uneasy taboo of silence that had cloaked these issues in the earlier post-war decades. Leading politicians too, CDU as well as SPD, have often set an outspoken example: one could cite Chancellor Brandt's public act of contrition at the Warsaw ghetto in 1970, and President von Weizsäcker's formidable speech to the Bundestag on the 1985 anniversary of May 8, when he told all Germans that only by continuing to remember the shame and horror of their past could they come to terms with it.

But how widely are his attitudes shared? One aspect of the ending of the long silence is that many elderly people who lived under Nazism are now much readier to try to justify themselves in public and to speak out their resentment at the stigma that has been branded onto their generation ('I was only doing my patriotic duty as a soldier', 'how could we have known what was going on in the concentration camps?', or even, 'the Nazis did some good things, as well as bad', are remarks one hears widely). And many younger people, however appalled they are by Nazism, resent being expected to go on feeling guilty for the sins of their grandparents. All in all, it is not easy for an observer to pick his way through the tangle of paradoxes and contradictions.

In the first years after the war, the Western occupying forces tried to carry through a programme of 'denazification' that included the removal of Nazis from public posts as well as the trial of the more actively guilty. This programme was ineptly executed, and it was far from consistent: in many firms and in some professions, there were found to be just not enough non-Nazis with the right ability and experience for the machine of German economic and public life to be set in motion again, and so a good many former party members or supporters were allowed to keep their posts. The most notorious case was that of Alfred Krupp, who at Nuremberg was sentenced to 12 years' prison for using slave labour, but three years later was set free and permitted to take over his steel-works again. Then after 1949 the Adenauer regime pursued the same erratic course as the Allies had done. And today, with hindsight, it seems very clear that first the occupiers and then the West German authorities were indeed too lenient towards a number of run-of-the-mill Nazis. True, the issue has been exaggerated by the Left, for there was never any widespread rehabilitation: but there were mistakes. In 1970 about half of the 15,000 magistrates and judges in West Germany had held legal positions in the Hitler era: probably few of them had been active Nazis, but even so the figure seems disturbingly high. Adenauer himself from 1953 to 1963 employed as his state secretary in the Chancellery a certain Dr Hans Globke, who had been a senior official in the pre-war Interior Ministry and was alleged by the Press to have drafted parts of Hitler's anti-Jewish laws. There was controversy over this at the time – as there was over the CDU's choice as Chancellor in 1966 of Kurt Georg Kiesinger. He was a modest and honourable man who had never been more than a minor time-serving Nazi: nonetheless, he had been in the party for twelve years and a great many Germans felt that this in itself should have disqualified him from high political office. As Professor Eberhardt Jäckel, a leading German historian of the Nazi period, commented to me in 1985, 'Whether these and other men were personally guilty is not the point. It was bad for German democracy, and it set a bad example to the younger generation, that people with *any* kind of Nazi record should have been given such posts. Adenauer and the other CDU leaders should have been more scrupulous.'

There was another and brighter side of this picture, for the Germans after the war also did a great deal to make amends for the Nazi crimes and to punish the guilty. By 1970, German courts had prosecuted 12,900 persons suspected of offences: 5,200 were imprisoned and seventy-six of these were given the maximum life sentence. Under a German–Israeli agreement of 1962, reparations worth more than 2.5 billion DM were made to Israel during the following years, while 15 billion DM were paid directly to individual Jewish victims or their families under Germany's Restitution Law. This was penance on a vast scale – even though money alone could never atone for the evils done. In addition, various private German bodies carried out their own reparations or publicly confessed their share of guilt – above all, the Protestant Churches. In the 1960s a Lutheran pastor in Berlin set up a 'penance corps' of young German volunteers (architects, carpenters and others) who built Jewish centres in Europe and Israel and restored buildings wrecked by the Nazis.

The 1950s and 1960s were an especially difficult time for the German conscience. A new generation grew up with the realisation that its own parents were the guilty ones, and this caused bitter rifts within families: fathers and sons were frequently not on speaking terms. Or, as one writer now in his fifties put it to me, 'You never knew who you were dealing with. If I went to a doctor, or met someone a bit older than me, I kept thinking, "I wonder if *he* was one of *them*."' Small wonder that the vast majority of Germans preferred to brush the troubling questions of the past under the carpet and to channel their thoughts and energies into the happier task of building up the *Wirt-schaftswunder* — itself a kind of atonement. One aspect of this situation was the very inadequate schoolroom teaching about Nazism, during that post-war period. Even though the convinced Nazis had been removed from the schools, many passive time-servers were still there, and they were far too involved with the problem of guilt to be able to teach about Nazism properly; there was also a lack of suitable textbooks, for it took some time to prepare new ones to replace those used under Hitler. My wife, who was at a *Gymnasium* in Munich in the mid-60s, says, 'We had new history books with a final chapter on the Nazi period, very dead-pan: but our teachers always left it out, saying that they didn't have time and anyway it wouldn't be needed for the *Abitur*. I think they were just embarrassed. They had no idea how to explain the subject and wanted to avoid controversy. I discovered about the Final Solution through talking to a Jewish schoolfriend.'

Over in the GDR, it was all much easier. There, the regime to its credit did winkle out former Nazis far more thoroughly than in the West. But it also dodged the issue of guilt. Right from the start it had taken the simple line, 'Nazism was the product of monopoly capitalism, and there is no reason why East Germans should feel responsible, for we are all good socialists here. The "bad" Germans are all over in the West.' This was the version fed to schoolchildren, who were not asked to feel any collective guilt for their elders' sins. And the GDR paid no reparations to Israel, for it claimed that it was not the successor to the Third Reich and so had no moral obligation. The May 8 anniversary was celebrated in the GDR as a day of 'liberation' by the gallant Red Army, and not one of humiliation and defeat. The Nazis were portrayed as an alien people, battled against by noble German Communists — and this led Leslie Collitt to comment in the *Financial Times* of April 25, 1985, 'At times it appears to younger East Germans as if East Germany itself had fought beside the wartime Allies to crush the Nazis.' Happily, one of the very first acts of the GDR's new democratic Volkskammer (parliament) elected in April 1990 was to issue a public apology to Israel and the Jews and to acknowledge east Germans' share of guilt.

In West Germany, there has been a most striking change in attitudes since around the early 1970s — as I have noticed on my own visits. When I was first in Stuttgart in 1969–70, researching *A Tale of Five Cities*, I found that very few people would talk to me about their feelings towards the Nazi period; and I, not wishing to alienate my useful new contacts, cravenly refrained from pressing them. But, during my long months in Germany in 1984–5, researching the first edition of this book, I had no such problems. People of all ages raised the subject spontaneously all the time; they talked openly and excitedly, even made jokes about it. Everyone notices this contrast. Of the many reasons for it, the most important is the obvious one of the sheer passing of time and the change of generations. Today's young people need no longer feel angrily ashamed of their parents, who themselves were too young to have been Nazis; and the grandparents are fast dying out. So families are no longer riven: guilt has become less personalised, more a general national legacy, and therefore easier to talk about. There have been other factors, too. The 1968 upheavals blew away the taboos on many subjects, this one included, and ushered in an era of much more open public discussion of all kinds of questions. Then in 1969 the Chancellorship passed from Kiesinger to Willy Brandt, the former Free Norwegian officer, whose approach was very different — witness his State visit to Warsaw in 1970, when he dropped on his knees and bowed his head in silent reverence at the memorial to half a million Polish Jews killed by the Nazis in the ghetto. Around the same time, teaching in schools was improving radically, and the media embarked on a far more frank and detailed scrutiny of the Hitler period. In 1979 Hollywood's *Holocaust* series was shown on German TV: vulgar soap it may have been (I agree with Reitz), but it did at least open German eyes far more widely than before to the truth about the Final Solution. It won very high audience ratings of about 40 per cent, and it prompted thousands of schools and colleges to organise discussions on the subject.

Many town councils too have followed the new trend: some have invited exiled former Jewish inhabitants to pay their first return visits since the 1930s, and have entertained them generously. Rather more daringly, by the early 1980s a number of big cities such as Munich had mounted elaborate exhibitions of local life under the Nazis. In 1984 I visited one of these at a museum in Stuttgart, initiated by Mayor Rommel himself, and it was mind-blowing — it included a big photo of the 1937 city council all in Nazi uniform giving the Nazi salute and others of happy gentle Swabian teenagers in their Hitler Youth garb. Such an exhibition would have been inconceivable only twenty years ago. Sadly, it was not visited by more than 70,000 people, half of them made up of compulsory school groups. But it passed off with no more than a few isolated protests from older people, some of them saying that it was wrong to rake up the past, or that the evils of Nazism had been exaggerated.

Now that this over-sixty generation has at last become readier to discuss the subject, out very often will come a jumble of mixed feelings of guilt and self-justification, suppressed for so many years. I had a vivid experience of this when Professor Jäckel, who teaches at Stuttgart University, arranged in 1985 for me to talk to some of his history students. He assembled about thirty of them: half were in their early twenties, doing a normal degree course; the others were 'mature' students attending his extra-mural class, most of them aged 65 or more (the men had all fought in the war). And the sparks flew! First I asked the older group whether they felt any guilt about the war and Nazism. 'No!' was the near-unanimous answer. 'It wasn't Hitler who started the war,' said one former *Panzer* lieutenant, 'it was you British, *you* declared it on us – Hitler wanted peace with Britain.' Other views followed from the others: 'Germany has suffered so terribly from the war, first bombed to bits and now split in two, that she has fully paid the price, and I for one have no more guilt;' 'we never knew about the killing of the Jews, how could we? – it wasn't our fault;' 'yes, I *did* know that Jews were being shot and deported, but I could do nothing, I was just not prepared to be a martyr;' 'I was in the Wehrmacht, merely doing my duty – it's very unfair that we soldiers should be asked to bear guilt for obeying orders.' Some of the group were patently nettled by a Briton asking them smug questions, and they hit back: 'What about Dresden? – that was just as bad – Winston must have drunk too much whisky;' 'what about the Versailles Treaty? – you created Nazism too.' And so on – a predictable mish-mash of classic reactions, all a bit depressing. And yet these sturdy veterans had been taking the trouble to attend the regular classes of a famous liberal historian known for his firmly anti-Nazi line – so there must have been some uneasy consciences lurking behind the gropings after extenuating circumstances. Then some of the more radical of the young students began to attack the old ones. 'You dreadful old fogeys, why do you try to justify yourselves?' said one Green girl; 'why did you fail to speak out against Hitler's war, while we now *are* speaking out against the threat of Reagan's war? If Germany were dragged into a conflict now, *we* would refuse to fight –

why did *you* not do so?' Tempers rose. 'You young people have no idea what it was like to live under a dictatorship,' said one veteran; 'no protest was possible. It's only because Germany today is free that *you* can enjoy the luxury of a Peace Movement. And besides, your dangerous pacifism is leading us straight into the Russians' arms.' So here was a horrifying phoney debate: one generation that had failed to stop a fascist Germany from aggressing, at odds with another that would refuse to defend a democratic Germany if aggressed.

At least, with the taboos now lifted, such arguments are today out in the open. And many respectable older citizens will cheerfully explain why at first they found Nazism attractive — 'Yes, of course I was a Nazi, it was the thing to be,' said a charming banker I met in Frankfurt. A great many men of his age, it must be stressed, experienced the better side of Nazism, more than its horrors: in the 1930s they witnessed a go-ahead new regime that restored national pride and confidence, and then during the dark war years they were away from Germany, fighting patriotically. Today, just like many British veterans, it is the camaraderie of those soldier years that they remember most vividly.

The late 1970s produced a wave of popular cult-like interest in Hitler, much of it commercialised in the form of films, records and photo-articles. To some older people it may have brought an element of nostalgia. Hitler, it is true, was generally portrayed as a lunatic megalomaniac: but, as one young German suggested to me, 'There's something dangerous in this obsession with Hitler and his cronies as a bunch of mad freaks who led the good German people astray. It tends to absolve that generation of their own share of responsibility. It's a comforting alibi.' In fact, an Allensbach survey in 1977 that put the question, 'Did the German population have any practical means of influencing Nazi policy, for instance over the concentration camps?', found only 4 per cent of the over-60s answering 'yes' and 86 per cent 'no' (among the under-45s, the replies were 16 per cent 'yes', 53 per cent 'no'). Another poll in the same year revealed that 41 per cent of those questioned felt that 'the positive aspects of Hitler's action' should not be forgotten, even though he had 'made numerous errors'. And a few people go much further. 'The Nazis had good ideas, it's a pity they got out of hand,' one sometimes hears; or, 'Hitler would have known how to deal with all those terrorists, punks and drop-outs;' or, 'at least *we* had an ideology that we cared about. The young today believe in nothing.'

Such views, still quite common among the old guard, surely represent little more than a muddled emotional reaction against the permissiveness of modern society, and a vague nostalgia for older and firmer values. They hardly constitute 'neo-Nazism', and it is doubtful whether many of these people would vote for a new Nazi party – as elections have shown. One small neo-Nazi party that survived the war was outlawed in 1952 as unconstitutional. Then in the mid-1960s, with the first breath of recession after the 'miracle' years, the newly-formed National Democratic Party (NPD) suddenly emerged in some strength. Its platform was extreme right-wing and twelve of the eighteen members of its executive had been active Nazis: but it managed to remain just outside the orbit of the Constitution's formal ban on parties 'aiming to overthrow democratic society'. It won some seats in *Land* elections and began to cause alarm among democrats both in Germany and abroad. But in the federal elections of 1969 it fell well short of the minimum 5 per cent vote needed to secure seats in the *Bundestag*; and after this it steadily declined. The NPD today has no elected representatives anywhere and is seldom in the news. In many ways NPD was less a genuine neo-Nazi movement than a vague reactionary protest movement, Poujadist in nature – just as the extreme-right Republikaner Party, which emerged briefly to prominence in 1989–90, is xenophobic and nastily nationalist but not really Nazi, though it does contain a neo-Nazi wing. By 1991 it seemed a spent force (see p. 432).

Neo-Nazism however still possesses a vocal mouthpiece in the form of the *National Zeitung*, a weekly published in Munich with a claimed circulation of 100,000. This pursues a stridently nationalistic line; it glorifies military leaders such as Dönitz, and, though it stops short of glorifying Hitler, it tries hard to minimise the Nazis' misdoings – 'They may have killed some Jews, but not six million, that's a wicked exaggeration put about by Germany's enemies,' is its common refrain. This paper, like *Bild*, is protected under the German code of Press freedom – and probably rightly so, for, if such views exist, it is best for them to be out in the open where they can be contested. They do however trouble the German conscience, and they have caused protests from Jews. This led the SPD in 1982 to table its much-contested Bill against the *Auschwitzlüge* (lies about Auschwitz), aiming to make it illegal to spread lies about Nazi crimes that insulted the memory of the Jewish dead. It was well intentioned. But a great many Germans, including some of the most liberal, felt that this legalistic approach was misguided and could prove counter-productive: it could provide a platform in the court for neo-Nazis and enable them to parade in public as martyrs deprived of free speech. After three years of debate, the law was finally passed in an amended form, its scope extended to protect victims of Soviet 'tyranny' (e.g. Silesian exiles, etc.) from similar slander. It was far from certain that this was the best solution.

Neo-Nazi activity today, insofar as it does exist, seems to be confined largely to the elderly and to the young – to those nostalgic for the past, and to young hotheads who never knew that past and are more often motivated by anti-Turk racism. The two elements are very different. On the one hand are the NZ readers and other ex-Nazis, including the associations of former SS: since they are war veterans like others, they are permitted to hold their regular reunions, and so they get together in beer-cellars or holiday resorts, where they sing the 'Horst Wessel' song and other Nazi favourites and talk over old times. Young Left-wingers come to demonstrate angrily outside the doors, demanding that the rallies be banned. But these old SS comrades today have no influence and will die out before long; many were forced to join the SS in their teens and were never really Nazi. It seems to me right that in a democracy they should be tolerated.

Far more malign are the small extreme-right groups composed mainly of men under 30, who in recent years have assaulted Turks and other foreigners and have even raided army garrisons – either to seize weapons, or because their xenophobia extends to a hatred of NATO. These groups are fairly similar to the extreme wings of the National Front in Britain or France: but because of the Nazi heritage they are less tolerated in Germany. They are illegal, and their cells are often raided by the police: one of their leaders, who had been training armed gangs of young Bavarians to fight Turks and Leftists, was recently imprisoned. Such groups are recruited mainly from the working class, and sometimes they will stir up soccer hooliganism, just as in Britain. Being of low mental calibre, they have made no impact in student circles. They remain a potential threat: but at present they are far too small and isolated to have any real influence. Their weakness was clearly illustrated at the time of Rudolf Hess's death in 1987. The funeral of the last of the Nazi leaders was an obvious occasion for the neo-Nazis to make a public display of their feelings and their strength. But little happened beyond a few minor demonstrations by small groups of thugs and hotheads. Very quickly the fuss died down. A report from the Ministry of the Interior at the time claimed that, while extreme-right organisations had a total membership of some 22,000, actively militant neo-Nazis probably numbered no more than about 1,500.

The younger generation as a whole seems today to be fairly level-headed and well-informed about the Nazi period — far more than a generation ago. Since the mid-1960s the *Land* authorities have made concerted efforts to improve teaching in schools, and with some success. A number of good history textbooks and audio-visual series are available which present the facts in a clear and truthful if somewhat unemotive manner, including details of the Final Solution. Much then depends on the interpretation given by the individual teacher and while of course this varies, the majority of them today do not shrink from depicting Nazism in its true colours. Some schools possibly err too much on the side of stressing the extenuating circumstances: 'We try to explain the facts that led to Nazism,' I was told at one *Gymnasium* near Stuttgart, 'such as the harshness of the Versailles Treaty, the faulty Weimar constitution and the impact of the Depression.' On the other hand, a number of schools have made excellent efforts to encourage pupils to do their own first-hand research into the period, by interviewing their own grandparents or writing to Jews in exile for details of what happened to the Jewish community in their town. This has yielded some remarkable results — and also reawakened some family tensions! Many schools also take senior pupils on compulsory visits to the concentration camps, notably Dachau and Belsen: Dachau receives some 6,000 school groups each year.

The reaction of a German child when he first learns about these horrors, and compares them with the decent, peaceful Germany that he sees around him, is quite often one of sheer disbelief. 'It *can't* have happened — someone is lying to us,' he may say. Some sensitive children will shut their ears, or else have depressions or nightmares — 'Please can you stop telling my daughter about the Holocaust, it's making her ill,' one mother in Munich told her headmaster. How much children retain of what they are taught about Nazism in school is hard to assess. In 1976 a Kiel educationalist, Dieter Bossmann, organised a survey in 110 schools over Germany that was later published in a book and made the subject of a lengthy *Spiegel* article — and it caused a sensation. Of the 3,042 essays he received on the theme, 'What I have heard about Hitler', some pupils thought that he was an Italian, or a Communist, or had fought in the Thirty Years' War, or had made the first moon landing, or had survived the war to become a CDU deputy in the Bundestag; one contribution affirmed that he had called his opponents 'Nazis' and sent them all to the gas chambers. No one doubted that these answers were genuine. But were they *so* alarming? —

the wiser experts soon pointed out that there is always a minority of youngsters who refuse to assimilate information not connected with their own lives, and that a similar survey in France or Britain would produce a handful of similar freak replies about de Gaulle or Churchill. Other German surveys have in fact given a more reassuring picture; and my own impression, from talking to young people, is that nearly all of them know perfectly well what Nazism was like and what it did. The result is that, even today, a number of them are not happy to be German (see p. 577). But of course there are others who try to put the whole subject out of their minds – 'Why should we be made to feel guilty for what happened all those years ago?' is a common attitude. Some of them even react against the surfeit of serious well-intended programmes and articles about Nazism in the media – 'Oh God, not bloody Hitler and the Jews *again*! – switch it off!'

For the Germans as a whole, the problem of coming to terms with the awful past is now quite largely a matter of time. It will all have fallen into place in another ten or twenty years, when the last of the guilty generation have died away. Yet the central dilemma will still remain: how to sublimate any personal guilt complex for events long past, without either whitewashing that past or evading a more general sense of collective historical responsibility. How far *is* a nation morally responsible for its history? – no one knows, not even the British when confronted with colonial Africa. At least in the past two decades the Germans seem to have to come some way towards digesting the legacy of Nazism without rejecting it – and they have done this with a much better grace than the Austrians, who even though Hitler came from their country have always tried to pretend that they were not to blame. Witness their election of Kurt Waldheim as their president in 1986, despite the strong evidence against him.

In Germany, reactions to the past are mixed. There are some who believe in sedulously keeping the memories alive, such as the ones who go on visits of penance to the concentration camps, now preserved as memorial parks: Dachau is the fourth most visited site in Germany, with one million visitors a year, and by no means all of them are foreign tourists or school groups. But there are many other Germans who feel that the past should not be raked up any more and that any survivors among the guilty should be left to die in peace. Take the case of Dr Aquilin Ullrich, an elderly gynaecologist living in Stuttgart, who in 1967 together with two colleagues was committed to trial on a charge of 'complicity in mass murder' for his part in the Nazis' euthanasia programme. The three doctors pleaded that they were just obeying orders, and thus got themselves acquitted. Then, much later, new evidence emerged (Ullrich was alleged to have carried out painful sterilisation experiments on Jewish women, without anaesthetics) and back they went on trial in 1986. But in Stuttgart the average reaction even among younger people was, in sum, 'The old boy has been such a kind and respected doctor in this town ever since: maybe he has had a change of heart, and he should not be prosecuted now, not at his age.' Ullrich was even able to produce letters in court from Stuttgart mothers who wrote that he dealt with their maternities so wonderfully and they just could not believe the charges against him. (This seems to me an example of the strange hiatus in Germany between public and private morality: if a man is your friend, or has done you a kind service, then you turn a blind eye to what he may have done to others – see p. 526.)

Or take the case of Anja Rosmus in the ultra-conservative Bavarian town of Passau (her story has been told in a well-known film, *Das Schreckliche Mädchen:* The Nasty Girl), who in the early 1980s courageously conducted an enquiry into the past of some of the town's most respected burghers – editors, councillors, priests, etc – and discovered that several had been active Nazi supporters but had managed to cover it up. For this she was locally ostracised, victimised, physically attacked – though she did also become a kind of national heroine and won several prizes. On some other occasions, indeed, when a politician's guilty past comes to light, he can be pressured into resigning. This happened also in Stuttgart, in 1978, when Hans Filbinger, the prestigious prime minister of Baden-Württemberg, was revealed to have signed death sentences on teenage deserters in the last days of the war, when he was a naval judge under Dönitz. At first he denied it, but then he was proved to be lying: so under pressure from the media the CDU had no choice but to force him out. But he went on living in his official residence and was still respected by the local establishment.

However, there are some German leaders who have set the most honourable example to the nation in urging it to accept its collective guilt and never to forget. Foremost among them, along with Willy Brandt, is Filbinger's CDU colleague Richard von Weizsäcker, born in 1920, who just before the war studied law and history at Oxford, Grenoble and Göttingen and then spent six years in the Wehrmacht. Elected Federal President in 1984, he made an inspiring and courageous speech to the Bundestag on the fortieth anniversary of the German surrender of May 8, 1945. It was, he said, 'a day that liberated all of us from the inhumanity and tyranny of the National-Socialist regime – the end of an aberration in German history.' He spoke of 'Germany's responsibility for the outbreak of the Second World War', and, after urging the nation to commemorate the six million murdered Jews, he added: 'The perpetration of this crime was in the hands of a few people . . . But every German was able to experience what his Jewish compatriots had to suffer . . . Who could remain unsuspecting after the burning of the synagogues . . .? Whoever opened his eyes and ears and sought information could not fail to notice that Jews were being deported . . . There was, apart from the crime itself, the attempt by too many people including those of my generation, who were young and were not involved in planning the events and carrying them out, not to take note of what was happening . . . All of us, whether guilty or not, old or young, must accept the past. We are all affected by its consequences and liable for it . . . Anyone who closes his eyes to the past is blind to the present. Whoever refuses to remember the inhumanity is prone to new risks of infection . . .'

Meanwhile, Chancellor Kohl was having rather more trouble with *his* May 8 anniversary. It is true that in 1984 he had gone honourably to Israel to deliver a *nostra culpa*: and at Belsen on April 21, 1985, he made a good speech, referring to Germany's 'never-ending shame' at the Nazi crimes. But then he bungled Bitburg. When he first invited Reagan to accompany him on a memorial visit on May 5 to the military cemetery at Bitburg, south of Bonn, he and his advisers did not know – or at least, it is still not clear whether they knew – that some of the graves were of young SS men. And, when this became public and caused an outcry on both sides of the Atlantic, Kohl refused to cancel the visit or change the venue. Kohl was not born until 1930, and his entire attitude since taking office had been distinctly different from that of the older von Weizsäcker: he claimed that he represented a new generation of German leaders, no longer tainted by guilt, and that this made the time ripe for reconciliation and normalcy. In this spirit he went to Bitburg. But it was a serious political misjudgement. He had reckoned without the wrath of America's Jews, very many of them exiles from Germany.

Compared with the 550,000 Jews in pre-1933 Germany, today west Germany has only 28,000, and generally speaking they are well accepted and assimilated. Just after the war there was still widespread anti-semitism, for the Nazis had done their indoctrination thoroughly;

and it took some years for this to wane, as the full truth about the Holocaust became more widely known. Meanwhile the West German authorities had made some attempts at atonement: in addition to the reparations, fifteen new synagogues were built with public money for the tiny new communities of Jews who had the courage to settle again in this land of horror. Today they are left in peace — even though, in Germany as elsewhere, so many of the new young radicals have become anti-Israel and pro-Arab. But this is not the same as anti-semitic racism (which in Germany is punishable by law). The Jews today are so few in number that most Germans have probably never met one, and they are so well assimilated that it is not easy to identify them — as a Jewish woman teacher in Karlsruhe told me: 'My friends and colleagues are vaguely aware that I'm Jewish, but it doesn't seem to interest them at all. They are neither pro- nor anti-semitic.' A healthy development, it seems to me.

Dig deeper, and of course one finds that the German conscience is still troubled. Older people in particular do not like to be brought up against reminders of Jewishness. Once at a dinner-party in Bonn I sat next to a sophisticated baroness who talked to me eagerly and flirtatiously. I then happened to mention to the company at large that my mother had been Viennese Jewish. My neighbour froze, and would hardly speak to me again. I have often reflected on this incident. I doubt that she was being anti-semitic as such: more probably she felt, 'This chap will make me feel guilty, or will ask me what I think about the Jews, and that I don't want.' Sometimes, among the war-time generation, old resentments will suddenly flare to the surface, fuelled maybe by the feeling that many Jews have done too nicely out of the restitution benefits and are now again too rich. There was a strange incident in 1986 in a small town near Düsseldorf where the CDU mayor, Graf von Spee (a descendant of the Kaiser's admiral), was reported to have jested to a council meeting that 'a few rich Jews' should be killed off to balance the town's budget. He was then pressured into resigning, and he made a public apology for 'the damage done to German/Jewish reconciliation'. This shows how sensitive the subject still is. But feelings ran higher twenty years ago: in 1970, after Brandt's visit to Warsaw, *Der Spiegel* sponsored an opinion poll which gave 48 per cent of people thinking that his gesture of atonement at the ghetto had been 'over-done', while only 41 per cent thought it 'suitable'.

The confusions and contradictions that are still latent in German thinking about the Jews were vividly illustrated recently by the furore in Frankfurt over Fassbinder's allegedly 'anti-semitic' play, *Garbage, the City and Death*. Frankfurt before the war had a very powerful Jewish community, especially in banking (Rothschild, etc.). Just a few of these Jews have since returned, one of them being Ignaz Bubis, who moved into property speculation and was responsible for many of the new skyscrapers: his brash redevelopment of the city was much disliked, but publicly the criticisms were muted by reason of his being Jewish and thus in a sense immune. Fassbinder in 1975 then made this the theme of his play, which daringly broke the German post-1945 taboo on speaking ill of Jews (*The Merchant of Venice* had remained unperformed for many years). He portrayed a property tycoon who was cruel, sex-crazed, power-hungry and Jewish. And he portrayed too the private local reactions to this character: one ex-Nazi says, 'I could sleep better if this bloodsucker had been sent to the gas-chambers.' When the text of this typical Fassbinder provocation was made available, the outraged Frankfurt press called him a 'Left-wing Fascist', and the hue and cry was such that plans for staging the play were dropped. But Fassbinder said to me in 1976, 'I'm *not* anti-semitic – how could I be? I simply wanted to show a reality that exists in Frankfurt, where developers make use of Jews to do their dirty work for them, because they're above criticism. The play is anti-hypocrite. And isn't it high time in Germany, after all these years, that we should be able to admit that even a Jew can be bad? – just as in Britain it ought to be possible, though it seldom is, to portray Blacks as bad as well as good, without being accused of racism.' This seemed to me a fair argument. But Frankfurt's Jewish community did not see it that way. When in 1985, after Fassbinder's death, the civic Kammerspieltheater made another attempt to produce the play, local Jews stormed the stage at the first night. The director claimed that in its heightened way the work was trying to show that Nazi views were still alive in Frankfurt, and his supporters made its production an issue of free speech. But its opponents alleged that some passages could be exploited by anti-semites and in any case they were intolerable for Jews to hear on a German stage. Most Frankfurt politicians sided with this view. The play was taken off, and a year later this modern Shylock was still off stage.

This was no more than an isolated incident. Mostly, German/Jewish relations have settled down very well, and for some years about thirty major cities – including Frankfurt – have been inviting former Jewish residents to pay return visits of one or two weeks as the guests of the council. This has been a success. So let me end my survey of the Nazi legacy on an upbeat note, by quoting from an article in the *Guardian* of June 26, 1985 by Joel de Haas, a former German Jew now living in

England, who was one of a group of seventy invited back to their home town of Oldenburg, near Bremen. The visit, he wrote, was well organised by the town's Association for Christian/Jewish Cooperation which has no active Jewish members but has worked for years to keep the memory of the Jewish residents alive and to maintain the Jewish cemetery in prime condition. 'More than £100,000 was collected from the citizens to make our visit possible. Every effort was made to make us personally welcome, and we were privately entertained by individual Oldenburgers. All of us were invited to visit our former school. I addressed about 300 students at the Alte Gymnasium, and my theme song was that it is the duty of survivors to tell the tale of the Holocaust. One girl asked, "Do you hate us?" I told them, "No." It was a wonderful and heartwarming experience to meet democratic young Germans.

'Quite different was my meeting and address at the Rotary Club. There for the first time I met my contemporaries. I told them straight of our past experience and our abhorrence of recent German history. I added that in their case we are hardly able to forgive, never mind forget. The leaders of the community were rather distant, if perhaps slightly hostile. It did not help that I reminded them that Rotary in Germany, before it even became legally necessary under Hitler, asked its Jewish members to resign.' But later, at a Jewish cemetery, 'the school children were waiting to give each of us a white rose, the original sign of resistance to Hitler. We were told that they had organised this of their own accord.' Finally there was a Sabbath inter-denominational service in a large and packed church: 'The Catholic and Protestant ministers gave sermons. Pastor Dierken said, "We have sinned, we have deserted our brethren in their hour of need. We stood apart in silence when you were persecuted, and mostly for having forgotten the teaching of the Jew, Jesus Christ, 'Love thy Neighbour'."'

## Political strengths and community weaknesses

Have the Germans changed since those Nazi days? This artless but crucial question has been posed countless times since the war, and it would seem to me that the answer is clear. Democracy has taken root so firmly, and is so well safeguarded by the Constitution, that any return to a totalitarian regime would be hard to imagine. This at least is the most widely held view – and it is an optimism that I tend to share, though with a few reservations that relate more to the Germans' community sense than to politics in particular.

The success of democracy since 1945 appears especially remarkable when set in the context not only of the Nazi period but of Germany's entire past. As every history book points out, feudal domination persisted far longer than in most neighbouring countries, and even in the nineteenth-century parliamentary forms of government were still only embryonic. The regime created by Bismarck in the 1860s had institutionally some democratic features including a parliament. But in practice it was highly authoritarian, allowing little scope for popular self-government; and ordinary citizens, so long used to rule by princes, generals and bureaucrats, lacked the tradition or the experience for exerting their influence. Then Weimar in 1919 marked the first proper attempt to set up a fully democratic system in the Western sense. But this young republic had everything stacked against it. It had to deal with a terrible economic situation, caused in part by the harshness of the Versailles Treaty; its leaders were inexperienced; and it was hamstrung by certain weaknesses in its constitution. One of these was the kind of proportional representation used, which led to a pullulation of parties, more than 15 in all; and as economic unrest grew it was the extremist groups, Communist and National Socialist, that came to dominate. In 1932 the Nazis polled 37 per cent of the votes and emerged as the largest party. Hitler was then able to exploit a clause in the Weimar Constitution that permitted him to take emergency measures, and thus he seized power.

After 1945, as I noted at the start of this book, several factors enabled the new regime in Bonn to avoid repeating the errors of Weimar. One was the much more constructive policy of the Western Allies, another the sheer totality of the defeat which gave a stronger impetus for a complete new start. In addition, the new Republic's Constitution, the *Grundgesetz*, has proved far more effective than Weimar's. It is a very liberal and well-balanced document that protects basic freedoms while allowing curbs to be placed on extremist parties, if necessary. One clause states that no amendments to the *Grundgesetz* can be made that would limit its guarantees of human rights or alter the country's democratic basis – and most experts believe that this would make it virtually impossible for an anti-democratic party to come to power legally, as the Nazis did. Backed by this security, and bolstered too by economic prosperity, German politics since the war have been able to show a high degree of stability. They have been helped by an intelligent system of semi-proportional representation, whereby half of the seats for the *Bundestag* (the total since unification is 636) are decided on a single-member first-past-the-post basis as in Britain, while the other half (plus a few extra ones) are shared between the parties according to their overall voting strength in each *Land*. This system enables smaller parties to be much more fairly represented than in Britain (in the 1990 elections, for instance, the FDP with 11 per cent of the vote won seventy-nine seats, whereas in Britain in 1983 the SPD/Liberal Alliance won twenty-three seats with 26 per cent of the vote): but, as any party needs to poll more than 5 per cent nationwide to gain any seats at all, there is some check on the kind of proliferation that was the ruin of Weimar. If one or more parties with extremist views did ever succeed in surmounting this barrier and then formed a bloc in the *Bundestag*, there could be dangers. Mercifully, this has not yet happened. The Rightist NPD in 1969 won only 4.3 per cent. The Greens (whom some might consider 'extreme' in their economic views) won 5.6 per cent of the votes and twenty-eight seats in 1983: but this was not enough to prevent the Centre-Right coalition from securing an overall majority. In general, the PR system allied to the German voters' distaste for extremism has produced a succession of moderate centre-inclined governments, with the FDP sitting in the middle and somewhat opportunistically switching its allegiance so as to make coalitions possible. As a result the alterations of power between SPD-led and CDU/CSU-led governments have always passed off smoothly and democratically, alike on the federal level in 1969 and 1983 and in the *Länder* on various occasions. In 1966–9 in Bonn there was even a 'grand coalition' of all the major parties and it was quite successful.

The bitter lessons of the past have driven the great majority of West Germans since the war to look for consensus in public affairs: this is reflected in the relative harmony of labour relations, and also in politics. Of course it is true that this outward avoidance of conflict does mask some very real differences of interest and of ideology; and in the past twenty years, with the rise of a more radical generation, the tensions have become all too apparent, in street demonstrations and in sectors such as the universities – but not nearly so much in parliamentary politics. Here, both at *Land* and federal level, the spirit of consensus has been much more marked than in France, or indeed than in Britain today, and this corresponds to a wide public desire for reason, prudence and the status quo. The SPD since 1959 has turned its back on Marxism and embraced the mixed market economy; the CDU and CSU, though they do contain some Thatcher-like elements, have generally lent their support to generous social welfare policies. Not only in the handling of the economy, but in foreign policy and at least till recently in defence, there has been a broad measure of agreement: as one example, Kohl in the 1980s actively continued the SPD's *Ostpolitik*, despite the initial CDU misgivings about it.

Journalists and politicians are continually analysing the merits and possible weaknesses of their democratic system and asking anxiously, 'Are we democratic enough?' To a foreigner it all seems a little self-conscious, but the reasons are understandable. The voting turn-out at federal elections has run consistently at between 78 and 91 per cent, one of the highest levels in the West. And the Allensbach Institute produced some remarkable findings on popular attitudes to politics in the period up to 1978 (it does not appear to have repeated these particular questions since then). According to these surveys, the numbers thinking that 'we need a parliament and deputies in Bonn and cannot manage without' rose from 69 to 83 per cent between 1956 and 1978 (even among the under-30s, the figures went up from 63 to 81 per cent in that period, despite the rise of an allegedly more sceptical generation). The percentage of people preferring a multi-party to a one-party system rose from 53 to 68 per cent between 1950 and 1978, while devotees of a one-party state dropped from 24 to 5 per cent. In 1978, the proportion thinking that the present German democracy is 'the best form of government' stood at 71 per cent, while only 11 per cent thought 'there is another that is better'. And, most curiously of all, the numbers thinking that the deputies in Bonn 'serve foremost the interests of the people' increased from 25 to 55 per cent between 1951 and 1978, while the answer 'they serve mainly personal, private interests' fell from 32 to 15 per cent, and 'mainly party interests' from 14 to 3 per cent. If these figures are to be taken literally, they show that, after the initial post-war period of pessimism, faith in democracy grew steadily.

But, since 1978, has this bright picture been sullied by a few Flicks of the corrupter's pen across his cheque-books (see p. 516)? Possibly so. While the Constitution and the institutions of democracy are still respected, there is some evidence that the public have been losing confidence in those who animate them – the politicians. Another Allensbach survey of 1978, somewhat at variance with those quoted above, found that only 9 per cent of respondents felt that the country's 'most capable people' went into politics, whereas 55 per cent thought they tended to be in business or the universities. Certainly one hears plenty of laments today that the average calibre of politicians has been deteriorating – not so much in the *Länder* as in Bonn, where they tend to live out of touch with the real life of the nation. This is not only due to the well-known artificiality of that little city. Another harmful factor is that most federal politicians nowadays tend to be recruited from within the ranks of the parties' permanent staffs, which they will probably have joined at a young age. They are thus little more than apparatchiks, with scant experience of ordinary life.

There also appears to have been some decline recently in the public morality of politicians. In the Adenauer/Erhard era, and in that of Brandt and Schmidt, seldom did any whiff of corruption emanate from the higher ranks of the leadership: but this is no longer so, as the Flick affair has shown. Maybe one reason is that German democracy after forty years is now so tried and solid that the leaders have become more prepared to take risks with it and less conscientious. However, let me emphasise that corruption is still largely confined to politicians and senior executives and it exists very little at the lower level of petty bureaucracy: this is not Italy, where so often an official expects his palm to be greased before he will sign a permit or grant other favours. And this probity is one of the great strengths of the traditional discipline and strict obedience in Germany's otherwise rather too overpowering civil service. But politics are a different matter. In Munich, there have been cases of property developers bribing local councillors to secure contracts; in one instance, Siemens managed to get one of its directors chosen as candidate for the city council, where once elected he was able to swing a big contract his firm's way, against competition from EMI. In Berlin and Frankfurt, too, there has been trouble. And even the SPD has not been immune. In 1982 Neue Heimat, the huge and prestigious property company owned by the DGB trade union federation, became the subject of a major scandal: it was revealed that some of its highest executives, SPD members, had been lining their own pockets with large sums channelled via 'phantom' holding companies, while some union leaders had used the same means to secure taxfree shelters. Albert Vietor, the firm's managing director, had to pay back 15 million DM.

The CDU and FDP were chortling to see the 'virtuous' Socialists so discomforted. But the laugh was soon on them, when in 1984 the long-simmering Flick crisis came to a head. This revolved around the issue of the funding of political parties. These in Germany receive some public subsidies for running their campaigns: but, in order to avoid the dangers of a 'bought' democracy, strict legal limits are set on the level of donations that they can receive from industry or similar sources. With party costs rising, it had become tempting to find ways of circumventing this rule. And reports began to filter out, via well-researched articles in *Der Spiegel* and elsewhere, that the Flick conglomerate, one of Europe's most powerful financial groups, had been secretly 'laundering' contributions to the parties via dubious charity foundations and other 'front' bodies, in return for tax concessions and other favours from ministers. Count Otto Lambsdorff of the FDP, at the time economics minister under Kohl, resisted these Press accusations for some months: but in June 1984 he resigned and in 1985 he went on trial, charged with having accepted some 140,000 DM for party coffers (not for his own pocket) in return for signing tax waivers of about 800 million DM on certain of Flick's investments. It was the first time since the war that an ex-minister had stood trial for corruption. And in October 1984 the president (speaker) of the Bundestag, the respected Rainer Barzel, also resigned, following allegations that in the 1970s he had received some 1.7 million DM from Flick as a reward for standing down as CDU chairman in favour of Kohl (Flick preferred Kohl to be the next CDU chancellor). The scandal spread, implicating Kohl himself who admitted to having taken cash from Flick in plain envelopes. The reports then began to incriminate the SPD too, leaving only the Greens in the clear — and at one point Franz Josef Strauss blithely admitted that, yes, it was quite usual to receive funds for one's party in this under-the-counter way.

The Kohl Government soldiered on, refusing to resign despite these blows to its reputation. However, the much graver aspect of the Flick affair was the question of what effect it might have on the Germans' faith in parliamentary democracy — and this has been not so easy to estimate. Some commentators began to liken Germany to some 'banana republic' where politicians are in pawn to powerful business interests. This aspect has possibly been exaggerated, for there is little evidence that the Flick money had gone into private pockets. Even so, public morality was put under scrutiny as never before since the war. Then in 1987 came another startling scandal when Uwe Barschel, the dynamic and popular young CDU Prime Minister of Schleswig-Holstein, was alleged to have conducted a vicious smear campaign against his SPD rival, Björn Engholm. The allegations were proved true, and Barschel killed himself. The affair caused waves of shock in a country still insecure about democracy and thus demanding high standards of behaviour from its politicians. Yet in a sense it was democracy that triumphed in the end, for in the *Land* elections a few months later the voters of this normally right-wing region showed their disgust by removing the CDU from power and giving Herr Engholm a handsome majority – a remarkable victory for justice over self-interest.

However, after all these scandals, Neue Heimat included, the public now does seem to accept cynically that a degree of corruption or malpractice in high places is part of the normal way of life – in this affluent society where money values count for so much. Ironically, maybe the rule of law itself is partly to blame. In Germany the laws and regulations are so heavy and complex that well-to-do people and businesses are continually searching for legal or semi-legal ways of bending them to their advantages, via tax-free shelters, front organisations and the like. And, if nepotism or other forms of influence are not formally illegal, then they tend to be accepted just a little too readily by a German conscience that reasons in legalistic rather than moral terms. And this leads us to a central dilemma of Germany today. Blind obedience led the Germans down a disastrous path, under Hitler. But if the opposite trend is now gaining ground – a questioning of authority, or a pragmatic bending of the rules – might not this also carry dangers, in a society that has little experience of this common-sense way of conducting its affairs?

'In Germany', so the old saying goes, 'everything is forbidden except what is specifically allowed. In Britain, everything is allowed except what is specifically forbidden. In France, everything is allowed, even what is forbidden. In the Soviet Union, everything is forbidden, even what is allowed.' Today, the Germans have been trying to shift away from their own model, towards the British one. But the move is not proving easy. And it carries some hazards.

The rule of law has a stronger tradition in Germany than in most Continental countries. And so does the rule of the judges who apply the law, and of the bureaucrats who have so long administered the whole system of state with impartial but coldly abstract authority. Even more than in France, laws and regulations have been seen as the best way of holding society together; and, much more than in France, submission to the law and to superiors has been seen as the citizen's most essential duty. The philosopher Immanuel Kant (1724–1804) wrote: 'The characteristics of a child must include, above all, obedience.

[518]

This obedience may be obtained by force – then it is absolute; or by confidence – then it is voluntary. The latter is important, but the former is an absolute necessity because it prepares the child for adherence to the laws he will have to obey as a future citizen, whether he likes them or not.'

After 1945 it was seen that Hitler's lawyers had managed to exploit and distort the system, and so the rule of law was clarified and in many ways strengthened, in order to prevent a recurrence of such abuses. Hence the massive role given to the Constitutional Court in Karlsruhe, which interprets the *Grundgesetz* – usually very fairly and liberally – and adjudicates on all kinds of grievances and disputes, inter-governmental or between state and citizen. This works quite well. As democracy was still on probation after the war, the instinctive German reaction was to provide it with an explicit legal basis and to give the citizen directives on how to be democratic: so all kinds of laws were devised to guide and nurture the new society, like the wires that bind a growing sapling to its stake. It was all very well meant, and it reflected the old German utopian belief that a wisely regulated society can create universal happiness. Today, nearly all these German laws and rules are individually well intentioned: they aim to protect the citizens' rights from abuse by others, and it could be argued that in some cases they make for better justice than the laxer British system.[1] But, cumulatively, they can be very irksome. Rigidly applied, they can force the individual to choose between mindless obedience or a sly evasion of the regulations that leaves him feeling uneasy: between these extremes, ordinary common sense finds too little outlet. As Professor Nikolaus Lobkowicz, former president of Munich University, suggested to me: 'The excess of law leads to opposition or to apathy and frustration. It tends to make people disillusioned with the process of democracy, which could be dangerous; or it drives them into a French-style *Système D* attitude where they try to find ways of dodging the

---

1. For example, a Hamburg lawyer once justified to me the German requirement that any change of domicile must at once be registered with the police: 'In Britain and America, the police do not keep a record of who lives where. This makes it harder for them to find adolescents who have run away from home, or to catch people charged with petty crimes who have failed to answer summonses, or ex-husbands who fail to pay child maintenance. If a German girl has a child by a GI, so long as he's here the US Army will see that he pays his maintenance. But once he's back home the police have no means of tracing him. Our system is more fair, and it makes crime harder.'

rules without being caught. And the Germans are psychologically unsuited to this. They are not Latins.'

There are by-laws and regulations in Germany for a thousand and one matters that in Britain would be left to the community common sense or individual goodwill. Some exist to answer the German craving for security. One of the best-known obliges a house-owner to keep the snow, ice and fallen leaves swept clear on the stretch of pavement in front of his property: if he fails to do so, and a passer-by slips and breaks a leg, he is responsible. Other laws are devised to fulfil the German passion for orderliness. The city of Hamburg recently had the good idea that street-numbers outside houses should be illuminated: so an elaborate by-law was passed, stipulating in the minutest detail how large each sign should be, how bright or dim, how high or low above the ground, and of what materials it could be made – German thoroughness run riot. Or a new law will aim to regulate the dissensions between different interest groups – for example in education, where the *Land* ministry decides in detail how each school should operate.

A torrent of ever more complex legislation keeps pouring from the ministries and parliaments in Bonn and in the *Länder*. One of its many victims, Mayor Rommel of Stuttgart, gave me his explanation: 'The trouble is that the bureaucrats and deputies have little else to do all day but prepare new laws. Many of them have a legal background, so it's their idea of fun. But it makes life hell for a city council. If I want to fight some red-tape decisions by a ministry, I can take it to court, but that will involve up to five years' delay, so it's usually simpler to give in. Politicians talk about the need to simplify the administration, but all they do is make it worse.' Nearly everyone today agrees that the nation's laws have become too cumbersome and omnipresent, but no one quite knows how to solve the problem. The CDU blames the SPD and its massive welfare legislation in the 1970s. Both the CDU and FDP are pledged to reducing the number of laws, and they claim that they have indeed abolished or simplified more than 200 of them. They even introduced a Bill to reduce bureaucracy, the *Entbürokratisierungsgesetz* – a law against laws. What its impact will be is not yet clear.

The effect of these long centuries of legalism upon the national character has been, firstly, to make the Germans extremely litigious – more so than any other people in Europe. And with post-war affluence this has increased, for they now have more money to spend on lawyers' fees. I have already quoted the case of a Berliner who sued a tennis-club next door – of which he himself was a member – because the ping of ball on racquet disturbed his repose. This is typical. If a neighbour is noisy or otherwise tiresome, he is more likely to receive a formal solicitor's letter than be remonstrated with informally. Plenty of matters do get settled before they actually reach court: but they still tend to be dealt with by lawyers rather than be argued out privately, as happens much more often in Britain. This may be something to do with the German trust in law; or, more probably, with the Germans' dislike of direct confrontation that one notices also in the formality of so much social contact.

Secondly, the legal instinct is so deeply ingrained that families, friends and neighbours will sometimes draw up their own private rules for their mutual conduct, for a written code of this kind makes them feel more secure. This can be seen in marriage. As in Britain, many couples ask their solicitor to help them devise a formal agreement on property and other rights, which can help to avoid wrangles in the event of their splitting up. But some couples, wed and unwed, go further: they draft and sign their own private treaty, which has no legal force but lays down clearly the day-to-day rights and duties of each partner. An architect aged 40, living with a girl of 22, told *Quick* magazine (September 26, 1985): 'Before we signed our document, we would constantly quarrel in the evening when the washing-up was still undone. Now it's clearly set out who does it when – and we have no more tiffs. It is also written down that we each have the right to go out on our own two evenings a week, with no questions asked.' Some couples sign treaties on the amount of sexual freedom they allow each other. It works like a charm.

A third effect of legalism is to make the Germans more inclined to follow the set rules than to do what is obviously most sensible, when confronted with some little problem. The cry is always, '*Sie müssen . . .*' In a sauna frequented by my wife in Stuttgart, there was a notice up, 'No bathing costumes', and if a newcomer put one on, the other women would say angrily, 'Can't you read? It's *verboten!*', whereas in Britain the appeal would probably be to reason: 'I think you'd find it nicer and healthier, dear, if you didn't wear it.' Similarly, in the most often-cited example, children at pedestrian crossings are taught to wait for a green light *because* that is the rule, rather than to use their common sense and look out for traffic. ('If reasons are given, how can you call it obedience?' said the well-known nineteenth-century peda-gogue Lorenz Kellner.)

It follows that the Germans still tend to mind your own business for you, if they see you breaking the rules in however minor a way, for this gives them a sense of unease. If you walk down the street with your shoelaces undone, in France or Britain no one will notice: in Germany, you will soon have it pointed out to you, and not just for your own safety's sake. *Ordnung muss sein*, in all ways. A German may perhaps break the law gently when no one can see him (e.g. tax evasion), but not if others are watching (e.g. at traffic lights), nor does he like to see others doing so. In Hamburg in 1976, early one Sunday morning, I stopped my car for three minutes opposite 'no parking' signs to read my map. There was little traffic about, on a six-lane urban ringway, and I was not causing the slightest obstruction. But the cars that passed hooted at me testily, and one of them stopped right behind me and blared its horn until I moved on.

This at least has been the traditional pattern of German attitudes. But over the past fifteen or so years it has begun to change under the impact of a new generation: please note that my Hamburg traffic incident was back in 1976, whereas in 1984–5 during ten months' driving around the country I encountered no other quite so irritating case of private officiousness, though I had been expecting some. The Germans are changing, I do believe, and so do others. The proportion of pedestrians who wait patiently for a green light at a crossing, when there is no oncoming traffic and no policeman in sight, is still much greater than in Britain or France, but it has been declining noticeably, especially among younger people: those who still obey the rule will often do so primarily to set a good example to children, rather than for the rule's own sake. In other words, the generations of 1968 and after are now beginning to use their common sense and to obey the spirit of the law rather than its every letter – and this seems positive. However, the general decline in law-abidingness does have its more negative side, as is seen in the spread of moonlighting and tax evasion (let alone petty crime), and this can be damaging to the moral fabric of society. So this is a central dilemma for the Germans today: how to become *less* legalistic but *more* morally responsible for each other.

Paradoxically, while bureaucratic legislation has increased, society as a whole has become much more permissive and just a little more tolerant – even in the rules that private citizens set for each other. This can be seen in flat leases. During the housing shortage of the postwar decades, landlords (never the most tolerant of breeds) would exploit their command of the situation by imposing draconian rules on tenants or sub-tenants. When my wife was a child in Munich in the early 1960s, living in rented rooms with her impoverished widowed mother, a refugee from Silesia, they were not allowed to flush the toilet at night, nor to smoke, nor play a musical instrument, nor open the window in cold weather. In those days even in self-contained flats it was commonly forbidden to have guests to stay overnight, to hold a party more than once a month or continuing later than 11 p.m., or to have children whose noise could be heard, and couples frequently had to give proof of being married before a lease would be granted. Even today, the rules against making a noise after 10 p.m., or against hanging up washing or other outward untidiness, are a good deal stricter than in Britain, and in some *Länder* they have the sanction of law. But in general the situation has become much more liberal – partly because housing is now so plentiful that a tyrannical or puritan landlord would not find tenants, and partly because social attitudes have changed.

There has also been an easing of relations between the authorities and the public: the average *Beamte* (petty official) or police officer (see p. 541), may still be at pains to enforce the rules, but unless provoked he is now much less likely to shout at people officiously in the way he used to do. His instructions are to be courteous. Politeness has even crept into some official notices. Outside the main hospital in Stuttgart I saw a picture of a dog with the words, '*Ich muss leider draussen bleiben*' (alas I must stay outside), whereas twenty years ago it would certainly have been simply '*Hunde verboten*'. Along with this goes a generally more relaxed public attitude to authority, less scared or servile than in the old days: this is no longer the Germany of heel-clicking or love of uniforms (see p. 564). The change is even reflected within official hierarchies. At a big public hospital in Munich, a senior doctor told me: 'Staff relations used to be very rigid in this hospital, but they have changed. Yes, we still prefer to stick to surnames: but there is now a great deal of easy-going democracy among the staff, and some pressure from the middle ranks for group decision-taking, which can create difficulties.'

Many of these changes derive from the new ideas of the 1968 period, which in various ways have been taken up by a younger generation including the Greens. And this is now affecting school education. Many younger teachers bred of 1968 no longer try to inculcate the virtues of formal obedience (as Kant recommended), but instead they encourage their pupils to examine the meaning of the rules and to question the authorities – officials, professors, and their future employers. Some of them even cast doubt on all authority, including the police and the courts: this can provoke a backlash from parents, and much will then depend on the headmaster's attitude. In a broader sense, too, the new trends are leaning to a number of problems. In some schools, there are conflicts between young teachers and older ones, who want to stick to the old ethos. More important, because of the Germans' past and their psychology it is not proving so easy to instil a new kind of social responsibility that does not depend merely on keeping the law. In Britain, France or the United States, there exists a generalised patriotism that spills over into a moral feeling for community, so that a teacher can tell his pupils that it is 'British' or 'good for Britain' to behave in this or that way. In Germany, for obvious reasons, it is much harder to appeal to this kind of idealism; some teachers will refer to Christian values, but these too are now in some confusion owing to the conflicts within the Churches. So pedagogues have to look for an ethic that is based neither on patriotism, nor on obedience/ legalism, nor merely on enlightened self-interest, but somehow on a warm sense of human responsibility to the community, and this does not come easily in Germany (especially with an education system that pays so little attention to practical civic training). Furthermore, the new approach to authority causes problems for the authorities themselves. When a young policeman sees pedestrians crossing on a red light (for which he could impose fines), he does not want to be unpleasantly officious: but his whole value-system is threatened if people no longer obey the rules, and he feels bewildered. Nearly all German authorities face this dilemma, in one form or another. How far can they safely permit the letter of the law to be flouted? Can they learn to be flexible?

The new questioning of authority has notably taken the form of trying to protect the citizen from the encroachments of computerised data-collecting. This is an issue in many countries today – and especially in Germany where memories of the Gestapo police files have made people wary of allowing the State or any other organisation to amass data banks that could be used against the individual. In 1983 the federal authorities prepared a new census: but in the ultra-thorough German manner they overloaded the forms with searching questions about sources of income, life-styles, and so on. There was a widespread outcry that this was an invasion of privacy, and some 300 'boycott' groups were formed. Fears were expressed that the data might be given to the police, or to local authorities hunting for tax dodgers or other social offenders, or that it might be made available for commercial purposes such as market surveys. Finally two bold women lawyers took the matter before the Constitutional Court which duly pronounced that, yes, the questions *were* excessive. So the census was postponed. Then in May 1987 it was re-introduced, this time with the questions worded more discreetly. Again the Greens and others waged a campaign for a boycott, using much the same arguments as before. This time they failed to prevent the enquiry from being held, but an estimated 5 per cent of those questioned either refused to fill in the forms (thus risking a large fine) or else deliberately gave false answers, and this somewhat reduced the value of the census.

A few years previously, Parliament had passed the famous *Datenschutzgesetz* (law on protection of data) which aims to guarantee the secrecy of personal dossiers collected by public or private bodies, and to prevent their misuse. Not only police bureaux but also tax offices, insurance companies, hospitals and doctors' surgeries, all build up files of this kind, and so indeed do newspaper cutting libraries. I have good relations with *Der Spiegel*, and I asked if I could consult their library for my research for this book (as I have done on many similar occasions in London and Paris). I was told politely that under the law only staff members had access to it. Luckily I knew a reporter there who was able to get photostats for me of the cuttings I needed. It was explained to me that such libraries are among the very few places that keep massive biographical files on all kinds of people; if an outsider was able to gain entry to them, the material could easily be misused for defamation or blackmail. The precaution seems eminently sensible. But it is characteristic that the Germans should feel the need to pass a law about it.

Authoritarianism may be on the wane: but I am not sure how far there has been any increase in citizen participation, that is, in the individual's continuing feeling of shared responsibility for the daily doings of government, local or federal. He is punctilious about going to the polls to choose his representatives (even local elections have a high 70 to 80 per cent turn-out): but, rather as in France, once he has chosen them he feels it is *their* business to get on with the job of government and he does not intervene. Only in rare cases does public pressure exert the same kind of regular constructive influence as in Britain. The *Beamte* is less aloof and feared than he used to be: but he is still one of 'them', while the citizen is 'us', as in the days when it used to be said that the average German believed that 'the state equals the officials'. In fact, the

Allensbach multiple survey of 1978, quoted above, found only 29 per cent of people considering that they were able to influence the decisions of the federal government, while 48 per cent felt they were powerless. This pattern may have changed a little since the arrival of the Greens with their local citizen initiatives: but even Greens very often tire of trying to alter official policy and retreat into their own circles.

It is often the simplest incidents of daily life that are the most revealing of the lack of communal responsibility or even of neighbourly help. My wife reports: 'At my sauna/fitness-centre in Stuttgart if an elderly woman needed assistance or a mother wanted her child minded for a few moments, the other guests would expect the staff to do it all and would not lift one finger. At a similar centre near our home in Kensington, where I now go daily, everyone helps spontaneously without bothering the staff. This is typical of all areas of life, and it is one of the most striking differences I have noticed between the British and the Germans. In Germany, if you ask a person you do not know for a small favour, she is likely to reply indignantly, "That's not my business — the officials are paid for that." But this is not so much nastiness as a kind of timidity, a fear of improvising or stepping outside one's role.' And, if this is true of guests at a fitness-centre, what is it like at a much higher level of civic or political responsibility?

This trait may in part derive from the newness of the democratic tradition in Germany, or even from the Germans' problems with their national identity (see p. 577). It is certainly also a by-product of the education system which, as we have seen, concentrates on the child's mind and not on training his character or giving practical lessons in civics and leadership: but this is a chicken-and-egg situation, for a different society would presumably have devised another kind of education. Another related and highly relevant factor, also noted earlier in this book, is the contrast between the warmth of German private life and the stiffness and coolness of public life, and the curious hiatus between the public and private morality. An individual will feel affection, loyalty and moral obligation to his family and friends and others whom he knows and trusts: towards other fellow-citizens he feels little sense of concern, even if they are in trouble, and to the state and local authorities his sense of duty tends to be cold and rational, a matter of self-interest and of wanting to help preserve order. To schematise, this means that those he cares for personally he will defend, whether innocent or not; those he does not know he will leave to their fate. I can give two illustrations from instances previously referred to. One was that of the Stuttgart gynaecologist and alleged former Nazi, warmly supported by his doting female patients who did not seem to care about his black past. And the other, very different, was that of Böll's poor Katharina Blum – a fictional case but one that rings true. This innocent girl, cruelly victimised by the *Zeitung* and arraigned by the police, was most lovingly and loyally supported by her own small circle of friends, and at great cost to themselves, for they became victimised too. But her neighbours and the general public, most of them also decent people, simply accepted the *Zeitung*'s line and joined in the persecution – *because they did not know her*. Böll's underlying message was that these good citizens were every bit as guilty as the gutter tabloid itself. It was a trenchant condemnation of an abiding flaw in the German social character.

Similar traits can be observed in German attitudes to the weak, the handicapped or the unsuccessful, in this competitive, success-geared society where failure carries a stigma and the frail or inadequate are sometimes shunned as though infectious. I quote again from my conversation with Hans Magnus Enzensberger: 'I think that the Germans have certainly become far more tolerant in accepting deviants such as homosexuals, punks or other rebels, who are considered a bit shocking but amusing and colourful and fairly innocuous: but once there is a price to be paid in terms of social responsibility for the weak, then the Germans as individuals remain much less tolerant and caring. I know of lots of little towns where people today will accept a gay bar, a porn-shop, maybe a mixed sauna or even a political cabaret making fun of the mayor and the bishop. But once it is proposed to open, say, a home for the handicapped, or for ex-drug-addicts, or for rehabilitating ex-prisoners, then they make a great fuss and say, "Oh no, we don't want that *here*." And this I find very unpleasant. Or let me give you another example. German popular comedy, unlike say Italian or Jewish, has no tradition of sympathising with the underdog. In Italy, the most popular comedians are losers – there's this little man who's always getting hit on the head, he tries very hard but he can't get the girl or the job that he wants, he's a bit of a fool, a bit innocent, and the audience laugh at him but they also identify with him. In Germany, to identify with a loser is still very, very rare. People don't want to know about the loser, or to admit to being a loser. And that's a problem today with unemployment – look at these men who lose their jobs and then go on pretending to leave for work each day because they don't want their friends and neighbours to learn the awful truth.'

It is not that officialdom itself neglects the weak: very far from it. Local authorities and the Churches lavish their funds and their kindly care upon excellent homes for the handicapped, among the best in Europe. But, just because the institutions do so much, the individual does not feel concerned; or, conversely, because individuals are so uncaring, the authorities must bear the full burden – it is the same old divide between public and private morality. Until quite recently, in the more pious rural areas, for parents to give birth, say, to a mongol or spastic was looked on as a kind of divine retribution for some sin they must have committed, and the hapless couple would try to avoid displaying their shameful progeny in public; these attitudes have now been modified, but even today, much more often than in Britain, a mentally handicapped child tends to be put into an institution where he is kindly cared for, rather than live in society with his family, if it is possible. Rather as with Turkish immigrants (see p. 284), people seem to take the view, 'Now, the mongol who lives next door, *he's* awfully sweet, we know him well – but handicapped people as a whole, oh no!' And even today a blind or crippled person will not find it easy to get lodgings, unless he applies via the welfare authorities, who will then put him somewhere suitable. This national trait is more than a dislike of weakness, it is a real fear of weakness as something abnormal, offending against the German desire for order and perfection. It reached its worst excesses under the Nazis' euthanasia policy, and it has still not entirely disappeared. In 1980 an elderly lady in Munich booked a package tour to a hotel in Greece, which she found to contain a big group of Swedish spastics. She was so angry at having her holiday 'ruined' that she sued the German travel firm: the court pronounced in her favour, and she got a big refund. Liberal papers such as *Die Zeit* and *Der Spiegel* were scandalised. All in all, it is hardly a happy picture. However, it must be stressed very strongly that attitudes are different among a younger generation that is less success-oriented and more caring. Young Greens and others will sometimes run day-nurseries where handicapped and normal children mix together; conscientious objectors frequently choose work in homes for the handicapped as their alterna-tive to military service. This seems to me one of the most sympathetic features of the new wave of Greenish idealism; as this generation grows older possibly Germany may become a kindlier community.

Meanwhile, the curious blind spot in public moral attitudes can sometimes extend to political figures, when they fall foul of the law. Consider, for example, the shocking affair of Otto Wiesheu, who in

1983 was secretary-general of the CSU and one of Bavaria's most respected politicians. One October night of that year he was driving his Mercedes blind drunk down an *Autobahn* near Munich when he rammed a small, slow car driven by a Jew from Poland, and killed him. The police took blood tests and questioned witnesses, and charged Wiesheu with drunken driving. Instead of resigning on the spot, he clung to his job, claiming that he was not really so very drunk and that it was partly the Pole's fault. What is more, the CSU stood by him solidly: Strauss said publicly, 'He's a very good man, one of our best,' and, on Wiesheu's next visit to the *Landtag*, he was loudly cheered from the CSU benches. The general view in the party was, 'This is a matter for the courts to decide. Meanwhile, we stick by him in his hour of need.' Some months later in face of a mounting Press campaign against him, Wiesheu did resign: but then the party found another good job for him, as head of a research foundation. A year after the accident, the lumbering legal system produced a trial, where Wiesheu was found guilty. He appealed, and the following year was given a suspended 11-month sentence, while also settling the civil claim by giving 30,000 DM to the Pole's next-of-kin. I am not suggesting, and nor has anyone, that the courts and the police were other than fair, or in any way corrupt. But what an Englishman may find disturbing is, firstly, that Wiesheu did not resign at once, as I think he would have done in Britain: instead of accepting his clear moral guilt, he stuck to his legal rights of being innocent until proved guilty and behaved as if nothing had happened. Secondly, I was shocked by the way that the CSU backed him and that public opinion (with the honourable exception of some local papers) failed to get indignant. In this *macho* society, many CSU stalwarts privately took the view, 'Well, we all drink too much beer sometimes, don't we? That's inevitable. It was just bad luck on old Otto. Such a good chap, such a pity.' Some of them in their cups even murmured that the Polish Jew should not have been driving so slowly down the motorway in such an old car. And, when in 1985 I met Wiesheu's successor in the CSU post, he spoke of 'this terrible thing that happened to our dear colleague'. But what about what 'happened' to the Pole?

Wiesheu's reactions were not so different from those of Count Lambsdorff in the Flick affair, who also refused to resign when the scandal broke, and did so only after the media campaign had made his position impossible. This is the practice in German political life: when accused you try to sit it out and to avoid admitting responsibility. And this seems to me to touch on the weak point of society that depends more on law than on individual conscience. The system of law in Germany may be as fair, and as fairly applied, as anywhere: but it takes too much precedence, and in public life people tend to act by what is legally permitted rather than by what is morally right. Maybe at this point, having quoted Enzensberger of the moderate Left, I could now usefully cite Professor Wilhelm Hennis, of Freiburg, a leading political scientist of the moderate Right, who gave me this critique: 'Not only are the Germans too obsessed with demanding their legal and social rights, but there is a lack of moral idealism in German society. It may have something to do with the lack of patriotic feeling. Leaders of other countries are always making moral appeals to a national ethic. It is hard to imagine this in Germany, where a Kohl or a Schmidt will base their appeals on much more practical arguments, on mutual self-interest or sound financial management. Brandt was the last idealist. But he was too much of a romantic, so he failed.'

I seem to have painted rather a severe picture of some of the weaker points in the German public character. So are we to conclude that democracy in the new Germany is still a fragile plant? There are some observers who believe so. They ask whether economic success is not perhaps the only cohesive force holding society together, and they point to recent signs of a decline in consensus – in labour relations and bipartisan defence policy, and through the emergence of the Greens with their challenge in the whole industrial system. The Germans tend to worry about such matters. Being still an insecure people, they do not find it easy to live with democratic conflict, and by temperament they grow uneasy when things become at all unstable. Hence the over-reactions against left-wing terrorism in the 1970s (see p. 537) and the fears sometimes expressed that it might take only a medium-sized crisis for latent anti-democratic forces to be mobilised, as in the 1930s.

It may very well be that these anxieties are excessive. Despite the reservations I have voiced, there is plenty of evidence that the democratic process has now become firmly established in Germany, where political consensus still remains a good deal stronger than in Britain, France or Italy. And total consensus anyway is inconceivable and undesirable – how boring it would be! Over the past two decades, society has become more open and informal, more tolerant of diversity, and this may have been due partly to the ferment of 1968 – as Enzensberger, amongst others, suggested to me: 'For me, 1968 was the watershed. Before that, we were still in the old Germany – not Nazi Germany, but a far older tradition, very rigid, authoritarian and hierarchical, especially in education or in the relation of bosses to employees and seniors to juniors. This had become more and more anachronistic and dysfunctional, sometimes to the point of black-and-white – as when Strauss tried to crack down on *Der Spiegel*. Then in 1968 we intellectuals took a leading role in trying to modify this structure, and we did have some influence. For us on the Left, it was both a victory and a defeat: we did not succeed at all in doing away with capitalism, but we did help to modernise society, towards more openness and participation. So Germany is a much easier place to live in than twenty years ago. But it's a porridge-like situation, very fluid and disparate, where the issues are no longer so clear-cut. And federalism, one surviving German tradition, suits the porridge very well.'

In this new and more flexible world, freedom of expression has increased, so the various tensions are now less suppressed and more out in the open – a healthy trend. In politics, the growth of tolerance is reflected in the way that marches and demonstrations, once considered so threatening, are now accepted as part of normal life; and the police (see p. 539) are finally learning how to deal with them sensibly without over-reacting. Of course the problem of extremist minorities still haunts and troubles the Germans, and Article 21 of the Constitution declares that 'parties which, by reason of their aims or the behaviour of their adherents, seek to impair or abolish the free democratic basic order' shall be unconstitutional if the court in Karlsruhe so decides. This is a right and proper safeguard, in view of Germany's past. But in practice it has rarely been felt necessary to invoke this clause. It was used to ban the West German Communist Party in 1956. But in 1968 a new Party was founded, the DKP, that tactfully jettisoned its predecessor's formal objective of revolutionary overthrow of society and so was allowed to exist normally as in other Western countries. But it has never had any real influence.

Popular support for extremist parties seems to have declined: according to Allensbach, backing for Communism was down to 2 per cent by 1988, while the numbers of those saying they would 'welcome and support' a new Nazi party fell from 5 to 2 per cent between 1953 and 1972. It is true that there remains a strong ground-swell of popular feeling that parties of this kind ought to be banned: quoting Allensbach again, in 1973 the numbers thinking that the DKP should be prohibited (39 per cent) were almost as great as those (43 per cent) who felt it should be allowed. Or, as one sceptic said to me, 'There are still plenty of diehards around who find the Constitution too liberal and cannot see the point of a democracy that is so permissive.' Fortunately however, governments and the Constitutional Court in recent decades have all wisely tended towards tolerating extremist parties and avoiding too indiscriminate a crackdown on terrorism that would impinge on the rights of ordinary people. As Bernard Levin wrote in an excellent article on Germany in *The Times* of October 4, 1985, 'It has come to be thought better, in a soundly-based democratic state, for anti-democratic organisations to be allowed to do their work in daylight rather than in the dark, where they may prove to be ultimately more dangerous . . . The Constitutional Court had shown itself to be very firm in its interpretation of the provisions under which a party may be banned; the upshot has been that even some of the vilest organisations have been left alone, provided they stay within the law.'

There is however one important exception to this pattern of watchful tolerance: the regulation that prevents extremists whose loyalty to the state is in doubt from being employed in the civil service or in other public posts such as teachers or railwaymen. This notorious and much-criticised *Radikalenerlass* (decree against extremism) was drawn up in 1972 by Chancellor Brandt and the *Land* prime ministers, with the aim of controlling the influence of the rebel student generation; and it has been widely applied, against Communists, the far Left and the far Right. Of course it is normal to expect loyalty from a civil servant, and indeed most democratic countries have ways of excluding undesirable elements from sensitive posts, notably those involving security; but they do so quite informally with no reasons given. In West Germany, characteristically, the problem has been tackled by legalistic decree – and this has caused difficulties, especially as the bureaucratic rules have not been suited to distinguishing between anti-democratic subversives and mere radical critics. So the measure has provoked rumbling allegations of 'McCarthyism'. Many teachers and scientists have been excluded. A driver with the state railways, though not dismissed, was refused promotion and the status of *Beamte* because he was a known Communist; he appealed to the courts, but lost. However, the *Länder* in SPD hands have recently become more lax about applying the decree, and in 1985 Saarland became the first to abolish it formally (as it had the legal right to do): its interior minister declared that the measure had created an atmosphere of fear and intimidation and had damaged West Germany's reputation abroad. In fact, today the view is spreading that German democracy is secure enough to be able to relax a formal control that is not totally democratic.

So this brings us back to the initial question. Is an anti-democratic regime, whether fascist or extreme-left, conceivable today? – could a new

Hitler ever come to power in Germany? Of course no categorical answer is possible. But Article 21 of the Constitution does provide stronger safeguards than Weimar enjoyed; and, more important, the Germans today are far more alert to any possible dangers. As I have tried to suggest, there may still be some traits in the German public personality and in legal and civic attitudes, that do not provide the firmest of bases for democracy: on the other hand, the institutions and the machinery of government have been working quite smoothly and are well accepted. It is true that the implications of the Flick affair are worrying, for if such practices were to become endemic, public faith in the democratic system could be undermined. It is true also that no really major crisis, economic or international, has yet arisen to test the solidity of the system. But some omens are favourable. After all, it was high unemployment above all else that fuelled the rise of Nazism, and in the 1960s many sceptics were predicting similar ugly tensions if the jobless total ever rose above a million or so: in the 1980s the figure remained above 2 million for several years, and on the labour front there was scarcely a murmur (fringe Leftist terrorism has quite other causes). In 1990, reactions to the economic upheaval of unification were similarly peaceful, despite the anxieties. It remains true that if the Western economy went into serious recession, or if some other crisis threatened peace in Europe, then the insecure and anxiety-prone Germans might react more violently and unpredictably than other NATO nations. This is hard to foresee.

In any event, much will depend on the new generations, those that have emerged since 1968. They appear to be more socially caring, more generous and informal than their elders: but they are also far more sceptical of Western industrial society and of its military defence. So are they to be regarded as a liability for the new German democracy, or as its brightest hope for the future?

## The Greens and their values: fundamental social change, or just another youth protest?

The past twenty years have been marked by a number of successive waves of youth protest and revolt against the established order. First came the student uprisings of the late 1960s, exploited by revolutionary leaders and sometimes marked by violence. Amid sporadic disorders on the campuses this movement lurched on into the 1970s, when a fraction of it moved underground to fuel the extreme-left terrorism of the Baader-Meinhof gang. Then in the late 1970s a very different trend emerged, far wider in its appeal, less directly political though still anti-capitalist, and much more peaceful though sometimes infiltrated by fringe violence. It was oriented towards ecology, pacifism, social informality, new life-styles and new anti-materialist values, and it found its sharpest identification in the setting up of the Green party, as well as through 'alternative' ventures such as communes, squats and workshops, extending also to punks, hippies, oriental sects and much else in this motley scene.

All these movements have been essentially middle rather than working-class. And they have had simultaneous counterparts in other countries – for example, the Sorbonne riots of 1968, the Red Brigade terrorists in Italy, and the various environmental and alternative groups in Britain and America. But the German youth protests, the Greens especially, have on the whole been more determined, more widespread and more enduring than elsewhere, and above all more strident in their condemnation of the older generation and its values. Indeed there is plenty of evidence to suggest that the gap between the generations has been wider in Germany than in other countries. One international survey in 1981 that put to under-25s the question, 'Do you have the same set of moral values as your parents?' found only 38 per cent of Germans answering 'yes', compared with 50 per cent of other Europeans and 77 per cent of young Americans. But today there are signs that the gap is narrowing.

What have been the reasons for this sharper generational conflict? It has sometimes been put down to the Germans' utopianism, to their dislike of compromise and tendency towards excess – but this view runs somewhat counter to the general post-war pattern of a search for political compromise. A more likely explanation could be that younger people, especially in 1968, have been reacting against the exceptional degree of conformism, formality and hierarchy in German society, and against the materialist ethos of parents who had rebuilt Germany after the war while rejecting all ideologies as 'dangerous'. The younger generation today can enjoy the fruits of their hard work: but they never shared in the triumphs and travails of the reconstruction, and they now prefer to concentrate on criticising its harmful effects on the environment and on human relations. They also feel themselves to be living in a society lacking in spiritual values. So the old German idealism, long buried since Nazism, has been coming back – for better or for worse. And thus, as the bourgeoisie in turn show a high degree of intolerance towards the new rebels, the contrast in Germany between two distinct sets of values and life-styles is much sharper than in most Western countries. It is far harder than in Britain to be somewhere in the middle, an easy-going and vaguely messy liberal but certainly not an *Alternativ*. You have to choose. If you hold the balance, each side will denounce you as belonging to the other.

There are other crucial questions to be explored. Do the new trends extend to the whole of the younger generation, or just parts of it? – and *which* generation? Among the very young, the under-22s, there are clear signs today of a return to more conservative values – how significant is this? Is the broad movement of the past fifteen years, epitomised by the Greens, just one more youth protest which its protagonists will slough off as they grow older and more settled? – or does it herald a more lasting and fundamental change in values and in society? As an American general said in Frankfurt (admittedly, in a different and more military context), 'The question is not so much, "how many Greens are there in Germany?" but "how Green are the Germans?"'

During the initial post-war decades, West German youth behaved with its habitual obedience and docility. Then the student revolt came as a bolt from the blue, and it was the first of its kind in Europe. Like the French uprising which followed a few months later, it began as a movement against an outmoded university system and the heavy authoritarianism of senior teachers – and some parents too. It started fairly moderately with some sensible proposals for reform: but it was soon taken over by the political extremists. Some were the children of ex-Nazis and this lent a special moral ferocity to their rejection of society. West Berlin was the powder-keg, as one might expect: when the Shah of Iran paid a visit there in June 1967, students demonstrated against him and the riot police then attacked them, injuring forty-seven and killing one with a revolver. This provoked a wider uprising, as students besieged the Axel Springer offices and staged campus sit-ins all over Germany. In April 1968 Rudi Dutschke, the best-known student leader though not the most extreme, was shot in the head by one right-wing fanatic (the resulting brain damage crippled him for life, and he died in 1979 aged only 39).

During 1968, rather as in France, the ideas of the reform movement spread outside the university world itself to embrace schools, hospitals, firms, public offices and other institutions, where pupils, nurses, clerks and other juniors began to demand 'participation' and a relaxation of the old rigid hierarchies. And to quite an extent they succeeded. The revolt did not prompt the same drastic official overhaul of the university system as in France: but it did reduce the tyrannical hold of professors, hospital directors and others, and generally throughout working life (as Enzensberger told me, see p. 530) it ushered in a more democratic and informal climate − often amid a certain confusion. But it did *not* break capitalist society as the extremists had intended, and so it left them highly disillusioned. After the wider upheaval had subsided, they formed into little Leftist groups and continued their physical agitation in the universities (see p. 246). Some of them created the so-called 'Red Cells', Communist-inspired, which in some places were still active in the 1980s, violent in nature but led by serious and dedicated intellectuals, now mostly in their forties. This was the unpleasant face of what has been dubbed 'German Left Fascism': these embittered activists were verbally as well as physically violent, and rather than try to convince people they would interrupt lectures and meetings with ferocious heckling and breathe hellfire on anyone who tried to debate with them reasonably. Their influence has never been great, and today it is minimal.

One small group, disavowed by most of the other new Leftists, resorted to brutal terrorism after 1968 − and they gave Germany a nasty fright. Their leaders, many of them women, were highly intelligent, educated and sensitive. Gudrun Esslin, the daughter of a Swabian pastor, was consumed with hate against a Church that she saw as the accomplice of capitalism. Ulrike Meinhof, a brilliant journalist and mother of two, was an uncompromising utopian crusader for equality and pacifism. Her lover, Andreas Baader, though a rougher personality, was none the less the son of a professor. So what was it that drove these young people, so disgusted with society, into a kind of romantic idealisation of violence as what they felt to be the only outlet left to them? It has never been clearly explained, though studies with such titles as *Hitler's Children*[1] have looked for clues in some atavistic irrational streak of visionary cruelty in the German psyche. In 1972, after a number of bomb attacks and bank robberies, the three main Baader-Meinhof leaders were arrested and later sentenced to life impris-

1. A book about Baader-Meinhof by an English author, Julia Becker (Michael Joseph, 1977).

onment. But this was by no means the end of the terrorism. In their wake a larger, more deadly and much more professional gang emerged, the *Rote Armee Fraktion*, and they stepped up the attacks. In all, between 1970 and 1978, the RAF, Baader-Meinhof and other groups between them killed 28 people, wounded 93, took 162 hostages, and seized 5.4 million DM in 35 bank robberies. In April 1977, after Meinhof's suicide in prison, terrorists took revenge by killing Siegfried Buback, the chief federal prosecutor. Two months later they murdered Jürgen Ponto, chairman of the huge Dresdner Bank: the chief accomplice, Susanne Albrecht, was the 19-year-old daughter of close friends of Ponto, and she coolly explained her motive – 'I'm tired of all this caviare guzzling.'

As the terrorist campaign developed, the public and politicians reacted with varying degrees of panic to what was seen as a threat to the very fabric of society. Armoured cars, sharpshooters and helicopters patrolled the centre of Bonn, where the *Bundestag* was encircled with barbed-wire. Many wealthy and prominent families took similar precautions against the wave of shootings and kidnappings – as Heinrich Böll described with a touch of satire in his novel *The Safety Net* (*Fürsorgliche Belagerung*, Solicitous Siege, 1977), about a tycoon and his family who become the virtual prisoners of their own police guards, scarcely able to move out of their house. Böll was one of a number of liberals who felt that the Germans were reacting hysterically to a real but strictly limited crisis. But he was shouted down by the cohorts on the Right who began to demand sweeping measures against the terrorists and other known Leftists, of a kind that would have curtailed human rights and led to a *de facto* martial law. This was precisely the kind of breakdown of democracy that the rebels themselves were aiming to provoke. But, fortunately, the Schmidt Government wisely kept cool. Then in October 1977 came the ultra-sensational climax. The RAF had kidnapped the president of the employers' association, Hans-Martin Schleyer of Daimler-Benz, a tough campaigner who seemed to represent all that they most disliked about capitalism. It was a great coup. But when they offered to exchange Schleyer for the release of 20 of their own imprisoned members, including Baader and Esslin, Schmidt refused point blank. Then the RAF hijacked a Lufthansa jet on a holiday flight from Majorca, and forced it to fly via Rome and other places to Mogadishu, in Somalia, where they threatened to kill all on board if their demands were rejected. But a crack German anti-terrorist squad stormed the plane at night, killing three of four hijackers and saving the hostages. A few hours later, it was found that Baader, Esslin and a third ringleader had committed suicide in their prison at Stammheim, outside Stuttgart (whether they did this genuinely in despair at the RAF's failure, or whether they were somehow 'helped' by their guards, was never made clear). The RAF at once retaliated by murdering Schleyer and leaving his body in the boot of a car.

This melodrama was to mark a decisive turning-point in German radical protest. The terrorists' methods had by now disgusted all but a handful of their original sympathisers and from now on youthful campaigners turned away from ideological violence towards more peaceful causes, mostly environmental. By 1980 most of the leading RAF outlaws had been caught and imprisoned. But the gang's violence still continued spasmodically, sometimes taking the form of bank robberies to obtain funds, and sometimes that of kidnapping or even killing – as when, near Munich in 1985, they murdered another senior industrialist, Dr Ernst Zimmermann. In November 1989 they proved they were still a force to be reckoned with, by murdering one of Germany's top bankers, Alfred Herrhausen, chief executive of the Deutsche Bank. Although six armed bodyguards were with him, his car was hit by a bomb as he drove to work. The RAF and other German terror cells had by now linked up with a new Europe-wide network whose main targets were NATO installations and military chiefs. Today, this has so far had only limited success. But posted up in police stations and other offices one continues to see crude snapshots of the most-wanted killers still at large – ghoulish young faces like some nightmare from German past. Hitler's children, indeed.

In June 1990, thanks to collaboration between the east and west German police, nine leading terrorist suspects were tracked down and arrested in east Germany: they included Susanne Albrecht herself (she was tried and jailed for twelve years), Inge Viett, a former cabaret dancer, and the aristocrat Ekkehard von Seckendorff. It emerged that in the years after the Schleyer affair they had fled to the GDR, where the Stasi had welcomed them, given them false identities and helped them find jobs: Viett was working in a steel plant in Magdeburg under another name. Some appeared to have renounced terrorism and 'retired', but others were still working for the RAF, with the Stasi's connivance. And the de Mazière Government expressed its shock at this 'devilish' link between terrorism and Communism: the Stasi had apparently told Albrecht that, while the GDR regime disapproved of the RAF's violence, it would condone it with the aim of 'damaging imperialist

West Germany'. Today, as the Herrhausen murder shows, the RAF is still capable of horrific acts. But it is not the force that it was. Two other assassination attempts in 1990 that badly wounded two senior politicians, Oskar Lafontaine of the SPD and Interior Minister Wolfgang Schäuble (CDU), were the work not of the RAF but of individual fanatics.

It is worth looking briefly at the role of the German police. They have had very great difficulty in learning how to deal with student and other demonstrations, let alone with terrorism. And the many stormy scenes of the past twenty-five years inevitably cast a harsh public spotlight on their methods and behaviour – in a land where since Bismarck's day they have held a certain reputation for brutal authoritarianism. Today, their dilemma has been that of how to adapt to the gentler role required of them in a liberal democracy, while also facing up to modern violence. How have they managed?

At first they just did not know how to cope with the new phenomenon of student riots and they over-reacted, as was seen clearly when the Shah visited Berlin. These clumsy excesses played into the extremists' hands, morally speaking: they were able to claim, 'Look, this fascist society is after all as evil as we've always said!' Even when the less violent demos and sit-ins of the 1970s began (anti-nuclear, anti-motorway or pro-squat), the police still reacted uncertainly, and they were badly trained for this kind of work. Various battles took place, with assorted crowds of young protesters pitched against the lines of grim-faced riot police with their shields and visors. The most notorious sieges were those of the Brockdorf nuclear plant in the later 1970s (see p. 144) and of the Berlin squats (see p. 555) and the Frankfurt airport extension, both in the early 1980s.

When it was decided to build a new runway for Germany's largest international airport, militant opposition came swiftly from various quarters – ecologists, claiming that forests would be pulled down and housing threatened; peacenicks (often the same people), furious that the enlargement would create added facilities for the US Air Force; and Leftists and anarchists of all kinds who eagerly jumped on the bandwagon thrilled at the prospect of a new crusade. Petitions and lawsuits caused several years' delay: but these ultimately failed in the courts, and in 1981 construction work began. So the protesters then took the law into their own hands: they set up a big camp on the site (a larger-scale Greenham Common), and they began massive daily demonstrations. Much of this activity was peaceful and legitimate (apart from a certain amount of arson, bombings, and tearing down of airport fences): but the ecologists were heavily infiltrated by veteran agitators from other German and foreign cities, who proceeded to provoke the police and to try to stir up fighting. Heavily outnumbered, and even hit by stones, the police on several occasions lost their tempers and charged the demonstrators, truncheons flailing. They were totally incapable of distinguishing between the peaceful and the violent elements, and thus a great many innocents were hurt. I met one young Green who was badly hit herself and also saw policemen beating up a girl of five and her parents. All this caused a great emotional outcry which filled the Frankfurt headlines for weeks – and it sharply polarised opinion, completely blurring the original issues of the runway itself. 'It was just not possible to take a fair dispassionate stance,' said a journalist I met on the liberal *Frankfurter Rundschau*; 'it was out of the question, for instance, to say that you were for the runway yet felt that the police had behaved disgracefully; or, conversely, that you were opposed to the runway but thought that the police had done their best under provocation. Tenable positions like that were treated with angry derision by both Left and Right. And, because they hated the Greens, the entire establishment here including the SPD swung their weight behind the police, so that its undoubted excesses were never examined publicly. It was shocking, shocking.' Frankfurt conservatives I met, while admitting privately that the police had behaved badly, said they felt that even the most peaceful demonstrations of this kind should always be banned, for they were bound to be exploited cynically by the *provocateurs* and the police could not be expected to tell who was who.

In recent years there have been some other cases of the police rough-handling suspects or pulling their triggers at them a little too readily and then claiming it was self-defence. In Stuttgart in 1976, when searching for a terrorist, they burst into the flat of an innocent British consular employee, fired at him and killed him; in Munich on another occasion, a policeman saw a schoolboy climbing through the window of a youth-club at night and shot him, thinking he was a criminal on the run. Maybe such mistakes are inevitable from time to time, in a climate where the police are made nervous by so much terrorism. But, when a public inquiry is held, the courts seem to be too prepared to uphold the police claim to have been acting in 'putative self-defence'; and the police will never admit any responsibility or give details as to whether an individual officer has later been disciplined.

However, such incidents have today grown rarer, now that terrorism has declined; and in the past 10 or 15 years the police have also been making concerted efforts to improve their image with the public and to behave more discreetly. Though they can still over-react in face of violence, they have finally learned how to deal sensibly with the more peaceful kind of demonstration – 'In the Kaiser's day,' Manfred Rommel told me, 'the police were used like an army and would shoot people in the streets. Now they have become more tactful, and ordinary citizens are no longer nearly so afraid of them.' This is true. The police still carry arms, as is general on the Continent: but they now keep a much lower profile. Back in 1974, when three teenagers on the spree began to parade naked in a Stuttgart public swimming-pool, the police were summoned and twenty men arrived bristling with sub-machine-guns to arrest the trio; ten years later, when a rather similar incident occurred, two officers came along with their revolvers well hidden and no arrests were made. This is a measure of the change. As a result, though the climate of mutual trust between police and public is still not as strong as in Britain, it has much improved and is certainly better than in France. The police are becoming more accepted – even by the Greens.

The 'Green' movement that began to emerge in the late 1970s has been widespread in its popularity and also extremely diversified both in its policy aims and in the nature of its support which includes quite a ragbag of differing elements. Though of course the Greens appeal more to younger than to older people, their hard core of strength has resided less in the very young than among an educated middle-class generation in its late twenties and thirties – many of them the former students of 1968 now trying to apply those ideals in other ways. They include those who founded the Green party in 1980: but the Green movement is far wider than this party, which has always been more successful at local than federal level and remains just the tip of the iceberg of a whole new wave of ideas, aspirations and life-styles.

The basic tenet of their ideology, common to all Greens, is ecological – a desire to conserve resources and protect the environment, a mistrust of modernism and especially of nuclear power, and a liking for a simpler and less materialistic way of life. With many Greens, all this takes a moderate and reasonable form. But some carry it much further, into a passionate hatred of all technology and a romantic yearning to return to some kind of agrarian society, coupled with vague pantheistic feelings about the purity of nature. Another dominant current is anti-militarist; and here again there is a difference between the reasoned anti-nuclear stance of the peace movement (see p. 566) and the minority of extreme pacifists who reject all forms of defence and want the Sermon on the Mount applied literally. In addition, the Greens have attracted a motley assortment of malcontents and single-issue devotees who have happily jumped onto the bandwagon to espouse their own particular cause; they include natural-food freaks, gay and lesbian liberationists, militant feminists, ex-Marxist deviants, doctrinaire anarchists and other political cranks, and even – to the embarrassment of real Greens – a few dotty racists who want to preserve 'aryan ecological purity'.

So why has the whole Green movement in Germany been stronger than its counterparts in most other Western countries? There are several clearly identifiable explanations. First, the peace campaign in the 1980s was lent a special force by Germany's exposed front-line position in NATO and more especially by the residue of German war guilt and the revulsion against militarism. As for the strength of ecological feeling in Germany, one reason for it is that this is a thickly populated country, not only bursting with industry but so tidily decked out, with forests planted in neat rows and hardly a blade of grass out of place; and this has created a certain claustrophobia, a desire for a more natural kind of nature, of the sort so much commoner in France (and if the Greens are so much weaker in France, maybe it is because there is so much more wild greenery, and far more tradition too, and rural warmth, all providing outlets that the frustrated young German cannot find so easily – and so he turns to dreams of forging a very different utopia). Another factor is that the Green party at its birth was fuelled by a growing disillusion with the older political parties, especially as the SPD after ten years in power had seemed to many radicals to be siding too cosily with the capitalist establishment. But more important than this, as I noted earlier, was the reaction against what appeared as the excessive materialism and bourgeois conformism of society – one Green activist, Carl Amery, spoke of the need to 'recapture the German warmth' of pre-Nazi days; 'people,' he said, 'are so afraid of the cold rigidity of German society.' And this swing of the pendulum carries more than a hint, too, of old-style German romanticism. Very many commentators have noted this, drawing parallels with the famous *Jugendbewegung* of the 1980s, an idealistic youth movement that, though less politically influential than the Greens today, was also anti-industrial and inspired by romantic notions about nature and the simple life.

The Greens have been pursuing their objectives along three main channels – through practical 'alternative' activities such as communes, farms and workshops; through rallies, sit-ins, citizens' initiative groups and other local actions; and, with some misgivings, through parliamentary politics. Their first direct political breakthrough came in the Bremen elections of 1979, where for the first time their candidates overcame the 5 per cent barrier and entered a *Landtag*. This was soon followed by similar successes in Baden-Württemberg, Hesse, Lower Saxony, Hamburg and Berlin, where in each case the Greens polled between 5 and 8 per cent, enough to make their presence felt; and in 1984 they entered the European Parliament, replacing the FDP as the third German party there. But their main sights were set on the *Bundestag*. Here they scored a disappointing 1.5 per cent in the 1980 elections, just after their party had been formed federally: but in March 1983 the figure rose to 5.6 per cent, and this brought them 28 deputies. Most were youngish and highly educated (several were professors) and more than a third were women. This assertive band set about shaking up the solemn world of the Bonn Parliament. They broke its unofficial dress code by entering the chamber in an assorted garb of jeans and gym-shoes, T-shirts and woolly jerseys, and they plonked pot-plants on their desks. 'We are the anti-party party,' declared their best-known leader at that time, Petra Kelly. Though it raised a good many eyebrows, this behaviour appeared sympathetic to many millions of Germans, and so did some other of the Greens' more unusual practices: for example, both in Bonn and the *Länder* their deputies kept for themselves only about a third of their large state-paid salaries and expenses, and the rest they would put into a special party fund, to be spent on Green causes. 'It's ideological,' explained a *Land* MP I met in Berlin; 'of my 5,000 DM monthly salary, I retain 2,000 DM which is roughly the wage of a skilled worker. It is all that I really need if I live simply.'

However, the Greens in politics soon began to fall victim to their own innate weaknesses and divergences. Their essential philosophy is libertarian, anti-authority, anti-discipline; and so it was inevitable that such an untidy coalition of people from different political backgrounds and with varying ideas should soon fall to bickering. Meetings became disorderly, mighty quarrels erupted in public. When I met a somewhat distraught Petra Kelly at the *Bundestag* in 1985, she confessed her dismay: 'Yes, we are a very diverse party, very chaotic and amateurish. Everything is so disorganised, and we keep wasting our energy on things that should have been settled ages ago. I don't want to create a party like the SPD, God forbid – but some degree of discipline *is* essential.' Kelly was perturbed in particular by the way the Greens were applying one of their cardinal principles, enshrined in their policy manifesto: that of the 'rotation' of deputies and other elected officials. Under this system, every elected person is required to give up his or her post after a stated period of time, usually two years, and make way for an understudy. The idea, well-intended in its way, is to allow as many people as possible to gain political experience, and to prevent the growth of elitism or authoritarian leadership. But of course there are drawbacks. It takes time to learn any political job, and to throw away that experience once it has been acquired is wasteful and inefficient – or so many Greens themselves have argued, including Kelly: 'Rotation has killed the dynamism of our parliamentary group,' she told me; 'I'm in favour of some rotation, but not every two years, which is far too quick.' Some other Green leaders, such as Otto Schily, came to feel that all rotation should be abandoned. But that was not how the purists saw it. And in March 1984 they staged a kind of *Putsch* against the six well-known leaders of the parliamentary group, including Kelly and Schily, ousting them as front-benchers and replacing them with six fairly obscure newcomers, all women and militantly feminist to boot.

Born in Bavaria in 1947 of a German mother and an ex-Polish father, Petra moved to America at the age of 13 when her divorced mother remarried an Irish-American army officer called Kelly. She became active in the American human rights movement, idolising Martin Luther King and Joan Baez, and then worked in Brussels with the EC Commission which nurtured her loathing of bureaucracy. Back in Germany, the Green party provided the perfect outlet for her passionate, crusading nature. Small and frail-looking but vivacious and highly-strung, she sleeps only four hours a night and the zealous intensity of her working life has taken its toll, bringing her several times close to breakdown. She talks very fast nonstop in a manic sort of way, yet has a wonderful sweetness and naturalness of manner that has not been spoilt by fame; and she inspired warm affection even in those who most disagree with her views – in her office, I noticed a letter from the US Ambassador, 'My dear Petra, ... Do take care of your health. Regards to Gert. Your good friend, Arthur Burns.' How I would love to have been a fly on the wall at their dinner-parties together. 'Gert' is Petra's intimate friend General Gert Bastian, a former *Bundeswehr* officer who joined the the Greens but then resigned from the party in 1984, irritated by their inefficiency and internal feuding, and by what he saw as too anti-American a bias in their peace campaigning. His departure was a blow for Kelly. But she, like him, was angered by some Green excesses, as when, for example, one activist threw blood into the face of a US general. Today Kelly is still devoted to Green causes: but she has grown disillusioned with the party itself, and over-tired, and she no longer plays a central role in it.

The overriding policy divergence within the party has always been that between the so-called realists ('Realos') and the so-called fundamentalists ('Fundis'). The Realos believe that the Greens in order to pursue their objectives have no choice but to enter into the fray of parliamentary politics and to aim for a share of power, even if this means making compromises with a democratic system that they dislike. The Fundis, of whom Kelly is one, are afraid that such compromises might alienate the Greens from their principles and weaken their credibility. They have always been wary of forming a political party, and they reject the strategy of trying to reform society via what Rudi Dutschke called 'the long march through the institutions': they want to remain a pressure-group outside formal politics, working at the grassroots and gradually changing society at that level until the hated institutions of democracy somehow wither away. The Fundis dominate the party organisation at grassroots level, and in 1987 they won eight of the eleven seats on the national executive: but in the Bundestag most Green deputies, by definition, have been Realos. And there have been heated debates between the two factions as to whether or not the party should enter a ruling coalition with the SPD when it gets the chance. This happened in 1985 in Hesse, where an SPD government with no working majority persuaded the hesitant Greens to join it. So the Greens for the first time formally entered a *Land* coalition, with Joschka Fischer, a prominent Realo, as minister for energy and the environment. But the two parties soon came to blows on the issue of nuclear power: the Greens demanded that nuclear stations in Hesse be closed down, and the SDP refused, whereupon the so-called 'Red–Green coalition' broke down. This led to new elections which brought the CDU back to power and left the Fundis saying, 'We told you so,' to Fischer.

The party's fortunes have veered about dramatically in the past few years. In the Bundestag elections of January 1987 it increased its share of the vote from 5.6 to 8.3 per cent, winning forty-two seats, and it seemed to be a growing force in federal politics. It had profited from the SPD's weaknesses and from the public's post-Chernobyl anxieties about nuclear energy. But then the Fundi/Realo quarrels got worse, filling the headlines, and in 1989 the influential Otto Schily left to join the SPD, annoyed at the failure to alter the rotation system. With Kelly too in the shade, the party had lost its two most charismatic leaders. Then in December 1990, in the first pan-German elections, the Greens in the west dropped just below the crucial 5 per cent barrier, thus losing all their Bundestag seats; the only Greens elected were two forming part of an 'alternative' coalition in the east that had there polled 6 per cent (see p. 432). If the western Greens had done so badly, it could be put down in part to the negative image caused by their feuding, or to the fact that the larger parties had by now stolen much of their thunder, by themselves taking up ecological causes. But above all the Greens had overplayed their hand by denouncing the '*Anschluss*' of unification and sharply attacking Kohl over this. It ran counter to the public mood. And their harping on classic environmental issues now seemed dwarfed by the gigantic new practical task of remedying pollution in the east, which was a matter of hard cash, not of innovative ideology. 'Amid all this Deutschland euphoria, the environment has gone out of fashion,' lamented one Green leader. This was not quite true but it did seem to many people that the Greens no longer had the most relevant answers.

And yet, despite this failure at federal level, in *Land* and city elections the Greens have continued to do well. In Munich in 1990, increasing their share of the vote from 7.9 to 9.5 per cent, they joined the SPD-led ruling coalition, as they had already done in Frankfurt; and in Hessen in January 1991, polling over 9 per cent, they again entered an SPD-led Government. The answer is simple: the Greens can address themselves well to precise local issues, such as traffic, green spaces, conservation, where local electors trust them: but they are often out of their depth on broader federal issues. Indeed, the Greens' future as a party seems clearly to lie more on a local than federal level, where in May 1991 a final break-up did take place between Realos and Fundis: the latter left the party but stayed in the broader movement. 'We're all heartily tired of this quarrel,' a young Realo leader said to me in Bonn; 'we shall now restructure the party and virtually start again. There's been a generational change, as the old post-1968 activists become exhausted, and we younger Greens want a more practical, less ideological approach. So do the voters.'

What is more, the big, established parties have been paying the Greens the compliment of appropriating many of their better ideas, and this has clearly been one of their major contributions to German public life: they have greatly influenced the other parties and have forced them to take stock of several important issues previously neglected, notably ecological ones. As we have seen (p. 148), the Kohl Government and most *Land* governments have themselves turned a pale green by embarking on expensive environmental policies, under the pressure of public opinion led by the Greens. The SPD has moved much closer to the Greens' position on nuclear power. And other Green-sponsored causes such as data protection and local democracy have also been finding more favour with the older parties. The Greens' less realistic utopian ideas are still rejected by the mass of German politicians and public: but their saner ones are becoming common coinage. For Fundis and Realos alike, this is something of a moral victory: but, ironically, as a national political force they may be losing out in the process.

On the more local level too, in towns and rural areas, the Greens' main political effect has been to act as a catalyst upon the older parties. They now have their representatives on many local councils, often in alliances with 'Alternative Lists' of other non-aligned anti-establishment radicals. The lady mayor of Tübingen is a Green. Their principal successes have tended to be conservationist. In Tübingen, for example, they torpedoed an earlier project for an urban ringway; and in one north Bavarian town they persuaded the CSU-led council to drop a plan for tearing down some half-derelict sixteenth-century timbered houses and to renovate them instead. This is valuable, as far as it goes: but, when it comes to more innovative or constructive schemes, the Greens often seem to be either short of valid ideas or else rather too fanciful and unrealistic − in a manner that irritates, rather than influences, the other parties. In 1985 an SPD politician in Munich gave me a typical reaction: 'The Green councillors here produce a stream of verbose documents which they expect us to read; or they protract the council meetings with long discussions about matters they don't understand, like city administration. They waste our time fearfully. Some of their ideas are sensible: but others are useless romantic ones about bringing back more streetcars to replace the Metro and car traffic. Some of them even want to abolish Munich airport, so that we'd all have to use Frankfurt. They're crazy.' That is one point of view: on the other hand, it could be argued that in some towns they have broken the cosy ententes between the older parties and forced a new appraisal of local needs. Hence their recent electoral success in Munich which belies the view quoted above. But the Greens' forte in local affairs lies not so much within the political arena as in extra-council activity – notably through their *Bürgerinitiativen* which proliferate everywhere. These are ad hoc citizen associations, again mainly environmentalist, which lobby local councils into improving waste disposal, building cycle paths, desisting from new road-building, sparing trees, and so on. A bearded art teacher in northern Bavaria gave me a picturesque example: 'A local property firm wanted to cut down a 150-year-old oak tree to make way for a new superstore. Twenty of us kept vigil by the tree for a fortnight, in a rota, day and night, and this so impressed opinion that the firm was persuaded to put the store elsewhere.'

It might be unfair to suggest, as some critics do, that the Greens are more concerned about trees than about people. None the less, there do seem to be a number of curious lacunae and confusions in their policies. While their environmental blueprint is so clear, on social and welfare matters their official programme is remarkably vague; and at a local level, whereas they will campaign vociferously for purer air or recycled milk-bottles, they have relatively few ventures aimed at helping the weak and lonely, or promoting a warmer sense of community, and so on. As individuals, Greens and other 'alternatives' are certainly more caring and spontaneous than the other generation (as I noted earlier): but even they seem still to suffer a little from the German inhibition against transferring private warmth into public responsibility, as far as social relations are concerned. One explanation given to me by several Greens was, in effect, 'Officialdom does this kind of welfare action so well that we are hardly needed.' But this is no valid argument – and the real difficulty lies elsewhere. It is simply that the Green movement is still profoundly split, ideologically, between an active Marxist or ex-Marxist minority that wants more state involvement, i.e. more socialism, and a liberal majority that certainly favours social justice but is deeply suspicious of *étatisme* and prefers grass-roots democracy. The debate goes on, and is unresolved. So there is no clear social policy, and this seems to inhibit even the Greens' more informal local ventures.

Environmentalism however poses no such problems, and with many Greens it has become an obsession – perhaps a little too much so. Concern about asbestos walls, toxic fluids or over-use of water supplies is of course legitimate and valuable: but some crusaders seem to have become fixated on such matters to the neglect of other even more important aspects of life. Take for example the tree issue. Of course the sickness of Germany's own forests is extremely serious: but there are other less populated and polluted areas of the world, such as Canada or

Scandinavia, where vast forests can easily be replanted, and in this respect an ordinary tree for use as paper or furniture is simply a replenishable practical commodity like wheat or flowers or livestock. It is not a sacred being to be preserved for its own sake (as might be true of some much-loved old oak or elm in a village square). And it could be argued that the recycling of paper, so much in favour with the Greens, uses up more resources (in terms of energy) than it saves. Yet in German schools the teachers tell their pupils to be as economical as possible with paper — 'Daddy,' one ten-year-old rebuked her journalist father, 'you shouldn't waste all that paper on your articles. One big sheet of it kills a tree, we're taught that in class.' Schoolteachers tend to be among the most assiduous of Greens, and they have been imbuing a whole new generation with their ideas — especially in the cities, for this nature-loving movement is essentially an urban phenomenon and few of its activists have real knowledge of the countryside. Some of the more ardent of them raise farmers' hackles (see p. 171) when they arrive with their missionary zeal to lecture them on how to sow organic crops or to return to the sublime purity of pre-industrial agriculture.

The Greens have also been much criticised for their views on the economy and on industry. They believe that each individual should receive a basic income, whether or not he or she works. And their policy manifesto says, 'Large corporations should be split up into manageable units and administered democratically by the people who actually work there.' The more moderate Greens prefer that this should happen gradually and without revolution: 'To go back to an agrarian economy would be impossible,' Otto Schily once told me; 'we cannot change industrial society completely, nor would we want to. We are not against modern technology: we simply want it humanised and prevented from damaging the environment. Yes indeed, we favour the spread of small-scale "alternative" firms, but we don't say that the whole economy should be changed to this system.' However, there are plenty of romantics that would like Germany to go back to some semi-rural utopia full of little communes and workshops, with scarcely a tractor, car or aeroplane. How they must regret that Roosevelt spurned Morgenthau! And they trumpet their ideals so loudly, claiming to speak for all Greens, that they give this serious movement a greater reputation for silliness than it deserves.

In other ways, too, the Greens are often the prisoners of their own ethos of total democracy and freedom of speech for all minorities. Their doors are wide open to all sorts – not only the food freaks, bra-burners, machine-haters and other relatively harmless fanatics, but others more sinister whose vocal presence damages the party's cause. At one *Land* election campaign meeting in Düsseldorf in 1985, an ultra-libertarian Green group was able to propose the legalisation of all non-violent sexual relations between adults and children: this filled the headlines ('Greens Favour Child Sex!') and was certainly a factor behind the party's poor showing in the North-Rhine-Westphalia poll. Some extreme-right and anti-Turk elements have also infiltrated the party, claiming that racial purity is 'ecological' and that 'the Nazis were really the first Greens'; not only because of their racism but because they too preached the virtues of the simple rural life and opposed technology. Such maniacs are few, but enough to cause embarrassment.

Even mainstream Greens will very often overstate their case – especially the Fundis – by dogmatically denouncing all aspects of bourgeois society and arrogantly shouting down anyone who disagrees with them. This provokes a polarising chain-reaction, for the more the older bourgeoisie intolerantly opposes the Greens, the more their own dogmatism increases. Even many pleasant and decent citizens see the Greens as a threat – or they criticise them for their hypocrisy. 'They reject industrial civilisation while enjoying its benefits,' is a common complaint, and quite well justified, for indeed it is easy to find young people from well-to-do families who drive to anti-nuclear demos in smart cars and extol their anti-capitalist ideals while playing with their expensive hi-fi and videos. But not all Greens are like that. Many sincerely try to practise the 'alternative' life.

A great many Green sympathisers, with ordinary jobs as teachers or civil servants, or even in banks or factories, will pursue an 'ecological' life-style as far as they can. I have friends in Munich who travel right across the city to buy organically-grown vegetables at a cooperative, and who together with eight other families have formed a rota whereby they take it in turns to drive deep into the country to get their milk from a farmer whose cows receive only pure feed – 'not that dreadful imported American stuff'. Many families also make a point of buying only recycled paper, 'bio' cleaning materials, and milk in bottles not cartons; they bicycle everywhere, using their car rarely or maybe giving it up; and some of them fix solar heating panels on their roofs or wear hand-knitted clothes and home-made shoes.

Some others choose to opt out of a regular job within 'the system' and to join the so-called 'alternative economy'. This extremely diverse and haphazard phenomenon spreads far wider than the Green movement itself; it embraces many people who are not necessarily Green, just as only a small percentage of Green voters are actively part of it. In strictly economic terms its impact has been minimal, for it has impinged hardly at all on capitalist and official structures: but in other respects it is one of the most interesting developments in modern Germany.

Like so much else, it was born of 1968 – or rather, of a reaction against the failure of 1968. Just as in France, many of the rebels of those days have now made their peace with society and have settled down as respectable bourgeois parents with secure jobs. But others are continuing the struggle in a new form. Not only were they disgusted by the way that 1968's bright idealism degenerated into violence and terrorism, but they soon became aware of the futility of Dutschke's proposed 'long march', that is, of the plan to reform society by infiltrating the institutions of government and bodies such as the universities, the Churches and the media. This proved impossible. Not only did a strong and entrenched society resist very skilfully (through the *Radikalenerlass* and other means), but the rebels themselves were too weak and divided to make much headway. So a number of them gradually decided instead – and this was the crucial change – to turn their backs on the hated system and to build up their own little counter-society, through a range of small-scale practical ventures. This is the essence of the 'alternative economy'. Compared with the big dreams and endless theoretical discussions of 1968, it is all very concrete, modest, and private. At first it led to the communes (*Wohngemeinschaften*) of the 1970s: but, as in other countries, these experiments in group living rarely proved successful, for they led to too much bickering over personal property, sleeping-partners, washing-up rotas, and the like. Today a few communes do still exist: but most *Alternative* now live more individually, maybe on a house-sharing or flat-sharing basis. They include a number of 1968 veterans now in their late thirties or forties, as well as many younger drop-outs from middle-class society who had failed at their exams, or wanted to avoid the career rat-race, or were impelled by some kind of anti-bourgeois idealism. Their ranks have been swelled recently by rising unemployment.

Numerical estimates vary widely. Brigitte Sauzay in her rather starry-eyed portrait of the new German trends, *Le vertige allemand* (Orban, Paris, 1985), said that some 500,000 people work directly in the 90,000 projects of the alternative economy, while another six million sympathise with it or support it with their custom. These figures may well be excessive. Even so, the movement is still very active. What these ventures have in common is that they are all very small, they are non-profit-geared, they are run as cooperatives whose members share out the revenue equally between them, they follow ecological principles, and as far as possible they all service and trade with each other in one vast closed-circuit relying on the outside world only for certain raw materials and for essential services such as telephone and electricity. A joint organisation called *Netzwerk*, based in Berlin, provides a certain coordination and helps to fund new projects. The scene includes publishing and printing houses, a daily newspaper (the *Tageszeitung* of Berlin), pubs and cafés, theatres and arts centres, shops and workshops of all kinds, organic farms, cooperatives of lawyers, architects, engineers, doctors, social workers and taxi-drivers, as well as infant schools run by mothers, and the *Frauenhäuser* for women in distress (see p. 195). So complete in fact is this network that in a big city it is possible to depend on it more or less completely, for all work and leisure needs, without dealing with the German mainstream except for paying taxes and utility bills. Of course the scene also includes a substantial fringe of zero-work freaks, drug addicts, psychopathic cases, and other less enviable drop-outs. But largely it is a serious and even high-minded movement.

I myself am rather attracted to the concept of this kind of pioneering social enterprise – and therefore I only wish that I could report more enthusiastically on its results, at least as I observed them in a number of places and notably in west Berlin, which is very much the central focus of Germany's alternative world. The city has traditionally been a magnet for every kind of outsider (see p. 45) and today its various free-lance activities include bakeries, potteries, weavers, an electrical workshop, and a farm for children with pigs, rabbits and horses in a former railway yard. The *Tageszeitung*, selling about 40,000 copies a day throughout Germany, is run as a cooperative, with all decisions taken collectively and all its staff drawing the same very modest salary. But if it possesses a headquarters it is Mehringhof, in Kreuzberg, known as 'the Alternative Rathaus'. This disused graphics factory was bought by a few pioneers for 2 million DM in 1979 and now it houses not only the offices of *Netzwerk* but some thirty cooperatives where about 200 people work. You enter through a gateway into one of those typical Berlin inner courtyards, enclosed by tall gloomy buildings. All has deliberately been kept shabby and derelict-looking, for that is part of the alternative ideology. Tattered posters, from this year or last year, advertise punk street-breakfasts, Turkish folklore fêtes, and the like. A few black-jacketed coxcombs sourly ask for a coin or a cigarette. Amongst much else, the buildings house a sort of cabaret, a bike shop, an adult education centre, an incredibly messy-looking kindergarten, a Turkish group, a shop run by feminists selling goods from Nicaragua, a big café where a rock band was practising lustily, and a publishing firm that produces the *Stattbuch*, a fat guide to the Berlin alternative scene. I was shown round by one of its editors, a Berlin philosophy graduate aged 30: 'I came here basically because I wanted to create my own work structure and not join an organisation. In our little firm we share equally all that we earn; and, as in many of the ventures here, we take it in turns to go "unemployed" so that some of us can collect dole money and thus add to our funds. We are anti-marriage and against private property, but not too much so: I even own an old car which I share with others. Above all, we feel that we are doing something useful and practical, whereas 1968 was merely destructive. Even the local CDU rulers grudgingly approve of us – they admire our spirit of self-help which accords with their own ideals, and they see that we are helping to keep unemployment down.'

This is certainly true. In the mid-1980s the CDU-led Establishment in West Berlin set about trying to woo and seduce the 'alternative' milieu – but this hardly benefited Mehringhof. The right-of-centre Senate, in welfare matters quite progressive, began to lavish funds upon many of the city's hundreds of self-help ventures and to utilise them for its own policies. If some Greenish group had set up a medical self-care centre, or was helping Turkish wives, or the aged, it could be sure of Rathaus aid. This policy was then continued by the SPD-led Senate in 1989–90, and it remains in force today, with the CDU back in power. The result has been a split in the 'alternative' milieu. Many little groups now collaborate with 'normal' society: they infiltrate it with their ideas and are less militantly political than ten years ago. And those few cooperatives that succeed commercially have now become normal businesses, no longer seeing themselves as 'alternative'. But Mehringhof is thus left stranded: formerly the moral leader and focus of the whole diverse movement, it now represents just the drop-out extreme, and this adds to its desolate air today. 'Advice Centre for Total Rejectors of Society', was a notice I saw there.

While I found the ambience of Mehringhof somewhat sad and

apathetic, the same, alas, was true of my visit to the UFA Fabrik, largest and best-known of Germany's still-surviving communes. This occupies the former UFA studios in Berlin's Tempelhof district, where *Metropolis, The Blue Angel* and other great movies were made, and then Goebbels' wartime propaganda films. The commune, previously existing in Kreuzberg, began squatting at UFA in 1979 and was then granted a contract by the city and allowed to stay. Sixty hippy characters now live there – 'we're a sort of kibbutz but less organised,' said one of them. In the barrack-like sheds, families have their own rooms but children aged over 3 sleep in dormitories. No one has an outside job; chores are shared; and the commune earns the money it needs by running a saddlery, a health-bread bakery, a cinema and a circus – 'So we're offering Berliners *panem et circenses*,' said one cultured inmate, 'plus a touch, too, of *pane, amore e fantasia*.' The circus itself is certainly full of *fantasia*: with its clever performing dogs it has become very well known and successful, and it travels all over Germany. Thirty-five of the inmates make up the troupe, as jugglers, acrobats and musicians: and the performance I saw was lively and talented. But the commune as a whole gave off vibrations that I found oddly depressing. In true hippy style it was quite astoundingly filthy, untidy and run-down-looking – and this appeared to be more a matter of attitudes than lack of funds, for to clean and tidy costs almost nothing. The inhabitants, once out of their circus-ring, seemed listless and passive. I was given a conducted tour by their spokesman, Yupi, a gentle young man with long ginger hair who called me *du*: 'We have no particular ideology here,' he said, 'save a feeling that society needs more leisure and quiet. We have a very loose collective structure with no real leadership. But this does lead to a certain amount of chaos, so now we're evolving towards more discipline.' I did indeed come away with the feeling that a community of this kind, to be successful, needs either a charismatic leader or else an ideology or some spiritual base. Compared with the various religious communes I have visited, such as Findhorn in Scotland, or the wonderful l'Arche in Languedoc, the UFA venture struck me as lacking in some crucial ingredient. On the other hand, its members are freely being what they want to be, and they have chosen it that way.

UFA also runs a school, for 5–13-year-olds who come both from the commune itself and from outside. This is a prolongation of the '*Kinderläden*' (child-shop) movement of the late 1960s, when in various German cities a number of young radicals decided to take education into their own hands by opening small junior schools in former retail shops (hence the name) where they did much of the teaching themselves. It was an anti-authoritarian initiative, influenced by the ideas of A. S. Neill in Britain. In the 1970s the movement began to gather momentum in Berlin, where it was actually encouraged by the very liberal-minded education ministry of the SPD-led city government, which officially recognised a number of the schools. But then things went badly – as I was told in 1985 by one kindly ministry official: 'At first we were sympathetic. But when our inspectors visited the schools, they began to find that very little class work was being done. The parents and teachers were sitting around chatting and smoking, or they had gone off to a café, and the kids were playing on their own. Academically they learned very little, so when later they went into the State system they could not cope. Today almost all these schools have been closed. UFA's still provisionally recognised by us, but we are not too happy about it.'

There has been a happier ending, however, to another and far more notorious saga of alternative Berlin – that of the squatters. By the late 1970s some 30,000 flats in the city were lying empty, most of them in large older tenement buildings owned by private landlords or by property firms such as Neue Heimat. Rather than pay the cost of repairs, these owners frequently preferred to let the properties run right down to the point where they could obtain state subsidies for pulling them down and then replace them with far more profitable middle-class housing: and the SPD-led *Land* government cynically connived at this, for its policy of low fixed rents was such that no landlords could be expected to pay for proper repairs. In some cases, demolition was also made difficult by the presence of sitting tenants in one or two flats. But many of the students and *Alternative* flocking into Berlin had nowhere to live, or they were in bourgeois flats paying more rent than suited them. So a mass squat became an obvious temptation, alike materially and politically. By the time it had reached its peak in 1981, some 170 partly or wholly abandoned buildings were occupied, most of them big tenement blocks with scores of flats in each. The squatters were of various kinds. Some were middle-class youngsters wanting a cost-free escape from the parental nest. Some – to an extent the same ones – were eagerly seizing this opportunity for spectacular political protest against capitalism and its iniquitous accomplices. And a smaller minority, as in the case of the Frankfurt airport drama, were *provocateurs* from extreme-left or anarchist groups, who came in from West Germany and further afield (and even from the GDR too, under orders), all too ready to stir up violence.

The squatters claimed that they were not really acting illegally, for West Berlin's constitution laid down that all housing, if not pulled down, should be kept in repair and made available for use – and thus it was the owners who were breaking the law. The city authorities at first wavered in face of this challenge. Then the CDU came to power in 1981 and under pressure from the landlords it ordered the police to start evictions. There followed a drama lasting several months that filled all the German headlines and many foreign ones too, as the Leftists seized their chance and led street demonstrations against police 'brutalities'. Repeated pitched battles took place in Kreuzberg and in the Ku'damm area, and one rioter was killed. As at Frankfurt airport, undoubtedly the police committed excesses and just as undoubtedly they were provoked. However, the city had meanwhile persuaded some owners to negotiate with the squatters for a legislation of their stay. This was quite a success, and finally about half of the intruders signed contracts, while the rest were evicted and the houses gradually pulled down. The squatters legally committed themselves to paying a nominal rent and to carrying out ad hoc improvements, which many of them did gladly – they set about repainting, re-wiring, re-plumbing, mending doors and windows, even re-roofing, and quite often the city helped to train them and to provide materials and expertise. It was an inspired and useful campaign of urban renewal. In 1985 I visited one big block in Kreuzberg whose young occupants had decorated the entire façade with a really lovely multi-coloured mural – 'It's a symbolic picture of liberation,' they said – 'look at the arrow pointing skywards.' Here in one renovated flat a group of students were living cheerfully and messily: it struck me as not especially 'alternative', more like a bohemian version of the kind of flat-sharing that is common in London even among Sloane Rangers. One gentle philosophy student, rather unpolitical, said, 'It's been a great moral victory; we've got the cheap housing that we need and we've proved that use *can* be made of these old buildings.' His flatmate, much more militant, added, 'Yes, but it's no real victory. We failed to boot the CDU out of power as we'd hoped.' Probably the great majority of the original squatters were nearer to the first than the second of those two views: elsewhere in Berlin I met another Leftist, an older man, who told me, 'During the battles against the police evictions, I tried hard to organise those young people to join the political cause and fight for their rights. But they were all so passive and apathetic, they seemed to have no ideas at all. I just could not communicate.'

In some other cities too, there have been squats and a few small ventures of the Mehringhof type. In rural areas, alternative activity more often takes the form of organic farming: the produce is sold to health-food stores, or direct to consumers' cooperatives formed by Greens and others. Some 1,500 farms are involved, 2 per cent of the German total and mostly very small ones. Their numbers have been growing recently, but the movement remains less widely developed than in some other countries such as Switzerland, Holland and Britain. This may seem strange, in view of the role of the Greens in Germany. Perhaps the problem is that, as one organic grower lamented to me, 'the Greens are so intellectual and dogmatic that the real farmers don't trust their ideas. And when they drop out from the cities and try to run their own little farms, it's usually a disaster.' Near Stuttgart I did however visit one professionally operated and old-established enterprise, run on 'bio-dynamic' principles: this was the main farm of the Demeter movement, created in the 1920s by none other than Rudolf Steiner who was almost as interested in bio-dynamic agriculture as in education (see p. 243) and saw it as a key element in his anthroposophical programme. Cereals and vegetables are sown and planted in relation to minerals in the ground and the positions of the moon and the stars. The results are claimed to be tastier and more nutritious than ordinary produce and to stay fresh longer: but as so much of the work has to be done by hand, and only at specific times, retail prices are up to 60 per cent higher. Perhaps this is why so many Demeter farms have failed since the war – though they have recently been given a new lease of life by the Greens' interest in them. I do not wish to scoff at scientific ideas that may be very sound: but it did seem to me that, in this domain, the great Steiner has been somewhat let down by his later apostles. In striking contrast to the splendid *Waldorfschulen*, the Demeter venture that I visited was most unimpressive – a draggle of dreamy cranks and apathetic hirelings, sitting around in unkempt greenhouses amid disorderly piles of mangy-looking carrots. More bio than dynamic, I felt.

Clearly it is not easy to pass any fair objective judgement on west Germany's alternative scene and its economy. What future can it have? Why in practical terms has it not made more impact, when so many young people subscribe to its values? Has it anything to teach conventional society, and might the two ever move closer together? One *Alternative* in Berlin raised the pertinent question, 'Are we a safety-valve for established society, or a destabilising factor?' And I heard an unexpected answer to this from the president of the West Berlin police, Klaus Hübner, the very man who had directed the squatter evictions: 'The alternative scene here is very peaceful now, and it's creating new structures which prevent the special crimes of our affluent society. This is because of its different attitude to property: no one wants to feather his nest at others' expense. So we have no police problems in Kreuzberg today. We all have to learn from this kind of social structure, made up of rich chaps who want to become poor. It cannot be the society of the future, but it can give impulses.'

There may well be truth in this. In all kinds of ways, the alternative world acts as a testing-ground for new ideas and thus influences society; and it provides valuable outlets for those who do not want to conform to the career rat-race. But it hardly constitutes any serious 'threat' to society (as some people believe), for even though it has been slowly expanding, in its present form it seems unlikely to grow so very much larger – as many of its more clear-eyed sympathisers will frankly admit. Above all, so it seems to me, this is because it is the prisoner of its own ethos, which is *anti-success* in the world's terms, even while claiming to be practical and concrete. Being anti-profit, anti-hard work, and even anti-organisation, most of these little economic ventures find it hard to compete with bourgeois enterprises if they try to do so; and there are limits to which they can flourish and develop within the closed circuit. Equally, they reject on principle the kind of discipline that they probably need if they are to survive, and this applies also to the communes and other social or cultural projects. One young non-Green spoke to me of a youth centre he had joined near Stuttgart: 'It was splendid when it first started ten years ago, but it's now developed into a messy and worthless shambles. This is because it's been taken over by a lot of Green types who refuse any leadership or organisation and believe that all members should be free to do what they want. So I and my friends have left.' Examples of this kind can be found every-where. Just as they reject bourgeois tidiness and swing to an opposite very un-German extreme, so on moral grounds the *Alternative* reject the usual German pattern of authority, self-discipline and methodical organ-isation. Without any of it at all, they can hardly succeed – but do they *want* to 'succeed'? Maybe, in their terms, their shambles *is* success, an ethical victory over other values. It is a dilemma that is still not resolved.

## The Greens and their values

They are of course of many different kinds, these *Aussteiger*.[1] Some, probably the majority at the grassroots level, are very passive, gentle, unambitious, lacking in willpower, not so dogmatically ideological. Another far more energetic minority, attracting much publicity recently, are the so-called '*Spontis*': these little groups are more existentialist or anarchist, and they believe in acting spontaneously, in going where the action is and having adventures. If there is a demo or strike or squat, or any other crusade, they will join in: but they reject all 'isms' and politics and are seldom violent. Thirdly, an important hardcore of Greens and other alternatives, few in number but influential, are very ideological, doctrinaire, intolerant and moralistic. Not only are they dogmatically anti-planning, anti-property, anti-American, anti-intellectual and pro-emotions, leisure and spontaneity, but they often have a Teutonic pessimism about the world, an apocalyptic doomsday philosophy – and this may help to explain their streak of wild and self-indulgent hedonism.

These are extreme examples of new currents in Germany today. But how far are they widespread or typical of a whole generation? More important than the Green party itself, or the alternative scene, seems to me the much broader emergence of new values and social attitudes among the post-1968 generation as a whole, in all classes. It is important to stress that many of these changes are quite moderate and non-revolutionary and they do not necessarily involve being an *Aussteiger*, or prophesying doom, or even voting Green or living the Green way. These changes have been noted repeatedly throughout this book, in different areas of life; and though they may contain some negative or disturbing aspects, they seem to me generally encouraging for the future of Germany – among them, the rejection by younger people of stiff social formality, the declining use of pompous titles, the greater individual concern for the weak and handicapped, the waning of hostility to children, the replacement of workaholism by a stronger emphasis on leisure and enjoyment (dangerous for Germany, if carried too far), the easier, more informal spirit in education (ditto), the questioning of authority (ditto) and the trend away from blind obedience towards more individual responsibility, the return to tradition and to *Heimat*, the fringe cultural scene, the street-festivals and other new

1. The term is less negative than the English 'drop-out' and applies to anyone who has taken some conscious decision to 'get out' (*aussteigen*) of conventional society. A worker at Mehringhof is an *Aussteiger* but not really a drop-out.

informal community activities ... Nearly everyone under about forty-five is involved in these changes to some extent or another. And younger ones especially, in their late teens or twenties, appear as in other Western countries to be returning to private personal values and to be disregarding politics (again, possibly dangerous). This is the generation of what has been called 'the new tenderness' – gentle and caring, with each other and towards animals. And their search for private individual fulfilment can very often take the form not only of hedonism but of a quest for spiritual satisfaction. Hence the revival of interest in Christianity among young people, as well as the popularity in Germany of the various 'oriental' cults that have arrived via the United States. To the inevitable alarm of many parents and teachers, Hare Krishna, Scientology, the Moonies and other sects have all held a certain appeal for young Germans wanting warmth and certainty and finding a spiritual emptiness in modern society.

The Baghwan Rajneesh movement was proportionately stronger in Germany than anywhere else, even in the United States and India, in the period before September 1985 when the bearded guru (now dead) was finally expelled from his Oregon headquarters and his ashrams around the globe were disbanded. In those days, in Cologne, Hamburg, Berlin and other cities, smiling sanyassin in their pink, red and purple clothes ran shops, cafés and discothèques open to the public – all exceedingly clean, bright and business-like, in striking contrast to most of the rest of the alternative scene. Why the special appeal of the Baghwan to young Germans? Some critics felt that it reflected a typically German love of a charismatic leader and father-figure whose word should be obeyed implicitly. But more probably these young middle-class people were involved in an equally Germanic search for the absolute, and in this very international movement they felt able to escape from soured German nationalism and find a new identity – at the Cologne ashram in 1984 I met a brilliant sanyassin aged 43 who told me, 'My father had been a Nazi, and I was haunted by guilt about the German past and a longing for a way out. So as a young man I went to Cambridge and became a don at St John's College. But this attempt to turn myself into an Englishman did not really work. Then I came across Rajneeshism, and ever since then I have this beautiful love-affair with Baghwan and my problem is solved.' I remain myself less blatantly scornful of this particular cult than most people, for I have a special interest which I should declare: my own son by my first marriage was with Baghwan for four years in Oregon and Poona, and through him I observed the good side of the movement and how it helped him to a far greater spiritual maturity and self-confidence.

In my own view, there have been other far more negative aspects to the youth revolt and the quest for new values or forms of escape. Like other Western countries, Germany has its share of punks and skinheads, and of young drug-addicts. The drug scene is worst in Frankfurt and Berlin, where it has thrown up a number of sensational case-histories, most notably that of one young girl, *Christiane F.*, as told in a best-selling book and film of the 1970s. She recounted how her loveless home background and her search for tenderness led her to enter a clique where she took marijuana, and then heroin, and then to pay for it she turned to prostitution and by the age of 15 was earning up to 4,000 DM a month. Much publicity has also been given to the problem of youth suicides: though the rate for the Federal Republic is not much above the Western average, in Berlin it is said to be the highest in the world. In 1985, four 16-year-olds in Aachen formed a suicide pact and tried to kill themselves with car exhaust: three of them succeeded and the fourth, who survived, said he would soon try again. Their motive was that they were all without jobs and they saw no future in life.

Incidents of this kind have lent some support to the view, much canvassed in the media, that the younger generation as a whole is riddled with *Angst*, insecurity and nihilism. Probably this has been much exaggerated. It is true that in the early 1980s there did appear to be a sudden new wave of pessimism: it was fuelled by rising unemployment and fears of the impending installation of missiles, and it was nourished as well by older anxieties about the difficulty of being German and by the feeling of being trapped both by geography and by the past. All of this was much analysed by the Press and in radio and TV debates. But it was also pointed out that for centuries the Germans have been more prone to *Angst* than most peoples. It is nothing new. It informs much of their literature, even the Grimms' fairy tales, and amongst artists and intellectuals it has long been a kind of fashion, even a token of respectability. Not to worry and be gloomy is not to be taken seriously as a thinker. But how far is German youth really coloured by this today? My own impression, and that of many others, is that German fears tend to go in mysterious cycles of obsession, and that in 1984 the wave of *Angst* subsided quite considerably, after the missiles debate ended and people had come to terms with the situation. During my own months in Germany in 1984–5, I found much less talk of *Angst* and 'No future' than I had expected, even amongst young people; and the same was still true in 1991, despite anxieties about the east German economy, about the Soviet Union's future and the Gulf crisis. One father with children aged 18 and 20 suggested to me: 'It may be a fashion among young people to display a certain pessimism and dislike of society, when talking with each other. But if you speak with them privately and individually, they are often much more positive and serene. It's just that they daren't show this side to their peer group, for if they seem to betray the youth cult of rejection, then they lose face.'

There are signs today that this new trend back towards acceptance of society goes much further still. Nearly all the observers of the youth scene – parents, educators, social scientists and others – seem to agree that the new rising generation now in its late teens or early twenties is more conservative and less anti-materialistic than its immediate predecessors. So the pendulum may be swinging back. Some outward signs are that very young people are manifesting more concern for private possessions, they are again dressing more elegantly and they show an aesthetic feeling for nice clothes; instead of straggly long hair they have neat hair-cuts; and they prefer smart, bright cafés to bohemian dives. More important, they are again becoming more career-minded, more keen on making money and a little readier to work hard for it, and they admire achievement and individual performance – their emulated prototype, you could say, is the young Boris Becker, just as Petra Kelly was that of an earlier generation. 'We too, as in 1968, are in revolt against our teachers,' said one 17-year-old *Gymnasium* pupil, 'but the other way round, for *they* are now the Leftist ones. They come to school in beards, sandals and woolly jerseys, so *we* turn up in smart clothes and we reject their propaganda.'

It is too soon to tell the real significance of this new trend. Many of these young people, especially the ones from richer homes, are clearly being self-centred, opportunistic, even snobbish. They know about the failure of earlier protest movements to refashion society – and so they are readier to accept the established order and get what they can out of it. But others, the more altruistic, are seeking to apply the lessons of Green and radical excesses by pursuing the path of change in a more moderate and realistic way: instead of totally opposing modernism, they try to give it a more human dimension. In any case, there has been no complete return to the old values by the new generation. Neat clothes and careerism may again be 'in': but the new informality, the new gentleness, the new questioning of hierarchy and authority, these remain. And so it is hard to answer what is perhaps the most important question: has the entire Green and alternative movement been just one more youth protest that will later fade away, or does it symptomise fundamental and permanent change in German society and values? Probably a bit of both. The least attractive aspect of the more militant Greens and other rebels is that too often they have spoilt their own cause through dogmatism, absolutism, refusal to compromise, intolerance of opposition, and other forms of Germanic excess, and this has prompted the question: the Greens may talk of radical change, but are they not simply perpetuating certain less pleasant German traits in a new guise? But these activists are not typical of German youth as a whole, which for the most part is more gentle and reasonable and has quietly been pursuing its own 'long march' through social values. The Greens and the 'alternative' minority have made an interesting contribution. But much wider than this is the tentative groping of young Germany towards a more tolerant, caring and informal society; and about this I am cautiously optimistic for the long term, even if Germans, now reunited, are again having to rethink the question of their national identity and of Germany's place in the world.

## Germany and the world: nationalism, or European integration?

The Germans' view of their role in the world has of course been affected by unification. With the addition of nearly 17 million citizens from the old GDR, and the removal of all remaining Allied constraints upon her sovereignty, Germany has become much the most powerful nation in Europe, aside from the huge but ailing Soviet Union. How will she use that power? Will she become unpleasantly domineering? Or, on the contrary, will she prefer to keep a low profile, reluctant to assume the greater world responsibilities that might now be expected of her? Both of these fears have been expressed simultaneously, not always with the best of logic, by certain potent voices in the Western world. And within Germany itself the same discussion has been taking place. Inevitably it centres round the new Germany's role in Western defence and world peace-keeping – as was shown most clearly during the Gulf War and the consequent debate on whether the Constitution should be amended to allow German troops to serve abroad.

[563]

Is it right for a country with such a warmongering record to be part of any military alliance, or even to take part in defensive operations? Should not Germany be neutral, like Sweden or Austria? Ever since 1945, such views have been voiced quite widely – oddly, more often by the Germans themselves, with their feelings of guilt, than by those they fought against. But if a neutralist trend, even a pacifist one, persists in Germany today, one has to remember that it was stronger in the earlier post-war years. When Adenauer in 1954–5 brought Germany into NATO and agreed with his Western allies to create a new German army, the *Bundeswehr*, he was greeted by a great wave of anti-militarism. It came not only from the SPD, the trade unions and a large part of the Protestant Church, but from sections of his own party and from much of German youth. These feelings were understandable, and morally speaking they were laudable – though in practical terms it might have been disastrous if they had proved strong enough to force Adenauer to change his plans. As it was, the *Bundeswehr* was gradually built up and today it is the largest European army in NATO. In 1991 the German armed forces comprised some 480,000 men. They were due to be scaled down to some 370,000 by 1994, in line with other NATO cuts in Europe. But this would still leave them in the first position.

Anti-militarist thinking has made its impact upon the style and the spirit of these forces. From the outset the Government agreed that the *Bundeswehr* should be a 'citizens' army', shorn of all goose-stepping and even of heel-clicking, based on persuasion and discussion rather than unthinking obedience, and closely integrated into society. Conscription was retained, partly because it is an old German tradition but also for more important reasons – it was feared that a purely professional army would never attract enough recruits, and that if it grew powerful it might become politically dangerous. Conscripts today serve fifteen months and at any one time there are 220,000 of them, nearly half the total under arms. This is much less than the full strength of the age-group: many young men are granted exemption for health, study or family reasons, while each year some 60,000 conscientious objectors are allowed to do an *Ersatzdienst*, usually in the form of heavy physical work in hospital or homes for the handicapped.

As far as is possible, conscripts do their service near to their own homeland, rather than be sent to some far corner of Germany. The aim of this policy has been to give them the sense that they are protecting their own homes and families – an important factor in a country where local feeling is often much stronger than national patriotism. In one battalion that I visited near the Czech frontier in 1985 most of the recruits were from northern Bavaria. It follows that nearly all of them go back to their families at weekends, and quite a number even commute daily from their homes: so, apart from the much longer hours, in some ways it is not so different from doing an office or factory job. This in fact is a rather sedentary modern army without much sense of adventure: as Germany has no overseas commitments and only just a few troops stationed in other NATO countries, for conscripts and regular soldiers alike there are not the outlets for service abroad, that the Americans or French can find, and this makes for a certain dullness. The conscripts I talked to were not hating their months under the colours, but they did not seem to be getting much real satisfaction from them. In many ways their life is made easy. If a soldier of any rank has a complaint of any kind, he can take it to a senior officer; and if that does not satisfy him, he can appeal to a kind of federal Ombudsman that deals with such cases. If a soldier commits a crime, he is tried by a civil court, for there are no more courts martial. This is all very decent and democratic, and it works well: but there are no legal provisions for any change in this system in time of war, to deal for example with mutineers or deserters, and several officers told me they were worried about what effect this might have on battle discipline – especially as so many young Germans today claim that they would not be prepared to fight for their country.

Relations between officers and NCOs, or between NCOs and other ranks, are today noticeably more informal and free-and-easy than in the British army, and salutes are just casual little gestures – so unlike the old *Wehrmacht* days. Some senior officers told me that, while they felt the change was necessary, they wondered if it had not gone too far. I spent two days on field exercises with a division in Bavaria, and was more impressed by the conviviality than the efficiency. When I checked in with military punctuality at its HQ in Regensburg, the officer due to receive me was not there and no one knew where he was, and I was kept hanging around for an hour while amiable corporals joked and smoked cigarettes in the corridors. The next day, the general gave me an appointment for 4 p.m. which I was later told was cancelled. At 4.30 he rang up the major I was with to ask where the hell I was – there had never been any cancellation. 'Sorry, old chap,' said the major in a Yankee drawl, 'we seem to have fouled this up along the line somewhere.' In a sense it came as a relief, in this relentlessly efficient

Germany to find at last a little corner of inefficiency – though not in the most suspicious or likely area. Perhaps these were untypical incidents, for the *Bundeswehr* as a whole has the reputation of being not only the best-equipped NATO force in Europe but one of the most effective.

Organised opposition to the *Bundeswehr* has come mainly from the peace movement, and it was inflamed in 1983 by the decision to allow the installation of American Cruise and Pershing II missiles on German soil, for the peace crusaders saw the German army as the accomplices of American aggressive interests in Europe. During the 1980s the peace movement was stronger in Germany than in most Western countries and was backed not only by the Greens but a great many Socialists, trade unionists and Church leaders. One of their main arguments was that Germany, being in the front line, was in danger of becoming a Russian-American nuclear battlefield in the case of war: and that, as both Germanies were forbidden under the Potsdam agreements to possess nuclear weapons of their own, then they should not provide bases for others. These feelings led to mass demonstrations during the 'hot autumn' that preceded the *Bundestag* debate on the US missiles in November 1983. On one occasion, 300,000 protesters paraded in Bonn; on another, a 'human chain' with hands joined was formed along the whole of the 55-mile route from Stuttgart to the American base at Ulm. The protests died down after the *Bundestag* voted in favour of the missiles, but they were renewed the next year when the dreaded weapons began to arrive: left-wing activists including the writer Walter Jens were arrested and fined for blocking the road to the US nuclear base at Mutlangen, near Stuttgart.

A small but militant minority within the peace movement also wanted Germany to leave NATO and become neutral. And quite often from young people one heard a view something like this: 'Reagan is a greater threat to world peace than the Soviets, he is almost as bad as the Nazis. So we must campaign to prevent his war, just as our grandparents failed to prevent Hitler's war' – the view that I heard from Professor Jäckel's younger students. But this minority anti-NATO view; was quite distinct from the far more widely shared anti-missile view, the two were sometimes confused. Opinion surveys in 1983–4 showed that the great majority of Germans – as many 86 per cent, according to one poll – were opposed to the deployment of Cruise and Pershing in Germany, but 75 per cent wanted the Federal Republic to remain in NATO and closely allied to the United States. Not to welcome foreign missiles on one's own soil was one thing, but to want neutrality was quite another; and the wave of anxiety in the early 1980s about growing German neutralism, voiced by Germany's allies and especially the French, was probably much exaggerated. The neutralist current had been stronger after the war. A poll in 1956 showed that 57 per cent of Germans wanted American troops to leave Europe: this figure fell to 11 per cent in 1979, then rose to 25 per cent in 1983 and levelled off at around 20 per cent – a proportion that NATO could live with.

The various events of the 1989–91 period have now created a new situation. First, the arms reductions in Europe agreed in 1989–90 between Moscow and Washington were greeted by the peace movement as a victory for its efforts – and not entirely without reason. The total number of foreign NATO troops on German soil was now to be reduced gradually from 400,000 to about 170,000 by the mid-1990s: the British were to halve their 50,000-strong Rhine army, the French were to withdraw all their forces, and the Americans were to make comparable major cuts, including the dismantling of many of their missiles bases. At the same time, under the 'two-plus-four' agreements on German unity, the Soviet Union was to withdraw progressively by the end of 1994 the whole of its 380,000-man army in eastern Germany.

All this meant that the peace movement had now lost much of its raison d'être. It reduced its campaign against the US missile bases, it became less active within Germany itself and instead turned some of its attention to the problems of the Third World. At the same time, however, popular feeling against the Bundeswehr increased. With the decline of the Soviet threat, the demise of the GDR and its army,[1] and with the Czech border now turned so friendly, some people began to ask, 'Do we need a Bundeswehr any more?', and the young complained more loudly against having to do military service. On top of all this, quite by coincidence German unification came at the same time as a very different event – crisis and war in the Gulf. And this aroused a whole new set of emotions and arguments. Germany's allies felt that

---

1. At unification, the East German army (see p. 396) was merged into the Bundeswehr. Most of it was disbanded, though some units were retained for work on dismantling the border defences and weapons dumps. Although quite a number applied, hardly any officers were allowed to join the Bundeswehr on a permanent basis. They were judged politically unreliable.

this new unified nation should be ready to play a major positive role in such a crisis: but the Gulf war showed how unready most German opinion was for international involvement of this kind. Once the fighting began, in January 1991, the anti-war demonstrations were greater in Germany than anywhere else in Europe, even though no German troops were involved. The peace movement had found a new cause. Many young people in particular felt a visceral hatred of any kind of war – 'There is no just war, only bloody wars against innocent people,' said one speaker. However, these peace rallies did not represent the majority, for polls showed that two-thirds of Germans supported the use of force against Iraq. But few of them would have wanted Germany's own troops to be involved.

Kohl therefore felt unprepared to lend military support to operations in the Gulf. He used the alibi that, under one interpretation of the Constitution, German forces could not be deployed outside the NATO area. Even so, he was criticised by his NATO allies, as well as by the *Bundeswehr* generals who felt humiliated and embarrassed. After the fighting ended, he came under pressure from them, and from much of the CDU, to seek amendment of the Constitution so that Germany could play a more active part in the future, if need be. He was himself in favour of this. But any change in the Constitution requires a two-thirds majority in Parliament, so Kohl needed the votes of the SPD. They were divided. At a congress in May, they finally agreed that German troops could join UN 'blue beret' peacekeeping missions: but they would not accept the use of German forces for UN-sanctioned war operations, such as that in the Gulf. Kohl, and Germany's allies, thought the SPD had not gone far enough. But politically he was blocked, and it seemed that the issue might drag on for years. The SPD were reflecting a widespread anti-militarist feeling in Germany. That it should still be so strong, forty-five years after the Nazis' war, was remarkable and in some ways laudable and reassuring. But some critics wondered whether Germans who felt like this were being entirely realistic. If the new Germany was to play a full responsible role in the world, commensurate with its power, could it afford to apply special rules to itself, as if it were a big Switzerland?

Some of the feeling against the Gulf operation was due to its being American-led. Much has been written, especially during the missiles affair of the 1980s, about alleged anti-Americanism in Germany – but just how strong is it today? Of all the people of Europe, only the British and Irish have a more 'special' relationship with America than the Germans, and today emotions towards the United States are as equivocal in Germany as anywhere. Some 5.5 million Germans emigrated to America between 1820 and 1920, followed later by the waves of Jewish and other refugees from Hitler; and today, if we exclude the Irish, Welsh and Scots, more Americans are of German than English origin. Small surprise that so many prominent Americans have German names. Maybe this helps also to explain why the two peoples are in some ways so similar: they may differ greatly in their degree of social formality, but they share something of the same business ethos, the same liking for thoroughness, efficiency and modernism and the same fondness for litigation.

After 1945, the Germans developed a sometimes obsequious admiration for the powerful nation that had both defeated and liberated them; and their bid to create a new and prosperous democracy was modelled much more consciously on the United States than on Britain. The British may have bequeathed the structures for broadcasting and the trade unions: but much of the inspiration for Germany's Constitution came from America, which also provided Marshall Aid and thus the impetus for the economic miracle. During those post-war years the Germans defined themselves in relation to America, which was also responsible for their defence, especially in Berlin. For better or worse, they copied and upheld many American values – freedom of speech, consumerism, the success ethic – and many of them saw America as the promised land. But then in the 1960s all began to change. The Vietnam war, the assassinations of Martin Luther King and the Kennedys, the growing student unrest – all this and much else produced a new image of America around the world. And it was the Germans, hitherto the greatest admirers, who inevitably now suffered the keenest disillusion. Typically, the swing of the pendulum was more sharply expressed in Germany than elsewhere, though in part it was merely an aspect of Germany's own youth revolt of the late 1960s. A new generation took up arms against consumerist values – and all too readily they identified these with America, forgetting maybe that part of young America was waging the same battle and sharing many of their ideals. America became the universal Aunt Sally for a lot of confused thinking. This new German generation, and the Green one that came after it, had never known the post-war era, the Berlin Airlift and Marshall Aid, and so they had less reason than their elders to feel grateful. This new mood of disenchantment found expression in some of the films of Wenders, and in Herzog's *Stroszek* (see pp. 336–9).

## Conclusion: how stable a democracy?

As elsewhere in Europe, a good deal of the hostile feeling in the 1980s was really a matter of the hatred of Reagan and his policies – and this hardly constituted anti-Americanism as such, any more than to abhor Thatcher was to be anti-British. Since the arrival of Bush, this feeling has diminished. It is true that even today some young Germans express a general distaste for all that they think America stands for: but, if they actually visit the United States, they usually like it more than they expected. They meet lots of young Americans who share their own critical view of society, and they find themselves admiring American informality and easy friendliness – 'One good thing about American influence,' said one student I met, 'is that it makes us uptight Germans less German.' Even so, a current of anti-American sentiment certainly exists in Germany, on the Right as well as the Left and in all age-groups; and I have noticed it especially among people now in their thirties and forties, the first generation that did not have direct experience of America's post-1945 help. In Munich I know a liberal publisher aged about 40, with many friends in New York, who told me: 'When I am in the depths of the English or French provinces, I can talk to the local peasants or workers and immediately sense common values. But in Oregon or Alabama I feel myself to be in an alien world with other values.'

As has often been pointed out, until a decade or so ago it was French intellectuals who were the most stridently anti-American in Europe, but that then changed with the decline of the Marxist Left and the rise of the *nouveaux philosophes*. Instead it was the German thinkers who in the 1980s became the more critical – as exemplified by Günter Grass, who has always been staunchly anti-Communist but told *Newsweek* in an interview in 1983: 'I see no difference between the Soviet Union's insolent, arrogant occupation of Afghanistan and the power-wielding of the United States in Central America ... America has been betraying its own ideals.' Nor were such feelings confined to the Left. In 1986 I met an industrialist also aged about 40, who breathed fire against the SPD and the unions and then added, 'America's NATO forces in Germany were foisted on us before we got back our sovereignty and we had no say in it. So, in a way, we're a colonised country. If an SPD government ever acted like de Gaulle and asked the American troops to leave, I bet they would refuse. That's because the Pentagon sees West Germany as far more strategically important than France.' These currents of thought certainly caused some anxiety, in those years, to senior US Army officers in Germany. When the demonstrators paraded outside the nuclear bases, American officers would sometimes tell them, 'Remember that we are here to protect your right to protest like this. Under Communism, you'd have no such right.' This message might not have always been appreciated: but confrontations between American servicemen and the peace protesters were generally free of any personal animosity — 'We like you and we have nothing against you as people,' the more responsible peaceniks would say, 'it's just your government's policy that we don't like.'

Today the anti-American feelings have waned, now that so many of the troops are leaving. And it would be wrong to give the impression that they were ever treated as harassed outcasts amid a hostile population, even at the height of the missiles crisis. Most of the US troops are in Germany with their families, and about half of them live 'on the German economy'; that is, in ordinary German rented housing and not within their own barracks: so opportunities for contact are numerous, and fraternisation is even discreetly encouraged. Of course there are some problems. Black GIs, as one might expect, are not always easily accepted by the Germans. And when GIs make certain pubs, restaurants and discos into their favourites, and crowd there together, the owners sometimes take fright that this will lose them their German clientele, and so they stick up 'Off Limits' signs — as legally they should not do. This has sometimes led to trouble. Generally the US commanders and the German local authorities collaborate in trying to persuade the publicans to remove the signs (some have even been taken to court) and generally this has met with success. Meanwhile, at officer and NCO level, an organisation called Kontakt arranges regular social gatherings and other activities between the German civilians and the Americans and their wives, and this works quite cordially — even extending to Christmas invitations to meals in German homes. I was told that 180 such visits had been made one Yuletide to families in one small Swabian town. All in all, human contacts of this kind are warmer and closer in the US zone of south Germany than in the British zone to the north, where the British Army of the Rhine though perfectly friendly is a little more reticent about fraternisation.

Anti-Americanism must therefore be seen in perspective. Like other German obsessions it seems to come and go in waves, and it is strongly tinged with emotionalism, irrationality, even petulance — almost the feeling of a spoilt child for its parent. And it must be viewed against the background of the strong links of friendship and sympathy between many Germans and Americans. Allensbach surveys, in response to the question, 'Which country in the world do you consider to be Germany's best friend?', have consistently put the United States ahead. In 1980, the last time this particular question was asked, the US scored 49 per cent, while France lagged second with 17 per cent, and Britain trailed fourth-equal at 2 per cent. On the other hand, in a poll of Germans east and west, published by the *Süddeutsche Zeitung* in January 1991 and asking the question, 'With which country should Germany in the next ten years have specially good and close relations?', 59 per cent said the Soviet Union, while only 44 per cent quoted the US, 36 per cent France, and 12 per cent the UK. This result might seem surprising. But it does not mean that the Germans want to abandon their Western alliances for a new one with Moscow. Rather, people feel that relations with the West are already good and sure, whereas their security will depend on building up better relations with the troubled colossus to their east. This view reflects especially the fear of uncontrollable mass emigration from the east into Germany, if the situation in the Soviet Union should further deteriorate.

Nor should these figures be taken to mean that the Germans are losing interest in the European Community. The official view at least, widely shared, is that there is no incompatibility between closer European integration, alliance with the United States within NATO, and growing links with eastern Europe. In the period of the creation of the EC, in the late 1950s, the surge of European idealism was stronger in Germany than anywhere else, for obvious reasons: the Germans were hoping to find a new identity within a United Europe, and an escape from their own past and their problems of nationalism. And to an extent the EC is still providing them with this. It is true that the European ideal has come under question in recent years. The Greens are 'European' in a broader sense, but are wary of an EC organisation that they see as too capitalist and industrial, and this view is shared by many younger Germans. At the same time, bankers and financiers do not like the way that rich Germany is expected by her partners to shoulder so large a part of the EC's budgetary burden. But of the stubborn clinging to national sovereignty, still so common in Britain, there is not so much sign in Germany – and unification has not altered this. The same *Süddeutsche Zeitung* survey that I quoted above gave 71 per cent of Germans – a very high figure – wanting to see a European federal state by the year 2000.

According to EC figures, some 53 per cent of Germans think that the '1992' single market will be a 'good thing', while 33 per cent are uncertain and 5 per cent are against it: these figures are about average for the EC countries, i.e. on a level with France, below Italy but well above Britain. Most businessmen welcome the challenge of '1992': but, as in other countries, some are wary for self-interested reasons, if their particular sector is ill placed to cope with the new open competition. In general, German enthusiasm for Europe is more political than economic, more a matter of emotion and instinct than of hard monetary reasoning. Most Germans back the Kohl Government's lead in pushing for a more democratic EC with stronger powers for the European Parliament, and they are annoyed at the foot-dragging, by France as well as Britain, on this issue. After all, the *Bund* already shares power with the *Länder*, so the *Bundestag* is less concerned than Westminster with guarding its sovereignty.

On the other hand, practical doubts about European Monetary Union have been growing among Germans recently – and this is the direct result of unification. Now that the German economy is faced with such huge domestic problems, many people agree with the Bundesbank's view that this might not be the moment to hurry into a venture that would expose the Deutschmark to weaker currencies. Germans may not care so much about political sovereignty: but they care mightily for their Deutschmark, which they see as the prime symbol of their post-war success. And they are afraid of its being weakened, if the Bundesbank were to merge into a new European Central Bank with maybe a single currency. They still accept EMU as a final goal: but they think that the problems of the eastern *Länder* should be settled first. This widespread feeling has put pressure on Kohl to waver in his own support for a strict EMU timetable – to the delight of London, and the fury of Jacques Delors and others. So a circle has to be squared here, for general support for the European ideal remains strong among all major parties. Most thoughtful Germans still see a tightly integrated Europe – leading maybe to a federal Europe – as the best long-term answer to the problem of German nationalism and the balance of power in Europe. Young people, who may not care greatly for the niceties of monetarism, are enthusiastic about such current developments as the abolishing of frontier controls between Germany and France. A Europe without frontiers seems to them right and normal.

The burying of the Franco-German hatchet, after three major wars in the space of 80 years, has been one of the greatest of Europe's post-war success stories; and personal relations today are fairly cordial, despite the differences of temperament between the two peoples. There are some 600 active twinnings between French and German towns and regions: Franconia, for example, has formed a successful one with Limousin where the village of Oradour-sur-Glane was in 1944 the scene of the worst of the SS massacres in France. The initiative for the various exchanges has tended to come more from the German than the French side, and many older Frenchmen were at first reticent or even hostile: but this feeling has diminished as war memories fade and the older generation die, and today the younger Germans and French get on perfectly easily, without complexes. This is seen especially in the very numerous school and youth exchanges, which have been fostered by the Franco-German Youth Office, set up in 1963 under the de Gaulle/Adenauer friendship treaty. Nearly five million young people have travelled on group visits to each others' countries under this scheme. A French Jew once said to me, 'You can't expect me to like the Germans, but rationally I'm in favour of the *rapprochement*. Germany and France are today like man and wife. Germany raped her in 1940, but then did the honest thing and married her. It's an uneasy marriage, but it works.' The unification at first caused some opposition amongst older Germans with wartime memories, or left-wing intellectuals, but this soon passed away.

Of a *mariage à trois* to include Britain there is still not much sign. The Allensbach surveys quoted above showed that between 1965 and 1980 the percentage of Germans seeing France as 'Germany's best friend' rose from 9 to 17, while in the case of Britain the figure fell from 6 to 2 per cent. The 1991 *Süddeutsche Zeitung* poll has borne out this picture. It is not that the Germans dislike the British, more that they sense that the British are not very interested in *them* – as the school twinnings show. A great many *Gymnasien* have active partnerships with *lycées*, where big groups of pupils go for two-week visits in term-time and are readily housed and entertained by French parents: exchanges with schools in Britain are far fewer, and many have collapsed, partly because the British show less interest in learning German, but above all because not enough British families are prepared to welcome the young visitors to their homes. The Germans today rather admire the British for their easy-going tolerance and social informality. But they scorn them for their class system, their inadequate social and public services (London Transport shocks any German visitor), and for their backward trade unions and continuing insularity. Recent British outbursts against Germany, such as Nicholas Ridley's in July 1990, are treated with sorrowful contempt, as revealing how little the British really try to understand modern Germany.

Yet the Germans in general remain very internationally-minded – again, the desire to escape from their past plays a big role. One sign is their readiness to learn foreign languages, notably English (one reason for this, admittedly, is the difficulty in getting foreigners to speak their own remarkably difficult tongue). Allensbach shows that the numbers able to speak English 'at least fairly well' rose from 22 to 41 per cent between 1961 and 1979; only 13 per cent could speak French. In 1989, 47 per cent could speak at least one foreign language; in the 20–29-year-old age-group, the figure was 65 per cent, and among the over-60s 25 per cent. That Schmidt and Giscard could not speak each other's language but conversed fluently in English at their meetings was entirely typical. However, I have noticed in the past year or two, since the *Wende,* that Germans have become a little less ready to talk English with foreigners who speak at least some German. This happened in several of my conversations, with people whose English is in fact better than my German. And others have shared my experience. Is it that those officials have become so absorbed by the inner German crisis as to have lost command, for a while, of other languages? Or, as some non-Germans might fear, is it a portent of a new German assertiveness? Yet if the Germans now follow the French in trying to uphold their own language, this does not seem to me unhealthy. Why on earth should everyone be expected to talk English together?

So finally, what will be the role of this new united Germany, in Europe and in the world? My own view, and many of the Germans I meet agree with me, is that unification will not change the picture as much as people abroad often suppose, or fear. Once eastern Germany's preoccupying crisis of adaptation has been solved, then the new larger Germany will follow a pattern not so very different from that of the Federal Republic hitherto.

Some fears were expressed during 1990, especially in Britain and France, that the new Germany might try to dominate and throw its weight around. But the Gulf War episode has indicated that this is nonsense, at least in the shorter term. The danger is much more the opposite, that Germany for some years will be too introverted, too obsessed by its own problems, to play a fully cooperative role in the wider world. This too has aroused some fears abroad, a little more realistically. But it is absurd to harbour both fears at once, of Germany the big bully and Germany the too-retiring flower. There is no doubt that Germans in public positions are today utterly absorbed by the crisis of the eastern *Länder* and how to pay for it: the press and media talk of little else. And this could make Germany less cooperative for a while, in EC and NATO matters.

But has unification changed the colour of what ordinary western Germans want from life? Have they become more nationalist, or expansionist? There is little sign of it. In the *Süddeutsche Zeitung* poll quoted above, its most significant finding was this: asked, 'Which country do you see as a future model for Germany?', far more people (40 per cent) quoted Switzerland than any other. Sweden, with its elaborate welfare system, came second with 29 per cent. France (8 per cent), the United States (6 per cent) and Britain (2 per cent) were well down the list. And throughout the survey, the portrait emerged of a German people concerned above all with ecology, peace, stability and tolerance – the solid post-war German virtues – and wanting to be left alone to enjoy the fruits of their hard work. True, this was only an opinion poll: but it does bear out the general impressions of anyone exploring Germany in depth today. Since the war the west Germans have built up a viable democracy, troubled only by sporadic terrorism, often the work of individual fanatics; the neo-Nazis remain a tiny lunatic fringe, and political ventures by extremist parties have come to nothing, as witness most recently the Republikaner. There seems little reason to doubt that the east Germans, given a few years, will succeed in adapting to this democratic system: they have already made a good start. The Germans still have their failings, like any people: but, short of some global disaster, I do not see any very likely recurrence of the worst of the old pre-war German faults.

There remains the question of whether Germany, by its sheer size and industrial prowess, will dominate Europe too much, even without trying to do so. Again, this is not an immediate problem. For several years, the eastern *Länder* will be too much of a liability, too much of a drain on Germany's resources, for it to be in full command of its strength. As for the further future, it is hard to say. But I think it would be wrong to talk as if Germany were now becoming a far greater colossus than before. In population terms, the new increase is only from 61 to 78 million, and in economic terms the new *Länder* have added only about 10 per cent to Germany's GDP. Already slightly larger and stronger than its main EC partners, the new Germany will now become a little more so – but not so much as to develop into the major super-power league. And European integration will act as a brake on any

German assertiveness. If there is an EC Central Bank that fixes interest rates, then the Bundesbank will have to take more account of the economic needs of Germany's EC partners.

So we come to the famous issue of the German national identity, which unification has again thrown into the limelight. For many years, in a stream of books, articles, lectures and debates in the media, the west Germans have talked and worried about this endlessly – 'What does it mean to be German?' 'Are we a real nation or not?' – and it often occurs to me that nothing identifies a German so much as this search for his identity. But we have to differentiate between national identity and patriotic feeling, for the two are not quite the same. The west Germans in my experience are intensely aware of being German (or how could they talk about it so much?): but what distinguishes them from many other peoples, such as the British or French, is that since the war they have taken little joy in being what they are. Some of the causes may lie deep in German history or even geography: but the principal one is obviously the Nazi legacy. So it is hardly surprising that the Germans have less patriotic pride than others. A Gallup international survey in 1982 put them firmly at the bottom of the table in this respect: asked, 'Do you feel very proud to be ... (American, British, etc.)?', 80 per cent of Americans said 'yes', 55 per cent of Britons, 41 per cent of Italians, 33 per cent of French (an unexpectedly low figure), 30 per cent of Japanese, and 21 per cent of Germans.

Anyone who travels around Germany as I did is likely to gain impressions that tend to the same conclusion. The people he meets may feel proud of German culture and local tradition, the German way of life, German economic or sporting achievements – but not of 'being German' in a patriotic sense. The national anthem is not often played (and it is worth pointing out, to those with poor German, that '*Alles*' does not mean 'everyone' but 'everything', so that '*Deutschland über Alles*' means 'Germany my first priority', not 'Germany supreme over other nations'). There is little equivalent of the kind of jokey jingoism so common in Britain, where people wear Union Jack T-shirts – that would be considered in appalling taste. The joyous celebrations that followed the World Cup victory in July 1990 were probably less fervent than they would have been in many countries, such as Britain. And the black-red-and-gold flag is seldom waved in the west for patriotic reasons: those who did so in the east, early in 1990, were simply signalling a desire for unification that was more economic than nationalist.

The younger generation in the west will often admit that being

German means little to them; and those who marry a foreigner are happy to exchange their nationality for another. Far more readily than the British or French they then adapt to the ways and attitudes of their spouse's country rather than expect the reverse. When young Germans visit London, they will sometimes envy the British their easy patriotism – but they have little desire to emulate it. And they possess few national heroes of their own: in one recent opinion poll, asked which famous figures they admired most, German or foreign, alive or dead, people put Albert Schweitzer head of the list (an Alsatian, born German, who later became French), followed by Mother Teresa and Lech Walesa. Postwar German politicians did poorly, and Luther, Bismarck and Frederick the Great were not mentioned.

Some trends in the mid-1980s, such as the wave of anti-Americanism and neutralism, and the Government's tougher stance on some EC matters, were taken by some observers at the time as signs of a revival of nationalism. But they really had quite other motivations. If there has been any nationalist trend in recent years, it has been not so much political as cultural in character. The Germans, or the more educated ones, are certainly very conscious of their culture, which they see as being bound up with a certain musical tradition and with their language and literature; and as such it is to them not solely German but something that they share with the Austrians and German Swiss – and this pan-Germanic culture they eagerly promote, as we have seen in the case of theatre. They have been returning also to their folk and other traditions, but mostly on a local and regional level. Whereas July 4 and July 14 are national fêtes in America and France, Germany has never till now had a national day, and *Karneval* and *Fasching* are local celebrations. 'The *Heimat* tradition may be reviving quite strongly,' one sociologist told me, 'but not in any national sense. There is a *Heimat Bayern*. But there was never a *Heimat Deutschland* – only a *Vaterland*, and that concept is still quite out of fashion.' Unification day, October 3, is now to become the German national day: but we shall see whether it arouses much enthusiasm.

Is this relative absence of patriotism to be regarded as an asset or a handicap for the Germans? Those old enough to remember the havoc of the Nazi period very often see it as the former: Marion von Dönhoff, for example, the co-editor of *Die Zeit*, said to me, 'I myself am glad about this lack of patriotic feeling, and I see it as a progress. We have quite enough to be legitimately proud of in Germany today, and we don't want nationalism too.' But there are others who argue that patriotism is not a quality that a people can lightly dispense with – that it provides an inspiration for all kinds of positive community feelings and that individuals with low national pride are generally the ones most lacking in other kinds of loyalty and positive motivation, towards democratic institutions or even towards work, friends and family. According to this view, some of the German sense of insecurity and rootlessness can be explained in this way. The problem is less acute for intellectual or richer people, who have wider horizons and more opportunities for travel abroad, and thus have less need of a national context; but, for the more ordinary citizens, the lack of a strong sense of nationhood, and of easy flag-waving outlets for expressing it, can build up frustrations and may help to account for the Germans' relatively weak sense of community responsibility and for the radical rejection of society by so many of the young.

There may be elements of truth in such a view. But, if the continuing shame about Nazism is the main cause of wariness over national pride, this will surely ease as the years go by. It could then lead to a revival of the less pleasant aspects of German nationalism. But as yet there is little sign of this: and it is important to stress that nationalism today is diluted and even transmuted by the new feeling for Europe, as it was not in the Nazi time. The young are not only less guilt-ridden about Nazism than their elders, but despite everything they have a stronger sense of European identity; and, like young Italians, French and others, they set less store by national frontiers. So I do not consider that the quest for national identity is the most serious of Germany's problems today.

Has unification changed this picture? It is too early to tell, but I doubt that it will have changed it much. The initial rejoicings on both sides of the border, after the *Wende* of November 1989, were prompted more by delight at the overthrow of Communism and a people's liberation, than specifically by patriotic joy. And by the time of unification itself, the rejoicing had given way to mutual resentments. But this too is temporary. I think that when the two parts of Germany have settled down and learned to live with each other, as they will, then the problem of the German identity will remain much as before – save that it will be shorn of one of its main components, based on the division of the country. People will have less cause to ask, 'Are we really a nation?' But German nationhood will still be balanced by the historical and cultural patchwork of the *Länder*, which is surely a source of strength. And the old German *Angst* and sense of insecurity will probably continue too, for these are deeply rooted in the German character. Some of those other, rooted German traits – mistrust of neighbours, polarisation of attitudes, legalism, inability to live with imperfection – may also continue to make it harder than in some Western countries to achieve an ideally stable and moderate democracy. And yet – at the risk of sounding patronising, as in this context an Englishman can so easily be – one must affirm that democracy has made enormous strides in this land that had little tradition of it, and that the younger German generation for all its follies and excesses is full of positive qualities that offer hope for the future. But the Germans, like all of us, cannot manage on their own and should not be allowed to do so. The best guarantee for this new Germany is that we all continue to strive towards the ideal of a united Europe. In that promised land I am confident that the troubled Germans will finally find their escape from Nietzsche's 'hidden paths to chaos'.

## Postscript, May 1995

Those last few pages, written in 1991, on the new role of Germany in Europe and the world, remain largely valid today. It is true that there has been some further waning of faith in the ideal of a United Europe. The growth of Euro-scepticism in other countries, notably in France, has made an impact on many Germans, who have come to reflect that even their great French ally may now be less than fully reliable, and that Germany should do more to depend on itself. One opinion poll in 1994 gave two-thirds of Germans as rejecting the idea of a federal European state, exactly the reverse of the 1991 *Süddeutsche Zeitung* poll which I quoted. *Bild Zeitung*, that self-proclaimed voice of the man-in-the-street, often carries headlines about the high cost of German net contributions to the European Union, and this cost prompts some west Germans to ask, 'When we pay so much for the east – can we be expected to pay for Europe too?'

Monetary union is a main sticking-point: the Bundesbank may be less fundamentally opposed to EMU than is often suggested, but it argues that it may have to be delayed, and that nations must not join unless their economies are strong enough, or the result will be chaos. As for the Bundestag, it ratified the Maastricht Treaty only with the proviso that it will have the right to vote again later on proceeding with EMU

– thus awarding Germany a *de facto* opt-out not so very different from Britain's.

In short, Helmut Kohl, that ardent 'European', has been forced on to the defensive at home since the Maastricht summit of December 1991, and he can no longer take German Euro-enthusiasm so much for granted. Even within his own coalition, some voices have been speaking up against further integration, notably in the CSU's Bavaria, where the Prime Minister, Edmund Stoiber, nicknamed 'Edmund Thatcher', has denounced Maastricht and the Euro-federal ideal. However, he was then upbraided for 'treason' by leaders of the CDU, nearly all of whom remain solidly behind Kohl. Two of the most influential of them, Wolfgang Schäuble and Karl Lamers, in November 1994 produced a policy paper that urged Germany, with France and a few other countries, to go ahead into a 'hard core' of monetary and political union, leaving the impossible British on the sidelines. The paper preached European federalism – but of course that word does mean opposite things to German and British ears. For the Germans, who already have a federal system, it means a devolution from the centre; for the British, with no federal experience, it means the reverse.

It is still the guiding light of Kohl's foreign policy that rapid European integration remains the best way of averting a return of German nationalism, whether isolationist or expansionist and in either case disastrous. For the moment, the FDP agrees with this, and the bulk of the SPD too, with some reservations: remarkably, Europe was not a major issue in the October 1994 election campaign. But many younger Germans have greater doubts; and as Jacques Delors, one of my great heroes, said to me in 1991, 'I have complete trust in Kohl, his views on Europe's future are the same as mine. But he might be the last German leader with this attitude. So we have to act quick to tie Germany into Europe irreversibly, or it could be too late.'

Neal Ascherson, another of my heroes and a superb analyst of modern Germany, has written recently in the *Independent on Sunday*:

> If Germany gives up on European union, all certainties collapse under us like a rotten floor and we plunge down into darkness ... The Germany that we now have is the best of all possible Germanies. For the moment, those who govern it still believe that united Germany is too big and powerful for the stability of a Europe of nation-states. They conclude that Europe must push ahead towards full political integration, so that the sovereignty of nation-states is

pooled. Stripped of its power to act alone, Germany could no longer overshadow and disturb its neighbours. This is the great window of opportunity for our times: the overwhelming argument for European union. The ghost of the 'German problem' can be laid for ever. Especially in Britain, we do not understand our incredible luck in having men and women with such ideas in charge of Germany. But windows can close. The opportunity could be missed, through short-sighted obsession with our own sovereignty or sheer xenophobia.

The issue today for the new, larger Germany is how to play a greater role in world affairs, as it must, without being seduced by ideas of supremacy. Abroad, there has been much talk about a revival of assertive German nationalism, but I find little more evidence for this today than in 1991. What I do find is a greater national self-confidence, a desire to stop being asked to feel guilty about the past, and to be treated as a normal nation (plus a chagrin that the British, so often, fail in this). As for assertiveness, alike in the EU and in NATO the new Germany has not been throwing its weight around and has seldom tried to go it alone. It is true that when in 1993 the Bundesbank served to break up the European Exchange Rate Mechanism, it was putting national interests first, as central banks do. And Germany has been much criticised for allegedly provoking the Bosnian conflict by pushing its allies into premature recognition of Croatia and Slovenia. But I am not sure that I accept this view. Yugoslavia would have broken up anyway, and by 1991 to keep it going artificially might have been impossible, except by force of Serb domination. Little Slovenia at least, a nation I know well and love, richly deserved to win full sovereignty at last.

Chancellor Kohl's Government today wants simultaneously to tighten EU integration and to intensify relations with countries to the east — 'Genscher is gone, long live Genscherism!', so it's said. Bonn may find that the two aims are not easily compatible, for it will be many years before those nations can reach western standards, and some kind of two-tier system will be needed. Germany wants closer links with countries like Poland and the Czech Republic, partly as a protection against possible chaos spreading from Russia, and partly for trade reasons: but Bonn is fully aware of Czech anxiety about excessive German invest-ment, and would genuinely like Germany's EU partners to invest more themselves. Politically, there is today no revanchism in Bonn about the

Czech border, or the Polish one along the rivers Oder and Neisse. Since the late 1940s, little groups of exiles in the west, notably Silesians and Sudeten Germans, have run *Heimatverbände* (homeland associations), campaigning for the recovery of their lost territories. They did so especially in 1989–90, feeling that their chance had come, after the collapse of Soviet power in those countries and in the GDR. This caused some embarrassment to Kohl's Government, and for a while it did waver (I can't resist quoting the pun I invented at the time: the German policy on the Polish border stinks, so what should it do? Make its odour nicer). However, all German politicians except the far-Right fringe are now firm in their commitment to those borders, and the subject is closed.

Fears are sometimes voiced, in countries such as Britain, about a revival of German militarism. But the truth is the opposite. A large part of German opinion has shown extreme reluctance, even to allow troops to go abroad for UN peace operations – to the annoyance of Germany's allies. Some British opinion simultaneously expresses alarm at the danger of 'German jackboots again on the march' and anger at German failure to take part in the Gulf War – not very logical.

The facts are (see p. 568) that the Kohl Government, backed by the armed forces command, realises that if Germany is now to play a fuller responsible role in world affairs, commensurate with its power, and is to gain a permanent seat on the UN Security Council, as it desires, then it must be prepared to take part fully in NATO outside-area ventures, and in UN operations both peace-keeping and peace-enforcing, like the 'normal' nation that it now claims to be. This is hardly 'militarism'. However, the SPD has always been reluctant, and its support is needed for any change in the Constitution, which under one interpretation would not allow German forces in activities outside the NATO area. But so unclear is this document on this issue that Kohl decided to test it by sending troops outside the NATO area, to see what happened. So in 1993 some 1,700 were deployed to help the UN in Somalia – mostly engineers and medical staff, but backed by 300 paratroopers for 'self-defence'. It was the first time since 1945 that German forces were used outside the NATO area. The SPD retorted by challenging the Government in the Constitutional Court, but they lost (it was suggested that some SPD leaders, agreeing with Kohl and ahead of the party's more pacifist rank-and-file, were using the Court as an alibi, to take a decision that would let them off the hook).

In July 1994 the Constitutional Court concluded that Germany has the right to use troops abroad exactly like any other NATO member.

But Parliament has to approve in each case, by majority vote and, of course, it is sensitive to a still wary public opinion. A poll in 1994 showed that barely more than half (52 per cent) of voters were now in favour of German forces taking part in UN and NATO peace-keeping operations. In the case of Bosnia, all political parties, backed strongly by public opinion, have ruled out sending ground troops there, for obvious reasons connected with Germany's Second World War role in the region – and this NATO fully accepts. When in December 1994 Kohl wanted to accede to a NATO request for the use of German high-tech Tornado planes in Bosnia, a poll suggested that two-thirds of voters were opposed. However, very many Germans support the view that the UN should use force against Serbia – and not only on the Right. In 1994 Danny Cohn-Bendit, the Green leader, and Freimut Duve, on the left of the SPD, both compared the UN soft line against the Serbs with the West's appeasement of Hitler before 1939. However, using Germany's own troops there is another matter.

In sum, the Germans today have plenty to worry about, not only abroad but within their own country, still in a sense divided by its own unseen border. For the past few years, west as well as east Germans have shown an increased anxiety and moroseness, an egotism and a greater intolerance alike towards foreigners and other Germans. But there are so many exceptions, and like Neal Ascherson I am a 'nervous optimist'. The much-discussed *Politikverdrossenheit* (disillusion with politics) is worrying in Germany, where democracy is still a tender plant, but it goes far deeper in Italy and France, where corruption at high levels has been much greater. In time, the east's economy will recover, and this will ease much of the anxiety: I do not believe, as some suggest, that the east will be a permanent Mezzogiorno, a poorer, underdeveloped region. The major problem remains the Germans' own temperament, their sudden *Angst*, their tendency to swing from one extreme to another when things go badly. But I can only repeat my pious hope of 1991, that a united Europe, where the Germans are loved and assured by true friends, will offer their best escape from Nietzsche's 'hidden paths to chaos'. That depends above all on the French, and on us.

# ACKNOWLEDGEMENTS

Many hundreds of people, of all kinds, gave up their time to help us with our field research, and in many cases were generously hospitable. They are too numerous for me to mention all by name. But first I wish to thank a few who were especially kind and helpful:

*In Bonn*: the late Brigitte Lohmeyer, Stefan and Cosima Sethe, Herr Richter, Elke Berger. *In Munich*: Anna Maria Schmitz, my mother-in-law, Jessica and Alan Stubbings. *In Stuttgart:* Heinz Krämer and Sigrid Stellwag, Kurt and Grete Hoffmann, Anthony Gibbs. *In Allensbach:* Professor Elisabeth Noelle-Neumann and her colleagues at the Institut für Demoskopie. *In Hamburg:* Marion and Hans Heibey, Charlotte Schoell-Glass, Henry Glass. *In Herleshausen*: Heino and Ursula Flemming. *In Rödermark*: Carmen Lakashus. *In Berlin:* Birgit Meyer and Jürgen Woycke, Georg and Irmgard Wittwer, Steffi Schappo, Helfried and Renate Liebsch, Reiner and Christina Oschmann, Nicholas Gay, Michael Brodersen and G. Buchholz of the tourist office. *In London:* Bernd von Waldow, Friedrich Gröning, Peter Gottwald, all past or present Press Counsellors at the German Embassy, also Hildegard Dunkl, Ulrich Maier; Günter Coenen and Elmar Brandt of the Goethe Institute and their staff; Günter Nischwitz, Rudolf Richter and Agatha Süss of the German National Tourist Office; the staff of Lufthansa.

Amongst others, my special thanks go also to:

*In Munich:* Christina Hederer of Inter Nationes; Herbert Winkler, Linda Baumgärtner and Gertrud Schaller of the city tourist office; Günter Wolfbauer and his colleagues at the Rathaus; Georg Welsch of the Greens; Tom Bryant and his staff at the British Consulate-General; Daniel Contenay, French Consul-General; George Bailey. Franz Münsterer; Richard Gaul of BMW; Peter Olfs and others of Siemens;

## Acknowledgements

Randolf Rodenstock. Prof. Nikolaus Lobkowicz, Prof. Wulf Steinmann, Eberhard Dünninger, Toni Schmid, Georg Knauss, Elizabeth Magana; Rupert Graf Strachwitz; Dr Jost Martinius; Carla Baran; Kirchenrat Paul Rieger, Pfarrer Turner. Hans Magnus Enzensberger, Lothar Menne; Wolfgang Ebert; Werner Herzog, Alexander Kluge, Margarethe von Trotta, Edgar Reitz, the late Rainer Werner Fassbinder; Jürgen Kolbe; Dieter Schröder and others at the *Süddeutsche Zeitung*; Richard Dill, Renée Goddard, Hano Frei. David and Birgit Kehoe, Gert and Ulla Pegler, Andrea and Jürgen Kölble (Dutton), Reinhardt and Utta Riemerschmid, Sue and Peter Kafka, Hella Schwerla, Jürgen Claus.

*Rest of Bavaria*; Major-General Wolfgang Odendahl and his Bundeswehr colleagues at Regensburg; at Ansbach, Rolf and Renata Fütterer; at Augsburg, Gerda Rutsche of the tourist office.

*In Stuttgart:* Lothar Späth; Manfred Rommel and his colleagues at the Rathaus; Frau Weber of Inter Nationes; Anneliese Schuhholz of the Baden-Württemberg tourist board; Brian Rose, former British Consul-General, and his staff; the late Bob Larson; General Galvin of the US Army. Hans Georg Kloos and his colleagues at Daimler-Benz; Wolfgang Knellessen, Rüdiger Stephan, and their colleagues at Robert Bosch; Alfred Krone. Prince and Princess Mainrad von Hohenzollern; Prof. Eberhard Jäckel, Prof. Georg Turner, Fritz and Pauline Hejl, Magda Meier and her colleagues at the Waldorfschule. Thomas Löffelholz, Erich Peter, Johann Kannicht and their colleagues at the *Stuttgarter Zeitung*; Jürgen and Susanne Offenbach; the late Roderich Klett, Hans Heiner Bolte and their colleagues at Süddeutsche Rundfunk; Klaus Hübner, Michael Maegraith; Peter Palitzsch; Marcia Haydee and her colleagues at the ballet. Liselotte Hoover; Frau von Egloffstein; Erwin and Ingrid Wartenburg, Graf and Gräfin zu Knyphausen.

*Rest of Baden-Württemberg:* in Tübingen, Prof. Walter Jens, Axel Markert. In Horb, Prof. Rainer Nagel and his wife; in Dornstetten, Erhard Eppler; in Konstanz, Hans Willauer; in Freiburg, the late Philip Ernst, Richard Farnsworth; in Baden-Baden, Sigrun Lang, Richard Schmitz; in Karlsruhe, Renate Stiehl, the Niemann family. Friedrich Karl Fürst zu Hohenlohe-Waldenburg and his wife.

*In Frankfurt:* Barbara Schander of Inter Nationes, Jost Enseling; Klaus Mehrens of IG Metall; Florian Schilling and other INSEAD alumni. Burkhard Schwarz; Prof. Iring Fetscher; Stephen Castles. Prof. Hilmar Hoffmann; Brian Michaels; Karlheinz Braun; Werner Hölzer, Peter Iden

## Acknowledgements

and others of the *Frankfurter Rundschau*. Prof. Klaus and Ellinor Lüderssen, Prof. Kurt and Ingrid Shell, the late Albert von Metzler.

*Rhineland-Palatinate:* Rudi Molz at Woppenroth, Hunsrück.

*In Bonn:* Michael Mertes, Rüdiger Thiele, Herr Geyer and others in the Chancellor's office; Carl-Dieter Spranger and others of the Interior Ministry; Lothar Ruhl, General Naumann and others of the Ministry of Defence; Marlies Jansen and Jürgen Aretz of the former Ministry for Intra-German Relations; the late Petra Kelly, Otto Schily and other Greens or former Greens; Ernst-Günter Pätzold of the federal Press office; Christopher Mallaby, the Ambassador, Catherine Pestell, Alistair Hunter, Alan Hatfull, Georges Chantrey, Tom Macan, Joan Link and others of the British Embassy; Dinnies von der Osten of BP. Detlef Kühn, Gerhard Müller, Dr Martin Friedrichs. Klaus-Peter Schmid, David Marsh, David Goodhardt, Michel Meyer. Armgard Rostowski.

*In Cologne:* Marianne Esch and others of the city tourist office; Robert Arbuthnot and Trevor Rutter of the British Council; Joachim von Mengershausen; Helga Ihlau; Carnival Prince Karl-Josef Kappes; Klaus and Lizzi Barisch.

*In Düsseldorf:* Prof. Reimut Jochimsen; the late Kurt Birrenbach of Thyssen; Ulrich Borsdorf and others of the DGB; Prof. Herbert Reuter, Fritz Conzen, the late Dame Lilo Milchsack.

*Rest of North-Rhine-Westphalia:* in Dortmund, Prof. Kurt Kosyk; in Bochum, Udo von Hagen and his wife; in Essen, Alfred Plitzko, Andreas Schlieper; in Buir, the Brecher family.

*In Hamburg:* Klaus von Dohnanyi and his colleagues in the *Land* Government; Dr Ingo von Münch; Freimut Duve; Michael Platte of the tourist office. Karl Freiherr von Hahn. Jil Sander; Eva Rühmkorf; Angelika Jahr, Mario Scheuermann, Karl Theodor Walterspiel, Wolfgang Schüler; Bishop Krusche, Siegfried von Kortzfleisch; Prof. Peter Fischer-Appelt. Rolf Liebermann, Peter Zadek, Eberhard Möbius; Marion Gräfin von Dönhoff, Theo Sommer, Christoph Bertram, Rudolf Walter Leonhardt, all of *Die Zeit*; Günter Gaus; Peter Scholl-Latour, Bernd Leptihn. Borries and Irmgard de Grahl, Hans Meckel and his family, Karl-Heinz Piepenbrink and his family, Albrecht and Regine Eggert, Sabine Skoruppa. Hans Eppendorf, Dennis Clark.

*In Bremen:* Hans Koschnik, Manfred von Scheven, Dieter Opper.

*In Schleswig-Holstein:* Günter Kunert; Beate Uhse; Hans Hermann Petersen and his family, Peter Rabe and his family, Dierk Boie and his family, Franz Hollmann; Senator Lund of Lübeck.

*In Lower Saxony:* in Göttingen, Prof. Rudolf von Thadden and his

## Acknowledgements

wife, Artur Levi, Gerd Pistohlkors. In Wolfsburg, Karl-Heinz Schüling of Volkswagen. The Abeln family of Dörpen, Emsland.

*In Berlin:* Eberhard Diepgen, Günter Rexrodt, Dieter Senoner, all of the city government. Gerhard Kohnen, Horst Winkelmann, Lothar Nass. Alex Bidder, Gerhard Buchholz of the tourist office. Michael Burton of the former British Military Government. Major Michael Hoover, Kurt Kasch. Barbara John, Cemalettin Çetin. Professor Werner Knopp, Professor Peter Wapnewski. Wim Wenders, Rosa von Praunheim, Romy Haag. Joachim Braun, Wolfgang Hauptmann, Donald Armour. Marlies Menge, Tony Allen Mills, Anne McElvoy, Peter and Isabella von Jena, Gisela Wille, Jan Schäfer, Michael Schöbel. Werner Krätschell, Helga Salier, Jens Reich, Heiner Müller, Hermann Kant, Ulrich Plenzdorf, Claus-Peter Flor, Geoffrey Deane, Robert Röntgen, Ekkehard Fahldieck.

*In the Potsdam area:* Herr Grasshof, Marguerite and David Morgan, Berndt and Marine Unger.

*In Dresden:* Martin Schneider, Michael Kinze, Johannes Heisig and his wife, Helge Budäus.

*In Leipzig:* Prof. Albert Neubert, Roland and Ilse Engel, Christa Heisig, Manfred Müller, Ulrich Seidel, Peter and Maritta Helbig.

*In the Eisenach area:* Mayor Hans-Peter Brodhun, Martin Kaspari, Superintendent Hans Herbst, Margot Friedrich, Helmut Schmidt, Marina and Karl-Heinz Faulstier, Horst Schmidt, Günther Fey.

*In Paris:* Charles Hargrove, Bernard Brigouleix, Brigitte Sauzay.

*In London:* Alex Hamilton, Victor Price, Barbara Beck; Richard and Jocelyn Mayne, Peter Fabian, Edith Rudinger, the late Erich Fried, Leonie Cohn, Alexander Wathenphul, Irene Hawkins, Angelika Sahla; Ian and Ruth Bell, Michael Balfour.

Last but far from least, my thanks go to my publishers in London, Peter Carson, Miranda McAllister and Mark Handsley of Penguin Books, and Andrew Franklin and Christopher Sinclair-Stevenson of Hamish Hamilton, who have been unfailingly helpful and encouraging.

# BIBLIOGRAPHY

(In the case of German books translated into English, only the English
  version is given)

**General and political:**

Luigi Barzini, *The Impossible Europeans*, Weidenfeld and Nicolson, 1983.
Bernard Brigouleix, *Les Allemands*, Balland, Paris, 1984.
Jonathan Carr, *Helmut Schmidt, Helmsman of Germany*, Weidenfeld and
    Nicolson, 1985.
David Childs, *Germany in the Twentieth Century*, Batsford, 1991.
Gordon Craig, *The Germans*, Putnam's, New York, 1982 and Penguin
    Books, 1984.
Marion von Dönhoff, *Foe into Friend*, Weidenfeld and Nicolson, 1982.
Timothy Garton Ash, *In Europe's Name: Germany and the Divided
    Continent*, Jonathan Cape, 1993
Timothy Garton Ash, *We the People, the Revolution of 1989*, Penguin
    Books, 1990.
Alfred Grosser, *Germany in Our Time*, Pall Mall Press, 1971.
Wilhelm Hennis, *Die missverstandene Demokratie*, Freiburg, 1973.
Walter Laqueur, *Germany Today*, Weidenfeld and Nicolson, 1985.
Rudolf Walter Leonhardt, *This Germany*, Penguin Books, 1966.
David Marsh, *The Bundesbank: The Bank that Rules Europe*, Mandarin,
    1992.
David Marsh, *The New Germany*, Century, 1990.
Richard Mayne, *Postwar*, Thames & Hudson, 1983.
Michel Meyer, *L'Allemagne inachevée*, Denoel, Paris, 1976.
Giles Radice, *The New Germans*, Michael Joseph, 1995.

# Bibliography

Joseph Rovan, *L'Allemagne du Changement*, Calmann-Levy, Paris, 1983.
Anthony Sampson, *The New Europeans*, Hodder and Stoughton, 1968.
Brigitte Sauzay, *Le vertige allemand*, Orban, Paris, 1985.
Michael Simmons, *Berlin*, Hamish Hamilton, 1988.
Ken Smith, *Berlin, Coming in from the Cold*, Hamish Hamilton, 1990.
Alan Watson, *The Germans, Who are They Now?*, Thames & Hudson, 1992
Werner Weidenfeld (ed.), *Die Identität der Deutschen*, Hanser, Munich, 1983.
Allensbach Institute, annual collections of opinion polls; also *Eine Generation später, Bundesrepublik Deutschland 1953–1979*, Saur, Munich, 1983.
Facts about Germany, Bertelsmann Lexikothek, Gütersloh.


## Society, including youth, Greens and immigrants:

Jillian Becker, *Hitler's Children*, Michael Joseph, 1977.
Fritjof Capra and Charlene Spretnak, *Green Politics*, Hutchinson, 1984.
Stephen Castles, *Here for Good: Western Europe's Ethnic Minorities*, Pluto Press, 1984.
Ralf Dahrendorf, *Society and Democracy in Germany*, Weidenfeld and Nicolson, 1968.
Hans Magnus Enzensberger, *Politische Brosamen*, Suhrkamp, Frankfurt, 1982.
Angelika Gardiner-Sirtl, *Gleichberechtigt?*, Brigitte, Hamburg, 1982.
Elim Papadakis, *The Green Movement in West Germany*, Croom Helm, 1984.
Günter Wallraff, *Lowest of the Low*, Methuen, 1988.


## Regions and cities:

John Ardagh, *The Shell Guide to Germany*, Simon & Schuster, 1991.
John Ardagh, *A Tale of Five Cities*, Secker & Warburg, 1979.
George Bailey, *Munich*, Time-Life Books, Amsterdam, 1980.
Hans Eppendorfer, *St. Pauli*, Hoffmann und Campe, Hamburg, 1982.
Bob Larson, *Your Swabian Neighbours*, Schaben International Verlag, Stuttgart, 1980.

Rudolf Walter Leonhardt, *Hamburg*, Süddeutscher Verlag, Munich, 1985.

Thaddäus Troll, *Stuttgart*, Belser, Stuttgart, 1969.


**Culture and media:**

Peter Iden, *Theater als Widerspruch*, Kindler, Munich, 1985.

Brian Keith-Smith (ed.), *Essays on Contemporary German Literature*, Oswald Wolff, 1966.

John Sandford, *The New German Cinema*, Oswald Wolff, 1980.

Günter Wallraff, *Der Aufmacher*, Kiepenheuer & Witsch, Cologne, 1977.

*Cultural Life in the Federal Republic of Germany* (various hands), Inter Nationes, Bonn, 1981.


**German Democratic Republic:**

Anthony Bailey, *Along the Edge of the Forest*, Faber & Faber, 1983.

David Childs, *The GDR: Moscow's German Ally*, Allen & Unwin, 1983.

Timothy Garton Ash, *Die DDR heute*, Rowohlt, Hamburg, 1983.

Günter Gaus, *Wo Deutschland liegt*, Hoffmann und Campe, Hamburg, 1983.

Anne McElvoy, *The Saddled Cow: East Germany's Life and Legacy*, Faber & Faber, 1992

Jonathan Steele, *Socialism with a German Face*, Jonathan Cape, 1977.

Christa Wolf, *Was Bleibt*, Luchterhand, Frankfurt, 1990.

# INDEX

Principal page references are in **bold type**. With the exception of Edgar Reitz's *Heimat*, which occurs so frequently, book, play and film titles are not indexed: see under name of author or director. Some general themes are indexed, i.e. 'unemployment' – but not where the location of the subject is evident from the Contents list (e.g. industry, women). Almost all German proper names are indexed: foreign ones are listed only when they are specially relevant.

# Index

# Index

# Index

# Index

# READ MORE IN PENGUIN

In every corner of the world, on every subject under the sun, Penguin represents quality and variety – the very best in publishing today.

For complete information about books available from Penguin – including Puffins, Penguin Classics and Arkana – and how to order them, write to us at the appropriate address below. Please note that for copyright reasons the selection of books varies from country to country.

**In the United Kingdom**: Please write to *Dept. EP, Penguin Books Ltd, Bath Road, Harmondsworth, West Drayton, Middlesex UB7 ODA*

**In the United States**: Please write to *Consumer Sales, Penguin USA, P.O. Box 999, Dept. 17109, Bergenfield, New Jersey 07621-0120*. VISA and MasterCard holders call 1-800-253-6476 to order Penguin titles

**In Canada**: Please write to *Penguin Books Canada Ltd, 10 Alcorn Avenue, Suite 300, Toronto, Ontario M4V 3B2*

**In Australia**: Please write to *Penguin Books Australia Ltd, P.O. Box 257, Ringwood, Victoria 3134*

**In New Zealand**: Please write to *Penguin Books (NZ) Ltd, Private Bag 102902, North Shore Mail Centre, Auckland 10*

**In India**: Please write to *Penguin Books India Pvt Ltd, 706 Eros Apartments, 56 Nehru Place, New Delhi 110 019*

**In the Netherlands**: Please write to *Penguin Books Netherlands bv, Postbus 3507, NL-1001 AH Amsterdam*

**In Germany**: Please write to *Penguin Books Deutschland GmbH, Metzlerstrasse 26, 60594 Frankfurt am Main*

**In Spain**: Please write to *Penguin Books S. A., Bravo Murillo 19, 1° B, 28015 Madrid*

**In Italy**: Please write to *Penguin Italia s.r.l., Via Felice Casati 20, I–20124 Milano*

**In France**: Please write to *Penguin France S. A., 17 rue Lejeune, F–31000 Toulouse*

**In Japan**: Please write to *Penguin Books Japan, Ishikiribashi Building, 2–5–4, Suido, Bunkyo-ku, Tokyo 112*

**In Greece**: Please write to *Penguin Hellas Ltd, Dimocritou 3, GR–106 71 Athens*

**In South Africa**: Please write to *Longman Penguin Southern Africa (Pty) Ltd, Private Bag X08, Bertsham 2013*

# BY THE SAME AUTHOR

**Ireland and the Irish**
Portrait of a Changing Society

Travelling everywhere 'from the small farms of Mayo to the slums of North Dublin and the hitherto violence-ridden ghettos of West Belfast', John Ardagh spoke to President Mary Robinson, Gay Byrne of Irish television, the disgraced ex-Bishop of Galway and countless others. Interweaving their insights with his own observations and analysis, he reveals how the rural-based society of the South has evolved into a prosperous modern state, closely involved in Europe and vibrant with its own Irish culture, while in the North, a resilient people may at last be emerging from their long conflict.

'He has conducted dozens of interviews in all the provinces of the island ... It is his intelligent presence at these interviews which enables him to create from them and from his study of prevailing social and economic trends his impressionistic "portrait"' – Robert Kee in *The Times*

*With new material*

**France Today**

*France Today* is a fully revised edition of John Ardagh's acclaimed *France in the 1980s*, which over the years has established itself as the standard work on modern France.

A new preface looks at the France of 1995, in the light of the presidential election. The rest of the book examines the profound changes in French society since the war, from the Fourth Republic via de Gaulle to the Socialists' years in power. In the course of preparing this ambitious and wide-ranging book, Ardagh talked with many of the new leaders of France. His main theme, however, is not politics but the lives and attitudes of the French as they look to the future. Exasperating and stimulating, the French personality emerges triumphantly from this portrait of a nation that has its eyes on the future but is also turning back to some of its deepest traditions.

*With a new Preface for the 1995 edition.*